Who Should Read This B

This book is for you if you've been wanting to take the dive into the world of 32-bit programming but didn't know where to begin. This book is aimed toward the beginner—the one who wants to learn what Delphi 2 is all about.

How This Book Is Structured

This book has been laid out as a seven-day, teach-yourself training course complete with exercises, chapter quizzes, and examples that you can try out on your own. To get the most benefit from the book, you should first attempt to keep to the pace set by the daily structure, and you should also attempt to complete all the exercises you are given.

teach yourself DELPHI 2

in 21 days

teach yourself DELPHI 2 in 21 days

Dan Osier
Steve Grobman
Steve Batson

201 West 103rd Street
Indianapolis, Indiana 46290

FIRST EDITION

International Standard Book Number: 0-672-30863-0

Library of Congress Catalog Card Number: 95-74783

99 98 97 96 4 3 2 1

Interpretation of the printing code: the rightmost double-digit number is the year of the book's printing; the rightmost single-digit, the number of the book's printing. For example, a printing code of 96-1 shows that the first printing of the book occurred in 1996.

Composed in AGaramond and MCPdigital by Macmillan Computer Publishing

Printed in the United States of America

Publisher and President Richard K. Swadley
Acquisitions Manager Greg Wiegand
Development Manager Dean Miller
Managing Editor Cindy Morrow
Marketing Manager John Pierce
Assistant Marketing Manager Kristina Perry

Acquisitions Editor
Christopher Denny

Development Editor
Angelique Brittingham

Production Editor
Johnna VanHoose

Copy Editors
Marla Reece, Gregory Horman

Technical Reviewers
Kurt Barthelmess
Steve Schafer

Editorial Coordinator
Bill Whitmer

Technical Edit Coordinator
Lynette Quinn

Formatter
Frank Sinclair

Editorial Assistants
Carol Ackerman
Andi Richter
Rhonda Tinch-Mize

Cover Designer
Tim Amrhein

Book Designer
Gary Adair

Copy Writer
Peter Fuller

Production Team Supervisor
Brad Chinn

Production
Stephen Adams, Michael Brumitt
Brian Buschkill, Jama Carter
Charlotte Clapp, Kim Cofer
Mike Dietsch, Jason Hand
Sonja Hart, Ayanna Lacey
Michelle Lee, Brian-Kent Proffitt
Bobbi Satterfield, SA Springer
Susan Van Ness, Mark Walchle
Todd Wente, Colleen Williams
Jody York

Indexer
Cheryl Dietsch

I would like to dedicate this book to my two brothers, Tim and Steve, for their perseverance in making it through the trials and tribulations of life and their unquenchable spirit.—DJO

This book is dedicated to my wife Ashlyn for her patience and support, and to my dog, Ada, who I hope forgives me for occasionally missing the evening walk.—SLG

To my beautiful and wonderful wife Sharon, who stands by me and supports me in all my dreams and endeavors, and my beautiful daughters, Alyssa and Amber who bring joy and laughter to my life; Sharon, Alyssa and Amber, I love you all—you're the best! Also to my brothers, Greg, Jeff, and Doug, and their families, who believed in me and supported me with encouraging words during this effort. To my relatives, Uncle Cliff, Aunt Mary, Joe and De De, my Grandmother, "BaBa" Gill—your words have been nothing but encouraging through this effort. To my extended family Lou & Pat, Elaine, Donald and Linda, Amber, and Scott, most of whom have seen me go from computer illiterate to where I am today; thanks for your patience and support over the years. To my friends and business associates, Anne and Paul Talbot and Bert and Jo Vanderlans, whose teachings, encouraging words, and unwavering belief in me over the years and during this project have meant a lot to me and made it possible for me to accomplish many things including this one. To all the other family and friends too numerous to list, but who have made a positive impact on my life. Finally, to my departed parents who always provided for, and supported, my brothers and me the best way they knew how; I wish they could be here to see this work. This is for you, Mom and Dad.—STB

Overview

Appendixes

Contents

Week 2 at a Glance 213

Acknowledgments

I would, as always, like to acknowledge the overwhelming contribution of love and support from my wife Diane, and my daughter Nathalia. They have made my life the wonder that it is. For the contributions of my life-long friend (and prior co-author) Robert Shaw, and the many hours he spent with me on the phone, discussing the finer points of "authoring." For the fabulous work of Jim and Darlene, my parents, in being the rudder that kept me on course.—DJO

I would like to thank Warren Grobman for being my first line editor and providing a wealth of advice.—SLG

To all the authors' families and friends for tolerating their mental and physical absence during this effort.

For the fine work of our acquisitions editor Chris Denny, who has the precarious job of cracking the whip with the precision of a surgeon.

For the speedy work of Angelique, Johnna, and Marla in making sure that the reader could actually read the book when we were done. We felt like we were in English class again, but it was worth it!

For technical editing by two people we knew only as TechEd and SAS. Thanks for ensuring the accuracy of the material, and for your graceful, yet poignant, comments.

To the folks at Stirling Technologies for providing the tools and support regarding the InstallShield product.

About the Authors

Dan Osier

Dan Osier is a senior systems programmer with Intel Corporation working on session encryption technology. Dan has also worked as a software engineer for the Air Force designing real-time aircraft simulations. After receiving his masters in Software Engineering, Dan taught graduate and undergraduate Computer Science classes at his alma-mater. Dan has been writing software since the age of 12 and had his first contract programming job at the age of 15. In his spare time, Dan enjoys playing classical guitar music. Dan's first love is virtual reality (it's so much cooler than reality), with Doom II running a distant second. You can reach Dan on CompuServe at `72724,710` or `72724.710@compuserve.com`.

Steve Grobman

Steve Grobman has used computers to do everything from creating three-dimensional models of goldfish retina to providing manufacturing support applications at IBM. He currently develops client/server, Internet, simulation, and security applications for a major semiconductor company. Away from work, Steve has done substantial work with computer graphics, multimedia, and artificial intelligence. You can reach Steve on CompuServe at `102202,3325` or `102202.3325@compuserve.com`.

Steve Batson

Steve Batson has worked with computer hardware and software for over 14 years. Steve gained an electronics background in the United States Air Force where he installed, repaired, and maintained a variety of electronic communications equipment. Steve then moved on to work for Intel Corporation where he currently works as a systems programmer/analyst supporting e-mail gateways and developing and supporting monitoring and maintenance process software applications in the company's Information Technology Organization. Steve got his start in computers doing hardware projects on a TRS-80 color computer (which many owners affectionately call "The CoCo"). Steve first learned to program in BASIC. Shortly after he joined Intel, Steve moved to IBM PC–compatible platforms where he went on to learn 8088 Assembler, Pascal, C, Visual Basic, and most recently, Delphi. Steve loves working with computers at work and as a hobby. He also enjoys older arcade games and occasionally tinkering with the old CoCo. While he loves the PC and all the new technologies that are available and spends most of his computing time on PC-related projects, one recent fascination is computer emulators (programs that allow the PC to run computer programs designed and written for other computers). He purchased an emulator that runs his old TRS-80 color computer software on his PC. "There is just this nostalgic warm feeling about the old classic computers," he says. Steve can be reached on the Internet at `sbatson@midtown.net`.

Introduction

About This Book

On these pages you find everything you need to use Delphi 2 to successfully create real, working windows applications. No prior knowledge of writing code is assumed. You will be taught how to use the visual programming tools to create a working application by Day 1. Each chapter explores features that you need to know to become proficient in Delphi 2.

Conventions

A Note box presents interesting pieces of information related to the surrounding discussion.

A Tip box offers advice or teaches an easier way to do something.

A Warning box advises you about potential problems and helps you steer clear of disaster.

A Type icon identifies Delphi code that you can type in yourself.

An Analysis icon identifies the explanation of the purpose and what was accomplished by the code presented earlier.

At A Glance

Week 1—Delphi Basics

On Day 1, you take a look at what Delphi is and how you can benefit from its RAD capabilities. RAD stands for Rapid Application Development. You get your feet wet in Delphi by going through a quick introduction as you touch on some basic programming topics common to all programming languages. In Day 2, you take a whirlwind tour of the IDE, Delphi's Integrated Development Environment. Days 3 and 4 come next where you get into some Object Pascal basics to give you the foundation you need to move on to Week 2 and beyond. On Day 5, you move on to the Project Manager and learn to stay organized as you develop applications. On Day 6, you take a look at some fundamentals of GUI (Graphical User Interface) design concepts to help you write windows applications that have the familiar standard “Look and Feel” that you have come to know and love. Week 1 finishes with an introduction to the concepts involved in Object-Oriented Programming on Day 7.

Week 1

Day 1

Overview of Delphi

In Day 1, you get an overview of Delphi 2 from a philosophical perspective. I offer you some insight into where the industry has been and what has driven the development of a tool as unique and powerful as Delphi. We breeze through some of the basics, and then write a quick application at the end to help you get your Delphi legs. In answer to the question this section poses, Delphi 2 is visual Pascal, and much more. Delphi 2 gives you the solid foundation of Borland's Object Pascal, plus the visual application building characteristic of products like Visual Basic. Delphi offers huge advantages over the competition, and can create some real productivity gains for the programmer.

Delphi is RAD, Man!

I may just sound like a gnarly teenager, but Delphi users mean more by RAD than just the fact that Delphi is a great product.

New Term The term RAD refers to Rapid Application Development. This is a term coined for a new breed of software development environments. In this new RAD world, programmers use tools that are more intuitive and visual. It is difficult to look at a piece of code that generates a window and visualize that window, as opposed to the ease of creating the actual window with a couple of mouse clicks.

In this new world of simpler, more visual interfaces, the first real player to show up was Visual Basic (hereafter referred to as VB). VB brought programming down from a mystical religion (only accomplishable by that guru in the back room that you feed Twinkies and Mountain Dew to), to something a mere mortal could handle. These new interfaces enable the software developer to "visually" construct the user interface with the mouse, rather than constructing it in code, and then having to compile and run the code just to see what it looks like! This is sort of like if the designers at Lamborgini cut the body molds for the Diablo (a new model) without ever making a clay model to first see what the end product should look like!

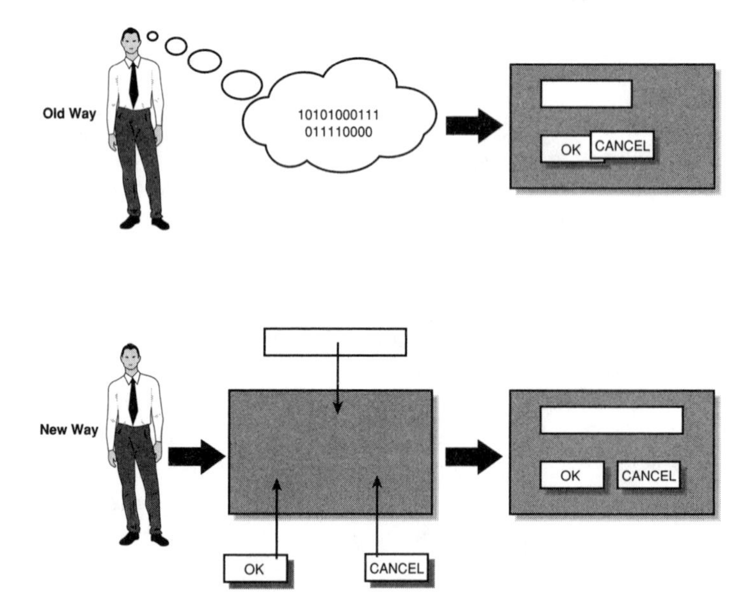

Figure 1.1.
The old and new paradigms.

Before we go too much further, I must mention that there is no substitute for a solid programming background. That guru in the back room more than likely generates better code with VB than my gardener. These RAD tools are only that—tools. A tool can be used for good or evil. I have seen horrible code written in VB, as well as code that brings tears of joy to my eye. To this end, I have included chapters on topics such as *object-oriented programming (OOP)* on Day 7, *GUI (Graphical User Interface)* design and database design on Day 6, which are the next steps toward being a well-versed software developer (that's YOU).

Although VB did well in the market and helped open the world of programming to us mortals, VB has also had its problems. The language itself did not really promote good design. VB lacked the mechanisms that promote highly structured, compact and well-refined code. It lacked the rigor of an object-oriented language (we will talk more about this on Day 7). VB even promoted bad programming (from our point of view) by enabling the developer to hack a quick solution and having "work arounds" for those pesky but good programming practices we should be observing. All three of this book's authors are good VB programmers (among other things); we have seen both sides of the fence (the VB/Delphi-OOP fence, that is) and feel we are finally standing back on the right side again.

Delphi is the next step in RAD development environments. It corrects most of the deficiencies found in VB, without adding too many new ones. We describe the strengths and limitations (there are not very many) of Delphi, and walk you through this new frontier. If you don't have goose bumps yet, you should. It's a great journey you're undertaking, with substantial rewards.

This Looks Like Visual Basic on Steroids!

We are not assuming that you have written code in any other language, but if you have written VB code in the past, you may look at the Delphi 2's development environment and say, "It's VB on steroids!". Well you're right! The Delphi developers have created a tool that may appear similar to VB 4 at first glance, but is in fact distinctly different (and superior to) the VB 4 environment. The IDE (Integrated Development Environment) is the portion of Delphi you see when you double click on the Delphi icon in Windows (you'll learn more in Day 2, "The IDE"). Although Delphi 2 bears a visual similarity to VB, the major difference between the two products is the language that exists "behind" the IDE. As I said earlier, the VB language tends to promote rapid development, rather than good development practices.

Delphi, on the other hand, uses Object Pascal as its foundation language. Borland's Pascal compiler (starting with Turbo Pascal 1.0) has been one of the fastest compilers in the business. Borland has added object-based extensions to the language to support good programming practices and more efficient code (get more done with fewer lines of codes). Object Pascal is a true object-based language with a rock solid compiler behind it.

The Benefits of Delphi

Several items have put Delphi head-and-shoulders above the competition. For those of you not familiar with VB, the MyApp.exe file that "is" your final VB application is not really a true executable. That .exe file is really compiled P-code. That means that MyApp.exe is really like a big macro or script file. A program called VBRUN300.DLL must accompany your .exe file in order to "run" that big macro. This is a serious nuisance; if you forget VBRUN300.DLL, or users erase the file because they do not think it is necessary, your application will not run.

When Delphi generates an .exe file it is a true executable. No support files are needed to make that .exe file run. This provides a cleaner application and one that is easier to distribute and maintain.

I attended the VBits '95 conference and saw a demonstration of the same application written in Delphi, VB, and Microsoft's Visual C++ (hereafter refered to as VC++). It was an interesting demo by Dan Appleman (the best VB developer ever; he walks on VB water—if you get my drift). He proved that a VB application could run just as fast as Delphi or VC++. The catch was, he spent hours optimizing the VB application, writing shared code, trimming to the core, just to get the VB application to run fast. However, the Delphi application was a quick throw-together with no optimization.

The point I am bringing up here is that Delphi provides an optimized compiler that gives you a fast application, without the programmer working harder to optimize the program than he or she did in writing the program in the first place.

Differences Between Delphi and Delphi 2

Although the Delphi 2 IDE may look pretty much the same (other than the Windows 95 GUI look), there are some major differences under the hood. Delphi 2 is capable of using OCX controls. If this is Greek to you, you're not alone. In the 16-bit world of Windows 3.1, Microsoft created the VBX. These were visual controls that were the building blocks of the VB RAD environment. These VBXs were added to the IDE, which placed them in a palette of tools that the developer could use. These controls served an important purpose. They were controls, such as buttons and text boxes, that provided visual feedback during the design process. This is what made the "visual" in Visual Basic. The VBX was really designed as a add-on. Bill Gates felt that the VB environment had to be extensible in order to be salable, and VBXs were the result.

The next generation of the VBX is the OCX. The OCX is the big brawny brother of the VBX. The VBX was a 16-bit afterthought. The OCX is a well-planned 32-bit OLE-based custom control. Although Delphi 2 enables you to add an OCX control to the tool palette (just as Delphi 1 allowed the addition of VBX), that is about all the attributes they share.

The OCX control is designed to work in the 32-bit world of Windows 95 and Windows NT. It enables you to "interact" with it the same way the VBX did. In that respect, their "behavior" is similar.

The OCX control is not the only way for you to use OLE in Delphi 2. Delphi 2 also allows you to create OLE automation servers and clients. These automation objects give you the flexibility of creating programs that perform tasks in the background and pass the results back to your application. These can be the work engines of your applications and can be shared between many applications running simultaneously. The OLE container control also provides the capability to put an OLE object in your application. An example would be including an Excel spreadsheet in your main form. This gives you the power of using an application's capabilities rather than having to reinvent them every time you write an application. These topics are covered in greater detail on Day 18.

NOTE

> Besides the OCX technology, Delphi 2, like Delphi 1.0, allows you to create native Delphi components and reuse them in all your projects. Where OCXs require you to distribute the OCX file along with your application, native components require no added files for distributing your applications. You learn how to write your own visual component on Day 20.

Another major boon for Delphi 2 is the ability to write multi-threaded applications. In the multitasking world of Windows 95 and NT, this is a necessary feature. As your applications become more complex, it becomes necessary to execute your application in separate pieces, each of which performs specific functions. These pieces are called *threads*. Delphi 2 supports the creation, use, and control of threads. I discuss these in greater detail on Day 8.

Delphi 2 has a significant performance advantage over Delphi 1.0 in the database area as well. With 32-bit drivers as well as a 32-bit executable, the execution speed is significantly better under Delphi 2. This helps Delphi 2 stomp on database front-end builders such as PowerBuilder.

What About This Delphi Client/Server? What's Up With That?

There are three different versions of Delphi: Delphi Desktop, Delphi Developer, and Delphi Client/Server (called CS from here on). These versions of Delphi offer different levels of connectivity with the outside world. Delphi Desktop comes with the ability to connect to dBASE and Paradox through the Borland Database Engine. The Developer Edition contains ODBC connectivity (for connecting any data source with an ODBC driver), and the CS Edition comes with SQL Links. The SQL Links product gives you high-speed 32-bit drivers for connecting to SQL server databases such as SyBase and Oracle.

The CS Edition is designed to compete with other client/server application development products. The main competition for Delphi CS is PowerBuilder. These products are typically used in a corporate environment to develop Windows-based front ends for network-based databases. I discuss much more about connecting to data sources on Day 13.

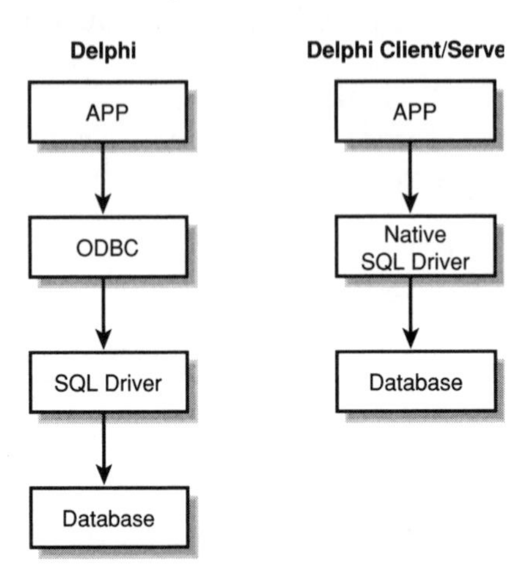

Figure 1.2.
Native database access with Delphi CS.

Another cool feature of Delphi CS is the visual query builder. If you have ever used Microsoft's Query or Access, you know the joys of building a data query by dragging and dropping fields onto a window, and playing connect the dots. This really helps those of us that are database illiterate. Delphi CS provides this little tidbit.

The last really cool thing about Delphi CS is the ReportSmith. In Day 16, you learn how to use this great report writing tool. In the Delphi CS edition, you get the SQL edition of ReportSmith, which can connect directly to SQL databases, as well as to local databases in Paradox, dBASE, and other database formats.

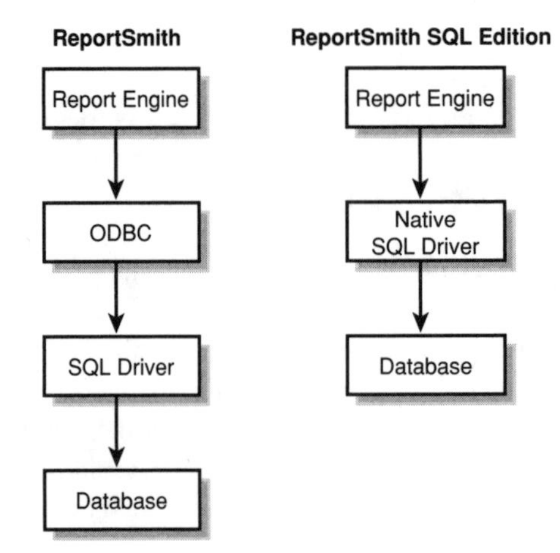

Figure 1.3.
SQL Server native access with ReportSmith SQL edition.

Delphi CS is meant to compete with other corporate-level database GUI builder front ends. It provides the same (if not better) features than other products costing more.

The VCL Replaces the VBX

Delphi also possesses its own native version of an VBX/OCX, called a Visual Component. A Visual Component (VC) is written in Delphi, and added to the Visual Component Library (VCL). The VCL is a repository of VCs that can be used by the developer to create Delphi applications. All the components in the VCL are displayed on the toolbar so they are easily accessible to the user.

The best thing about VCs is that you can construct your own (and you will on Day 20) and then add your new VC to the toolbar. This also promotes code reusability, a vital component in high productivity programming. The construction of a VC is also covered in the Component Writer's Guide help file that accompanies the Delphi 2 product.

Variables and Constants

For those of you who have done no programming before, a few concepts may be foreign to you. A *constant* in the programming sense is just that—constant. If you decide you are going to use the state tax in your program, you could type 0.0775 (7.75%) into all the formulas throughout your application. If the tax rate changes, you would have to go back and find every 0.0775 and change it to 0.08 (another new tax—figures!). This is miserable, not to mention that there is a high probability that you could make a typing error in the entry of 0.08 forty times in your application.

Constants to the rescue! You can define a constant, say `StateTax` to equal 0.08, and then use `StateTax` in those forty places. Now an important note is that constants cannot be changed during program execution. So, we could not ask the user for the new state tax and then place that user-defined value into `StateTax`. `StateTax` must be defined in code, and cannot be changed at runtime.

```
Const
StateTax = 0.08;
```

The idea of a constant is that the name (`StateTax`) is a direct substitute for 0.08. This means anyplace that you could have used 0.08 in your application, you can now use the constant name. It may look weird seeing `YourTax := YourPurchase * StateTax;` but it works.

That preceding line of code, `YourTax := YourPurchase * StateTax;` brings up the next interesting topic, *variables*. Do you remember your algebra classes in school? Those evil y=mx+b formulas. Remember the teacher saying, "It's easy, just solve the equation for y!"

Well, you were using variables then, so let's try it again. A variable is a placeholder for a value. Where constants remain the same throughout the execution of the program, a variable can be changed at any time.

If we defined a variable `FederalTax` as a Single number, that `FederalTax` variable is now capable of holding one Single number. The Single data type is a real number capable of representing a number between $1.5 * 10^{-45} - 3.4 * 10^{38}$. This type is big enough for our needs.

```
Var
FederalTax : Single;
```

The preceding declaration denotes that you have created a variable called `FederalTax` and that it is of type `Single`. Now in your program, you can get the user's input and place that input into the `FederalTax` variable.

```
FederalTax := {Put the user input code here};
```

The great thing about a variable is that we *can* change the value of `FederalTax` during the programs execution. Variables are a reusable asset. They are much more flexible than constants.

There is a dramatic difference between a constant and a variable, not only in functionality, but also in the use of each within the compiler. Because a constant is a substitute for a value, when you compile your application, Delphi goes out and simply un-substitutes all of your `StateTaxs` and replaces them with 0.08. This is done only in the executable that Delphi generates, and your source code is not altered. A variable is handled quite differently. Because the value of a variable can change during the program's execution, the application must allocate a place in memory for the value of that variable to be stored. It must have a memory location to store `FederalTax` in to remember it from one minute to the next and to hold the new value of `FederalTax` when it is changed during the program's execution. Constants and variables will be discussed in more depth in Day 3.

Procedures, Functions, and Events

When you first start writing programs, you will probably develop a bad case of von Neumann-ism. John von Neumann was the father of sequential computing. In the mindset he developed, everything happens sequentially from beginning to end, in a straight path. Let's look at how that mindset can be changed.

You have written a program that displays a hello world message on the screen three separate times. To write this program, you would probably write something similar to Listing 1.1. We have done it here in pseudocode, just to give you an idea of how it would work.

NEW TERM *Pseudocode* is an English-like interpretation of events that simulate or imitate the code. We use it in the listing to show the general form of a program without using the actual Object Pascal code.

TYPE

Listing 1.1. A simple on-screen message.

```
program Hello;

begin
{create the window}
{write "HELLO" to the window }
{destroy the window}

{create the window}
{write "HELLO" to the window }
{destroy the window}

{create the window}
{write "HELLO" to the window }
{destroy the window}
end.
```

This program writes "HELLO" to the screen three separate times. In case you did not notice, the program repeated itself a little. The program has the same bit of code three separate times. This way the programmer also had three times as many chances to make mistakes typing in the same bit of code. There must be a better way, and there is.

Procedures

A *procedure* is nothing more than a logical grouping of program statements into a single program block. That block of code can then be activated by executing a procedure call. Now for the English version of what I just said: If you take those three lines of code and put a wrapper around them, give a name to that wrapper, and then when you want to call those lines of code, you simply call that code block by the name you gave it. Look at the example in Listing 1.2.

TYPE

Listing 1.2. A simple procedure.

```
procedure SayHello;

begin
{create the window}
{write "HELLO" to the window }
{destroy the window}
end;
```

The lines of code are now in a `procedure SayHello` (our wrapper). Now when you want to open a window, print "HELLO" to the screen, and destroy the window you simply call `SayHello`. Look at your new program now, as shown in Listing 1.3.

TYPE **Listing 1.3. The finished program (using a procedure).**

```
program Hello;

procedure SayHello;
begin
{create the window}
{write "HELLO" to the window }
{destroy the window}
end;
begin
      SayHello;
      SayHello;
      SayHello
end.
```

As you can see, you can create the `procedure SayHello` once and then call it three separate times. There is less chance for error in the `SayHello` procedure because you only typed it once. You could also reuse this code by cutting and pasting the `SayHello` procedure into another application. Pretty slick, huh?

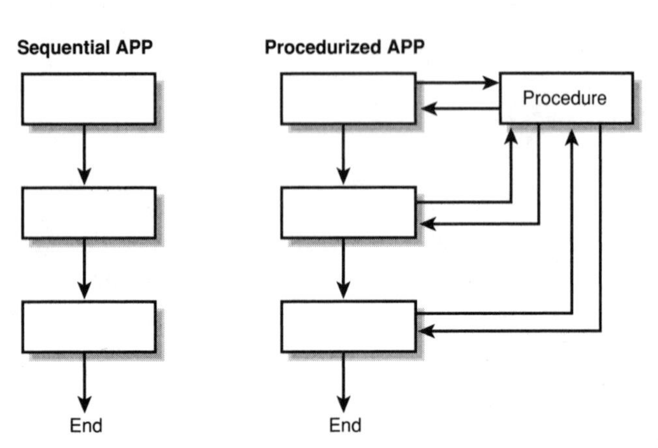

Figure 1.4.
Procedures and Code Reuse.

Functions

Functions are a slightly different beast. They are procedures that return a single value. Let's look at an example to illustrate. Take the equation y=cos(6). The cos (cosine) function takes 6 as its operand, calculates the cosine of 6, and then returns that value back to the equation. That returned value is then placed into the y variable. These are the same concepts learned in algebra. The concept of solving for y is a fundamental one. Notice that the cosine function

is called from within the mathematical expression. Yes, that's right. The great thing about a function is that the function call itself becomes the answer after the function call returns. So in your expression, the flow of events is as follows:

Original Equation: y=cos(6)

1. cos(6)
2. cos(6) function calculates the cosine of 6 and returns .99
3. The equation then is y=cos (with cos=.99)
4. y=.99

Functions are handy because you cannot call a procedure in the middle of an expression. "Why?" you ask. The main reason is a procedure can be set up to return multiple values as a result of the procedure call. Having multiple values in a mathematical expression wouldn't work very well. Functions are the practical alternative, because they are designed to return a single value.

Events

The last item in this section to address is an *event*. The entire concept of event-driven programming is described in Day 8, "Exceptions and Events," but let's just give you a flavor of what is to come. The method of single thread sequential programming has been transformed and improved upon in the world of Windows. Windows is a dynamic system that responds to events. For example, after you start Windows 95, it just sits there, right? It is waiting for something to happen. When you click the mouse on the Start button (on the task bar), a menu pops up. Windows has responded to a `mouseclick` event on the start button. This is what makes Windows development so challenging. Making sure that you are prepared for everything a user might do is a tall order. Day 8 helps guide you through this process.

Units—Reusable Code

Oh yes! Units are the greatest thing since sliced bread! Well, maybe a close third behind cellular phones, and Doom II. Anyway, *units* are a grouping of related functions and procedures. Just as you can group a series of Pascal statements and wrap them in a procedure or function, you can group those functions and procedures into the next "level" of wrapper, the unit.

Let's look at a sample unit that provides three functions, `SayHello`, `SayBye`, and `SayNothing`. The code is in Listing 1.4.

TYPE **Listing 1.4. A simple unit.**

```
unit SayStuff;
begin
procedure SayHello;
begin
{create the window}
{write "HELLO" to the window }
{destroy the window}
end;
procedure SayBye;
begin
{create the window}
{write "BYE" to the window }
{destroy the window}
end;
procedure SayNothing;
begin
{create the window}
{write "NOTHING" to the window }
{destroy the window}
end
end; {of unit SayStuff}
```

The only thing you have done here is to put three procedures into a common grouping called `SayStuff`. When you want to reuse this code in your new project, you simply tell your program to `Use SayStuff`. If that unit is in your path (in other words, if Delphi can find the `SayStuff` unit), then it enables you to call those three functions. Pretty cool, huh? You can create the wheel once and then use it over and over again. This looks pretty good after years of reinventing the wheel every time to write a new program. This is another way in which Delphi (and object Pascal) promote software reuse.

The Form

The heart of every Delphi Windows application is the form. You may have come to know the form as a "window." The window is that base object upon which the rest of the Windows environment is built. If you do not change the defaults, Delphi assumes that you have a form in every project and displays a blank one every time you start Delphi. You can, however, choose some of the desktop options in Tools | Options. You can save the position of your windows, as well as which code windows you had open last time. This is done on a project-by-project basis.

You may have seen the form in many of its different roles. Forms can exist both in the modal and modeless state. You have seen both I am sure. The modal window is one that stays on top of all other windows and must be closed before other windows can be accessed. A modeless window can be moved aside, and dealt with anytime. We will explore the creation of forms, in all their forms (yes, a pun), throughout the book. These are the foundation of a Windows application.

What Are Form and Component Properties?

When you hear about properties, what do you think of? Land? Do you think of the properties that a candle has while lit? When we speak of properties in the Delphi sense, it means the attributes a particular object has. A person for instance, has height, weight, eye color, and Social Security Number as attributes (among others).

In Delphi, all forms and all Visual Components (as well as OCXs) have properties, as well. A form (or window) has a size (height and width), a background color, a border, as well as less "visual" attributes, such as a name. We control the look and feel of these objects by changing or manipulating their attributes or properties.

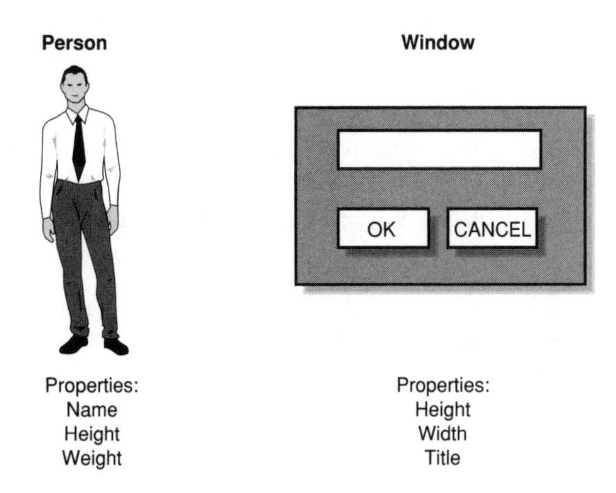

Figure 1.5.
Everything has properties.

An interesting example of a visual control would be one that controls a virtual reality headset. This headset would be similar to the ones found in many arcades today. This headset visual control would have some properties that would be quite interesting. A refresh rate (like a computer monitor), a screen resolution (maybe different for each eye to correct for your 20-50 vision), and so on. Then, while you execute your Doom VI program, you could constantly adjust the headset to the conditions of the game by changing the properties of the headset object. We will deal with properties at great length in this book, and you will come to see their usefulness.

A Simple Delphi Application

To get you on your way to being a Delphi developer, this section shows you how to construct your first Delphi application. I will assume you have already installed Delphi on your Windows 95 system. Follow these steps:

1. Run Delphi by selecting the Delphi 2.0 icon from the Start | Programs | Delphi 2.0 menu.
2. After Delphi starts, you should see a blank form titled FORM1. If this does not appear, you must select File | New Application from the Delphi main menu bar.
3. Choose the Standard tab from the Component Palette.
4. Click on the Button control.
5. Click on the middle of the form. A button should appear there.
6. Double click on the button. At this point, a code window should appear with the cursor sitting between a `Begin` and `End` line of code.
7. Enter the line of code:

```
Canvas.TextOut(20, 20, 'Delphi 2 makes Windows programming a breeze');
```

8. You have created your first Delphi application. Press the F9 key or choose Run | Run form the Delphi menu to compile and run your application.

You should see a window appear (that ever-present form we spoke about). The button you placed on the form should be there. Click it. You will notice that the phrase you entered in the `Canvas.TextOut` displays on the window. That is all the more difficult it is to create a working Delphi application. When you are done looking at your newly created application as it runs, press the close button on the window (the button with the X on it).

You can now do a File | Exit, and answer no when Delphi asks you if you wish to save changes to your project.

Summary

In this chapter, you have taken the first step toward understanding the Delphi environment. You have seen how RAD is more than just a teen slang, how VBX, OCX, and VCs are tools that you can use, and how VCs can also be created using Delphi. An overview of constants, variables, functions, and procedures started you on the road to understanding Object Pascal. You were given a primer to the world of event-driven programming, seeing how Windows 95 reacts to things around it. And last, you learned properties and what they mean to Delphi. The simple application you wrote will get more challenging as the book continues. Let's press on to Day 2 and talk about Delphi's IDE.

Q&A

Q Why do we need OCXs, as well as visual controls?

A The real issue here is extensibility. Delphi is great now, but what happens when we all get our virtual reality headsets? We would like to have a Delphi Visual Component for our VR headset control. By being able to add new functionality to Delphi in the form of toolbar add-ons, we extend the life and usefulness of the product.

Q I bought Delphi Client/Server. I have heard of "similar" products like PowerBuilder. How is Delphi different?

A Delphi Client/Server is really different in a number of critical ways. The sales brochures can tell you most of it. In my mind, there are two things that really stick out. Object Pascal as the base language really puts Delphi head and shoulders above the rest. If the foundation is solid.... Second is the speed. I have seen PowerBuilder applications running, and they seem visually slower. Delphi executables are faster and smaller (generally) than their PowerBuilder equivalents.

Workshop

The Workshop provides quiz questions to help you solidify your understanding of the material covered and exercises to provide you with experience. Please try to work through both before continuing to the next day.

Quiz

1. What are two benefits of using a RAD development environment as opposed to a regular compiler?
2. How do native Delphi 2 Visual Controls differ from OCXs?
3. What language are native Delphi Visual controls written in?

Exercises

1. Read the page in the introduction in the Object Pascal Language Reference Guide that describes a syntax diagram. Syntax diagrams are important to understand. If you cannot read them, it will be tough to look up a particular command or expression syntax to see how it works.
2. Create an application with two buttons and have the text from `button1` overwritten with some new text from `button2` (your new button).

Week 1

Day 2

The IDE

We have given you an overview of why Delphi exists, and why you are here. Now that you are here, let's see what's around you. The Delphi environment has been laid out in a very usable and organized fashion. The goal of this chapter is to familiarize you with Delphi's Integrated Development Environment (IDE). It also covers how to customize the IDE for your personal tastes and to help you organize your desktop and programming style.

New Term IDE, Integrated Development Environment, is an environment in which all the tools necessary to design, run, and test an application are present and well connected to ease program development. In Delphi 2, the IDE consists of a code editor, debugger, toolbar, image editor, and database tools, all of which operate in an integrated fashion. This integration gives the developer a set of tools that operate in harmony, and complement one another. The result is faster and more error-free development of complex applications.

The Basics

The first step is to start Delphi. When Delphi is finished loading, your desktop should look like Figure 2.1.

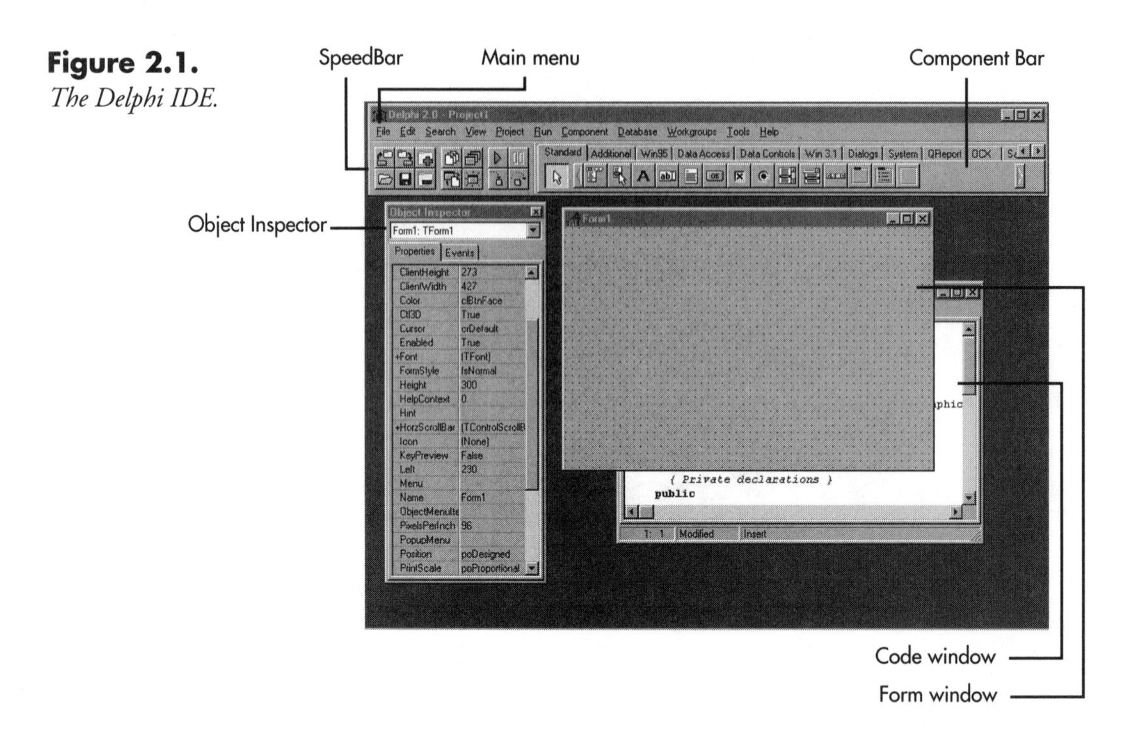

Figure 2.1.
The Delphi IDE.

If you do not have a window labeled Form1 in the middle of your screen, choose File | New from the Delphi main menu. The IDE is composed of several major pieces, and the Delphi menu bar is broken up into two major pieces.

SpeedBar

The *SpeedBar* shown in Figure 2.2 is designed to help you get to your most-used functions easily and quickly. The default setup gives you 14 of what Borland considers to be the most-used items. They are items that are also available from the Delphi menu, and are only put on the SpeedBar to speed your access to them. We will discuss each of these in detail when we cover the Delphi menu structure.

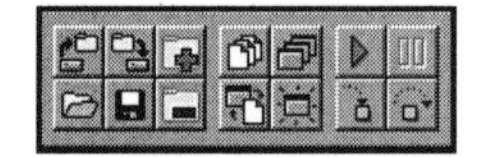

Figure 2.2.
The Delphi SpeedBar.

Component Palette

The component palette is the "visual inventory" of your Visual Component Library (VCL). It allows you to categorize your visual components into groups that make sense. By default, the components are grouped on functional lines, that is, with all the data access components together, and so on. These groupings or *pages* are denoted with labeled tabs. The default pages are

Standard
Additional
Win95
Data Access
Data Controls
Win 3.1
Dialogs
System
QReportOCX
Samples

The following icon represents the *pointer button.*

We will only describe the pointer button once because it is present on every component page. It is usually in the depressed position. This allows you to move about the forms and windows in order to manipulate the Delphi environment. When you select an item from one of the component pages, you find the pointer button is not depressed. This means you have entered a state in which Delphi thinks you are going to place a component onto a form. Once a component has been selected, placing that component onto a form is as simple as clicking on the form itself.

As a second method of placing the component onto the form, you can double-click the component, and it is automatically placed onto the form. If you select a component and then change your mind, you can simply press the pointer button, and you are placed back into Normal mode. Think of this button as a Cancel button for placing components. This pointer button is always present on the left end of the component palette regardless of what component page you have selected.

The following sections give a short description of each tab in the VCL. An entire chapter is dedicated to the VCL components, so we will defer the specifics of each component until then.

Standard Component Page

The Standard component page in Figure 2.3 is well named because it contains the items most necessary for a fundamental Windows application. These components are the core of most Windows applications in existence now. If you have other questions about the use of a particular component, click the component on the component bar and press the F1 key for help. One of my favorites is the `TPanel` control. This control allows you to give portions of your screen that 3D look by lowering or raising the inner or outer edges of the panel. This variety of edge treatments enables you to get creative and make a great looking application. Now look at few components Borland threw in to make your life easier!

Figure 2.3.
The Standard component page.

Additional Component Page

Now that you have seen the basics, let's move on to some cooler toys. The components on the Additional page (see Figure 2.4) provide some great features. These are some great add-ons to the standard palette. Don't take these components lightly; they could save you years of work. (Remember that when you are writing code, one hour of real-world time is equal to two months in programming time. At least it may feel like it.)

Figure 2.4.
The Additional component page.

Win95 Component Page

This page (see Figure 2.5) contains standard Windows 95 common controls. These controls are ones that you will find on most Windows applications. They help provide a common look and feel to all applications. They contain slider bars, progress meters, tab controls, and much more.

Figure 2.5.
The Win95 component page.

Data Access Component Page

The Data Access component page in Figure 2.6 contains a set of tools that enable you access to multiple data sources and destinations. With these tools you can natively connect your application to Paradox, dBASE, and InterBase databases, as well as connect (via ODBC) to

any database format that you have an ODBC driver for. These components are discussed in more detail on Day 13, "Databases in Delphi."

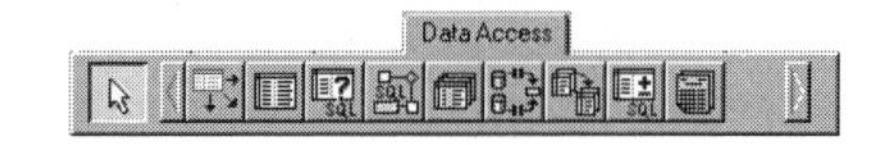

Figure 2.6.
The Data Access component page.

Data Controls Component Page

This page contains a number of components that enable you to control the content and flow of data from the data access controls. (See Figure 2.7.) This page also contains components that are called data aware. Data-aware components can hook their data input streams to the data output stream of particular data-access controls. This means your control (like a DBEdit control) could change its data automatically when a data-access component changes tables. These components are discussed in more detail on Days 13 and 14.

Figure 2.7.
The Data Controls component page.

Win 3.1 Component Page

The components in Figure 2.8 comprise the legacy components made available under Delphi 1. These components have been superceded by the controls on the Windows 95 page but are provided here for backward compatibility.

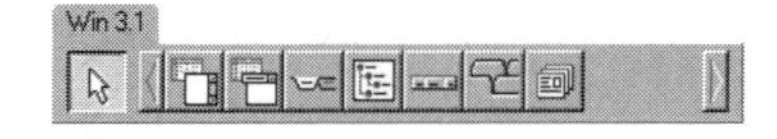

Figure 2.8.
The Win 3.1 component page.

Dialogs Component Page

The Dialogs component page shown in Figure 2.9 provides easy access to a number of standard Windows 95 dialog boxes. Did you really think you were going to have to rewrite the Open File dialog box you saw in Windows! No way! None of the components are interactive (or visual). This is because these components are nothing more than shells to Windows 95 system calls.

Figure 2.9.
The Dialogs component page.

System Component Page

This page holds some interesting components (as shown in Figure 2.10). Here you can find the OLE container control used to include an OLE server in your application, as well as DDE controls to enable your application to speak to other applications. Timer controls and even the media player (used on Day 11) are in this page as well. You will read more detail about these components on Day 9, "The Visual Component Library."

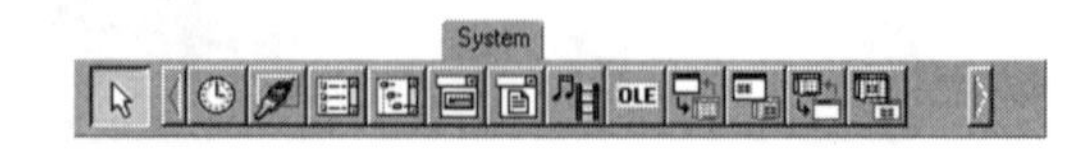

Figure 2.10.
The System component page.

QuickRpt Component Page

The Quick Report components shown in Figure 2.11 were added by Borland to provide a fast and easy way to generate simple reports without the overhead of ReportSmith. You learn more about these components on Day 16, "ReportSmith Fundamentals."

Figure 2.11.
The Quick Report component page.

OCX Component Page

You may have read that OCX technology was going to make VBXs obsolete, and it happened. These OCXs were provided to show how Delphi can interface to them. This author feels that native components are the way to go. They all compile into the executable and keep version control problems to a minimum. But there will be times when the power of OLE is needed, and when it happens, OCXs will come to the rescue. Read more about OCXs on Day 18, and see Figure 2.12 for the OCX component page.

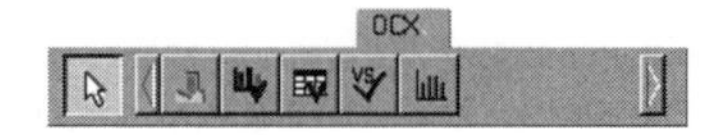

Figure 2.12.
The OCX component page.

Samples Component Page

The sample components shown in Figure 2.13 are provided to show you what kind of components you could write.

Figure 2.13.
The Samples component page.

Form

The basis of nearly every Delphi application is the form. You may know the form as a window: the kind of windows you see in Word, Paradox, or other Windows-based applications. In Delphi, the form is a foundation on which you place other Delphi components. It is the backdrop of your Windows application. A typical blank Delphi form is shown in Figure 2.14.

Figure 2.14.
A Delphi form.

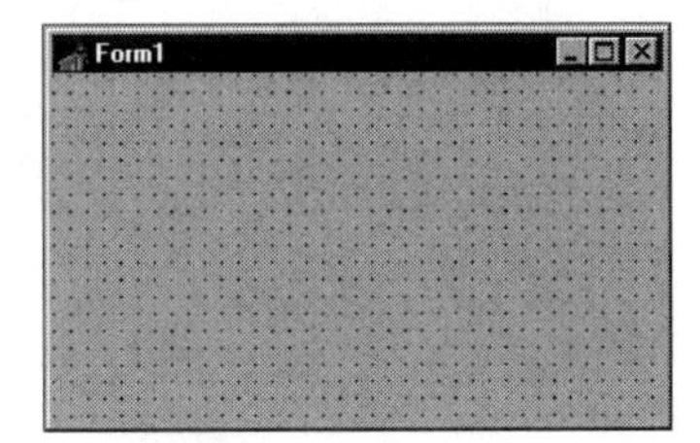

A form in Delphi has the same properties that you would find in any other Windows 95 window. It has a control menu (in the upper-right corner of the form), the title bar across the top, and the maximize, minimize, and close (or kill) buttons in the upper left corner of the form. You can hide these form attributes if necessary, or limit their use.

NOTE

> Although nearly all Delphi applications are based on the form, you can use Delphi to write Windows 95 DLLs in which a form may or may not exist at all in the DLL. Delphi can also be used to write visual components in which no forms are present.

Edit Window

One of the most essential pieces of the Delphi environment is the edit window. The edit window provides the mechanism for the developer (that's you) to input your Delphi code. The Delphi code editor is a great full-featured editor (as shown in Figure 2.15). With color syntax highlighting (which helps you spot those code errors quicker), Brief-style editor commands (Brief is the programmer's editor, for the purists), and the ability to "undo" from now until the cows come home!

Figure 2.15.
The Edit window.

Notice that the title bar displays the name of the file currently being viewed. Along the top of the window you see the tab(s) indicating the pages that are currently available. There can be many source files to Delphi applications, and the tabs help you navigate through them. Along the bottom of the edit windows are three other items of interest. At the left-most position is the line/column indicator. This helps you figure out where you are in the code. The second item is the modified indicator. When you start a new project, the code that Delphi brings up for you is not saved. You must save it yourself. Because this code has changed since the last time it was saved to disk (never), the word "modified" appears next to the line/column indicator. This always shows you if the code you see is not what is on the disk. The last item is the insert/overwrite indicator. This is a standard feature of most editors, showing you if you are inserting text or overwriting any existing text.

Object Inspector

You will find the Object Inspector essential to your work in Delphi. It provides an easy-to-use interface to change the properties of a Delphi item, as well as to control the events to which an object reacts.

Properties Tab

The properties portion of the Object Inspector (see Figure 2.16) enables you to look at and modify an object's properties. Click the empty form window, then observe the attributes present in the Object Inspector's Properties tab. An item of interest: When you see a property with a plus sign next to it, it means the property has subproperties nested beneath it.

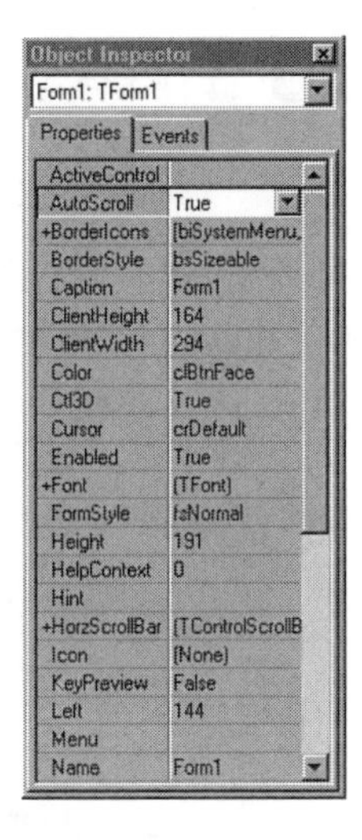

Figure 2.16.
Properties tab of the Object Inspector.

For example, notice that after you have selected the form, the Object Inspector has a `Font` property with a plus sign next to it. If you double click the `Font` property, it opens into more properties like `Color`, `Height`, `Name`, and others. This format is a clean, simple, and efficient means for changing an object's attributes.

Events Tab

The Events tab is the other half of the Object Inspector's life. (See Figure 2.17.) It relates to the programmer and different events that this object can respond to. For instance, if you need an application to do something special when the window closes, you can use the form's `OnClose` event to do that. Events and event-driven programming are covered in more detail in a later chapter.

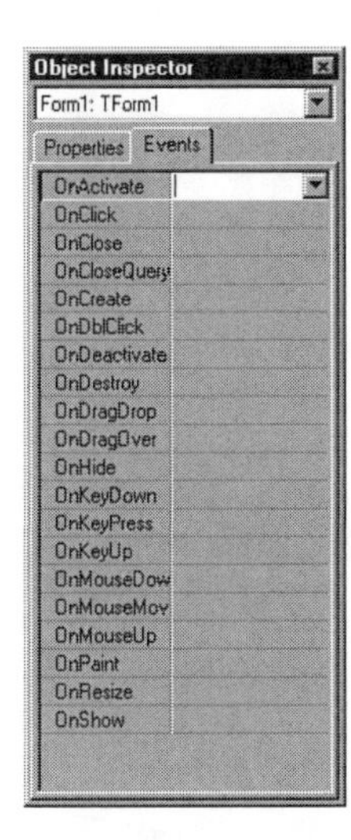

Figure 2.17.
Events tab of the Object Inspector.

Delphi Menu Structure

The Delphi menu structure gives you access to a rich set of tools that can aid you in more of that RAD development we all need. Take a look at each of the menu items in Delphi and what they do. We give only a casual glance to those items explained in detail in other chapters. See Figure 2.18 for the Main menu bar upon which all the menus discussed are based.

NOTE

> The actual menu items you see depends on the version of Delphi you have. The client/server version has some extras that we are covering here. Please refer to your documentation or call Borland if you need to know the differences with the three versions of Delphi 2.

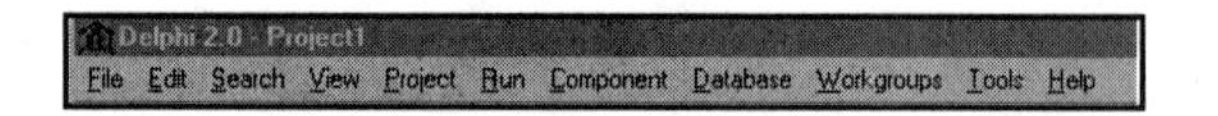

Figure 2.18.
The Main menu bar.

File

The File menu is the top-level menu for the items described in the following section, and is shown in Figure 2.19.

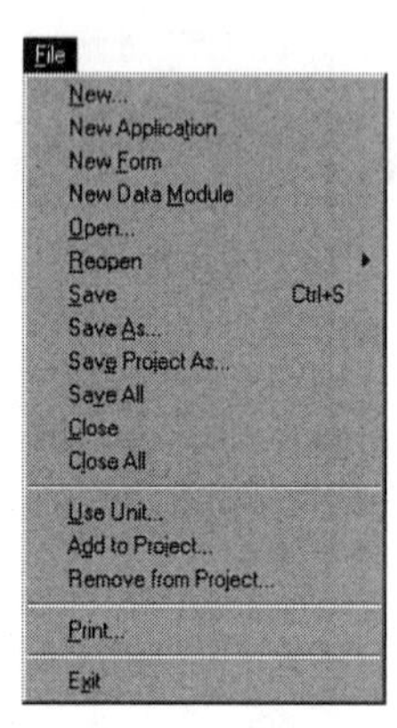

Figure 2.19.
File menu.

New

Selecting this menu option tells Delphi that you want to create a new object. This object can be any member of the object repository, including a new project.

New Application

Selecting this menu option tells Delphi that you want to create a new project. If you have no project currently open, or the project you have open is up to date (has been saved to disk in its current state), Delphi closes out the current project, and creates an entirely new one; this includes creating a new code editor window (with a newly created Unit1.PAS file), new Form object (Form1), and brings up the Object Inspector.

New Form

Selecting this menu option tells Delphi you want to create a new form. By default, the form is a blank form (as opposed to one of the special forms in the Object Repository).

New Data Module

Selecting this menu option tells Delphi you want to create a new *data module.* A data module is a non-visual form that you can use to house all your data controls. This is important because you need a form from which all the visual forms can get their data. This form serves that very purpose.

Open

Selecting this menu option tells Delphi you want to open an object. The object may be a code module, or an entire project. The directory in which Delphi first looks for a project is the working directory assigned during Delphi's installation.

ReOpen

This option is sort of like a favorites list that shows the last few projects or files you opened. This is just to make things faster for you.

Save

Selecting this menu option causes Delphi to save the current module you are working on.

Save As

Selecting this menu option causes Delphi to save your current module under a new name. You may want to do this if you are going to radically alter a piece of code. (If you are using the client/server version of Delphi, you can also use the PVCS version control software.) This allows you to keep revisions and go back to old code if you make a mistake in the new code.

Save Project As

Selecting this menu option causes Delphi to save your current project under a new name. This allows you to save an entire project off to the side for later use.

Save All

Selecting this menu option saves everything that is open—project files and all.

Close

Selecting this menu option closes the currently selected code module or associated form. If you have not saved your module in its current state, Delphi queries to find out if you want to save your changes.

Close All

Selecting this menu option closes the current Delphi project. If you have not saved your project in its current state, Delphi queries to find out if you want to save your changes.

Use Unit

Selecting this menu option puts a uses statement into your current code module for the unit you want to use. This is an easy way for you to include units in your code without manually inserting the unit name into the code.

Add To Project

Select this menu option to add an existing unit and its associated form to the Delphi project. When you add a unit to a project, Delphi automatically adds that unit to the uses clause of the project file.

Remove From Project

Select this menu option to remove an existing unit and its associated form from the Delphi project. When you delete a unit in a project, Delphi automatically deletes that unit from the uses clause of the project file.

Print

Selecting this menu option from the dialog box shown in Figure 2.20 prints the current selected item in Delphi. If that item is a form, Delphi prompts for printing options.

Figure 2.20.
Print Form dialog box.

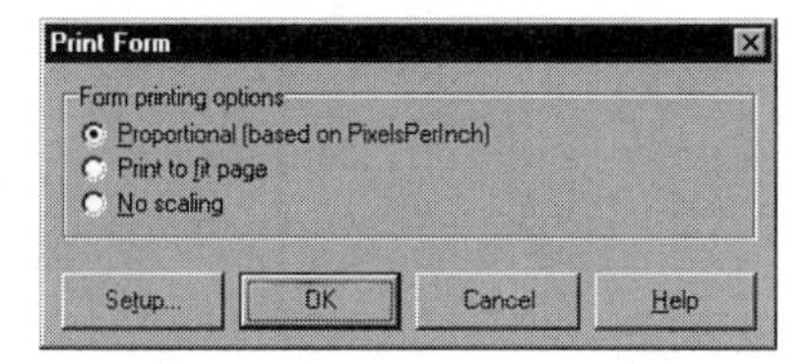

You choose how you would like the form printed. Proportional, fit to page, and no scaling are the options. If the item you have selected is a code window, you are given a number of print options including printing line numbers, printing selected text only (assuming you have selected a portion of text), as well as others as seen in Figure 2.21.

Figure 2.21.
Print Selection dialog box options.

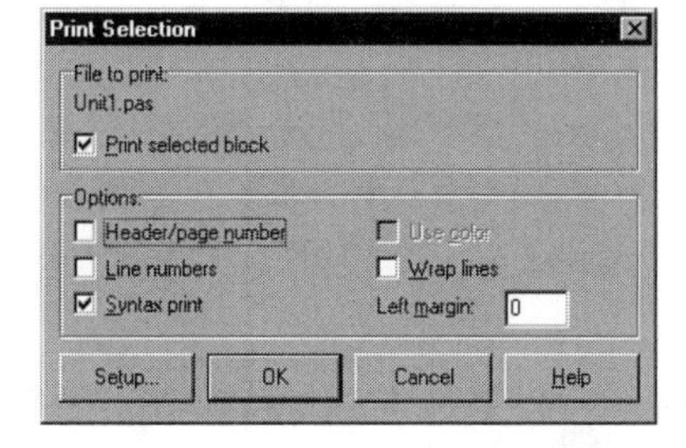

Exit

Selecting this menu option of course exits the Delphi IDE. If your project has not been saved in its current state, Delphi asks if you want to save the project before you exit.

Edit

The Edit menu is the top-level menu for the items described in the following section, and is shown in Figure 2.22.

Figure 2.22.
Edit menu.

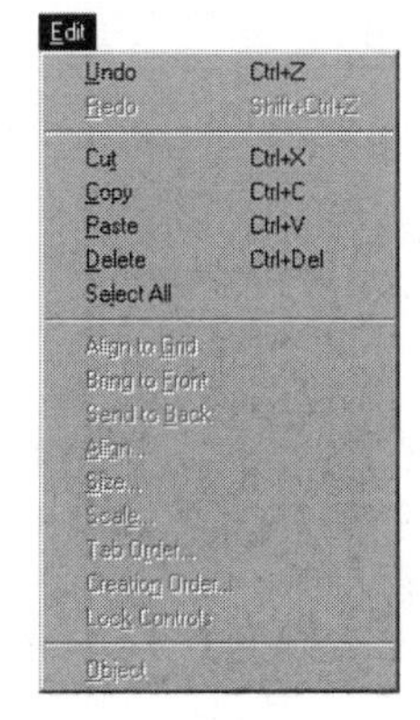

UnDelete/Undo

This menu option appears as either UnDelete or Undo depending on the previous action you have taken. If you have just deleted an object or some code using the Delete key, or using the Delete option on the Edit menu, this option reads UnDelete (seems logical, huh?). If you have just added code or components to your project, this selection reads Undo. This allows you undo your last additions (good for those of us who can't make up our minds).

Redo

Redo is the opposite of Undo. Redo backs you out of any number of Undos you have performed.

Cut

Selecting this menu option cuts the currently selected item (component(s) on a form or text) to the Clipboard. The selected item(s) are removed from the current form or code unit.

Copy

Selecting this menu option copies the currently selected item (component(s) on a form or text) to the Clipboard. The selected item(s) are *not* removed from the current form or code unit.

Paste

Selecting this menu option places the item in the Clipboard into the current form or code unit.

Delete

Selecting this menu option deletes the currently selected item. There is a reprieve though; the Undo feature can still undo any mistake you made with the Delete menu selection.

Select All

Selecting this menu option selects all components on the current form, or all code in the current unit, depending on which one you have selected.

Align to Grid

If you have the Snap to Grid option selected in the Options | Environment | Preferences tab, this menu selection is unnecessary. All components placed on the page automatically align themselves to the grid on the form. This menu selection is necessary if you want a component to align itself to the grid.

Bring to Front

This is like bringing the best pupil to the front of the class. When you place a number of components on a form, in some instances you layer them one on top of another. In this instance, you may find one component buried beneath another when it should be on top. By selecting the component and then selecting this menu option, the component is moved in front of all other components.

Send to Back

This has the opposite effect of the Bring to Front option. Choosing this moves the currently selected component(s) behind all other components. I would like to point out that windowed and non-windowed controls are considered separately. All non-windowed controls are "behind" all windowed controls.

Align

Selecting this menu option brings up the Alignment dialog box. (See Figure 2.23.) This option allows you numerous vertical and horizontal ways for aligning components on a form. You must select any items you want to align prior to choosing this menu option.

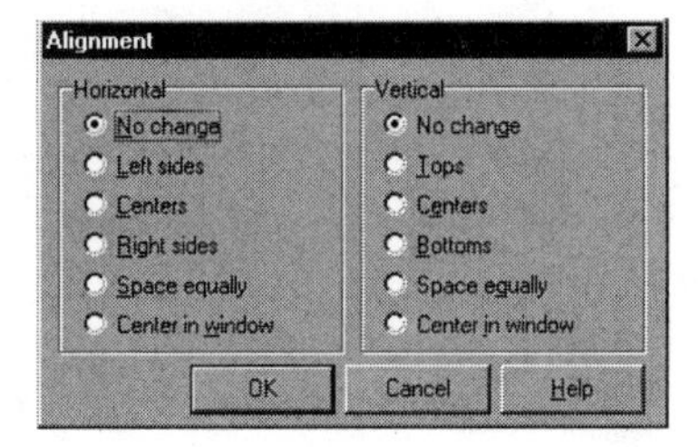

Figure 2.23.
Alignment dialog box.

Size

Selecting this menu option enables you to size a component to specific width and height. (See Figure 2.24.) If you select multiple components, this menu selection enables you to grow all components to the size (horizontal, vertical, or both) of the largest selected component on the page, or shrink all components to the size of the smallest one.

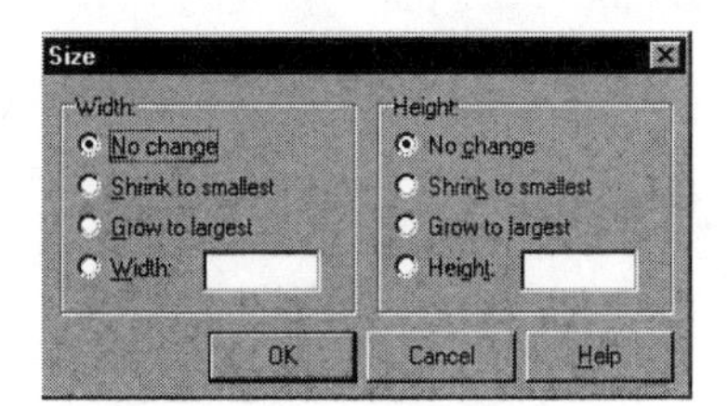

Figure 2.24.
Size dialog box.

Scale

Have you ever created a form only to realize that all the components on the form are too big or too small? Now, by using the Scale option, you can proportionally scale the entire contents of the form. Choosing a number over 100 increases the size, and choosing one under 100 decreases the size.

Tab Order

Delphi allows you to adjust the tab order by placing the names of all the components on the form into a list box and visually ordering them. (See Figure 2.25.) A much better method than having to set a property for each control manually.

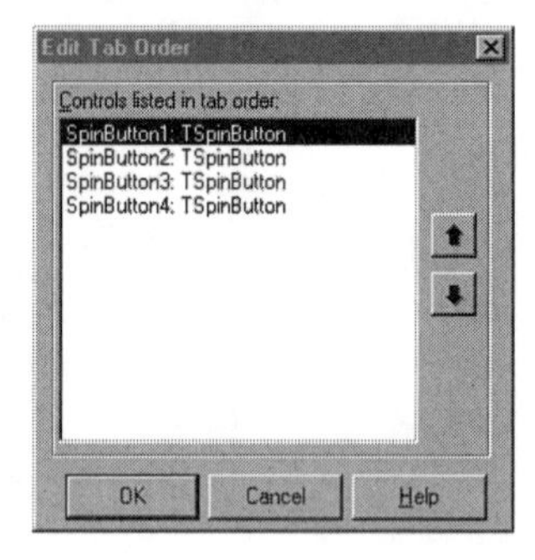

Figure 2.25.
Tab Order dialog box.

Creation Order

This option allows you to control the order in which non-visual components are created. Now you may ask yourself, "Why do I care?" The answer is simple; some of your non-visual components could rely on other non-visual components being present and initialized. If the components are not created in the right order, you have the cart-before-the-horse syndrome.

Lock Controls

Once you design your screen and place your controls, you probably will want to spend some time adjusting properties and events. It is very easy to perform a "mouse-misfire" and end up moving one of your precisely placed controls. If you select the Lock Controls option, all the controls are locked in place on the form. You can click on them to change properties and events without worrying about moving them. A truly handy option!

Object

This selection is used to convert or to edit an OLE object you have placed on a Delphi form. We discuss more about this on Day 18.

Search

The Search menu is the top-level menu for the items described in the following section, and is shown in Figure 2.26.

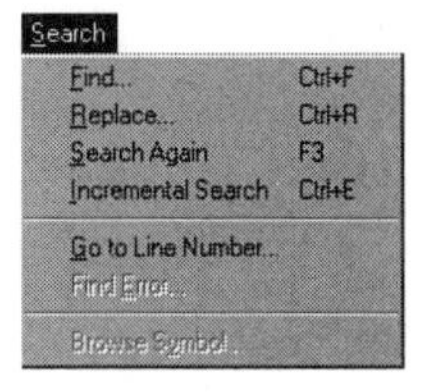

Figure 2.26.
Search menu.

Find

Delphi implements a first-rate find. The dialog box gives you numerous options in case sensitivity, search direction, and others. (See Figure 2.27.)

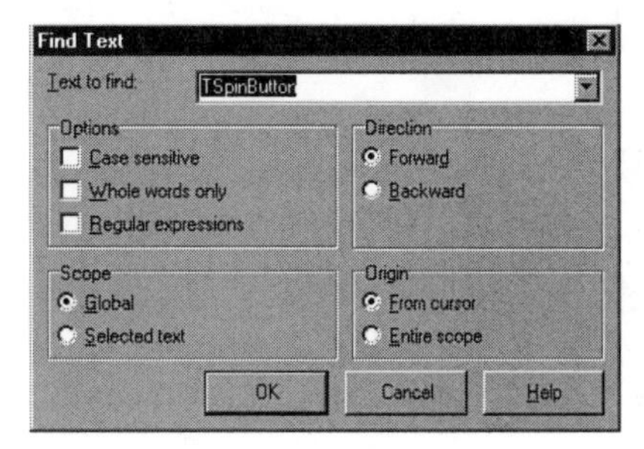

Figure 2.27.
Find Text dialog box.

Replace

The Replace dialog complements the Find dialog box mentioned previously. The difference being that the Replace dialog box has a Replace With edit box, so you can replace one piece of text with another.

Search Again

This option repeats the last find you did.

Incremental Search

This is one of the neatest options that Borland implemented in their editor. Select this menu item, then start typing a word. As Delphi finds the letters you type, it takes you to the first occurrence of that set of characters. A wonderful tool when you know approximately what you are looking for.

Go to Line Number

Selecting this menu option enables you to enter a line number (only up to the number of lines in your application), and it takes you there.

Find Error

Through this menu selection, you can enter the location of your last run-time error. Delphi then compiles your application, and stops at the line of code that would be at that location. It's also an easy way to track down run-time errors. This is a feature that has been part of Borland's Pascal for years.

Browse Symbol

After successfully compiling your application, you can actually look at any of the symbols in your application. For instance, if you have a form called Form1 in your application, you could type Form1 into the Browse Symbol dialog box, and Delphi brings up the Object Browser with that symbol loaded.

View

The View menu is the top-level menu for the items described in the following section, and as shown in Figure 2.28.

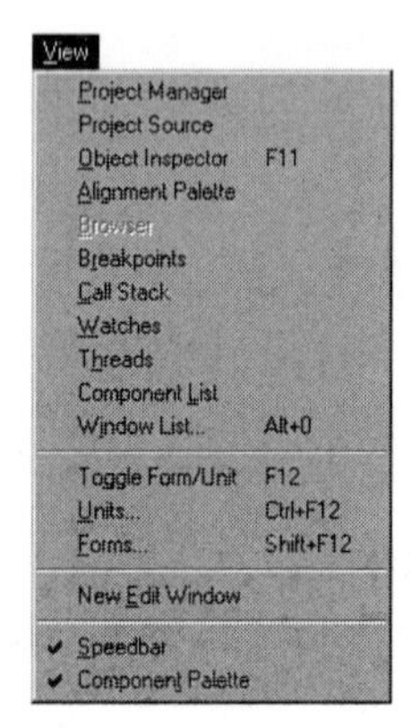

Figure 2.28.
View menu.

Project Manager

Selecting this menu option brings up the Project Manager window. This is explained in detail on Day 6.

Project Source

Under normal circumstances you do not see the main Delphi routine that starts the Delphi application. It is hidden because it is usually maintained and modified automatically. You can view the source code for this piece, but it is not advisable to change it unless you know what you are doing.

Object Inspector

Selecting this menu option brings up the Object Inspector, which we have described previously.

Alignment Palette

Selecting this menu option brings up the Alignment palette. The Alignment palette is the visual version of the Alignment dialog box under the Edit | Align menu option. You simply select the items you want to align, then bring up this palette and select what you want to do. The hints will help you if you don't understand what the picture is saying.

Browser

Selecting this menu option brings up a window that enables you to look at the inheritance model and the relationships of objects. This browser is a very powerful mechanism to help you understand the true object foundations of Delphi. It enables you to look at the hierarchy of Delphi's object model.

Breakpoints

Selecting this menu option brings up a Breakpoint List dialog box. It shows you all the current debugger breakpoints that have been set. If you right click the dialog box, a menu appears that enables you to add, modify, or delete debugger breakpoints.

Call Stack

Selecting this menu option brings up the Call Stack dialog box. This dialog box shows you the order in which procedures and functions are being called in your application. You would use this during a debugging session.

Watches

You can view and set watches to look at specific variables, or to create expressions based on these variables. When you set a particular watch, you can also specify how the result of your watch will be displayed. Delphi is smart enough to display your watches in their appropriate types (integer displayed as a decimal number, and so on).

Threads

Selecting this menu option displays a list of the current threads that are running. Because Windows 95 and NT are both multitasking kernels, you can launch several threads from your application to perform many tasks independently.

Component List

Selecting this menu option displays the Component List dialog box shown in Figure 2.29. You can search for components by name, or scroll through the list. If you see a component you want to use, simply press the Add to form button, and that component is placed on your screen.

Figure 2.29.
Component List dialog box.

Window List

Sometimes you may have a large number of windows open at the same time, and finding a particular one is difficult. When you select this option, a dialog box appears that lists all the windows Delphi has open. You can pick the windows you would like to see, and Delphi moves that window to the front.

Toggle Form/Unit

When you are working on a particular form, you may want to see the code associated with that form, or vise versa. This option toggles you between the two.

Units...

Selecting this menu option brings up a dialog box that shows all the units in your project. You can then click the unit you want to see, and the code editor displays that unit.

Forms...

This option operates the same for forms as the previous menu item did for code.

New Edit Window

Selecting this menu option opens a new edit window, leaving the old one in place. The current unit at the front of your edit window is displayed in the new edit window. This enables you to see two units of code at the same time.

SpeedBar

Selecting this menu option makes the SpeedBar visible if it isn't already.

Component Palette

Selecting this menu option makes the Component palette visible if it isn't already.

Project

The Project menu is the top-level menu for the items described in the following section, and as shown in Figure 2.30.

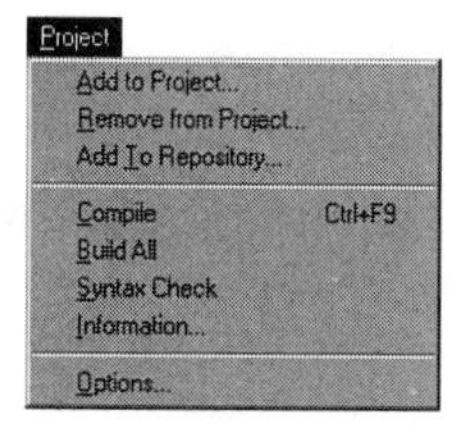

Figure 2.30.
Project menu.

Add to Project

Selecting this menu option performs the same function as File | Add To Project does.

Remove from Project

Selecting this menu option performs the same functions as File | Remove From Project does.

Add To Repository

Selecting this menu option adds the current form to the Object Repository. This enables reuse, and cuts your development by using common forms over again.

Compile

Selecting this menu option compiles all the files that have changed in your current project since the last executable you produced.

Build All

Selecting this menu option rebuilds all the components, units, forms, and everything regardless of whether they have changed since the last executable you produced.

Syntax Check

Selecting this menu option is great way to check to ensure correct syntax in your Delphi application without linking your program to an executable program.

Information...

Selecting this menu option gives you information about your Delphi compilation and information on memory consumption.

Options

Selecting this option brings up the Project Options dialog box, which enables you to set options for the compiler, linker, and directories.

Run

The Run menu is the top-level menu for the items described in the following section, and as shown in Figure 2.31.

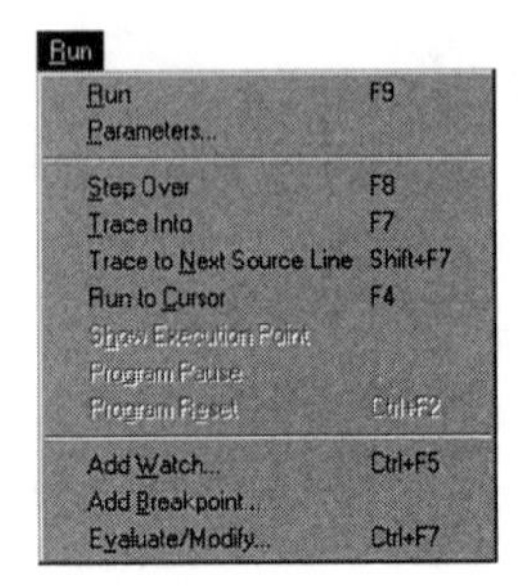

Figure 2.31.
Run menu.

Run

Selecting this menu option runs your Delphi application. If a current compilation does not exist, Delphi compiles the application first.

Parameters...

Selecting this menu option enables you to feed command-line parameters to your application. (See Figure 2.32.)

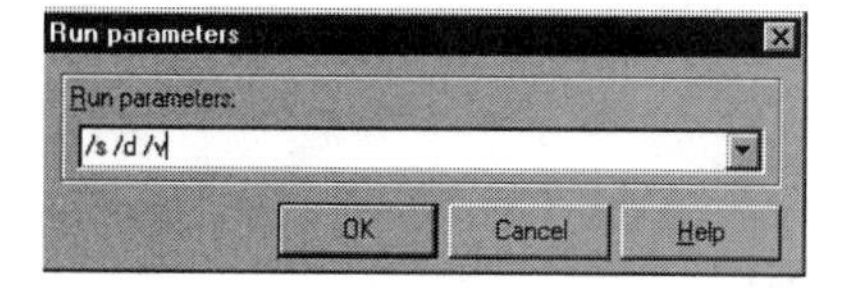

Figure 2.32.
Run parameters dialog box.

Step Over

Selecting this menu option executes your application one line of code at a time, but executes procedure and function calls as if they were one line of code. This comes in handy if you want to see how your application behaves but don't need to see the internals of each of the procedure and function calls.

Trace Into

Selecting this menu option also executes your application one line of code at a time, and it also executes procedure and function calls one line of code at a time. This comes in handy if you want to see all the gruesome details.

Trace to Next Source Line

Selecting this menu option allows you to see which line of code will be executed next. A complementary function to Trace Into.

Run to Cursor

Selecting this menu option executes your application up to the point in the source code where your cursor resides. At that point you may want to use the Watches window to evaluate a variable that you have doubts about.

Show Execution Point

Select this menu option if you have closed the edit window and are in the middle of single stepping through your application in debug mode. This brings you back into an edit window with the cursor on the next line of code to be executed.

Program Pause

Selecting this menu option pauses your application so that you can do some cool Watch stuff.

Program Reset

Selecting this menu option stops a paused program and releases it from memory.

Add Watch

Selecting this menu option is another way to add a watch to the watch list.

Add Breakpoint

Selecting this menu option is yet another way to add a breakpoint to the breakpoint list. It also toggles on a little red stop sign in your source code showing where the breakpoint is.

Evaluate/Modify

You cannot only look at variables, but you can (through this menu option) modify the value of a variable on-the-fly. In addition, you can also type in an expression based on variables from your application, and it will evaluate that expression for you instantly. Now if it would only do calculus...

Component

The Component menu is the top-level menu for the items described in the following section, and is shown in Figure 2.33.

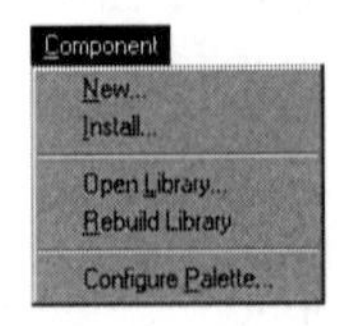

Figure 2.33.
Component menu.

New

Selecting this menu option brings up the component export that helps you create a new Delphi component. We discuss more about component creation on Day 20.

Install

This component enables you to add new Delphi visual components as well as new OCX files to the Delphi toolbar. You can view a list of currently installed components and use the Add button to add new ones.

Open Library...

If more than one programmer is using Delphi, you may want to save your own component setup. You each may use different components. You can save and load custom component libraries. This menu option allows you to open a library that has been saved previously.

Rebuild Library

This menu selection recompiles the existing component library. This can be done without closing Delphi down, but it must close any open work. This is why Delphi prompts you to save changes to any open project you are working on, before doing the actual rebuild.

Configure Palette

Selecting this option enables you to add or delete components from the VCL tabs. This gives you the option to avoid looking at components that you do not plan to use in your projects.

Database

The Database menu is the top-level menu for the items described in the following section, and is shown in Figure 2.34.

Figure 2.34.
Database menu.

Explore

Selecting this menu option fires up the Database Explorer. The Explorer enables you to browse database structures. You see more of this on Day 13.

SQL Monitor

Selecting this menu option gets the SQL Monitor program up and running. This monitor allows you to see queries going on as they are executed in your application. You will see this on Day 14.

Database Form Expert

This assists you in the creation of database entry screens. It works by opening the database you are going to hook to and then helps you to design the screens around the data in the files. We discuss more about this in the database chapters.

WorkGroups

The WorkGroups menu is the top-level menu for the items described in the following section and is shown in Figure 2.35. This menu item only exists if you have the Delphi Developer Edition (and have purchased PVCS separately) or the Delphi C/S version that comes with PVCS.

Figure 2.35.
Workgroups menu.

Browse PVCS Project

Selecting this option brings up the PVCS project window. Here you can browse the files that have previously been checked into the version control system.

Manage Archive Directories

This lets you manage the directory structure in your PVCS archives. You can create directories to support moving and organizing files.

Add ProjectX to Version Control

This is how you add the project that you are currently working on to the PVCS version control system.

Set Data Directories

Here you can set your public and private working directories.

Tools

The Tools menu is the top-level menu for the items described in the following section, and is shown in Figure 2.36.

Figure 2.36.
Tools menu.

Options

Selecting this menu option brings up the Environmental Options dialog box. This dialog box enables you to change the settings for the editor, the display, and the palette, as well as browser options. It even allows you to set autosave options so you don't lose your work.

Repository

This option allows you to view the objects that you could have placed here by using the Project | Add To Repository menu selection. Here you can add and delete them as well.

Tool

This options allows you to customize Delphi by adding tools to the Tools menu bar item. You can fire up your favorite applications from here if you want.

Image Editor

This menu selection brings up Borland's Image Editor that enables you to create bitmaps, icons, cursors, and more. This editor is a quick and easy way to fulfill your graphical design needs without going out and purchasing a separate product.

Database Desktop

Selecting this menu option brings up the database desktop (a product of Paradox 7), which we go into on Day 13.

Help

The Help menu is the top-level menu for the items described in the following section, and is shown in Figure 2.37.

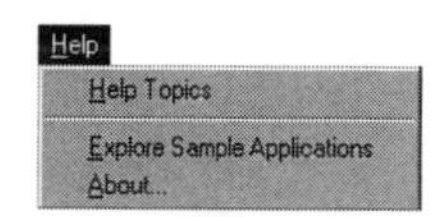

Figure 2.37.
Help menu.

Help Topics

Selecting this menu option gives you the main Delphi 2 help file in Windows 95 help format. All search capabilities are in the help engine, so no extra menu selections are needed.

Explore Sample Applications

This menu selection allows you to look at some of the demo applications that come with Delphi 2.

About...

Selecting this menu option shows you the version number of the Delphi software. If you want to be amused, while this window is up hold down the Alt key, and type **DEVELOPERS**. See what happens.

Customization

To customize Delphi to the way you work, there are several things that you can change. The three areas are listed in this section.

SpeedBar

You can add to or delete items from the SpeedBar by right-clicking the SpeedBar and selecting configure from the popup menu. This allows you to customize the SpeedBar to suit your personal needs.

Component Palette

The Component palette can also be customized by right-clicking the Component palette and then choosing configure from the popup menu. This brings up the same dialog box as if you had selected Options | Environment | Palette tab. This enables you to add, rename, or delete a tab, and add to the component palette.

Edit Window

The Edit window itself can also be customized by using the Windows 95 convention of right mouse clicking on the Editor window, and choosing properties. Here you can change everything from the syntax and color highlights to the actual keystrokes the editor uses. The editor supports Brief-style editor commands (Brief is a commercial editor). Changes to keyboard mappings and smart tabbing are just a few of the ways you can make the editor work for you.

Summary

In this chapter we have taken a look at the Delphi Integrated Development Environment (IDE). Now you may have wondered why we went through this in sort of a laundry-list style. Well, it's simple. In order for you to fully utilize the Delphi toolset, you need to know what

tools are available. As we explore Delphi throughout this book, I will show you the different tools and options, and how to use them more completely. After you finish the quiz and exercises, we will move on to the next chapter and talk about Object Pascal!

Q&A

Q How do I manage all these windows I have up?

A Sometimes I wonder that too. The best thing to do if you are doing lots of software development, is get a big monitor. To us, a 17-inch monitor is the minimum to really stare at all day long. (All three of the authors of this book actually have 21-inch monitors. We're called monitor snobs.)

Quiz

1. What is syntax highlighting?
2. How do you add a new VC or OCX control to the toolbar ?

Exercises

1. Run the tutorial and go through all the lessons.
2. After the tutorial is complete, go back and try to re-create some of the exercises they did. (See how well you watched.)

Week 1

Day 3

Object Pascal, Part I

Now that you have seen how Delphi's IDE can help you, let's look at the language that is the foundation of all that you do—Object Pascal. Object Pascal has a long and distinguished heritage starting as Turbo Pascal 1.0. Throughout its evolution, Turbo Pascal has come to be known as one of the richest languages (not to mention fastest compilers) in the business. When Borland later introduced the object-oriented extensions to Turbo Pascal 5.5, a new generation of compiler was born. What you see in Delphi 2 today is the culmination of years of effort to create the perfect language. In this chapter, you will look at the fundamentals that make up the language. You will then continue the study of Object Pascal on Day 4, "Object Pascal, Part II."

NOTE

You can enter the code listings in this Day and the next by following these steps:

1. Start Delphi 2.
2. If a new project is not automatically opened, choose File | New Project from the Delphi 2 menu.
3. Choose Project | Options | Linker and check the Create Console Application checkbox, then press OK. This tells Delphi that the application you are creating is not a windowed application, but a "DOS window" type of application.
4. Choose View | Project Source. The actual master source of the project becomes visible in the code editing window. Although you usually don't edit this code, in this case, you will replace this code with your own listing. This is a simple way to create a program.
5. When you run the program it appears in a window of its own. To close the output window, select Alt+F4, or click the X on the upper-right corner of the output window.

An Object Pascal Reference Manual comes with Delphi 2, which explains all the concepts covered here and more. We thought by including Day 3 and Day 4 that this book would provide an overview, or "Readers Digest" version of the reference manual. In learning Object Pascal, a different view or wording can sometimes make the difference between confusion and understanding. Enjoy!

Constants

As we briefly talked about on Day 1, when you start programming, you find that some of your programs require you to use the same value over and over. An example would be a point-of-sale program. You would probably have the local sales tax rate in your application several times. Now this is not a problem, you simply put 0.075 (7.5%) in your application five times. The problem is when they change the tax rate. You have to remember to change it in five places. This also means that you have a high probability of missing a change or making a typo on your 0.075.

That's where constants come in. Constants are nothing more than a name for a value you use in your program. In the example, the name `TaxRate` would be easier to use than the number

0.075. Constants are declared in the `const` section of your application. Here is the new declaration.

```
const
   TaxRate = 0.075;
```

This constant declaration serves several purposes. First, it makes the number easier to remember. If you see 0.075 in the middle of a code listing, you may not remember what that number represents. Second, it is much easier for someone to maintain your code. The odds are that you (the creator of the application) will not be the maintainer of that code. If someone else goes into your code to change the tax rate (another new tax), then seeing the `TaxRate` constant is much more intuitive than seeing 0.075 in five or more places. So, the two main reasons for using constants are readability and maintainability.

TIP

It is important that your variable and constant names be as descriptive as possible. Identifier names can be any length, but only the first 63 characters are recognized. An identifier name's first character must be an underscore or a letter. Subsequent characters must be letters, numbers, or an underscore.

Constants in Action

Constants can take many forms and encompass many types of data.

```
const
   MyName = 'Joe Smith';
   Age = 32;
   Wage = 6.50;
   Address = '1400 West Third Street';
```

The first constant, `MyName`, is an example of a string constant. In Delphi 2, everything between the single quotes, including the spaces, is part of `MyName`. In the second example, you are setting `Age` equal to the integer value 32. In the third example, you are setting `Wage` equal to the real number 6.50, and the fourth is another example of a string value.

Let's look at the lifespan of a constant. Remember the previous example of `TaxRate = 0.075`. In this scenario, when you tell Delphi 2 to compile your application, Delphi 2 looks at your constant declaration of `TaxRate = 0.075` and then goes and finds every occurrence of `TaxRate` in your application and replaces it with `0.075`. The trick is that it does this during the compile only and does not change your source code. So, you see that constants are really for your benefit only, not Delphi's. Delphi 2 knows that your constant declarations are simply a big substitution table!

Now that you have seen what a constant is, let's look at something that is not so constant.

Variables

You have seen how constants can be useful in replacing a piece of data that you use over and over again in your application. The problem with a constant is that its value cannot change during the execution of the program. So constants have to remain—constant! Their usefulness is limited to things that will not change. The problem is, how many things in this world stay constant besides death and taxes!

Variables to the rescue! A variable is similar to a constant in that it is a name given to a value. However, there is a big difference. The value of a variable can change during the program's execution. The value can vary! These names make real sense, don't they? A variable must be defined to be a certain *type.*

Let's look at the different types of data in Delphi 2. In the last couple of paragraphs, we referred to `real`, `integer`, and `string`. These are some of the data *types* available. Let's look at them in more detail.

Simple Data Types

The form that data takes plays an important role in how you perceive that data. If your friend asks you for the time, you do not tell them 2,345,567 seconds past midnight on 1/1/1970, you say 11:30 a.m.

The point is that the form data takes is very relevant to understanding the data. It can make the difference between understanding and confusion. In the programming sense, the way data is entered and saved has another implication. With a finite amount of memory in a computer, it is essential that you do not waste memory. For instance, if you are trying to store the number 10, you would not place it in a memory location that is big enough to hold 1,999,999,999. This would be a little wasteful. If you did this many times (mismatched data and where the data is stored), you could burn up a lot of memory. To decide how much storage to allocate, you also need to look at the possible range of values that a variable may have.

Types also relate to another concept. The Object Pascal language is known as a *strongly typed* language. This means that Pascal ensures that data of various types can interact with each other in a very well-structured way. This strong typing ensures that your Delphi 2 application does not try to add your age to your name and place the result in your telephone number! These types of things are much easier to do in less rigorous languages. The joke is, "Strongly typed languages are for people with weak minds." I disagree. Strongly typed languages help to ensure that your application does things right. It limits the programmer to what he should do, not what he could do. Let's look at the different types of data, and what Delphi 2 uses them for.

Integer Types

The integer data type is used to represent whole numbers (integers, as you learned in math). There are several different `integer` types (in other words, types that are capable of storing an integer value). Table 3.1 shows these types and their ranges.

Table 3.1. Integer data types.

Type	Range of Values	Bytes of Memory Required	Signed (Can hold a negative number)
`Byte`	0–255	1	No
`Word`	0–65535	2	No
`ShortInt`	–128–127	1	Yes
`SmallInt`	–32768–32767	2	Yes
`Integer`	–2147483648–2147483647	4	Yes
`Cardinal`	0–2147483647	4	No
`LongInt`	–2147483648–2147483647	4	Yes

Notice that the different integer types have dramatically different storage capabilities. Also note that everything comes with a price. The amount of memory that is required goes up with an increase in storage capacity. This is a good time to mention memory sizing and terms.

Memory space is counted in bytes. One byte can hold eight bits of information. A bit is a binary `1` or `0`. This means that the integer type `Byte` requires one byte, or eight bits, of memory to store its data. This is `0000000` to `11111111` binary, which is zero to 255 in decimal. Is this as clear as mud or what? It will become more clear as you move on.

Integer is one of two generic types in Delphi 2. *Generic* types are those that are affected by the particular CPU or operating system the compiler is implemented on. Under a 32-bit operating system such as Windows 95, the generic types take their respective storage capacities based on the OS.

Integers in Action

Let's look at a simple example of how to use an integer type. The code in Listing 3.1 shows you how to define three variables, `Pay`, `OverTimePay`, and `TotalPay`.

Listing 3.1. Integer demo program.

```
program MyIntegerDemo;

uses
  Forms;

var
  Pay : Integer;
  OverTimePay : Integer;
  TotalPay : Integer;

begin
  Pay := 500;
  OverTimePay := 100;
  TotalPay := Pay + OverTimePay;
  WriteLn ('The Total Pay is $', TotalPay);
Readln {To keep the window from closing until you press enter}
end.  {MyIntegerDemo}
```

In this example, you are declaring three variables of type `integer`, assigning numeric values to `Pay` and `OverTimePay`, and then adding `Pay` and `OverTimePay` together and placing the resulting value into `TotalPay`. Lastly, you use the `WriteLn()` procedure to send the output to the screen.

Real Types

The next logical step is to investigate the real data types. These real data types are designed to hold a number that has a fractional part. In the integer code sample (Listing 3.1), you assumed that your paycheck would be in even dollars. This is rarely the case. In the real world, you get paid dollars and cents, and you therefore need data types to mimic the real world. This gets back to our discussion on using the correct data type for the job. You can choose from several varieties of real data types, as shown in Table 3.2.

Table 3.3. Real data types.

Type	Range	Bytes of Memory Required
`Real`	$\pm 2.9 * 10^{-39}$ to $\pm 1.7 * 10^{38}$	6
`Single`	$\pm 1.5 * 10^{-45}$ to $3.4 * 10^{38}$	4
`Double`	$\pm 5.0 * 10^{-324}$ to $1.7 * 10^{308}$	8
`Extended`	$\pm 3.4 * 10^{-4932}$ to $1.1 * 10^{4392}$	10
`Comp`	-2^{63} to 2^{63-1}	8

3

The range of values variables of these types can hold is staggering. If you can generate a number that overflows $1.1*10^{4392}$, you're doing better than me.

NOTE

> The `Comp` type is really a big integer, not a real number. The reason it is included in this table is that it is implemented in the same "style" as the floating point types. It is really a 64-bit integer.

Reals in Action

Now that you know what real data types are, let's use them in a sample program. You can now revise your pay program to make the scenario more realistic. Look at Listing 3.2.

3

TYPE **Listing 3.2. A simple program using real types.**

```
program MyRealDemo;

uses
  Forms;

const
  TaxRate := 0.0075;

var
  Pay : Single;
  OverTimePay : Single;
  GrossPay : Single;
  NetPay : Single;

begin
  Pay := 500.55;
  OverTimePay := 100.10;
  GrossPay := Pay + OverTimePay;
  NetPay := GrossPay - (GrossPay * TaxRate);
  WriteLn ('The Total Gross Pay is $', GrossPay);
  WriteLn ('The Total Net Pay is $', NetPay);
Readln {To keep the window from closing until you press enter}
end.  {MyRealDemo}
```

You have made this application more like real life. You now have a `GrossPay` variable that stores just that. The `NetPay` is now the result of `GrossPay` minus the percentage of taxes defined in `TaxRate`. Notice that you have used the constant `TaxRate` as you defined it in the previous discussion of constants.

NOTE

When possible, use `Single` or `Double` data types instead of `Real`. `Reals` are slower (they are not a native type for the floating-point unit in the processor, so every operation requires conversion) and either use more storage or provide less precision than `Single` or `Double`.

The Currency Type

A new data type that warrants some discussion is the Currency type. Up to now in most languages, the developer has had to use a Real data type (of one sort or another) for representing monetary values. Delphi 2 now provides a Currency type specifically for that use. This type is a floating point type that is assignment-compatible with all other floating point types, including the `Variant` type discussed later. The Currency type has a precision of four decimal places, and is stored as a 64-bit integer (where the four least significant digits represent the four numbers to the right of the decimal place.

Currency Type in Action

You can rewrite your program MyRealDemo (Listing 3.2) to use the `Currency` type for monetary items. It should look like the code in Listing 3.3.

TYPE **Listing 3.3. A simple currency demo program.**

```
program MyCurrencyDemo;

uses
  Forms;

const
  TaxRate := 0.0075;

var
  Pay : Currency;
  OverTimePay : Currency;
  GrossPay : Currency;
  NetPay : Currency;

begin
  Pay := 500.55;
  OverTimePay := 100.10;
  GrossPay := Pay + OverTimePay;
  NetPay := GrossPay - (GrossPay * TaxRate);
  WriteLn ('The Total Gross Pay is $', GrossPay);
  WriteLn ('The Total Net Pay is $', NetPay);
Readln {To keep the window from closing until you press enter}end.  {MyRealDemo}
```

You may ask, "Why should I use this? What does it do for me?" Those are fair questions. The `currency` type provides two main benefits:

- The Currency type has a greater precision for holding large numbers.
- The Currency type is used in the `CurrencyField` and other components. It is compatible with database types representing money.

This type will be used more throughout the book.

Boolean Types

The Boolean data type is one of simplest and most used types around. Variables of this type represent a logical quantity, for example `TRUE` and `FALSE`. Knowing this, you may wonder why Table 3.3 lists five different Boolean types. The answer is "compatibility." In some instances, Windows requires a Boolean value that is one word in size. Instances such as these are when other Boolean types can be of use.

Table 3.3. Boolean data types.

Type	Range	Bytes of Memory Required
`Boolean`	Preferred 1 Byte Boolean	1
`ByteBool`	Byte-sized Boolean	1
`Bool`	Word-sized Boolean	2
`WordBool`	Word-sized Boolean	2
`LongBool`	Double word-sized Boolean	4

The last thing we will mention about the Boolean type is its use. Think of anything that is a YES or NO, TRUE or FALSE, ON or OFF. Any of these situations can be represented with a variable of the `Boolean` type.

NOTE

If you use a `ByteBool`, `WordBool`, or `LongBool` in a place where a `Boolean` type is required, Delphi 2 will now generate code so that all non-zero values of variables of this type are converted to `1` (`TRUE`). This enables you to use the types nearly interchangeably. Another way that the compiler keeps us rolling ahead.

Booleans in Action

Boolean types can be used for a great number of things, as we mentioned earlier. Listing 3.4 is a sample program in which you play with various aspects of Boolean variables.

TYPE **Listing 3.4. A simple boolean demo program.**

```
program MyBooleanDemo;

uses
  Forms;

var
  OKtoGo : Boolean;
  MyFlag  : Boolean;

begin
  OKtoGo := FALSE;
  MyFlag := not OKtoGo;

  WriteLn ('OKtoGo flag is set to ', OKtoGo);
  WriteLn ('MyFlag is set to ', MyFlag);
  WriteLn ('These two flags logically or'ed is  ', OKtoGo or MyFlag);
  WriteLn ('These two flags logically and'd is  ', OKtoGo and MyFlag);
Readln {To keep the window from closing until you press enter}
end. {MyBooleanDemo}
```

One of the most important things to note is that variables of type Boolean can accept the `and`, `or`, and `not` operators. This gives you additional flexibility as a developer.

Listing 3.4 shows how to create two variables, `OKtoGo` and `MyFlag`, both of type Boolean. These variables are the assigned a value; `OKtoGo` is set to `FALSE`, and `MyFlag` is set to the opposite of `OKtoGo`, `TRUE`. The output shows the user the value of both variables, and then logically `or`s and `and`s them (on-the-fly in the `WriteLn()` statement) on the way to the screen. Although this example is fairly simple, it illustrates the use of the `Boolean` type in a real application. You will use this type much more in the coming days.

Character Types

The `Char` type is probably very familiar to those of you who have programmed in C or C++. The `Char` data type was designed to store one character only. A character is one byte in length. If you do your math you will see that 2^8 (one byte) is 256 different characters that could be placed into a variable of type `Char`. If you look in the ASCII chart in Appendix B of this book, you can see that there are ASCII characters from 0 to 255 (computer stuff usually begins counting at zero, not one).

One of the things that is new for Delphi 2 is the addition (or really the redefinition) of the character types. Type `Char` is now the equivalent of the type `ANSIChar`. `ANSIChar` is still an 8-bit ANSI character. A third character type, `WideChar`, gives you a full 16-bit character type. Now you may ask why you need three different character types. The answer is "compatibility." Delphi 2 supports the Unicode standard, as shown in Table 3.4. The `WideChar` data type is the result of that support. A Unicode character uses all 16-bits of the `WideChar` type. If you place a normal `ANSIChar` value into a variable of type `WideChar`, the high order byte will be zero, and the ANSI character is stored in the low-order byte. Although Windows NT is fully Unicode compliant, Windows 95 is not. If you are writing applications that are going to be used on both, be sure to use the `SizeOf()` function and do not assume that characters are only eight bits.

NOTE

> At press time, Borland has defined the `Char` data type equivalent to the `ANSIChar` type. It was hinted that `Char` may be switched to be equivalent to the `WideChar` type. This would mean that all programs that use the `Char` data type, would default to being Unicode compliant.

Table 3.4. Character data types.

Character Type	Size in Bytes	What It Can Hold
`ANSIChar`	1	1 ANSI Character
`WideChar`	2	1 Unicode Character
`Char`	1	Currently equal to `ANSIChar`. In future versions of Delphi 2 may be equal to `WideChar`.

You may have noticed that many things in Delphi 2 are equal to the ANSI definitions now but are poised to move to their Unicode equivalent. As the industry moves away from Windows 3.1, and as Windows 95 and Windows NT eventually merge into one product (Microsoft's prediction), the world of 32-bit NT will arrive. When that happens, software developers will need a development environment that supports Unicode in all its glory. By that time (if not earlier), all the data types in Delphi 2 will be Unicode compliant. It all fits pretty well, doesn't it?

Character Types in Action

For a example of how the character type works, look at the code in Listing 3.5.

TYPE **Listing 3.5. A simple character demo program.**

```
program MyCharDemo;

uses
  Forms;

var
  Answer : Char;
  Question : Char;

begin
  Question := 'A';
  Answer := 'B';
  WriteLn ('Question is ', Question);
  WriteLn ('Answer is ', Answer);

  Answer := Question;
  Question := #66;

  WriteLn ('Question now is ', Question);
  WriteLn ('Answer now is ', Answer);

  Readln {To keep the window from closing until you press enter}

end. {MyCharDemo}
```

There are several points of interest here. After declaring two variables of type `Char`, `Answer` and `Question`, you assign each of them a value. Your assignment statement assigned the literal character `'A'` to `Question` and the literal character `'B'` to `Answer`. After writing those out to the screen, you pull a fast one. You then assign the value in the `Question` variable to `Answer`. You can do this because both variables are of the same type.

The piece of this that may look funny is the line:

```
Question :=#66;
```

Remember that a variable of type `Char` can hold one character only. If you look up ASCII character number 66, you will find the letter "B." You can use the `#` sign to tell Delphi 2 that you wish to use the decimal representation of a character, rather than the character itself. The character data type is very useful and will bring you into the next type of interest, the `String` data type.

String Types

The String data type tends to be a little more useful than the `Char` data type. The String data type in Delphi 1 was a concatenation of up to 255 individual characters. Another term for this is an array of characters. Delphi 2 is quite different in how it handles strings. Let's look at the four string types available in Delphi 2 (see Table 3.5).

Table 3.5. String types.

String Type	Length	Element It Holds	Null Terminated
`ShortString`	255	`ANSIChar`	No
`AnsiString`	up to ~3GB	`ANSIChar`	Yes
`String`	either 255 or up to ~3GB	`ANSIChar`	Yes or No
`WideString`	up to ~1.5GB	`WideChar`	Yes

Delphi 2 now contains long string support. This support is enabled by using the `$H+` compiler directive. This directive is on by default. When this directive is used, a variable of the `String` data type in Delphi 2 can hold a string of nearly unlimited length (about 3GB).

Once again, Borland has given the developer the option to remain compatible with Delphi 1.0 or move ahead. The type `String` is by default (`$H+` on) equal to the type `AnsiString`. The `AnsiString` type is a null-terminated string that is dynamically allocated. The real benefit of a variable of this type is the dynamic allocation of that variable. As you place longer strings into this variable, Delphi 2 reallocates the memory for that string. If you plan to change the length of your string greatly, you can also use the `SetLength()` function to allocate the appropriate memory required for your variable. The other advantage of using the `AnsiString` type is that it is already null terminated. This means you do not have to use the old `StrPCopy()` type commands to convert between Pascal style and null-terminated strings.

You may ask, "Why null-terminated strings?" The answer again is "compatibility." In most of the calls to system routines, such as the `Win32 API`, calls need to be passed null-terminated strings. With the old style Pascal string (now called `ShortString`), it was not null terminated and required conversion before used for a API call.

Delphi 2 stills maintains compatibility with Delphi 1 by offering the `ShortString` type. This gives you the equivalent of the old type `String` in Delphi 1. You can still define a string of specific length, even when the `$H+` directive is invoked. See the following example:

```
{$H+} {Long strings are now turned on}

var
   MyNewString : String; {This is a null terminated, dynamically allocated
                          string}
   MyOldString   : String[20];  {By qualifying the length of this string, Delphi
                                 2}
                                {automatically makes MyOldString a type
                                 ShortString,}
                               {with a max length of 20 characters.}
```

Delphi 2 VCL components now use the `AnsiString` type for all properties and events parameters. This simplifies your interactions with VCLs and APIs to make them more uniform in the way they behave. This helps your applications work and play well with others (sort of like kindergarten).

String Types in Action

Let's use a couple of strings to get a feel for how they work. Look at the program in Listing 3.6.

TYPE **Listing 3.6. Simple string demo program.**

```
program MyStringDemo;


uses
  Forms;

var
  LastName : String;
  FirstName : String[5];
  NewFirstName : String[30];

begin
  LastName := 'Smith-Mistier';
  FirstName := 'Susan';
  NewFirstName := 'Angelica';

  WriteLn ('First name is ', FirstName);
  WriteLn ('Last name is ', LastName);

  FirstName := NewFirstName;

  WriteLn ('The changed first name is ', FirstName);

Readln {To keep the window from closing until you press enter}
end. {MyStringDemo}
```

You have defined a variable `LastName` of type String. Because you have not specified a length, you will get an `AnsiString`. The variable `FirstName` you have defined as a String of length five (the `5` in the `[]` bracket denotes the string's length), which is automatically converted to a `ShortString[5]`. This string now holds a maximum of five characters. And finally, `NewFirstName` has been defined as a String of length 30, also converted to `ShortString` automatically.

Now there is a problem with your code. Can you spot it? Look at the line:

```
FirstName := NewFirstName;
```

The output should also tell you something. In the end, when you wrote out the `FirstName` to the screen for the second time, her name was Angel, not Angelica. Why?

The answer is in the definition of the variables. Remember that you defined `FirstName` as `String[5]`. This means that it can only hold five characters. When you took the contents of `NewFirstName` (which was eight characters long) and placed it into `FirstName` (which can only hold five characters), it put as much in as possible and truncated the rest. Remember that computers do what you ask, not what you want. The obvious answer is to define both of them as type String and use the `AnsiString` dynamically allocated capability. These variables would then hold anything you put into them.

The last tip to give you about String data types is how to empty them, although you have probably figured it out by now. If you want to empty the variable `NewFirstName`, you would write the following line of code:

```
NewFirstName := '';
```

By setting `NewFirstName` to an empty set of quotes, you are saying, "Set this variable to an empty string"; pretty easy, huh?

Data Structures

So far, the types of data we have looked at are used to store a single value, whether it is an integer, real number, or Boolean value. Now you are ready for the big time. Data structures represent a grouping of related data items that resides in memory. This grouping of items can be processed in its individual pieces (or items), although many operations can also be performed on the data structure as a whole. Object Pascal gives you type declarations that enable you to "roll" your own data structures from simple data types. You will explore three different data structures: arrays, records, and sets. In the next sections, you will learn how and why they are used, and what benefits they provide.

NOTE

> A `String` data type falls into both categories depending on your point of view. If you view the data in the string as one entity, it is a simple data type. If you view a string as an array of characters (see arrays below), then it is a data structure.

Arrays

Arrays are a wondrous tool. They provide a way for you to associate a single variable name with an entire collection of data. You can move the entire array around in memory, copy it, and so forth—all by referencing a single variable name.

If you wish to process a single element of the array, you identify it by the name of the array with the element being processed; that is, `Names[2]` would identify the second element of the `Names` array. The real benefit of the array is reuse. With a single variable, if you put a value in, the old value is written over. In the case of an array, you can store each new value in an array element for use later. This preserves the old values as well as the new ones. Each array element is stored in a separate memory location and is unaffected by its neighbor.

As stated earlier, you identify which element of the array you wish to deal with by using the array subscript. This subscript "fingers" the item in the array. Look at the array definition in Listing 3.7.

TYPE **Listing 3.7. Simple array demo program.**

```
program MyArrayDemo;

Uses
  Forms;

type
  MyArrayType = array [1..5] of Real;

var
  PersonScores : MyArray;

begin

  PersonScores[1]:=55.6;
  PersonScores[2]:=79.7;
  PersonScores[3]:=42.2;
  PersonScores[4]:=100.0;
  PersonScores[5]:=34.9

WriteLn (PersonScores[1]);
WriteLn (PersonScores[2]);
WriteLn (PersonScores[3]);WriteLn (PersonScores[4]);
WriteLn (PersonScores[5]);

Readln {To keep the window from closing until you press enter}

end. {MyArrayDemo}
```

In this scenario, you have created a data type called `MyArrayType`. Using this data type is no different than `Integer`, `Real` or any of the simple types, except that you created it yourself.

NOTE

> Those who say programming is not a creative process are wrong. If nothing else, just dreaming up cool variable names takes a lot of thought!

A variable of `MyArrayType` would be able to hold five `real` values. The `[1..5]` part of the type definition means that there will be five elements, numbered from one to five. You may think this is pretty obvious, but you could have an array of five elements labeled `[6..10]`. Although this seems a little weird, it could be done.

You then load up the elements of the array with data. Because the array holds real values, you assign a specific element in the array (`array[item]`) a real numeric value. Notice how you have to load each element of the array separately. This is necessary because each element is truly independent, although the entire data structure is referenced through one name (`PersonScores`).

To show you how an array could be used, let's take a couple of examples in Table 3.6.

Table 3.6. Sample array uses.

Sample Statement	What It Is Doing
`WriteLn ('First score is ',PersonScores[1]);`	Displays the value of `PersonScores` array, element 1, which has a value of 55.6, in a string of output text to the screen.
`Total := PersonScores[2] + PersonScores[5]`	Adds the values of elements 2 and 5 (79.7 and 42.2) and places the result in a variable named `Total`.
`Total := Total + PersonScores[4]`	Adds element 4 (100.0) to the `Total` variable.
`PersonScores[5]:=PersonScores[3] + PersonScores[1]`	Takes the third and first elements of the PersonScores array and places the sum into element number 5.

These are just a few examples of how arrays are used. Now it's time to get spatial.

Multidimensional Arrays

Just as in real life, arrays are often used to store a matrix of data. Look at a spreadsheet. A spreadsheet is nothing more than a two dimensional array. The cells can hold data, just like an array.

You can define multidimensional arrays as well. Think of these as nothing more than a map to get to your data. If you have ever played Bingo, you know that they call out using coordinates such as B-7 and D-3. In an array, the same principle applies. When you define your array type, you need to tell Delphi 2 what the "matrix" looks like. It is a grid of 3 by 3 cells, like a tic-tac-toe board. See Listing 3.8 to see how you dimension (or define) a two-dimensional array.

TYPE Listing 3.8. Simple array demo program.

```
program MyTrippyArrayDemo;

uses
  WinCrt;

type
  SuperArrayType = array [1..3, 1..3] of char;

var
  SuperArray : SuperArrayType;

begin
SuperArray[1,1] := 'X';
SuperArray[2,2] := 'X';
SuperArray[3,3] := 'X';
SuperArray[3,1] := 'O';
SuperArray[1,3] := 'O';

WriteLn (SuperArray[1,1], ' ', SuperArray[2,1], ' ',  SuperArray[3,1]);
WriteLn (SuperArray[1,2], ' ', SuperArray[2,2], ' ', SuperArray[3,2]);
WriteLn (SuperArray[1,3], ' ', SuperArray[2,3], ' ', SuperArray[3,3]);

Readln {To keep the window from closing until you press enter}

end. {MyTrippyArrayDemo}
```

Judging from the output on your screen, who won the tic-tac-toe game? This program is really not much different from the one-dimensional array program. You still need to create a type that defines what your array will look like. The difference is in the array type definition itself. You need to define the limits in two dimensions now. Think of it as length×width, or length×height, row×column, or anything else that will get you thinking spatially.

The definition `array[1..3, 1..3] of char` means "Please define an array that has dimensions of three cells wide (labeled 1, 2, and 3), by three cells in length (labeled 1, 2, and 3), and let each cell hold a piece of data of type `char`." With the type defined, you create a variable, `SuperArray`, of that type. You can now start loading values into the array. Since you have to specify each cell to load into it, you must use the Battleship B-2, D-5 method. You identify the row and column of the array that should be modified. By saying `SuperArray[1,1] := 'X'`, you are saying "Please take the character `'X'` and place it into the array `SuperArray` at row 1,

column 1." After you fill several of the cells in the array with Xs and Os, the WriteLn statements dump the whole tic-tac-toe board out to the screen.

You can, of course, take this many steps further, defining arrays of many dimensions. A five- or seven-dimensional array is not out of the question; the definition of the type could be:

```
type
  MegaArrayType = array [1..5, 1..5, 1..5, 1..5, 1..5] of integer;

var
  MegaArray : MegaArrayType;
```

With this definition in place, when you wanted to place a value (in this case an integer value), you would simply reference which cells, in five dimensions. The following line would work.

```
  MegaArray[3,2,4,2,1] := 2;
```

This would place the integer value 2 in the cell at row 3, column 2, depth 4, time continuum 2, and cosmic measurement 1. This can get really weird trying to name the many dimensions of an array, but you get the point. Before you fly of into the multidimensional galaxy, remember that memory for all the cells, even the empty ones, is allocated at runtime. This means your MegaArray, all 3,125 cells (that's 5^5 cells) will be allocated. Each one of those 3,125 cells will be given enough space to hold an integer value. If an integer is 4 bytes, that's 12,500 bytes—just for one array. The motto is "Do not forget, use memory wisely."

Records

Another data structure that is ever so useful is the record data type. Like an array, the record is used to store a group of related information. Unlike an array, the items in a record do not have to be of the same type. Records are great for storing information about things such as people or places. You can put someone's name, address, phone number, and weight in a record. You can then pass that entire group of information around under one name, similar to an array. Let's create an sample program, as shown in Listing 3.9.

TYPE **Listing 3.9. A simple record demo program.**

```
program MyRecordDemo;

uses
  Forms;

type
  PersonRecordType = Record
        Name : String[30];
        PhoneNumber : String[13];
        Age : Integer;
        Sex : Char
```

continues

Listing 3.9. continued

```
 end; {PersonRecordType}

var
  Person : PersonRecordType;

begin
  Person.Name := "Dan Osier";
  Person.PhoneNumber := "(916)555-1212";
  Person.Age := 32;
  Person.Sex := 'M';

  WriteLn ('The person''s name is ', Person.Name);
  WriteLn ('The person''s Phone number is ', Person.PhoneNumber);
  WriteLn ('The person''s age is ', Person.Age);
  WriteLn ('The person''s sex is ', Person.Sex);

Readln {To keep the window from closing until you press enter}

end. {MyRecordDemo}
```

Note

Notice that we used two quote characters in succession in the `WriteLn` statement. In a literal string, two quotes together mean an actual quote mark is in the string.

You start by defining your record type. This type is a data structure that consists of several parts. The first line `PersonRecordType = record` tells Delphi 2 that the lines of code to follow will be items in the `record` type definition. Now you must list the variables (and their types) that will be a part of the record. You have `name` as a `String` of length `30`, `PhoneNumber` is a `String` of length `13`, `Age` is an `Integer`, and `Sex` as a `Char` type (M or F). The end of your record definition is signified by an `end;` line.

At this point, you have a `record` type only. When the variable `Person` is declared (of type `PersonRecordType`), then you have actually allocated memory for one instance of your `record` type.

Now that memory is allocated, let's put some data into the record structure. You cannot say `Person := 'Dan'`, because Delphi 2 does not know in which item in `Person` to place the string `'Dan'`, so you need to qualify your entry to `Person.Name := 'Dan Osier'`. This tells Delphi 2 which field within the record you wish to access. This *dot notation* (putting a dot or period between the record name and field selector) is fundamental not only to records, but to the object-oriented programming that we discuss later. Through the next several lines of the program you use the dot notation to select and fill up the different fields of the `Person` variable with data.

Once you have loaded the `Person` variable, you can extract the data, one field at a time. Notice that in the `WriteLn()` procedure, you are specifying which field you wish to print. `WriteLn` could not discern which field(s) to print if you simply said `WriteLn (Person);`. The whole concept of records is a useful one. To make your application easy to write, it is important that you use data types that reflect real world data. The record is a natural evolution, storing attributes about a thing, person, or other object.

Brain Buster

Now that you have seen both arrays and records, what if you put them together? You may think this could blow a fuse on your thinking cap, but it's really straightforward. An array holds lots of things that are of the same type, right. Well, your `PersonRecordType` is a type. Couldn't you define the array to be `array [1..3] of PersonRecordType` ? Think about it. An array that holds three records. Yes, it works. Now each of those five records can hold information about a person, such as name phone number, and so on. The result is the program and code in Listing 3.10.

NOTE

When entering the code in Listing 3.10, there are a number of lines that are very similar. Instead of typing them all individually, use cut and paste in the editor window and just change the array element number. This will save wear and tear on you.

TYPE **Listing 3.10. Array-Record demo program.**

```
program MyArrayRecordDemo;

uses
  Forms;

type
  PersonRecordType = record
        Name : String[30];
        PhoneNumber : String[13];
        Age : Integer;
        Sex : Char
 end; {PersonRecordType}

  MyArrayType = array [1..3] of PersonRecordType;

var
  PersonArray : MyArrayType;
```

continues

Listing 3.10. continued

```
begin

  PersonArray[1].Name := 'Dan Osier';
  PersonArray[1].PhoneNumber := '(916)555-1212';
  PersonArray[1].Age := 32;
  PersonArray[1].Sex := 'M';

  PersonArray[2].Name := 'Susie Smith';
  PersonArray[2].PhoneNumber := '(916)555-9999';
  PersonArray[2].Age := 38;
  PersonArray[2].Sex := 'F';
  PersonArray[3].Name := 'Pat';
  PersonArray[3].PhoneNumber := '(916)555-7766';
  PersonArray[3].Age := 30;
  PersonArray[3].Sex := '?';

  WriteLn ('Person 1 name is ', PersonArray[1].Name);
  WriteLn ('Person 1 phone is ',PersonArray[1].PhoneNumber);
  WriteLn ('Person 1 age is ', PersonArray[1].Age);
  WriteLn ('Person 1 sex is ', PersonArray[1].Sex);

  WriteLn ('Person 2 name is ', PersonArray[2].Name);
  WriteLn ('Person 2 phone is ',PersonArray[2].PhoneNumber);
  WriteLn ('Person 2 age is ', PersonArray[2].Age);
  WriteLn ('Person 2 sex is ', PersonArray[2].Sex);

  WriteLn ('Person 3 name is ', PersonArray[3].Name);
  WriteLn ('Person 3 phone is ', PersonArray[3].PhoneNumber);
  WriteLn ('Person 3 age is ', PersonArray[3].Age);
  WriteLn ('Person 3 sex is ', PersonArray[3].Sex);

Readln {To keep the window from closing until you press enter}

end. { MyArrayRecordDemo}
```

Under your type declaration section, you first put the definition of the PersonRecordType record, and then use that type in the MyArrayType definition.

NOTE You must define something *before* you try to use it. Trying to use the `PersonRecordType` and then defining it later will not work.

Look at the `MyArrayType` type definition carefully. Now, your `PersonArray` variable is an array of records. To address `PersonArray`, you now have to give it the array subscript (the number that identifies which array item you want), and the field identifier within that array subscript that you wish to process or view. Therefore, the statement `PersonArray[3].Name := 'Pat';` is saying "For the `PersonArray` variable, take the third array element, the `Name` field within that third array element, and set it equal to the string `'Pat'`."

Brain Buster II

Arrays of records are pretty cool, but how about one more? What about a record with other records inside of it? Yes, a record of records. This has some real benefit in specific applications.

As you remember, a record is used to hold a grouping of related data, not necessarily of the same type. One of those components could easily be another record. Why, you ask? Let's look at an example. An employee tracking application you are creating has information about you as an employee. The record probably contains the standard stuff, as shown in the following lines:

```
type
  PersonType = record
    LastName : String[20];
    FirstName : String[10];
    EmployeeNumber : Integer;
  end; {PersonType}
```


Now you need to add the address. Well, this person may have a home and work address. A more convenient way to construct the record is by making a universal address record type, and reusing it. Look at the type you can create in the following segment:

```
type
  AddressType = record
    Street : String [50];
    City : String : [20];
    State : String [2];
    ZipCode : String [10]
  end; {AddressType}
```

The nice part about this type is that you can use it in several places. Now your home and work address variables can both be of type `AddressType`. Let's look at the finished code (Listing 3.11) for loading up me as a customer.

TYPE **Listing 3.11. Record demo program II.**

```
program MyRecord2Demo;

uses
  Forms;

type
  AddressType = record
    Street : String [50];
    City : String : [20];
    State : String [2];
    ZipCode : String [10]
  end; {AddressType}

  PersonType = record
```

continues

Listing 3.11. continued

```
    LastName : String[20];
    FirstName : String[10];
    EmployeeNumber : Integer;
    HomeAddress : AddressType;
    WorkAddress : AddressType
  end;

var
  Employee : PersonType;

begin

  Employee.LastName := 'Osler';
  Employee.FirstName := 'Don';
  Employee.EmployeeNumber := 16253;

  Employee.HomeAddress.Street := '1313 Your St.';
  Employee.HomeAddress.City := 'MyTown';
  Employee.HomeAddress.State := 'CA';
  Employee.HomeAddress.ZipCode := '95630-0011';

  Employee.WorkAddress.Street := '14 Big Business Road.';
  Employee.WorkAddress.City := 'NoOzone';
  Employee.WorkAddress.State := 'CA';
  Employee.WorkAddress.ZipCode := '95636-2211';

  WriteLn(Employee.LastName);
  WriteLn(Employee.FirstName);
  WriteLn(Employee.EmployeeNumber);

  WriteLn(Employee.HomeAddress.Street);
  WriteLn(Employee.HomeAddress.City);
  WriteLn(Employee.HomeAddress.State);
  WriteLn(Employee.HomeAddress.ZipCode);

  WriteLn(Employee.WorkAddress.Street);
  WriteLn(Employee.WorkAddress.City);
  WriteLn(Employee.WorkAddress.State);
  WriteLn(Employee.WorkAddress.ZipCode);

Readln {To keep the window from closing until you press enter}

end. {MyRecord2Demo}
```

In your `PersonType` record are two variables, `HomeAddress` and `WorkAddress`, that are both record variables of `AddressType`. Because these are records, you need to specify the entire path to get to the actual variable values. Therefore, specify the variable (`Employee`), dot, the field (`HomeAddress`), dot, and because `HomeAddress` is also a record, the field within `HomeAddress` (`Street`). The result is `Employee.HomeAddress.Street`, and this points to a single string value! This method may seem long, but it sure is easy to read exactly what another programmer is doing. Now you have loaded up the `Employee` variable with all the information, including two

sets of addresses. To print the information out to the screen, you have to retrieve each piece of information separately, and then `WriteLn()` it out to the screen.

Using the dot notation is sort of like your address. You say "I live in the United States, state of California, city of Sacramento, Fifth Street, Number 3423." Do you see what you are doing? You are narrowing the scope until you can be pointing at only one thing.

The only way you can make this whole thing a little more concise is to use the `with` clause. The `with` clause sort of sets a default, such as having an implied "I live in the United States," so all your searches start in the United States, instead of on a world level. The statement: `Employee.WorkAddress.ZipCode := '95636-2211';` is not bad, but using the `with` statement it looks like:

```
with Employee do
  WorkAddress.ZipCode := '95636-2211';
```

Did you notice that you did not have to specify `Employee` in front of the `WorkAddress.ZipCode` line? The with statement implied it. Now this may not amuse you too much, and to make matters worse, the `with` only works on the next line of code. "One line?" you say. "Worthless," you think? Not really. If that next line happens to be a `begin` statement, then everything from the `begin` to its matching `end` gets the implied `with`.

Your program could benefit a little from this new idea. The code could now be changed to what is in Listing 3.12:

TYPE **Listing 3.12. Record demo program III.**

```
program MyRecord3Demo;

uses
  Forms;

type
  AddressType = record
    Street : String[50];
    City : String[20];
    State : String[2];
    ZipCode : String[10]
  end; {AddressType}

  PersonType = record
    LastName : String[20];
    FirstName : String[10];
    EmployeeNumber : Integer;
    HomeAddress : AddressType;
    WorkAddress : AddressType
  end;

var
```

continues

Listing 3.12. continued

```
  Employee : PersonType;

{The code is the same so far, but now it changes}

begin
 with Employee do
  begin {the with stuff}
    LastName := 'Osler';
    FirstName := 'Don';
    EmployeeNumber := 16253;
  end; {with Employee}

with Employee.HomeAddress do
  begin
    Street := '1313 Your St.';
    City := 'MyTown';
    State := 'CA';
    ZipCode := '95630-0011';
 end; {with Employee.HomeAddress}

with Employee.WorkAddress do
  begin
    Street := '14 Big Business Road.';
    City := 'NoOzone';
    State := 'CA';
    ZipCode := '95636-2211';
  end; {with Employee.WorkAddress}

 with Employee do
   begin {the with stuff}
     WriteLn(LastName);
     WriteLn(FirstName);
     WriteLn(EmployeeNumber);
   end; {with Employee}

with Employee.HomeAddress do
  begin {the with stuff}
    WriteLn(Street);
    WriteLn(City);
    WriteLn(State);
    WriteLn(ZipCode);
  end; {with Employee.HomeAddress}

with Employee.WorkAddress do
  begin {the with stuff}
    WriteLn(Street);
    WriteLn(City);
    WriteLn(State);
    WriteLn(ZipCode);
 end; {with Employee.WorkAddress}

Readln {To keep the window from closing until you press enter}

end. {MyRecord3Demo}
```

Do you see how clean it makes the code? Notice that the `with` statements also go one level deeper and apply to `Employee.HomeAddress` instead of just `Employee`. This helps to funnel Delphi 2 more toward where you want it to go and to also make the code the easiest to read. The result is some clean code. Use the `with` statement auspiciously, and it can improve the readability of your code.

Subranges

Before we talk about Object Pascal sets, we need to discuss subranges. When you think of a range, maybe you think of it in a mathematical sense. A range of numbers could be from 1 to 10, 30 to 30,000 or something else. A range of letters could be “a” to “z,” or “A” to “F” (remember in Delphi 2 a lowercase “a” is different from an uppercase “A,” because they are two different ASCII characters).

In Delphi 2, ranges and subranges mean nearly the same as their counterparts in the real world. When you are writing your program, and want to compare input from the user to see if they typed in a lowercase letter of the alphabet, subranges are your ticket.

A *subrange* type is a range of values from an ordinal type called the host type. A subrange must always define the smallest and largest value in the subrange.

The subrange type can be easily constructed and used. Look at Listing 3.13; it shows you how subranges can benefit you.

Listing 3.13. Demo program using a subrange type.

```
program MyRangeDemo;

uses
  Forms;

type
  LittleLetter = 'a'..'z';

var
  GoodLetters : LittleLetter;

begin
  GoodLetters := 'b';
  WriteLn (GoodLetters)
Readln {To keep the window from closing until you press enter}
end. {MyRangeDemo}
```

In this example, you use a subrange to define what values are permissible to assign a variable of type `LittleLetter`. The variable `GoodLetters` is then created of `LittleLetter` type. This variable can now hold a single character between `a` and `z`.

You may be wondering why we are bothering to use these subranges. Why not just make `GoodLetters` a `char` type and get it over with! Well, there actually is a reason. Object Pascal has the ability to do range checking. This means that during the execution of your program, when you do an assignment statement such as `GoodLetters := 'b';` Pascal checks to see if the value you placed into `GoodLetters` is legal for its type (or subrange). If the value is out of bounds, a range error occurs. This enables you to quickly detect an error that may have eluded you otherwise. Variables that hold things such as day of the month (1..31) or months of the year (1..12) are great candidates for a subrange. This enables you to have built-in checking of the values you are passing around your program. As soon as you perform an illegal assignment, your program raises the error. How do you get this, you ask?

For only $49.95 plus tax, you can have this feature—just kidding! It's free with every copy of Delphi 2. You invoke this feature by putting an `{R+}` in your code where you want the range checking to start and an optional `{R-}` where you want it to end. It is also available as a checkbox in the project options dialog, under the compiler tab.

NOTE

> The only rule to defining subranges is that they must be an ordinal type, although only a subset of integer is OK. The other rule is that the ordinal value of the first entry needs to be less than the ordinal value of the second entry. So a subrange of `z` to `a` would not do, it would have to be `a` to `z`, since `a` has a smaller ordinal place than `z` does.

Sets

Sets are even more fun than subranges. Sets can use subranges in their definitions. A set is a group of elements that you want to associate with a single name and to which you can compare other values for inclusion or exclusion from the set. An example could be a set that contains all the possible single character responses to a Yes/No question. The four responses are `y`, `Y`, `n`, and `N`. You could create a set that would encompass all four: `['y', 'Y', 'n', 'N']`. Once this set has been defined, you can then use it to see if something else is in the set or is not in the set.

You look for set inclusion by invoking the `in` statement. If you create the statement `MyInput in ['y', 'Y', 'n', 'N'] then`, you are saying that if the value of the variable `MyInput` is one of the items in the set `'y', 'Y', 'n', 'N'`, then this statement evaluates to a `Boolean TRUE`. If the value in `MyInput` is not in the the set, then this statement is `FALSE`. A set can contain almost anything, as long as the set members are of the same ordinal type or of compatible ordinal types.

Not only can sets contain single values, they can also contain subranges. For instance, if you had a telephone simulator, you would want to allow the numbers 0 through 9, and the * and # keys. The set for this would be `[0..9, '*', '#']`. As the user pressed keys, you could check for inclusion in the set using the `in` statement. Listing 3.14 is just one of the ways you can use sets.

TYPE **Listing 3.14. Sets.**

```
program PhoneDemo; Set Demo Program

uses
  Forms;

type
  KeysType = set of  [0..9, '*', '#'];

var
  Keys : KeysType;
  UserInput : Char;

begin
  Read(UserInput);
  If UserInput in Keys then
    WriteLn ('That key was OK')
  Readln {To keep the window from closing until you press enter}
end.
```

Arrays and records can be both useful and fun. It is much easier to understand how things are done, if you can see the reasons behind them. You will use these structures more in later days.

Typed Constants

The concept of a *typed constant* is a strange one. Think of a typed constant as a preinitialized variable. You can define a typed constant and give it a value in a single statement.

```
Const
  Max : Integer  = 88;
  Name : String[10] = 'Dan';
  Digits : Set of '0'..'9';
```

This may seem a little confusing at first. (You thought the constant declaration section was for declaring constants.) This exception does confuse the rule, but the result is a unique opportunity. You can now define a variables type and give it a default value in one statement. The placement of these statements may be confusing, but the result is good. The typed constant is initialized only once with the default value, no matter how many times the module containing the declaration is called.

Typed Constants In Action

Using typed constants is easy. Look at Listing 3.15 and see how it uses typed constants just like variables.

TYPE **Listing 3.15. Typed constant demo program.**

```
program TypedConstantDemo;

uses
  Forms;

const
  MyName : String = 'Dan Osier'

begin
  WriteLn (My Name is ', MyName);
  MyName:= 'Jim Fischer';
  WriteLn('My new Name is ', MyName);
  Readln {To keep the window from closing until you press enter}

 end. {TypedConstantDemo}
```

Enumerated Types

Enumerated types are one of the things that can really add to the readability of your code. Although you may know what your code does, the next guy may not. Let's say you are writing a program to control stop lights (what would the D.O.T. say?), and you need to represent the colors red, yellow, and green in your application. You could assign each one of the colors a number, 1 for red, 2 for yellow, and 3 for green. Then, in your application, you could say, `if 3 then TurnLightGo`? That doesn't sound very intuitive, does it? What about the poor person who has to change your application after you are famous? He/she looks at `if 3 then TurnLightGo` and says "Huh?" Enumerated types to the rescue!

Enumerated types enable you to define a group of objects that belong in a set, and then use them. This is what is known as a user-defined type. There is a limit of 255 items that can be defined as part of an enumerated type.

Enumerated Types in Action

Now that you know how to declare an enumerated type, write a program that uses them. See Listing 3.16 for a code example using enumerated types.

TYPE **Listing 3.16. Enumerated type demo program.**

```
program MyEnumeratedDemo;

uses
  Forms;

type
  StopLightColors = (Red, Yellow, Green);

var
  MyLight : StopLightColors;

begin
  MyLight := Red;
  WriteLn (My light is currently ', Integer(MyLight));
  MyLight :=Green;
  WriteLn('The new light is ', Integer(MyLight));
  Readln {To keep the window from closing until you press enter}

 end. {MyEnumeratedDemo}
```


As you can see in Listing 3.16, I have created an enumerated type called `StopLightColors`. This type has its members Red, Yellow, and Green. The variable `MyLight` is then defined as type `StopLightColors`. From that point, you can use the variable `MyLight` and assign any of the three colors values to it as you do in the first line of code `MyLight := Red;`. Enumerated types are not for the benefit of the end user, but rather a way for the developer to make his or her code more readable and maintainable. Although the use of these types is limited to inside the code, it does help foster understanding for the maintainer of that code. Notice when you read the code how clean and easy to read it is. This is the real benefit of using enumerated types.

The Variant Type

If you have programmed in Visual Basic, you may have become accustomed to using the `Variant` type. This type is great, because you can place just about any value in it, from an integer to a string. The problem with the `Variant` type in VB is the memory that was required for a variable of this type. Microsoft suggested using this type only when necessary (due to resource requirements).

Delphi 1 did not have a `Variant` type because, as the author sees it, Object Pascal is a strongly typed language, and the `Variant` type lends itself to some "loose" programming practices. But as a result of popular demand, and because of some new requirements, Delphi 2 includes a `Variant` type.

Variant Types in Action

The Delphi 2, the `Variant` type can hold an integer, string, or floating point value. The use of this type is as varied as the type suggests. The `Variant` type is defined as shown in Listing 3.17:

TYPE **Listing 3.17. Variant types.**

```
program MyVariantDemo;

uses
  Forms;

var
   MyInput : Variant;

begin
  MyInput := 3.5555;
  WriteLn (MyInput);

  MyInput := 'Hello, my name is Dan.';
  WriteLn (MyInput);

  MyInput := 4;
  WriteLn (MyInput);
  Readln {To keep the window from closing until you press enter}
end.
```

The `Variant` type is capable of holding many different types of values, as demonstrated in Listing 3.16. The `Variant` type is a 16-byte structure that holds not only the value, but type information as well. The real value of using the `Variant` type is in dealing with OLE automation. In this instance, you may receive values back from an OLE server that would not mesh with the more rigid Pascal data types.

Operators

Now that you have learned about the data types, you need to know how to compare and evaluate variables of those types. In order to do that, let's look at the operators supported by Delphi 2.

Arithmetic Operators

These operators enable you to do binary and unary arithmetic operations. Tables 3.7 and 3.8 in this section describe the operations, what types are allowed, and what the resulting type is, for example, remember that if you divide an `Integer` by an `Integer`, the result is a `Real` type. This is sometimes forgotten.

Table 3.7. Binary arithmetic operations.

Operator	Operation	Types Used	Resulting Type
+	Addition	Integer	Integer
		Real	Real
-	Subtraction	Integer	Integer
		Real	Real
*	Multiplication	Integer	Integer
		Real	Real
/	Division	Integer	Real
		Real	Real
Div	Integer Division	Integer	Integer
Mod	Remainder	Integer	Integer

Table 3.8. Unary arithmetic operations.

Operator	Operation	Types Used	Resulting Type
+	Sign Identity	Integer	Integer
		Real	Real
-	Sign Negation	Integer	Integer
		Real	Real

Logical Operators

Logical operators are divided into two categories: logical operations and boolean operations. The logical involves shifting or comparing things at a bit level, and boolean operations involve comparing or manipulating values at a `TRUE` or `FALSE` level. (See Tables 3.9 and 3.10.)

Table 3.9. Logical operations.

Operator	Operation	Types Used	Resulting Type
not	Bitwise negation	Integer	Boolean
and	Bitwise and	Integer	Boolean
or	Bitwise or	Integer	Boolean
xor	Bitwise xor	Integer	Boolean
shl	Operation	Integer	Boolean
shr	Operation	Integer	Boolean

NOTE

If you use the `not` operator on an `Integer` type, the result will be of the same `Integer` type. If both operands of an `and`, `or`, or `xor` are `Integer` types, the resulting type will actually be the common type of the two operands.

Table 3.10. Boolean operations.

Operator	Operation	Types Used	Resulting Type
not	Negation	Boolean	Boolean
and	Logical and	Boolean	Boolean
or	Logical or	Boolean	Boolean
xor	Logical xor	Boolean	Boolean

Relational Operators

You will find these items in Table 3.11, necessary for comparing the values of two variables. Although we have not used all the types in Table 3.11, I thought it necessary include this table for reference. Some of the types in the table are discussed in future days. For your operators, just remember your high school math!

Table 3.11. Relational operations.

Operator	Operation	Types Used	Resulting Type
=	Equal	Compatible simple, class, class reference, pointer, set, string, or packed string types	Boolean
<>	Not equal to	Compatible simple, class, class reference, pointer, set, string or packed string types	Boolean
<	Less than	Compatible simple, string or packed string types, or PChar	Boolean
>	Greater than	Compatible simple, string or packed string types, or PChar	Boolean
<=	Less than or equal to	Compatible simple, string or packed string types, or PChar	Boolean
>=	Greater than or equal to	Compatible simple, string or packed string types, or PChar	Boolean
<=	Subset of	Compatible set types	Boolean
>=	Superset of	Compatible set types	Boolean
in	Member of	Left operand, any ordinal type; right operand, set whose base is compatible with the left operand	Boolean

Precedence of Operators

Just as in mathematics, you have to know how to evaluate an expression. To do that, you need to know in what order to evaluate the different parts of the expression. The precedence of operators does affect the outcome of the code, just as it does in mathematics. See Table 3.12.

Table 3.12. Precedence of operators.

Operators	Precedence	Categories
@, not	First	Unary operators
*, /, div, mod, and, shl, shr, as	Second	Multiplying operators
+, -, or, xor	Third	Adding operators
=, <>, >, <, <=, >=, in, is	Fourth	Relational operators

The order is fairly simple, just remember three other key points:

- An operand between two operators is bound (or attached) to the operator of higher precedence.
- An operand between to equal operators is bound to the one on the left.
- Expressions within parentheses are evaluated prior to being treated as a single operand (work from the inside parentheses out, just as in math).

Summary

In this Day, you have looked at the first portion of the Object Pascal language. You have explored the different data types that are offered and hopefully gotten a start into understanding how the language works. The best way for you, the reader, to become more familiar with Object Pascal is to use it. Look at all the examples provided with Delphi 2. Read through the source code, even if you do not understand everything that is going on. In Day 4, we will continue our discussion of the Object Pascal language and talk about the structure of a Delphi 2 program.

Q&A

Q Can I convert a variable from one type to another type?

A Yes. There is a concept called variable typecasting that enables this. See Exercise 1 in the next section.

Q Is Object Pascal the same as the Pascal on other platforms and by other vendors?

A There is an ANSI standard Pascal. Borland has many enhancements to the standard Pascal that make it much more useful. The benefits of going beyond the ANSI standard outweigh the drawback of not being only ANSI compliant.

Workshop

The workshop provides quiz questions to help you solidify your understanding of the material covered and exercises to provide you with experience. Please try to work through both before continuing to the next day.

Quiz

1. At a fundamental level, how do constants and variables differ?
2. Why is precedence of operators necessary?
3. What is the advantage of using typed constants?

Exercises

1. In order to help solidify the use of `Variant` types, write an application that uses an `Integer` and `Variant` type. Make sure that you move the `Integer` value into the `Variant` variable. Try writing both values to the screen to see that the `Variant` type really holds other data types (`Integer` in this case).
2. Write a program that makes use of enumerated types. Try making a type called `FamilyMember` that has all the members of your family as elements. Try inputing ages for each one and then printing the whole thing.

Week 1

Day 4

Object Pascal, Part II

On Day 3, you learned about the data types in Delphi 2 and what they are used for. In today's lesson, you will begin to explore controlling the application. Some powerful commands are available in Object Pascal to control the behavior of your application. We will talk about modularization of your application to decrease errors and improve code reliability. Pointers and their uses will also be covered, as well as parameter passing.

Control the Flow

The heart of programming stems from your application's ability to make decisions, based on input or other criteria, and then perform a given task or operation. This capability is commonly called conditional execution. Object Pascal provides several commands that offer this "conditional" capability. Let's look at each of these, and how they can be used.

If...Then

The `If...Then` clause is the most fundamental of the conditional statements. It provides a way for the software developer to pose a question and based on the answer, perform a given operation or task. If you plan to take an input from the user and want to tell the user if that input is incorrect, how would you do it? Let's look at a sample program in Listing 4.1.

TYPE **Listing 4.1. Simple program with user input.**

```
program IfDemo;

Uses
  Forms;

var
  UserInput : Integer;

begin
  Write ('How old are you ?');
   ReadLn (UserInput);
   WriteLn ('Being ', UserInput, ' years old is great!');
   ReadLn {To keep the window from closing until you press enter}
end.
```

ANALYSIS This is simple sample program. Let's go through it one line at a time. You declare a variable `UserInput` of type `Integer`. This is used to store the age of the user upon input. The `Write` line asks the user how old he/she is. You use the `Write()` function instead of `WriteLn()` because it leaves the cursor at the end of the line. The `ReadLn()` function line takes input keystrokes from the user until the Enter key is pressed. The input is placed into the `UserInput` variable, and the execution of the program continues. The `WriteLn()` at the end lets the user know that being their age is great.

This program has more than a few problems with it. It does no range checking to see if the age entered is reasonable (that is, negative ages or ages of 130+). So let's use the new `If...Then` clause to fix that. The syntax of the clause is as follows:

```
If <Expression1> then <Expression2> else <Expression3>;
```

The first expression must evaluate to a logical `TRUE` or `FALSE`. The second expression is the action that should be taken if the first expression evaluates to a `TRUE`. The third expression is optional, and is what should be done if the first expression evaluates to a `FALSE`.

So let's test for the age range. The statement would be "If the age is less than 1, or if the age is greater than 130, then they are lying, otherwise tell them their age is great." Now let's put that expression into code form. Look at the new program in Listing 4.2.

TYPE **Listing 4.2. Demo program using the `If` statement.**

```
program IfDemo2;

Uses
  Forms;

var
  UserInput : Integer;

begin
  Write ('How old are you ?');
   ReadLn (UserInput);
   If (UserInput < 1) or (UserInput > 130) then
      WriteLn ('You are not telling the truth.")
   else
      WriteLn ('Being ', UserInput, ' years old is great!');
  ReadLn {To keep the window from closing until you press enter}
end.
```

Remember that the first expression is everything between the `If` and the `Then` reserved words. The expression `(UserInput < 1) or (UserInput > 130)` must evaluate to a `TRUE` or `FALSE`, and it does. If the age is less than one, the first part `(UserInput < 1)` becomes `TRUE`. If the age is greater than 130, then the expression `(UserInput > 130)` becomes `TRUE`. Either way, with a logical `or` between them, if either part is `TRUE`, the whole thing evaluates to `TRUE`. If the first expression evaluates to `TRUE`, the second expression is executed. If the first expression is `FALSE`, then the third expression (the `WriteLn()` after the `Else` statement)is executed. This is a simple but effective example of the basic building blocks.

Case...of

Before the luxury of masked edit controls, if a programmer wished to limit the user's input of characters, as well as respond to them, the programmer needed to analyze every character individually. After each character was entered, the code would check to see what the character was and how to respond to it. The `Case` statement is very useful in this regard. The `Case` statement enables the programmer to compare an input to a predefined set of "cases," and respond accordingly. Look at the code example in Listing 4.3.

4

TYPE **Listing 4.3. `CaseDemo` program.**

```
Program CaseDemo;

uses
  Forms;

var
  UserIn : Char;

begin
  Read (UserIn);
  Case UserIn of
    'a'       : WriteLn ('That is a small a');
    'z', 'Z' : WriteLn ('That is a small or capital Z')
  else
    WriteLn ('That is a character other than an a, z, or Z.');
  ReadLn {To keep the window from closing until you press enter}
end.
```

ANALYSIS In this example, the user is given a chance to input a character from the keyboard (no Enter key is required since `Read` takes in only what it needs and requires to Enter). Then the user's input (now in the `UserIn` variable) is compared to the first constant. If that constant (the character `'a'`) is a match to the data in `UserIn`, the statement to the after the colon on that line is executed. That statement could be a call to a function or procedure (which we will cover later in this chapter), or a series of statements with a `begin` and `end` around them. At this point, after the statement for the `'a'` line has been executed, the rest of the `Case` statement will not be executed because a match was found.

If the `'a'` line is not a match, then the next constant line of the `Case` statement is compared to `UserIn`. If this is a match, the statement line associated with that constant is executed, and so on. If no match is found, the `else` statement will be executed (if present). It is wise to use the `else` as a part of any `Case` statement to help catch those "what if" sorts of things. This is another way to help bulletproof your application.

A couple of rules of the `Case` road (I know you hate rules):

- If you use more than one constant on a comparison line, they must be separated by commas unless you are denoting a range of values like ("a" through "z").
- The expression or the constant being compared to the expression must be `byte`- or `word`-sized ordinal types, so you cannot use a `String` or `LongInt` type as your arguments.
- The constants you are comparing your expression to (in this case `UserIn`) cannot overlap. That means that the following `Case` statement would not work:

```
Program EvilCaseDemo;

Uses
   Forms;
```

```
var
  UserIn : Char;

begin
  Read (UserIn);
  Case UserIn of
    'a'         : WriteLn ('That is an small a');
    'a', 'z', 'Z' : WriteLn ('ThatI''s a  Z or z, or it could be an a.')
  else
    WriteLn ('That is a character other than an a, z, or Z.');
  ReadLn {To keep the window from closing until you press enter}
        end.
```

- If you try to run this application, you get a `duplicate case label` error from the compiler. This is good because even if the compiler allowed this program to run, it would not make any sense. In order for the `Case` statement to run correctly, all the values must be unique. Having a duplicate `'a'` would give two possible alternatives.

Do It Again!

Sometimes you may want to perform a set of instructions over and over again until a certain condition is met. Object Pascal provides a set of looping instruction to accomplish this. There are three main commands, and they all accomplish about the same thing. However, they have some differences.

4

repeat...until

The functionality of the `repeat...until` is very straightforward. The statements between the repeat and the until are repeated until the condition defined after the reserved word `Until` evaluates to `TRUE`. Look the code example in Listing 4.4.

TYPE **Listing 4.4. `RepeatDemo` program.**

```
program RepeatDemo;

Uses
  Forms;

begin
  repeat
      Write('Enter a value: ');
      Read(I);
  until (I = 'q') or (I = 'Q');
  ReadLn {To keep the window from closing until you press enter}
end.
```

The program in Listing 4.4 continues soliciting characters from the user until the user presses either a capital or small letter `'q'`. At first, this may confuse some programmers because no `begin/end` is needed around the statements being executed. The `repeat` and `until` serve as the markers to show which code is being run in the loop.

As you can see from Listing 4.4 above, the code segment between the `repeat` and the `until` statements is executed once prior to checking the condition, in this case the `(I = 'q') or (I = 'Q')`. You must make sure that the code segment can handle one iteration prior to checking its state. If your code cannot be bulletproofed without that checking, use one of the other looping constructs available. The other item of interest is how many times will this loop run. The answer is unknown. This loop could run one time or one thousand times, depending on the user's input. This is something else to consider when using this command.

While...Do

Another interesting looping variation is the `While...Do`. This command pair has a similar function, but with a twist. You can use the `While...Do` to accomplish the same goal as the `Repeat...Until`. The difference is twofold:

1. The conditional statement is checked prior to entering the loop.
2. If the condition is `False`, the loop will not be executed again. (Note that this is the reverse of the `Repeat...Until` logic.)

Look at how you might accomplish the same goal in Listing 4.5 as the `Repeat...Until` example did in Listing 4.4.

TYPE **Listing 4.5. Demo program using `While...Do`.**

```
program WhileDoDemo;

Uses
  Forms;

var
   I: Char;

begin
  While (I <> 'q') or (I <> 'Q') Do
     begin
       Write('Enter a value: ');
        Read(I);
     end;
  ReadLn {To keep the window from closing until you press enter}
end.
```

Notice that you had to reverse the logic from `(I = 'q') or (I = 'Q')` to `(I <> 'q') or (I <> 'Q')` in order to get the loop to work. This is due to a change in attitude. You went from a "Do this until ____" to a "While ___ is true do ___" mentality. There is a fundamental change in the logic. As with the `Repeat` loop, there is no way to anticipate the number of times the loop is going to be executed. The execution is all dependent on the user's input.

One problem with your program is that you are doing an evaluation of the value of `I` without specifically putting anything into it first. If you get a portion of memory to hold a single character of data, it could have junk in it from the last program that used that memory. It could even have a `q` or a `Q` in it, and would therefore execute the `(I <> 'q') or (I <> 'Q')` condition prior to where you think it should. The resulting failure may occur once every 100 times, leading to a hard-to-diagnose intermittent problem. The answer is to insert a value into `I` first. (See Listing 4.6.)

TYPE **Listing 4.6. `WhileDoDemo` with `I` initially declared.**

```
program WhileDoDemo;

Uses
  Forms;

var
   I: Char;

begin
  I := ' ';
  While (I <> 'q') or (I <> 'Q') Do
     begin
       Write('Enter a value: ');
        Read(I);
     end;
  ReadLn {To keep the window from closing until you press enter}
end.
```

This way you know the value in `I` prior to entering the loop. This helps minimize the number of weird problems.

For...Do

The `For...Do` loop is one of the simplest of the looping constructs. Use this one when you know how many times you want the loop to be executed. Let's look at a sample program in Listing 4.7 just to get you started.

TYPE **Listing 4.7. `ForDemo` program.**

```
program  ForDemo;

uses
  Forms;

var
  Count : Integer;

begin
  For Count := 1 to 10 do
    WriteLn ('Hello');
  ReadLn {To keep the window from closing until you press enter}
end.
```

ANALYSIS In Listing 4.7, you define a variable `Count` of type `Integer`. The `For` loop is set up as follows:

- The `Count` variable holds the current value of the loop.
- `Count` initially is set to the initial value `1`.
- The statement after the `do` is executed once (if that statement is a `begin`, all the code is executed until a matching `end` is found).
- `Count` is incremented by one.
- If `Count` is greater than the ending value (`10`) the loop is done, and execution continues at the statement *after* the `For` loops statement line (in this case, after the `WriteLn`).
- If `Count` is not greater than the ending value (`10`), then the statement after the `do` is executed again.

You need to heed a couple of rules. The variable you are using to hold the current value of the loop (in this case, `Count`), needs to be in scope (which we talk about later in this chapter). Simply put, this means that `Count` needs to be a valid variable local to the block in which the `For` loop occurs. The second rule is that the initial value (`1`) must be smaller than the final value (`10`). This makes sense because the `For` is incrementing `Count`. You cannot use `Count` as a formal parameter to a procedure. You cannot modify the value of `Count` within the `For` loop itself. The only other rule is that the control variable `Count` must be assignment compatible with the initial and final values (`1,10`). Delphi 2 must be able to place these values, and every value in between them, into `Count`. You must also remember that `Count` is undefined once control leaves the `For` statement, so do not try to use its current value for anything outside the loop.

There is only one other variation of the `For` loop you need to look at. You also have the ability to decrement the `Count` variable by using another variation of `For`. Look at the code example in Listing 4.8.

TYPE **Listing 4.8. `ForDemo2` program.**

```
program  ForDemo2;

uses
  Forms;

var
  Count : Integer;

begin
  For Count = 10 downto 1 do
    WriteLn ('Hello');
  ReadLn {To keep the window from closing until you press enter}
end.
```

It looks the same as the `ForDemo` example except the `to` reserved word is replaced by `downto` and the initial and final values are reversed. The `For` loop works the same way except `Count` starts out as `10` and gets decremented by one until it reaches `1`, and the loop ends. Is this fun or what?

Looping Summary

As you can see, we have covered all the looping contingencies. We can really summarize the use of loops in the following table:

Table 4.1. Looping constructs.

Looping Construct	When Do I Use It?
`For`	If you know how many times you want the loop to repeat itself
`While...Do`	If you want to test the conditional part before entering the loop
`Repeat...Until`	If you want the loop to iterate through at least once before the conditional part is tested

Branching

Another capability that must exist in a language such as Object Pascal is the ability to *branch* in the code. What we mean by this is the capability to jump to another piece of code when necessary. Several mechanisms are available to help the developer accomplish this.

Goto

The Goto statement enables you to jump ahead from where you are now, to a specific prelabeled line. A *label* is defined by using the reserved word label to define a new label name. That label name can then be assigned to a line of code by placing the label, a colon, and then the line of executable code. Look at the code example in Listing 4.9.

TYPE **Listing 4.9. GotoDemo program.**

```
label ThePlace;

Program GotoDemo

uses
  Forms;

var
 Answer : String;

 label ThePlace;

 begin
   ThePlace : WriteLn ('Hello world');
   WriteLn ('Would you like to run this again?');
   ReadLn (Answer);
   If (Answer = 'y') then
      Goto ThePlace;
   ReadLn {To keep the window from closing until you press enter}
 end.
```

ANALYSIS You have defined a label named ThePlace for use in your code. The label is defined outside the executable code area, and after other definitions such as const, var, type, and so on. The 'Hello There' line will always be executed. The WriteLn asks the user if they want to run the program again. If the user answers 'y', then the Goto ThePlace is executed. Otherwise, the last ReadLn is executed, and when the user presses Enter, the program ends.

The concept of labels is very old and has been used widely. I am sure that you could have found a number of other ways of coding this example without the Goto in there at all. That is just the foundation of a long, on-going argument over its use. Many developers feel that the use of Goto only compensates for bad programming practices, and that a more rigorous examination of your code would turn up a more graceful way of doing things. Others feel if you have the tool, use it. The author's opinion is not any more relevant than your own, so make up your own mind and press on.

Break

Let's say you are in the middle of one those fancy `For` or `While` loops and you find a condition for which it is imperative that you exit that loop. It is pretty tough to get out of. The `Break` statement gives you a way to cease the execution of the loop entirely. Let's look at an example of how this might work in Listing 4.10. Let's take the `WhileDoDemo` from earlier and give it a working over.

TYPE **Listing 4.10.** `BreakDemo` **program.**

```
program BreakDemo;

Uses
  Forms;

var
   I: Char;

begin
  I := ' ';
  While TRUE Do
     begin
       Write('Enter a value: ');
        Read(I);
        If (I = 'q') or (I = 'Q') then
          Break;
     end;
   {The Break will cause execution to end up here!}
   ReadLn {To keep the window from closing until you press enter}
end.
```

ANALYSIS This is a strange bit of code, but it does illustrate a point. The `While` loop will continue forever because the expression evaluates to a `TRUE`. The only way this loop will end is through the use of the `Break` statement. So, after reading the user's input in the `Read`, the `If` statement determines if the key the user pressed was a small or capital "Q." If it was a "Q," then the `Break` is invoked. The execution drops to the line indicated in the code, and execution of the rest of the application continues.

Continue

The opposite condition can also exist where you do not want to jump out of the loop, but simply want to end what you are doing in this iteration of the loop and start the next iteration. The `Continue` command performs this task. When used inside a `For`, `While`, or `Repeat` loop, the `Continue` statement stops the processing in the current iteration and returns control to the loop itself to continue the next iteration. See the code example in Listing 4.11.

TYPE **Listing 4.11. `ContinueDemo` program.**

```
program ContinueDemo;

Uses
  Forms;

var
   I: Char;
    Count : Integer;

begin
  I := ' ';
  For Count = 1 to 100 Do
     begin
       Write('Enter a value: ');
        Read(I);
        If (I = 'q') or (I = 'Q') then
          Continue;
        WriteLn (' This will only be executed if the
        ➥user's input is not a q or Q.')
     end;
  ReadLn {To keep the window from closing until you press enter}
end.
```

ANALYSIS In Listing 4.11 you have a `For` loop that runs 100 times. Within that loop, you are gathering a keystroke from the user. If that keystroke is a "q" or "Q," then the `Continue` statement is invoked and execution is returned to the `For` line which increments the variable `Count` by one and moves on. This is just another mechanism for you to use when constructing your software masterpiece.

NOTE

After the control variable (`Count`) is incremented, it is also tested. You might use both the `Break` and `Continue` mechanisms if you encounter an error condition in your loop; use `Continue` to proceed with the next item or `Break` to skip the remaining items.

Exit

The name implies the `Exit` statement's full function. `Exit` is used to exit the current block of code. If that block is the main program, `Exit` causes the program to terminate. If the current block is nested, `Exit` causes the next outer block to continue with the statement immediately after the statement that passed control to the nested block. If the current block is a procedure or function (which we will cover later in the `Functions` and `Procedure` sections), `Exit` causes

the calling block to continue with the statement after the point when the block was called. An example follows in Listing 4.12.

TYPE **Listing 4.12. Demo program using `Exit`.**

```
program ExitDemo;

Uses
  Forms;

var
   I: Char;
    Count : Integer;

begin
    repeat
       Write('Enter a value: ');
        Read(I);
        If  I := 'Q' then
           Exit;
    Until FALSE;
    ReadLn {To keep the window from closing until you press enter}
end.
```


In this case, you have created an endless loop by setting the `Until` portion of the loop to `FALSE`, and therefore it can never end. The only way for the loop to cease to operate is for the user to enter a "Q" at which time the `IF...Then` evaluates to `TRUE` and the `Exit` command fires off. Because the block of code you are in is the main program, the program ceases.

Halt

`Halt` is not just what they shout in those old German movies but a useful command in Delphi 2, as well. It enables you to halt the execution of your application at will. Wherever you place the `Halt` command, that is where the application ends. Before placing this command in your application, ask yourself a few questions:

- ☐ Did I leave any databases or files open? They may get corrupted if I quit here.
- ☐ Did I allocate a bunch of memory that I have not freed up, and therefore am I wasting memory by quitting now?
- ☐ Place your concern here!

The point being that you should be careful with such a powerful command. It could get you in trouble. You might use this command when your application encounters a fatal error condition. Some of the return codes from Windows calls as well as Delphi calls let you know that something bad has happened. These could be memory- or disk-related problems. It is up to your discretion to halt the application, rather than exiting gracefully. I would recommend to always try to shut down your application gracefully. Use this only as a last resort, and even then think twice. If you halt your application it can leave files open, memory allocated, and lots of other stuff hanging in the wind. Here is a very short example of `Halt` in Listing 4.13.

TYPE **Listing 4.13. Demo program using `Halt`.**

```
program HaltDemo;

Uses
  Forms;

var
   I: Char;
   Count : Integer;

begin
   repeat
      Write('Enter a value: ');
       Read(I)
       If  I := 'Q' then
          Halt;
   Until FALSE;
end.
```

In Listing 4.13, when the user types in a "Q," the program quits instantly. Not a very smooth transition out of the application, but it will due in a pinch. Under normal circumstances (and a more complex application), you would want to have some code that gets executed on the way out that cleans up your environment before you leave.

RunError

This is a good one! If you don't like waiting for Delphi 2 to spit those runtime errors out at you, now you can create your own. That's right! Anytime during program execution, you can invoke the `RunError` command with an `Integer` parameter, and it halts the execution of the program and spits out the error number you entered as the reason for the program's failure. Here is a short example in Listing 4.14.

TYPE **Listing 4.14. `RunErrorDemo` program.**

```
program RunErrorDemo;

Uses
  Forms;

var
```

```
   I: Char;
   Count : Integer;

begin
   repeat
      Write('Enter a value: ');
       Read(I)
       If  I := 'Q' then
          RunError (600);
   Until FALSE;
   ReadLn {To keep the window from closing until you press enter}
end.
```

I have set up the program to generate a runtime error `600` (my own new error I just raised) every time that the user presses "Q" as an input. If I have my debugger running, I can see that runtime error coming out. This may come in handy, especially if you think your application is not generating enough runtime errors on its own.

Programs

As you have progressed through the first days in this book, we have given you somewhat of a "baptism by fire" on learning about the structure of a Delphi 2 application. Although we will go into the details of what files constitute your project and how to manage them on Day 5, "Files and the Project Manager," it is necessary for us to talk about your application from an internal structure perspective. You have seen (and hopefully been typing in) the sample programs provided. Let's dissect one of them now.

The one thing common to all Delphi 2 applications is that each has a segment of code that is the main point from which all the rest branches. That code segment starts with the word `Program`. This is the point at which your application begins executing. The `Uses` clause usually comes next. This section is used to include other units of code (which we will cover in the "Units" section). After the `Uses` section comes the declaration section. The reserved words `const`, `type`, and `var` are the statements normally present in this section. Here, global data types, variables, as well as constants are defined. Lastly, you have the `begin...end` pair, with a period behind the `end` statement. This `end` with a period signifies the end of the executable code, and there can only be one of these in the main executable. The only other place an `end`-period combination can appear is in a `unit`, or a DLL (covered on Day 19).

So a program looks as follows in Listing 4.15.

TYPE **Listing 4.15. Main program demo.**

```
Program ProgDemo;

Uses
   Forms;

const
  Taxes = 7.75;
  Death = TRUE;


var
Employee : String;

begin
  If (Taxes > 0) and Death then
    Employee := 'Me';
  WriteLn ('R.I.P.')
  ReadLn {To keep the window from closing until you press enter}

end. {ProgDemo}
```

In case you did not get the joke, notice there are only two constants: death and taxes. Everything between the `begin` and `end` is executed in order from top to bottom, and the program ceases when it hits the end with the period. Very straightforward isn't it? Now that you think you have everything under control, let's push on.

Procedures

I believe procedures to be greater than the discovery of the light bulb—well, almost. They do provide a serious increase in the quality of your programming life (the procedures I mean). Let's see how procedures can increase productivity, clarity, and decrease bugs in your code.

In the throes of programming, you often overlook the obvious. If you have a need to write a program that prints out a checkerboard, you might be tempted to do this:

TYPE **Listing 4.16. `CheckerPrint` using `WriteLns`.**

```
program CheckerPrint;

Uses
  Forms;

begin
  WriteLn ('   ¦  ¦   ');
  WriteLn ('--------');
  WriteLn ('   ¦  ¦   ');
```

```
  WriteLn ('--------');
  WriteLn ('   |   |   ')
end.
```

Now this will work (a lame checkerboard, sorry) but it gets the point across. The program is direct and gets the job done. Do you see the repetition in this? You are doing the same thing over and over. Now the concept of a procedure comes into play. Let's look at a revised example in Listing 4.17, and then we will talk.

TYPE

Listing 4.17. CheckerPrint using procedures.

```
program CheckerPrint;

Uses
  Forms;

{normally any Uses, Const, Var, Type and other declarations would go here.}

    procedure DoVerticals;
      begin
        WriteLn ('   |   |   ');
      end;

    procedure DoHorizontals;
      begin
        WriteLn ('------------');
      end;

begin
  DoVerticals;
  DoHorizontals;
  DoVerticals;
  DoHorizontals;
  DoVerticals;
end.
```

What you have done here is to take a section (or in this case, a line) of code that you use often and put a wrapper around it, give that wrapper a name, and then use that name to access the code inside that wrapper anytime you wish. You have done this by creating two procedures: one that prints the horizontal lines, and the other that prints the vertical ones. Notice that the procedures were declared between the reserved word `program`, and the beginning of the executable code (the `begin` statement).

The first thing you do to create a procedure is create a procedure heading. The heading consists of the reserved word `procedure` and a unique name for that procedure. In this case, `procedure DoVerticals;` is the procedure heading. The heading is very similar to the `program CheckerPrint;` line for your main program. The similarities between the main program and the procedure do not end there. The procedure is sort of a mini program and has the same format. After the heading, you can have a `Const`, `Type`, `Var` section, or even another procedure. A procedure can have another procedure nested inside of it. After all this, the procedure, of course, has an executable section marked by the `begin…end;` statement pair.

Now that you have created this procedure named `DoVerticals`, you can call that procedure in your code. When you call that code by its unique name, control will be passed to that procedure. When the procedure is finished executing, it will return control to the line of code *after* the line that called the `procedure`.

Procedures are a way of modularizing code and making it useable over and over. The other benefit is in code reliability. If you write the same piece of code six times in your application, you have six chances of making mistakes. If you use a procedure, you write the code once, test it once, and then use it repeatedly. You have a lesser chance of making mistakes, and your code quality is better overall.

Parameter Passing

Procedures are only of limited use considering how you have used them to this point. A procedure that prints a row of dashes is not really very useable. To help increase the worth of procedures, you need to make them more flexible. The most useful way is to be able to pass additional data into the procedure as you execute it, giving it additional direction or purpose. The way to accomplish this is through the use of parameters. Let's rewrite the `DoVerticals` procedure to include a parameter that varies the number of times it prints the lines.

TYPE **Listing 4.18. `DoVerticals`.**

```
procedure DoVerticals (HowManyTimes : Integer);

var
  Count : Integer;

     begin
       for Count := 1 to HowManyTimes do
        WriteLn ('    ¦   ¦    ');
      end;
```

Now the new procedure allows for some flexibility. You have incorporated a variable `HowManyTimes`, that is fed into the procedure. The `(HowManyTimes : Integer);` code is called a formal parameter list. This is a laundry list of the data that should be given to this procedure every time it is called, and what type(s) that data is. In this case, you want to pass an `Integer` variable into the procedure that will control the number of times the `WriteLn` is executed. By giving that variable a name, you are essentially doing a variable definition, not in the `var` section of the procedure. Now the procedure `DoVerticals` has a variable `HowManyTimes` of type `Integer` that can be used anywhere within that procedure.

Now remember that because this variable was defined inside this procedure, it can only be used inside this procedure (see the scope discussion later in this chapter). As you can see, you then use `HowManyTimes` as the end count of the `for` loop that executes the `WriteLn` as many times as you need. This makes the procedure much more flexible. The second part of this is now calling the procedure.

Now that you have created a formal parameter list as part of the procedure declaration, you need to change how you call the procedure. You can no longer just say `DoVerticals` and off it goes. For every formal parameter you identify, you must have a matching actual parameter when you make the call. There *must* be a one-to-one mapping between formal and actual parameters. Your procedure heading was `procedure DoVerticals (HowManyTimes : Integer);` and so you must have one `Integer` number to pass this procedure when you call it. The new code is shown in Listing 4.19.

TYPE

Listing 4.19. `ParamDemo` program.

```
program ParamDemo;

Uses
  Forms;

var
  Number : Integer;

   procedure DoVerticals (HowManyTimes : Integer);

   var
     Count : Integer;

     begin
       for Count := 1 to HowManyTimes do
        WriteLn ('    ¦   ¦    ');
      end; {Procedure DoVerticals}

begin
   WriteLn ('How many vertical lines would you like to print :');
   ReadLn(Number);
   DoVerticals (Number);
   ReadLn {To keep the window from closing until you press enter}
end. {program ParamDemo}
```

You may have noticed that when you called the `DoVerticals`, you passed it the variable `Number`. This is called an actual parameter. The contents of `Number` is copied into the procedure `DoVerticals` and lands in the locally defined variable `HowManyTimes`. At that point, the procedure has the data from the global variable `Number` in `HowManyTimes`, and goes on its way. When `DoVerticals` finishes its processing, the data in `HowManyTimes` disappears because the local variable is destroyed upon exiting the procedure.

When passing multiple parameters to a procedure, the order is most important. The only way that Delphi 2 can tell the matching of actual to formal parameters is by the order in which they are passed in. Let's look at another parameter example.

```
Procedure Junk (Number : Integer; Stuff : String);

begin
   WriteLn ('The number is ', Number);
   WriteLn ('The string is ', Stuff)
end; {procedure Junk}
```

This procedure takes two parameters, one is an `Integer` value, and the other is a `String` value. When you call this procedure, you must make the procedure call and pass it an Integer and a String, in that order. The program will not compile otherwise. You would call this procedure as shown in Listing 4.20:

TYPE **Listing 4.20. `JunkDemo` program.**

```
program JunkDemo;

Uses
   Forms;

var
  UsersNumber : Integer;
  UsersString : String;

Procedure Junk (Number : Integer; Stuff : String);

begin
   WriteLn ('The number is ', Number);
   WriteLn ('The string is ', Stuff)
end; {procedure Junk}

begin
  Write ('Enter your string :');
  ReadLn (UsersString);
  Write ('Enter the number :');
   ReadLn (UsersNumber);
   Junk (UsersNumber, UsersString)
  ReadLn {To keep the window from closing until you press enter}
end. {program JunkDemo}
```

As you can see, you are passing two parameters to `Junk`, making sure you pass them in the right order. You can also pass literal data to the function, as opposed to variable. An example would be calling `Junk(3,'Hello World');` which would pass the literal data into the local variables for processing.

Visibility and Scope

As your applications get broken up into smaller and smaller pieces, you need to become aware of how the lives of your variables are affected. With the move to procedures, functions, and units, there is more potential for things to overlap, so let's talk about two things that come to mind: visibility and scope of variables. Let's create a sample program (Listing 4.21), and then look at how variables are seen.

TYPE **Listing 4.21. `VisibleDemo` program.**

```
program VisibleDemo;

Uses
  Forms;

var
  A : Integer;

   procedure Outer;

      var
       B : Integer;

       procedure Inner;

       var
         C : Integer;

        begin
        C := 3;
        B := 8;
        A := 4; {I can see A from the main program declarations}
        end; {Procedure Inner}

     begin
        B := 5;
        C := 5; {this would be illegal, I can see only out, not in}
        A := 9 {I can see A from the main program declarations}
     end; {Procedure Outer}

   procedure AnotherOne;

     var
        D : Integer;

    begin
      D := 9;
      A := 55; {I can see A from the main program declarations}
      B := 4; {this would be illegal, I can see only out, not in}
      C := 5; {this would be illegal, I can see only out, not in}
    end; {procedure AnotherOne}
```

continues

Listing 4.21. continued

```
begin
   A:= 1
    {I can not reference any of the local variables in any of the procedures
      from here.  None are visible.}
end. {Main program VisibleDemo}
```

In this demo program, you have an application that has a nested procedure. There are two rules that describe which portions of your programs can see which variables.

Rule 1: Variables are only visible (which means you can access that variable) in the block in which they are defined.

Rule 2: In nested procedures or functions, you can always see from the inside out. This means procedures that are nested the deepest can see the variables defined in their parent procedure and it in its parent, and so on.

NOTE

Now you may say "Doesn't Rule 2 directly contradict Rule 1?" The answer to that question is no. This is based on the definition of block. Because a nested procedure was defined within its parent's block of code, the visibility is there, and if that parent is defined within the code block of its parent, the most deeply nested procedure can see all the way out. Just remember that you can always see outward (towards your parents) but not inward.

If you apply these rules to Listing 4.21, you can draw some conclusions.

- Because variable `C` was created in procedure `Inner`, it is only visible within that procedure.
- Because variable `B` was defined in procedure `Outer`, it is visible in that procedure, as well as visible to procedure `Inner`, which is looking "out" from a nested child procedure.
- Because variable `A` was defined in the main body, it is visible to every procedure and function in the main body. It is the parent of all the child procedures. The main body also has no visibility into any variable in those child procedures, because it cannot look "in," only out.
- Since variable `D` was defined in procedure `Another`, it can only be seen by `Another`, because there are no child nested procedures to see it. `Another` also has visibility to variable `A`, a variable in its parent.

Besides the visibility of a variable, you have its scope. In other words, where is it valid to use a variable. The rule here is simple. A variable does not reach beyond the block in which it is defined. Variable `C`'s scope is only within procedure `Inner`. It literally does not exist outside that procedure. Assignment to variable `C` outside procedure `Inner` (for instance, in procedure `Outer`) would gain you a wonderful compile time error that would let you know that variable `C` is undefined (in procedure `Outer`).

This is sometimes referred to as global versus local variables. Global variables are defined in the main program body and are visible to the entire application. Local variables are defined in procedures and functions, and are visible to certain portions of the application, depending on that procedure's nesting.

Functions

You may ask yourself "Why not just use procedures? Could there be anything better?" The answer is yes. As you see from our previous discussion, procedures play an important role in Delphi programming. There is another side to this argument, though. Let's say the world is full of nothing but procedures. Doing math in Delphi would be very interesting to say the least. If you had a square procedure it would look something like this:

```
procedure Square (The_Number : Real; Var The_Result);

  begin
    The_Result := The_Number * The_Number
  end;
```

Now this looks simple enough. To use the new procedure you would call it as shown in Listing 4.22.

TYPE **Listing 4.22. `FunctionDemo` program.**

```
program FunctionDemo;

Uses
  Forms;

   procedure Square (TheNumber : Real; Var TheResult : Real);

     begin
       TheResult := TheNumber * TheNumber
     end;

var
  UserInput , TheAnswer : Real;

begin
```

continues

4

Listing 4.22. continued

```
  Write ('Enter the number you want to square :');
  ReadLn (UserInput);
  Square (UserInput, TheAnswer);    {Here we called our procedure}
  WriteLn (UserInput, ' squared is equal to ', TheAnswer)
  ReadLn {To keep the window from closing until you press enter}
end. {FunctionDemo}
```

NOTE

> Notice how we put a `Var` before `TheResult` in the formal parameter list of the `Square` function call.

Now this works out OK, but you have to create a separate variable, `TheAnswer`, just to hold the result of the squaring operation, when all you want to do is to print the result out immediately after you calculate it. There is a better way.

A function is similar to a procedure in that you pass parameters to them both. The difference is that a function is designed to return a single value. This may not be a big revelation because you have designed procedures that return a single value as well. The difference is that the function returns that single value in the function name itself. The function name itself becomes a temporary variable in which the function's result is passed back to the calling code. Let's use an example to illustrate the point. In Delphi 2, there is a `Sqr()` function that you can use to square a number. Look at how to use this function in Listing 4.23.

TYPE Listing 4.23. `FunctionDemo2` program.

```
Program FunctionDemo2;

Uses
  Forms;

var
   UserInput : Real;

begin
   Write ('Enter the number you want to square :');
   ReadLn (UserInput);
   WriteLn (UserInput, ' squared is equal to ', Sqr(UserInput))
end. { FunctionDemo2}
```

As you can see, Listing 4.23 uses the `Sqr()` function and calculates the user's result right in the line that prints the answer out. A procedure would not work here two reasons. You do not have a place to put the result from a square procedure, and you cannot call a procedure

from within another procedure call statement. Let's rewrite the `Square()` procedure as a function and see how it differs.

```
Function Square (TheInput : Real) : Real;

  begin
     Result := TheInput * TheInput
  end;
```

There are two differences here between the old procedure and this function. The first is the function definition line. You pass the user's input into the function through the `TheInput` parameter. You are going to pass the result of the function back through the function name, associated with it, like any other variable. The `:Real` at the end of the function definition defines the return type of the function variable `Result`. Notice that in the function itself you have the line:

```
Square := TheInput * TheInput
```

Before your function can finish, you must assign a value to the variable `Result`. This special variable name is used to pass the result of your function call back to the calling code. `Result` is simply a transport mechanism to get your result back to the calling code. You need to set `Result` equal to a value of type `Real` (remember the `:Real`), before the function ends. Then, when control is returned back to the program that called the function, the function name `Square` actually has the function result in it. Now, this is a Cinderella story. The function name `Square` remains a temporary variable only in the line of code that called the function in the first place.

4

Once that line of code is done executing, the name `Square` has no value, and now is referencing a function call that requires parameters and the like. Rewrite the demo program showing how the function call is of a temporary nature. (See Listing 4.25.)

TYPE **Listing 4.25. `FunctionDemo3` program.**

```
Program FunctionDemo3;

Uses
  Forms;

    Function Square (TheInput : Real) : Real;

      begin
         Square := TheInput * TheInput
      end;

var
   UserInput : Real;
```

continues

Listing 4.25. continued

```
begin
   Write ('Enter the number you want to square :');
   ReadLn (UserInput);
   WriteLn (UserInput, ' squared is equal to ', Square(UserInput));
   {If we try to print the value of Square out after the line that called it
     we will get a compile time error.  This program will not run.}
   WriteLn ('In case you did not get it the value of the square is ', Square)
end. { FunctionDemo2}
```

The second `WriteLn` in Listing 4.25 will not compile. The word `Square` has no value at that point and is back to meaning the name of a function. The compile tells you that you are missing parameters for that function call. This does not diminish the value of functions, just limits their use. You will find functions throughout Delphi 2. Functions are invaluable as tools for doing math, graphics, and other interesting things.

Units

One of the reasons that software development progressed so slowly in the early years (I make it sound like the Stone Age, when dinosaurs roamed the earth and programmers used Microsoft C 7.0), is that everyone wanted to reinvent the wheel every time they developed a new application. "I have to do it my way." The number of times programmers wrote bubble sort routines could not be counted, it was so great (a slight exaggeration). With the advent of new development tools came new ideas.

Creation of the unit allowed the programmer to write and compile his bubble sort routine (maybe along with other routines) into a unit of code. That unit could then be reused and distributed to other developers. Because the unit is compiled, other developers could use my code without seeing the source code and my secret bubble sort algorithm.

The Format of a Unit

The *unit* is constructed similarly to a Delphi main program. A unit has the general form:

```
Unit YourNameHere;

  interface
      Uses ....

      const ...
      type ...
      var ...
      procedure ...
      function ...

  implementation
      Uses ...
```

```
      Label ...
      const ...
      type ...
      var ...
      procedure ...
      function ...

  initialization {optional}
     begin
       ...
     end;

  finalization {optional}
     begin
       ...
     end;

end. {End of the unit}
```

The `interface` section of the unit comes first. Here, you define any variables, constants, types, or other goodies that you want to make available to the project or other units with this unit is their `Uses` statement that has your unit name in their `Uses` statement. This gives you the option to include predefined structures to help the developer use your unit. The next item that is placed into the `interface` section is the procedure and function headers of all the procedures and functions you have implemented in your unit. This is how Delphi 2 tracks what is available to the application, from your unit.

Now that you have made public your intentions (in the `interface` section), you implement the functions and procedures you have described there in the `implementation` section. Here, you weave your magic as you implement your super secret `XOR` encryption algorithm that will earn you international fame (and maybe a movie deal).

In the implementation section, you place any variables, constants, and so on, that will be used by functions or procedures within this section. The variables that you define here cannot be used outside this section. You can also create procedures and functions that are used locally by those procedures and functions you have specified in the interface section. As the last item in the implementation section, you implement the functions and procedures that you have described in the `interface` section. The parameter lists must match exactly, or the unit will not compile.

Two other sections in the unit also deserve some attention. The first is the `initialization` section. You are able to define variables and such in the `interface` section. The problem is that because the interface section has no executable area, you can not initialize those variables with a value. The `initialization` section affords you the opportunity to do so. Here, you can initialize your variables, record structures, file variables, and anything else that could use an initial value. This enables you to "prime the pump," as it were. You can also initialize variables in the `begin...end` block at the end of the unit.

The `finalization` section is just the opposite. This section enables you to do some house cleaning prior to shutting the application down. It enables you to close files, deallocate memory, and perform other clean-up activities. Once the `initialization` section of your unit has been executed, the code in your `finalization` section is guaranteed to run prior to the application's closing. Another brilliant and necessary stroke is that Delphi 2 executes the finalization of the units used, in reverse order from what the initialization code has run. If you initialize the units X, Y, and then Z, it makes sense to close them down in Z, Y, and X order. This may be necessary as well, if units have other units in their `uses` statement, the dependent units will have to wait until their `finalization` sections have executed.

NOTE

It is important to understand the order in which the different pieces get executed in a unit, so we will recap it. When your application starts, the initialization section begins executing in order of the unit names in your `Uses` statement in the main program. From that point on, the code in the units is executed as it is called from your main program. When the user ends your application, the finalization section of each unit is called in the opposite order the initialization sections were in at the beginning of the program.

Here is an example of a unit you might create to do a couple of simple math functions. The applicability of this unit is in question, but it will help illustrate the structure and function.

```
Unit MathStuff;

interface
  function AddTwoNumbers (One, Two : Integer) : Integer;

  function SubtractTwoNumbers (One, Two : Integer) : Integer;

 function MultiplyTwoNumbers (One, Two : Integer) : Integer;

  procedure PositiveKarma;

implementation

  function AddTwoNumbers (One, Two : Integer) : Integer;

    begin
       AddTwoNumbers := One + Two
    end;

  function SubtractTwoNumbers (One, Two : Integer) : Integer;

     begin
        SubtractTwoNumbers := One - Two
     end;
```

```
  function MultiplyTwoNumbers (One, Two : Integer) : Integer;

      begin
         MultiplyTwoNumbers := One * Two
      end;

   procedure PositiveKarma;
      begin
         WriteLn('You can do it, math is not hard!')
      end;

end. {MathStuff Unit}
```

This simple unit illustrates the form of a unit. You have defined the functions and procedures that are available to the user of the unit in the interface section. In the `implementation` section, you actually create the items you "advertised" in the `interface` section. I threw in the `PositiveKarma` procedure for those of you who hate math. You will see units used extensively in Delphi 2.

To call this unit you must simply include it in the `Uses` section of your main program. An example of calling the `MathStuff` unit appears in Listing 4.26.

TYPE

Listing 4.26. `MathDemo` program.

```
program MathDemo;

uses
  MathStuff;

var
  A, B : Integer;

begin
  A := 1;
  B := 2;
  WriteLn ('The sum of  ', A, ' and ', B, ' is ', AddTwoNumbers(A,B));
  ReadLn {To keep the window from closing until you press enter}
end. {program MathDemo}
```

You have used one of the `MathStuff` functions, `AddTwoNumbers` to demonstrate the use of units. It really is that simple.

Reusability

The concepts of software reusability and component libraries have come to light in recent years. The Unit is a natural extension of this theory of reuse. The Unit provides a way for a software developer to create a set of library routines and wrap them into a piece of code that can be set aside and used at any time.

The `Uses` statement allows you to include your own units in your application. Delphi 2 provides a standard set of units that perform general functions, such as file I/O, forms, graphics, buttons, and so on. (A full list of standard units is available in Delphi's online help.) You'll find several advantages to using the unit model for developing software. Because most of the functionality of an application can be divided into groups or areas, it only makes sense that you have a programming model that supports that concept.

`Units` also help in the debugging process. If you are having a problem with your self-derived math formula, you would look in your math `unit` to debug the function, rather than looking through your entire application for the defective math function. The ability to break your program up into pieces enables you to group such things as functions and procedures into units and better organize your project. In a large project involving many people, you may even want to assign a code librarian to keep the latest versions of your `units`, and distribute them to those who need the units.

Distribution Security

I assume that you are writing software (and reading this book) because you have a love of developing software. I also assume that many of you are trying to make money doing it as well. As with authoring books, writing software is creating something from nothing. That creative effort needs to be protected. If you were to come up with an encryption algorithm that can speedily encrypt data, you would more than likely wish to protect that code. You will also probably want to sell that code as well. This creates a problem—how to sell your code to other developers without giving them the source code and compromising your algorithm.

Units provide a feature necessary to everyone who wishes to distribute their code and keep it safe from piracy. Delphi units can be compiled into binary files and distributed for use by others. When a unit is compiled, Delphi gives it a .dcu extension. This designates the file as a Delphi Compiled Unit (hence the .dcu extension). From that point on you can distribute that .dcu file to others, and they may use that unit in their applications, by including it in the `Uses` statement, but they will never see the source code itself. This enables you to develop your code and sell it with more security and peace of mind.

In order for developers to use your unit, they must know what functionality it provides. It is necessary for you to detail the functionality in an accompanying document. Many developers simply copy the `interface` section of the `unit` and distribute that. Remember, now that your unit is compiled, the `interface` section is not humanly readable anymore. Selling add-on units, DLLs, and VCLs is big business, and there is no reason you cannot play along, too.

NOTE

> It should be known that to date, this concept of distributing units has not worked well between versions. It is usually necessary to recompile units for every version of Pascal/Delphi. For this reason, many programmer's make their source code available (for a price) along with the compiled unit.

Team Development

Another benefit of breaking your project into units is the ability to assign different developers to create those units. Once you have divided the application into math, graphing, and file I/O units, you can assign a developer to create each unit. Assign a developer who is math wise at doing the math unit, a graphics-type developer to the graphics unit, and so on. Most applications are getting too large to be written by a single developer (in a reasonable period of time). It becomes more important than ever to find ways to divide the work among several developers, and get the work done faster.

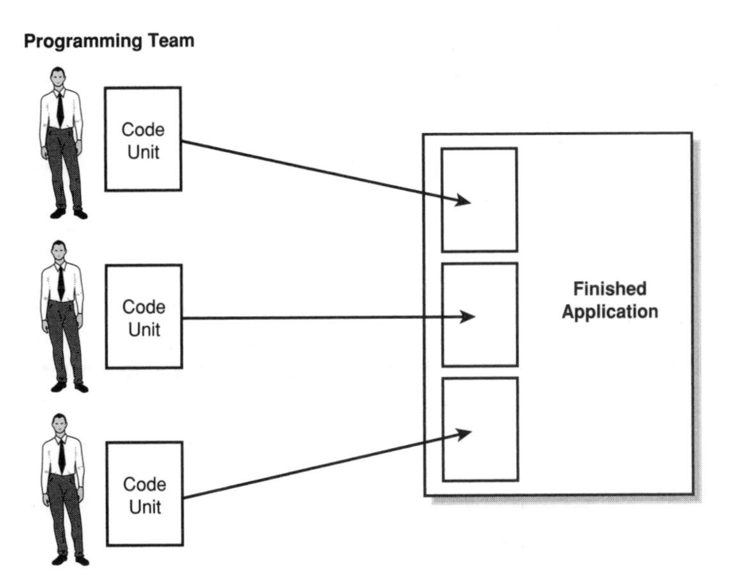

Figure 4.1.
The team development concept.

Pointers

The concept of pointers is probably the single most difficult topic for programmers to learn. We will give you an introduction to pointers here, but do not feel badly if you are not a pointer expert by the time you finish reading this. It may take some time working with them before you are comfortable.

When you create data structures in Delphi 2, they are allocated memory. That memory is needed to hold the data in your structure. Many of the data structures (such as records and arrays) can become arbitrarily large. For that reason, as well as others, allocate only the memory that you are going to use.

A pointer variable is capable of storing the address of a data structure (such as an array or record) in it. This is similar to a looking up something in the white pages in the phone book. You can give other procedures and functions this "pointer" to your data instead of the data itself. Now you may not see the immediate benefit of this approach. Think of a map. You don't bring the whole store home to give to your neighbor, but you give the neighbor directions—or a pointer to the store.

Procedures make extensive use of pointers. You use pointers every time you make a function call and use the `var` designator in the formal procedure declaration. When you pass parameters using the `var` designator, this actually passes a pointer to the data into your procedure. That is why, when you change the data in a `var` parameter variable in your procedure, that data is changed outside your procedure as well. You are really changing the outside data directly, using that "handle" to the data.

There is a real benefit to doing business this way. If you do not use the `var` designator in the formal parameter list of a procedure call, every time you pass something into the procedure, Delphi 2 has to make a local copy of the data to work on. By not using `var`, you are saying "Do not touch my original," so it makes a copy. Can you imagine how much memory is used by making copies of 10,000 record arrays. The payback for using pointers is very real.

NOTE

> Pointers do not mean that everything is free. Pointers also take resources in the system. To reference the data, Delphi has to de-reference a pointer each time. At best that may double or triple the number of CPU cycles it takes to complete the operation. The rule of thumb is use only what you need.

Using Pointers

To use a pointer, you must first define one. Let's take a simple example of a pointer to a real number, as shown in Listing 4.27.

TYPE **Listing 4.27. PointerDemo program.**

```
program PointerDemo;

Uses
  Forms;

type
  RealPointer = ^Real;

var
  P : RealPointer;

begin
  New (P);
  P^ := 21.6;
  WriteLn (P^ :5:1);
   Dispose (P)
  ReadLn {To keep the window from closing until you press enter}
end.  {PointerDemo}
```


Listing 4.27 demonstrates the fundamentals of using pointers. You begin by creating a type called `RealPointer`. `RealPointer` is a pointer to `Real` number. The caret (`^`) denotes "pointing to." Therefore, the line would read, "`RealPointer` is a pointer to real number." After you define the pointer type, you must create a variable of that type for use. So you create the variable `P` of type `RealPointer`. Now, you have a variable that is a pointer to a real number.

As you begin the execution of the program, you must first allocate memory for `P`. Right now, `P` is capable of pointing to a real number, but is currently pointing to nothing. By using the `New()` procedure call, you are having Delphi 2 assign a block of memory capable of holding a `Real` number and put that memory address into `P`. Now `P` is pointing to a memory location that can hold a `Real` number. The line `P^ := 21.6;` should be read, "Set the place that `P` is pointing to equal to 21.6." This is called *dereferencing* a pointer. In other words, you are taking the value `21.6` and placing it into the memory location pointed to by `P`.

When using the `WriteLn` to print out the value of what is pointed to by `P`, you again must use the caret to say, "Write to the screen what `P` is pointing to, and format it in 5 digits with one digit to the right of the decimal." After you have no more use for `P`, you must use the `Dispose()` procedure call to free the memory that `P` is pointing to and give it back to the free memory pool. Then, you end the program.

You can also use pointers to point to things more complex than just a `Real` number. In Listing 4.28, you create a record and use a pointer to it to access that record's fields.

TYPE **Listing 4.28. `PointerDemo2` program.**

```
Program PointerDemo2;

Uses
  Forms;

type
  PersonType = RECORD
     LastName  : String;
     FirstName : String;
     Age          : Integer
          end; {PersonRecord}

 PersonPointer = ^PersonType;

var
  Person : PersonPointer;

begin
  New (Person);
  Person^.LastName := "Smith";
  Person^.FirstName := "James";
  Person^.Age := 35;
  WriteLn ('Well ', Person^.FirstName, ' ', Person^.LastName, [ic:ccc]', you are
', Person^.Age, ' years old.');
   Dispose (Person);
ReadLn {To keep the window from closing until you press enter}
end. {PointerDemo2}
```

Listing 4.28 is a little more complicated. You create a type called `PersonType` that is a record, consisting of a last name, first name, and an age. Second, you create a `PersonPointer` type that is a pointer to the record you created earlier. The creation of a `Person` variable is the next step. That variable is of `PersonPointer` type. When the execution of the main program begins, you go through the same motions as with the `PointerDemo` program. Allocation of memory is done with the `New()` command. You place values into the record pointed to by `Person` by using the ^ to dereference the pointer and show which field of the record to place the data in. After assigning values to the record, the results are written to the screen in a string that ends up similar to "Well, James Smith, you are 35 years old." Using the `Dispose()` command frees the memory allocated to `Person`. This example is very similar to the `PointerDemo` in how the pointers are dealt with. The difference is what data structure you are pointing to.

The evil reality of it all is that Windows is full of pointers. Many of the ways programs exchange data is by exchanging pointers. In languages such as C++, pointers are it. This has only been a cursory introduction, and many pages could be spent talking about the intricacies of using pointers. Read all the material you can about pointers and look at examples. Delphi has gone to great lengths to hide as much of the implementation of pointers from you as it could. You will have to investigate anyway.

Summary

In this chapter, you have looked at the Object Pascal language. Hopefully, you have been introduced to the concepts necessary for developing modular programs. The idea of team development and the benefits of units, procedures, and functions were covered. On Day 5, we will talk about managing your Delphi 2 application from a file perspective, what files make up your Delphi application, and how to use the Delphi 2 environment to organize your project.

Q&A

Q Why does OP provide constructs such as `Goto` if it is considered bad programming practice to use them?

A The subject is not really closed (and probably never will be) on proper use of things such as `Goto`. The tool will still be there until it is wise to dump it, if ever.

Q What would happen if a procedure returned execution control to the line of code that called the procedure and not the line after it?

A It would not work. Every time the procedure finished, it would return control to a line code that simply called the procedure again. It's like calling the IRS and asking for an audit—not a good idea!

Workshop

Quiz

1. How many times is the `WriteLn()` statement executed in the following example?

```
Program Quiz4-1;

var
  Count, Count2 : Integer;

begin
  For Count := 1 to 10 do
    For Count2 := 1 to 10 do
       WriteLn ('Hello!');
end.
```

2. Which looping construct do you use if you would like to test your conditional prior to entering the processing loop?

3. What is the fundamental difference between a procedure and a function?
4. What is the advantage of using pointers in an application, as opposed to passing the real data around instead?

Exercises

1. Write an application that counts to 33, prints out the number as it counts, and uses two `For` loops to do it.
2. Try writing an application that has several units. To get a feel for the `Uses` statement, have your main application use a unit, and have that unit use yet another unit. As long as they compile, the units can be simple.
3. Write a procedure that has several parameters, both passing by reference and passing by value. See how changing the values around can generate different compile time error messages.

Day 5

Files and the Project Manager

What Actually Makes Up a Delphi Application?

In this chapter, we take a look at the various pieces that make up a Delphi application or better put, a Delphi project. The Delphi application will ultimately be an executable or group of executables and DLLs. If you used OCXs they will become part of it as well. That's all fine, but what we are really interested in here are actual files, forms, units, components, resources, and so on that are built by you the programmer or by Delphi.

At first glance, a simple program may look as though it is made up only of a project file and a unit. Actually, several other files are created for you behind the scenes as you work on your program. You may be wondering why you would concern yourself with files created by Delphi. You wouldn't want to accidentally delete or move files that are needed by that new Boss Key. ...I mean, database front end you have been working so hard on, now would you? In any case, it is a good idea to become familiar with what makes up a Delphi project, where all these extra files that you didn't create came from, and what they all do.

This chapter outlines several important topics, several of which could use an entire chapter of their own, but the purpose here is to help you understand the basics of a Delphi project. When you need more detail on a topic than is provided in this chapter, you should refer to the online help, the Delphi Manuals, or elsewhere in the book, as appropriate. In this chapter, I want to give you the big picture in an easily digestible format.

Once you have a good idea of what makes up a Delphi project, you will move on to managing Delphi projects. The Delphi IDE has a Project Manager to help you with this task. However, there is more to Delphi project management than just a menu. If you want an organized and well-managed project, you need to give some thought to setting up a directory structure to store your code using appropriate names for the files, forms, components, and variables. The best approach is to get your projects organized from the start and keep them that way through their completion.

Projects

A Delphi project consists of forms, units, option settings, resources, and so on. All this information lives in files. Many of these files are created by Delphi as you build your application. Resources such as bitmaps, icons, and so on, are in files that you obtain from some other source or create with the many tools and resource editors available. In addition, files are also created by the compiler. Let's take a quick look at some of these files.

A Delphi *project* consists of forms, units, option settings, resources, and so on.

The following files are created by Delphi as you design your application.

- Project file (.dpr)—This file is used to keep information about forms and units. You'll find initialization code here as well.
- Unit file (.pas)—This file is used to store code. Some units are associated with forms; some store only functions and procedures. Many of Delphi's functions and procedures are stored in units.
- Form file (.dfm)—This is a binary file that is created by Delphi to store information about your forms. Each Form file has a corresponding Unit (.pas) file. For example, myform.pas has a file called myform.dfm associated with it.
- Project option files (.dfo)—Project option settings are stored in this file.
- Resource file (.res)—This binary file contains an icon that the project uses. This file should not be changed or created by the user, because Delphi is continually updating or re-creating this file.

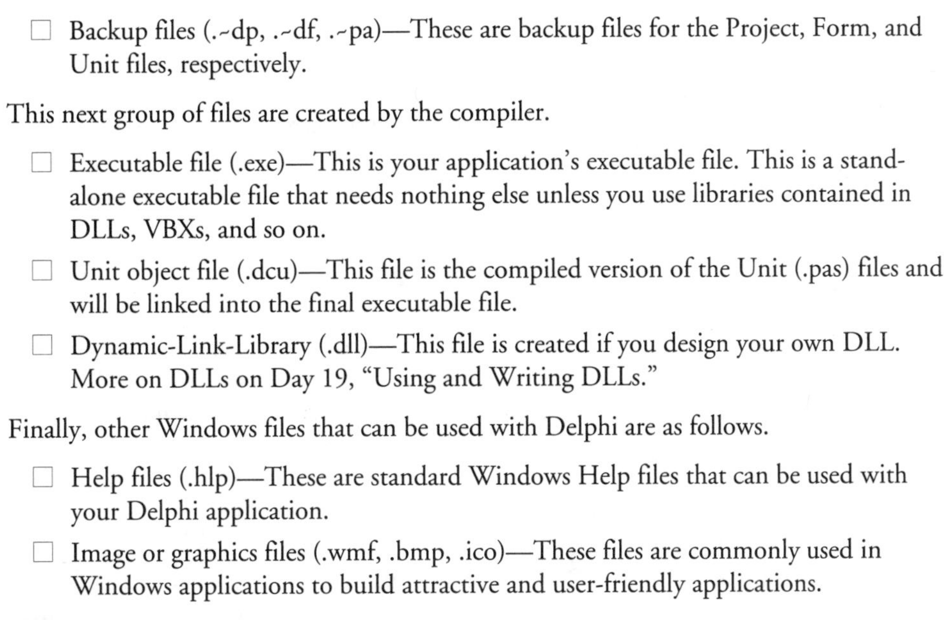

- Backup files (.~dp, .~df, .~pa)—These are backup files for the Project, Form, and Unit files, respectively.

This next group of files are created by the compiler.

- Executable file (.exe)—This is your application's executable file. This is a stand-alone executable file that needs nothing else unless you use libraries contained in DLLs, VBXs, and so on.
- Unit object file (.dcu)—This file is the compiled version of the Unit (.pas) files and will be linked into the final executable file.
- Dynamic-Link-Library (.dll)—This file is created if you design your own DLL. More on DLLs on Day 19, "Using and Writing DLLs."

Finally, other Windows files that can be used with Delphi are as follows.

- Help files (.hlp)—These are standard Windows Help files that can be used with your Delphi application.
- Image or graphics files (.wmf, .bmp, .ico)—These files are commonly used in Windows applications to build attractive and user-friendly applications.

NEW TERM The project file (.dpr) itself actually contains Object Pascal code and is the main part of your application that actually gets things started when you execute your application. The funny thing is, you can build an entire Delphi application and never need to look at this file. It is created and modified automatically by Delphi as you build your application. Whatever name you give your project file will also be the name of your executable file. The following code is an example of what a project file would look like if you started a new project and did not change the filenames or form names.

```
program Project1
uses
  Forms,
  Unit1 in 'UNIT1.PAS' {Form1};

{$R *.RES}

begin
Application.CreateForm(TForm, Form1);
Application.Run(Form1);
end.
```

NOTE

> Notice the word `program` in the first line? This tells Delphi that this is the main program code. `program` can be replaced with `library` if you plan to build a DLL.

5

Again, the project file is maintained by Delphi automatically. You should not typically need to modify a project file. I would recommend leaving it alone unless you are building a DLL or doing some other advanced programming.

Forms

One of the greatest things about Windows programs is the form. Before I started writing Windows programs, I was using mostly C for DOS-based applications. C is a great and powerful language, but not very easy or forgiving when it comes to Windows programming. Then I took a C++ class, a Windows programming class and went off to write Windows programs in C/C++. Ouch!!! I spent hours just trying to create a basic form with a button on the screen and to understand what I had done and how the code worked. The amount of source code involved in C to create just one window is huge. In C++, it is a little better if you use a development kit such as Borland's OWL or Microsoft's MFC, but you still need a good understanding of OOP and the language to know what's going on and how to use it all. Even the latest and greatest C++ compilers on the market today cannot perform the visual programming that Delphi does so well. Delphi basically gives us "mere mortals" a chance to create real Windows programs that blow the socks off programs developed in other visual environments. Delphi programs will run at speeds close or equal to a program written in C++. Delphi does much of the work for you and enables you to focus on the code specific to your application.

New Term As you know, a Windows program is made up of a window or series of windows commonly referred to in Delphi as *forms.* When you start Delphi, it automatically creates a form for you to use. Forms are used to house your controls, components, and so on.

The Delphi application (as well as most Windows applications) is centered around the form. Although other programs can use the concept of windows or forms, for an application to achieve a true Microsoft Windows likeness, it must comply to Microsoft's guidelines for the layout and structure of its appearance. You'll learn more about the look and feel of Windows programs in Day 6, "Fundamentals of GUI Design." The information for Delphi forms is stored in two files: the .dfm and the .pas file. The .dfm file actually contains information about your form's appearance, size, location, and so on. This is one of those files that you do not need to worry about or maintain. I just want you to be aware of how the .dfm file is used.

The form's code and the code for its controls are stored in the .pas file, also known as a *unit.* This is the file you spend most of your time in as you write a Delphi application. Each time you add an event handler for a form or double-click on a control to add code to it, this file is updated, and Delphi puts the cursor in the correct spot to add or modify your code. When you add additional forms, they also have their own .dfm and .pas files.

Another thing you need to know about forms is that they have properties. These properties can be set to control the appearance and behavior of the form. With these properties, you can change form color, size, location, centering, visibility or invisibility, whether it is located at the position set at design time, and more. A form also has a number of *event handlers* (segments of code you can add to execute when specific form-related events occur). You can include event handlers for events such as a mouse click or form resize.

NOTE

> You have just read about all the files that make up a Delphi project. For the most part, these files will be kept synchronized by Delphi as you make updates. You should always use Delphi to change filenames or update the files to prevent files getting out of synch. If you do not, you may get errors when you try to load or compile your programs. In other words, if you click on a component and delete it, let Delphi remove the associated code. Don't delete it in the editor. Delphi cleans up after itself very well.

Units

There are three types of units: units associated to forms (the most common), unit files used to store functions and procedures, and unit files used to build components.

NEW TERM *Unit files* are source code files with the .pas extension. As you work with Delphi, you will become intimately involved with units.

Let's look at a basic unit associated with a form (see Listing 5.1). The unit name is on the first line following the word `unit`. Following the `unit` header is the interface part which contains the `uses`, `type`, and `var` clauses. Lastly, the `implementation` part contains functions and procedures for your controls (event handlers), as well as your own functions, procedures, and code to be used in the unit.

5

TYPE **Listing 5.1.** `Unit1.`

```
unit Unit1;

interface

uses
 Windows, Messages, SysUtils, Classes, Graphics, Controls, Forms, Dialogs;

type
  TForm1 = class(TForm)
    procedure FormCreate(Sender: TObject);
  private
    { Private declarations }
  public
    { Public declarations }
  end;

var
  Form1: TForm1;

implementation

{$R *.DFM}

procedure TForm1.FormCreate(Sender: TObject);
begin

end;
end.
```

ANALYSIS Believe it or not, the preceding code, along with the project file code, is all you need in Delphi to create an executable that opens a window. It won't do much at this point, but it is a functional Windows program in its simplest form.

Look at the names in the `uses` clause in Listing 5.1. These are names of other units. If you decide to write a bunch of handy functions and procedures, you could create your own unit, put all your handy work in the unit, and compile it for future use. Each time you want to use your homegrown unit, you simply add the name to the `uses` clause. Let's look at the parts that make up the `unit` in Listing 5.1.

- Unit header—A unit header identifies the code as a `unit` and is followed by the name that will also be the filename for the `unit` with an extension of .pas. (See Listing 5.1.)
- `interface`—This marks the start of the `unit interface` part that is used to declare variables, types, procedures, and so on. The `interface` part determines what in this `unit` is available to other units and parts of the program. The `interface` portion of the `unit` ends with the start of the `implementation` part. (See Listing 5.1.)
- `uses`—The `uses` clause tells the compiler which libraries of functions and procedures need to be compiled into the final executable. Delphi automatically puts several of these in for you. If you write your own unit, you need to remember to

include the unit name in the `uses` clause when you need to use functions contained in the unit. (See Listing 5.1.)

- `type`—The `type` declaration section is used for creating user-defined types. These types can then be used to define variables. (See Listing 5.1.)

Visibility specifiers follow the `type` clause in the interface part (see Listing 5.1). The following specifiers are used to control how objects appear to other programs and objects:

- `private`—Declarations in this section are treated as public within the module, but will be unknown and not accessible outside the unit.
- `public`—Declarations in this section are visible and accessible outside the unit.

The following two specifiers (published and protected) are used for creating components (these are not needed and do not appear in Listing 5.1 and will be covered in more detail on Day 20, "Writing Your Own Visual Component"):

- `Published`—This used to create components. Published properties are displayed in the Object Inspector to allow you to modify them at design time.
- `Protected`—A component. Fields, methods, and properties that are declared as protected are accessible to descendants (descendants are discussed on Day 7, "Object-Oriented Programming") of the declaring type (types were discussed on Day 3, "Object Pascal, Part I").
- `var`—Used to declare variables and object variables. In a form unit, `var` is used in the interface part (Delphi puts this declaration here for you) to declare the form as an instance of the `TForm` object (see Day 7, "Object-Oriented Programming" for more info on objects). `var` is also used to declare variables in the implementation part as well as in procedures in functions.
- `implementation`—This is where all the functions and procedures that were declared in the `interface` part will actually be placed. Any declarations that are made here are `private` to the `unit` (not available to other units).
- `{$R *.DFM}`—In a form unit, Delphi inserts the `$R *.DFM` entry for you. This is very important, as it ties the form to its .dfm file that we talked about earlier. *Do not remove* this from your program, or you will have problems.

The following code block executes when your form is created. You should put any startup code here that needs to be executed when the form starts to load. To create this procedure, use the Object Inspector to view the Events menu for the form and then double-click the `OnCreate` event. The Object Inspector is discussed in more detail on Day 9, "The Visual Component Library." Event handlers are discussed in more detail on Day 8, "Exceptions and Events."

```
procedure TForm1.FormCreate(Sender: TObject);
begin

end;
```

5

Add, of course, the final `end`—and notice that it has a (.) or period after it. This signifies the end of the unit.

```
end.
```

Finally, there are two additional optional parts you can add to your unit: *`initialization`* and *`finalization`*. The `initialization` part is used to run any code that you might need to run to initialize and prepare for your unit to be run. The `finalization` part allows you to do any cleanup before your unit completely exits. Please refer to the online help or Delphi manuals for more information on these.

This concludes the discussion on a `unit` associated with a form. It is important to keep headings, clauses, and so on, in the correct place. Delphi pretty much takes care of this for you because it creates the unit and code as you make changes to the form. You simply add your code to the correct section as needed. The remaining two unit types, units associated with a component and units used to store functions and procedures are not covered here. The unit used to store functions and procedures is very much like a form unit without the form-related declarations; see the Delphi manual or online help for more information on "Unit files for Procedures and Functions." A component associated unit is discussed on Day 20, "Writing Your Own Visual Component."

The Visual Component Library

The Visual Component Library (VCL) is made up of a rich selection of objects that are written in Delphi's Object Pascal for use as controls (or components) on the Delphi forms. There are two basic types: visible and invisible. Visible components are placed and programmed for the user. Invisible components give special control or programming interface to the programmer. A timer is an example of an invisible component while the edit box is an example of a visible component.

The different categories of components include buttons, listboxes, labels, edit boxes, data aware, timers, image boxes, selection boxes, and the list goes on. You will come to know and love these components because they are the building blocks of your Delphi application. Each of these components has quite a bit of code associated with it to make it work, and you don't have to write or maintain any of it. You simply drop the components on the form, and they are ready for your use. Components have properties, events, and methods, all of which enable the programmer to use a component and control the way it behaves. We will look at the Visual Component Library in much more detail a little later in the book.

Optional OCX Components

An *OCX* is a 32-bit, OLE-based, predesigned Windows control or component that can be used by Delphi 2 or any language with OCX support. OLE is discussed on

Day 18, "OLE 2, A Primer." The OCX will mostly likely have been developed by a third party vendor or programmer, and created in C++.

Delphi 2 supports OCXs. This is both good and bad. On the good side, a ton of third-party controls are on the market and available for you to purchase. You can find an OCX that will do just about anything you want from fancy tabs to calendars to full-blown communications controls. The downside to using OCXs is that they are not compiled into your executable, so you must ship them with your application. The important thing to remember here is, if you really need an OCX and find one that works with Delphi and meets your needs, go for it. The desirable way to add-on to your application is with Delphi components. As time goes on, a number of vendors will be producing Delphi components for purchase as opposed to OCXs for use in Delphi.

User-Created Procedures, Functions, and Event-Handler Code

User-created procedures, functions, and event handlers are an important part to your application. As you build your application, you create forms using the components, but you eventually need to tie them all together with your own code. All those components are pretty useless if you don't have some way to access them for information or instruct them as to what to do. The Object Pascal Language behind Delphi has a great selection of tools to help you build your programs. You will also want to write your own routines using Object Pascal. All this code is the "engine" under the fancy exterior. Without the engine, nothing is going to happen.

Resources Such As Icons and Bitmaps

We can't forget about all the good stuff—the graphics! You can't build an attractive application without some pretty graphics. Delphi comes with some sample icons and bitmaps, but you will obviously want to start your own collection as well. When you choose an icon for the program, Delphi stores it in the .res file. However, icons are not the only resources a Delphi program uses. Cursors, bitmaps, and Windows metafiles (.wmf) are also resources. These all become part of your executable, but they are resources that start outside of your source code. You usually choose the resources you want by setting properties in a component or specifying a filename. This causes the component to load the bitmap, icon, or other graphic. The graphic or resource is then loaded into the project and prepared to be used when you select run or compile.

Organizing Your Delphi Project

Now that you know what makes up Delphi projects, you should think about organizing and managing them. You may be able to work on simple little programs or projects without much thought about project management, but if you are not careful, it is possible to delete or overwrite files that you didn't want to lose. It is also easy to get confused as to which files go with which project, if you aren't organized. So, as you go through the rest of this chapter, you'll learn more about how to start off well organized and how to stay that way. It really does not take much effort, but it will save you time and effort later if you know where everything for a project is when you decide to work on it, delete it, back it up, and so on.

Creating Separate Directories

Let's start off with the basics. I like to create a source directory under the compiler directory. In my case, it is c:\program files\delphi 2.0\source. Underneath the source directory, I usually like to create a separate directory for each of my projects. This makes it easier to find projects, easier to make backups, and it protects files from being changed accidentally. If you had a project that used a unit called mainmenu.pas and another project were copied into the same directory with a mainmenu.pas... Yep, you guessed it. You have just lost your original mainmenu.pas. Not fun—I know, because I have done it! Consider the following directory structure:

```
C:\PROGRAM FILES\BORLAND\DELPHI 2.0\
                                 |
                                 SOURCE\
                                       |
                                       PROJECT1
                                       |
                                       PROJECT2
```

If you set up a structure like this, projects will be fairly safe from each other. When you select File | Open or File | Save As from the File menu options in Delphi, the directory you selected displays. Another benefit to this is that you always know where your updated files and executables go (assuming you have not changed to the wrong directory or set Delphi to put output files someplace else). This structure makes backups a breeze. You can use Windows Explorer, File Manager, or a backup utility to backup c:\program files\borland\delphi 2.0\source and all its subdirectories.

Naming Conventions

Another practice that will help you keep organized (and be able to look at your Delphi source files and know what they are) is to use some kind of naming convention for your filenames. In other words, don't use the default names, such as project1.dpr and unit1.pas. (This is

something most of us are guilty of at some time or another.) Probably the easiest way to break this habit is to immediately do a Project | Save As when you start a new project. Give the unit1.pas and project1.pas files new names when prompted for them. Of course, each time you add a form, you need to give it a new name when you save. However, if you name all these when you start out, you can occasionally save the project without the need to deal with filenames, and so on, and you enjoy the benefits we have been talking about. If you don't do this, think about how fun it will be if you come back 6 months later and start wondering what unit1.pas and unit2.pas do in project1.dpr. Of course, if you have a lot of these in various directories, it really gets fun—NOT!

Actually, a good naming convention should apply not only to your files, but also to forms, components, and variables you use in your application. It is easy to use all the default names for forms and components as you design your application. However, once you have given the files unique names, you can still end up with a messy project if it gets big enough. Imagine looking over your project and seeing FORM1, FORM2, FORM3 each with its own set of BUTTON1, BUTTON2, BUTTON3.... I think you get the picture. You'll see examples of code like this all the time, including examples in this book. For one form and a few components, it is not a big deal, but as your projects grow in size, this will cause you to waste time going back to look and see what a form or component is called or does. If you get in the habit of giving unique and descriptive names to your files, forms, components, and so on, you will save time and frustration.

Let's compare two listings, and you will see what I am talking about. The first is a listing (see Listing 5.2) that creates a form on the screen designed to get a user's name. All of the filenames, caption, and name properties have been changed from their defaults to something more descriptive and meaningful.

NOTE

> Filenames must follow the rules for length and valid characters for the target operating system (for example, Windows 95 or Windows NT). Captions may be up to 255 characters long and must be a valid Pascal string. Names may be up to 63 characters long and must follow the rules that apply to Pascal identifiers (see the online help for more information on identifiers).

TYPE **Listing 5.2. Readname.**

```
unit Readname;

interface

uses
 Windows, Messages, SysUtils, Classes, Graphics, Controls, Forms, Dialogs

type
  TGetUserName = class(TForm)
    Button_GetName: TButton;
    Edit_Getname: TEdit;
    procedure FormCreate(Sender: TObject);
    procedure Button_GetNameClick(Sender: TObject);
    procedure Edit_GetnameChange(Sender: TObject);
  private
    { Private declarations }
  public
    { Public declarations }
  end;

var
  GetUserName: TGetUserName;

implementation

{$R *.DFM}

procedure TGetUserName.FormCreate(Sender: TObject);
begin

end;

procedure TGetUserName.Button_GetNameClick(Sender: TObject);
begin

end;

procedure TGetUserName.Edit_GetnameChange(Sender: TObject);
begin

end;

end.
```

Now, let's look at identical code, but with all the default names Delphi creates for the unit (see Listing 5.3).

TYPE

Listing 5.3. `Unit1` (default names).

```
unit Unit1;

interface

uses
  SysUtils, WinTypes, WinProcs, Messages, Classes, Graphics, Controls,
  Forms, Dialogs;

type
  TForm1 = class(TForm)
    Button1: TButton;
    Edit1: TEdit;
    procedure FormCreate(Sender: TObject);
    procedure Button1Click(Sender: TObject);
    procedure Edit1Change(Sender: TObject);
  private
    { Private declarations }
  public
    { Public declarations }
  end;

var
  Form1: TForm1;

implementation

{$R *.DFM}

procedure TForm1.FormCreate(Sender: TObject);
begin

end;

procedure TForm1.Button1Click(Sender: TObject);
begin

end;

procedure TForm1.Edit1Change(Sender: TObject);
begin

end;

end.
```


ANALYSIS The differences should be pretty obvious. Listing 5.2 is much easier to follow because names describe what each item is and what it does (`Button_Getname`, for example). It is pretty obvious that this button is supposed to get a name—much easier to figure out than `Button1`. With all this information behind you, you are ready to move on to the Project Manager.

Sample Project

Let's build a small project from the ground up. As you go, you'll learn to put some of the ideas we have been talking about into practice. You'll also be introduced to the Project Manager and other Delphi features you need to know about when working with projects. You'll create a simple Delphi application with two forms that interact with each other. To get a good start, let's set up an organized directory structure to work with.

1. Create a source directory under the Delphi directory (if you don't already have one); for example, c:\program files\borland\delphi 2.0\source.
2. Create a directory to store your project in. Let's call it `Formtalk` (c:\program files\borland\delphi 2.0\source\formtalk). If you are wondering why it is called `Formtalk`, it's because one form talks to another, or in this case it simply updates information on another form.
3. If Delphi is not already running, start it up. Create a new project using File | New, select the Application Icon from the New Item Menu, and click OK. (See Figure 5.1.)

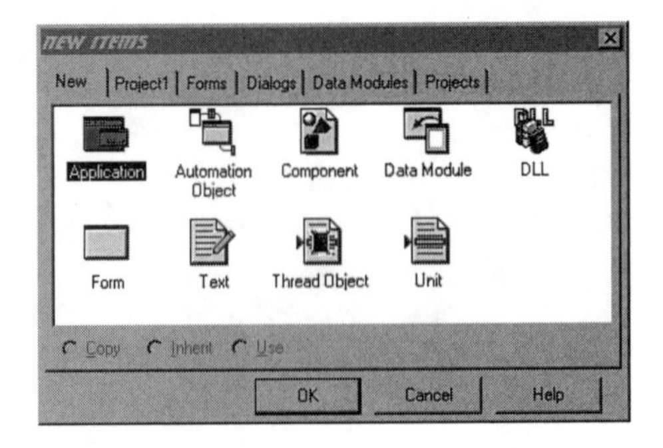

Figure 5.1.
New Item dialog box with the Application icon highlighted.

4. Now, save the project using File | Save Project As (see Figure 5.2). Select the directory and filename to save unit1.pas, but change unit1.pas to c:\program files\borland\delphi 2.0\source\formtalk\input.pas (see Figure 5.3). This will be the Input form that will take information from the user.

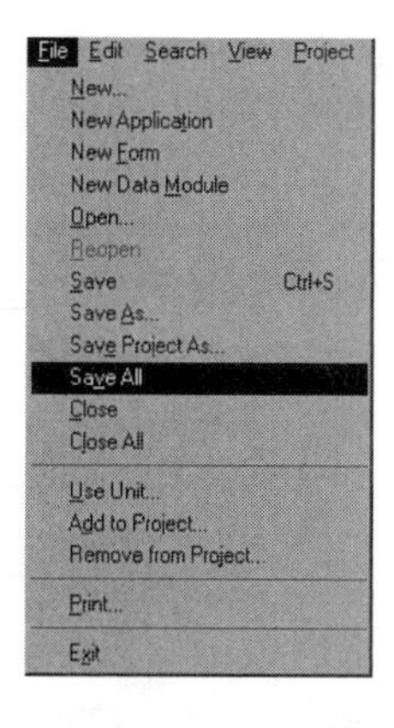

Figure 5.2.
File | Save Project menu option.

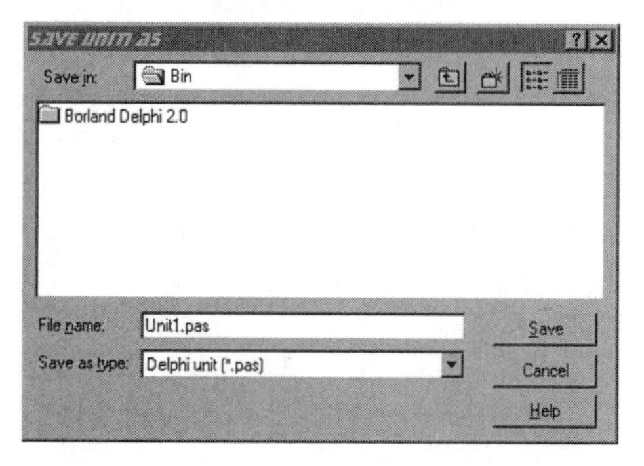

Figure 5.3.
Save Unit As dialog box.

5. Save the project file from project1.dpr to c:\program files\borland\delphi2\formtalk\source\formtalk.dpr (see Figure 5.4).

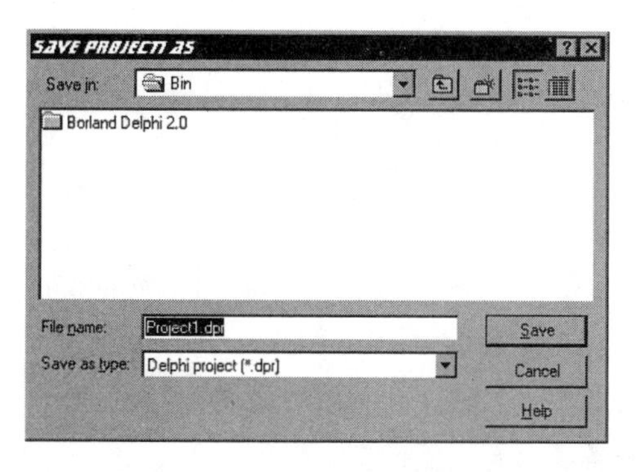

Figure 5.4.
Save Project As menu

6. OK, now you need to change some properties on the form and its components so you stay organized. Use the Object Inspector to change the caption property of your form to `Input Form` and the form name property to `InputForm`. (The Object Inspector was covered on Day 2, "The IDE").

7. Next, you need to add another form to the project. You do this by using File | New Form or the new form icon on the SpeedBar.
8. Using the Object Inspector, change the form caption for this new form to Output Form and the name property to `OutputForm`. This form receives the output from the Input form when the program is run. Data is transferred here after data is input and sent by pressing the Send button.
9. Now, make sure to save the form. Because you have already saved the project file and the first form to new names, all you need to do is make your new form the active window by clicking on it. Then do a File | Save File As. Save to your project directory (C:\program files\borland\delphi 2.0\source\formtalk\output.pas, if you've been following that example.)
10. Add an edit box to each of the forms and a button to the input form (on Day 2, you learned to place components on a form; The VCL tabs and components are covered in more detail on Day 9). Next, clear the text property on both edit boxes by using the Object Inspector and deleting the text from the text property.
11. Set the name for the edit box in the Input form to `InText`. Set the name for the edit box in the Output form to `OutText`. Set the button caption in the Input form to "Send" and its name property to `SendText`.
12. To make sure that both forms come up visible, you need to use the Object Inspector to change the visible property of any forms you add (excluding the first form created when you start a new project) to `True`. (You'll see another way to do this with the Project Manager shortly.)
13. Double-click the Input form to bring up the code window for the unit, add "`OutPut`" to the `uses` clause (you need to scroll up to the top of the code window). This is required so you can reference the Output form unit from the Input form unit. (Refer to Listing 5.5 to see what the `uses` clause should look like.)
14. Now, let's add a line of code to the button and make your program functional. Double-click on the Send button and add this line of code:

    ```
    OutputForm.OutText.Text:=InputForm.InText.Text;
    ```

15. Now, let's look at your program and see what it looks like. Listing 5.4 contains the source code that is created and stored in your project file. Use View | Project Source to show the contents of the project file.

TYPE **Listing 5.4. `Formtalk`.**

```
program Formtalk;

uses
  Forms,
```

```
  Input in 'INPUT.PAS' {InputForm},
  Output in 'OUTPUT.PAS' {OutputForm};

{$R *.RES}

begin
  Application.CreateForm(TInputForm, InputForm);
  Application.CreateForm(TOutputForm, OutputForm);
  Application.Run;
end.
```

ANALYSIS In the project source code (see Listing 5.4) the `uses` clause includes the Forms unit (which is Delphi's code used to create windows), and the Input and Output units (which contain the code for the forms you created). After execution begins you will notice the `Application.CreateForm` method statements. These methods excute the necessary code to start and create your forms. Simply put, methods are sections of code contained in an object (our form) that is executed when the method is called as you have done here. We discuss more about methods and their use on Day 9. The final statement is `Application.Run`. This actually starts up our application and executes the code associated with our forms (remember, some code is added by Delphi and some is added by you). The project source is updated by Delphi for you as you add or delete forms.

Next, double-click on the Input form to see the code there. (See Listing 5.5.) Notice how nice it is to read the code because you have been using descriptive names.

TYPE **Listing 5.5. `Input` unit.**

```
unit Input;

interface

uses
  Windows, Messages, SysUtils, Classes, Graphics, Controls, Forms, Dialogs,
  OutPut, StdCtrls;

type
  TInputForm = class(TForm)
    InText: TEdit;
    SendText: TButton;
    procedure SendTextClick(Sender: TObject);
  private
    { Private declarations }
  public
    { Public declarations }
 end;
```

continues

Listing 5.5. continued

```
var
  InputForm: TInputForm;

implementation

{$R *.DFM}

procedure TInputForm.SendTextClick(Sender: TObject);
begin
     OutputForm.OutText.Text:=InputForm.InText.Text;
end;
```

ANALYSIS Look at the code for the Output form (Listing 5.6). As you study the code for the Input and Output forms, you should find it easy to read because you have used descriptive names for files, captions, and names. Imagine a complex project with many forms and controls. The good habits you have been practicing here will help you tremendously with that complex project. It is easier to remember many of the names you create for the various forms and components saving time when you go to look for them in a sea of forms.

TYPE Listing 5.6. `Output` unit.

```
unit Output;

interface

uses
  Windows, Messages, SysUtils, Classes, Graphics, Controls, Forms, Dialogs,
  StdCtrls;

type
  TOutputForm = class(TForm)
    OutText: TEdit;
  private
    { Private declarations }
  public
    { Public declarations }
  end;

var
  OutputForm: TOutputForm;

implementation

{$R *.DFM}

end.
```

ANALYSIS The code in Listing 5.6 was created by Delphi when you created the Output form. Because we use this form only to display data sent by the Input form, it contains no user-created code. You should be familiar with the sections of code that are present from earlier in today's lesson.

The Project Manager

Now that you have a project to work with, let's see what the Project Manager and other options in Delphi have to offer. Let's open the Project Manager and take a look. Use View | Project Manager to pull up the Project Manager user interface (Figure 5.4).

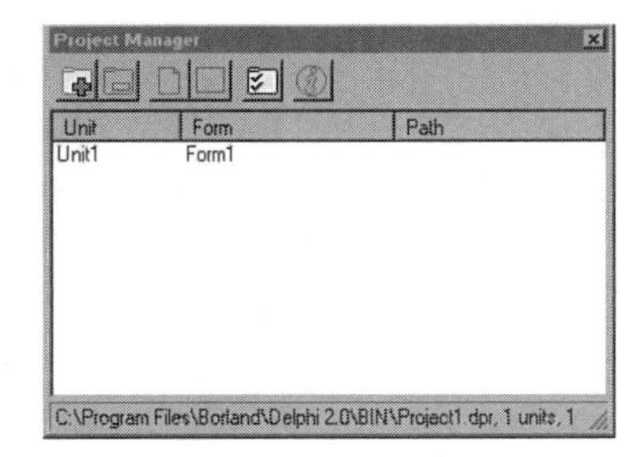

Figure 5.5.
Project Manager user interface.

In the Project Manager user interface, notice that you see the names of each of the units in the list (Input and Output in this case), the form name, and the path (which is empty in this case because you did not set it). Just below the title bar, you have a SpeedMenu with some handy features.

Take a look at the Project Manager SpeedMenu options and their functions. Because most of these options affect the selected unit, make sure that you select the correct one before clicking a button on the toolbar.

Add Enables you to add a unit file. This is nice because you may have a form that you designed for another program that will work well for the current project. You simply add the form to the project. When you click on the Add Form button, you are presented with the standard file selection box you have seen many times by now. Simply browse through the directories and select the form file you wish to add.

Remove Removes the selected unit from the project. (The file is not deleted, just removed from the project file.)

View unit Takes you to the code for the selected unit.

View form Displays the form associated with the selected unit.

Options Takes you to Project Options, which is a tabbed dialog box with several options. (We'll discuss this in more detail in the next section.)

Update A button that is disabled unless you have manually changed something in the project file. This button synchronizes the forms and units listed in the Project Manager with the project file.

It is not recommended that you change anything in the project source file unless you are writing a DLL or doing some advanced programming. Delphi will make most changes needed to the project source file for you.

As you can see, the Project Manager enables you to quickly move around in your project, add and remove files, and go to the Project Options dialog box. In addition to the Project Manager, you will use the File, View, Project, Workgroup (Workgroup is available only if you install the optional PVCS support that is not covered, but mentioned briefly at the end of today's lesson) and Tools menus, as well as the SpeedBar (which enables you to access project-related functions), as you work on your project in opening, creating, deleting, and closing project and related files, and so on. You should be familiar with the IDE at this point, so we'll focus on those options and features particular to managing the project.

Project Options

The Project Options tabbed dialog box enables you to set many options for your project. This information will be saved in the .dfo file we defined earlier. The Project Options tabbed dialog box has five sections, as shown in Figure 5.6. These sections include Forms, Application, Compiler, Linker, and Directories/Conditionals. Let's take a look at each of these tabs and the options you have available. You'll also check the settings for your `Formtalk` project.

The Forms Tab

The first tab is the Forms tab (see Figure 5.6). This is the active tab when you open the Project Options dialog box. At the top, you have the Main Form drop-down list. This enables you to select the project's Main Form. The Main Form starts up first along with the code in its `OnCreate` event. Normally, the first form you create is the Main Form. For this project, it should be `InputForm`. If you click on the down arrow of the drop-down box, you see that you could choose `OutputForm` (which, in this project, is the only other form so far).

Also on the Forms tab are the Auto-Create Forms and Available Forms listboxes. Forms appear in the Auto-Create Forms listbox by default. Available forms are part of your project but will need to be moved to the auto-create section if you want them created on startup. Otherwise, you need to activate them at runtime before they can be used. When a form is

added to the Auto-Create listbox, the proper code is added to the project file with a statement such as `Application.CreateForm(TInputForm, InputForm);`.

NOTE You can't reference a form until it has been created.

To move forms between the two listboxes, you can use the controls (the single- and double-arrow buttons) between the two listboxes. You may also drag-and-drop to move files between the two boxes or change their order.

If you look at the project you have been working on (`Formtalk`), `InputForm` should be the Main form, `InputForm` and `OutputForm` should both be in the Auto-Create listbox, and the Available Forms listbox should be empty. Assuming you have the `Formtalk` project debugged and running, move `OutputForm` to the Available Forms listbox. Now, run the application. Enter **`test`** in the Input Form textbox and click the Send button. You should get an error. This is because your application could not find the Output form. Move `OutputForm` back to the Auto-Create listbox and run the program again. The program should run without error.

Finally, the Default checkbox is used to set the current options to be the default options for all new projects. You probably don't want to use this when you are working on a specific project unless you want all future projects to use the same settings.

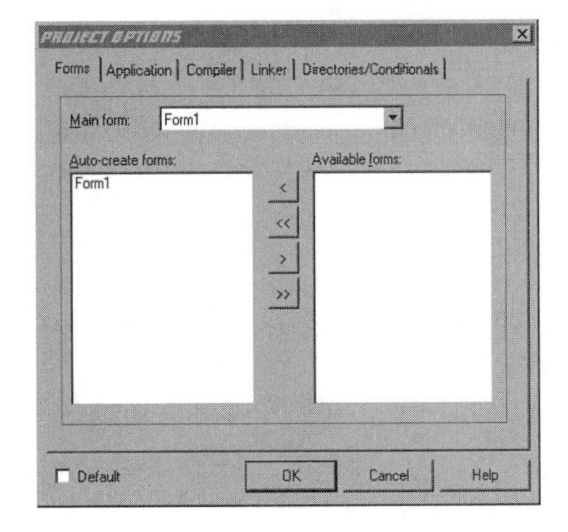

Figure 5.6.
The Forms tab.

The Application Tab

This section enables you to set the Application Title, Icon, and Help file, as shown in Figure 5.7. These should all appear blank when you come to the screen for the first time. These fields are optional, but fill them in as you read along.

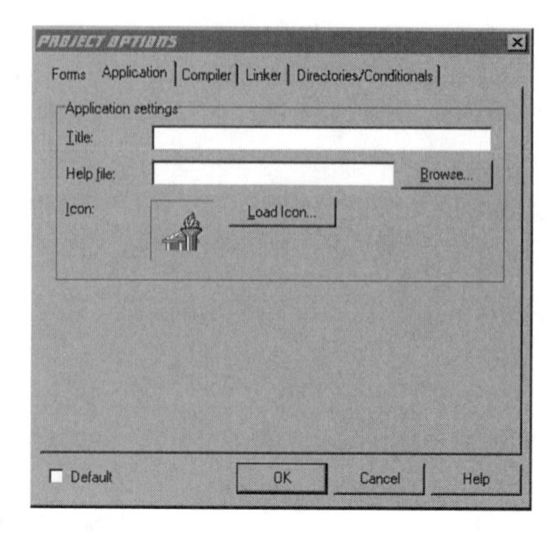

Figure 5.7.
The Application tab.

First is the Application title. This is the text that Windows displays with the icon when the application is minimized. If you leave this blank, the application displays the project name. Add the name **`Form Talk Application`**. This will add the following to the project source code. Use View | Project Source to see a line such as the following code:

```
Application.Title := 'Form Talk Application';
```

Run the project and minimize it. You should notice Form Talk Application as the application title on the Windows 95 Task Bar and the icon appearing to the left. If you delete the text from the Project Screen and run it, you will notice that it uses the Project Name, `Formtalk` in this case. Make sure you have `Form Talk Application` in the textbox before you move on.

Just below the Application Title textbox is the Help file textbox and Browse button. You may select a standard Windows Help file to associate with your application. Just to try it out, click on Browse. Move to the \program files\borland\delphi 2.0\help directory (depending on what you entered during your Delphi installation, your installed directory names may be different, for example, \program files\borland\delphi 2.0\help) and select any of the .hlp help files (for example, delphi.hlp). View the project source code again. Notice the following line of code has been added:

```
Application.HelpFile := 'c:\program files\borland\delphi 2.0\help\delphi .hlp;
```

This doesn't do much for you in your program, but the Help file is attached to the project. If you were to set the proper Help context numbers in the forms and components, pressing F1 would bring up the Delphi Help screen for the Help context set for the selected component or form. The purpose here is only to show you how to set the Help file to be used by the project.

Next is an image box that contains the default or selected icon which appears below the Help file edit box and is followed by a Load Icon button. The Load Icon button brings up a file selection box for you to choose the application icon. The application icon is displayed when you minimize the application main form. Click on the Choose Icon button and select c:\program files\borland\delphi 2.0\images\icons\chip.ico and click OK. This displays a computer chip in the image box.

Run the application again. Minimize it and you should see the new icon (the Computer Chip) and the title `Form Talk Application`. Do a File | Save Project.

NOTE

> You are not required to set any of these, but it is recommended because it gives a more finished look to your application. The checkbox is used to set the current options to be the default options for all new projects.

The Compiler Tab

Available sections (see Figure 5.8) in the Compiler tab include Code generation, Runtime errors, Syntax options, Debugging options, and Messages. Each of these sections includes a number of options that you may toggle on or off. For most projects, the defaults will be fine. The checkbox is used to set the current options to be the default options for all new projects.

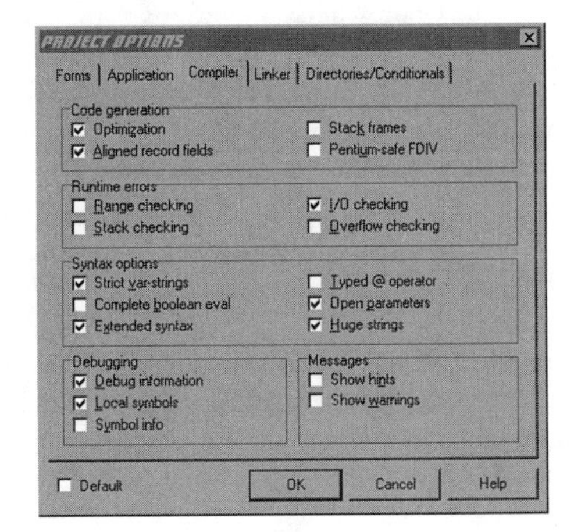

Figure 5.8.
The Compiler tab.

The Linker Tab

Linker options (see Figure 5.9) include Map file, Linker output, EXE and DLL options, Memory sizes, and EXE Description. As with the Compiler tab, you find options here that are out of the scope of this book. You should refer to the online help and the manuals for more info on Linker Options. Again, default options should be fine for most projects.

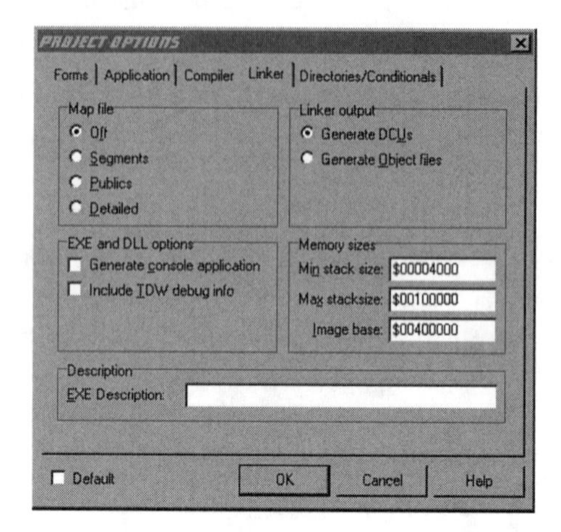

Figure 5.9.
The Linker tab.

The Compiler Dialog Box

Compiler options are out of the scope of this book. However, as an example, notice under the Code generation options that there is an option called Pentium-safe FDIV. This option compiles code that checks for a Pentium processor with the floating-point divide flaw and prevents the flaw from occurring. If you know your application will not be run on a Pentium system with the flaw, you simply turn this option off, and your code will be a bit more compact and faster because it doesn't need the extra code or time. I'd recommend leaving this option on. There will probably be some people out there that won't take Intel up on the free replacement of the flawed unit. You might as well let Delphi protect you from the problem. I simply point this out to give you an idea of the type of control you have with the compiler options because they affect executable size and speed. You may use Delphi's online help by pressing F1 at this tab for more info or refer to the Delphi manuals.

The Directories/Conditionals Tab

In the Directories (see Figure 5.10) section, you find the Output directory and Search path textboxes. The Output directory enables you to specify where you want your compiled units and executables to be placed (.dcu and .exe). I usually leave this directory blank and move the

tested executable to another directory when I am done. When left blank, .dcu and .exe files are stored in the same directory as the source code. The Search path option enables you to specify where to look for .dcu files. When you compile your program, the compiler looks only in the search path defined here, the library search path, and the current directory. As with the DOS path, you can have multiple search path entries separated by a semicolon (;) and limited to 127 characters. You would use the Search path option if you want your project to use files that are in a directory other than those just mentioned. Keep in mind that you will get an error if the source files can't be found when you try to compile.

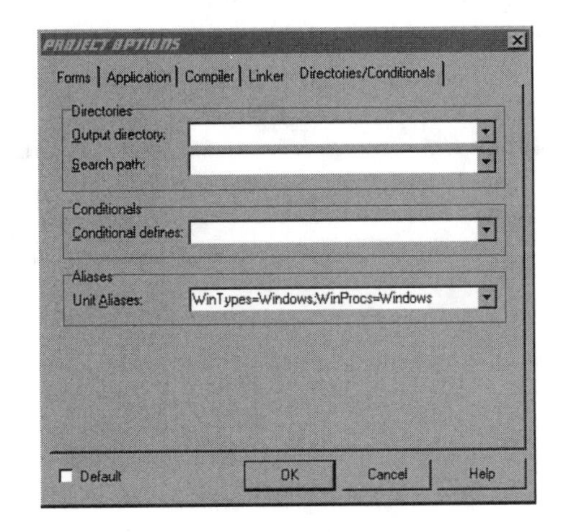

Figure 5.10.
The Directories/ Conditionals dialog box.

The Conditional defines drop-down listbox enables you to enter or select from a previous list of compiler conditional directives and symbols (see Figure 5.10). These symbols control how your program compiles, depending on certain conditions. See Delphi's online help or the manuals if you need more information on compiler directives and symbols. The checkbox is used to set the current options to be the default options for all new projects.

The Aliases box enables you to enter aliases to other units. Notice that the following entry appears:

```
WinTypes=Windows;WinProcs=Windows
```

This allows backward compatibility because the Windows and WinProcs units have been replaced with the `Windows` unit. Of course, you can add aliases of your own here as well.

TIP

> Now that we have talked about the various options used in managing your project, look at the File, View, Workgroup, and Tools menus, as well as the various SpeedBar options. You should see some pretty nice shortcuts.

Creating a Project

The remainder of today's lesson is devoted to Delphi's project-related features. You should supplement your reading here with Delphi's online help and documentation. If you are coming from Delphi 1.0, you will notice a number of new items, name changes, and new menu locations. When you start Delphi, you are usually presented with a new blank form and project. The blank form and project are default settings that are installed with Delphi. These settings can be changed and are discussed shortly. By now you are familiar with the default form and code, so let's move on and talk about other options you have when creating a new project. Under the File | Menu option, you will find a menu that is now called the New Items menu. Here you find five very useful tabs as seen at the top of Figure 5.11.

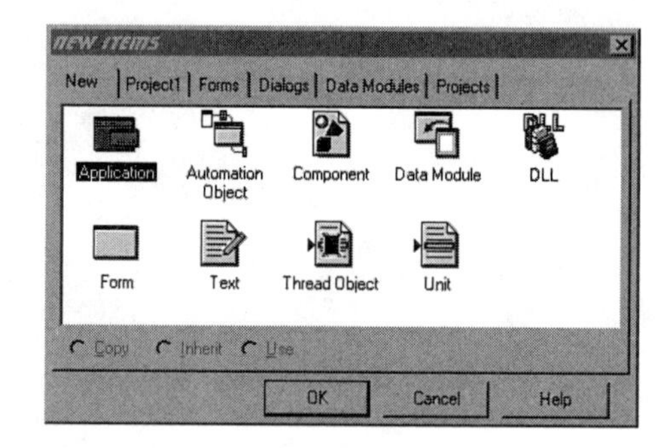

Figure 5.11.
The New Items menu.

OK, take a quick look at what's available in each of these tabs.

I won't be going into great detail on most of these items. If you need more information, please refer to Delphi's help or documentation.

The New Tab

The New tab is used to create new applications, forms, units, automation objects, text editor object, components, and DLLs. You make your choice and select OK. If more information is needed for the object you select, you will be prompted with a dialog box.

The Forms Tab

The Forms tab gives you a choice of form templates to use when creating a new form. You may create your own templates and make them available here.

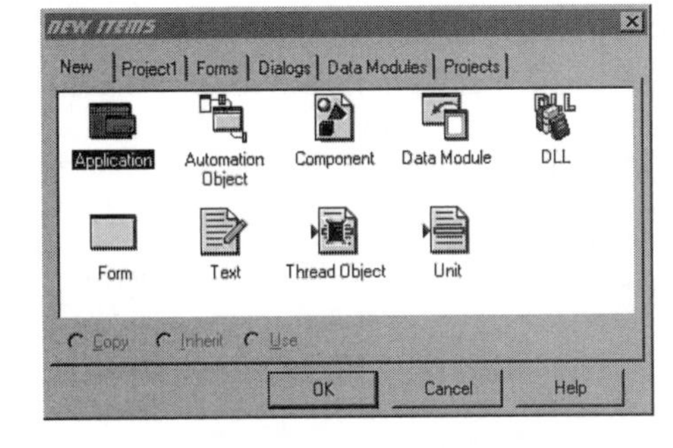

Figure 5.12.
The New tab.

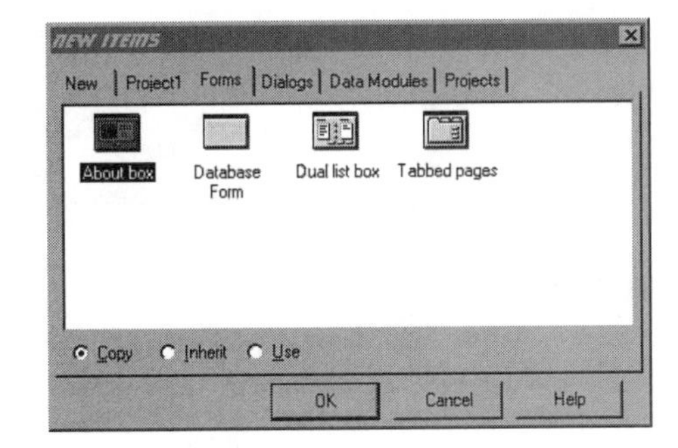

Figure 5.13.
The Forms tab in the New Items menu.

The Dialogs Tab

Like the Forms tab, the Dialogs tab contains templates with prebuilt dialog boxes. As with the Forms, you can create templates and make them available here.

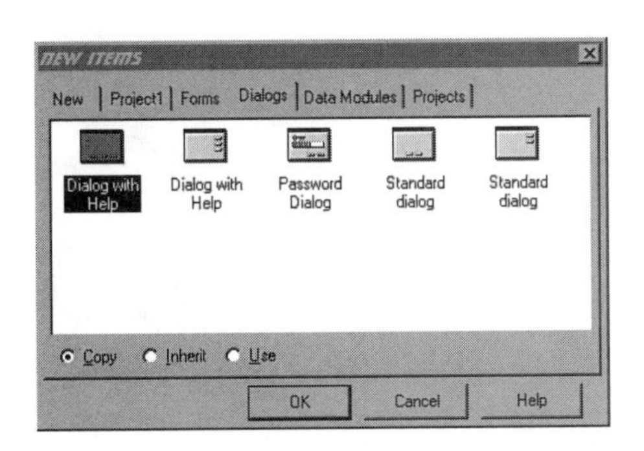

Figure 5.14.
The Dialogs tab in the New Items menu.

Data Modules

The Data Modules tab is used to store objects containing predefined data tables. A sample customer module is provided, but you may want to create your own from information in the database chapters. See the Delphi help and manuals for more information.

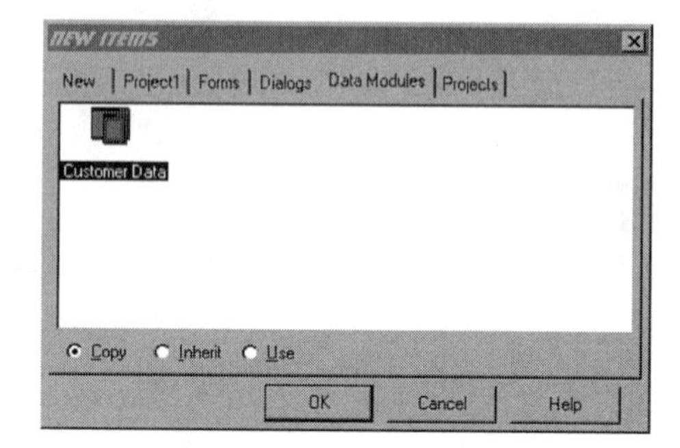

Figure 5.15.
The Data Modules tab in the New Items menu.

The Projects Tab

The Projects tab contains project templates. You can save time by using predefined projects that are provided or by creating your own.

One final note: notice that if you are working on a project, it will be added to the New Items menu just following the New Tab. This allows you to see what you have added as well as to select from it if you need to create a new form or object similar to one already in the project.

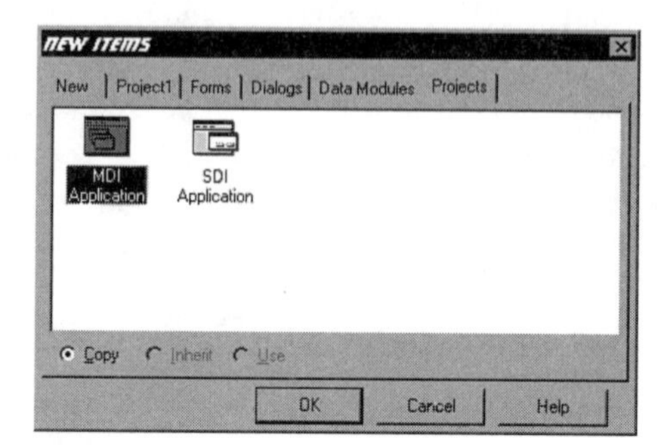

Figure 5.16.
The Projects tab in the New Items menu.

The Object Repository

In Delphi 1.0 the Gallery was used to store templates and experts. The Gallery has been replaced with the Repository in this version of Delphi. The Object Repository Options menu can be found in the Tools | Repository menu shown in Figure 5.17.

Figure 5.17.
The Object Repository Options Menu

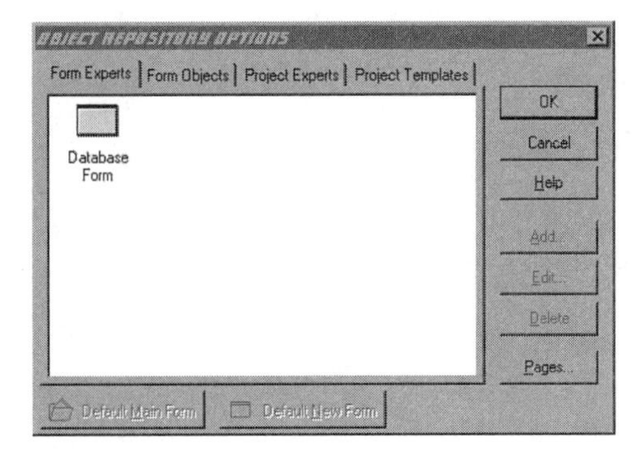

Here you will find four tabs: Form Experts, Form Objects, Project Experts, and Project Templates. In this menu you can add, delete, and edit selections as well as change defaults that will be used when you create a new form or project.

The Repository really enhances your ability to reuse code in Delphi. As you can see, commonly used features are already made available to you but you greatly extend your options by creating your own templates and adding them to the Repository. Next you'll move on to creating and using templates and experts. This will help us tie up some loose ends and get a feel for how all this works.

Experts and Templates

As you probably know, an expert is a program installed with Delphi that takes you through a series of questions and choices and builds you a framework to start with for a complex form or project. This can be a great time saver. Templates are similar in that they have much of the repetitive work done for you but you don't need to answer questions. You are essentially taking a copy of what you need and inserting it in your new project. Both experts and templates show up in the Net Items menu, so you will have easy access to them.

Experts

There are two types of experts: Form Experts and Project Experts. To view what is available, you can go to the Object Repository and click on the appropriate tab. The available experts are displayed in the appropriate tabs. To use an expert you simply select New and from the New Items menu select the desired expert. Once the expert starts, you are prompted for information. Finally, the expert creates a form or project and you are ready to add your code and changes. Just to get a feel for starting an expert, do a File | New. Then from the New Items menu, select the Forms tab. At this point, the Database Form Expert starts. (See Figure 5.18.)

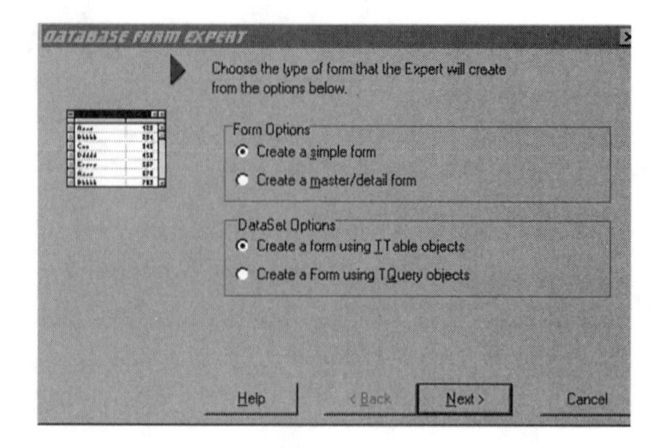

Figure 5.18.
The Database Form Expert.

As you can see, at this point you start making your selections and entering information. The Database Form Expert is explored in more detail in the database section. Here, we are just concerned about where experts are started.

Creating and Using Templates

A template is simply a project, form, or some code framework that has been prebuilt and is ready for you to use. When you select a template, it is simply copied into your project and you add to it as needed. For example, if you came up with a really cool splash screen form that you wanted to use for all your programs, you could create a splash template with your logo, colors, and so on. Then all you need to do to use it in your programs is save it into the Object Repository. Now create a simple template and use it in a project.

Create that splash screen and turn it into a template. Create a form with an OK button in it and a label that says My Cool App! Make sure to save your work by doing a File | Save All and naming appropriately. Then right-click on the form and select Add to Repository. You are prompted with the Add to Repository screen. From here, enter the name of the template you want to add, in this case, My Splash Screen. (See Figure 5.19.) You can leave the description blank or fill it in with a description you want to be shown when the template is selected in the New Items Menu or the Repository. Select Forms from Page combobox. Now press OK. You have just created your first template.

Now, to use your new template, you simply do a File | New, select the Form tab, and your template should be added to the tab. From here, all you need to do is select the new template and it is ready to use.

As you get more familiar with Delphi and get an idea of the types of tasks you want to do, you may want to spend some time creating some commonly used forms and dialogs to convert to templates. As your collection of templates grows, your time spent on routine work will shrink.

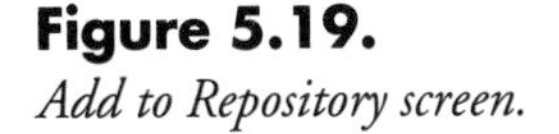

Figure 5.19.
Add to Repository screen.

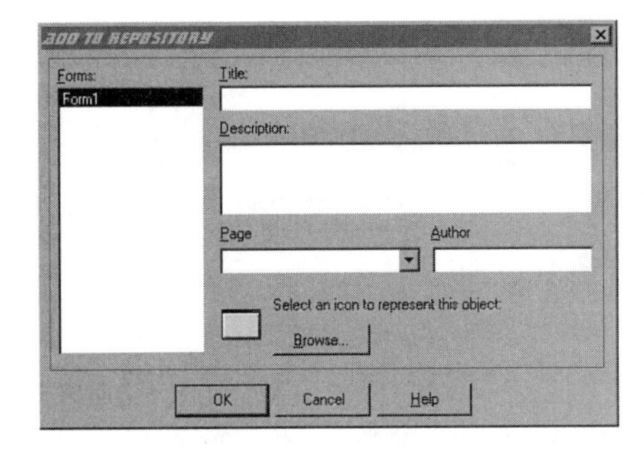

Version Control

Until now, we have discussed what makes up a project, how to get organized, how to work with the Delphi Project Manager, and project-related features. We have even talked about how to save a lot of time using experts and templates. Now let's talk about version control. It may be fairly simple to keep yourself organized without version control software, but what if you have multiple programmers working on the same project? What if you have multiple flavors of a project that you must support?

A version control system allows you to manage projects in a highly organized and safe manner. For example, if you had a group of programmers working on the same project, a version control system allows you to lock portions of code that you don't want changed or to check out a portion of code and prevent others from making changes to it until you have finished working. You may keep archives of previous versions so that you don't lose the ability to revert back or look at code for a previous version.

Delphi supports the Intersolv PVCS Version Manager 5.1 or later, which is included in the client/server edition. Version control features are available in the Workgroups menu and require that you follow a simple procedure that can be found in the online help to activate it. Use of the version control system is not covered here (see the documentation for the version control software), you just need to be aware that it exists and what some of the benefits are. If you are a single developer with the regular version of Delphi, you can use smart project management practices by keeping separate directories for each version, or using a standard set of templates to accomplish pretty much the same effect. If you are a team of programmers working on the same projects, you should seriously consider using version control software.

Summary

In this chapter, you learned about all the various files that make up a Delphi project—both design time–created files and compile time–created files. You learned about forms, units, VCL, and OCXs as part of your projects, as well as how to include user-created functions, procedures, and event handlers as a part of your project. Resources such as bitmaps, icons, and so on were also covered. You then moved on to organizing your project by learning how to set up a directory structure that makes it easy to find, maintain, and back up your files. You learned about the Project Manager and how to move about in your project, as well as how to add and delete files. You learned about the Project Options tabbed dialog boxes, which give you many options about how your project will be compiled. Next, you moved on to the Object Repository and its various options. We talked about how to use the Object Repository to choose various experts and templates as defaults. You learned how to use experts to create forms and projects. We talked about how to choose a template when creating a new form or project, and we also talked about how to create your own templates and add them to the Object Repository for use later. Finally, we talked about Delphi's capability to use the Intersolv PVCS Version Manager and what its advantages are.

Q&A

Q Can I create my own experts?

A Though I am sure it is possible, Delphi does not provide a way to easily create an expert. Experts are add-on products.

Q How do I create a project template?

A From Project Manager, you simply right-click and select Save as Template. You are presented with the Save Project Template screen. Just as you did when creating a Form template, you simply fill in the title, description and select what page it is to be added to in the Object Repository. Once this is done you select OK and a project template is created.

Q Why isn't the PVCS version control system or its Workgroup menu option available from the Delphi IDE menu?

A The PVCS system is an optional product and must be installed separately. To activate it, use help to search for PVCS and follow the instructions for activating it.

Workshop

Quiz

1. Which files are created by Delphi at design time? At compile time?
2. What are the parts that make up a unit?
3. How do you add a form to a project? How do you delete a form from a project?
4. If you delete a form from the project does it delete the form file?

Exercise

Create a project template that has a main form with File and Help menus. The Help menu should have an About option in it. Also, create an About box form with code in the OK button to remove the form from memory.

Day 6

Fundamentals of GUI Design

One of the principle benefits of being a Windows user is that most of the applications we use have a similar look and feel. After you have used several (or in my case, several hundred) applications, you will find that you can almost anticipate where a particular function exists within that new application you just purchased. This goes for everything from the installation (I just stick Disk 1 into the A drive and type SETUP, and I rarely read instructions), to the fact that the Help menu selection will always be the right-most selection on the main menu bar. You probably have been doing this too, but not knowing why things felt the way they did.

Microsoft has provided design specifications for Windows software in an effort to change the user's paradigm. That shift in focus is from learning the nuances of interfacing with your application to being productive with your application instead. Microsoft is enforcing these guidelines in what is called the Win95 Logo program. Under this new program, your application must meet Microsoft's logo program criteria before you can place the "Designed for Windows 95" logo on your packaging. When you see that logo on a piece of software or hardware, you can be sure that the product will run well under the Windows 95 environment and is designed properly using the design guidelines. Delphi 2 is designed to help you develop applications that meet the Windows 95 logo requirements. Borland has given you the tools, but much is still up to you. As we journey through this chapter, I point out some of the ways you can design your application to improve its usability and help meet the logo requirements as well.

Why GUI?

First off, why do we need graphical user interfaces (GUIs) anyway? The answer is we do not. Users have survived using the command prompt for a number of decades, and we could have indefinitely. Before you get ruffled, that does not mean, however, that we would be happy doing it! Time and time again, I have seen the transformation of DOS users as I move them (and their computers) to Windows 3.1 or Windows 95, and have seen the light in their eyes as they see the potential there for improved productivity.

New Term *Graphical user interface* (GUI) is a type of display format that enables a user to choose commands, start programs, and view lists of files and other options by pointing to pictorial representations (icons) and lists of menu items on the screen. Choices can generally be activated either with a keyboard or a mouse. An example of GUI interface is Windows 95.

GUIs exist because we need them to. I need access to as many as 12 applications on a daily basis (that's on a light day). With only a command prompt, I would spend most of that day starting and shutting down applications and not doing real work. The word for the day here is productivity. We can be more productive by having simultaneous access to several applications. Switching between cc:Mail, Delphi 2, WinZip, WinCim, Explorer, and so on, becomes trivial in the Windows environment. I don't have to shut down any application to access another one. What a time-saver this is!

Rapid Prototyping and Development

New Term You may have heard the term *rapid prototyping*. This refers to the practice of creating working models of your application's GUI interface early in the design process.

You can then present this interface to customers and get feedback about the feel, object placement, and inclusion of features, as well as give customers an overall warm fuzzy because they feel you are catering to their needs. Over the years, several products have emerged to cater to this growing trend. These rapid prototyping tools build "false" front ends with no data processing on the back. You get the look and feel, with no "guts." Things have changed.

With the advent of a new generation of Rapid Application Development (RAD) tools such as Delphi 2 and Visual Basic 4, these rapid prototyping tools are no longer necessary. You can now use the RAD tools themselves to create these ghost front ends to show your customer. Nowhere is this concept easier to implement than in Delphi 2. As you saw on Day 5, "Files and the Project Manager," Delphi has provided you with a set of Visual Components that enable you to create your screens first, and then implement the data processing later. You can also include OCXs purchased from third-party vendors in your new front end. Many of these can exist in your application for demo purposes with little or no coding (just drop them onto your window).

NEW TERM *Rapid Application Development* (RAD) is just what the term implies. Using a set of the latest generation tools (such as Delphi 2), the programmer develops applications quickly with very little turn-around time. This is accomplished by having tools that allow the programmer to make large leaps in functionality with a small amount of work. An example would be using the Windows 95 Open and Save common dialog boxes, instead of writing them from scratch or using the OLE container control to embed an Excel spreadsheet into the application, rather than creating the spreadsheet functionality in Delphi itself. Delphi 2 is a prime example of a RAD development environment, giving you the tools to create great applications in a short period of time and with a minimum of coding.

The disadvantage that has been overcome here is the problem of duplication of effort. When you created your front end using one of those rapid prototyping tools, as soon as your customer approved the interface, you had to recode the interface in the tool you were using to generate the real application. What a waste of time. With Delphi 2, you can develop the front first, get the customer's approval, and then finish the application within the same environment. This is another huge productivity enhancer.

In order for your GUI design to work well, you should consider another item—your GUI development team. You may be working alone now, but as the products you develop get larger and more complex, you will need help. When creating a GUI development team for your product, do not gather up a group of programmers! Programmers are the worst designers because they take for granted many of the things a regular user wouldn't know. Your GUI development team should consist of people from diverse backgrounds. Writers, human interface experts, usability specialists, as well as computer users of varying skill levels should be involved. I understand that you may not have the access (or the money) to get all these people on your team, but you get the point. Your team is essential for developing a user interface that is usable.

Once your product has been coded, usability testing will show you how good your design is. The best person to test your software is your non-computer-literate mother. Another good candidate is someone who is afraid of computers. The point here is that you should not have the computer whiz sitting next to you at work test your software, unless that's the user base for whom you are constructing the software.

Putting the User First

When you are constructing your killer application, it's important to remember the principles upon which Windows 95 was written. Microsoft has seven user-centered design principles that it employs. Let's look at each one of these.

The User Is in Control

None of us likes being controlled by others. We especially do not like being controlled by our computers. The user must always feel in control of what is happening on the screen. Users should always feel they are the ones initiating an action, rather than reacting to the computer's whims. If you are going to provide a high degree of automation in your application, ensure that the user has control over that automation process.

Users are individuals. They each have their own preferences and needs. It's important that you provide a way to personalize your application. For example, notice how easy it is to customize the Windows 95 interface. Your ability to change fonts, colors, icons, and so forth, makes Windows a more personal experience. Many of these attributes within Windows are accessible programmatically to you, the developer. Take advantage of these and enable your program to follow the color schemes and font selections of the rest of the system. If you do not, your application will seem rigid and inflexible.

Have you ever looked at how a good application interacts with the user? A good application tells you what it is doing or what "state" or "mode" you are in. If you are in overwrite mode in Microsoft Word, the letters OVR appear on the status bar. Your application should be as interactive as possible. It should be responsive and not leave your user wondering what is going on.

Directness

Enable users to directly manipulate objects in their environment. The phrase "A picture is worth a thousand words" becomes more true every day. It is so much easier to remember what something looks like, than its command syntax. Countless times I have seen users who remember accomplishing a task by saying, "I drag this thingy and drop it on that thingy, and it prints!" Even if *you* don't, this is the way most people think. Try to design your software to be visually intuitive. Let users see how the actions they take affect the objects on-screen.

One of the most direct ways users can interact with a computer is through the use of metaphors. Metaphors are what made the Macintosh such a popular computer and are partially responsible for its success. The concept of a folder makes much more sense than a directory or file. For those of us in the business world, we can comprehend a "filing cabinet," "folders" inside it, and "documents" inside the folders. This makes perfect sense to us and makes the transfer of these concepts to the computer much easier. Metaphors support the concept of user-recognition rather than user-recollection. Users can usually remember the meaning associated with an object more easily than a command.

Consistency

This is one of the most important aspects of developing a Windows application. Consistency is one of the main reasons why the Windows 95 logo program was developed. If all applications are consistent in how they present data and in the way they interact with the user, the user can spend time accomplishing tasks, not learning the differences in the way your application interacts with them. This consistency extends to several areas you should consider:

- Ensure that your application acts very similarly to the Windows operating system. The user can then easily transfer skills they have learned in Windows to your application.
- Ensure that your product is consistent within itself. If you support Ctrl+C as your copy shortcut on one screen, do not use a different paradigm on another screen (such as Ctrl+D).
- Ensure that your metaphors are consistent. If a Black Hole icon is the same as the Recycle Bin, users may think that they can retrieve documents from the Black Hole icon, as well. (Your Black Hole is actually an application that places those files in the same place as your socks that get lost in the dryer.)

We will talk about consistency more later in this chapter when we discuss the use of menus, toolbars, and other common controls.

Forgiveness

I don't know about you, but I spend a great deal of time just exploring new applications. (Pushing buttons and seeing what happens.) In most well-written applications, this very rarely presents a problem. If I am about to perform an action that will format my hard drive, a dialog box would come up and alert me to that fact. I can then press the Cancel button supplied, and nothing is lost.

This is the concept of forgiveness. You need to let users explore your application. All actions the users take need to be reversible or correctable. Users need to be made aware *before* hand that the actions they are about to perform are destructive. It is also possible for a user to make a mouse-o (a mouse-o is a type-o, but done with a mouse). People make mistakes. You must allow for this and require confirmation for all destructive actions, using either the keyboard or the mouse, in case they were initiated in error.

TIP

> You may want to enable your application's user to shut off some of the confirmation for certain actions once they become accustomed to using it. An options tabbed dialog box offering users the ability to shut off confirmation of customer deletes, file deletes, and so on, may be a useful addition for the professional user of your application.

Feedback

There is nothing most users hate more than a computer that just sits there. You don't know what it is doing, and it's not telling you a thing. This is a cardinal rule: Let your user know what is happening. Provide feedback to the user in a timely fashion. You can use a combination of visual, as well as audio cues to let users know you are aware of them.

It is important that the feedback be near the point at which users are working. If they are inputting data on the top of the screen, do not present an error message at the bottom (unless you have a specific status bar line defined). You can change the cursor shape to indicate a condition (such as the infamous hourglass we all love). Users will not tolerate a dead computer for more than a couple of seconds. (Would you?)

Aesthetics

Your application must also be visually pleasing to the customer. This means several things. Besides using the system colors for your screens (so your application blends with the environment), the design of the screen itself is extremely important. The placement of objects determines how usable your screen is, as well as the number of items on the screen itself. When possible, use the "seven rule." Give the user only seven choices (plus or minus two). This number of five to nine choices comes from research on how many things the brain can comprehend at one time. More than nine choices and people tend to get confused and suffer from brain overload. We will talk more about screen design later in this chapter.

Simplicity

The last design principle is simplicity. Your application should be easy to learn and easy to use. You need to balance two things that work against each other: one, access to all the functionality and information in the application; and two, keeping the interface and the use of the product simple. A good application balances these two principles and finds the happy medium.

Try not to be to wordy when creating your screens. When using labels on data entry fields put "Last Name" not "The Last Name of the Customer." Try to use the least number of words that communicate the meaning correctly. Microsoft also recommends the concept of progressive disclosure. This means presenting data as needed. For instance in a phone book program, you may show the person's name and phone number on the initial screen, and the user will have to push a button that reveals all the other information about that person.

Data-Centered Design

You may have already used an application based on a data-centered design and didn't even know it.

NEW TERM *Data-centered design* refers to the user's ability to act on specific pieces of data without having to bring up external editors or programs. As the user begins to operate on the data (either browsing or editing the data), the appropriate tools become available to the user automatically.

This concept comes to life in applications such as Microsoft Word. Notice that when you click on a drawing, the drawing toolbar appears at the bottom of the screen with all the tools you need to perform drawing operations.

The concept of a document helps to solidify concepts in a user's mind. The document-centric view of things is easy to remember. Now, you may think that documents apply only to word processing–type applications—not so. Many applications make use of a document-centric view of non–word processing items. In some communications packages, file transfers are even referred to as "document transfers."

Which Model Is Right for You

A topic we need to discuss early on is windows management. There are two different application models, the Single Document Interface (SDI) and the Multiple Document Interface (MDI). By choosing File|New|Projects Tab, and either SDI or MDI application, you can create a skeleton application. If you haven't dealt with MDI applications you may not understand the benefits or the conditions under which a MDI application should be used over a SDI application.

In almost all instances, an application can be interfaced to the user through a single primary window. If additional information needs to be displayed or gathered, a secondary window can be used. A good example of an SDI application is Explorer. Explorer has a single, primary window that reflects nearly all the information needed for its use. When you need to do something such as view a property, a secondary window is brought up. The other benefit of an SDI application is that it is easier for you, the developer, to manage the one-to-one relationship between a screen and the data on it.

An MDI application, on the other hand, has some real benefits, too. Microsoft Word is a good example of a MDI application. An MDI application has a parent window (the primary) and a number of child windows (also called a document). There are times when it is more efficient to display information in multiple windows that share interface elements (such as a toolbar or menu bar). The document windows are controlled or clipped by the parent. If you size the parent window down, the child windows can be hidden from view.

The conditions under which an MDI application should be used are few. First, MDI should only be used when all the child windows will be used to hold identical objects—like documents or spreadsheets. Don't use MDI if you plan to have different types of child windows (like documents and spreadsheets together.) Don't use MDI if you want to control which child window is on top by using the "stay on top" property, or if you want to control the size of the children, or if you want to hide and show a child. MDI was designed for a very narrow application niche, like Word or Excel where the children are all uniform. Trying to make it accommodate anything else will not work, cause the developer unknown grief, and generally make life miserable for all. Finally, it should be noted that Microsoft discourages development of new MDI applications (mainly because so many people have been writing poor MDI applications in previous Windows versions).

Parts of the Whole

I know this may seem somewhat basic, but a review of the basics helps us get focused. A typical window consists of a frame and a title bar identifying the name of the application in the window, or the name of the item being viewed in the window. If the item being viewed is larger than the window, scroll bars appear to enable the user to scroll around the entire window.

Figure 6.1.
Generic window.

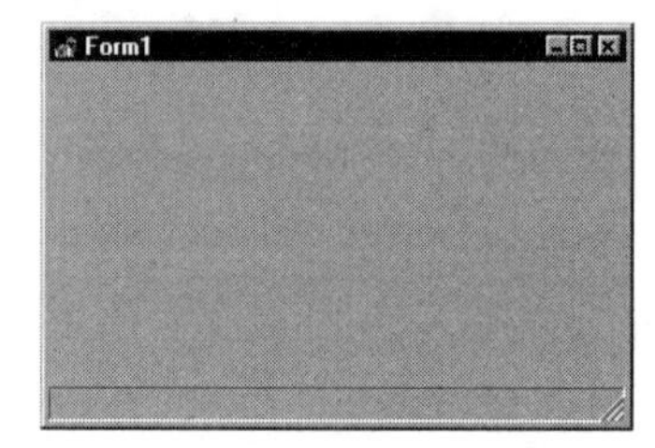

The window frame (if sizable) should include a size grip in the lower-right corner of the window. In addition to the title bar, there are a number of other elements that may be present on the window. These items can include menus, toolbars, status bars, and more. Let's discuss each of the items in a window, focusing on how the items are constructed to conform to the requirements for a clean design.

Title Bar Icons

When you construct a Windows application, your primary window should have a small version of your application icon on it. This icon would represent the product, if that product were a utility or tool of some sort that did not create or view documents of any kind.

Figure 6.2.
Utility or Tool title bar.

If the primary window is used to view documents of some sort, you want to place a document icon, instead of the application's icon, in the upper-left corner of the window. Place the document icon there, even if the user has not saved the document she is creating or viewing. This is done purely for consistency's sake. Remember that we are trying to make the applications uniform and consistent in their presentation of data and in their form.

Figure 6.3.
Document title bar icon.

MDI document interfaces are a special case. In a MDI application, the applications icon is placed in the primary window, and the document icon is placed in all child windows within the parent. Delphi 2 takes care of a lot of the default items as far as the behavior of windows and enables you to leave most of the basics up to Delphi 2.

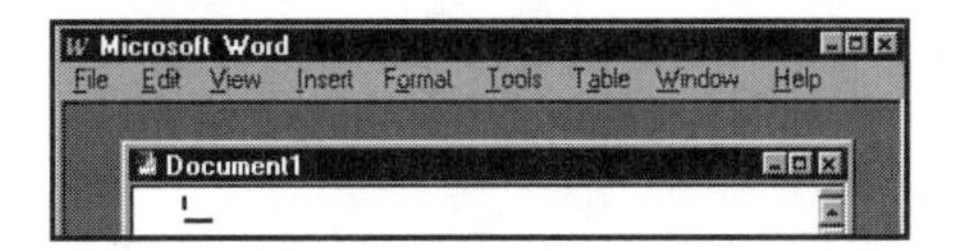

Figure 6.4.
An MDI application.

Title Bar Text

The main function of the title bar is to identify the name of the document being viewed in the window. For instance, if the user opens a document called "My Resume" in a MDI application, the title bar should have the document icon representing that document type, followed by the name of the document "My Resume." In addition, you can include the name of the application after the document name. If you include the application name, you must include a dash between the document and application name.

In Windows 3.1, the specification was to place the application name first and the document name second. The new method of placing the document name first is suited more for a document-centric view, instead of application-centric.

Figure 6.5.
Sample title bar text order.

If the application is a utility or tool and does not have a particular document name associated with it, you can use the application icon, followed by the application name only. An example of this would be the Windows Calculator. In the case of an application such as Explorer (where it is browsing a wide variety of things), you can place the application's name, followed by some text that specifies what is being viewed currently.

MDI applications again are a special case. In this instance, you display the name of the application in the parent window, and the document name in the child window. When the user maximizes the child, the parent window follows the same convention as a Utility, with the application name first, a dash, and then the document name.

New Documents

Several issues are related to the titling of windows. If your application enables the user to create new documents, the application should automatically name the windows using the type of file followed by a unique identifier. For example, using document1 or sheet1, such as Word and Excel do, provides a quick way to continue after the user has created a document. You never want to ask users for a document name when they create the file. The user should be asked for a filename when the document is saved for the first time.

When your application creates the temporary window (and filename), it is also important that the name be unique. That is why many applications simply increment the unique number at the end of the file type name (for example, document1, document2, and so on). It is very important that the name not conflict with the name of any other open window. That temporary name (document1) should be the title of the document window until such time as the user is asked for a permanent name for the document. At that point, the user-designated name should be substituted for the temporary one.

Title Bar Buttons

The last item to discuss in relation to the title bar is the title bar icon. Windows 95 has a revised set of buttons that may confuse Windows 3.1 users. The buttons that are now supported by Windows 95 appear in the following table:

Button	*Command*	*Function*
	Close	Closes the current window

	Minimize	Minimizes the current window
	Maximize	Maximizes the current window
	Restore	Restores the current window to its original size, after a minimize or maximize

The new button that seems to confuse most Windows 3.1 users is the Close button. The X symbol seems to suggest minimize to some people. This button closes the current window, just the same as selecting Alt+F4 does. The Close button should always be the right-most button, separated by a space from the other buttons. The Minimize button should always precede the Maximize button, and the Restore button should replace the Minimize or Maximize button after that button has been used. As the programmer, you are able to control whether these buttons appear on your forms by changing the `BorderIcons` attributes for that form.

Opening and Closing Windows

One of the nicest features in any Windows application is being able to save your settings when you leave your application. This saves the size and position of the application window. When the program is run the next time, it comes up in that same place and size. You can make your own entries in the registry to store the size and position information. Another method for sizing is to get the size of the screen and make your application window the size of the entire screen or a portion of the screen size, centered on the screen.

The behavior of a Windows application varies according to its design. For instance, a NotePad-like program would enable multiple instances of the program to run at the same time. When the application is run from the Start menu, another instance is run. When the application is something such as Delphi 2, if the user tries to start another copy, the instance running is simply brought to the foreground. This type of response works well for applications in which only a single instance can be run. You can also bring up a dialog box and give the user the option to bring to the front the running application or run another application.

Window Colors

The use of color in your application can add some real sparkle. The use of too much color can also make it look as if a paint store exploded. Delphi 2 provides the system colors in the palette so you can have your application colors match the overall Windows color scheme. If you look for colors in the Object Inspector, you will find colors such as `clWindowActive`.

These are the current system colors that have been chosen by the user. If you pick these colors to be your application's colors, as the user changes the overall color scheme, your application will change to match. You can also make your colors *static* (your application colors do not change when the user changes the Windows color scheme). When you create a new form or add components to a form, Delphi 2 sets the colors of these items to match the Windows 95 color scheme. You have to manually change the colors with the Object Inspector, if you wish to override Delphi's behavior.

There are several reasons why you should not override the system colors in favor of your own. The user's color choices may have a functional purpose, such as power management (black backgrounds consume less battery power). Visibility may also play a role (the user picked greyscale because he is color blind). There are many instances in which you may not know best. If you do change the colors in your application, try to stick with the 16 basic colors. If you try to use 256 (or worse yet 16,000) colors it has a tendency to slow down your application, and may not look right on users' machines that are using 16 colors.

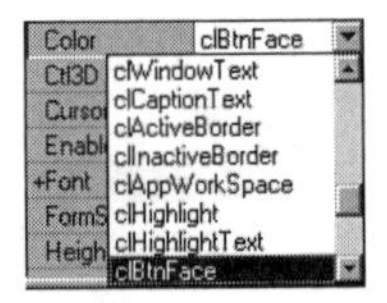

Figure 6.6.
The Object Inspector color palette.

Menus

We have all used menus in Windows applications at one time or another. They are a convenient way for us to access a program's functionality by recognition (we all know the File | Open routine) rather than having to remember some cryptic command syntax. There are several different types of menus including pop-up menus, drop-down menus, and cascading menus. Let's take a look at each one of these types of menus and what they have to offer.

The drop-down menu exists mostly in the context of a menu bar. The menu bar is a part of most applications we use today. The menu bar contains elements called menu titles. These titles, when selected, provide access to drop-down menus. Those drop-down menus then contain the next level of selection—menu items.

Figure 6.7.
Typical menu bar.

The visual controls provided with Delphi 2 enable you to construct your own menu bar and associated drop-down menus. The actual menu choices you give your user depends on the functionality of your application. It is possible for you to enable the user to change or customize the menus in your application. If you decide to go this route, make sure that you

give the user access to the standard set of choices through a standard mechanism, such as pop-up menus and toolbars. This way users do not customize the interface to the point where they cannot use it.

TIP

If you select File | New | Projects Tab | SDI application, you get a minimal menu structure consisting of File and Help commands. If you create an MDI application you get a more extensive menu bar including the Edit and Window menu titles.

The File Menu

The File menu is the primary way the user accesses the major commands in your application. Usually, you would include a New, Open, Save, and Save As command set if your application opens documents of any kind. A new feature for Windows 95 is the Send To command that could also be included here. If your application provides a printed output capability, a Print command would go here as well. If your application supports the Exit command, it should be the last selection on the File menu. If the application remains active even when the window is closed (such as the Volume control on the taskbar), use the Close command in place of the Exit command.

It is important that menu items be in the same place every time so the user does not have to learn the basics over and over again with each new application. File | Exit or File | Print should be natural reactions for the user, and should be the same every time.

NOTE

You may have noticed that each command has one underlined key or a combination of keys next to it. You'll learn how to establish these accelerator keys in the section titled "Menu Labels, Shortcuts, Access Keys, and Types" later in this chapter.

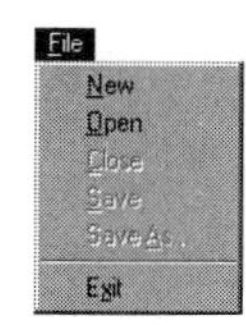

Figure 6.8.
Typical File drop-down menu.

The Edit Menu

The Edit menu is critical in applications where documents are being edited or viewed. This menu usually contains the Cut, Copy, and Paste commands. You can place OLE object commands into this menu, as well as several of the more "deluxe" commands found in some applications. These commands could include Undo (for reversing the last action), Repeat (to repeat the last action), Find and Replace (for searching for and replacing text), Delete (for removing the currently selected item), and the Duplicate command for creating a copy of the currently selected item. The Select All command also comes in handy for selecting an entire document.

Figure 6.9.
Typical Edit drop-down menu.

The View Menu

The View menu provides a way for users to change their view of the data. This change could be something such as zooming in or out (sizing), or could be the viewing of additional items on the screen (such as a ruler or toolbar). In this menu, you should support the selection of items, such as a Ruler, with a checkbox to show that it has been selected.

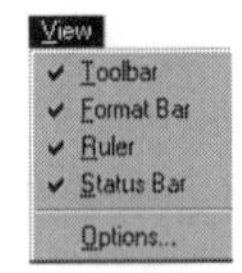

Figure 6.10.
Typical View drop-down menu.

The Window Menu

The Window menu is usually present only in an MDI application where it is necessary to control more than one window. This menu would usually support the New Window, Tile, Cascade, Split, and Minimize All functions, as appropriate. The purpose of this menu is to provide a way for the user to manage a number of windows at one time. In this menu you may also want to provide the user access to all windows that are currently open. Usually this is done with a list of windows, by name, at the bottom of the Window drop-down menu. This enables the user to access any window by simply choosing it from the menu.

TIP

> Delphi 2 automatically includes the current window list feature as part of the standard MDI application skeleton generated by choosing File | New | Projects Tab | MDI Application.

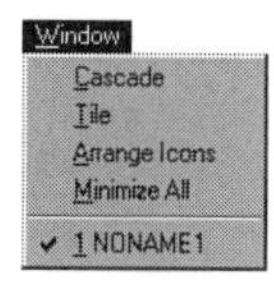

Figure 6.11.
Typical Window drop-down menu.

The Help Menu

One of the most important of all the menus is the Help menu. This menu provides you with the first line of defense against the user calling you with simple questions that are more efficiently answered online. As a standard part of the Windows Help, you should provide a Help Topics command that provides access to the Help Topics browser, as well as possible individual items such as Topic Search and any Help Wizards (such as in Microsoft Word). If you are going to include any information about the version number or your company, you should include the information in an About dialog box that is accessed through the Help | About menu selection. Remember that the better your help system is designed, the fewer calls you will have to answer.

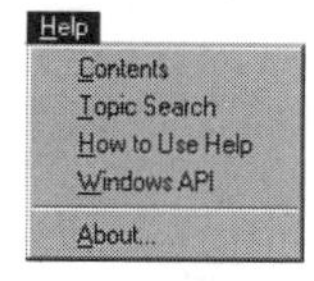

Figure 6.12.
Typical Help drop-down menu.

Pop-Up Menus

Pop-up menus did not really exist in the mainstream of Windows computing prior to Windows 95. The right (or alternate) mouse button has taken on a whole new meaning in Windows now. The right button offers users a set of functions that can be performed on the object they right-click on. For instance, when you right-click on the background in Windows 95, a pop-up menu appears that gives you all the functions you can perform in relation to the display (the screen).

The nice part about pop-up menus is that they provide only those choices that are relevant to, the object that is currently selected. You should always include a pop-up menu for the user if you provide a menu bar (this is assumed because some of the items on the menu bar are assumed to be relevant to specific objects in your application.

As far as the organization of the pop-up menu goes, use as few items as possible on the menu itself. The selections should be kept short, and individual properties should never be listed. Always use a Properties menu choice and let the user navigate through a separate screen instead. It is permissible for a pop-up menu to contain items that are not part of the regular menu bar commands, and vice versa, but make sure that your pop-up menu is not the only way in which the user can access commands in your application.

Figure 6.13.
Typical pop-up menu.

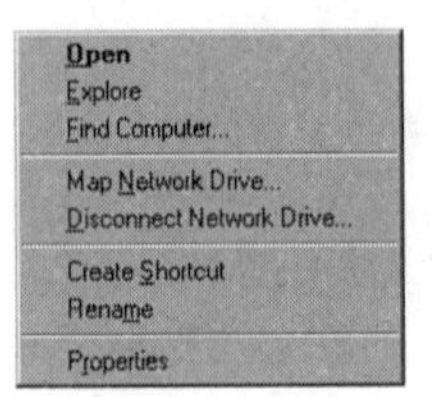

The order of the items is critical (in order for the common look and feel). Starting from the top, the first commands should be the primary functions that are performed on that object, such as Open, Explore, Run, Print, and Play. The transfer commands, such as Send To, should go next, as well as the "What's This?" command, if supported by your application. Cut, Copy, and Paste should be placed in that order. And finally, the Properties command should be the last item on the pop-up menu.

Pop-up menus are used extensively in the Windows environment. If you right-click on your application's executable file in Explorer, you will notice that several choices are available for you. It is possible for you to add specific menu items to support your application. For instance, if you install WinZip for Windows 95 (an indispensable product), you will see that WinZip places an Add To Zip command in the Explorer. This enables the user to add any file in Explorer to a Zip file from within Explorer, without having to start WinZip first. This is just one example of how to use pop-up menus to help users be more efficient at their tasks.

Cascading Menus

You have probably used an application that has cascading menus in it (Delphi 2 is one of them). Child menus (another name for cascading menus) are used to help minimize the confusion of overburdening the user with too many choices on a single menu. Think for a minute of the File menu in Delphi 2. Look at all the menu choices under the File submenu. Can you imagine how confusing it would be to place all these choices at the highest menu level, instead of separating each into its own child?

If you want a good example of how child menus should be used, look at Delphi 2. The presence of a child menu is indicated by a triangular arrow on a menu item in the parent menu. An example of its use in Delphi 2 is the File | Reopen menu choice.

WARNING

Although child menus are available, use them sparingly. They have a tendency to add complexity by forcing the user to make several directional changes with the mouse. Even Delphi2 itself makes scarce use of this feature in its menus.

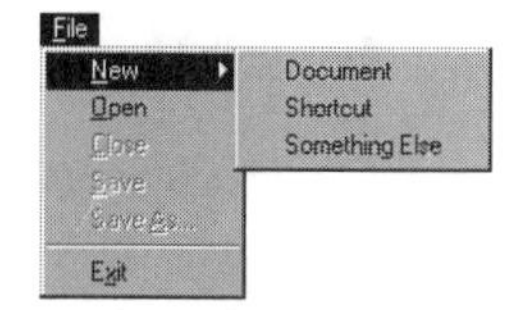

Figure 6.14.
Typical submenu layout.

Also try to limit the number of levels. Try not to put a commonly executed task under five levels of submenus. That would make for some very unproductive time for the user.

Menu Labels, Shortcuts, Access Keys, and Types

When creating your menus, you should also consider several concepts that bear some discussion. The first concept is the labels used in a menu. The items on the main menu bar and all submenus should be single word identifiers, if possible. The names should be succinct and clearly understandable. Do not use phrases or more than two words because it adds complexity and takes the user longer to scan the menu to make his choice.

Two alternate methods (besides using the mouse) to select functions from the menu are to use a shortcut or to use an access key combination.

NEW TERM A *shortcut* is when you assign a key combination such as Ctrl+F4 to execute a menu command.

Shortcuts enable the user to do things such as a "fast save" of the current document by pressing F2 (as used in Word). You can assign shortcut keys to just about any task, as long as you do not reassign crucial key combinations such as Alt+F4 (close the current window), and so on In the Delphi 2 menu visual control, you can assign shortcut keys by changing the shortcut attribute of each menu item. Delphi gives you a listing of all available shortcut keys, and you simply pick one.

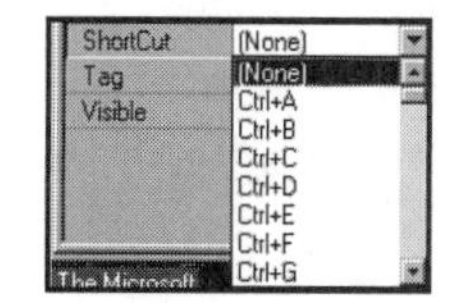

Figure 6.15.
Shortcut Property drop-down box.

Besides the assignment of shortcut keys, you can also use access key combinations.

Access keys are used in combination with the Alt key on your keyboard. For instance, in Delphi, you can access the New Items dialog box by simply pressing Alt+F, N.

The keys you can use in combination with the Alt key are underlined. If you see the word File with the F underlined, you know that the Alt+F combination can be used. When using the menu visual control, you can place an access character (the one that is underlined) in the title by placing an ampersand (&) in front of the letter in the menu item name that you wish to highlight. For example, the word File with the F highlighted would be written `&File`.

> When using access keys in multiple layers of menus, the Alt key should be held down only for the first access key. After that selection, just the letters themselves need to be entered.

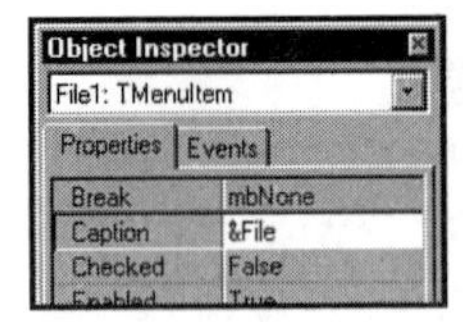

Figure 6.16.
The menu item caption property.

Many things need to be taken into consideration when creating the menu system for your application. We have covered some of the major areas here. Usability testing helps bring out the deficiencies in your design. Don't hesitate to take input from those who will use the product, and your product will be a great one!

Controls

In order for your applications to be useful, they must interact with the user. This is done through the use of controls. Controls provide a method for the user to control the actions or properties of other objects. Controls come in many forms (no pun intended) and in many styles.

Controls are usually activated by using the mouse pointer in conjunction with the left mouse button. Most controls have what is referred to as the "hot zone." This hot zone is an area that is sensitive to left mouse clicks and activates the control when a mouse pointer is clicked in that area. Some controls' hot zones are very apparent, such as the hot zone on a button, which corresponds to the area inside the border of the button. Other controls may have hot zones that are smaller or larger than the control itself. A checkbox, for instance, has a hot zone that is larger than just the checkbox itself, because the label for the checkbox is included.

Labels are important so that the purpose of your controls can be quickly ascertained by the user. Labels, just like menu items, should be concise and to the point. As with menus, it is important to provide access keys for controls so that the user can use the keyboard directly, instead of relying entirely on the mouse.

Command Buttons

Several types of buttons are used in Windows 95. The first is the command button. The command button is used to activate a command associated with that button. The usual behavior is for the command button to be pressed. When the button is released, if the mouse pointer is on the button, the command associated with the button is executed. If the mouse pointer is off the button, the command is not executed. This enables the user a second chance to cancel the command after the button has already been pushed.

This second chance works only if you are using the mouse to visually activate the button. If the button has the current focus and you press the Enter key, that's it. The button has been activated. There is no second chance mechanism.

NOTE

> When we use the term "press" in relation to buttons on forms, we mean two separate things. A button can be visually pressed or activated by using the mouse. The button appears to be pushed in when you click that primary button on your mouse. You can also press, or activate, the forms button by making sure the button has the focus, and then press the Enter key. They both accomplish the same thing: pressing the button.

Besides the command button, Windows 95 makes good use of the unfold button. This is a command button that expands a window to a larger view when activated. When you use a command button as an unfold button, placing the double greater than signs (>>) signifies that the button will expand the current view. This enables the user to view only primary information and then press the unfold button to review additional information.

If your command button requires additional information in order for its associated command to execute correctly, place the ellipses (...) after the command button's label. This indicates to the user that more information needs to be given (usually in the form of a dialog box) by the user for the button's command to execute successfully. When command buttons are unavailable, they should be grayed out. This can be accomplished by setting the `Enabled` property for that button to False.

Radio Buttons

Radio buttons are another control that assists the user in selected options in your application. This is why radio buttons are also referred to as option buttons. Radio buttons are shown as small round circles and should be presented in groups of two to seven. If you need more items than that, consider using another control such as a listbox. The radio buttons can be presented in two ways. The first is in exclusive mode (their most common use). In this state, only a single button in the group can be selected at any given time. Uses would be anything in which each option is mutually exclusive.

Figure 6.17.
Radio buttons in exclusive mode.

A second state radio buttons can be used in is called mixed-value appearance. This means that more than one radio button can be selected at any given time. This would be useful for something such as selection of file attributes where a file can be read-only, hidden, and archived all at the same time.

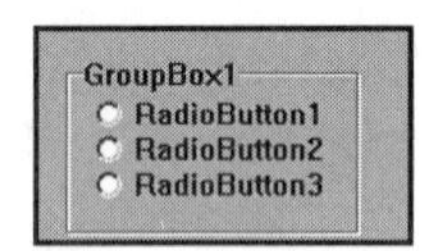

Figure 6.18.
Radio buttons in mixed-value mode.

Most Windows users assume that radio buttons are used in exclusive mode, which means that one button is always checked. During the design of the application, the programmer usually picks the button that is checked. The programmer accomplishes this by setting the value attribute to True for one of the buttons. You make the radio buttons act as an exclusive group by placing them into a RadioGroup, Panel, or Bevel control. These controls ensure that only one radio button is ever active at any given time. If you are going to use the radio buttons in mixed-value mode, simply do not place them in a group box control. This enables the radio buttons to act independently of one another. In this instance, you could set the value attribute of all the radio buttons to False and let the user choose them at will.

NOTE

> Using radio button controls in mixed-value mode is highly discouraged. In that instance, checkboxes should be used in their place.

As with any other Windows control, it is important that you assign access keys to the controls as shown in the two previous examples. This enables the user to select a specific radio button

from the keyboard directly. Another method for selecting any radio button is to tab around the screen until that control is highlighted and then press the space bar to select it.

NOTE

There is an alternate method of accessing radio buttons short of assigning them all individual access keys. If you assign an access key to the GroupBox, or other control in which the radio buttons are a part of, when you press the access key for this group control, the focus jumps to the radio buttons in the grouping control. Then you can use the arrow keys on the keyboard to activate the correct radio button.

Checkboxes

Checkboxes provide another mechanism for the user to select options in your program. The checkbox exists in several states. The state attribute determines whether the checkbox is checked or not by setting the `State` property to either `cbChecked` (the checked state), `cbUnChecked` (the unchecked state), or `cbGrayed` (a state where the box is checked but grayed out). This last state is provided for your own use, and your application would have to define what that state means.

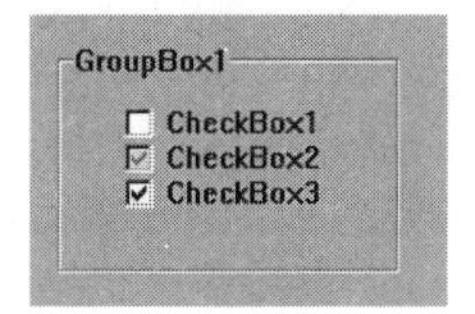

Figure 6.19.
Checkboxes in all three states.

When using checkboxes, group related checkboxes together. This helps the user see the relationship between the checkboxes. As with other controls, use access keys to enable the user to interact with the checkboxes directly from the keyboard. Like the other controls, if you check a checkbox with the mouse, your selection can be undone by removing the mouse from over the control, prior to releasing the mouse button. This leaves your selection unchanged. You can also gray out the entire checkbox control by changing the Enabled attribute to `FALSE`. This would make the control unavailable to the user, regardless of the state.

Listboxes

Listboxes are a convenient and succinct way for you to display a number of items to the user. The benefit of a listbox is that the items can vary in both number and form. Unlike checkboxes and other controls, if a selection is not available, it should not be shown in the listbox at all. This differs from the graying out concept of other controls. The contents of the listbox can be arranged a number of different ways. Use the method that best fits your user's browsing needs. For example, names would probably be arranged alphabetically, numbers in ascending order, and dates in chronological order.

Figure 6.20.
Sample listbox (listed alphabetically).

NOTE

It is important that you use the Listbox and Combobox controls for what they are intended for. If you have your 4GB database, do not load all that data into one poor Listbox control. That method is slow and unwieldy. Think of how long it would take you to use the vertical slider bar to roll through 4GB of data! Instead, you may want to use an Edit control and a search button to narrow the choices down to something reasonable.

A listbox does not have a label associated with it. If you create a label for the listbox, ensure that it is disabled whenever you disable the listbox (by setting the Enabled attribute to `FALSE`). The Delphi 2 version of the listbox has the Multiselect attribute which enables that listbox to be used as a single or multiselect listbox. The single select means just that—the user can select only one item from the listbox. If the Multiselect attribute is set to `TRUE`, the user can select multiple items from the listbox. If the list of items in the listbox is longer than the window height, a vertical scroll bar appears.

View Controls

There are two different types of view controls in Windows 95. The first is a listview control. This control allows for a list of items to be viewed in a similar fashion to the right window in Explorer. The list can be viewed in one of the four following ways:

- Icon View—The items appear as full size icons with the label underneath the icon.
- Small Icon—Each item appears as a small icon with the label to the right of the icon.
- List—Same as small icon except the icons appear in columns and are sorted.
- Report—The items are displayed in column format. All but the left-most column must be supplied by the application displaying the listbox.

TreeView Controls

TreeView is another form of the list view control. The major difference is that the tree view is more conducive to showing information of a hierarchical nature. There are some major benefits to this approach. The tree view control enables you to associate icons with each of the items in the "tree." The icon for an item can even change when it is collapsed, as opposed to when it is expanded.

The tree control enables lines to be drawn between items, to help reinforce to the user the hierarchical relationship among the items. A prime example of using the tree control is in the Explorer. The left window within the Explorer is a tree control. Notice how the drive icons represent each drive, and folder icons represent each directory within the drive, and so on. This control helps gives a clear display method to something that would usually be a little more confusing.

Text Entry and Display

Text can be displayed in two ways using Delphi 2. The first is using a label control for displaying static text. This method is used frequently when displaying information that the user cannot change, such as a customer serial number or social security number.

Microsoft guidelines say that we need to ensure that the label control does not receive focus when tabbing between controls on the screen. Delphi 2 goes one better. The label control has no tab order, so it does not receive focus. In addition, if you set the `FocusControl` attribute to the control that should have the focus, when the user presses the access key for that label, the item pointed to by the `FocusControl` receives focus instead! Here you gain the ability to both label controls and provide proper focus for those controls.

The edit box is the other method for displaying data. The added benefit of this control is that you can edit the data as well. The Delphi 2 edit control supports the `MaxLength` attribute which enables you to limit the length of a user's input. The basic editing techniques of insert, overwrite, and delete are supported.

The Memo control is another control that provides similar capabilities. The Memo control is really a multiline edit control. It has a `MaxLength` property as well. The Memo control also has a `Lines` property under which you can set the value of each line in the control.

Tabbed Page Controls

The tabbed dialog box is the newest, trendiest thing to hit Windows 95. Think of the filing cabinet in your office (if you have one). The tabbed separators help to organize your information into "buckets," which enable you to find information more easily. Follow the same guidelines for naming the tabbed pages as with menu items. The tabbed pages themselves are usually aligned in a single row. If necessary, you can place several rows of tabbed pages on one page. Each tabbed page contains pieces of data, and to access the data on a tabbed page, simply click on the tab.

NOTE

There are several use and design considerations that go into tabbed dialog boxes. Depending on whether you place your OK and Cancel buttons on the tabbed page itself or on the form holding the tabbed pages makes a statement to the user. If it's on the page itself, the inference is that the OK locks in changes on that page only. If the only OK button is on the form itself, then the user should be able to go back and forth and change all tabbed pages, using the OK button at the end to commit those changes.

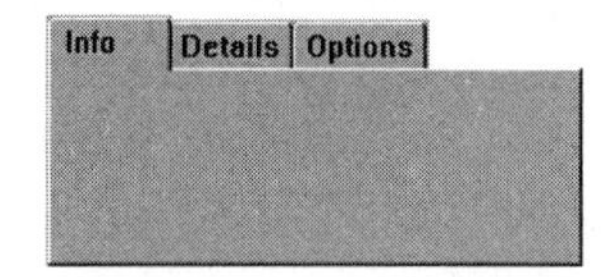

Figure 6.21.
Typical tabbed page.

Sliders

Sliders are another way to control the adjustment of data values. You must assign a minimum and maximum value for the slider using the `Min` and `Max` properties. This control is ideal for adjusting values such as contrast, volume, and so on. Anything that lends itself to a knob in the real world does very well here. You can control the orientation of the slider (horizontal or vertical), the presence and number of increments, and the size of the slider itself.

NOTE

Even though the slider bar needs `Min` and `Max` values set, you can translate those into other options. For example, Windows 95 uses the slider in the display properties dialog box to set the screen size, where each increment is 640×480, 800×600 or 1024×768. You assign from one to three values on the slider to match these screen resolution settings. The result of this mapping of values makes the slider more useful.

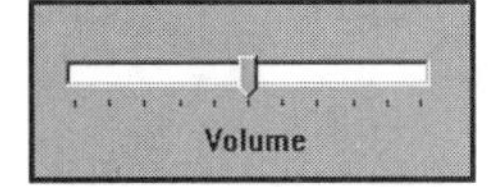

Figure 6.22.
Typical slider.

Tooltips

Tooltips are an important innovation of Windows 95. They provide a quick reference for the user in identifying control and its function. Delphi 2 provides a "hint" (the Delphi equivalent of a tooltip) for all relevant controls. You can set the `Hint` attribute for a control, and set the `ShowHint` attribute to True, and the hint appears when the user places the mouse pointer over a control and leaves it there.

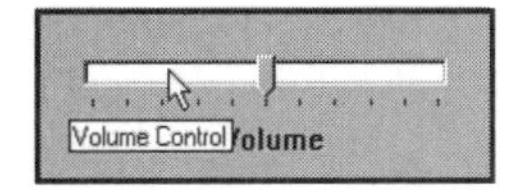

Figure 6.23.
Tooltip (hint) in action.

Progress Indicators

When your application performed a lengthy operation in Windows 3.1, you would have used the hourglass icon to tell the user that something was happening. Under Windows 95, a more informative way has been found. The use of a progress indicator shows the user that something is happening and approximately how much of the operation has taken place. Users will usually be much more patient when they know something constructive is going on.

Figure 6.24.
Typical progress bar.

Toolbars

Toolbars are a wonderful way to enhance the productivity of the user. They enable fast access to commonly performed operations in your application. There are many different names for toolbars, such as ribbons, palettes, and tool boxes. In Delphi 2, a toolbar is usually implemented using a panel control and a number of speed button controls. These buttons are placed on the panel and usually appear under the menu bar. If you select File | New | Projects and SDI or MDI application, you get, as part of that default project, a toolbar. Look at the controls carefully and what they represent.

Figure 6.25.
Default toolbar in an SDI application.

Designing Your Screens

When we say "A picture is worth a thousand words," we aren't kidding. Visual images can have dramatic impact on our minds and emotions. The visual images we as software developers present to users can have a number of effects. They can range from inspiration to distraction. This is why it is important to design your applications to inspire the user, without distracting them from the task at hand.

When it comes to actually designing your screens, you can leverage a lot of information from companies, such as Microsoft, which have done a great deal of research in this area. In this next section, we will go over some of the things Microsoft has learned. All this information is part of the Windows 95 design specifications or is on the Microsoft Developer Network (MSDN) CD-ROM. I hope this will give you ideas on how to proceed in your development effort.

Organization

There are really six organizational principles that Microsoft has outlined as being important. Let's look at each one of them and what they mean.

Readability and Flow

The principle of readability and flow asks you to arrange your design to communicate your ideas directly and simply with minimal visual interference. To minimize visual interference and increase readability and flow, ask yourself the following questions when designing a dialog box or window:

Is this idea being presented in the easiest manner possible?

Can the user easily step through this dialog the way I have designed it?

Does everything in this window have a reason for being here?

Structure and Balance

Structure and balance refer to the idea that without a sturdy foundation, the house will never last. The structure of your application is a little esoteric but refers to how your overall application is put together. Without a good structure there is a lack of order and meaning. The relationship between screens and the information on those screens all play a part in how the application feels to the end user. Balance refers to how your information is balanced on those screens. If too much information is on one screen and not enough on another, the application will feel lopsided or out of balance. A lack of structure and balance makes it more difficult for the user to clearly understand the interface.

Relationship of Elements

It is important for you to visually show the relationship that exists between elements of your application. If a button expands information in a listbox, it is important that those two items are connected to each other visually so that the relationship is obvious to the user. This may involve having both the button and the listbox in close proximity on the screen, or having them both in the same bevel control. If your screen is nothing more than a random grouping of buttons, that is exactly what it will look like.

Focus and Emphasis

The concept of focus refers to identifying the central theme or idea your screen revolves around. The concept of emphasis refers to choosing the central controls or theme and making them stand out so that the user understands which things on the screen are most important. These two concepts reinforce the principles of structure and balance as well. If your application has a solid focus, the structure of the application will seem strong to the user. You do not want your application to be a floor wax *and* a desert topping (sorry, an old comedy joke). It should focus on accomplishing one task, and doing that task well. An example of a well-focused program is WinZip. All that program does is compress and uncompress files. It does not have a disk defragmenter, an Explorer, or a checkbook balancing program built-in. It focuses on the task of file compression and does it well. The user interface is concise and focused, and gets the job done.

Hierarchy of Information

The concept of a hierarchy applies to screen design, as well as to data (as in the TreeView control). You must decide what information is the most important and should be on the initial screen, what is on the second screen, and so on. There are a number of questions you can ask yourself to help decide the structure of your hierarchy: What is the most important information to the user? What things does the user need to do first, second, and so forth? What things should the user see on the first screen, second,...? You also need to understand what the priorities of the user are going to be. Will your screen organization help or hurt the user, and which portions do you wish to emphasize?

Unity and Integration

This is sort of the 30,000-foot view. How does your application fit into the overall desktop and how does it interact with other applications? If your application stands out like a sore thumb, it may be heading for trouble. If you follow some of the guidelines in this chapter, you will find that your application behaves more like a standard application.

Oh the Colors!

As mentioned earlier in this chapter, you can create your application using a rainbow of colors available in Windows. Color provides some mental cues for us, as well as helps draw our attention to particular areas of the screen. We also seem to associate color with a particular state.

If we do not practice good color management, color can have a negative effect. Too many (or not the right) colors can distract the users or confuse them and make it difficult to work. Here are few other things to remember when choosing colors:

- Associating color with a particular meaning is not always obvious to the user. In the United States stop signs are red, but stop signs in other countries could be other colors as well.
- Other people may not have the good taste in color you do; therefore, it's good to use the system colors for your application whenever possible. The user can then change the overall color scheme in Windows, and your application will follow.
- There may actually be someone out there with a monochrome monitor that wants to use your application.
- Colors have different meanings in different countries. It would be a shame to create a really cool utility, only to have half the world not use it, because its color scheme has a negative connotation.
- Microsoft estimates that nine percent of the adult male population has a color-confusion problem.

Color should be used to add to a display not as the primary way to disclose information to the user. Shapes, patterns, and other methods can be used to help distinguish information on your screen. Microsoft even suggests building your screen in black and white, and then adding color later.

Using a limited number of colors also includes using the *right* color combinations. Using bright colors, such as red, on background colors such as green or black , makes it hard for the user to focus. The use of opposite colors is not recommended. A neutral color, such as light gray, is often the best background color (as is evident in most of Microsoft's product line). Remember also, that light colors have a tendency to jump out at you, whereas dark colors recede back into the screen.

Layout

One of the things I found most interesting is a statement in the Windows design guidelines that says one of goals is to make a predictable environment. As a user, that is what I like to

feel is the ability to be able to predict where a menu choice will be (About is always the last choice on the Help menu). I think this goal strikes at the very core of your goals. Using your application should be fun, not a chore.

The spacing, font usage, and placement of controls and information on your screen will make or break your application. Font usage in screen design is critical. There are some fonts that are better to use than others. MS San Serif eight-point is Microsoft's font choice for all system-related items. There are other factors to take into consideration, as well. An italicized font is much harder for the eye to see—the edges are more jagged than a regular font. It is best to use the default system font whenever possible.

It is possible for the user to change the default font, so you should not make any assumptions that MS Sans Serif will always be the system font. Your application should try to adjust for new fonts whenever possible. Another factor to take into consideration is that the fonts will show up worse on the screen than they would in printed form. This is especially true for low resolution monitors. These are all things to consider when choosing your font.

The Unit of Measure

In its specifications, Microsoft uses dialog base units as the unit of measure. This system is used because it is a device-independent measurement system, based on the size of the default system font. This compensates for the variations in screen size that different systems may have. There is a `GetDialogBaseUnits()` function call in the Win32 API that returns a 32-bit value that contains the dialog base units, based on the current system font. The low-order word of the return value contains the horizontal dialog box base unit, and the high-order word contains the vertical dialog box base unit.

The horizontal base unit is equal to the average width, in pixels, of the characters ["a".."z","A".."Z"] in the current system font; the vertical base unit is equal to the height, in pixels, of the font. Each horizontal base unit is equal to four horizontal dialog units, and each vertical base unit is equal to eight vertical dialog units. Therefore, to convert dialog units to pixels, your application would use the following formulas:

```
PixelsInX = (DialogUnitsX x BaseUnitsX) / 4

PixelsInY = (DialogUnitsY x BaseUnitsY) / 8
```

And to convert from pixels to dialog units, your application would use the following formulas:

```
DialogUnitsX = (PixelsInX x 4) / BaseUnitsX

DialogUnitsY = (PixelsInY x 8) / BaseUnitsY
```

The multiplication is performed before the division to avoid rounding problems if base units are not divisible by four or eight. The `PixelsInX` and `PixelsInY` let you know what your

6

multiplier is for spacing, and so on. There are some general recommendations for the size of different items. Edit boxes, labels, spin boxes, and buttons should be 14 dialog base units in height. This gives you just the right amount of space, both above and below the lettering.

Grouping and Spacing Elements

When developing your screens, it is important to provide the proper spacing for the elements on your screen. It is also important to maintain a constant margin (seven dialog base units) around the entire window. There should be at least four dialog base units between controls. The exception to this rule is when you are trying to group sets of toolbar buttons together. In this case, related buttons should be directly adjacent to one another with no space in between them.

You should always group related elements together. The group box control is a good way to accomplish this, although just spacing works, too. Group boxes help the user focus on a particular set of elements. It is not recommended to group controls using color (such as a colored shape behind the controls). This method is distracting, and if the user changes the color scheme, it could really get ugly.

Figure 6.26.
Grouping controls for focus.

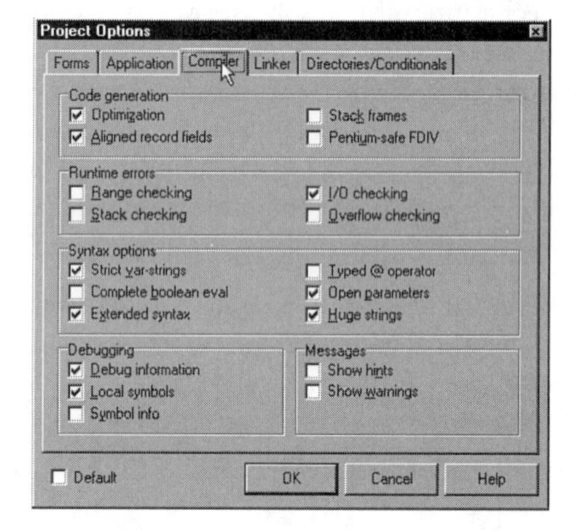

NOTE

Our discussion of base dialog units is to give you an understanding of where Microsoft is coming from. Delphi 2 uses device units (pixels) for spacing and alignment, not base dialog units. The pixel measurement is easier for the programmer to understand and work with.

Alignment of Elements

You can use several ways to position data on your screen. In western countries, we usually read from left to right, and top to bottom. The most important piece of data is usually in the top-right corner. When the data (or elements) are positioned vertically, the left edges should be aligned. If you attach labels to these controls, the labels should be placed above or to the left of the controls, and be left aligned as well. This applies to controls like the edit, listbox, and combobox control. The exception to this is the Radiobox and Checkbox controls. For these controls, the controls are normally left aligned, with the labels to the right of the control itself.

Using the alignment palette provides an easy way to align controls in Delphi 2. By selecting the controls you wish to align and then choosing the alignment option from the alignment palette, you can quickly move the controls into position. Using the Lock Controls feature under the Edit menu in the IDE also keeps the controls from moving once you have them aligned properly.

When you place command buttons on a window, if the command button is in a group box, it is implied that the button only effects the information within that group. If the command button appears outside any group boxes, the implication is that it effects the entire window.

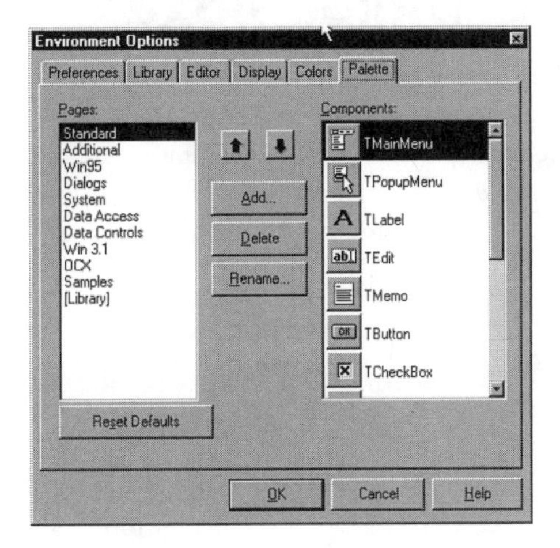

Figure 6.27.
Command buttons (local and global).

Use of Tabbed Dialog Boxes

Tabbed dialog boxes are extremely useful and aid in keeping your interface clean and simple. When creating tabbed dialogs, you should keep the tabs themselves all the same size (if possible) to give a uniform appearance. Tabs can be arranged on a functional basis, where each tab control has information about a specific topic. A good example of a tabbed dialog box is under Tools | Options in Delphi 2. Look at how organized the information is on those tabbed dialog boxes. This new habit in Windows 95 of using tabs helps your interfaces stay neater, and it is easier for the user to use.

Capitalization

When you display text on buttons, labels, tabs or in menus use headline capitalization. This means that you capitalize the first letter of every word, unless it is a preposition or article that does not appear at the beginning or end of the phrase or name. The other instance when a word may not be capitalized is if the word's conventional usage is not capitalized. Some examples are:

Save As
Insert Object
Always on Top
Add to Project
Syntax Check
Database Form Expert

These are just a few examples from Windows and Delphi 2. You can see that capitalization can help add flair to a menu or control.

Modal Dialog Boxes

The first thing we need to define in this section is what a modal dialog box is. It is a window that pops up to provide or request information. Modal dialog boxes can display supplemental information related to information found on a primary window. It is not, however, your application's primary window. This dialog box has (or lacks) several items found on a primary window. The following list outlines some of these features:

- It does not have minimize or maximize buttons.
- It can have a Close button to dismiss the window (although it's not required).
- The title bar text describes what the window does.
- The title bar does not have an icon on it.
- It does not include a status bar.
- It can have a What's This? button to give the user help on the components on the window.

When displaying modal dialog boxes, the recommendation is that they not be larger than 263 dialog base units by 263 dialog base units. If a secondary window is a property sheet, the three recommended sizes are 218×227, 215×212, and 212×188 dialog base units. These sizes have been determined to give ample viewing area without becoming too big for the screen (especially at lower resolutions).

Play Nice

Your dialog boxes have to learn how to act in this multiwindowed environment. There is a standard behavior for dialog boxes. They appear under two instances. The first is that a dialog box is created as a response to a command chosen in primary window. An example would be a Find dialog that comes up in Microsoft Word 7. In this circumstance, when you shut the primary window, you would want all the dialog boxes associated with it to close as well. When the primary window is restored, the dialog boxes return to their positions and Z order.

NEW TERM *Z order* is the layered relationship for a set of objects such as windows. The Z order in Windows is the order in which windows are drawn on the screen. The window at the top of the Z order is also the window that will appear on top of all other windows on your screen. (Another term for which window is on top, second, third, and so on).

The second example of a dialog box would be one that is generated from the system, or outside your application. An example of this would be the Display Properties window for the Windows 95 display. In this instance, you want that properties window to stay open when you minimize your application window. These behaviors are part of the Delphi environment. When you minimize your Delphi application, all the child (for MDI) and secondary windows are minimized as well.

Dialog boxes should not appear on the taskbar in Windows 95. Only the primary window should appear there (think of how crowded the taskbar would get if all application windows showed up there). The Delphi applications you generate also provide for this behavior. If you add a dialog box to your project and set the `FormStyle` attribute to the value `sStayOnTop`, you can minimize the primary window, the secondary window will minimize with it, and only the primary will show up on the taskbar. Windows that stay on top can be fairly annoying to the user, so use them sparingly.

If you provide for cascading windows in your application (where a secondary window opens another secondary window), keep two things in mind. First, limit the number to three windows (the primary, the secondary, and the subsecondary). Do not take the levels any further than that. It gets really confusing for the user. Second, make sure when you open the secondary and subsecondary windows that are set off and below and to the right of the primary window. This gives the windows a natural cascading effect and lets the user know they are getting deeper into the windows layers.

We talked earlier about unfolding windows. This is where you have a secondary window, you press a button that has a >> next to the label, and the window expands to reveal additional information. This method is very useful for revealing information in stages. If the user is satisfied with the information on the smaller page, that's fine. If more in-depth information is needed, they can expand the window.

You can also open secondary windows in two modes: modal and modeless. If you open the windows in modeless mode, the user is still able to access the other windows in your (and other) applications without dismissing the window first. If you open a secondary window in modal mode, then the user must dismiss that window first before gaining access to the windows in your application. This is one of those cases where you are forcing the user to do something (such as enter a password to continue), and you know how people hate being told what to do. Use the modal dialogs and windows sparingly; they tend to slow productivity.

Summary

In this chapter, we have explored some of the concepts involved in developing a graphical user interface. We have looked at some of the different ways in which you can put users in control (or at least make them feel that way), as well as design techniques to help keep your screens uncluttered and easy to read. Although we can barely scratch the surface of this topic (the entire topic would be a book of 1000 pages plus), I hope you have been able to glean a little idea of what designing a good GUI interface takes. It makes me appreciate applications such as Delphi 2 a lot more, now that I see what GUI designers have to contend with. Good luck on your GUI design project!

Q&A

Q I'm getting ready to write an application and I think it might be a candidate for an MDI application. How would I know?

A That's a good question. As discussed earlier in this chapter, Microsoft is discouraging you from creating MDI applications because most people are not very good at writing them. If you think you should use one, remember that all the children have to be identical. No mixing of document types (documents, spreadsheet, and so on) as children. You also must give up controlling the windows and let the user do that. It's a lot to give up for MDI!

Q This chapter is good, but I feel like I need to know more. Where can I get additional information?

A There are several sources. The Microsoft Developer Network CD has a wealth of information about the Win95 logo requirements, as well as GUI design. Another great book is *The Windows Interface Guidelines for Software Design* (from Microsoft Press).

Workshop

The Workshop provides quiz questions to help you solidify your understanding of the material covered and exercises to provide you with experience. Please try to work through both before continuing to the next day.

Quiz

1. What is the primary purpose of the right mouse button in Windows 95?
2. Why does Microsoft specifically recommend that you use one of the two secondary window sizes?
3. Why is it important to have the standard menu layout in your application?

Exercises

1. Go through the color palette in Delphi 2 and see if you can find out what all the system colors are used for. If you need help, try to place several types of controls onto a form and notice the default color given to each item.
2. Look at some of the mainstream Windows 95 applications and see how they use pop-up menus to present choices to the user.
3. Look at some the applications you use every day. How do they measure up to standards we have talked about in this chapter?

Week 1

Day 7

Object-Oriented Programming

Many of you who purchase this book may be learning Delphi (or Object Pascal) for the first time. Many of you may also have little or no formal training in software development or software engineering. This is significant because learning to be a good computer scientist involves more than learning the syntax of a particular language like Delphi.

There are many other aspects of the software field that really bear little connection to the actual act of writing code, but are equally important to the act itself. This chapter covers several topics you may not have dealt with before, but will affect your career as a software developer. These include the software crisis, software lifecycle, and software engineering.

Now you may be saying, "Come on, I just want to learn Delphi!" To that I answer, "A man who lives with blinders on, is soon hit by reality from the side, which he cannot see" (an ancient Chinese proverb I just made up). The point here is that if you plan on developing software for money, and you have real customers that expect

- ☐ your software to work out of the box,
- ☐ your software to be done on time,
- ☐ your software to be bug free,
- ☐ your software to be inexpensive,

then you need to read this chapter. Let's talk about the problems today, and then about potential solutions, and how Delphi 2 supports the solution.

Software Crisis

I know what you're thinking: Crisis, what crisis? There has been a software crisis for so long now that most people think it's normal. People have been programming computers (at least what we think of as computers) for only a handful of decades. But, as anyone who has been around computers can tell you, even a couple of years is a long time in technological terms (think of computer years the way you do dog years). Times and technology change: people don't. The method of programming has changed very little from those early beginnings. Although, rather recently, there has been a large shift in the accepted programming doctrine.

In the old days (prior to 1990), when a programmer was given a task, he or she plopped down in a chair in front of a PC and started coding. The tasks were small and the coding was fast. These were the good old days. It was a time when, if you needed to get something done, you could just sit up all night and get it done. It was a time of thousand-line programs—good programs, too. It was a time when a single person, could tap along and come up with a million-dollar program! It was, literally, the golden age of programming. But all good things must come to an end, and there is no better example of this than in the arena of programming.

Software Complexity

As computers became more sophisticated, so too did their users. The tasks foisted upon the programmer became larger and so did the associated coding time. Then a funny thing happened. After a program reached a certain size, the time it took to code turned out to be much longer than expected (based on smaller programs). If a program was twice as long as another program it was assumed that it would take twice as long to code (we thought the curve was linear). It actually turned out to take more than twice as long! Whether it was the fundamental unfairness of the universe or Murphy's Law, the fact of the matter was that when a program reached a certain size, the human brain couldn't keep track of all the complexity. Complexity was the culprit all right, and there was nothing we could do about it (at least not directly). It was a hard truism to accept, but case after case, program after program, it was proven to be true.

Figure 7.1.
Software size vs. complexity.

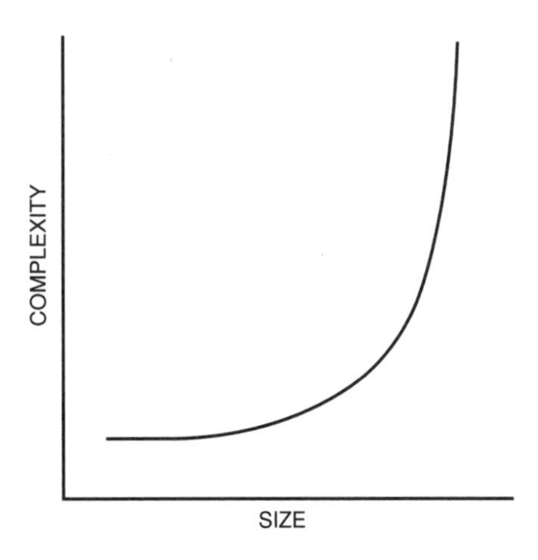

As you may have noticed, there are quite a few very complex programs running about around your local software store. We must have beaten complexity...right? Well, yes and no. Complexity is like the sea, you can't tame it or beat it. You have to ride out complexity, take advantage of calm times, and take shelter in protected harbors when you can. Okay, okay, I've milked that analogy for as much as I can. But the essence is true: you can't beat complexity. How many of those whiz-bang, very complex programs are error free? Very few! A bug is complexity's way of telling you that you haven't beaten it. And just think, we even find bugs in small programs. Only after quite a bit of work, can we say that even the smallest program is truly error free. What hope can we have of putting together a large program that doesn't fall apart at the seams? Well, the trick to beating complexity is to write small "error free" programs and put them together building a large "error free" program. Of course, this is easier said than done, but this modular approach helps us manage complexity in programming. Note that I put quotes around "error free." "Error free" is much the same as "100% pure"—for any non-trivial sample, there is no such thing!

The Need to Plan

The obvious thing here is that we figured out that more was needed than just sitting down and coding. We needed to apply scientific analysis to the problem and not just undisciplined artistry (hacking). Like every great battle, there is a battle plan, a set of tactics and weapons to use on the enemy. Software development is no different. You will now look at the two things that have helped us, not only with the battle but the war. Those two weapons are the software lifecycle and software engineering.

Software Lifecycle

The software lifecycle is a roadmap. A series of steps that should be taken, and taken in order. Using this disciplined approach, the developer can generate a better end product and spend lees time maintaining the product as well. This is not a panacea, but just another tool in the fight against lousy software.

The software lifecycle is broken into six major areas. As you read through these, they will really seem like common sense. You would be surprised how many developers skip several steps and go right to the coding, and then skip all the steps after that! Look at each step and the implications of each.

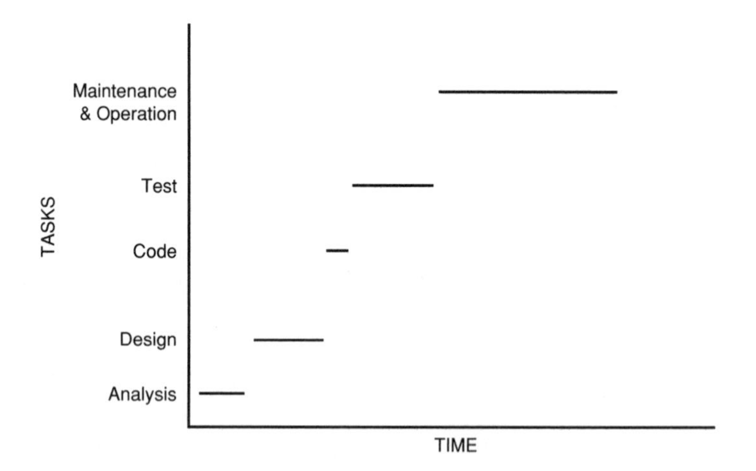

Figure 7.2.
The software lifecycle.

Analysis

During the analysis phase of your development, you try to better define the problem at hand. At this point, one thing that needs to be determined is whether a software-based solution is even right. There are many things that can be better accomplished by two columns on a piece of paper rather than a complete software application.

Now you may call me a traitor. No, not really. I am sure that you too have seen applications requiring more work from you, to input your data, than the results you get out of the application (a poor return on investment). This is called a "time sucker." It sucks all of your useful time from your body with no return on your investment. You just need to make sure that a computer-based solution will help the problem, not add to it.

During this phase of development, you also need to determine what type of resources you will need to complete the project. It may be just you and your PC and Delphi 2. For larger

projects, you may require the assistance of several other developers, technical writers, and the like. At this point you usually do not select a language. This is because until you understand the problem, and design a solution, how do you know which language best supports your solution.

In the big league, usually the result of this phase of development is the creation of a system specification. This specification helps define the system as whole. It maps out the system functions that need to be performed.

Requirements

In this phase you take the functions defined in the analysis phase, and determine detailed requirements for each. The system specification is the input to this phase, and the output is a functional software specification. What are the functions that the software will perform? Here you are not designing the complete solution but only the functions the software will perform.

At this point you may want to think of functions in terms of Delphi units, functions, and procedure declarations. If you have decided early on to use the language, using Delphi's syntax for everything helps create a documentation set that is more maintainable and integrated with the solution.

Design

This phase is where all the design details are ironed out. Because you had a good idea from the requirements phase of the functions your software was going to perform, you can take that next step. Here you develop a detailed design of your software solution including a definition of the relationships among units and a detailed procedural flow.

As you drill down (a term used often with spreadsheets to describe getting to finer and finer levels of detail), you need to figure out and document how everything will work. Things like screen layouts, button placements, report contents and types are looked at here.

It is important to realize that your customer will not know all the details up front (customers rarely know what they want, they just know that they want). This is an iterative process. If this is happening to you, it is a good thing. It means that you and your customer are communicating, and getting things out on the table.

One of the benefits of using Delphi as your development language is that during theses phases you can use it as a high-level definition language to show general logic. Because Delphi is a very "English-like" language, it is more self-documenting than most other languages. That has been one of aspects I love most about this language: the ability to read the code from top to bottom and have it read like a book!

Code

Ah, the coding phase! Get that case of Mountain Dew and those Twinkies, and let's get to work. This phase of development starts now and ends… never. Coding exists throughout the rest of the development cycle and continues as you make changes to the code through the rest of the product's lifecycle.

If you have done a good job of designing your software and defining the interfaces for the different modules, the code should literally fall out of this phase. I know what you are saying. Yea, sure! Well I have actually witnessed the code falling right out of the detailed design document. If you follow the steps with great rigor, the code almost writes itself.

The product from this phase is twofold. The first of course is the code itself, but nearly as important is a complete product specification that details the product "as built." This will serve as a tool for testing and may also serve as the basis for the user's manual.

Test

The real purpose of this phase is to test the "as built" product against the requirements agreed upon in the development specification. Here is where you will know whether you have done a good job at mapping those requirements to reality. There should be mapping of each function in the software to a requirement in the requirements documentation. If there is no requirement for the function, then the function should not exist.

Testing is usually done in two steps. The first is *unit testing*. This is where you take individual units of code, write drivers stubs for each, and test the functionality and reliability of each module. The second step is *integration testing*. Here you put the tested units together and make sure they behave in the manner you assumed they would.

Software testing is an art form in itself. If you're writing a fairly simply application, the testing may be simple. With larger programs, the testing becomes very unwieldy if you don't pay close attention. There are a number of good books on software testing out there, so you will have some good reference material to work with.

Maintenance and Operation

So you think you are home free. The product is out the door, and boy are you happy! Just remember that 80 percent of the effort and money is spent in this phase. Now you will follow this software as it services customers, as they find undocumented features (bugs), and as the software slowly moves to the grave.

Sound dismal? Well the truth is, maintaining a program is not nearly as fun as creating it, but someone has to do it. How do you think that new guy you just hired is going to maintain your application after you become vice president of engineering at your company?

All that wonderful documentation: the user's manual, design document, product specification, and test manual will assist that new lad in getting up to speed on your application. That's right, doing your job right means working yourself out of that job so you can move on to greener pastures. Invention is the spice of life! The discipline to build these pieces using software engineering principles and goals is what got you there.

Where Now?

Now that you know some of the steps necessary to get a disciplined approach down, you need to talk about the next level of consciousness. What you needed in the old days (and some say what's still needed today) was a programming discipline. A set of rules to guide the troubled programmer, help us use the lifecycle process, and refine it with other "rules" to achieve an even more stable environment.

Software Engineering

Enter *software engineering*. A software engineer is very different from a programmer. A software engineer talks to the intended user and formally writes down what the user needs from the software. He or she then formally writes down what must be done to build this piece of software. Then, and only then, will the software engineer start writing code.

Sounds dull? Sounds like a lot of work? Sounds like it will make very clean, very robust code? Yes, yes, and sometimes (if the software engineer knows what he is doing). It's a lot more fun to sit down in front of the computer and start hacking out code, but for large systems it's a lot more fun down the road to have a working product. At any rate, software engineering is the disciplined approach to programming.

Software Engineering Goals

If you are going to pursue this avenue of disciplined development, you need to have a goal; something you are trying to achieve. If you don't know where the finish line is, it will be hard to win the race. The most straightforward goal of software development is to make the finished product match the requirements specification. You need to break this down into something more manageable. Some smaller or more precise set of goals that are both attainable and easy to remember.

Remember that the one thing that is always constant is change. As we had discussed earlier, your application will spend the majority of its lifecycle in the maintenance phase. It's important then, for us to have a set of goals that transcend change. The four generally excepted goals of software engineering are modifiability, efficiency, reliability, and understandability.

Modifiability

In your software product's lifecycle, it will probably need to be modified many times. This may be the result of a bug that you or your customer found or a feature request or enhancement that your user(s) requested. Either way, it is important that the work you have done in your well-thought-out design need not perish when you make a change.

You should be able to make changes to your application without wrecking the foundation you built. This goal implies controlled change in which some parts of your application change while others stay the same, and you get the result you sought. This is hard to do. Many languages do not support this very well and are very "touchy" or abrasive to change.

The Object Pascal language however, provides a very readable language. It also provides an environment that allows you to easily make changes. With the string typing errors are harder to make. These attributes provide an environment that promotes our goal of modifiability. A thought that should always be in your mind when making a change to your application is making that same change in your documentation. You could (or should) go as far as adding that new user requirement to the requirements document, then trace that requirement through your design document, and finally make the change to the code last. It sounds a little dull, but it will help to make your design more stable.

Efficiency

This is one that is very straightforward. Your application should use the optimally available resources. In the days of 64K computers we had very little memory to play with, but because PCs were multitasking, at least you had most of that memory to yourself.

Today, many applications share memory space and run simultaneously on your PC. This is why it is important that your application be resource friendly and work and play well with others. By *resources*, we are referring to two types, time and space. Your application may have requirements to execute in a given time frame, if it is gathering time-sensitive data or live network information. Also, a time requirement could mean that you must leave some CPU cycles for someone else! Your application should be good at sharing that time with other applications. If it is hoarding CPU cycles, look at the `Application.ProcessMessages()` function for help.

The other resource requirement for efficient operation is space. As you have probably noticed, software is getting larger and larger. Most software now comes on a CD-ROM because it is too expensive to supply forty floppies! Seriously, it is also important that you use disk space efficiently. Just like anything else, take only what you need, and be frugal.

Reliability

This is probably the most important goal, especially if your application is responsible for some critical function. Applications that operate for long periods of time without human intervention must be stable and able to recover from problems automatically. Can you imagine an operator of a nuclear power station getting a "Cannot open configuration file, program terminated" error from your application? What a nightmare!

The problem here is that the cost of failure is too high to let you have anything but the highest reliability software. You must design reliability into your software from the ground up. There are many ways to make sure you don't get `numeric overflow` or `invalid record` messages in your applications. Object Pascal's strong typing helps you avoid many of the mistakes you could make with "looser" languages. Also with things like range checking turned on, you can avoid other potential problems. Range checking allows you to help validate that the values you think are going into your variables, really are. This should help you in the testing phase to iron out any bugs in your software and make sure that your bulletproofing is really working.

Understandability

This goal is one that is born from the world of object-oriented programming. For your application to be understandable, and therefore maintainable, it must be easy to understand. This is a difficult goal in a complex system: to understand all the pieces.

One way in which this goal is attainable, is by making sure that your applications design and implementation models the real world. If your application's objects are modeling real-world objects, you can relate the two in our minds more easily. This is why we use object-oriented design in our applications, so we can relate code to the world more easily.

One of the ways your code is also understandable, is a basic readability level. The use of good coding techniques, styles, and commenting add to the understandability of the end product. The objects in the code should be easily discernible.

Software Engineering Principles

The goals discussed above are ones that should apply to any software project. The next question is, "How do you get there?" You must define a set of principles that you stand by that help you achieve these goals. Here are a set of principles to help guide you.

The Seven Software Engineering Principles

1. Modularity
2. Localization
3. Abstraction

4. Information Hiding
5. Confirmability
6. Uniformity
7. Completeness

When I was getting my Master's degree in Software Engineering, one of my professors (Mr. Shepherd) had us memorize these principles for practically all of our tests. It only seems fair that you at least see them. Shepherd—what better name for a teacher guiding his flock through the perils of programming.

These principles are supported in the Delphi class structure. Some are a natural consequence of classes, while others must be consciously introduced by the programmer.

Modularity and Localization

Modularity and localization come easily from the class structure. Classes are inherently modular, and localization refers to keeping modules logically organized—each module should be a grouping of logically related code. When you are actually constructing your code, if you write small autonomous modules, they are easily transportable to other software projects as well. This is no more evident than in the object repository.

The object repository holds objects that can be used over and over again. By simply doing a File | New in Delphi, you have access to much work done by others. The key to the success of this paradigm is the modularity of the code and the lack of dependency on outside code.

Abstraction and Information Hiding

Abstraction and information hiding have very good support in the Delphi classes. The `private` and `protected` keywords allow two levels of support for hiding information from objects outside a particular class. Abstraction is supported through information hiding and through the interface/implementation nature of class files. You allow only the abstracted nature of the class to be public. The implementation details are hidden.

An example of this is how you work with text files in Delphi. When you open a file, you specify the file you wish to open, and the mode (mode specifies whether you are opening the file for read or write). Now Delphi does not demand that you know the exact sector on which the file resides, nor which head will read the data off the hard drives platter. The implementation details of the file system are hidden from you. This allows you to read data equally from either a hard drive, floppy drive, or CD-ROM, even thought the physical structures of each storage media is different.

Confirmability

Confirmability is attained through a combination of strong type checking and the building of testable modules. Type checking is a way for the compiler to confirm that a given variable is used properly. Delphi provides string typing as part of the language. Testable modules allow the programmer to logically test individual modules for accuracy. Remember, it's a lot easier to build small, error-free programs than large, error-free programs. All code modules should be submitted to the code repository accompanied by driver programs that test the module. Confirmability implies that you must be able to break your applications down into modules that are testable.

Uniformity and Completeness

Uniformity and completeness fall totally under the domain of the programmer. Code is easier to read and maintain if it is written and commented in a uniform manner. Modules that are complete when originally written do not need to be rewritten or appended when a new need arises—and new needs always arise. Completeness, is a lot like error free, it's hard to attain. But, if you're mindful of the need for completeness, you can maximize the adaptability of your code and minimize changes that are needed later. Changes are an open invitation for errors to come into your application.

Every one of the Software Engineering Principles is intended to fight complexity. When you build your classes, keep these principals in mind, they will help you and your code. Also keep them in mind when you're looking at the Delphi classes. Now and again, you'll find yourself asking why Borland did a such an odd thing in a class. You can usually find the answer in the Software Engineering Principles (sometimes not—Borland is human too). The Delphi Class Library is a good example of software engineering. Why Delphi classes? Because it's a method of programming in Microsoft Windows that is well founded in software engineering.

Coupling and Cohesion Issues

Part of the benefits to the modular approach is that you can extract a module of code from one application and place it into another and it will work. An example would be that you have written a Delphi unit that does data encryption. You can provide it with a filename, and it will read that file, encrypt it with a key, and write the file back out to disk.

By writing this unit of code as an independent entity, you can use this in any number of applications simply by calling functions in the unit and getting the results.

When we speak of cohesion, we mean that the internal function of your code modules should be tightly integrated. Strong cohesion is good (sort of a self reliance). The second aspect is coupling. Your modules should be loosely coupled to their neighbors (in other words, very few, or no dependencies). If your unit depends heavily on other units, then it isn't portable to other applications without carrying a lot of baggage. So your code should be string cohesive and loosely coupled. This is an attainable goal, although you will have to work at it.

Object-Oriented Design (OOD)

If you look at the real world, our language has two primary components: nouns (objects) and verbs (operations). In order for our applications to map to reality, our computer language needs the same. Most languages have a large variety of operations you can perform, but have a small set of nouns to describe the objects. Even for those languages that have object capabilities, they are usually flat (they cannot inherit attributes from their parents). This of course does not model the real world. In the real world things are very 3D. We need language that supports. Delphi provides a very 3D set of nouns that allow us to describe objects.

Define an object. This word has been seriously overused. According to Grady Booch (God of all that is Object Oriented) and author of *Software Engineering with Ada*, an object is "an entity that has a state; that is, it has some value...the behavior of an object is defined by the actions it suffers and vice versa... every object is actually an instance of some class of objects." There is the first answer, for the first question, of your first quiz, in your first graduate Software Engineering class.

The goal of object-oriented design is that each module on the system represents an object or a class of objects in the real world. Grady Booch said "A program that implements a model of reality may thus be viewed as a set of objects that interact with one another." You can design a system using this object-oriented mentality by following these steps:

1. Identify the objects and their attributes.
2. Identify the operations that affect each object, and the operations that each object must initiate.
3. Establish the visibility of each object in relation to the other objects.
4. Establish the interface for each object.
5. Implement each object.

The Objects

When identifying the objects in our problem space, you usually think in terms of the nouns in your problem. In a heating control system, you would have a heat source, temperature sensor, thermostat, solenoid, or the like. These nouns become the main objects in your system. Objects may be very large and consist of smaller objects. For instance, a car is big object. You would break that down into smaller objects like the engine, drive train, and body.

The Operations

Here you need to identify the operations that each of the objects defined earlier perform or have performed on them. For instance, a thermostat may be adjusted, a solenoid may be activated, or a temperature sensor may take a temperature reading. You also would define which operations would come first on an object. A well-designed automobile would start itself when you shift from park to drive.

The Visibility

Here you define the topology of our design. You need a map telling you which objects are seen and can be seen by other objects. In the heating control system, the temperature sensor needs to be seen by the thermostat, but the temperature sensor does not need to see the thermostat.

The Interfaces

Here you define how your objects will interface with other objects. This step is extremely important to designing a system that is truly modular. You need to define exactly how other objects will talk to your object. Here you may use function or procedure call statements to define the interface for your object. You can do this if, and only if, the language you are using supports a readable format (like Delphi).

Implement the Objects

In this step you implement each object in your solution. This means writing the code interfaces for each object. You may opt not to write the complete object code, deferring the code bodies until later. If your object is a complex object (an object made up of smaller objects) you need to decompose your object into its component objects. With each one of these objects, you need to go through the same steps to determine their operations, visibility, and interface. Once you create functional skeletons with well-defined interfaces, the body coding can be done anytime.

Using these steps, you can design a system that is cohesive and well thought out. Because Object Pascal has the facilities to let you code the way this method works, so much the better.

OOP

Object-Oriented Programming has been around for a number of years and has reared its head (bet you thought we were going to say ugly head) in such programming languages as Ada,

Smalltalk, C++, Borland Pascal (various versions) and finally in Delphi. This magical term "object" has conjured up such a name for itself, that the mere mention of "object," especially in the same sentence with the words "software engineer," makes IS managers drool with anticipation.

The reality is just that, reality. We have seen object-oriented code that is far worse than any standard Pascal code could ever be. We have also seen beautiful object-oriented code. OOP is a means to an end, a tool to be used for good or evil.

There are several components in Object Pascal that make it object oriented. Look at the basic class definition and a couple of other goodies that help Object Pascal take on that object-oriented look.

Classes

Delphi provides a reserved word: *class*, that enables you, the developer, to define an object. When you create a new project in Delphi, if you look at the declarations in `unit1`, you will find a class declaration for the form itself.

```
type
 TForm1 = class(TForm)
public
    { Public declarations }
protected
    { Protected declarations }
private
    { Private declarations }
  end;
```

This is how you define an object. From the interface section, use your type name (`TForm1`) and then the base class from which it is derived. All objects must be derived from `TObject` or one of its child objects.

The public section is reserved for those declarations that you want the world to have access to. There is a private section in which you can declare variables, procedures, and functions that are used within your class only. The protected section gives you the best of both the private and public sections in one. Components declared as protected are accessible only to descendants of the declaring type.

As with private components, you can hide implementation details from end users. However, unlike private components, protected components are still available to programmers who want to derive new objects from your objects without the requirement that the derived objects be declared in the same unit.

Create your own data object to store a bank card PIN code in the object. The declaration will read

```
Secret = class(TObject)
  private
    FThe_PIN : Integer;
end;
```

Notice that not only have you created a class called `Secret`, but you have a `private` data variable that holds the value of the PIN itself. We called this variable `FThe_PIN`.

Properties

The reserved word property enables you to declare properties. A property definition in a class declares a named attribute for objects of the class and the actions associated with reading and writing the attribute. The attribute you have created is `FThe_PIN`. You do not want to allow the programmer to directly affect a change in that value. You want to take input and validate that the change is correct. This is part of the information-hiding principle mentioned earlier.

Use a property called `GetThe_PIN` to be the go-between in dealing with your value. When you call the property `GetThe_PIN`, you get the value of `FThe_PIN`. The difference here is that variable `FThe_PIN` is protected from outside modification. Only through the `Change_PIN` procedure can we modify the value of `FThe_PIN`.

```
Secret = class(TObject)
  private
    FThe_PIN : Integer;
  protected
     procedure Change_PIN (New_PIN : Integer);
     property GetThe_PIN : Integer read FThe_PIN write Change_PIN;
  end;
```

Now you can query the value of the PIN number without changing it. Selectors are a necessary part of the object model. If you cannot see the data in an object, then it is no good.

Inheritance

NEW TERM *Inheritance* is one of the most powerful features of an object-oriented language like Delphi. It allows child classes to take on the properties of their parents. They inherit the fields, properties, methods, and events of their parent class. In addition to having the attributes of their parents, the child class can add new components to those it inherits. This allows you to take a class that has nearly all the fundamental pieces you need and add new objects that customize that class to fit your needs exactly.

If you compile even a new project, you can then go to View | Browser and view the entire object base in Delphi. (See Figure 7.3.) The Inspector pane (the left window) allows you to pick a particular class in your project. You can see by the tree view what classes are parents of the object you have selected. By using the Inheritance tab you can see all descendent and ancestor objects related to the class you selected in the inspector pane.

Figure 7.3.
The Object Browser.

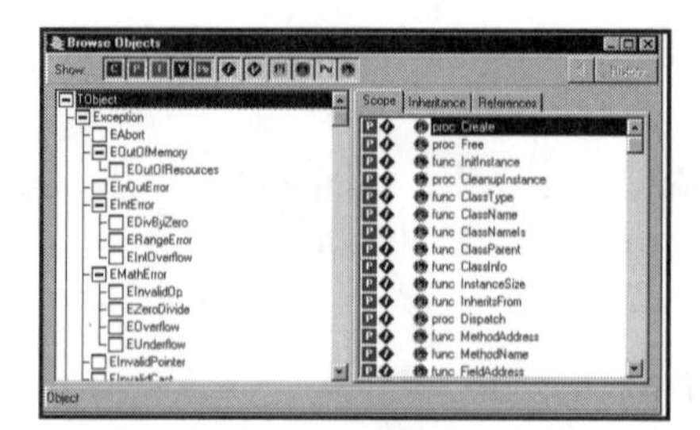

OK, maybe OOP won't solve the worlds problems, but it can make a contribution toward the common good. The object mentality is a good one, filled with promise of a more organized and orderly world. We have shown you how Borland has jumped on the object bandwagon, and has provided the foundation for you to grab your OOT (Object-Oriented Trumpet, a little band humor) and do the same.

Summary

In this chapter you have looked at some of the fundamentals of software engineering, both the principles and the goals of the discipline. You have looked at the software lifecycle and given you a better understanding of your creation's evolution. And finally, I have given you a brief tour of the land of objects. I realize that this chapter only touches on subjects that are worthy of better consideration, but this book would need to be on CD-ROM to cover all the topics in detail. I hope that we have lit a flame of curiosity, and that you will search out other information on these subjects.

Q&A

Q Can't we make gains using the software engineering principles using a non-object-oriented language?

A Yes. Anything is possible. The problem here is that if your language provides a poor mapping of its structure to the real world, then it will be difficult to achieve. Also, maintenance of the code will be equally challenging, because the mapping will not be intuitive to the application's maintainers.

Q Can you do object-oriented programming without doing object-oriented design?

A Yes, but again, the benefits of using one methodology throughout the product lifecycle bring a sense of uniformity to the process. In the long run an all or nothing approach is better (the all being preferable).

Workshop

Quiz

1. What are the goals of Software Engineering?
2. How does Object Pascal support information hiding?
3. How does inheritance help Object Pascal succeed at modeling the Windows environment?

Exercise

Create your own object called `Person` that holds information about a person (name, address, phone number, for example). Now create a property that retrieves the values in `Person` and method for changing the values in the `Person` object.

In Review

Week 1—Delphi Basics

In the first week, we tried to give you a good feel for the foundations of Delphi 2. We introduced you to the product on Day 1 and gave you a feel for what the product has to offer. On Day 2 the IDE was the topic, and you examined the different portions of the environment. Days 3 and 4 should have given you an understanding of the Object Pascal language, and how to use it. Day 5 was there to help you learn to manage your code development in Delphi 2. Day 6 provided you with some the fundamentals of designing your own GUI interface, and we finished out this week with an introduction to the latest development paradigm: OOP!

At A Glance

Week 2—Putting Delphi to Work

Day 8 brings you to event-driven programming as compared to linear programming that many programmers grew up on. Event-driven programming takes a bit of getting used to, but don't worry, you'll be up to speed in no time! Day 8 also brings you up to speed on exception handling. Exception handlers allow you to trap errors and deal with them appropriately. On Day 9 you take a good look at the Visual Component Library. This library has a rich selection of components, many of which would be add-on products in Visual Basic. On Day 10 you decide to have some fun and play with graphics. You learn about pens, brushes, drawing, painting, and so on. You also learn how to save and load your graphics. On Day 11 you explore the fun side of Windows 95 by looking at the multimedia and animation support in Delphi 2. You move on to Day 12 and learn how to work with text and binary files and their various modes. On Day 13 you learn how to work with various databases using the supported database selections as well as non-supported databases with ODBC. You even create your own simple database! Week 2 finishes with some basics about SQL and how to talk to a database using SQL on Day 14.

Week 2

Day 8

Exceptions and Events

Event-driven programming, exception handling, and the concept of threads are three of the most difficult concepts for a beginning programmer to grasp. This chapter takes an introductory look at all of these three areas, which are vital to being an effective Delphi 2 application developer. Some of the material in this chapter is slightly advanced but don't be scared to read on, I swear it does get easier! Get what you can out of it. In many places it covers what is going on behind the scenes in an attempt to make your programming more efficient and robust.

Event-Driven Programs

What is an event-driven program? An event-driven program is composed of blocks of code that are executed when an event or action occurs. Some examples of events include mouse clicks, keystrokes, and an application starting. In a graphical environment, where applications are running on the same desktop, an event-driven model is an effective way to respond to user input and interaction with the surrounding environment. You begin by examining a non-event-driven model.

A Non-Event-Driven Example

In this example, you use Delphi's console application option to create a console application that prompts the user for his name and then comments on the length of his name. The short listing follows.

```
program NonEvent;

var
   Name : String;

begin
  write('Hello There - Please enter your name -->');
  readln(Name);
  if (length(Name) < 7) then
    writeln('You have a short name.')
   else
    writeln('Your name is pretty long!!');
end.
```

Notice that the program flow is well defined. First it asks for the user's name. You can now wait for the user to input his name and not have to worry about any other inputs or actions occurring in the environment. After the name is entered, an `if` statement defines what the program should do next: print out either `You have a short name` or `Your name is pretty long!!`. Finally the program terminates. The logic in this linear program is straightforward and sequential. An event-driven program uses a different paradigm. The event-driven model cannot use *beginning-to-end flow control* because the application must be able to handle all possible actions or events. Now take a closer look at the event-driven model.

The Event-Driven Model

An event-driven application actually does nothing—unless an event occurs. That's right, an event-driven application does not have a logical beginning or ending point. It simply needs to know how to respond to different types of events. This does not mean that you can't have an event that occurs when the program starts or when it is about to close; however, you need to think about your programming model in a different manner. In the previous example, you knew exactly what actions the user would take—type in his name. However, think about a Windows-based word processor application. There is no way to know whether the user will type a sentence, choose an option from the menu, or click a button in the speed bar. Regardless of which action the user takes, the application needs to be robust enough to respond to the event. Let's start with a simple example using Delphi. Create a new application containing only one simple form. Look at the Events property page on the Object Inspector.

Figure 8.1.
The Properties page for a form.

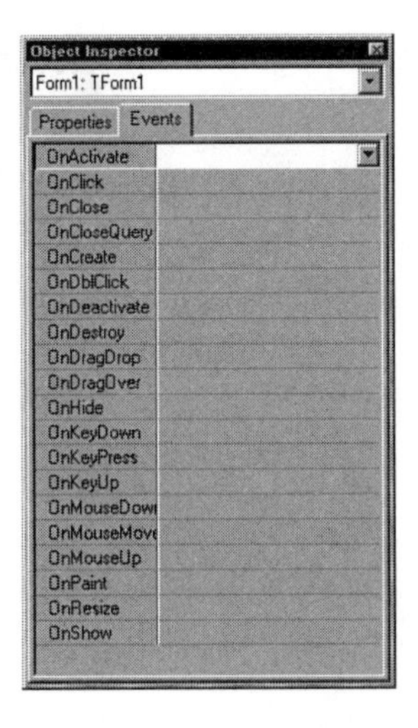

This is a list of all of the events that are predefined for a form. (You can add other events yourself if you need to.) If you leave all of them undefined, your application will compile and run fine; however, it will not perform any customized actions when any of the events occur. Delphi automatically creates the implementation to respond to some events. For example, when you click on the minimize button, the form is already programmed to respond to this event by becoming minimized. Create an application that handles an event. For starters, you can indicate the mouse coordinates on the form whenever the user clicks the mouse button. Therefore, you are setting up an event handler for the form that is executed when the user presses down on the mouse. To implement this, double-click to the right of the OnMouseDown label in the Object Inspector on the Events page. This tells Delphi that you would like to add code (the event handler) that should be executed when the event occurs. In this case you are going to add code that is executed when the user presses down on the mouse button while the cursor is on the form. Note that Delphi sets up a procedure skeleton and shows you the parameter that it will pass. In this case you need to add only one line of code. The event handler appears as follows:

```
procedure TForm1.FormMouseDown(Sender: TObject; Button: TMouseButton;
  Shift: TShiftState; X, Y: Integer);
begin
   Form1.Canvas.TextOut(X,Y,'Mouse At '+inttostr(X)+','+inttostr(Y));
end;
```

By adding this one line of code, you now have an application that actually does something. Run the application and try it out.

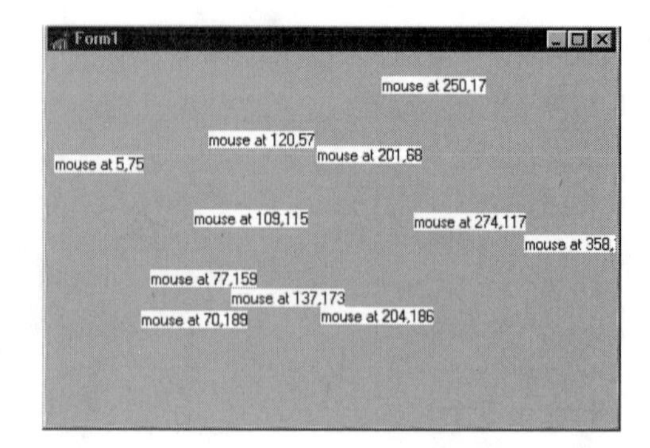

Figure 8.2.
An application that responds to MouseDown events.

In this example you have looked at events that can occur on a form. There are also events associated with every component added to a form, and even with the application itself. It is up to the developer to determine to which events it is necessary to respond. One important thing to remember is that you can't make any assumptions about the order in which a user will cause events to occur. To get a better understanding of how events and components work together, take a look at the events associated with a standard component, the TButton. Recall that components contain properties, methods, and events. The events are placeholders for procedures the developer can write when certain things occur. The TButton has the following events:

- **OnClick** signals when a user clicks on the button.
- **OnDragDrop** is called when an object is dragged onto the button and dropped.
- **OnDragOver** is called when an object is dragged over the button.
- **OnEndDrag** is called if the button itself is being dragged, and then when the button is either dropped or the drag is ended without a drop.
- **OnEnter** is called when the button receives the focus.
- **OnExit** is called when a component loses its focus.
- **OnKeyDown** indicates that a key has been pressed. This includes non-printable keys such as Shift, Alt, and Insert. This event handler is called only when the button has the focus.
- **OnKeyPress** indicates a printable key has been pressed (does not include Shift, Alt, and Insert). This event handler is called only when the button has the focus.
- **OnKeyUp** is signaled when a key is released. This event handler is called only when the button has the focus.
- **OnMouseDown** is called when one of the mouse buttons is pressed while the button is focused.

- **OnMouseMove** is called when the cursor is moved over the button.
- **OnMouseUp** is called when the user releases a mouse button while the cursor is over the button.

This may seem like a large number of events for a simple button component; however, remember that it is necessary to write event handlers only for events to which the program needs to respond.

Working with Parameters in Event Handlers

The earlier example displays the coordinates of the mouse whenever the user clicks on the form that calls the OnClick event handler. This means that the part of the Delphi runtime library that called the event handler passed it a series of parameters. One of the powerful features of Delphi is that the developer does not need to know what parameters are passed to an event handler. The procedure header is automatically filled in when the developer double-clicks the event on the Object Inspector. Parameters are used in Delphi for two reasons: to pass the event handler information, or to request that the event handler return data when it is called. Look at the first case in which you pass data to the event handler. This is the case that you have already seen in which the X and Y coordinates are passed to the OnMouseDown event handler. Note that X and Y are declared as integers and are *value parameters*. This means that the X and Y variables can be freely used and modified in the event handler and there is no danger that the true position of the mouse can be changed by manipulating X and Y. Sometimes an event handler has the option to pass back information to the underlying procedure that called it. For example in the OnKeyPress event in an editbox, the event handler header is

```
procedure TForm1.Edit1KeyPress(Sender: TObject; var Key: Char);
```

In this case, the `Key` variable, which contains the value of the key the user pressed, is listed as a `var` parameter. Recall that this means that any changes made to the variable are passed back to the calling procedure or function. What does this mean in the context of an event handler? Remember that behind the scenes something is calling each event handler routine (either the Delphi runtime library or a visual component). Therefore, if the calling routine wants the event handler to pass back data, it sets up a parameter as a `var` parameter. The key press event handler allows the routine to modify what key is returned to the caller. For example if you wanted an editbox that automatically converted any lowercase letter a user typed to uppercase, you could write the following event handler:

```
procedure TForm1.Edit1KeyPress(Sender: TObject; var Key: Char);
{ This routine forces every key that is returned to be uppercased}
```

```
begin
      Key := AnsiUpperCase(Key)[1];
end;
```

ANALYSIS In this procedure, the original key pressed is passed to the procedure. The `AnsiUpperCase()` function is used to convert the character to an uppercase value. `AnsiUppercase()` operates on a string, therefore you need to use the `[1]` to specify a single character.

To this point, you have looked at two major types of event handlers. The first type is used to respond to an event. The second is used to respond to an event and optionally pass back data to the caller. There are also events whose main purpose is to perform a subtask of a complex control. Consider the following situation: You want to have a listbox containing a list of boxes and balls; however, you want to display a symbol representing each ball or box in the listbox along with the text "ball" or "box". How can this be done? Unfortunately there is no component called ListBoxBallandBox that would do this automatically. Therefore, you need a mechanism to enhance the functionality of a standard listbox. The solution lies in a special kind of event. From your application's point of view you can think of most events as "when something happens, I will call the proper event handler." There are also events with a slighrly different tone—that is "I don't know how to do everything, so when I need additional help, I will call your event." The latter type of event enables you to solve the ball and box listbox problem because you can use an event that the program treats as follows: "I understand that you need to do some special work when I display each cell in the listbox. Therefore whenever I need to draw a cell I will call your event handler and tell you where to draw the cell, however you are responsible for what goes inside the cell." To accomplish this task, first set the `Style` property of the listbox to `lbOwnerDrawFixed`. This setting informs the listbox component that that you want to draw the cells yourself and that you want an event to occur whenever it's time for you to draw a cell. Therefore, whenever the component needs to draw an item, it calls the OnDrawItem event. The OnDrawItem event has the following header:

```
procedure TForm1.ListBox1DrawItem(Control: TWinControl; Index: Integer; Rect:
  TRect; State: TOwnerDrawState);
```

For our purposes you will only look at the `Index` and `Rect` parameters. The `Index` parameter tells the procedure which item needs to be drawn, and the `Rect` parameter tells the procedure where it should be drawn. The use of graphics is covered in detail in a later chapter, but for now you can still illustrate how to use this event to create your customized listbox.

```
procedure TForm1.ListBox1DrawItem(Control: TWinControl; Index: Integer;
  Rect: TRect; State: TOwnerDrawState);
begin
 with ListBox1.Canvas do
   begin
    if ListBox1.Items[Index]= 'Ball' then
     {Draw a ball in the listbox cell}
     Ellipse(Rect.Left,Rect.Top,Rect.Left+(Rect.Bottom-Rect.top),Rect.Bottom);
```

```
    if ListBox1.Items[Index]= 'Box'  then
     {Draw a box in the listbox cell}
     Rectangle(Rect.Left,Rect.Top,Rect.Left+(Rect.Bottom-Rect.top),Rect.Bottom);
    {In ether case write out the text}
    TextOut(Rect.Left+(Rect.Bottom-Rect.top)+10,
            Rect.Top,ListBox1.Items[Index]);
  end;
end;
```

ANALYSIS The procedure determines if there is a box or a ball in the item it is drawing and makes the appropriate calls to draw a circle or a square in the boundaries described in the `Rect` parameter. In either case the text is written out. This example illustrates the use of the customized listbox.

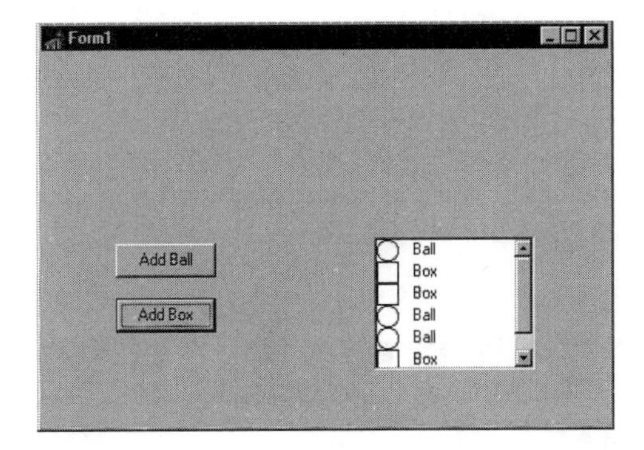

Figure 8.3.
Using specialized events to customize a listbox.

Don't Do Too Much (Unless You Know What You Are Doing)

Each event handler in Delphi is a procedure with a beginning and an end. It is important not to write an event handler that takes a long time to execute because it can make the application appear to hang (there are ways around this that we will cover later in this chapter). Create a new application, place a Tbutton component on the main form, and add the following code to the OnClick event handler:

```
procedure TForm1.Button1Click(Sender: TObject);
var
 X : integer;
begin
 for X := 1 to 100000000 do; {100 Million}
 Application.MessageBox('Done','I am Finished',MB_OK);
end;

end.
```

Run the application and press the button. What happens? The application appears to be dead for a while. It cannot be moved or resized, and if a different window is placed in front of the application and moved away, the form doesn't make itself look correct (repaint itself). Finally, the Done message box is displayed and the application appears to be OK. Why does the application do this? Some people might say "I want my money back! Windows 95 is supposed to be a preemptive multitasking operating system." Windows 95 actually is (notice that although the application appears to be dead for a while, all your other applications should function as usual). The bottom line is that, unless you use specialized programming tasks (which are covered later in the chapter), an application can do only one thing at a time. Therefore, while the application is busy counting to 100 million (on the author's machine about 4 seconds) the piece of code that calls other event handlers and performs normal maintenance such as moving the window cannot function. The traditional way to solve this dilemma in Windows 3.1 or earlier was to create an event handler that performed one small task at a time. (The other way was to put a piece of code in that told the operating system that it could "do anything else.") For most applications that you write in Delphi, you can still use the method of performing only a small chunk of work in each event handler. As this example illustrates, counting to 100 million takes only a few seconds, so most routines will be acceptable. If you run an application and it appears to hang, make sure it's not doing too much work somewhere else.

Going Behind the Scenes—A Look at Messages

NEW TERM All right, you now know how to deal with events, but what exactly is calling my event handler and what makes it all work? The event handler is called from either the Delphi runtime library or a visual component's implementation. Input in a windowed Delphi application is fed to the program from the operating system through objects called messages. A *message* is a structure that the Windows 95 or Windows NT operating system passes to the application to indicate that an event has occurred. In many other programming languages it is actually necessary to place code in the application to receive messages and to dispatch the proper event-handling routines. Luckily, Delphi has encapsulated this functionality and hides it from the developer. An example of a typical message that might be passed would be "The 'A' key was pressed in window 0x4E." Although you do not need to worry about messages directly, it is helpful to know that they exist and that something is taking care of them.

Good-Bye Windows—Hello Win32!

To fully capture the resources available in a Win32 programming environment, it's necessary to have a basic understanding of important operating system concepts. True Windows NT and Windows 95 have some very powerful features that can be utilized and need to be mentioned to make applications robust and powerful.

What's All This Business About 32 Bit versus 16 Bit Anyway?

Many software consumers will say they would like to migrate to 32-bit applications. However, most consumers don't know what a bit is and why 32 of them is better. The number of bits describes the amount of data that the computer can move in a single instruction. Therefore, to multiply two 32-bit integers in a 16-bit operating system takes many more instructions than in a 32-bit operating system. The end result is that the 32-bit system is much faster. (Of course, how much performance improvement an application receives is also very application-specific.)

A Better Memory Model

In my opinion, one of the greatest advantages to Win32 is the new memory model. In Windows 3.*x* and DOS you were stuck with a complex memory implementation consisting of 64K segments. Furthermore, this limited the amount of memory for a single piece of data to 64K. Win32 has a much simpler model. Win32 uses a flat memory model where each program or process has a virtual memory space. The operating system performs the task of mapping a process' virtual memory to physical memory locations and also performs the functionality required to swap memory to disk in order to provide more virtual memory than is physically installed on a machine.

Managing Applications with DOS, Windows, Windows 95, and Windows NT

Each of the major operating systems that Microsoft has released manages how applications interact with the operating system and other applications in a different way. We will give an overview of how each one works with applications.

In the beginning there was DOS. If DOS were a person, Mr. DOS, he might make the following statement to an application:

> "You are the only program that I am going to run. Therefore I am going to give you complete control of the computer. Take your time, do what you want to. When you are finished I will be happy to take over and let the user load and run the next program."

This was a rather easy environment in which to develop applications because a program could have a known starting point. The program controlled exactly what the user could do and how to respond to the user's actions. What made people move to Windows? Each DOS application seemed to have its own look and feel. It was difficult to run more than one application at a time. Applications could not communicate with each other. Microsoft had a wonderful idea—"We will write a DOS program that can run other programs within it. We will also address many of the things that people dislike about DOS programs. Let's call it Windows."

Mr. Windows had a bit of a different attitude toward applications than Mr. DOS. Mr. Windows would say:

> "You can load into my operating system, however there are some very serious ground rules. I am the boss! I will tell you what is going on around you. When something happens, it is your job to respond to it and take appropriate action. I am trusting you not to take too long. If you do take too long, I will not stop you; however, other applications will be unable to run until you relinquish control."

Windows is a cooperative, multitasking operating system. This means that it is up to the application (and therefore the application developers) to write applications that respond to events and take appropriate action. One of the major problems with Windows was that if one application was not "well behaved," then it could cause problems for all the other applications that are running. Take a simple example of an application to factor numbers (this is computationally intensive). In a Windows application, if the developer set the application up so that the user could enter a number into an editbox and then click a button to factor it, the developer might simply put the factor code in the equivalent of an OnClick event. The mathematical code would be invoked, and if the number was large the entire system would appear to be hung. This was a major problem with Windows. Any misbehaved application can disrupt, crash, or severely tie up the entire operating system and all the programs running in it.

Finally Mr. Win32 came along. He runs programs in Windows 95 and Windows NT. Mr. Win32 is a tough cookie. He allows a program to do whatever it wants, but if any program takes too long performing a task, Mr. Win32 says:

> "You have taken too long. I am going to freeze you just where you are and let some other programs perform tasks for a little while. After each one has its turn I will restore control to you in the exact state that you were in."

This is called preemptive multitasking. Each program is given a time slice in which to perform its task, but the operating system stays in control at all times. You can see why this is more crash-proof. Each application continues to run regardless of other applications executing in the operating system. This still doesn't solve the problem of performing a computationally intensive task within an application and the application appearing to hang. This is because by default each application is executing code in one piece of that application at a time. Therefore, if you are performing a computationally intensive function, the other parts of the application (including the maintenance routine to size and move windows) cannot be executed. Fortunately there is a way in Win32 to execute more than one piece of an application simultaneously. This process is the use of something called *threads*.

An Introduction to Threads

NEW TERM In Windows 95 and Windows NT each 32-bit program that is running is called a *process*. A process deals mainly with ownership issues. For example, a process owns its memory space. As far as execution of code is concerned, the operating system uses a new object called a *thread*. When a new process is started, it is automatically given one thread which starts executing code in the appropriate routine. Threads are used by the operating system to schedule processor time. What does scheduling time mean? Scheduling is the method used to allocate time to each thread (you don't say process because a process can have more then one thread). The operating system looks at all the threads that are in a runable state and chooses one to run. The scheduler also determines the time slice, or amount of time it gives to each thread to execute.

We have mentioned that there can be more than one thread executing in a process at any time. What are the properties of each thread? Each thread executing maintains its own stack to local variables and a copy of the state that it is in. All the threads in a process can access any global memory object; therefore, a word processor program might have one thread dedicated to proofreading the text while the main thread performs all other tasks. Enough talk, let's see how this works. Take a slightly more practical application that can be processor intensive for a single task and use threads so that the application doesn't appear to hang while it's doing its work.

Recall that a prime number is a number that cannot be divided evenly by any number except one and itself. Examples of primes are 2, 3, 5, 7, 11, 100857, 100913, and 100927. Examples of numbers that are not prime are 4, 9, and 22. There are efficient complex algorithms to determine if a number is prime, but there is also a very simple one that is extremely inefficient. To determine if a number is prime, you can simply start at two and count toward the number. At each iteration, you determine if the count variable divides evenly into the number being tested. If it does divide evenly, then the number is not prime and you can quit. If you reach the target number with no hits, then the number is prime. There are more prime numbers than many people think (actually there are an infinite number of primes).

Now write a program to find all the prime numbers in a given range. Your first attempt uses the algorithm described above to create a simple Delphi application to loop through a range of numbers and to place the primes it finds into a listbox.

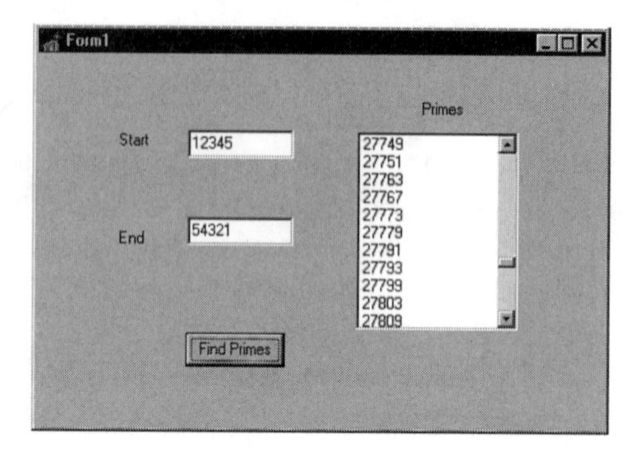

Figure 8.4.
An application to find prime numbers.

Your first implementation does not use threads, and simply executes the algorithm when the user clicks on the button.

TYPE **Listing 8.1. A single-threaded version of the program to find primes.**

```
unit main;

interface

uses
  SysUtils, Windows, Messages, Classes, Graphics, Controls, Forms, Dialogs,
  StdCtrls;

type
  TForm1 = class(TForm)
    PrimeList: TListBox;
    Min: TEdit;
    Max: TEdit;
    Label1: TLabel;
    Label2: TLabel;
    Primes: TLabel;
    Button1: TButton;
    procedure Button1Click(Sender: TObject);
  private
    { Private declarations }
  public
    { Public declarations }
  end;

var
  Form1: TForm1;
```

```
implementation

{$R *.DFM}

procedure TForm1.Button1Click(Sender: TObject);
var
  Low,High,Count,Count2 :integer;

begin
  {Clear out the Listbox}
  PrimeList.Items.Clear;
  {Get the loop boundaries from the Editboxes}
  Low := strtoint(Min.Text);
  High := strtoint(Max.Text);

  {Loop through all numbers in the range}
  for Count := Low to High do
   begin
     Count2 := 2;
     {Determine if the number divides evenly or if we have }
     {reached the limit}
     while (Count2 < Count) and not(Count mod Count2 = 0) do
       inc(Count2);
     {if the number is prime add it to the listbox}
     if (Count=Count2) then
       PrimeList.Items.Add(inttostr(Count));
   end {for}
end; {procedure}
end. {program}
```

This program works quite well for finding small primes (less then 50,000). Try using this program to find large prime numbers. For example, find the prime numbers between 100,000 and 110,000. Notice that your application suffers from the "apparent hang" syndrome. How can you make this better? You can modify your application slightly to use a separate thread to perform the factoring work. This lets the main thread in the application remain available for all maintenance functions, and the application does not appear to hang. What information would the scheduler need to launch a new thread? The main piece of information that the scheduler needs is "where do I start the new thread executing." There is other information that can optionally be passed, but a starting place is the main thing that needs to be supplied. This is done by writing a function to become the starting place of the new thread.

Creating a New Thread

Be forewarned, the subject of multitasking is complex and has many components. The example given here is to give the reader a sample of the power with which threads can be used. There are many new issues that you need to worry about when you deal with multithreaded applications. One example is the issue of two threads trying to access the same part of memory simultaneously. Don't attempt to do elaborate multithreaded programming without consulting additional sources. With that disclaimer behind us let's go!

Step 1 is to create the function at which the new thread will start. This is a special function in that it should return an integer and accept a single pointer as a parameter. To perform your factoring set up a function header as follows:

```
function DoFactor(NotUsed:Pointer):integer;
```

In this case you do not need to use that parameter so call it `NotUsed` for clarity. The rest of the function is simply whatever the thread needs to do.

To create the thread itself, use the `CreateThread` Win32 API call. This call takes six arguments; however, the only required two are the address function in which to start the new thread and a variable in which to put the thread's ID. The other parameters are as follows:

Table 8.1. Create thread parameters.

Number	Name	Type	Comments
1	Thread Attributes	SECURITY _ATTRIBUTES (`var` parameter)	Used by Windows NT for security, can be nil.
2	Stack Size	DWORD	Initial stack size. The stack in threads grows dynamically, therefore this can be 0. Other values can be used for optimization.
3	Start Address	Pointer	The address of the function to start the new threads' execution.
4	Parameter	Pointer	You can pass a single pointer to the thread function using this parameter. It can also be nil.

Number	Name	Type	Comments
5	Flags	DWORD	Additional information. For example, to start the thread in a suspended state. This can be 0.
6	Thread ID	DWORD (var parameter)	Thread ID placed in variable.

To implement your prime number identification program with threads, you need to make a few minor changes. First, move all the logic to a new function, which will be where the thread starts. Next you need to modify all your references to objects to include Form1. For example, the PrimeList listbox component will not be in scope as PrimeList; therefore, you need to identify it as Form1.PrimeList. Finally, add the `CreateThread` API call to the OnClick event handler of the Button1 component. The call is

```
CreateThread(nil,0,@DoFactor,nil,0,THID);
```

This means that you want to start a new thread. There is no security information, and the stack size will be dynamic. The new thread should start in the `DoFactor` function where there is no argument to pass. Don't set any flags, and return the thread id in the `THID` variable. The only thing that may look a little funny is the `@DoFactor`. The `@` means to take the address of the function as opposed to calling the function itself and returning its result. Hopefully this example clarifies how threads can be used to make applications better. The listing for the multithreaded version of the prime number identification program is shown in Listing 8.2.

TYPE

Listing 8.2. The multithreaded version of the prime number identification program.

```
unit main2;

interface

uses
  SysUtils, Windows, Messages, Classes, Graphics, Controls, Forms, Dialogs,
  StdCtrls;

type
  TForm1 = class(TForm)
    PrimeList: TListBox;
    Min: TEdit;
    Max: TEdit;
```

continues

Listing 8.2. continued

```
    Label1: TLabel;
    Label2: TLabel;
    Primes: TLabel;
  Button1: TButton;
    procedure Button1Click(Sender: TObject);
  private
    { Private declarations }
  public
    { Public declarations }
  end;

var
  Form1: TForm1;

implementation

{$R *.DFM}

function DoFactor(NotUsed:Pointer):integer;
var
  Low,High,Count,Count2 :integer;

begin
 {Clear out the Listbox}
  Form1.PrimeList.Items.Clear;
 {Get the loop boundaries from the Editboxes}
  Low := strtoint(Form1.Min.Text);
  High := strtoint(Form1.Max.Text);

 {Loop through all numbers in the range}
  for Count := Low to High do
   begin
     Count2 := 2;
     {Determine if the number divides evenly or if we have }
     {reached the limit}
     while (Count2 < Count) and not(Count mod Count2 = 0) do
       inc(Count2);

    {if the number is prime add it to the listbox}
     if (Count=Count2) then
       Form1.PrimeList.Items.Add(inttostr(Count));
   end; {for}
end;{procedure}

procedure TForm1.Button1Click(Sender: TObject);
var
  THID : DWORD;
begin
      CreateThread(nil,0,@DoFactor,nil,0,THID);
end; {procedure}

end. {program}
```

Exceptions

In a perfect world of perfect people, programmers, and programs nothing would ever go wrong. Unfortunately, things do go wrong. It's important that applications are robust enough to handle a problem when one arises. What's the wrong thing to do? Remember the infamous "General Protection Fault" in Windows 3.*x*? What's a normal user supposed to do with that information except curse and become frustrated? Delphi includes support to handle errors in an elegant manner as opposed to simply crashing the application whenever something goes wrong.

Overview of Exceptions

Computers are not magical devices. They usually do what you tell them to do. However, programmers often think that they are telling a computer to do one thing, when, in fact, they are telling it to do something else. Remember that exceptions occur at runtime, not at compile time. Let's examine a simple example. You would like to use an array of integers in a procedure. You declare the array and use a `for` loop to set each value to 0. This is the code that is used:

```
procedure TForm1.Button1Click(Sender: TObject);
var
  IntArray:array[1..10] of integer;
  Count : integer;
begin
  {First Let's Clear the Array}
  for Count := 1 to 11 do
    IntArray[Count] := 0;
  {now we will do our work....}
end;
```

The code is syntactically correct; however, there is a big problem with it. When the `Count` variable gets to 11 it tries to set a value in the array that doesn't exist. The result is that an exception, or error, is raised.

Figure 8.5.
Exception raised for trying to write to memory that does not exist.

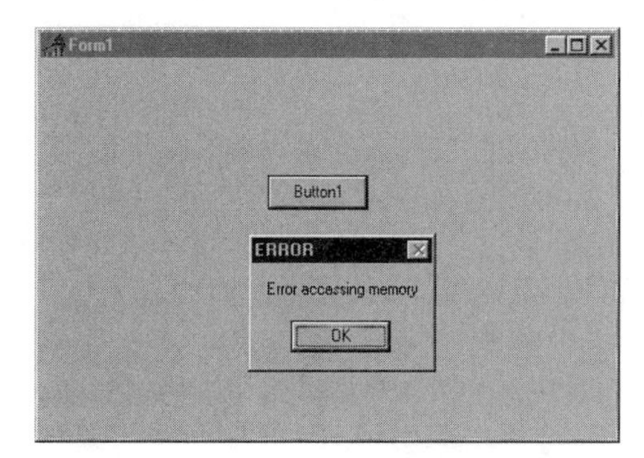

This is the type of error that a programmer likes because it is consistent and it is likely that the bug would be identified and corrected quickly. There are many times when an error occurs only under certain runtime conditions. Consider the following console application that prompts a user for a number and divides 100 by the number given.

```
program err1;

uses
  forms;
{$R *.RES}
var
  X : integer;
  Y : integer;

begin
  writeln('Enter a number, I will divide 100');
  writeln('by the number you give me');
  readln(Y);
  X := 100 div Y;
  writeln('The result is ',X);
end.
```

Under normal testing the program functions fine. However, what if the user enters a 0? The program attempts to execute `100 div 0` and causes a division by 0 error. Why can't you simply add a line of code to determine if Y is going to be 0 before you divide?

```
{…}
 readln(Y);
  if Y=0 then
    writeln('I cannot divide a number by zero!')
  else
   begin
    X := 100 div Y;
    writeln('The result is ',X);
   end;
{…}
```

You can! This is the best thing to do when you see the potential for an error because you can control exactly how the logic flows. For example, you could add a `while` loop to keep asking your users for a number until they supply something other then 0. The problem is that as the code gets complex it is not always possible to see every error that will be generated. Another key benefit of using exception handlers is that it allows you to protect code in a DLL or component library that you did not write. If you call a routine in a DLL and it does something that it shouldn't you can trap the exception. This allows a developer to terminate the application gracefully as opposed to displaying a cryptic error message. Delphi supports the ability to protect an entire block of code against an error as opposed to protecting a single routine. This is done by using a special block of code called a `try…except` block.

Protecting a Block of Code With try and except

The try...except block is used to define a piece of code that will be executed if an error occurs anywhere in a block of code. The format for the try...except block is

```
try
    {Code to execute}
except
    {Code to execute if we get an error}
end;
```

In the except portion of the block, you can also identify what error occurred. Therefore, you could have performed the same error checking in the division program using a try...except block as follows.

```
begin
  try
    writeln('Enter a number, I will divide 100');
    writeln('by the number you give me');
    readln(Y);
    X := 100 div Y;
    writeln('The result is ',X);
  except
    writeln('I cannot divide a number by zero!')
  end;
end.
```

One of the things to note here is that you protected all the code within the block. What would happen if the user typed in "A"? Well this certainly causes an exception, but in your current protection scheme you assume you know what the error was. It looks like you need a way to distinguish which exception was raised. To check the exception, the on statement is used. The syntax for the on statement is

```
on <type of exception> do <statement>;
```

To improve your error handling routine add on statements to handle the two conditions that you know might occur.

```
begin
  try
    writeln('Enter a number, I will divide 100');
    writeln('by the number you give me');
    readln(Y);
    X := 100 div Y;
    writeln('The result is ',X);
  except
   on EDivByZero do
    writeln('I cannot divide a number by zero!');
   on EInOutError do
    writeln('An invalid number was entered!')
  end;
end.
```

Another advantage of using the on statement is that for any exception that your exception handling routine does not take care of, the default routine will be invoked. Your final console application is robust and can gracefully handle almost any situation. It should be noted that trapping all exceptions can hide problems in your code.

Nested Exception Handling

What happens when there are multiple exception handlers nested as in the following situation?

```
procedure DoDiv;

var
  X : integer;
  Y : integer;

begin
  try
    writeln('Enter a number, I will divide 100');
    writeln('by the number you give me');
    readln(Y);
    X := 100 div Y;
    writeln('The result is ',X);
  except
   on EDivByZero do
    writeln('I cannot divide a number by zero!');
  end;
end;

begin
 try
  Writeln('***********');
  Writeln('* WELCOME *');
  Writeln('***********');
  DoDiv;
 except
  writeln('An Error has occured')
 end;
end.
```

ANALYSIS In this case, the DoDiv procedure uses an exception handling block to protect against division by zero. There is also a try...except block in the main routine that has the call to DoDiv within the try block. What happens if there is a division by zero? What happens if some other error occurs in DoDiv such as invalid input? The answer is that the innermost exception handling block that covers a condition is used. In the case of division by zero in DoDiv, only the exception handling routine in DoDiv would be invoked. If something other then division by zero occurs in DoDiv, it is handled by the exception handler in the main routine. If there were no handler in the main routine, then it would be handled by Delphi's default exception handler routine which displays the error in a message box.

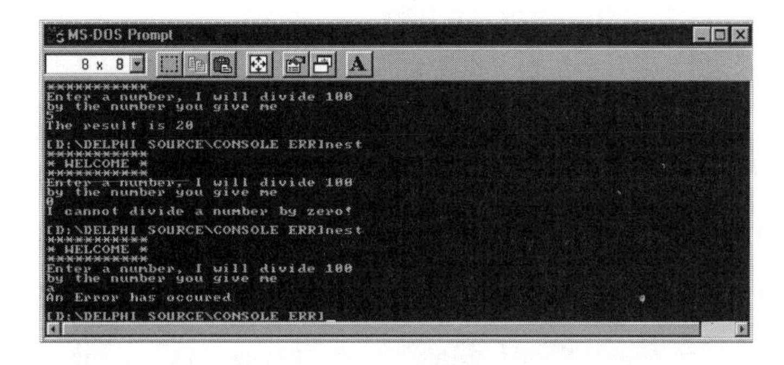

Figure 8.6.
Running the nested console division application to trap errors.

Differences Running Inside and Outside the IDE

When running a Delphi application in the IDE with the debugger enabled, the program pauses when it hits an exception.

Figure 8.7.
The execution pauses when an exception is hit.

At this point you can use the debugger to step through your code and help determine what type of error is occurring and if it is possible to defend against it or fix it. For exception handling routines, it is advisable that you test them with the Break on Exception option disabled. To disable this feature, choose Tools | Options from the main menu and uncheck Break on Exception in the debugging portion of the Preferences dialog box. When you get ready to ship, it is also advisable that you fully test your code outside of the IDE completely just as your customers will use your application.

Creating and Calling Your Own Exceptions

Now that you know how to handle exceptions, you will look at what it takes to create your own exceptions. Why should you create exceptions? Creating exceptions allows us to signal an error condition in a standard manner. For example, suppose that you have written a genealogy program. One of the routines is to enter information about a family member. An example of a call to the routine would be

```
GetPersonInfo(Name,BirthDate,Spouse,Mother,Father);
```

If successful, the routine returns the pertinent information in the variables that were passed. However, suppose that the user entered an invalid birthdate such as February 30? Or what if the user omitted her mother's name? One way to handle this would be to have all the checking logic and procedures to correct it within the GetPersonInfo procedure. However, suppose that you wanted to call the routine from different parts of your application and respond differently to improper input. One thing you could do is to set up GetPersonInfo as a function that returns an error code or a numeric code indicating success. This would work, but you could not take advantage of the mechanisms for protecting an entire block of code, and the function would use a different protocol from all other standard Delphi components and features. The answer is clear that you need a way to raise custom exceptions.

Creating a New Exception Class

All exceptions are built as a subclass of the Exception class. This means that all exceptions contain all the same properties and methods as the Exception class, and also can add additional information specific to a particular exception (additional information is not usually necessary). To declare a new Exception class, you use a type declaration in the Type portion of a unit. For example to create a new exception type called ENoMotherSpecified you would use

```
type
  ENoMotherSpecified = class(Exception);
```

Once the new type of exception is declared, you need to be able to signal that an exception occurred. This process is called raising an exception.

Raising an Exception

To raise an exception, you use the keyword raise and then create a new exception object. One key part of raising an exception is how the constructor works for an Exception class. The constructor takes one parameter, which is the message that is associated with an exception. This can be used to provide additional information about an exception. For example, the EAccessViolation exception reports which memory address was accessed illegally. An example of raising the ENoMotherSpecified exception is

```
Raise ENoMotherSpecified.Create('You Must Have a Mother');
```

Exception objects are automatically deleted by the exception handler, therefore you never need to delete an exception object.

A Complete Example of Using Custom Exceptions

In the following code, you implement a program that displays a dialog box requesting information about family members and inserts a row into a string grid for each family member. The program is composed of two primary units. The `person` unit implements the dialog box and all the error handling routines. The only procedure the main unit needs to call is `GetPersonInfo`, which returns all the information about a person. If invalid data is supplied in the dialog, either an `ENoMotherSpecified` or `EInvalidDOB` exception is raised. One of the interesting things to note is that you can use an exception handler to determine if you need to raise a custom exception. This method is used to determine if the birth date is valid. Delphi provides a function to convert a string to a date. If this function raises an exception then you know it is not a valid date and you raise the `EInvalidDOB` exception. Note that we use the `TOKRightDlg` that is contained in OKCANCL2, which is part of the form repository that comes with Delphi 2. Unit `person` is shown in Listing 8.3.

TYPE **Listing 8.3. `person.pas`.**

```
unit person;

interface

uses
  SysUtils, Windows, Messages, Classes, Graphics, Controls, Forms, Dialogs,
  OKCANCL2, Mask, StdCtrls, ExtCtrls;
type
  {Declare New Exception Types}
  ENoMotherSpecified = class(Exception);
  EInvalidDOB = class(Exception);

  TPersonForm = class(TOKRightDlg)
    pName: TEdit;
    pFather: TEdit;
    pMother: TEdit;
    pSpouse: TEdit;
    Label1: TLabel;
    Label2: TLabel;
    Label3: TLabel;
    Label4: TLabel;
    Label5: TLabel;
    pDOB: TMaskEdit;
  private
    { Private declarations }
  public
    { Public declarations }
  end;

{Add GetPersonInfo to the interface portion of the unit so that it is}
{accessible from other units }
procedure GetPersonInfo(var Name,BirthDate,Spouse,Mother,Father:string);
```

continues

Listing 8.3. continued

```
var
  PersonForm: TPersonForm;

implementation

{$R *.DFM}

procedure GetPersonInfo(var Name,BirthDate,Spouse,Mother,Father:string);
var
  ReturnCode : integer;
begin
  {Call the dialog box}
  ReturnCode := PersonForm.ShowModal;
  {Check to see which button the user pressed}
  if ReturnCode = mrCancel then
   begin
    {if they canceled, set the name to blank and leave the proc}
    Name := ''; {blank out the name}
    exit;
   end;
  {Set the variables passed to the Edit.Text values}
  Name := PersonForm.pName.Text;
  BirthDate := PersonForm.pDOB.Text ;
  Spouse := PersonForm.pSpouse.Text ;
  Mother := PersonForm.pMother.Text ;
  Father := PersonForm.pFather.Text ;
  {Check to see if we need to raise any custom exceptions}
  {check to see if a mother was specified}
  if length(Mother) = 0 then
    Raise ENoMotherSpecified.Create('You Must Have a Mother');
  {Check to see if it is a valid birthdate}
  try
    StrToDate(BirthDate);
  except
   on EConvertError do
    Raise EInvalidDOB.Create('Error Converting Date of Birth');
  end;
end;

end. {unit}
```

ANALYSIS The main unit in this application (see Listing 8.4) has two primary functions. It manipulates the string grid by initializing it and inserting valid data into it. Also, the unit handles what happens when a custom exception is raised. Note that if an exception other than one of the custom exceptions occurs, then the unit allows the default exception handler to process the exception.

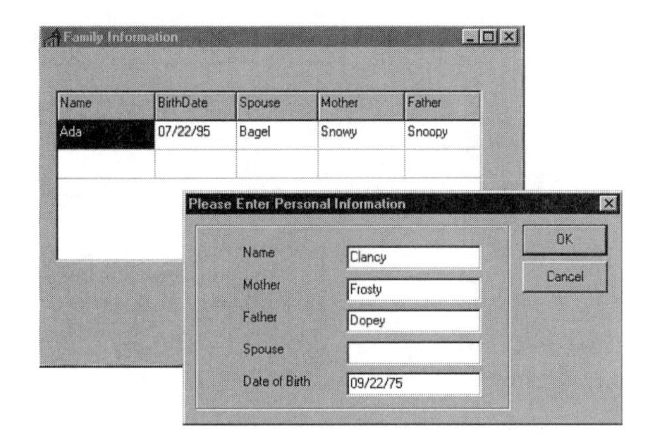

Figure 8.8.
Dialog for entering personal information.

TYPE **Listing 8.4** `main.pas.`

```
unit main;

interface

uses
  SysUtils, Windows, Messages, Classes, Graphics, Controls, Forms, Dialogs,
  StdCtrls, Grids;

type
  TForm1 = class(TForm)
    AddPerson: TButton;
    TheFamily: TStringGrid;
    procedure AddPersonClick(Sender: TObject);
    procedure FormCreate(Sender: TObject);
  private
    { Private declarations }
  public
    { Public declarations }
  end;

var
  Form1: TForm1;

implementation
{important! we must add the "uses person" clause for this to work}
uses person;

{$R *.DFM}

procedure TForm1.AddPersonClick(Sender: TObject);
var
 Name,BirthDate,Spouse,Mother,Father:string;
 TmpRowCount : integer;

begin
 try
```

continues

Listing 8.4 continued

```
  {with in Try block get and process a new family member}
   GetPersonInfo(Name,BirthDate,Spouse,Mother,Father);
   if length(Name) > 0 then
    Begin
      { Offset rowcount by -1 so we start at 0}
      TmpRowCount := TheFamily.RowCount-1;
      TheFamily.Cells[0,TmpRowCount] := Name;
      TheFamily.Cells[1,TmpRowCount] := BirthDate;
      TheFamily.Cells[2,TmpRowCount] := Spouse;
      TheFamily.Cells[3,TmpRowCount] := Mother;
      TheFamily.Cells[4,TmpRowCount] := Father;
      TheFamily.RowCount := TheFamily.RowCount + 1;
    end;
  except
    {Check to see if it is one of our customized exceptions and if so}
    {take appropriate action}
    On ENoMotherSpecified do
      MessageDlg('You must specify who your mother is',mtError,[mbok],0);
    On EInvalidDOB do
      MessageDlg('You specified and invalid Date of Birth!',mtError,[mbok],0);
  end;
end;

procedure TForm1.FormCreate(Sender: TObject);
begin
   {on creation of the form set the top of the grid with labels}
   TheFamily.Cells[0,0] := 'Name';
   TheFamily.Cells[1,0] := 'BirthDate';
   TheFamily.Cells[2,0] := 'Spouse';
   TheFamily.Cells[3,0] := 'Mother';
   TheFamily.Cells[4,0] := 'Father';
end;

end.
```

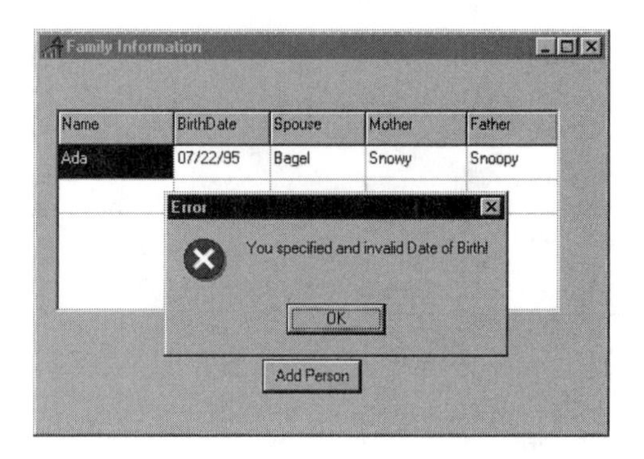

Figure 8.9.
Custom exception message in the Family Information program is displayed.

Reraising an Exception

What if you would like to perform an action when an exception occurs, but let the exception handler in the next layer handle the exception as well? This can be accomplished by reraising an exception. To reraise an exception, simply execute the `Raise` keyword without any additional parameters after customized processing has been done.

In Listing 8.5 you use a simple program to request a number and divide 100 by it. The block is protected with a `try...except` block. If an exception is raised, then a custom dialog is displayed telling the customer to call the technical support line. You also reraise the exception to tell the customer exactly what happened (a division by zero or invalid input entered in the `readln`).

TYPE **Listing 8.5. Reraising an exception with `reraise.dpr`.**

```
program reraise;

uses
  Forms,Dialogs;

{$R *.RES}
Var
  X : Integer; {use static allocation}

begin
   {Execute the "protected" statments}
   try
     Writeln('Enter a number');
     readln(X);
     X := 100 div X;
     Writeln('Result is ',X);
   {For our exception routine simply display a custom dialog}
   except
     MessageDlg('Error - If problems persist call 1-800-4BEAGLE'
               ,mtError,[mbok],0);
     raise; {Let default exception handler also do its thing}
   end; {exception block}
end.
```

Ensuring Cleanup Code is Executed With `try` and `finally`

One of the most powerful features of exception handling is the capability to safeguard resources and ensure that cleanup code is executed even if something goes wrong. Consider the following simple program:

```
program TryFin;

uses
  Forms;

{$R *.RES}
Var
  X : ^Integer;

begin
   {Dynamically Allocate Storage for Integer X}
   new(X);
   Writeln('Enter a number');
   readln(X^);
   X^ := 100 div X^;
   Writeln('Result is ',X^);
   {Free Memory used By X}
   Dispose(X);
end.
```

ANALYSIS The program uses variable X which is a pointer to an integer, and calls `new(X)` to allocate memory for it. From here, the program reads an integer into the memory space pointed to by X and divides 100 by it. After the division, the program writes the result to the user and then frees the memory allocated to X. What happens if a user types a 0? You know that it will cause an exception, but what happens to all the code following the location at which the error occured? It isn't executed! Therefore, if there is a problem dividing the number (or reading the number) then the `Writeln('Result is ',X^)` and `Dispose(X)` functions are not executed. So what? Four bytes of data are lost; what's the big deal? In this situation there is likely no harm in bidding the lost memory farewell. However, consider a program that dynamically allocates memory to store a bitmap image and in which an error occurs while processing the image. That would be a big deal in that a few megabytes of memory could be lost. There are many other cases such that if you start something you will want to finish it. For example, consider opening a text file; you always will want to close it. The question becomes how do you ensure that your crucial cleanup code is executed even if an error occurs? The answer is a `try…finally` block.

A `try…finally` block has two parts. One code block executes statements that should be protected. The other block of code is executed regardless of whether or not an exception occurs. Therefore you could modify your sample program so that it ensures that the memory allocated to variable X is freed.

```
{…}
begin
   {Dynamically Allocate Storage for Integer X}
   new(X);
   {Execute the "protected" statements}
   try
     Writeln('Enter a number');
     readln(X^);
     X^ := 100 div X^;
```

```
    Writeln('Result is ',X^);
  {Ensure that we free X}
  finally
    {Free Memory used By X}
    Dispose(X);
  end;
end.
```

One important thing to note is that the try…finally block is completely independent of a try…except block. Therefore, if you also want to perform exception handling, you need to "wrap" the block in a try…except block. In the example, you combine a resource protection block and an exception handling block.

```
{…}
Var
  X : ^Integer;

begin
   {Dynamically Allocate Storage for Integer X}
   new(X);
   {Use our own exception Handler}
   try
     {Execute the "protected" statements}
     try
       Writeln('Enter a number');
       readln(X^);
       X^ := 100 div X^;
       Writeln('Result is ',X^);
     {Ensure that we free X}
     finally
       {Free Memory used By X}
       Dispose(X);
     end; {resource protection block}
   {For our exception routine simply display a custom dialog}
   except
     MessageDlg('Error Processing Data!',mtError,[mbok],0);
   end; {exception block}
end.
```

Using the initialization and finalization Sections

To protect resources within a block of code, try…finally blocks work very well. There is a way to globally allocate and initialize resources as well as globally ensuring that they are disposed of properly. This is accomplished with two special sections of a unit called the initialization and finalization sections. The following example is a windows-based implementation of the division program that uses dynamic memory allocation. In this case, the memory is allocated when the form is loaded by using an initialization section of the unit. When the form is unloaded, the finalization portion of the form that is executed in this case frees the memory allocated to X. To illustrate what is going on, the form also displays dialog and message boxes when it enters an `initialization` or `finalization` section of the unit.

TYPE

Listing 8.6. Illustrating the use of `initialization` and `finalization` sections with `main.pas`.

```
unit main;

{$R *.DFM}

interface

uses
  SysUtils, Windows, Messages, Classes, Graphics, Controls, Forms, Dialogs,
  StdCtrls;

type
  TDemInitFin = class(TForm)
    NumIn: TEdit;
    DoDiv: TButton;
    Rsult: TEdit;
    Label1: TLabel;
    procedure DoDivClick(Sender: TObject);
  private
    { Private declarations }
  public
    { Public declarations }
  end;

var
  DemInitFin: TDemInitFin;

implementation

var
  X : ^Integer;

procedure TDemInitFin.DoDivClick(Sender: TObject);
begin
  {perform division}
  X^ := strtoint(NumIn.Text);
  Rsult.text := inttostr(100 div X^);
end;

{always do this code when the form loads}
initialization
MessageDlg('In initialization Code',mtInformation,[mbok],0);
new(X);

{always execute this code when the form is unloaded}
finalization
MessageBox(0,'In finalization Code','Info',mb_ok);
```

```
Dispose(X);

end.
```

Exceptions Aren't the Only Thing You Need to Check

Checking exceptions will get you most of the way, especially if you stick with object Pascal and visual components. However, once you begin to make DLL calls or calls into the Win32 API, the method for indicating failure or that an error occurred may be different. For example, most of the Win32 API calls return an integer value to indicate status. Let's consider the `MessageBox` API call. This call takes four parameters: a handle to a window, the text for the caption, the text for the message, and the buttons to display. Conveniently, it is possible to pass 0 as the first parameter so that it uses the desktop as the parent window. What happens if you pass the API call a bogus handle? No exception is generated, the function simply returns a 0. You often don't even check which return code the `MessageBox` API returns because you assume that it works (and it almost always does). Listing 8.7 shows how you can cause an error to occur in the Win32 API and that the only way you know an error occurred is to check the return code.

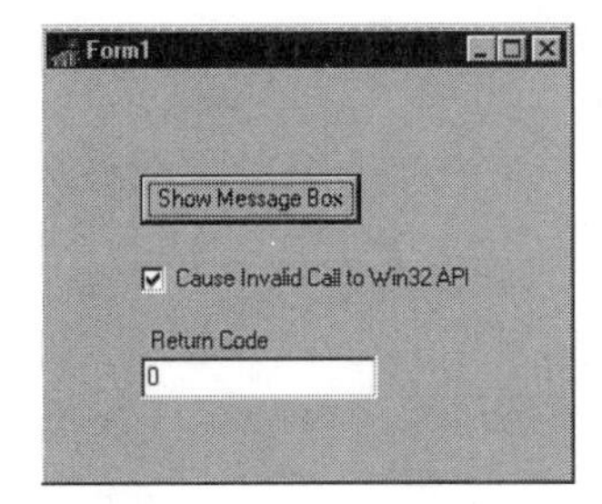

Figure 8.10.
Testing invalid API calls.

TYPE

Listing 8.7. Procedure to cause an invalid API call—check return codes!

```
procedure TForm1.Button1Click(Sender: TObject);
var RetCode:integer;

begin
    if CauseInvalid.Checked then
      RetCode := MessageBox(10,'Test','Invalid Message Box',mb_ok)
     else
      RetCode := MessageBox(0,'Test','Valid Message Box',mb_ok);
    RetValue.Text := inttostr(RetCode);
end;
```

Summary

You have covered the fundamentals of how Delphi works and what techniques can be used to build robust applications. You also examined the advantages that Windows 95 and Windows NT have to offer and how not to fall into common pitfalls. Event-driven programming is a state of mind more than anything else. You can't make any assumptions about what the user will do. I have noticed that no end user ever uses a product exactly as the developer had in mind. Never think "Oh, they won't do that; it would be illogical." They will! You took a quick look at threads and multitasking. This allows your application to appear as if it were performing multiple tasks simultaneously. One of the drawbacks to multithreaded programming is that it adds an extra layer of complexity to an application. Finally you examined how to make your application robust with exception handling routines and resource protection blocks. These are important concepts and become increasingly helpful as the complexity of applications grows. One final recommendation is to revisit this chapter after you have looked through the rest of this book. Many of the concepts will become more clear; however, it is the chicken-and-the-egg scenario where information in this chapter is essential for building a foundation for future topics.

Q&A

Q If Windows 95 and Windows NT are both 32-bit preemptive multitasking operating systems, why is there a difference?

A Windows 95 has quite a bit of 16-bit code, but in some cases is more backward compatible with DOS and some Windows applications. In general, Windows NT is slightly more robust. Windows NT is a true 32-bit operating system and also has certain security and server features that are not available on Windows 95. Windows NT cannot run some DOS and Windows 3.1 programs, and, therefore, is often less backwardly compatible. Today the two operating systems target different audiences; however, one day they could be merged into one.

Q How can I prevent threads from accessing the same memory location simultaneously?

A The Win32 API has a series of calls that allow you to protect blocks of code and resources. Some of these include mutual exclusion zones and semaphores.

Q If I use exception handling religiously is it possible for my application to crash or to crash the operating system?

A Never say never. I have managed to crash both Windows 95 and Windows NT. Nothing is totally bulletproof.

Workshop

Quiz

1. Why can't you write a graphical Win32 program that uses `readln` to get keyboard input?
2. Although an application may have multiple threads, is it possible for the computer to actually execute more then one instruction simultaneously? What if the computer is running Windows NT with more than one CPU?
3. If you want to perform special processing for an exception, but also want to call the default exception handler, how do you do this?
4. How can you cause a customized exception to occur?
5. How can you ensure code is executed in an application?

Exercises

1. Write an application that fills a listbox with the numbers 1 through 100. If the user clicks a number in the listbox, display a message indicating which number the user clicked.
2. Look at how menus can be used in an application and how to respond to events when a user chooses a menu item.
3. Write a program that causes an exception. Use a `try...except` block to call an exception handler when the error occurs.

Week 2

Day 9

The Visual Component Library

The wonderful thing about Delphi is its rich library of prebuilt components. Up to this point you have covered some basics with the Delphi IDE as well as programming basics including OOP. You have used some examples from the VCL (Visual Component Library) but really have only scratched the surface. Today, you take a complete tour of the VCL. You learn what is available as you go through every tab on the VCL palette, and take a look at properties and event handlers. You put many of these components to use as you build demo programs. Some components such as Database, OLE, and QuickReport are mentioned, but are covered in more detail in other chapters. By the end of today's lesson, you will have a good idea of what components are available and will have had the opportunity to use several of them. So without any further delay, grab your library card, fire up Delphi 2.0, and get to it!

What is the VCL?

NEW TERM So, what is the VCL? Well, VCL stands for *Visual Component Library.* This library is made up of prebuilt objects known as components. Simply put, these components are to Delphi what the OCXs are to Visual Basic 4.0. Unlike OCXs however, the components in the VCL are written in Delphi's Object Pascal and stored in a single library, not individual files. Any that you use become part of your executable. These components save you many hours—if not weeks or months—of coding and testing by providing you with the ability to visually design your application. By selecting components, dropping them on a form, and setting some properties, you can actually create some applications with little or no code. The VCL is made up of components that provide commonly used features found in most Windows applications. Because of all the components provided in Delphi, you are able to focus on creating your application rather than reinventing the wheel in creating your GUI, database functions, and program-to-program-communication (OLE and DDE). With the power built into Delphi's Object Pascal, you can easily design in record time just about any type of Windows application you can dream up. Your code essentially "glues" the components together. It's like building a prefabricated home versus building one from scratch. Building a home from scratch requires many pieces of wood, nails, materials, and so on, as well as a lot of preparation of the wood. By contrast, the prefabricated home comes with walls and other major components of the home already cut and assembled. The pieces are simply connected and the home takes much less time to build. It still has all the basic components, but the builder doesn't have as much to worry about. Also, unlike Visual Basic and OCXs, you can create your own visual components in Delphi and add them to the VCL palette for later use. As you go through the various components in the VCL, they are referred to by the name that shows up when you position the mouse pointer over the component (for example, Button). The components' names actually start with a T (for example, TButton) which is the name you see in the Object Inspector as well as the online help. So from this point on, if you see Form, think of TForm, if you see Edit, think of TEdit, likewise, if you see TEdit, you can think of Edit.

What actually happens when you drop a component onto a form? Delphi automatically generates code necessary to use the component and updates the project appropriately. You then only need to set properties, put code in event handlers, and use methods as necessary to get things working.

Hey, That's My Property!

You have these nice components, but you need a way to tell them how to appear and behave. Delphi components, like the OCXs in Visual Basic, have properties. These properties allow you to change many things about a component's size, shape, visibility, position, and more. To access these properties, use the Object Inspector. (See Figure 9.1.) The Object Inspector has two tabs: the Properties tab and the Events tab. For now, let's focus on the Properties tab.

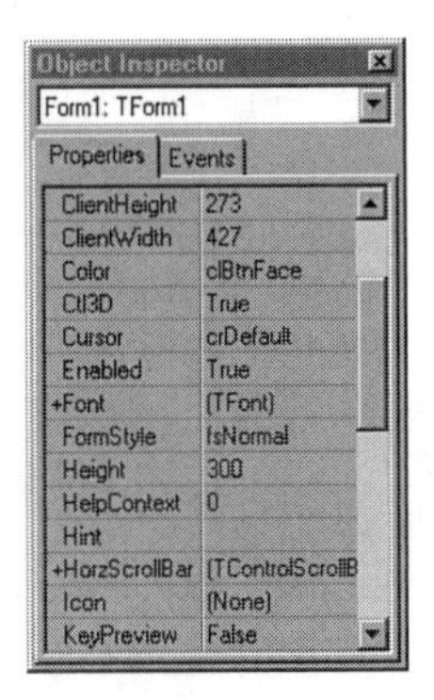

Figure 9.1.
The Object Inspector Properties tab.

Many properties are common among components, however, not all properties are found in all components. Also, some properties are specific to a component or group of components. It's impossible to cover every property of every component in this book, so we'll take a look at some of the more common properties as well as the types of properties and how to use them. Take a look at properties for a component you have used already: the Button. In Delphi, open a new project. Go to the Standard tab on the component palette. Select the button by clicking it and then click on the form. This adds a new Button component to your form. The Object Inspector with the Properties tab selected is shown in Figure 9.2.

As you can see, there are a number of properties that can be set for the Button component. Some properties have number values for their settings, such as the `Height` property. Some properties have a combobox that allows you to select from a list of predefined settings (constants defined in Delphi) such as the `Cursor` property. Still, other properties give you a true/false selection such as the `Default` property. Some properties take plain old text as their setting such as the `Caption` property. Finally, some properties have pop-up menus and editors that you use to make changes.

Figure 9.2.
The Object Inspector Button Properties tab.

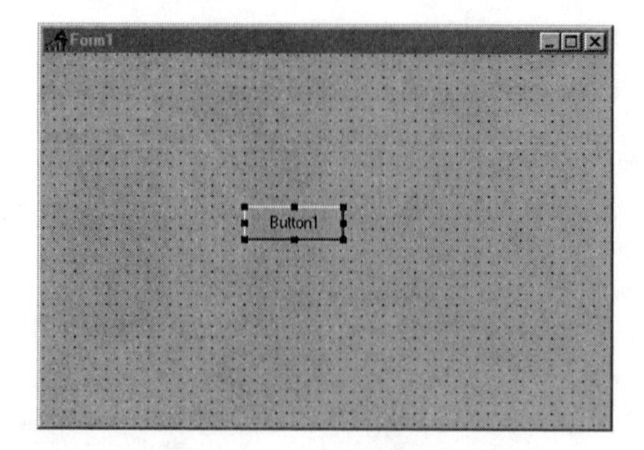

There is another type of property that you need to be aware of: the nested property. A nested property is always preceded with a "+", like the `+Font` property. Basically, a nested property is a property of a property. When you double-click on a property with nested properties, it expands, showing you the nested properties. The "+" changes to a "–". Nested properties can go down several levels. The "+" and "–" are used the same for each level. To collapse a nested property list, double-click the "–" and the list is collapsed and the "–" changes back to a "+". Take a look at the following list of properties for the Button component. All the nested properties have been expanded.

```
Cancel
Caption
Cursor
Default
DragCursor
DragMode
Enabled
+Font
    Color
    Height
    Name
    Pitch
    Size
    +Style
        fsBold
        fsItalic
        fsUnderline
        fsStrikeOut
Height
HelpContex
Hint
```

```
Left
ModalResult
Name
ParentFont
ParentShowHint
PopupMenu
ShowHint
TabOrder
TabStop
Tag
Top
Visible
Width
```


By changing these properties you can control the appearance, size, behavior, color, font, and more. One of the most commonly used properties for components such as the button, is the `Caption` property. If you are creating an OK button, you change the button `Caption` property to OK. Then your button displays OK. Likewise, you might want to have your button's `Name` property something like MyOKButton to make the code in the unit file more readable. As mentioned earlier, there are far too many properties to cover them all in this book. Go through this chapter and the rest of the book, and you will be introduced to a number of properties. When you need information about a particular property, all you need to do is click on it and press F1. The online help explains each property in detail. A good study assignment for you would be to spend a little time each day going through some of the properties for components and reading the online help for each of them. Don't forget, forms have properties too.

Another thing you should know is that some properties are dependent on the settings of other properties. An example of this is the `Hint` property. You set `Hint` to a text message you want displayed when the mouse cursor is left over the control for a short period of time. This won't work unless you have set either the `ShowHint` property on the control to True or the parent form or containers (for example, a `GroupBox`) `ShowHint` property to True. This is because the control's `ParentShowHint` property is set to True by default, which passes down the default setting of False to the child controls. Another example is the `ParentFont` property. If `ParentFont` is set to True, the component gets its font information from the parent form or container. You can see that there are many, but rest easy in the fact that the defaults for most of these properties are fine for most projects. As you work with Delphi, these become second nature. The names are fairly descriptive, so you should be able to figure out a lot of them just by looking at the names. When all else fails, help is just an F1 key away.

The Big Event

As mentioned earlier, Delphi components have a number of events or event handlers associated with them. As you know, any code you store in these event handlers is executed when a specific event occurs (for example, mouse move, mouse click, and so on). Take a look at the Object Inspector Events tab for the Button component. (See Figure 9.3.)

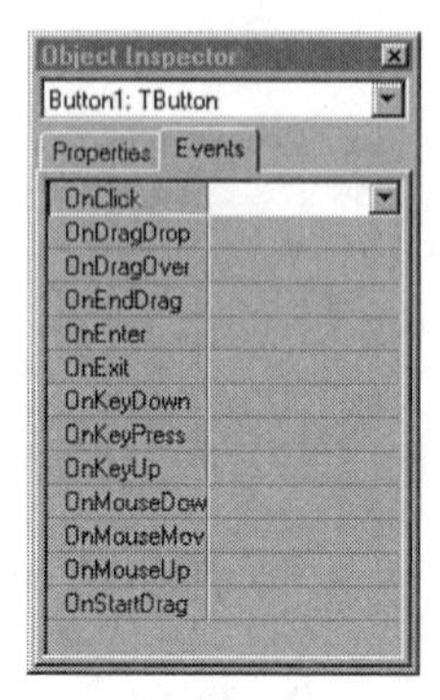

Figure 9.3.
The Object Inspector Events tab.

To create an event handler, simply double-click the event you want to create and you are placed inside the handler and are ready to enter your code. If you decide not to use the event handler, Delphi deletes it for you the next time you compile, assuming you have no code stored in it. As with the Properties tab, you can click an event you need help with and press F1 for a description. Also notice that when you click the box to the right of an event in the Object Inspector, you get a combobox. When you click the down arrow you get a list of currently defined and available events. This allows several controls and/or events to share the same event handler. That should save some space and typing on some of your projects.

Methods

There are several types of methods, but what you are interested in here are the methods associated with the various components and how they affect them. Methods give you a another way to control components. Because components are objects, they can have functions and procedures declared in them. That is what a method is: a public function or procedure declared inside an object that you can call. Take the example of your Button component. If you wanted to make it invisible, you could execute a line of code like `Button1.Hide`, and the button would become invisible. To find out about the methods available for a particular component or object, click the component or object and press F1. In the online help, click on Methods and you will be presented with a list of methods available. You can then click on the method for which you need information and view its help.Take a look at the following list of methods available for the Button component.

```
BeginDrag
BringToFront
CanFocus
ClientToScreen
Create
Destroy
Dragging
EndDrag
Focused
Free
GetTextBuf
GetTextLen
Hide
Refresh
Repaint
ScaleBy
ScreenToClient
ScrollBy
SendToBack
SetBounds
SetFocus
SetTextBuf
Show
Update
```

Like properties, the names are fairly descriptive and usually give you an idea of what the method does. Unlike properties, methods are not accessible in the Object Inspector. To find out about methods, you must use the online help. If you click the component for which you need help and press F1, you find the help screen for that component. Click on methods and you are given the list of methods available. Of course, clicking any of the methods listed gives a description of what it does and how to use it. This is another area where it would be good for you to make a practice of regularly looking through the help to learn about the available methods and what they do. You don't need to memorize all this, but once you know what is available to you, it will be much easier to create with less effort applications that do what you want. You don't want to reinvent the wheel or do without because you didn't know a method existed to do just what you want.

Visual and Nonvisual Components

You will find two types of components in Delphi: visual and nonvisual. The visual components are those you use to build your user interface. Both types of components appear at design time but nonvisual components are not visible at runtime. `Button`, `Edit`, and `Memo` are examples of visual components. Nonvisual components are used for a variety of different tasks. `Timer`, `OpenDialog`, and `MainMenu` are examples of nonvisual components. `Timer` is used by the programmer to activate specific code at scheduled intervals and is never seen by the user. `OpenDialog` and `MainMenu` are nonvisual components that ultimately produce visible and usable results on the screen, but the components themselves are not visible to the user. Nonvisual components are easy to spot because they can't be resized and look just like the button that you used to select them when you drop them on a form. Visible or not, all the components are very useful and save you much time and effort.

The Library

The library is broken into nine logically grouped tabs. In addition, there is an OCX tab and a Samples tab. These extra tabs have sample OCXs and VCLs in them for you to experiment with. This gives a total of 11 tabs. Features are accessible by selecting the appropriate tab. While it is not possible to cover and use every component and its properties, you will see all the components and learn about some of the properties as you go. You'll build demo forms for some of the tabs covered. The online help is great help in determining what a particular component is used for. You can move the cursor over a component and look at the hint. If you need more information about a component, simply click on it and press F1. The Help screens give you information about what a component is for and how to use it. You are never more than just a few clicks and a key press away from the help you need with the library. Take a look at each of these tabs and build an application using some of these components. This application is not going to do anything useful; its only purpose is to demonstrate the use of components. You will no doubt get some ideas for use in other projects as we put this demo application together. Open a new project and save UNIT1.PAS as STANDARD.PAS. Save the project as VCLDEMO.DPR. Go through the Standard tab and start on the VCLDEMO application.

The Standard Tab

Here in the Standard tab you find the most commonly used components. This tab is the default when you start Delphi. There are 14 components here. Take a quick look at them and then build the first form of your demo application using some of them. (See Figure 9.4.)

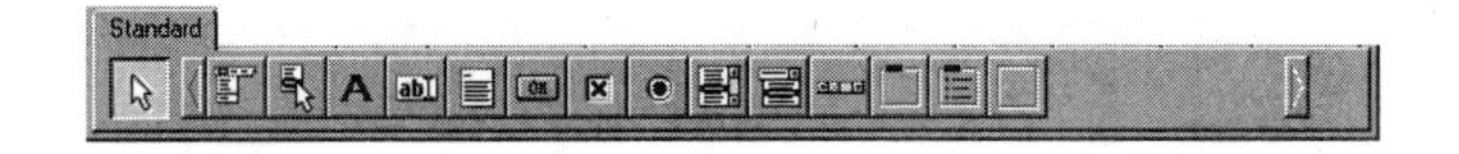

Figure 9.4.
The VCL Palette's Standard tab.

The MainMenu component allows you to design and create your form's menu bar and dropdown menus. This is a nonvisual component.

The PopupMenu component allows you to design and create popup menus that appear when the user clicks on the right mouse button. This is a nonvisual component.

The Label component is used to place text in forms and other containers that cannot be changed by the user. This is a visual component.

The Edit component is used to input single lines of text from the user. The Edit component can also be used to display text. This is a visual component.

The Memo component is used to input and/or display multiple lines of text. This is a visual component.

The Button component is used to create buttons that the user will use to select options in an application. This is a visual component.

The Checkbox component is used to allow the user to select or deselect options by clicking on the checkbox. This is a visual component.

The RadioButton component is used to offer a set of options in which only one option in the set can be selected. A set is any number of RadioButtons in a container such as a form, panel, and so on. This is a visual component.

The ListBox component is the standard Windows listbox that allows you to create a list of items that the user can select from. This is a visual component.

The ComboBox is a component that is like the ListBox component but adds the benefits of an Edit component. The ComboBox component gives the user the option of either selecting from a list or entering the text into the box. This is a visual component.

The ScrollBar component is the standard Windows scrollbar used to scroll forms or controls. This is a visual component.

The GroupBox component is a container used to group related controls and containers, such as the RadioButton, CheckBox, and so on. This is a visual component.

The RadioGroup component is a combination of a GroupBox and RadioButtons designed specifically for creating groups of radio buttons. Multiple radio buttons can be set up, but no other controls are allowed here. This is a visual component.

The Panel component is another container to group controls or containers. Panels can also be used to build status bars, tool bars and tool palettes. This is a visual component.

Now that you have gone through all the components on the Standard tab, start work on the demo application and put the VCL to work. In your VCLDEMO.DPR project that you created earlier, change the form caption to read "The Standard tab". You are going to create a very busy form using at least one of every component on the Standard tab. Take a look at Figure 9.5 and refer back to it as you add components to the form to make sure you place the components in the correct location and get the proportions close to the example.

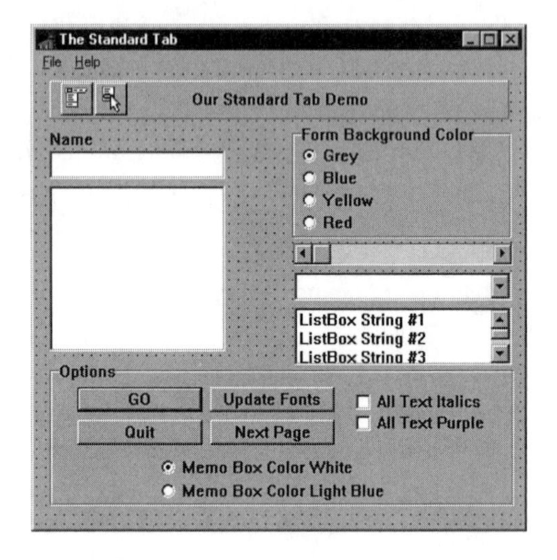

Figure 9.5.
The VCLDEMO Standard tab form.

Start by changing the `Name` property to read Standard tab. Next, add a Panel component to the top of the screen. Stretch it out like a banner. You'll use this to label your form with a title. Set the `Caption` property for the Panel component to read "Our Standard tab Demo." The Panel is very useful for creating labels with a 3D look, but it also works great as a container for other controls. Next, add a label to the screen and change its caption to Name. The label component has a property called `AutoSize`, which is set to True by default. `Autosize` causes the label to increase or decrease in size as you change the caption, font size, etc. If the label's background color is the same as the form (which is the default), you may lose track of your label if it shrinks down to no characters and is not selected. If this happens, you can easily find it by going to the Object Inspector and using the combobox to pull down a list of components and selecting it from the list. (See Figure 9.6.) You can then type the text you want into the `Caption` property. Now add an Edit component under the label. Use the Object Inspector to delete all the characters from the Edit component's `Text` property. Add a MainMenu and PopupMenu component to the form. Remember, these are nonvisual components, so it really doesn't matter where you place them. You will probably find it easy to just move them into a corner out of the way so they are not distracting you as you add other components. Next, add a Memo component.

Figure 9.6.
Object Inspector Name window.

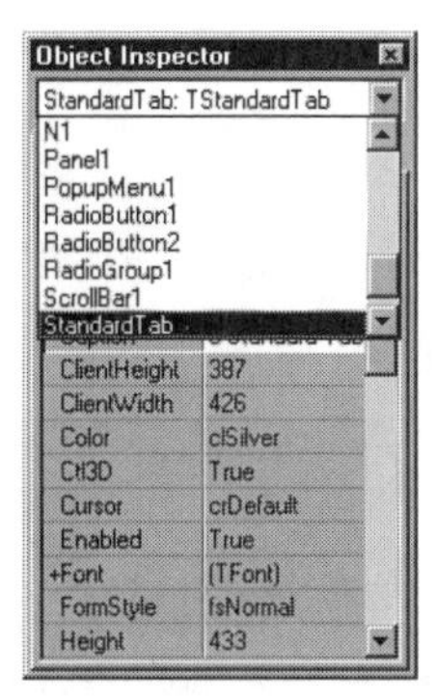

Take a minute and look at some of the properties available for the Memo component (for example, `ScrollBars`, `WordWrap`, `WantReturn`). Use the online help to view the descriptions of some of these properties. The Memo component is a pretty powerful component allowing you to design your own text editor. You won't use many of the properties that Memo has available in this example, but you should know they exist. In the Object Inspector, double-click the `Lines` property and delete the text, "Memo1." Press Enter four times. This adds space to the Memo component's text buffer (you need at least three or four lines available to modify for this demo and this creates them). If you don't do this, the demo will not work. Now add RadioGroup, ScrollBar, ComboBox, and ListBox to the form. Make sure all the components you have dropped onto the form look like that in Figure 9.6.

Double-click the RadioGroup component that you placed on the form and add the following code to its OnClick event:

```
procedure TStandardTab.RadioGroup1Click(Sender: TObject);
begin
     If RadioGroup1.ItemIndex=0 Then StandardTab.Color:=clSilver;
     If RadioGroup1.ItemIndex=1 Then StandardTab.Color:=clBlue;
     If RadioGroup1.ItemIndex=2 Then StandardTab.Color:=clYellow;
     If RadioGroup1.ItemIndex=3 Then StandardTab.Color:=clRed;
end;
```

Now double-click the ScrollBar component and add the following code to the ScrollBar component OnChange event:

```
procedure TStandardTab.ScrollBar1Change(Sender: TObject);
begin

     RadioGroup1.ItemIndex := ScrollBar1.Position;end;
```

Drop a GroupBox onto the form and make sure it has room for some components on it. Add four buttons, two radio buttons, and two checkboxes to the GroupBox. Change the `Caption` property on each of the buttons to Go for `Button1`, Update Fonts for `Button2`, Quit for `Button3`, and Next Page for `Button4`. These are all the components you will use on this form.

Adjust the component locations and sizes until your form looks as close to Figure 9.5 as possible. Now, add some code to these buttons. Here is the code for the `Button1` OnClick event:

```
procedure TStandardTab.Button1Click(Sender: TObject);
Var
   x : Integer;
begin
{Clear the current contents of the TMemo}
     Memo1.Clear;
     {Copy the text typed in the Name Box (Edit1) to the Memo}
     Memo1.Lines.Add(Edit1.Text);
     {Copy the text from the text box in the Combobox to the Memo}
     Memo1.Lines.Add(ComboBox1.Text);
     {Copy the selected text from the list box to the memo}
     Memo1.Lines.Add('ListBox String
        #'+IntToStr(ListBox1.ItemIndex+1));
     If RadioButton1.Checked then Memo1.Color:=clWhite;
     If RadioButton2.Checked then Memo1.Color:=ClAqua;
end;
```

And code for the `Button2` OnClick event:

```
procedure TStandardTab.Button2Click(Sender: TObject);
begin
     If CheckBox1.State = cbChecked then
        StandardTab.Font.Style:=[fsItalic]
     else StandardTab.Font.Style:=[];
     If CheckBox2.State = cbChecked then
        StandardTab.Font.Color:=clPurple
     else StandardTab.Font.Color:=clBlack;
end;
```

And the code for `Button3`'s OnClick event:

```
procedure TStandardTab.Button3Click(Sender: TObject);
begin
     Close;
end;
```

The code for `Button4`, which is used to hide this form and display the next, will be added shortly after you have created a second form for the additional Tab.

Remember that when you double-click a component, it creates the procedure declaration with the `begin` and `end` keywords. You simply need to fill in the code from the examples given. Also, remember that you will not see code for all of the controls. Delphi cleans up empty event handlers that get created when you double-click on a component each time it compiles. In fact, it is best to let Delphi clean up unused event handlers as you can cause problems if you delete them yourself.

Finally, add code for the MainMenu and PopupMenu components. Look at the MainMenu component. At first, this component and the way it is used may seem a bit strange, especially if you come from a Visual Basic background. You may be wondering where the Menu Designer is. One way it is activated is via the `Items` property in the Object Inspector for the MainMenu component. (See Figure 9.7.)

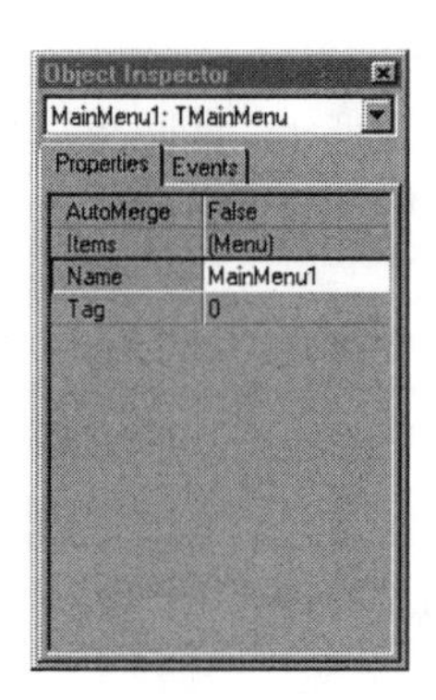

Figure 9.7.
Object Inspector for MainMenu component.

If you double-click the property value for the `Items` property where it says (Menu), you are presented with the Menu Designer. (See Figure 9.8.) You can also click the MainMenu component on your form and use the speed menu by clicking the right mouse button. The Object Inspector changes to accommodate the Menu Designer. (See Figure 9.9.) Here you simply change the caption to the menu selection you plan to add. Change this to `&File`. The "&" tells Delphi to underline the character following and set up the hot key sequence for the menu selection. In the example, pressing Alt and F keys brings up the File menu option when the program is running. After you have added the File menu option, notice that a box appears to the right of it. This allows you to click on it and add another menu option by changing the Object Inspector `Caption` property as before. You may also click on existing menu options to add the submenu options. Click on File and a box appears below it. Click on the box and it is highlighted and the Object Inspector is ready to change its caption. Add an Exit option to the File menu. Change the `Caption` property in the Object Inspector to `E&xit` and you should see Exit added below the File menu option.

Notice the blank boxes below the Exit and to the right of the File menu options in the menu box. You click on these as you want to add options. If you don't click on them, they will not appear on your menu. Add a Help menu with a Help option, a separator line, and an About option. Add the Help menu, then a Help option by entering **`&Help`** into the caption properties as you did with the File and Exit menu options. To create the separator line, simply add a hyphen (-) to the caption property of the submenu, in this case just below the Help option under the Help menu. As soon as you do this, you will see the separator. Next, add an About option by adding **`&About`** below the separator line. (See Figure 9.10.) When you are done designing the menu, double-click on the control box for the Menu Designer screen. The

Menu Designer closes and you see your menu options on your form. You can then go through them as you would in a regular menu by clicking on an option, holding the mouse button down, and dragging through the options. To add code to any of the options, simply select the menu option as if the program were running and you are put into the proper event handler code section. Here, you could do a Select File | Exit on your new menu option and add the following code to close it. Instead, use the existing event handler you have already created. From the Object Inspector, select Exit1 (your File | Exit Menu option) using the combobox. Next, select the Events tab in the Object Inspector and click the down arrow on the combobox for the OnClick event to show the available options. Select Button3Click. In this case, you have saved only one line of code, but in a large event handler, you could save quite a bit.

Figure 9.8.
Main Menu Designer.

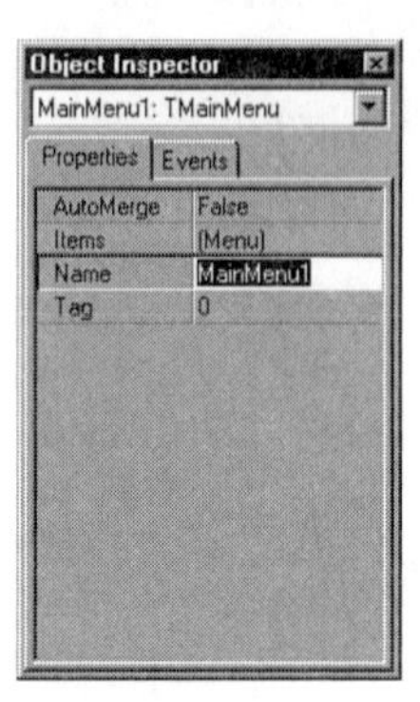

Figure 9.9.
Object Inspector for the Main Menu Designer.

This simply closes the application. You don't need to add code to the other options; this was just an example of how to create menus. Later in your exercises, you get a chance to come back and fill in the code for the Help and About menu options under the Help menu.

NOTE

If you did not leave much room at the top of your form, you will notice that the menu might cover up some of your components and that scroll bars have appeared. This isn't desirable in our case, so resize the form so everything fits by making the form longer and moving the components down a bit to make room for the menu if necessary.

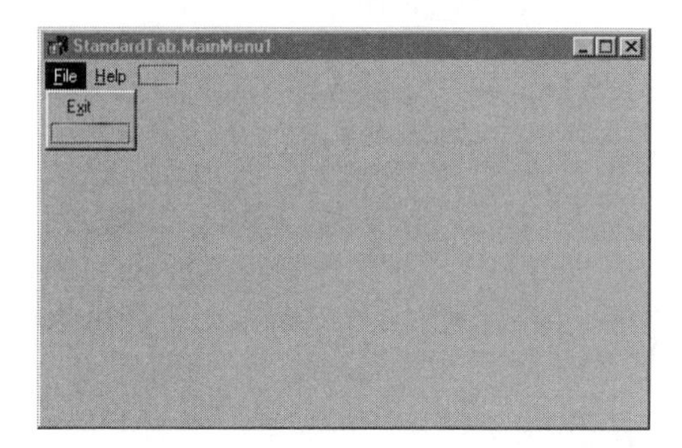

Figure 9.10.
Menu Designer with menu options.

Add the pop-up menu and you'll be done with the form. Click the PopupMenu component that you placed on the form earlier. Right click the mouse to bring up the speed menu. Select Menu Designer... from the popup menu. This Menu Designer works identically to the MainMenu Designer with the exception that all the menu options run vertically down a single box. To add code to the menu options in the popup menu, you must select the menu option in the menu designer. You are then put into the event handler code. Add two options: Go and Update Fonts. When you are finished, exit the Menu Designer. Use existing methods for these just as you did with the File | Exit menu option. From the Object Inspector, select Go and select Button1Click for the OnClick event. Next, use the Object Inspector to select UpdateFonts1 and select Button2Click for the OnClick event. This saves some more code and gets the popup Menu working.

If everything went well, you should be done with this part of the VCLDEMO application. Make sure to save your work. Take a look at the complete code you should have for this form unit.

```
unit Standard;

interface

uses
  Windows, Messages, SysUtils, Classes, Graphics, Controls, Forms, Dialogs,
Menus, StdCtrls, ExtCtrls,Addition;

type
  TStandardTab = class(TForm)
```

```
    MainMenu1: TMainMenu;
    PopupMenu1: TPopupMenu;
    Panel1: TPanel;
    Label1: TLabel;
    Edit1: TEdit;
    RadioGroup1: TRadioGroup;
    GroupBox1: TGroupBox;
    Button3: TButton;
    Button2: TButton;
    CheckBox1: TCheckBox;
    CheckBox2: TCheckBox;
    ScrollBar1: TScrollBar;
    Memo1: TMemo;
    ComboBox1: TComboBox;
    ListBox1: TListBox;
    Button1: TButton;
    Button4: TButton;
    RadioButton1: TRadioButton;
    RadioButton2: TRadioButton;
    File1: TMenuItem;
    Exit1: TMenuItem;
    Help1: TMenuItem;
    Help2: TMenuItem;
    N1: TMenuItem;
    About1: TMenuItem;
    Go: TMenuItem;
    UpdateFonts1: TMenuItem;
    procedure RadioGroup1Click(Sender: TObject);
    procedure ScrollBar1Change(Sender: TObject);
    procedure Button3Click(Sender: TObject);
    procedure Button2Click(Sender: TObject);
    procedure Button1Click(Sender: TObject);
    procedure GoClick(Sender: TObject);
    procedure UpdateFonts1Click(Sender: TObject);
    procedure Button4Click(Sender: TObject);
  private
    { Private declarations }
  public
    { Public declarations }
  end;

var
  StandardTab: TStandardTab;

implementation

{$R *.DFM}

procedure TStandardTab.RadioGroup1Click(Sender: TObject);
begin
     If RadioGroup1.ItemIndex=0 Then StandardTab.Color:=clSilver;
     If RadioGroup1.ItemIndex=1 Then StandardTab.Color:=clBlue;
     If RadioGroup1.ItemIndex=2 Then StandardTab.Color:=clYellow;
     If RadioGroup1.ItemIndex=3 Then StandardTab.Color:=clRed;
end;
```

```
procedure TStandardTab.ScrollBar1Change(Sender: TObject);
begin
     RadioGroup1.ItemIndex := ScrollBar1.Position;
end;

procedure TStandardTab.Button3Click(Sender: TObject);
begin
     Close;
end;

procedure TStandardTab.Button2Click(Sender: TObject);
begin
     If CheckBox1.State = cbChecked then
        StandardTab.Font.Style:=[fsItalic]
     else StandardTab.Font.Style:=[];
     If CheckBox2.State = cbChecked then
        StandardTab.Font.Color:=clPurple
     else StandardTab.Font.Color:=clBlack;
end;

procedure TStandardTab.Button1Click(Sender: TObject);
Var
   x : Integer;
begin
     {Clear the current contents of the TMemo}
     Memo1.Clear;
     {Copy the text typed in the Name Box (Edit1) to the Memo}
     Memo1.Lines.Add(Edit1.Text);
     {Copy the text from the text box in the Combobox tp the Memo}
     Memo1.Lines.Add(ComboBox1.Text);
     {Copy the selected text from the list box to the memo}
     Memo1.Lines.Add('ListBox String#'+IntToStr(ListBox1.ItemIndex+1));
     If RadioButton1.Checked then Memo1.Color:=clWhite;
     If RadioButton2.Checked then Memo1.Color:=ClAqua;
end;

procedure TStandardTab.GoClick(Sender: TObject);
begin
     Button1Click(StandardTab);
end;

procedure TStandardTab.UpdateFonts1Click(Sender: TObject);
begin
     Button2Click(StandardTab);
end;

procedure TStandardTab.Button4Click(Sender: TObject);
begin
     StandardTab.Hide;
     AdditionalTab.Show;
end;
end.
```

If you have not done so already, save your project and test it out. When you run the project, the form should come up looking like Figure 9.11. The only menu option that does anything at this point is File | Exit. When you make changes to the Edit, ListBox, or ComboBox components and click the Go button, updates are shown in the Memo component. When you select Go, the background color is also updated to the color selected by the radio buttons at the bottom of the form. You can change the color of the form background by using the scrollbar or selecting the color you wish from the radio buttons in the RadioGroup. Form font colors can be changed to purple and the font to *italic* by checking the checkboxes and clicking the Update Fonts button. Finally, you can select Go or Update Fonts from the pop-up menu by right-clicking the mouse from anywhere on the form.

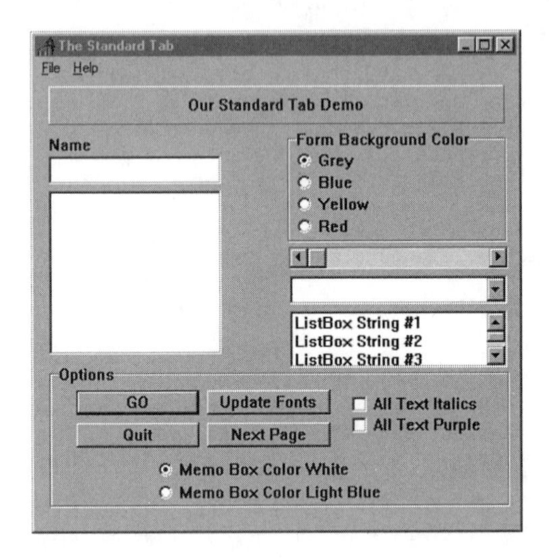

Figure 9.11.
The VCLDEMO Standard tab form.

You have just covered every component on the Standard tab and tested your application to see how they work. You should notice that you really didn't write much code or need to change many properties to get it all working. This really demonstrates the power available to you in the Delphi VCL.

The VCL Palette's Additional Tab

The Additional tab has another group of components you might want to use often. In version 3.0 of Visual Basic, some of these would have been add-on products. You have nine components to choose from here. Look at them and put some of them to work in a second form in our VCLDEMO project. (See Figure 9.12.)

Figure 9.12.
The Additional tab.

The BitBtn component is used to create a button with a bitmap graphic on it (an OK button with a checkmark, for example). This is a visual component.

The SpeedButton is a specialized button designed to work with the Panel component. The SpeedButton is used to create toolbars and specialized sets of buttons including buttons that stay pressed. This is a visual component.

The MaskEdit component is used to format for data or require proper character input. This is a visual component.

The StringGrid component is used to display string data in rows and columns. This is a visual component.

The DrawGrid component is used to display information other than text in rows and columns. This is a visual component.

The Image component is used to display graphics such as icons, bitmaps, and metafiles. This is a visual component.

The Shape component is used to draw shapes such as squares, circles, and so on. This is a visual component.

The Bevel component is used to draw a rectangle that can appear inset or raised. This is a visual component.

The ScrollBox component is used to create a display area that is scrollable. This is a visual component.

Now that you know what components are on the Additional tab, build the second page to your VCLDEMO application and learn how to tap into their power. Add a new form to our VCLDEMO project. Change the form's `Name` property to `additionaltab`. Change the caption to read the Additional tab. Do a File | Save As and save the new form as ADDITION.PAS. Make this form come up centered on the screen. To do this you need to set the `Position` property. By default, this property is set to `poDesigned`, which means it shows up in the position at which it was designed. Click once on `poDesigned` and you get a combobox. Select `poScreenCenter`. This setting takes effect when the form is activated. As you add components to the form, refer to Figure 9.13 for approximate size and location. You will also need to add `Addition` to the original (Standard) forms uses clause. Before you move on, you need to go back to the StandardTab form and add code to allow you to access your new page when you test the program. From the menu, select View | Forms to bring up the Forms menu and select `StandardTab`. Double-click on `Button4` (Next Page) and set its Click event code to read:

```
procedure TStandardPage.Button4Click(Sender: TObject);
begin
     StandardPage.Hide;
     AdditionalPage.Show;
end;
```

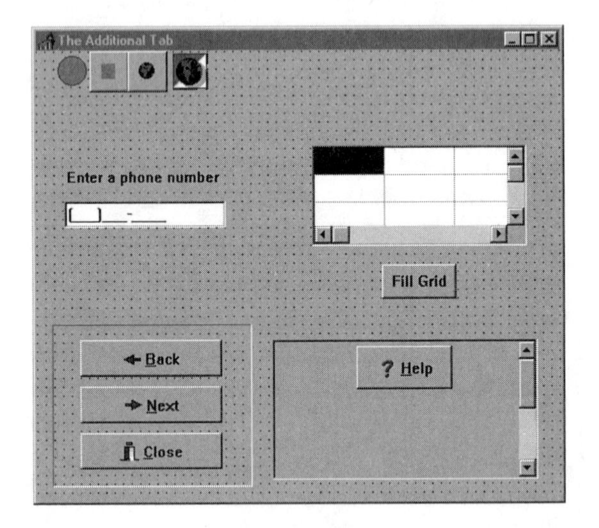

Figure 9.13.
The VCLDEMO Additional tab form.

First up is the BitBtn component. Drop three of these in the lower right corner of the form. For `BitBtn1` and `BitBtn2`, set the `Kind` properties to `bkCustom`. Set the caption property for `BitBtn1` to `Back` and `BitBtn2` to `Next`. The BitBtn component allows you to set a graphic on the button called a glyph. Glyphs are simply small bitmaps that can contain multiple images that can be displayed depending on the state of a BitBtn or SpeedButton. You can use one of the predefined glyphs that come with Delphi, or you can create your own using the Image Editor found in the Tools menu. For our purposes, use the glyphs provided with Delphi. For `BitBtn1`, double-click on `Tbitmap` in the `Glyph` property. This brings up the Picture Editor. (See Figure 9.14.) This screen does not actually allow you to edit the picture, it simply lets you select the filename of the glyph you wish to load and view it before you add it to the button. Click on the Load button and you are presented with the file selection dialog box. Change to the c:\program files\borland\delphib2.0\images\buttons directory assuming that is where you have Delphi stored and select ARROW1L.BMP. You should see a red arrow pointing to the left as well as a white arrow. The red arrow is displayed when the button is in the enabled state. The white arrow is displayed in the disabled state. This gives the grayed-out effect. You can toggle the `Enabled` property for the button between True and False to see

the difference. Make sure that the button's `Enabled` property is set to True when you are done. Now repeat the steps you used for `BitBtn1` and set the glyph for `BitBtn2` to ARROW1R.BMP. Setting up `BitBtn3` is going to be easier because of a predefined type that you use in the `Kind` property. For `BitBtn3`, click on `Kind` and select `bkClose`. This sets the button's glyph to an open door and the `Caption` property to `Close`. For future reference, notice that the `Kind` property has 10 predefined types and one type called `bkCustom` that enables you to create your type of button.

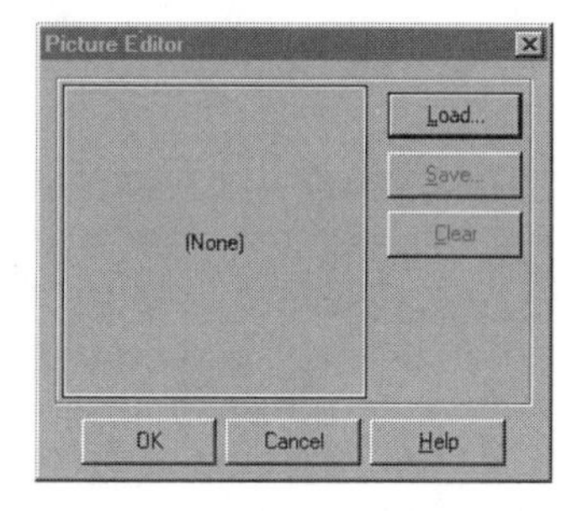

Figure 9.14.
The Picture Editor.

```
bkAbout
bkAll
bkCancel
bkClose
bkCustom
bkHelp
bkIgnore
bkNo
bkOk
bkRetry
bkYes
```

The names are self-explanatory. These types are commonly used buttons in Windows applications. The `bkCustom` is of course used when you need to create a new button type as you have already done. Give your buttons a nice grouped appearance by adding a Bevel component. Select the Bevel component on the Additional tab and draw it around the box. This gives you a box with an inset appearance around your buttons. Add some code to the buttons by double-clicking `BitBtn1` and adding the following code to its Click event:

```
procedure TAdditionalTab.BitBtn1Click(Sender: TObject);
begin
   Standard.StandardTab.Show;
   AdditionalTab.Hide;
end;
```

We will come back to BitBtn2 later, but for BitBtn3, add this code:

```
procedure TAdditionalTab.BitBtn3Click(Sender: TObject);
begin
  Standard.StandardTab.Close;
end;
```

To make the Close button work properly, add the following code to the form's Close event:

```
procedure TAdditionalTab.FormClose(Sender: TObject;
  var Action: TCloseAction);
begin
     Application.Terminate;
end;
```

If you do not add the code, the form will close when the Close button is selected, but the application will remain in memory wasting resources. Now create a toolbar. For this, you need to use a Panel component from the Standard tab as the container for your buttons. Add a Panel near the top left corner of the form large enough to hold two square buttons. Now add two SpeedButtons to the panel from the Additional Page. The SpeedButtons enables you to do things you can't do with other buttons. For example, you can create buttons that stay pushed in, you can group buttons together, and even create buttons that change the glyph depending on the state of the button. The states available for a SpeedButtons are Up, Disabled, Down, and Stay Down. These states cause the proper part of a glyph to be displayed. To take advantage of these states, you can use the Image Editor to create a four-image glyph for use with your button. The Image Editor was briefly touched on in Day 2, "The IDE" so we won't go into much detail here (if you need more info on the Image Editor, please refer to the online help or documentation). The Image Editor is a simple draw program designed for creating resources, icons, bitmaps, and so on. (See Figure 9.15.) If you have ever used any type of Windows Paint or Draw type program, you should have little trouble using the Image Editor. If you are not ready to use Image Editor at this point, feel free to skip over it and come back to it later.

Basically, you want to create a bitmap that is 16×64 with 16 colors. The image will have four equally sized square boxes each a different color. Going from left to right, you can color them green, gray, purple, or red. I decided on this example because even those of us with no artistic abilities can participate in this example. Moving right along, when you are finished you can do a File | Save as, set the file type to BMP, and save your glyph to the name of your choice (I called it GRNRED.BMP). Using the same procedure as you used for setting the BitBtn component's `Glyph` property, set the `SpeedButton1` component's `Glyph` property to the GRNRED.BMP file you just created. Set the `Glyph` property of `SpeedButton2` to \pprogram files\borland\delphi 2.0\images\buttons\globe.bmp (if this is where you installed Delphi 2.0). For `SpeedButton1`, make sure the `NumGlyphs` property is set to `4` (4 is the default). This tells it that there are four glyphs available for each of the states you mentioned earlier. Set the `GroupIndex` property to `1`. This tells the button that it belongs to group number 1. Only one button in a group can be in the down position at any given time. Just like the `RadioButton`,

if you press down one button in the group, the other buttons are forced to the up position. Set the `GroupIndex` property for `SpeedButton2` and its `NumGlyphs` property to `2`. Set the `Visual` property for `SpeedButton2` to `False`. This completes the design of your toolbar; now add the code.

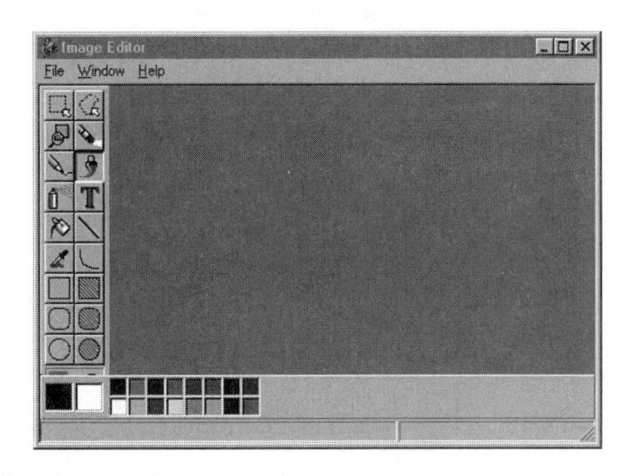

Figure 9.15.
The Image Editor.

Double-click `SpeedButton1` and make its Click event look like this:

```
procedure TAdditionalTab.SpeedButton1Click(Sender: TObject);
begin
     If SpeedButton1.Down=True then
        Begin
           Image1.Visible:=False;
           Shape1.Brush.Color:=clRed;
        end;
end;
```

And Click event code for `SpeedButton2` should look like this:

```
procedure TAdditionalTab.SpeedButton2Click(Sender: TObject);
begin
     If SpeedButton2.Down=True then
        Begin
           Image1.Visible:=True;
           Shape1.Brush.Color:=clLime;
        end;
end;
```

Now add a Shape component to the left of the toolbar. Draw it about the same size as the SpeedButtons on the toolbar. Set its `Shape` property to `stEllipse`. Double-click the `Pen` property to expose its nested properties. Set the `Color` property to `clGreen`. Double-click the Brush property to expose its nested properties and set its `Color` property to `clLime`. The `Pen` properties are used to set attributes used when drawing the shape (for example, color of the line, and so on). The `Brush` properties are used to set attributes used to fill the shape.

Next, add an Image component to the right of the toolbar. Make the Image component about the size of SpeedButton just as you did with the shape. The Image component can display graphics such as an icon, bitmap, or metafile. For our purposes, use an icon. Double-click the `Picture` property and you are presented with the Picture Editor. Load an icon file \delphi\images\icons\earth.ico. The code you added to the SpeedButton is used to affect the appearance of the Shape and the Image components.

On `SpeedButton1`, use another property that is available on all visual components: the `Hint` property. The `Hint` property stores a string of text that will be displayed when the user leaves the mouse pointer over the component for a short period of time. Change the `Hint` property to read My SpeedButton Hint. To enable the `Hint` property, you must set the `ShowHints` property to True as it is False by default. You'll test this at runtime.

Add a Label component to the form with the `Caption` property set to `Enter a Phone Number`. Next, just below the label, add a MaskEdit component. Double-click the `EditMask` property to bring up the Input Mask Editor. Click on Phone and then press OK. This sets the EditMask component to only accept numbers in the form of an area code and phone number.

Put a StringGrid component on the form. Set the `StringGrid1, RowCount, and ColCount` properties to `3`. Set the `FixedCols` and `FixedRows` to `0`. Adjust the size of the StringGrid so that only the nine cells are visible. Add a button to the form and set its caption to read Fill Grid. Double-click the button and add the following code:

```
procedure TAdditionalTab.Button1Click(Sender: TObject);
var
  x, y: Integer;
begin
  with StringGrid1 do
    for x := 0 to ColCount - 1 do
      for y:= 0 to RowCount - 1 do
        Cells[x,y] := 'Cord. '+ IntToStr(x)+'-'+IntToStr(y);
end;
```

And finally, the last component covered on this tab is the ScrollBox. Draw the `ScrollBox` on the form in the lower right corner and size it appropriately as in Figure 9.14. You will add a few components to it to demonstrate its ability to scroll components that may not fit in the area in which they need to be used. Add a BitBtn to the scrollbox, and set its `Kind` property to `bkHelp`. Add a panel to the scrollbox. Notice that if you drag the Panel down below the bottom border of the scrollbox, scrollbars appear. Temporarily stretch the scrollbox from top to bottom two to three times longer than you will need it. Place the button at the top and the panel at the bottom. Set the `Caption` property on the panel to read Panel in ScrollBox. Now resize the scrollbox to fit on the form as shown in Figure 9.13. Double-click on the Help button in the scrollbox and add the following code to its Click event:

```
procedure TAdditionalTab.BitBtn4Click(Sender: TObject);
begin
     ShowMessage('Testing Help Button in Scrollbox!');
end;
```

Now double-click on `BitBtn2` and add the following code:

```
procedure TAdditionalTab.BitBtn2Click(Sender: TObject);
begin
     ShowMessage('This feature not active');
end;
```

You are done with the Additional tab form and ready to test. The complete source code for the Addition unit created as you built your form should look like this:

```
unit Addition;

interface

uses
  Windows, Messages, SysUtils, Classes, Graphics, Controls, Forms, Dialogs,
Buttons, StdCtrls, ExtCtrls, Grids, Outline, Mask,
  TabNotBk, Tabs;

type
  TAdditionalTab = class(TForm)
    BitBtn1: TBitBtn;
    BitBtn2: TBitBtn;
    Panel1: TPanel;
    SpeedButton1: TSpeedButton;
    SpeedButton2: TSpeedButton;
    Bevel1: TBevel;
    Image1: TImage;
    Shape1: TShape;
    ScrollBox1: TScrollBox;
    BitBtn3: TBitBtn;
    BitBtn4: TBitBtn;
    Panel5: TPanel;
    Label1: TLabel;
    MaskEdit1: TMaskEdit;
    StringGrid1: TStringGrid;
    Button1: TButton;
    procedure BitBtn1Click(Sender: TObject);
    procedure BitBtn3Click(Sender: TObject);
    procedure Button1Click(Sender: TObject);
    procedure SpeedButton2Click(Sender: TObject);
    procedure SpeedButton1Click(Sender: TObject);
    procedure FormClose(Sender: TObject; var Action: TCloseAction);
    procedure BitBtn4Click(Sender: TObject);
    procedure BitBtn2Click(Sender: TObject);
  private
    { Private declarations }
  public
    { Public declarations }
  end;

var
  AdditionalTab: TAdditionalTab;

implementation

Uses
     Standard;
```

9

```
{$R *.DFM}

procedure TAdditionalTab.BitBtn1Click(Sender: TObject);
begin
   StandardTab.Show;
   AdditionalTab.Hide;
end;

procedure TAdditionalTab.BitBtn3Click(Sender: TObject);
begin
  StandardTab.Close;
end;

procedure TAdditionalTab.Button1Click(Sender: TObject);
var
  x, y: Integer;
begin
  with StringGrid1 do
    for x := 0 to ColCount - 1 do
      for y:= 0 to RowCount - 1 do
        Cells[x,y] := 'Cord. '+ IntToStr(x)+'-'+IntToStr(y);
end;

procedure TAdditionalTab.SpeedButton2Click(Sender: TObject);
begin
     If SpeedButton2.Down=True then
        Begin
           Image1.Visible:=True;
           Shape1.Brush.Color:=clLime;
        end;
end;

procedure TAdditionalTab.SpeedButton1Click(Sender: TObject);
begin
     If SpeedButton1.Down=True then
        Begin
           Image1.Visible:=False;
           Shape1.Brush.Color:=clRed;
        end;
end;

procedure TAdditionalTab.FormClose(Sender: TObject;
  var Action: TCloseAction);
begin
     Application.Terminate;
end;

procedure TAdditionalTab.BitBtn4Click(Sender: TObject);
begin
     ShowMessage('Testing Help Button in Scrollbox!');
end;

procedure TAdditionalTab.BitBtn2Click(Sender: TObject);
begin
     ShowMessage('This feature not active');
end;

end.
```

Save the project and test it out. You should be able to go through the two forms and experiment with the components you have placed on each page. Click on the toolbar (`SpeedButton`) buttons and observe the results. Use the scrollbar to view the Help button and the panel. Click on the Help button in the scrollbox to see a message box. When you are satisfied, click Close and the program exits.

You have just gone through a lot of components, done a lot of work, and not built anything useful. Remember, the point has been to get you familiar with the VCL and give you some exercise with it. About now you are probably thinking, "Four more tabs plus the OCX tab and the sample tab to go, I'm tired!" Rest easy, you have a majority of the work behind you for this chapter. The Data Access and Data Controls are only briefly mentioned here (they are covered in detail later in the database section). We will touch on the Win95 tab, Dialogs tab, and System tab. Several of the components in the System tab are also covered in other sections of the book. You will not be covering anything in the OCX and Sample tabs because they are only samples and not officially supported or documented. So, let's quickly go through the rest of the tabs here and build another small application to test out some of the remaining components.

The VCL Palette's Win95 Tab

The Win95 tab contains 11 components that enable you to create applications with the Windows 95 look and feel (see Figure 9.16). Several of these controls are similar to those that can be found in the Win 3.1 tab.

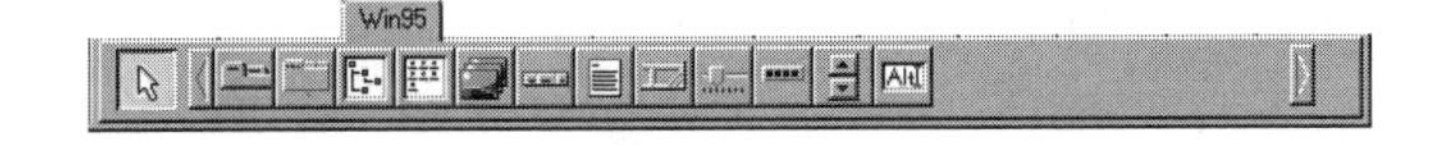

Figure 9.16.
The Win95 tab.

The TabControl is a Windows 95–style tab component allowing tabs to be added to a form for user selection. This is a visual component.

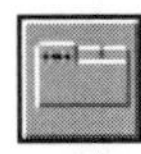
The PageControl is a Windows 95–style component used to create pages that can be changed using tabs or other controls to conserve desktop space. This is a visual component.

The TreeView is a Windows 95–style component that views data in a hierarchial format. This is a visual component.

The ListView is a Windows 95–style component that visually displays lists in columns. This is a visual component.

The ImageList is a new object provided for working with image lists. See the Delphi documentation for more information. This is a nonvisual component.

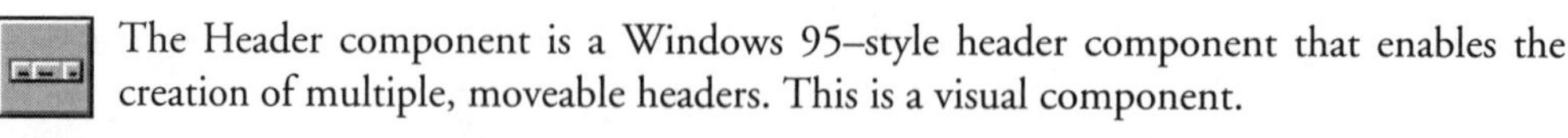
The Header component is a Windows 95–style header component that enables the creation of multiple, moveable headers. This is a visual component.

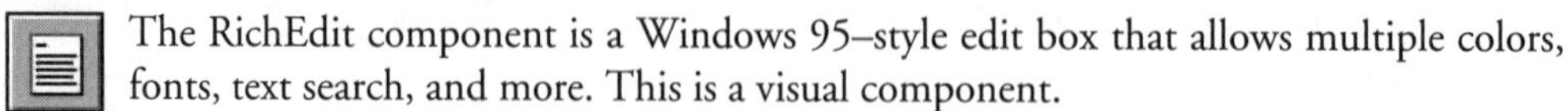
The RichEdit component is a Windows 95–style edit box that allows multiple colors, fonts, text search, and more. This is a visual component.

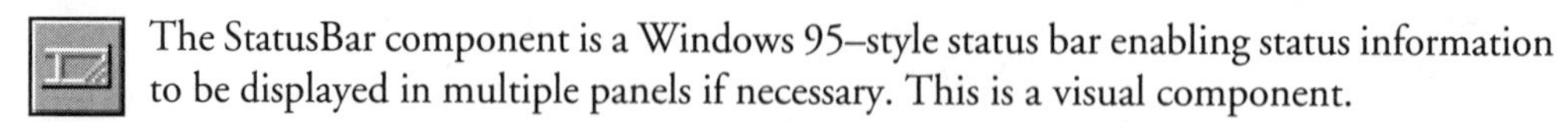
The StatusBar component is a Windows 95–style status bar enabling status information to be displayed in multiple panels if necessary. This is a visual component.

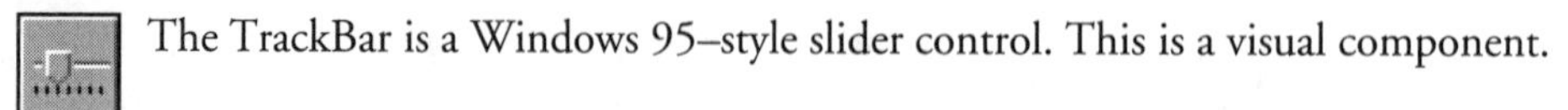
The TrackBar is a Windows 95–style slider control. This is a visual component.

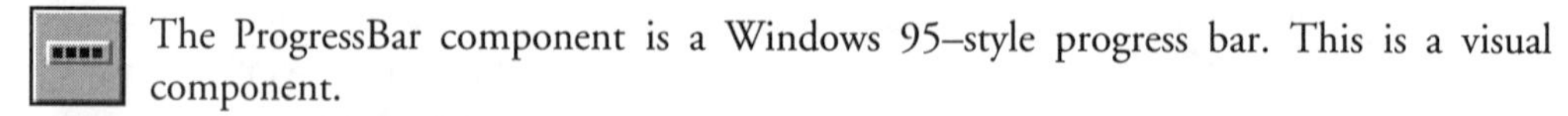
The ProgressBar component is a Windows 95–style progress bar. This is a visual component.

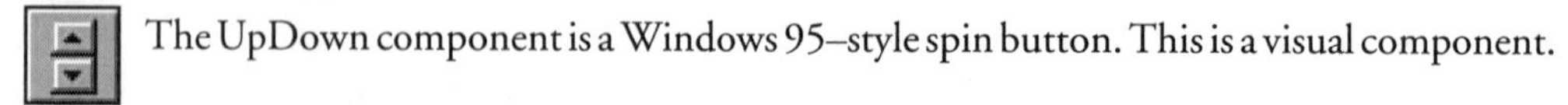
The UpDown component is a Windows 95–style spin button. This is a visual component.

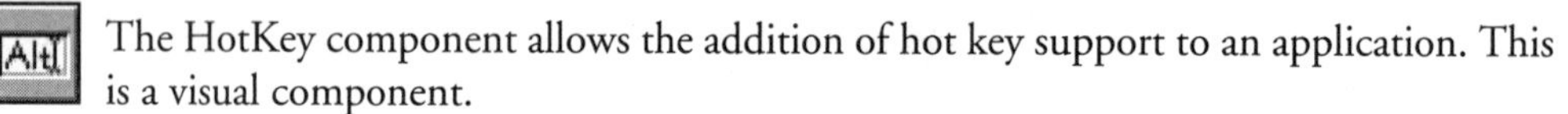
The HotKey component allows the addition of hot key support to an application. This is a visual component.

The VCL Palette's Data Access Tab

The Data Access tab contains components to link to, and communicate with databases. These components are not covered here because they are discussed in detail, later in the book. See Figure 9.17.

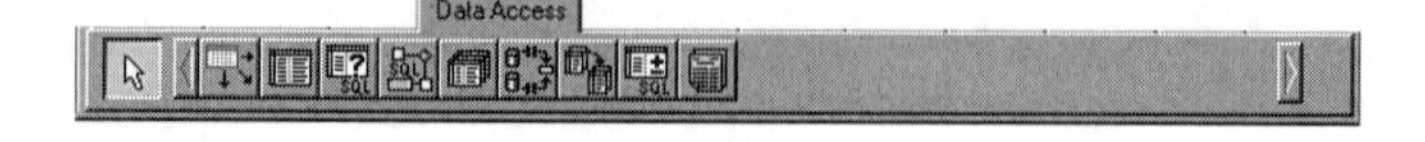

Figure 9.17.
The Data Access tab.

The DataSource component is used to connect the Table or Query components to data-aware components. This is a nonvisual component.

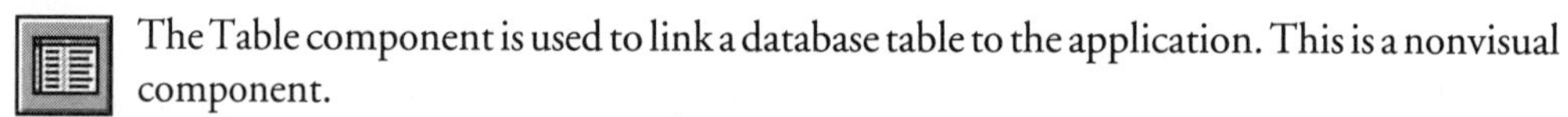
The Table component is used to link a database table to the application. This is a nonvisual component.

The Query component is used to create and execute SQL queries to a remote SQL Server Database or a local database. This is a nonvisual component.

The StoredProc component is used to execute procedures that have been stored on a SQL Server. This is a nonvisual component.

The Database component is used to make connections to remote database servers. This is a nonvisual component.

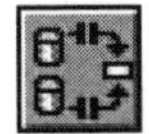
The Session component is used to provide global control over an application's database connections. This is a nonvisual component.

The BatchMove component allows you to perform work on records and tables locally and then move the updated information back to the server. This is a nonvisual component.

The UpdateSQL component is used to make updates to a SQL Database.

The Report component is used to create and print reports via ReportSmith. This is a nonvisual component.

The VCL Palette's Data Controls Tab

The Data Controls tab contains several data-aware components. Most of these components are data-aware versions of commonly used components found in the Standard and Additional tabs. These are covered later in the book. (See Figure 9.18.)

Figure 9.18.
The Data Controls tab.

The DBGrid component is used to create a data-aware grid where data can be displayed in rows and columns. This is a visual component.

The DBNavigator component is used to create a control that navigate through the database with the ability to edit data. This is a visual component.

The DBText component is a data-aware version of the Label component. This is a visual component.

The DBEdit component is a data-aware version of the Edit component. This is a visual component.

The DBMemo component is a data-aware version of the Memo component. This is a visual component.

The DBImage component is a data-aware version of the Image component. This is a visual component.

The DBListBox component is a data-aware version of the ListBox component. This is a visual component.

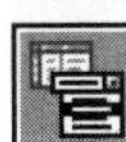
The DBComboBox component is a data-aware version of the ComboBox component. This is a visual component.

The DBCheckBox component is a data-aware version of the CheckBox component. This is a visual component.

The DBRadioGroup component is a data-aware version of the RadioGroup component. This is a visual component.

The DBLookupListBox component is used to create a look up ListBox that is data-aware. This is a visual component.

The DBLookupComboBox component is used to create a look up ComboBox that is data-aware. This is a visual component.

The DBCtrlGrid component is used to create a data grid that is data-aware. This is a visual component.

The VCL Palette's Win 3.1 Tab

The Win 3.1 tab stores components that have been replaced by newer components. These components are here for backward compatibility when porting applications between Delphi 1.0 and 2.0. Components in this tab should not be used with 32-bit applications. (See Figure 9.19.)

Figure 9.19.
The Win 3.1 tab.

The DBLookupList component is a Windows 3.1 data-aware control used to look up a value in a lookup table using a listbox. This is a visual component.

The DBLookupCombo component is a Windows 3.1 data-aware control used to look up a value in a lookup table using a combobox. This is a visual component.

The TabSet component is used to create notebook tabs. This is a visual component.

The Outline component allows the creation of a tree-like control used for visually displaying data in a hierarchical format.

The Header component is used to create a control that displays text in resizable sections. This is a visual component.

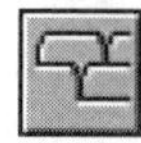
The TabbedNoteBook is used to create multipage forms with tabs. This is a visual component.

The NoteBook component is used to create a stack of pages that can be used with the TabSet. This is a visual component.

The VCL Palette's Dialogs Tab

The Dialogs tab contains eight components used to create the various dialog boxes that are common to windows applications. Dialogs are used to specify files or select settings. Using the dialog boxes provided in Delphi can save you time and help give a consistent look and feel to your applications. For detailed information on any of these components, click the component on the palette and press F1. (See Figure 9.20.)

Figure 9.20.
The Dialogs Tab.

The OpenDialog component is to create a File Open common dialog box. This is a nonvisual component.

The SaveDialog component is used to create a File Save common dialog box. This is a nonvisual component.

The FontDialog component is used to create a Font dialog box. This is a nonvisual component.

The ColorDialog component is used to create a Color dialog box. This is a nonvisual component.

The PrintDialog component is used to create a Print dialog box. This is a nonvisual component.

The PrinterSetupDialog component is used to create a Printer Setup dialog box. This is a nonvisual component.

The FindDialog component is used to create a Find dialog box. This is a nonvisual component.

The ReplaceDialog component is used to create a Replace dialog box. This is a nonvisual component.

The VCL Palette's System Tab

The System tab contains 12 more important components to take advantage of Windows features. The PaintBox, MediaPlayer, DDE, and OLE components are not covered in any detail in this chapter because they are covered elsewhere. Examples for components from this tab are included in our final application for this chapter. (See Figure 9.21.)

Figure 9.21.
The System tab.

The Timer component is used to activate procedures, functions, and events at specified time intervals. This is a nonvisual component.

The PaintBox is used to create in an area the form that can be painted. This is a visual component.

The FileListBox component is used to create a list box for displaying the files in the selected directory. This is a visual component.

The DirectoryListBox component is used to create a list box for displaying directories on the selected drive. This is a visual component.

The DriveComboBox component is used to create a combobox that is used to display and/or choose a drive. This is a visual component.

The FilterComboBox component is used to create a combobox that can display and/or select the file filter(s). This is a visual component.

The MediaPlayer component is used to create a control panel that looks like that of a VCR. This control is used to play sound and video files. This is a visual component.

The OLEContainer component is used to create an OLE client area. This is a visual component.

The DDEClientConv component is used by a DDE client to set up a conversation with a DDE Server. This is a nonvisual component.

The DDEClientItem component is used to specify client data that will be sent to a DDE server during a conversation. This is a nonvisual component.

The DDEServerConv component is used by a DDE server application to set up a conversation with a DDE client. This is a nonvisual component.

The DDEServerItem component is used to specify data that will be sent to DDE client during a conversation. This is a nonvisual component.

The VCL Palette's QReport Tab

The QReport tab contains 11 components for use in report generation. These components are covered on Day 16, "ReportSmith Fundamentals." (See Figure 9.22.)

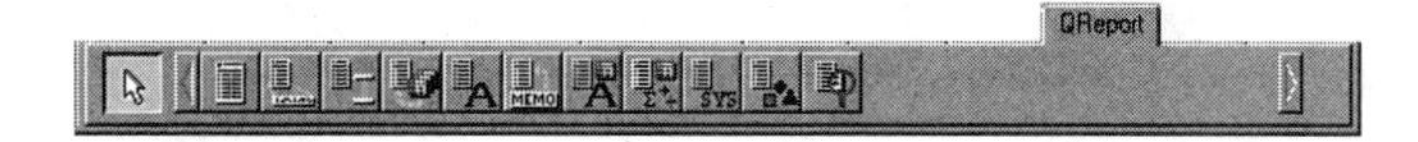

Figure 9.22.
The QReport tab.

The QuickReport component is used to add QuickReport printing capabilities to applications. This is a nonvisual component.

The QRBand component is used to build reports by placing printable components on it. This is a visual component.

The ORGroup is used to create data groups. This is a nonvisual component.

The QRDetailLink is another component used to create reports. This is a nonvisual component.

The QRLabel component is used to put text on a report. This is a visual component.

The QRMemo component is used to put multiline text on a report. This is a visual component.

The QRDBText is a data-aware component for placing text on a report. This is visual component.

The QRDBCalc component is used to perform simple calculations of your data fields. This is a visual component.

The QRSysData component is used to display system data. This is a visual component.

The QRShape component is used to draw a shape on a report. This is a visual component.

The QRPreview component is used to create preview forms for viewing reports onscreen. This is a visual component.

The VCL Palette's OCX Tab

The OCX tab contains four sample OCX controls (these are not part of the Delphi VCL, but samples with minimal documentation). This area is also where OCXs you add to Delphi are stored. Delphi VCLs are the better way to go (in my opinion) for your Delphi projects, but if you really need to use an OCX control, by all means do so. Remember however, that if you use an OCX in your Delphi application, you must include it with your application when you distribute it. These components are not covered in detail because they are samples. (See Figure 9.23.)

Figure 9.23.
The OCX tab.

The ChartFX OCX is used to add charting capability to a Delphi application. This is a visual control.

The VCFirstImpression OCX is used to add 3D graphing capability to a Delphi application. This is a visual control.

The VCFormulaOne OCX is used to add spreadsheets to a Delphi application. This is a visual control.

The VCSpeller OCX is used to add spell-check features to a Delphi application. This is a nonvisual control.

The GraphicsServer is another OCX used for generating graphs. This is a visual control.

The VCL Palette's Samples Tab

The Sample tab contains six sample VCLs, but like the OCX tab, they are provided only as samples with minimal documentation. Source code for them can be found in the \delphi\source\samples directory. (See Figure 9.24.)

Figure 9.24.
The Samples tab.

The IBEventAlerter is an event alert component.

The Gauge sample component is used to create a progress indicator that can appear as a bar, text, or pie-shaped gauge. This is a visual component.

The ColorGrid sample component is used to create a grid of colors from which the user can make a selection. This is a visual component.

The SpinButton sample component is used to create spin buttons. This is a visual component.

The SpinEdit sample component is used to create an edit box combined with the features of a spin control. This is a visual component.

The DirectoryOutline sample component is used to create a display of the selected drives directory structure. This is a visual component.

The Calendar sample component is used to display a calendar that can be used to display or retrieve date information in a standard, monthly calendar format. This is a visual component.

Finishing Up with the VCL

Now that we have all the tabs out of the way, let's build a small application to demonstrate some of the components not used in the VCLDEMO.DPR project. You'll tap into the Win95, Dialog, and System tabs. From the Win95 tab, you'll use the ProgressBar and TrackBar, as well as the TreeView and TabControl. From the Dialog tab, you will use the OpenDialog component. You'll also use the Timer component from the System tab along with a few other components you have already used on the Standard tab.

Now, build your final application for the day, test it out, and get finished up. This project is called MOREVCL.DPR and the unit is MORE.PAS. Follow Figure 9.25 as you build the form. On the left side of the form starting at the top and working down, drop the following components on the form. TabControl, Panel (place it on the TabControl), ProgressBar, and TrackBar. Drop a Timer and OpenDialog component on the form (anywhere, remember these are nonvisual). In the upper right corner, draw a Panel. Working down on the right side, drop a Label, TreeView, Label, Edit, and Button component.

To get this thing working, you need to set up a few properties and add some code. For the TabControl component, double-click on the `Tabs` property in the Object Inspector and bring up the `TStrings` editbox. Here, you can type the names of the tabs. Each tab name starts on a new line. Enter `Tab 1`, `Tab 2`, and `Tab 3`. For the panel you placed in the TabControl , edit its caption to read **`Tab = 1`**. Next set the `Max` properties for the ProgressBar and the TrackBar to `10`. Add the following code to the TrackBar OnChange event:

```
ProgressBar1.Position:=TrackBar1.Position;
```

Now double-click on the timer and add the following code to the `OnTimer` event:

```
Panel1.Caption:=TimeToStr(Time);
```

Change the label just above the TreeView to read **`TreeView`** and the label below the TreeView to read **`FileName Selected`**.

For the TreeView component's properties, double-click to the right of the `Items` Property where it says `TTreeNodes` and this brings up the TreeView Items Editor. Here you can add items and subitems to build your TreeView. Add an item called Level 1. Next add a subitem for Level 1 called Level 2 and then a subitem of Level 2 called Level 3.

Finally, add the following code to the OpenDialog button:

```
OpenDialog1.FileName := '*.*';
  if OpenDialog1.Execute then
    Edit1.Text := OpenDialog1.FileName;
end;
```

When you are finished, the code should look like the following listing:

```
unit more;

interface

uses
  Windows, Messages, SysUtils, Classes, Graphics, Controls, Forms, Dialogs,
  ExtCtrls, ComCtrls, StdCtrls, Buttons;

type
  TForm1 = class(TForm)
    Timer1: TTimer;
    Panel1: TPanel;
    OpenDialog1: TOpenDialog;
    TabControl1: TTabControl;
    TrackBar1: TTrackBar;
    ProgressBar1: TProgressBar;
    Panel2: TPanel;
    Button1: TButton;
    TreeView1: TTreeView;
    Label1: TLabel;
    Edit1: TEdit;
    Label2: TLabel;
    procedure Timer1Timer(Sender: TObject);
    procedure TrackBar1Change(Sender: TObject);
    procedure BitBtn1Click(Sender: TObject);
    procedure TabControl1Change(Sender: TObject);
    procedure Button1Click(Sender: TObject);
  private
    { Private declarations }
  public
    { Public declarations }
  end;

var
  Form1: TForm1;

implementation

{$R *.DFM}

procedure TForm1.Timer1Timer(Sender: TObject);
begin
     Panel1.Caption:=TimeToStr(Time);
end;
```

```
procedure TForm1.TrackBar1Change(Sender: TObject);
begin
     ProgressBar1.Position:=TrackBar1.Position;
end;

procedure TForm1.BitBtn1Click(Sender: TObject);
begin
     Application.Terminate;
end;

procedure TForm1.TabControl1Change(Sender: TObject);
begin
     If TabControl1.TabIndex=0 then Panel2.Caption:='Tab = 1';
     If TabControl1.TabIndex=1 then Panel2.Caption:='Tab = 2';
     If TabControl1.TabIndex=2 then Panel2.Caption:='Tab = 3';
end;

procedure TForm1.Button1Click(Sender: TObject);
begin
  OpenDialog1.FileName := '*.*';
  if OpenDialog1.Execute then
    Edit1.Text := OpenDialog1.FileName;
end;

end.
```

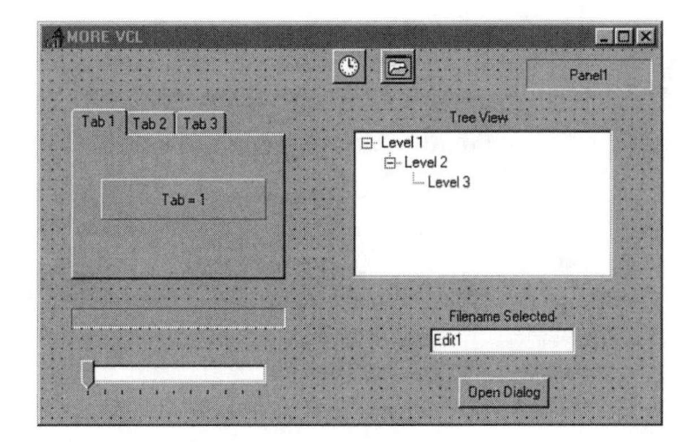

Figure 9.25.
The MOREVCL demo form.

Save the program and run it. If all went well, you should be able to move the TrackBar and watch the ProgressBar follow along. You should be able to select from the three tabs on the `TabControl` and watch the Panel caption change to reflect the tab number selected. You should also be able to open the TreeView down three levels by clicking on each item as it is displayed. Finally, you should be able to pull up the OpenDialog by pressing on the button and selecting a file. The file's name should display in the editbox. If you have any problems, go back and check the code and properties; if not, the application is complete.

While we have covered a lot of components, we have not covered all of them. As we discussed earlier in the chapter, there are far too many components as well as properties, methods, and so on to cover everything in detail. But you should be fairly comfortable with the VCL at this point and be able to use the online help to quickly find the information you need to be productive. You know where to look and what is available. You should now be ready to start building applications that actually do something.

Summary

In this chapter, we learned what the VCL is and what it is used for. You learned about properties, events, methods, and so on. You learned how to use the online help to quickly find valuable information for each of these topics. You briefly talked about every component in the VCL including the sample OCXs and sample VCLs. As you went, you built a "do-nothing application" to demonstrate as many of the commonly used components as possible from the Standard tab and Additional tab. You also built yet another do-nothing application using components from the Win95, Dialogs, and System tabs. In short, you had a pretty good work out! Take some time to finish up with Q&A and the Workshop, pat yourself on the back, and take a rest; you deserve it.

Q&A

Q What's the difference between the 32-bit Delphi VCL and the 16-bit version?

A Delphi 1.0 has 75 components and Delphi 2.0 has over 100. Delphi 2.0 supports OCXs instead of VBXs.

Q Can I recompile my 16-bit applications from Delphi 1.0 to 32-bit with Delphi 2.0?

A Yes. Because Delphi components are written in Delphi, you simply need to recompile your application with the new 32-bit version to convert from 16- to 32-bit.

Workshop

Quiz

1. What is the difference between a visual and nonvisual component?
2. What is a nested property?
3. What is a method?
4. What are events?
5. What component would you use if you wanted to accept input from a user in a particular format?
6. What component would you use if you wanted to run a procedure or task every five minutes?

Exercises

1. Go back and fill in code for Help and About Menu options in the VCLDEMO. *Hint*: You can use the `ShowMessage` procedure for this.
2. Write a Windows Alarm Clock application. Your application should be able to display the time, allow you to set an alarm and display a message when the selected time arrives. *Hint*: Use Timer and Panel as well as any other components that you like to complete the project.

Day 10

Introduction to Graphics

Sit through *Jurassic Park*, and you might believe that Steven Spielberg actually had a cast of dinosaurs on the payroll. How did they make those dinosaurs look so real? The answer is computer graphics. People seem to be amazed by graphics. Windows and Windows 95 have been very successful in part due to the graphical user interface they use. Graphics are an important subject even if you do not plan to write a game such as DOOM or work at Industrial Light & Magic on *Jurassic Park II.*

The Graphical Elements

Programmers should understand how to display images in applications and how to manipulate points, shapes, lines, and colors. Windows 95 and Windows NT offer some advanced features to enable high-performance graphics applications to use system resources effectively. Delphi offers a rich set of graphical components and methods that hide many of the operating system implementation details from the developer. This is extremely useful to a programmer who is new to graphics because he can concentrate on how graphics work rather than learn how to manipulate complex operating system calls.

Coordinates

NEW TERM You probably have a pretty good feel for what a coordinate is. All the visual components have a `Top` and `Left` property. The values stored in these properties determine where a component is placed on a form. Another way to say this is that the component is placed at coordinate X,Y where X is referring to the `Left` property and Y is referring to the `Top` property. The values for X and Y (or `Left` and `Top`) are stored in pixels. A *pixel* is the smallest region on a drawing surface that can be manipulated.

All Coordinates Are Relative

Consider the following situation. A man is flying in a plane 20,000 feet above the earth. You want to describe the height (or Y coordinate) of the man's nose. Do you measure from the bottom of the airplane or the earth below? There is no right answer; you can measure from either, as long as the person to whom you are giving this information is aware of the reference point for the measurement. If you do not specify that you are measuring from the ground, you could generate quite a bit of confusion when you state that the Y coordinate of the man's nose is at 20,005 feet. Delphi coordinates work the same way. You usually state component coordinates in relation to the form on which they reside and a form's coordinates in reference to the screen. You can also define an area of a form that takes on its own coordinate system. As a result, you report the coordinates of anything drawn on that portion of the form in relation to the specified region.

The Canvas

The `Canvas` property is the drawing area on forms and many other graphical components. The `Canvas` property enables Delphi code to manipulate the drawing area at runtime. One main feature of the `Canvas` property is that it consists of properties and methods that make using graphics in Delphi relatively simple. All of the overhead and bookkeeping that is done is hidden in the implementation of the `Canvas` object.

The next section covers the basic functions you need to perform graphical operations in Delphi by using the canvas.

Pixels and Points

Conceptually, all graphical operations boil down to setting the color of pixels on the drawing surface. In Delphi, you can manipulate pixels individually. In the ancient days of computers, a pixel was considered on or off, so it was either black or white (or green or amber). Luckily,

in today's world of computers pixels can take on a wide range of colors. Before I give an example of how to manipulate individual pixels in Delphi, you need some background in color theory.

The Colors of the Rainbow (Plus a Few Million More)

You might have heard the term 8-, 12-, 16-, or 24-bit graphics. What does this mean? The number of bits that a graphics environment supports indicates how many different colors can be displayed on the screen at any one time. In ancient days, when pixels were either on or off, it required *x* number of bits, which equals the number of pixels on the screen, to hold the screen image. If the screen had a resolution of 200 × 300 pixels, it took 60,000 bits (or 7,500 bytes) to store an image. With every bit per pixel you add, you double the number of unique colors that the screen can display; however, you also increase the amount of memory needed to store the screen image.

For example, if you represent your screen with two bits instead of one, it takes 200 × 300 × 2 bits to store the image—120,000 bits (or 15,000 bytes). However, you can use four simultaneous colors. How does this work? With two bits, there are four permutations of the bits being on and off (00, 01, 10, and 11). You can arbitrarily assign colors to each bit pattern (00=Black, 01=Blue, 10=Red, and 11=White). The numbers are amazing when you consider a modern display with a resolution of 720 × 1024 that supports 24 bits per pixel; this requires over 17 million bits. Such a system can display 16 million colors simultaneously (that is a lot!).

Palettes and "True" Color

The question now becomes, "Which bit patterns represent which colors?" Of the two methods for handling this, one approach is using a palette. Just as a painter's palette has a set of colors that the artist can use, a *palette* in graphics is the set of colors that can be used on the screen. The palette can have as many colors as there are unique bit patterns (which is equal to 2 to the *x* power where *x* is the number of bits the graphical environment supports). To use a new color that is not on the palette, you have to replace one of the colors on the palette. It is only possible to manipulate the palette under certain graphics modes in Delphi. The palette can only be manipulated in 256 (or 8-bit) color mode.

NEW TERM The other approach is using *true* color. True color is defined as the 16 million colors that can be created by adding together all the combinations of red, green, and blue. Computers that can use 24-bit color have the option of storing the value representing the color of each pixel instead of using a color lookup or palette setup. Each primary color can range in intensity from 0 to 255. The number of permutations for all possible combinations of red, green, and blue (where each color ranges in intensity between 0 and 255) is $256^3 + 256^2 + 256 = 16,843,008$. Using this approach, any color is possible by specifying a number between 0 (which indicates black) through 16,843,008 (which indicates white). Table 10.1 lists some other common colors in RGB (Red, Green, Blue).

Table 10.1. The RGB color values.

Color	Red Value	Green Value	Blue Value	RGB Value
Red	255	0	0	255
Green	0	255	0	65,280
Blue	0	0	255	16,711,280
Yellow	255	255	0	65,535
Purple	255	0	255	16,711,935

With 16 million possible colors this table could be huge, so instead of trying to fill it in, write a Delphi program to display RGB colors. If your environment does not support true 24-bit color, Delphi picks the color closest to the RGB value selected. Most PC graphics systems use a palette for their display mode.

In this example, provide three scrollbars to enable the user to change the amount of red, green, and blue in the color of the form's background. Use the `RGB` function to automatically build the requested color based on the amounts of red, green, and blue. Add one additional scrollbar to demonstrate grayscale intensity. Moving the final bar sets the red, green, and blue values to the same value (which is gray). Each scrollbar indicates an intensity. Listing 10.1 shows the sample code.

TYPE **Listing 10.1. main.pas.**

```
unit Main;

interface

uses
  SysUtils, WinTypes, WinProcs, Messages, Classes, Graphics, Controls,
  Forms, Dialogs, ExtCtrls, StdCtrls;

type
  TForm1 = class(TForm)
    ScrollBar1: TScrollBar;
    ScrollBar2: TScrollBar;
    ScrollBar3: TScrollBar;
    Red: TLabel;
    Green: TLabel;
    Blue: TLabel;
    Clr: TLabel;
    ScrollBar4: TScrollBar;
    Label1: TLabel;
    procedure ScrollBar1Change(Sender: TObject);
    Procedure UpdateAll;
    procedure ScrollBar4Change(Sender: TObject);
  private
```

```
    { Private declarations }
  public
    { Public declarations }
  end;

var
  Form1: TForm1;

implementation

{$R *.DFM}

Procedure TForm1.UpdateAll;
BEGIN
  Form1.Color := RGB(ScrollBar1.Position,
                     ScrollBar2.Position,
                     ScrollBar3.Position);
  Red.Caption := 'Red='+Inttostr(Scrollbar1.Position);
  Green.Caption := 'Green='+Inttostr(Scrollbar2.Position);
  Blue.Caption := 'Blue='+Inttostr(Scrollbar3.Position);
  Clr.Caption := 'RGB Color='+Inttostr(Form1.Color );
END;

procedure TForm1.ScrollBar1Change(Sender: TObject);
begin
  UpdateAll;
end;

procedure TForm1.ScrollBar4Change(Sender: TObject);
begin
  ScrollBar1.Position := ScrollBar4.Position;
  ScrollBar2.Position := ScrollBar4.Position;
  ScrollBar3.Position := ScrollBar4.Position;
end;

end.
```

10

ANALYSIS Three of the scrollbars represent the intensity of the colors red, green, and blue. As the user moves any of these scrollbars, the `TForm1.UpdateAll` event handler is called. The `UpdateAll` procedure sets the form's color equal to the color represented by combing the intensities shown on the scrollbars. If the user moves the "greyscale" scrollbar, each of the red, green, and blue scrollbars are set equal to the value of the greyscale scrollbar. With an equal mix of red, green, and blue, you will always build a shade of grey. This application is shown in Figure 10.1.

In addition to the capability to assign an RGB value to a color property, Delphi can also use predefined colors. The predefined colors are either a constant color used frequently, such as `clBlue`, or a color indicating a color in the environment, such as `clBackground`, which indicates the background color of the desktop.

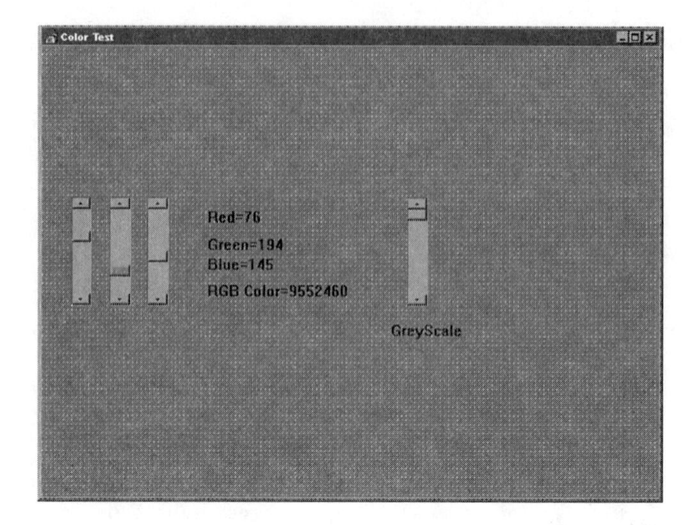

Figure 10.1.
RGB color application.

Back to Pixels

Now that you see how colors work, jump back to the basic unit of graphics measurement, the pixel, and examine how pixels are set and how you can obtain the color of a pixel. To access the pixels on a form, use the form's `Canvas` property and the `Pixels` property of the canvas. The `Pixels` property is a two-dimensional array corresponding to the colors in the canvas. `Canvas.Pixels[10,20]` corresponds to the color of the pixel that is 10 pixels to the right and 20 pixels down. Treat the pixel array as any other property; to change the color of a pixel, assign a new value. To determine what color a pixel is, read the value.

Using Pixels

In the following example, we use the `Pixels` property to draw a sine wave in the main form. The only component on the form is a button that draws the sine wave when it is clicked. We use the form's `Width` and `Height` parameters to scale the sine wave to fit into 70 percent of the form's height and all of the form's width. The code that produces the sine wave is shown in Listing 10.2. Figure 10.2 shows the sine program running.

TYPE **Listing 10.2. main.pas.**

```
unit Main;

interface

uses
  SysUtils, WinTypes, WinProcs, Messages, Classes, Graphics, Controls,
  Forms, Dialogs, StdCtrls;
type
  TForm1 = class(TForm)
```

```
    Button1: TButton;
    procedure Button1Click(Sender: TObject);
  private
    { Private declarations }
  public
    { Public declarations }
  end;

var
  Form1: TForm1;

implementation

{$R *.DFM}

procedure TForm1.Button1Click(Sender: TObject);
const
  PI = 3.14159;
var
  X  : real;
  Y  : real;
  PX :longint;
  PY :longint;
  HalfHeight : longint;
begin
{ Determine Halfway down the form}
HalfHeight := Form1.Height div 2;
for PX:=0 to Form1.Width do
  BEGIN
    {Scale X interms of 2 PI to do 1 full sine wave}
    X := PX * (2*PI/Form1.Width);
    Y := SIN(X);
    PY := trunc(0.7 * Y * HalfHeight) + HalfHeight;
    {Set pixel to black (0 intensity of RGB)}
    Canvas.Pixels[PX,PY] := 0;
  END;
end;
end.
```

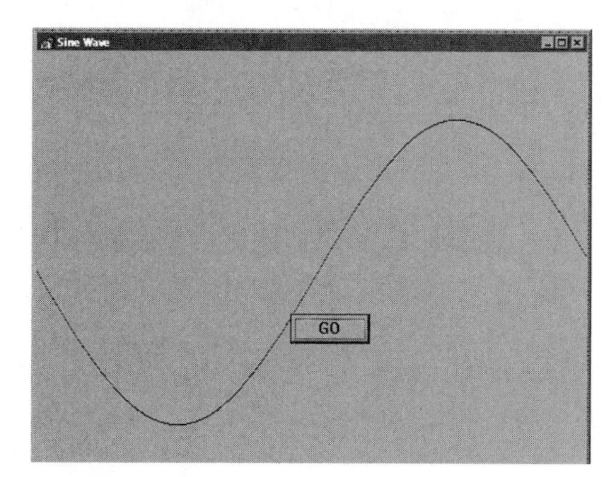

Figure 10.2.
Sine wave program using the `Pixels` property.

The Pen

Every canvas has an imaginary pen it uses to draw lines and shapes. Think of the pen on the canvas as a real pen on a piece of paper. Of the two ways to move the pen, one method is to touch the paper and leave a mark. The second method is to lift the pen above the paper so that moving it does not leave a mark. In addition to its different actions, the pen also has attributes associated with it. For example, it has a distinct color and width. Furthermore, the pen has methods that enable it to draw shapes such as a rectangle. To move the pen without actually drawing, you use the `MoveTo` method. The following line of code moves the pen to the coordinates 23,56.

```
Form1.Canvas.MoveTo(23,56);
```

Drawing Lines

To draw a straight line from the pen's current position to another position, you use the `LineTo` method. `LineTo` simply needs the coordinates of the pen's destination, and it draws a straight line from the current position to the new position.

WARNING

> Of course, you could write a function to draw a line using the `Pixels` property; however, this would have a severe impact on performance. Although it is possible, accessing the `Pixels` property directly involves a great deal of overhead.
>
> The two main reasons not to use the `Pixels` property concern the best use of your resources. First, most drawing functions have been implemented in methods. The developer does not need to waste his time writing an algorithm to draw a line, circle, or shape. The second reason is performance. Using methods to draw shapes, lines, and pictures is much quicker then writing algorithms that interface to the `Pixels` property.

You can compare the two line-drawing methods yourself. Write a simple program to fill a box with a color by looping through each pixel and setting its color using the `Pixels` property. Next, accomplish the same feat by iterating through every line in the box but calling the canvas methods `LineTo` and `MoveTo`. Listing 10.3 shows these procedures.

TYPE **Listing 10.3. Timing the `Pixels` property and `LineTo` method.**

```
procedure TForm1.DrPixelsClick(Sender: TObject);
var
 X: integer;
 Y: integer;
 Start: real;
 Finish : real;
begin
  Start := time;
  For X := 0 to Form1.Width do
   For Y := 0 to Form1.Height do
    Canvas.Pixels[X,Y]:= 255;
  Finish := time - Start;
  Form1.Caption := floattostr(Finish);
end;

procedure TForm1.DrLinesClick(Sender: TObject);

var
 X: integer;
 Start: real;
 Finish : real;

begin
  Start := time;
  For X := 0 to Form1.Width do
   begin
    Canvas.MoveTo(X,0);
    Canvas.LineTo(X,Form1.Height);
   end;
  Finish := time - Start;
  Form1.Caption := floattostr(Finish);
end;
```


ANALYSIS What were the results? On my computer, it took 7.35 seconds to fill the box using the `Pixels` property and 0.06 seconds using the `LineTo` and `MoveTo` methods, which is 115 times faster. (There is actually a quicker way to fill a box by using the `FillRect` method which is covered later in the chapter.)

Look at the simple procedure in Listing 10.4 that uses the `LineTo` property to draw a neat pattern. This program is shown in Figure 10.3.

TYPE **Listing 10.4. An interesting line pattern.**

```
procedure TForm1.Button1Click(Sender: TObject);
const
  PI = 3.14159;
var
```

continues

Listing 10.4. continued

```
  X  : real;
  Y  : real;
  PX :longint;
  PY :longint;
  Offset : longint;
  HalfHeight : longint;
begin
{ Determine the coordinate Halfway down the form}
HalfHeight := Form1.Height div 2;
Offset := 0;
For OffSet := -10 to 10 do
BEGIN
     PX := 0;
     While PX < Form1.Width  do
       BEGIN
           {Scale X interms of 2 PI to do 1 full sine wave}
           X := PX * (2*PI/Form1.Width);
           Y := SIN(X);
           PY := trunc(0.7 * Y * HalfHeight)
            + HalfHeight + (Offset *10);
           IF (PX = 0) Then
             canvas.MoveTo(PX,PY);
           canvas.LineTO(PX,PY);
           PY := trunc(0.7 * Y * HalfHeight) +
              HalfHeight + ((Offset-1) *10);
           canvas.LineTO(PX,PY);
           PX := PX +15;
       END;
END;
end;
```

ANALYSIS The program is almost identical to the previous sine wave program except that now we are providing gaps between the points and connecting them with lines. On the first iteration (when PX=0) we use the `MoveTo` method to go to the first point. After moving to the first point, we only need to use `LineTo` to move to all subsequent points.

Polygons

In addition to methods for drawing straight lines, the canvas also has methods for drawing shapes. You draw some shapes, such as a rectangle, using the shape's own method, but you draw others using a series of points. These shapes are known as polygons. Delphi has separate methods to draw filled-in shapes; for now, I discuss only outlined polygons until I cover how to fill graphical objects (covered later in this chapter). Some polygons you recognize include triangles, octagons (like a stop sign), or trapezoids. See Figure 10.4, which shows some common polygons.

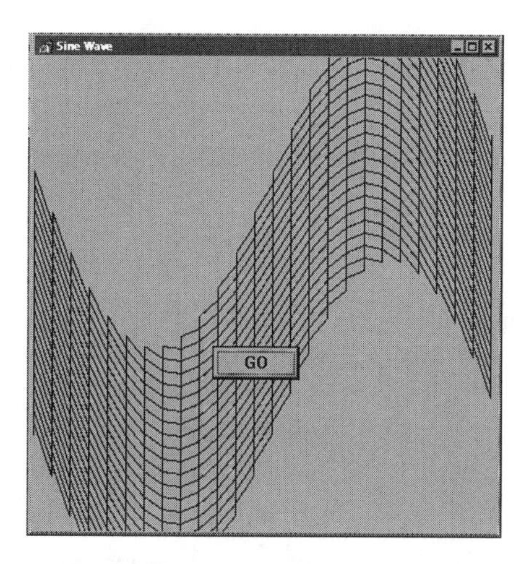

Figure 10.3.
Neat pattern drawn using `LineTo` *and* `MoveTo`.

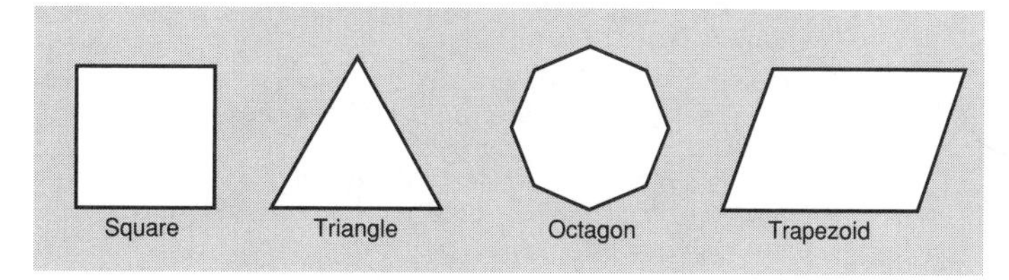

Figure 10.4.
Some common polygons.

To draw a polygon, you pass the `PolyLine` function a series of points, which the function then connects with lines (just like connect-the-dots).

You simply pass the `PolyLine` function an array of points; this is a new concept. Up until now, you did everything with coordinates; you passed the `LineTo` function an X and Y value.

Delphi also has a type `TPoint`, which encapsulates the X and Y value into a single record called a *point*. The easiest way to create a point is using the `Point` function. `Point` simply takes an X and Y value and returns a `TPoint` record. Note that the first and last points are not automatically connected, so the last point must be the same as the first point to form a complete polygon. For example, the following call to `PolyLine` draws a triangle:

```
Form1.Canvas.PolyLine([Point(10,10),Point(100,100),Point(50,75),Point(10,10)]);
```

You can expand on this to create a procedure that draws a symmetric polygon with an arbitrary number of sides, which the user enters. If the user enters `8`, the procedure draws an octagon; entering `6` draws a six-sided polygon. To do this, use some basic geometric principles to put the vertices on a circle. Listing 10.5 shows the source code.

TYPE

Listing 10.5. An arbitrary-sided polygon.

```
procedure TForm1.DrawPolyClick(Sender: TObject);

Const
 PI = 3.14159;

var
  Sides : integer;
  Count : integer;
  PolyArray : Array[0..15] of TPoint;

begin
    Sides := strtoint(NumSides.Text);
    For Count := 0 to Sides do
    BEGIN
     {Using Points From A circle, choose Vertices for points}
     PolyArray[Count] :=
       Point(TRUNC(SIN((2*PI)*COUNT/Sides)* 30)+(Form1.Width div 2),
             TRUNC(COS((2*PI)*COUNT/Sides)* 30)+(Form1.Height div 2));
    END;
     {Hook Last point back to the first point and set all }
     {remaining points equal to the first point           }
    For Count := Sides+1 to 15 do
     PolyArray[Count] := PolyArray[0];
    {Draw the Polygon}
    Form1.Canvas.PolyLine(PolyArray);

end; {Procedure}
```

ANALYSIS This procedure calculates evenly spaced points on a circle depending on how many sides are selected. The points are connected by using the `PolyLine` method on the canvas. To close the polygon simply set the unused points equal to the starting point. Figure 10.5 shows the polygon application executing.

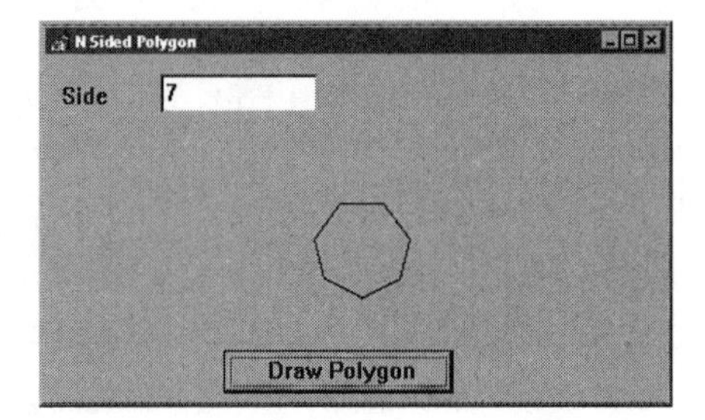

Figure 10.5.
Arbitrary-sided polygon program.

Modify the Pen Attributes

All of the shapes that you have drawn to this point used the default pen. It is possible to change the color, width, and style of the pen. In Delphi, you access the pen through the canvas, which has a `Pen` property. The main properties used with the pen are `Color`, `Width`, `Style`, and `Mode`.

Color

You can set the pen's color using the same methods you used to set the form's color. For example, to set the color of the pen to blue, you could execute the following:

```
Form1.Canvas.Pen.Color := clBlue;
```

You could also use the following line:

```
Form1.Canvas.Pen.Color := RGB(0,0,255);
```

To show all of the possible intensities of gray that your computer can show, you could use the following procedure:

```
procedure TForm1.DrawGreyClick(Sender: TObject);

var
  Count : Integer;
begin
  For Count := 0 to 255 do
  BEGIN
   Form1.Canvas.Pen.Color := RGB(Count,Count,Count);
   Form1.Canvas.MoveTo(Count,0);
   Form1.Canvas.LineTo(Count,100);
  end;
end;
```


`Width` and `Style`

The `Width` property sets the width of the pen in pixels. The `Style` property enables the pen to draw various styles such as dashed or dotted lines. Valid values for the `Style` property are `psSolid`, `psDash`, `psDot`, `psDashDot`, `psDashDotDot`, `psClear`, and `psInsideFrame`. If you wanted your pen to be red, three pixels wide, and dotted, you would execute the following:

```
Form1.Canvas.Pen.Color := clRed;
Form1.Canvas.Pen.Width := 3;
Form1.Canvas.Pen.Style := psDot;
```

`Mode`

Another pen property is `Mode`, which enables the pen to interact with its environment. For example, indicating a mode of `pmNot` causes the pen to draw the inverse color of the background (therefore the inverse of each bit). The pen uses the mode `pmCopy` by default, which causes the pen to use the current color. You can determine the color of the pen by checking the `color` property. One example of using the `Mode` property is performing simple animation. You create animation by slightly redrawing a picture and showing the changes in a sequence. It appears to the human brain that the object is moving or changing. For simple animation, you can use the `pmXor` or `pmNotXor` mode to draw an object and then remove it without changing the background. Remember that each pixel stores a color as a sequence of bits. Changing a pixel by `XOR`ing the current pixel with a color changes the color. Doing this again sets the pixel back. The following steps illustrate this process:

1. The background pixel has a value of 0110011.
2. You XOR it with the value 1111000.
3. The new pixel has a value of 1001011.

When you want to erase the pixel and set the background back, you simply perform the same steps again.

1. The pixel currently has a value of 1001011.
2. You XOR it with the value 1111000.
3. As a result, you get 0110011 (wow! your original color).

The advantage of using this process is that you do not need to store the background information; it is done automatically. The disadvantage is that you can't get exactly the picture you want because you are embedding information into your pixel's color. In the procedure in Listing 10.6, you use this technique to animate a triangle flying across a form. Note that there is also a red box on the form. The blue triangle will fly through the box but not disturb the box.

TYPE Listing 10.6. Simple animation using the Mode property.

```
procedure TForm1.SimpleAnimationClick(Sender: TObject);

var
   Count : Integer;
   Pause : real ;
begin
{ Draw a Box }
Form1.Canvas.Pen.mode := pmCopy;
Form1.Canvas.Pen.Color := clRed;
Form1.Canvas.PolyLine([point(50,10),
                        point(100,10),
                        point(100,200),
                        point(50,200),
                        point(50,10)]);
{Set the Pen}
Form1.Canvas.Pen.Color := clBlue;
Form1.Canvas.Pen.mode := pmNotXor;
For Count := 0 to (Form1.Width div 5) do
BEGIN
 {Draw the Triangle}
 Form1.Canvas.PolyLine([point(Count*5,100),
                        point(Count*5+10,100),
                        point(Count*5+5,110),
                        point(Count*5,100)]);
 Pause := Time;
 while (Time-Pause) < 1e-12 do; {nothing}
 {Erase The Triangle}
 Form1.Canvas.PolyLine([point(Count*5,100),
                        point(Count*5+10,100),
```

```
                            point(Count*5+5,110),
                            point(Count*5,100)]);
end;  {end While}
end;  {end Procedure}
```

Analysis The program first draws a red box by setting the pen mode to `pmCopy` and the color to `clRed`. Next, the program moves a triangle across the screen by using the `pmNotXor` pen mode. It is necessary to draw the triangle twice in each position. The first time the triangle is drawn, the second time the triangle is removed.

The Brush and Filled Objects

Rather than use only the outlines, you can fill some of the graphics objects that Delphi provides. The `Brush` property determines how an object is filled. The three main properties that affect the brush are `Color`, `Style`, and `Bitmap`. There are two ways to use the brush—either with the `Color` and `Style` properties or with the `Bitmap` property.

When you use the `Color` and `Style` properties, the overall color of the fill comes from the value of `Color` property. The `Style` property defines the style of the fill. In the same way you use the `PolyLine` method for outlined (unfilled) objects, you use the `Polygon` method to draw filled polygons. The sample program shows all the available styles in eight different triangles. Listing 10.7 shows the source code for the procedures used to draw the triangles. The triangles are displayed in Figure 10.6.

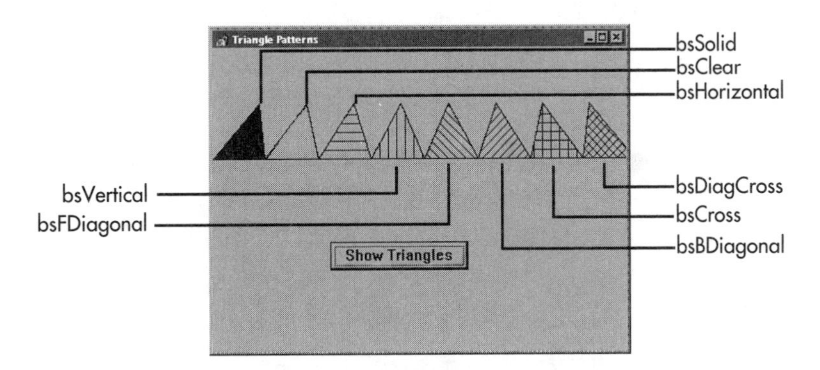

Figure 10.6.
Triangles filled with different styles.

Type

Listing 10.7. Drawing triangles filled with different patterns.

```
procedure Triangle(Iteration : Integer);
BEGIN
Form1.Canvas.Brush.Color := clBlue;
```

continues

Listing 10.7. continued

```
Form1.Canvas.Polygon([Point(TRUNC((Iteration/9)*Form1.Width),50),
                      Point(TRUNC((Iteration/8)*Form1.Width),100),
                      Point(TRUNC(((Iteration-1)/8)*Form1.Width),100),
                      Point(TRUNC((Iteration/9)*Form1.Width),50)]);
END;

procedure TForm1.ShowTrianglesClick(Sender: TObject);
begin
  Form1.Canvas.Brush.Style := bsSolid;
  Triangle(1);
  Form1.Canvas.Brush.Style := bsClear;
  Triangle(2);
  Form1.Canvas.Brush.Style := bsHorizontal;
  Triangle(3);
  Form1.Canvas.Brush.Style := bsVertical;
  Triangle(4);
  Form1.Canvas.Brush.Style := bsFDiagonal;
  Triangle(5);
  Form1.Canvas.Brush.Style := bsBDiagonal;
  Triangle(6);
  Form1.Canvas.Brush.Style := bsCross;
  Triangle(7);
  Form1.Canvas.Brush.Style := bsDiagCross;
  Triangle(8);
end;
```

ANALYSIS You create a generic procedure to create triangles in one of eight regions of the screen. The `ShowTrianglesClick` procedure sets the brush to various settings and calls the `triangle` procedure passing the position that the triangle should be drawn in.

In addition to using the predefined styles and colors for a brush, you can also use a bitmap to define the pattern that a brush uses to fill objects.

NEW TERM A brush bitmap is an 8-pixel-by-8-pixel bitmap that defines the pattern with which all objects are filled.

To use a bitmap for a brush, you must first create a bitmap, assign it, and then free it when you're done. Creating and manipulating bitmaps are discussed later in this chapter.

Drawing Filled Rectangles

Just as a TPoint type specifies a set of coordinates in Delphi, a TRect data type specifies a rectangular part of a form or graphical area. You specify a rectangular region by giving coordinates for the top-left and bottom-right corners. You use the function `Rect` to create a TRect type from coordinates. Many of the functions that deal with rectangular regions use TRect types as parameters. For example, you use the `FillRect` method to draw a filled rectangle. The following code line is an example of the `FillRect` method. Note that you need to use the `Rect` function to specify the coordinates.

```
Form1.Canvas.FillRect(Rect(20,20,100,100));
```

In addition to the `FillRect` procedure, the `Rectangle` procedure draws a rectangle using the attributes from the current brush for the fill and the attributes from the current pen for the outline. Although it is inconsistent in the way that parameters are passed, the `Rectangle` procedure takes all four points as parameters as opposed to a TRect type. The following code line is an example of the `Rectangle` procedure.

```
Form1.Canvas.Rectangle(20,20,100,100);
```

Drawing Circles, Curves, and Ellipses

Everything that you have drawn so far has used either single points or a combination of straight lines. The world would be a pretty dull place without curves. Delphi offers a number of methods for drawing circles, ellipses, arcs, and slices. A circle is simply an ellipse that has a constant radius. To draw an ellipse in Delphi, you supply the rectangular region of the drawing surface (or canvas) within which the ellipse is contained. To draw a perfect circle, you execute the following:


```
Form1.Canvas.Ellipse(100,100,200,200);
```

To draw an ellipse that has a width greater than its height, you execute the following:

```
Form1.Canvas.Ellipse(100,100,300,200);
```

Drawing part of an ellipse is slightly more complex. The method takes eight parameters. The first four parameters are exactly like the parameters for drawing a complete ellipse. The final two parameters are points that indicate the percentage of the ellipse that should show. For example, the following line draws the quarter of a circle shown in Figure 10.7.

```
Form1.Canvas.Pie(100,100,200,200,100,100,100,200);
```

Figure 10.7.
Quarter circle using the pie method.

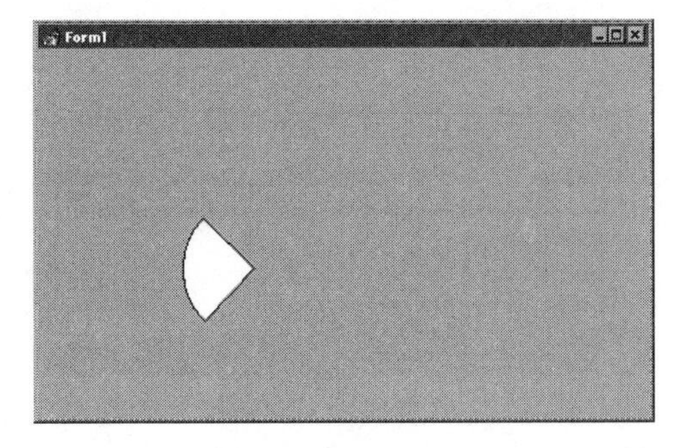

An arc is exactly like a pie slice except that it is not filled. The following code shows only an arc for the same part of a circle drawn by the preceding pie method.

```
Form1.Canvas.Arc(100,100,200,200,100,100,100,200);
```

OnPaint...Unfortunately, Things Change!

In the days of old, a graphics program used the entire screen and assumed that any change on the screen was caused by the program's own action. In a Windows 95 or Windows NT environment, many applications can run simultaneously on a display. What happens when a window is covered by another window or resized? One option that the operating system has is to keep a copy of what the screen looked like in memory and perform in memory any changes to the screen that are out of view. This method requires a lot of overhead, especially if there are many applications running. Instead, the operating system notifies the application that something has changed and that it is the application's job to fix it. Whenever an update is needed, an OnPaint event occurs.

NEW TERM Delphi redraws only the part of a canvas that has been corrupted, which is known as *invalidation.* When part of a form is invalid, Delphi calls the procedure specified in the OnPaint event handler to redraw the invalidated part of the form.

The example in Listing 10.8 places code that draws a quarter circle on the form in the OnPaint event handler. It also rigs up an edit box to display the number of times that the form has been repainted. When you execute this program, you see from the updated iteration every time the `OnPaint` handler is called.

TYPE **Listing 10.8. Demonstration of OnPaint event handler.**

```
unit Main;
{Used to illustrate the OnPaint Event }
{the Iteration counter is incremented }
{every time the form is repainted, and}
{an edit box is updated to show the  }
{iteration                            }

interface

uses
  SysUtils, WinTypes, WinProcs, Messages, Classes, Graphics, Controls,
  Forms, Dialogs, StdCtrls;

type
  TForm1 = class(TForm)
    Edit1: TEdit;
    procedure FormPaint(Sender: TObject);
    procedure FormCreate(Sender: TObject);
  private
    { Private declarations }
  public
    { Public declarations }
  end;

var
```

```
  Form1: TForm1;
  Iteration : Integer;  {Incremented every time the form is repainted }

implementation

{$R *.DFM}

procedure TForm1.FormPaint(Sender: TObject);
begin
  {Increase Iteration}
  Iteration := Iteration + 1;
  {Draw Something}
  Form1.Canvas.Pie(100,100,200,200,100,100,100,200);
  {Update the TextEdit box}
  Form1.Edit1.Text := inttostr(Iteration);
end;

procedure TForm1.FormCreate(Sender: TObject);
begin
  {On startup initialize Iteration}
  Iteration := 0;
end;

end.
```


The TPaintBox Component

All drawing that you have performed to this point has been on the canvas of a form. It is often useful to confine a graphic to a rectangular region of a form. Delphi offers a component for doing this, the TPaintBox component. Try the following exercise:

1. Drop a TPaintBox component on a form.
2. Drop a `TButton` on a form.
3. Add the following for the OnClick event of the button:

   ```
   PaintBox1.canvas.Ellipse(0,0,2*PaintBox1.Width,2*PaintBox1.Height);
   ```

4. Compile and run the application.

What happened? You asked for an ellipse, but Delphi drew only an arc. This happened because the ellipse is bigger then the TPaintBox component, which is the only area that Delphi can draw in. The rest of the ellipse was *clipped.* Imagine the extra complexity you would need to add to an application to ensure that nothing is drawn outside of a region. The TPaintBox handles this for you. The coordinates in a TPaintBox are relative to the TPaintBox, not the form. This also means that as long as an OnPaint event handler is responsible for drawing the TPaintBox, you can move the image on the form by changing the `Top` and `Left` properties of the TPaintBox. The TPaintBox uses the Align property to keep the image at the top, left, bottom, or right of the form. It also forces the TPaintBox to fill the client area of the form.

The TShape Component: Losing Some Complexity

What if you want to manipulate simple shapes but don't want to deal with events to handle repainting; are there any controls that can make this easier? Of course! The TShape component encapsulates many of the drawing methods in its properties and methods. The TShape component has properties to represent its brush, pen, and shape. The shapes that the component can become include a circle, ellipse, rectangle, rounded rectangle, square, or rounded square. The real advantage to using TShape is that all the code to draw and repaint the object is hidden. The sample program in Listing 10.9 uses a timer, a TShape component, and two simple procedures to animate a bouncing ball. The TShape component handles all the painting and drawing routines. You can set all the other properties at runtime. To get the circle to move, you simply change the coordinates of the component. To implement this using methods, you would need to erase the previous circle every time it moves and also keep track of the background.

TYPE

Listing 10.9. Animate a bouncing ball using the TShape component.

```
unit Main;
{Bouncing Ball:                                      }
{Uses a Timer and TShape to illustrate a bouncing ball }

interface

uses
  SysUtils, WinTypes, WinProcs, Messages, Classes, Graphics, Controls,
  Forms, Dialogs, StdCtrls, ExtCtrls;

type
  TForm1 = class(TForm)
    Shape1: TShape;
    Timer1: TTimer;
    procedure Timer1Timer(Sender: TObject);
    procedure FormCreate(Sender: TObject);
  private
    { Private declarations }
  public
    { Public declarations }
  end;

var
  Form1: TForm1;
  XPos : Integer;
  XMult: Integer;
implementation

{$R *.DFM}

procedure TForm1.Timer1Timer(Sender: TObject);
begin
```

```
  if XPos > Form1.Width-(2*Shape1.Width) then XMult := -1;
  if XPos < 1 THEN XMult := 1;
  XPos := XPos + (XMult * 10);
  Shape1.Left := XPos;
end;

procedure TForm1.FormCreate(Sender: TObject);
begin
   XPos  := 0;
   XMult := 1;
end;

end.
```

When the OnTimer event handler is called, the program determines the new coordinates for XPos. If it is necessary for the ball to change direction, then the value of XMult is set to 1 if its current value is -1 and -1 if its current value is 1.

Shapes Are Okay, but How Do I Put Up a Picture?

Using the graphical methods and components works well for many types of applications, but sometimes a developer wants to add a predrawn graphic image or picture to an application. This would be cumbersome if the only method available was using the graphical components. For example, the Bonzo Soda Pop Company wants to have its founder's picture on every application the company uses. Doing this with the graphical methods would be an eternal nightmare. Instead, you simply take a photo of Frank Bonzo and scan it into the computer using a digital scanner. The scanning program stores the picture in a special format that Delphi can understand and simply displays the picture. Another time that it does not make sense to use the graphical methods is if an artist designs an image in a drawing program and wants to incorporate it into a Delphi application.

Delphi provides native support for working with three types of images: bitmaps, icons, and metafiles. All three types of files store images; the difference is how the images are stored internally to the file and what sorts of tools can manipulate and access the images. When you calculated the memory requirements to store an image on the screen, you had to multiply the color depth (in bits) by the resolution. You can think of a bitmap as a snapshot of a piece of the screen and all of its associated information. This is true in the sense that a bitmap only knows the colors of every pixel in the image but not what the image represents. For example, if you take a bitmap of a red square on a blue background, the only information in the bitmap is that all the pixels are blue except for the pixels in the square with vertices (10,10) in the upper-left corner and (100,100) in the lower-right corner, which are red.

Windows, Windows NT, and Windows 95 have standard file formats for what a bitmap file should look like. Bitmaps on Windows, Windows NT, and Windows 95 are device-independent bitmaps, which means that the information is stored in such a way that any computer can display the picture in the resolution and number of colors that it is configured for. This does not mean that the image looks the same on every computer! It obviously looks better on a screen with 1024-by-720 resolution and 24-bit color than on a standard VGA screen. The important thing is that users of both computers can view the image. It would definitely be a drag if every Windows 95 programmer had to understand what each byte in the .bmp file represented.

Luckily, the details of the bitmap file format are encapsulated in the operating system and Delphi. The easiest way to display a bitmap in Delphi is to use the TImage component. The TImage component can display different types of graphical images. The TImage component can load a bitmap from a file and then contain the bitmap in the application. This enables you to ship the application without including the bitmap with the software as a separate file. Icons are simply very small bitmaps. Icons are placed in a separate category because they are generally used to display a shortcut to an application or a minimized view of some information. Internally, icons are stored in a fashion similar to that of bitmaps. Metafiles, on the other hand, are stored completely differently. A metafile stores information about how a picture was created rather than the series of bits that form the picture. For example, a metafile might contain the following encoded information:

```
BACKGROUND WHITE
RED SQUARE FROM (02,99)-(222,999) FILL BITTPATERN 0x45ef333
        BLUE CIRCLE RADIUS 100 COORD (45,33) FILL NONE
```

Windows can then analyze, display, and manipulate this information. Think of a metafile as a set of instructions to draw a picture. This example gives a command to draw a square and then a circle. If this same picture were described as a bitmap, each pixel would be represented.

When should an application use a bitmap, and when should an application use a metafile? Many drawing programs use metafiles because a person can edit the image more easily. For example, to change the radius of the circle in the previous example, an application simply needs to change the data that represents the radius. A bitmap has no information to indicate that a circle even exists! A bitmap is well suited for realistic images or any images that you don't need to change. For example, it is very difficult to scan a photograph with a scanner and store the image as a meaningful metafile. In this case, a bitmap would be a better choice because it is more compact.

To display an image using the TImage component, place a TImage on a form and double-click the `Picture` property. This brings up a dialog box that enables you to view, load, and save a bitmap into the image. Click on Load and choose any valid .bmp or .wmf file. The bitmap or metafile that you choose is displayed in the TImage component.

Stretching and Sizing Images

By default, an image is displayed at its native resolution, and you see only the part of the image that is displayed within the TImage component. Two key properties affect the way that an image appears in a TImage component. The `Autosize` property causes the size of the image contained in the component to match the size of the component. Setting the `Stretch` property to `True` forces the image to fit into the dimensions of the TImage component. If you set the `Stretch` and `Autosize` properties to `False`, the image is centered in the component by default. To force the image to be displayed with the top-left corner in the component, set the `Center` property to `False`.

Loading an Image from a File at Runtime

You have examined how to use the TImage component to display a bitmap, metafile, or icon by setting the image at design time. You can also load a bitmap from a file at runtime with the `LoadFromFile` method. The following line loads the Windows 95 setup bitmap into your image component.

```
Image1.Picture.LoadFromFile('C:\WIN95\SETUP.BMP');
```

Note that the method operates on the `Picture` property of the image component and not the component itself. The image uses most of its properties to describe how the image interacts with the application. The `Picture` property holds information about the image itself so you need to load the image into the `Picture` property.

Getting Fancy: Creating Your Own Bitmap!

Earlier in this chapter, I describe how to draw on a form's canvas and a paintbox's canvas. Can you also draw on a bitmap's canvas? The answer is yes. In Delphi, a `TBitmap` object has a canvas that you can manipulate like a canvas in a TPaintbox or on a TForm. One of the differences is that the bitmap is stored in memory as an image. The canvases on a form and paintbox are not. When drawing on a bitmap, you don't have to worry about `OnPaint` events to redraw the scene when it is invalidated. You can simply reload the image from memory—but only when the bitmap is stored in a TImage component. A disadvantage of using a bitmap is that it requires more system resources because the image is stored in memory. In Delphi, a bitmap by itself has limitations because it is difficult to display; however, when you use a bitmap in conjunction with an image component to display the bitmap, everything works quite well.

Creating a Bitmap from Scratch

To create a new bitmap, you need to declare a variable of type `TBitmap` and then use the `Create` method as a constructor to allocate space for the bitmap.

```
Var
   MyBitmap : TBitmap;

BEGIN
    MyBitmap := TBitmap.Create;
```

At this point, the bitmap is created but empty. The next step is to define the dimensions for the bitmap. Use the `Height` and `Width` properties.

```
   MyBitmap.Height := 100;
   MyBitmap.Width  := 200;
```

Before you draw the bitmap, add some graphics to it—in this case, a diagonal line.

```
  MyBitmap.Canvas.MoveTo(200,100);

  MyBitmap.Canvas.LineTo(0,0);
```

To display a bitmap, you can use the `Draw` method. The `Draw` method copies a bitmap onto a canvas. All other manipulation of the bitmap is done in memory. To draw the bitmap on Form1 at coordinates 100,100, use the following line:

```
   Form1.Canvas.Draw(100,100,MyBitmap);
```

When you are through with the bitmap, you should free its system resources using the `Free` method.

```
  MyBitmap.Free;
```

The other way that you could display the bitmap is setting an image component's picture to the bitmap that you created.

```
   Image1.Picture.Graphic := MyBitmap;
```

One advantage of using the image component is that you don't have to worry about the image becoming invalidated because the component takes care of redrawing the image if it becomes invalid. Also, you don't need to free the bitmap because the image does that when it is destroyed.

Saving a Bitmap to a File

In addition to loading and manipulating bitmaps, you can also save a bitmap back to a file. To save the bitmap, simply use the `SaveToFile` method.

```
MyBitmap.SaveToFile('C:\CoolStuff\MyBitmap.BMP');
```

Putting Bitmaps to Work with a Sample Program

In this example, you use Delphi's graphics functions to create a program to manipulate bitmaps. A user loads a bitmap into the program, clicks the Mixup Bitmap button, and creates a new bitmap, which is built from random pieces of the original. Figure 10.8 shows the mixup program in action.

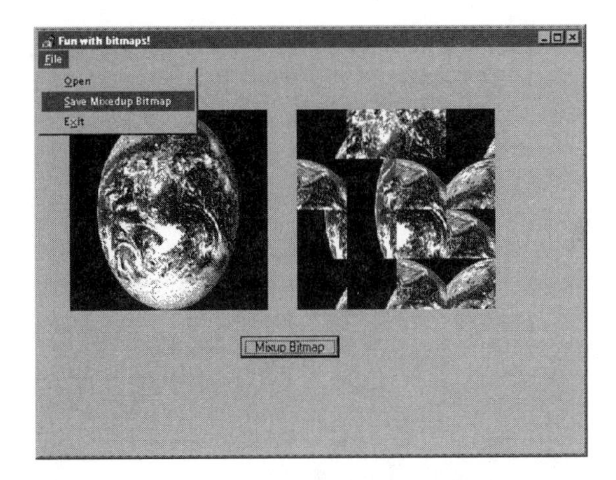

Figure 10.8.
Mixup sample program.

Take a look at how this program works. First, you use the following components:

- Two image components to display the original image and the mixed-up image
- A OpenDialog component to access the common open dialog box
- A SaveDialog component to access the common save dialog box
- A menu and standard button to trigger events

Figure 10.9 shows the component layout.

When a user selects the File | Open option from the menu, the program displays the common open dialog box. When the user chooses OK, the program loads the bitmap file that the user selected into the `Orig` image component with the following code:

```
Orig.Picture.LoadFromFile(OpenDialog1.FileName);
```

Next, the user clicks the Mixup Bitmap button. This invokes the `MixupBitmapClick` procedure to scramble the bitmap. The steps to build a new bitmap and pull in random pieces from the original are as follows:

1. Build a new bitmap by executing the `Create` method on a bitmap object.

   ```
   NewBitmap := TBitmap.Create;
   ```

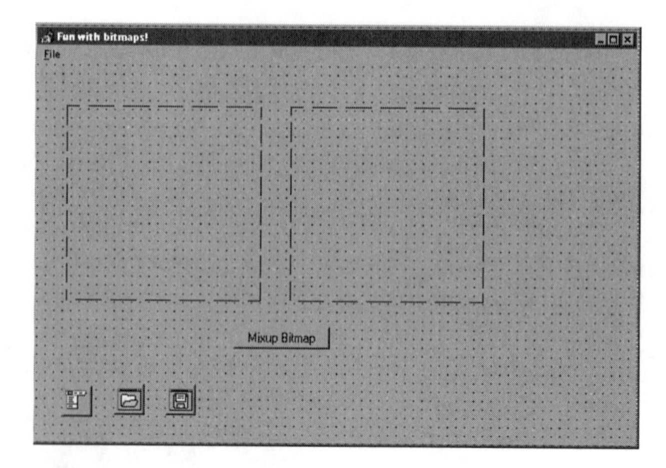

Figure 10.9.
Mixup component layout.

2. Set the dimensions of the bitmap equal to those of the original picture. Note that you use the `Picture.Bitmap` instead of the `Picture.Graphic` to obtain the bitmap dimensions.

```
NewBitmap.Height := Orig.Picture.Bitmap.Height;
NewBitmap.Width := Orig.Picture.Bitmap.Width;
```

3. When the original bitmap is divided into 16 pieces and the new bitmap reassembled, you need to know how big each chunk is. Calculate an integer value of four pieces in each direction. Assume that the possible loss of three bits per section is acceptable (for example, if the bitmap had a width of 43 pixels, `ChunkX` would be only 10 pixels).

```
ChunkX := NewBitmap.Width div 4;
ChunkY := NewBitmap.Height div 4;
```

4. Loop through each sector and select a random piece to put into the new bitmap. This is accomplished by setting up a nested loop to choose each piece of the bitmap to create. You select a random piece from the original bitmap by using the `random` function to select random X and Y coordinates. You can draw on a bitmap by using any canvas function. One of these functions is `CopyRect`, which copies a rectangular region of one canvas to a rectangular region of another canvas.

```
For X := 0 to 3 do
   For Y := 0 to 3 do
    BEGIN
      NewX := random(3);
      NewY := random(3);
      NewBitmap.canvas.CopyRect(
         Rect(X*ChunkX,Y*ChunkY,(X+1)*ChunkX,(Y+1)*ChunkY),
         Orig.Picture.Bitmap.Canvas,
         Rect(NewX*ChunkX,NewY*ChunkY,
              (NewX+1)*ChunkX,(NewY+1)*ChunkY));
    END; {For Y}
```

5. When the program creates the new bitmap, it displays it by setting the `Picture.Graphic` property of the new image equal to the bitmap.

   ```
   NewImage.Picture.Graphic := NewBitmap;
   ```

To save the image, the program uses the common save dialog box when the user selects File | Save from the menu. If the user gives a valid file, the program uses the `SaveToFile` method on the NewImage component.

```
NewImage.Picture.SaveToFile(SaveDialog1.FileName);
```

Listings 10.10 and 10.11 show the complete code.

TYPE Listing 10.10. mixbit.dpr.

```
program bitmix;
{**************************************************}
{Program: Mixup            Version: 1.0            }
{Created: August, 27 1995                          }
{**************************************************}
{ Sample program to illustrate bitmap manipulation }
{ in Delphi32. This program allows a user to load  }
{ a bitmap from a file and then generate a new     }
{ bitmap which is created from random pieces of the}
{ origional.  Finally, the user is able to save the}
{ new bitmap back to a file.                       }
{**************************************************}


uses
  Forms,
  main in 'main.pas' {Mixup};

{$R *.RES}

begin
  Application.CreateForm(TMixup, Mixup);
  Application.Run;
end.
```

TYPE Listing 10.11. main.pas.

```
unit main;

interface

uses
  SysUtils, Windows, Messages, Classes, Graphics, Controls, Forms, Dialogs,
  StdCtrls, ExtCtrls, Menus;
```

continues

Listing 10.11. continued

```
type
  TMixup = class(TForm)
    MainMenu1: TMainMenu;
    File1: TMenuItem;
    Open1: TMenuItem;
    Save1: TMenuItem;
    Exit1: TMenuItem;
    Orig: TImage;
    NewImage: TImage;
    MixupBitmap: TButton;
    OpenDialog1: TOpenDialog;
    SaveDialog1: TSaveDialog;
    procedure Exit1Click(Sender: TObject);
    procedure Open1Click(Sender: TObject);
    procedure MixupBitmapClick(Sender: TObject);
    procedure Save1Click(Sender: TObject);
  private
    { Private declarations }
  public
    { Public declarations }
  end;

var
  Mixup: TMixup;

implementation

{$R *.DFM}

procedure TMixup.Exit1Click(Sender: TObject);
{ Menu Item to terminate the application}
begin
  Application.Terminate;
end;

procedure TMixup.Open1Click(Sender: TObject);
{Use the open common dialog to select a bitmap to open}
begin
  if OpenDialog1.Execute then
   Begin
      Orig.Picture.LoadFromFile(OpenDialog1.FileName);
   End;
end;

procedure TMixup.MixupBitmapClick(Sender: TObject);
{ Divide the origional bitmap into 16 pieces.  Create}
{ a new bitmap by randomly selecting one of the 16}
{ pieces for each piece of the new bitmap           }

Var
  NewBitmap       : TBitmap;  {Bitmap to create}
  X,Y,NewX,NewY : integer;  {Used to index the pieces}
  ChunkX,ChunkY : integer;  {X and Y dimension for each piece}
```

```
begin
  {Allocate resources for a new bitmap}
  NewBitmap := TBitmap.Create;

  {set the dimensions equal to the original}
  NewBitmap.Height := Orig.Picture.Bitmap.Height;
  NewBitmap.Width := Orig.Picture.Bitmap.Width;
  NewImage.Stretch := true;

  {Calculate the dimensions of each section}
  ChunkX := NewBitmap.Width div 4;
  ChunkY := NewBitmap.Height div 4;

  {Build the new bitmap}
  For X := 0 to 3 do
   For Y := 0 to 3 do
    BEGIN
      NewX := random(3);
      NewY := random(3);
      NewBitmap.canvas.CopyRect(
         Rect(X*ChunkX,Y*ChunkY,(X+1)*ChunkX,(Y+1)*ChunkY),
         Orig.Picture.Bitmap.Canvas,
         Rect(NewX*ChunkX,NewY*ChunkY,
             (NewX+1)*ChunkX,(NewY+1)*ChunkY));
    END; {For Y}

  {Display the new bitmap by setting the picture of the new image}
  NewImage.Picture.Graphic := NewBitmap;
end; {Procedure}

procedure TMixup.Save1Click(Sender: TObject);
{Use the save common dialog to save the bitmap}
begin
  if SaveDialog1.Execute then
    Begin
      NewImage.Picture.SaveToFile(SaveDialog1.FileName);
    End; {if}
end; {Procedure}

end. {main.pas}
```


Using Graphics in Listboxes and DrawGrids: Moving Past OnPaint

The OnPaint event signifies that a canvas has become invalid. It is the developer's task to write code to redraw the image. Components can use this technique to perform specialized tasks. For example, a DrawGrid will contain an event, DrawCell, which is called to place the image in a cell in the grid displayed. Note that the internals of how the DrawGrid component works are still completely shielded from the developer using the VCL. You can examine how to use a specialized draw event by writing a children's math program to teach arithmetic.

To begin, create a non-graphics program to teach math. In this program, the user enters the multiplication table that he wants to view and a range of multipliers. For example, to view the 2s multiplied by 1 through 15, he would enter these parameters into the application and click the Go button. The resulting multiplication table fills a listbox . Figure 10.10 shows the ap-plication.

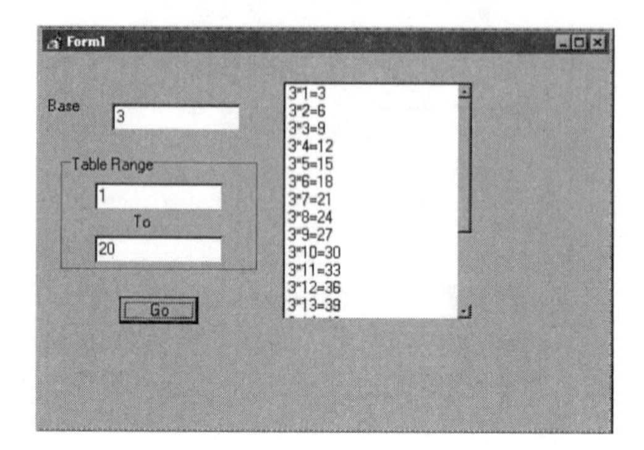

Figure 10.10.
Non-graphical multiplication program.

The main code to do this is for filling the listbox when the user clicks Go, as shown in the following segment:

```
procedure TForm1.GoClick(Sender: TObject);
var
 RL,RH,Count : integer;

begin
   MainList.Items.Clear; { Remove everything from List}
   RL := StrToInt(RangeLow.Text); {Convert entries to ints}
   RH := StrToInt(RangeHigh.Text);
   For Count := RL to RH do
     MainList.Items.Add(Base.Text+'*'+Inttostr(Count)+
            '='+IntToStr(Count * StrToInt(Base.Text)));
end;
```

When the application is executed, the listbox displays `2*1=2`, `2*2=4`, and so on, because the `ListBox` style is set to `lbStandard`. This indicates that you want the component to take care of displaying each item in the list. Children seem to learn easier with visual displays, so require that each item in the list shows next to the equation a set of circles equal to the answer of the equation. For example, the item that has `2*2=4` will also have four circles.

To accomplish the task of drawing circles along with the text, you first need to inform the listbox that you will draw each item. This is done by setting the `Style` property to `lbOwnerDrawFixed`. The listbox calls the function specified in the OnDrawItem event whenever it is necessary to draw an entry. Basically, the component takes care of scrolling and item management but calls your routine whenever an item needs to be drawn. The following code shows the procedure to draw an item in the list:

```
procedure TForm1.MainListDrawItem(Control: TWinControl; Index: Integer;
  Rect: TRect; State: TOwnerDrawState);
```

```
var
  Answer : integer; {Number of objects to draw}
  Count  : integer; {Loop through Object}
  ChunkX : integer; {width of each ellipse}
begin
    Answer := StrToInt(Copy(MainList.Items[Index],
                   Pos('=',MainList.Items[Index])+1,4));
    MainList.Canvas.TextOut(Rect.Left+2, Rect.Top+2,
                            MainList.Items[Index]);
    ChunkX := ((Rect.Right-Rect.Left)-50) div Answer;
    For Count := 0 to Answer-1 do
      MainList.Canvas.Ellipse(Rect.Left+50+(Count*ChunkX),
                              Rect.Top,
                              Rect.Left+50+((Count+1)*ChunkX),
                              Rect.Bottom);
end;
```


The first thing to notice is the parameters passed to the `MainListDrawItem` function. The `Rect` parameter defines the area on the canvas that you should draw the cell in. The `Index` specifies which cell you are drawing. You want to display the entire equation in each cell, so store values such as `2*3=6` in the `Items` property of the listbox. This causes a small amount of inconvenience because you need to know how many circles to draw, which means that you must pull the value after the `=` in the string and convert it to an integer. You can access the items in the list by using the `Index` that is passed. This is accomplished with the following code:

```
Answer := StrToInt(Copy(MainList.Items[Index],
                   Pos('=',MainList.Items[Index])+1,4));
```

The next step is writing the equation into the listbox; you do this with the `TextOut` method. Pass the `TextOut` method the top-left coordinates of the item plus two pixels for some padding.

```
MainList.Canvas.TextOut(Rect.Left+2, Rect.Top+2,
                        MainList.Items[Index]);
```

To determine the size available for each circle, subtract 50 pixels to account for the text, and divide the remaining size by the number of circles.

```
ChunkX := ((Rect.Right-Rect.Left)-50) div Answer;
```

The final step is drawing the series of circles. Set up a loop drawing each circle 50 pixels away from the left of the entry plus its offset. The offset is determined by the width of each circle and the count of the loop.

```
For Count := 0 to Answer-1 do
      MainList.Canvas.Ellipse(Rect.Left+50+(Count*ChunkX),
                              Rect.Top,
                              Rect.Left+50+((Count+1)*ChunkX),
                              Rect.Bottom);
```

To appreciate what the listbox is doing for you, consider the effort that would be involved if you had to set up the scrollbar, determine which entries were showing, and support list management capabilities.

Figure 10.11 shows the final product. Upon executing, the program shows a series of circles corresponding to the result of the equation.

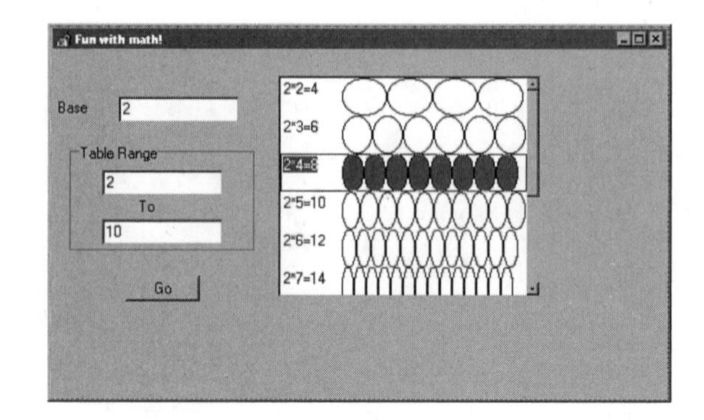

Figure 10.11.
Graphical version of multiplication program.

Summary

Graphics development is one of the hottest and most exciting topics in the computer industry. Delphi is an excellent development language for using the graphical features in Windows 95 and Windows NT. The primary drawing surface in Delphi is the canvas. The canvas enables an application to draw on a form, a paintbox, or a bitmap. In this chapter, I discuss different ways to manipulate a canvas. I also cover specific aspects of working with images and bitmaps, as well as underlying graphics theory. Numerous examples illustrate the graphical techniques used. After finishing this chapter, the application's developer will be able to use Delphi to create graphical applications without knowledge of the Win32 API.

Q&A

Q How can my application use Win32 graphics APIs with graphical components in Delphi?

A Most Delphi components and objects have properties that you can use to link to their underlying handles. For example, the `TBitmap` class has a `Handle` property that you can access to perform bitmap APIs. Also, the canvas's device context (DC) is available through its `Handle` property.

Q What are some of the advantages of drawing a bitmap off screen and then copying it to the display?

A When you're drawing to an off-screen bitmap, the image does not experience any flicker. Also, you can maintain multiple images and swap them rapidly to a section of the screen.

Workshop

Quiz

1. In the simple animation example, what happens if `pmCopy` is used for the pen mode instead of `pmNotXor`?
2. Clipping is useful to confine a drawing to a particular portion of a form. What Delphi components could you use to automatically clip a drawing to a region of the screen?
3. What are the significance of red, green, and blue in terms of colors that you can create with Delphi? What is a color palette?
4. How can an application use a method to load a bitmap into an image? How could an application copy a piece of the bitmap to a paintbox?

Exercises

1. Confirm that when a window containing a graphic object does not redraw itself after being covered, the image in that portion of the window is erased.
2. Modify the mixup program such that the newly created bitmap has the pieces arranged in a specific order, instead of being random (for example, so the X and Y pieces are transposed).

Day 11

Multimedia and Animation

What exactly is multimedia? The *American Heritage Dictionary* describes multimedia as "Including or involving the use of several media of communication, entertainment or expression." How does this apply to computers? Simply put, today's computers can express information in ways other than still images on a screen. We can view full motion video and listen to sounds. Users find it intriguing to hear a narration or view a video. This chapter shows how Delphi can exploit the power of multimedia to build applications that can perform audio and visual functions. Much of this chapter focuses on integrating prerecorded audio and video into your applications; however, it also covers techniques that allow you to use real-time animation.

Why is multimedia possible? One of the biggest reasons is new developments in computer hardware. Audio and video can be stored on disk; however, usually these files are quite large. It wasn't until people could store audio and video on CD-ROM that multimedia became popular. Imagine that you wanted to load a new application, but the installation said that it would install

650M on your hard drive, and worse yet that the application came as 300 1.4M floppies. No one would buy such an application. Other advances were also necessary, such as faster processors and sound cards to hear audio.

This chapter covers three ways that a Delphi developer can use multimedia and animation. The first is to use specialized functions available in the Win32 API to perform multimedia effects. Second, there are visual components available that perform multimedia functionality. You explore how these components can be integrated into applications. Finally, you examine how to create a smooth animation using methods and API calls.

NOTE

This chapter contains code that works only if the user's system has hardware to support specific functions. For example, to play MIDI files, the user needs to have a sound card. This is becoming less of an issue because most new systems are capable of performing multimedia tasks.

A Quick Start—Using Sound in Your Applications

There are many ways to play sound in an application; start by examining a very simple one that starts you on your way to using multimedia from within Delphi, the `PlaySound()` API call. The `PlaySound()` API call can play sounds from different sources and with different options. For example, you can use the `PlaySound()` API call to play a WAV file or to play one of the default system sounds. There are also many options for how the sounds interact with your application. For example, you can play a sound and pause the program's execution until the sound is completed, or you can play a sound and continue to execute other Delphi commands while the sound is played.

Let's begin with a simple example. Create a new application and add a single button on the main form. In the main form's unit, two steps are necessary to play a sound. First, the `mmsystem` unit needs to be added to a uses clause in the implementation part of the unit. Next, the `PlaySound` API call needs to be added to the OnClick event handler on the TButton visual component. For the first example, you simply play one of the WAV files that comes with Windows 95. You also specify that the sound should be played synchronously, which means that the application pauses until the sound has executed. The listing for this unit is shown in Listing 11.1.

TYPE

Listing 11.1. Using sound in a Delphi application with the `PlaySound()` API call.

```
unit mult1;

interface

uses
  Windows, Messages, SysUtils, Classes, Graphics, Controls, Forms, Dialogs,
  StdCtrls;

type
  TForm1 = class(TForm)
    Button1: TButton;
    procedure Button1Click(Sender: TObject);
  private
    { Private declarations }
  public
    { Public declarations }
  end;

var
  Form1: TForm1;

implementation
{Note that we need to include mmsystem for this to work}
uses mmsystem;

{$R *.DFM}

procedure TForm1.Button1Click(Sender: TObject);
begin
     {Replace C:\WIN95 with Wherever your Windows 95 Directory is}
     PlaySound('C:\WIN95\MEDIA\The Microsoft Sound', 0, SND_SYNC);
end;
```


ANALYSIS In this example, we simply play the wave file that is in the c:\win95\media subdirectory called "The Microsoft Sound." The sound is played synchronously, which means the program pauses until the sound completes.

The three parameters that the `PlaySound` API call takes are as follows:

Parameter 1 is a variant parameter that can either be the name of a file, a memory address, or a system event.

Parameter 2 is used in special circumstances where the sound is stored in a resource file. The chapter does not cover this case, so assume parameter two to be 0.

Parameter 3 specifies all the options including how to play the sound, and what type of parameter the first parameter should be treated as. Remember that the Win32 API is not object oriented, so there cannot be multiple forms of a call that automatically detect the type of data presented in the first parameter. The constants used for parameter 3 are defined in the `mmsystem` unit. The bit wise `OR` operator can be used to combine multiple options. For example, the following call plays "The Microsoft Sound" asynchronously (allows execution to continue while the sound plays) and plays the sound over and over until another call to `PlaySound` is made.

```
PlaySound('C:\WIN95\MEDIA\The Microsoft Sound', 0, SND_ASYNC or SND_LOOP);
```

System events are predefined sounds that occur when a program or the operating system is trying to make a statement clear to the user. For example, to play the effect used when the system starts, you can use

```
PlaySound('SystemStart', 0, SND_ASYNC OR SND_NODEFAULT);
```

If you want to play a sound frequently and don't want to access the disk, you can also play a sound that is stored in a memory location. This is not usually necessary because the operating system is usually good at caching disk information. One advantage of playing a file from memory is that your end users don't have access to the file (if you don't want someone to steal the cool sound your application uses). Listing 11.2 shows how a WAV file is loaded into memory when the form loads. When the user clicks the button, it plays the sound from memory. To keep the program short, assume that the WAV file is less then 30K. Note that the data is stored in a data member of the form. This allows you to have multiple instances of the form in which each one has its own copy of the data. One final point is the `SND_MEMORY` flag is used to tell the `PlaySound` API that we are passing a memory location instead of a file name.

TYPE **Listing 11.2. Playing a sound from memory.**

```
unit mult1;

interface

uses
  Windows, Messages, SysUtils, Classes, Graphics, Controls, Forms, Dialogs,
  StdCtrls;

{We know roughly how big the file is so }
{Hard coding the size is OK here.       }
const
     MAX_WAVE_FILE_SIZE = 30000;

type
  TForm1 = class(TForm)
    Button1: TButton;
    procedure Button1Click(Sender: TObject);
    procedure FormCreate(Sender: TObject);
  private
```

```
    { Private declarations }
    ChordDat : Array[0..MAX_WAVE_FILE_SIZE] of char;
    procedure LoadWavFile;
  public
    { Public declarations }
  end;

var
  Form1: TForm1;

implementation
uses mmsystem;

{$R *.DFM}
procedure TForm1.LoadWavFile;
var
   f: THandle;   {Handle To File      }
   size : DWORD; {Number of Bytes Read}
 begin
    {Use Win32 API calls to load file into memory               }
    {Replace C:\WIN95 with Wherever your Windows 95 Directory is}
     f := CreateFile('C:\WIN95\MEDIA\CHORD.WAV',
                     GENERIC_READ,0,nil,OPEN_EXISTING,0,0);
     if not(f=INVALID_HANDLE_VALUE) then
     begin
      ReadFile(f,ChordDat,MAX_WAVE_FILE_SIZE,size,nil);
      CloseHandle;
     end;
 end;

procedure TForm1.Button1Click(Sender: TObject);
var
  PToChord : PChar; {Pointer to the sound data}

begin
     {Play the Sound from a memory location instead of a file}
     PToChord := ChordDat;
     PlaySound(PToChord, 0, SND_ASYNC or SND_MEMORY);
end;

procedure TForm1.FormCreate(Sender: TObject);
begin
     LoadWavFile;
end;

end.
```

Different Types of Media Files

New Term The `PlaySound` API used a special kind of file called a *wave* file. You already know that a wave file can store a sound, but how exactly does it do it? A waveform file stores a digital representation of the pitch and volume over the length of the sound clip. The wave file does not have any knowledge of what the sound is, therefore a wave file needs to store a great deal of information to store a sound clip.

Another common type of multimedia file that is used is called a *Musical Instrument Digital Interface (MIDI)* file. A MIDI file is usually used to store a musical selection. A MIDI file stores the sound by saving data about which instruments are playing what notes for how long. If you are familiar with music, this would be the digital equivalent of the conductor's score. One of the key advantages of a MIDI file is that the files are much smaller. One analogy that can be used is that a wave file is to a MIDI file as a bitmap is to a metafile. In each case, one file format understands the data that it represents, and the other simply contains the raw data that is sent to an output device.

Wave and MIDI files can store only sound or audio. What about video or animation? There are multiple file formats that can store video: two examples of these are AVI and MPEG files. Most of the video files also support a track for sound so that the audio is played in sync with the picture. Now that you know about all of these file formats, how can you use them in Delphi? The answer is the Media Player visual component.

The Media Player Visual Component

The *Media Control Interface (MCI)* is a high-level command interface for controlling media files built into the Windows 95 and Windows NT operating system. Delphi provides a visual component that encapsulates the command interface into a visual component resembling a VCR or tape recorder.

Figure 11.1.
The Media Player component.

The Media Player component can be used in two ways. First, the component contains a user interface that can be enabled and the end user can manipulate media functions through a set of buttons such as "Play," "Stop," "Record," and "Rewind." The second way is to hide the component and manipulate media files by executing the component's methods from within a block of code. Start by creating a simple yet powerful application that lets the user load a WAV, MIDI, or AVI file and then be able to play and manipulate the file through the Media Player component interface. The application is quite simple; it requires three components: a TMainMenu component, a TOpenDialog component, and a TMediaPlayer component. Add the capability of choosing the "File | Open" selection to the menu component. The other two components need to be placed on the form.

Figure 11.2.
Component layout for simple Media Player.

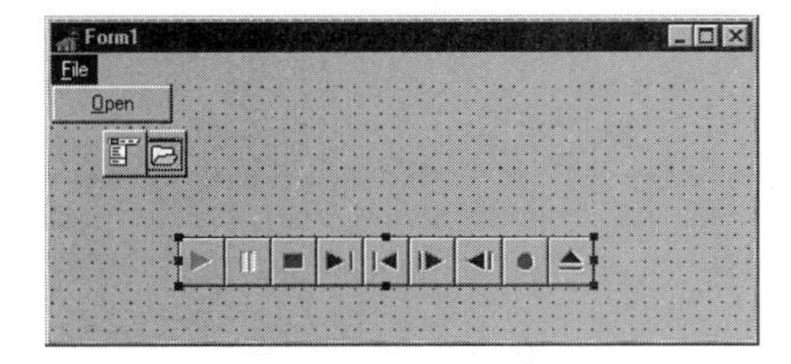

Add the following code behind the File|Open event on the menu:

```
procedure TForm1.Open1Click(Sender: TObject);
begin
 if OpenDialog1.Execute then
 begin
  {Set the file name}
   MediaPlayer1.FileName := OpenDialog1.FileName;
   {Open the file using the open method}
   MediaPlayer1.Open;
 end;
```

You now have a functioning application that can play audio and video files through an easy-to-use interface.

Figure 11.3.
The simple Media Player playing an AVI file.

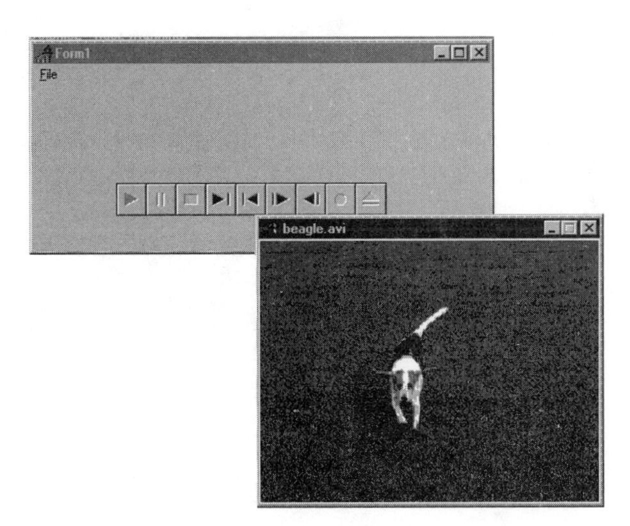

It's possible to change how the Media Player interacts with media files by setting the properties of the component. For example, if when the player plays an AVI file, it plays the video in its own window, this behavior can be modified by setting the `Display` property on the media player. The `Display` property tells the component where to play a video file. The value can be any form or component derived from a `TWinComponent`. There is also a `DisplayRect` property that can be used to specify the region of the new window in which to play the video file.

The `DisplayRect` property is slightly confusing. The confusion comes from the way it accepts its parameters. The `DiplayRect` property is set to a TRECT type, which you might think is the region to display the image in; it is not. The top left parameter does indicate where to position the image; however, the bottom right parameter is used to specify the width and height. Therefore

```
MediaPlayer1.Display := Form1;
MediaPlayer1.DisplayRect := RECT(10,10,200,200);
```

indicates that you wish to play the video on Form1 between coordinates 10,10 and 210,210 (not 10,10 to 200,200).

Using these two properties, create your next sample application, shown in Listing 11.3, which allows the user to load a video file and play it just as before; however, now the image will be shown on part of the main form instead of in its own window. Furthermore, you add a special button that lets the user capture a particular frame. The captured frame is held even if the video continues.

Figure 11.4.
The frame capture application.

TYPE

Listing 11.3. Playing video on a form.

```
unit Ex1;

interface

uses
  Windows, Messages, SysUtils, Classes, Graphics, Controls, Forms, Dialogs,
  Menus, MPlayer, ExtCtrls, StdCtrls;
```

```
type
  TForm1 = class(TForm)
    MediaPlayer1: TMediaPlayer;
    MainMenu1: TMainMenu;
    File1: TMenuItem;
    Open1: TMenuItem;
    OpenDialog1: TOpenDialog;
    Capture: TButton;
    Exit1: TMenuItem;
    PaintBox1: TPaintBox;
    procedure Open1Click(Sender: TObject);
    procedure CaptureClick(Sender: TObject);
    procedure FormPaint(Sender: TObject);
    procedure Exit1Click(Sender: TObject);
    procedure FormCreate(Sender: TObject);
    procedure FormClose(Sender: TObject; var Action: TCloseAction);
    procedure PaintBox1Paint(Sender: TObject);
  private
    { Private declarations }
    ImgBitmap : TBitmap;
  public
    { Public declarations }
  end;

var
  Form1: TForm1;

implementation

{$R *.DFM}

procedure TForm1.Open1Click(Sender: TObject);
{open the file and set the display to form1}
{also set the region to display from (10,10,210,210)}
begin
 {Use the OpenDialog component to find a video file}
 if OpenDialog1.Execute then
 begin
   MediaPlayer1.FileName := OpenDialog1.FileName;
   MediaPlayer1.Open;
   MediaPlayer1.Display := Form1;
   MediaPlayer1.DisplayRect := RECT(10,10,200,200);
 end; {if}
end; {procedure}


procedure TForm1.CaptureClick(Sender: TObject);
{when the capture button is pressed, use the CopyRect method to copy the image}
{to a bitmap in memory}
begin
   ImgBitmap.Canvas.CopyRect(Rect(0,0,200,200),Form1.Canvas,Rect(10,10,210,210));
     PaintBox1.Invalidate;
end; {procedure}

procedure TForm1.FormPaint(Sender: TObject);
{When the form is invalidated redraw the background rectangle}
```

continues

Listing 11.3. continued

```
begin
  Canvas.FrameRect(Rect(8,8,212,212));
end; {procedure}

procedure TForm1.Exit1Click(Sender: TObject);
{When exit is chosen on the menu, EXIT…}
begin
  Application.terminate;
end; {procedure}


procedure TForm1.FormCreate(Sender: TObject);
{when the form is created we allocate resource for the bitmap and}
{set the initial size.  The bitmap is also cleared               }
begin
  ImgBitmap := Tbitmap.create;
  ImgBitmap.Height := 200;
  ImgBitmap.Width  := 200;
  ImgBitmap.Canvas.Rectangle(0,0,200,200);
end; {procedure}

procedure TForm1.FormClose(Sender: TObject; var Action: TCloseAction);
{When we leave, clean up by freeing the bitmap}
begin
  ImgBitmap.Free;
end; {procedure}

procedure TForm1.PaintBox1Paint(Sender: TObject);
{when the paintbox which displays the captured image is invalidated, copy the}
{bitmap from memory into the paintbox.  This prevents us from losing the image}
begin
 PaintBox1.Canvas.CopyRect(Rect(0,0,200,200),ImgBitmap.Canvas,Rect(0,0,200,200));
end; {procedure}

end. {program}
```

ANALYSIS To load the media, you set up an Open option on the Main menu. The event handler, which is called when the user opens a new file, loads the file, determines where the video file will be played, and enables the Media Player component. To determine which file to open, use the OpenDialog component. When the `execute` method is executed on the OpenDialog component, it displays the standard open dialog and returns a Boolean value that indicates whether the user has chosen "OK" or "cancel." If the user chooses a valid file, then set the `FileName` property on the Media Player equal to the `FileName` property of the OpenDialog component.

```
MediaPlayer1.FileName := OpenDialog1.FileName;
```

Next, open the file and enable the Media Player by calling the `Open` method.

```
MediaPlayer1.Open;
```

The final step in preparing the video clip to run is to specify that you want the image to run on Form1, and that the picture should be confined to a well-defined rectangle. This is necessary so you know from where to capture the image.

```
MediaPlayer1.Display := Form1;
MediaPlayer1.DisplayRect := RECT(10,10,200,200);
```

The sample uses the interface provided with the Media Player to allow the user to control the media that is loaded. Therefore, the user can perform functions such as play, stop, rewind, fast forward, and pause. The application uses this interface to control the player; however it adds a new button (Capture) which takes the current frame and copies it into a bitmap in memory.

Why use a bitmap? You could simply copy the image to another part of the main form, or a paint box; however, if another window was dragged over the captured frame and then moved away, it would be erased. By copying the image to a bitmap, you have stored the image into a part of memory that you control. Using a bitmap does add some complexity to the program. Where do you store the bitmap? Only procedures and functions that are used in the form need to access the bitmap. Therefore, we can add the bitmap in the `Private` portion of the `TForm` class declaration. Although the bitmap is referenced in the form, you still need to call the `Create` method and specify the dimensions of the bitmap when the form is loaded. This code can be placed in the OnCreate event handler of the form. Similarly, you need to clean up by deleting the bitmap when the form is closed. Note that storing the image in a bitmap does not display the image anywhere on the form. This is accomplished by placing a PaintBox component on the form and using its OnPaint event to copy the bitmap into the PaintBox whenever an OnPaint event is called.


```
procedure TForm1.PaintBox1Paint(Sender: TObject);
begin
  PaintBox1.Canvas.CopyRect(Rect(0,0,200,200),ImgBitmap.Canvas,Rect(0,0,200,200));
end;
```

Therefore, whenever the operating system determines that the image needs to be redrawn, it calls the `PaintBox1Paint` procedure to reconcile the windows.

Using Methods to Control the Media Player

Sometimes, you will want to use multimedia capabilities in an application, but not want to display the Media Player component. You can do this by setting the `Visible` property to False on the media player component and perform all the functionality through the media player's methods. There are methods corresponding to all the buttons on the Media Player component's interface as well as methods to provide additional functionality that is not included in the user interface. An example of a method not in the user interface is the `Open` method, which is used to open a file.

It is common to hide the media player component when you want to show a video clip during an application; however, you don't want to confuse the user or add clutter to the interface. For example, consider a cookbook application. You may have a feature that allows a user to click on an icon and show a video clip of a chef preparing a recipe. In this case, there is no need for the entire interface to be displayed, the user simply wants to see how the meal is prepared.

Create a sample application shown in Listing 11.4 that demonstrates how to develop a multimedia application without the media player interface. This application would be used by a college to inform returning students of any new information that they need to be aware of. The application will be used by many people, so we want to keep the interface as simple and straightforward as possible. There is a group of radio buttons that designate the class the student is in and a button that plays a media clip from the dean directed at each class.

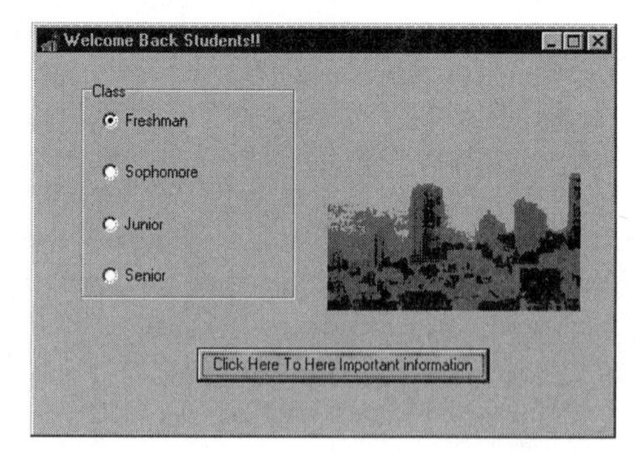

Figure 11.5.
The student information application.

TYPE **Listing 11.4. The student information application.**

```
unit main;

interface

uses
  Windows, Messages, SysUtils, Classes, Graphics, Controls, Forms, Dialogs,
  StdCtrls, ExtCtrls, MPlayer;

type
  TForm1 = class(TForm)
    MediaPlayer1: TMediaPlayer;
    RadioGroup1: TRadioGroup;
    Freshman: TRadioButton;
    Sophomore: TRadioButton;
    Junior: TRadioButton;
```

```
    Senior: TRadioButton;
    DisplayScreen: TPanel;
    ImpInfo: TButton;
    procedure ImpInfoClick(Sender: TObject);
    procedure FormCreate(Sender: TObject);
  private
    { Private declarations }
  public
    { Public declarations }
  end;

var
  Form1: TForm1;

implementation

{$R *.DFM}

procedure TForm1.ImpInfoClick(Sender: TObject);
{determine which radio button is selected and play the appropriate clip}
begin
   If Freshman.Checked then
      MediaPlayer1.FileName := 'F:\DELPHIU\FRESH.avi';
   If Sophomore.Checked then
      MediaPlayer1.FileName := 'F:\DELPHIU\SOPH.avi';
   If Junior.Checked then
      MediaPlayer1.FileName := 'F:\DELPHIU\JUNIOR.avi';
   If Senior.Checked then
      MediaPlayer1.FileName := 'F:\DELPHIU\SENDIOR.avi';
   MediaPlayer1.Open;
   {Set the display area on the panel component}
   MediaPlayer1.DisplayRect := RECT(0,0,
                                  DisplayScreen.Width,DisplayScreen.Height);
   MediaPlayer1.Play;
end; {procedure}

procedure TForm1.FormCreate(Sender: TObject);
{on initialization, set the media player to use a panel component}
{as the screen to display the clips                             }
begin
   MediaPlayer1.Display := DisplayScreen;
end; {procedure}

end. {program}
```

Analysis The main logic in this application is contained in the OnClick event handler of the ImpInfo button. When a user clicks on the button, the application checks which radio button is selected. Based on the selection, the proper filename is set on the media player component. Although the media component is not visible, it is still fully functional. After the filename is set, open the file using the `Open` method just as you have done in previous examples. The big difference in this example is that instead of the user clicking on the play button, you execute the `Play` method to show the video clip.

```
MediaPlayer1.Play;
```

NOTE

One final note about this application deals with setting the display. You set the display property equal to a Panel component in the OnCreate event handler of the form because it needs to be set only once and it would be unnecessary to set it every time the button is pressed. This is not true for the `DisplayRect` property. `DisplayRect` needs to be set each time a new file is opened, therefore it is placed in the OnClick event handler.

Responding to Media Player Events

Although the media player component has many properties and methods, there are relatively few events. The events that are included provide hooks into the user interface provided as well as notification as to when a media task is complete. One of these abilities is to execute custom code when a user clicks one of the buttons, and to tell the media player whether it should execute the requested task.

Use this event to set up an application that allows a user to load a video clip and play it. Your application has an enhancement such that you scan the name of the file to play and if it contains "RatedR," then you display a dialog box warning the user of the "R" rating and ask them if they wish to continue. This assumes that the rating is in the filename, but it demonstrates the functionality of the OnClick event. Listing 11.5 shows this application.

TYPE **Listing 11.5. The movie view application.**

```
unit main;

interface

uses
  Windows, Messages, SysUtils, Classes, Graphics, Controls, Forms, Dialogs,
  Menus, ExtCtrls, MPlayer;

type
  TForm1 = class(TForm)
    MediaPlayer1: TMediaPlayer;
    Panel1: TPanel;
    MainMenu1: TMainMenu;
    File1: TMenuItem;
    Open1: TMenuItem;
    Exit1: TMenuItem;
    OpenDialog1: TOpenDialog;
    procedure FormCreate(Sender: TObject);
    procedure Open1Click(Sender: TObject);
```

```
    procedure MediaPlayer1Click(Sender: TObject; Button: TMPBtnType;
      var DoDefault: Boolean);
  private
    { Private declarations }
  public
    { Public declarations }
  end;

var
  Form1: TForm1;

implementation

{$R *.DFM}

procedure TForm1.FormCreate(Sender: TObject);
{Set the screen to a panel component}
begin
    MediaPlayer1.Display :=  Panel1;
end;

procedure TForm1.Open1Click(Sender: TObject);
{Open a new file and set up the display area}
begin
   if OpenDialog1.Execute then
     begin
       MediaPlayer1.FileName := OpenDialog1.FileName;
       MediaPlayer1.Open;
       {fit exactly into the panel}
       MediaPLayer1.DisplayRect := RECT(0,0,Panel1.Width,Panel1.Height);
     end;{if}
end;{procedure}

procedure TForm1.MediaPlayer1Click(Sender: TObject; Button: TMPBtnType;
  var DoDefault: Boolean);
{Check to see if the user is playing, and if the movie has an R rating}
var
  DialogRC : integer;

begin
   {ignore case and check to see if the string contains ratedr}
   {also be sure that they clicked play as opposed to a different button}
   if (pos('RATEDR',UpperCase(MediaPlayer1.FileName))>0) AND
      (Button = btPlay) THEN
   begin
      DialogRC := Application.MessageBox(
                         'This Clip is Rated R. Do you still wish to see it?',
                         'Warning!',
                          MB_YESNO);
      If DialogRC = IDNO then
        DoDefault := FALSE;
   end; {if}
end; {procedure}

end.
```

11

Analysis The OnClick event handler is passed two parameters that you need. The `Button` parameter notifies the procedure of which button was clicked. The `DoDefault` parameter is a `var` parameter. The procedure should set this to False if you want to abort the specified action. In your application you determine if the play button was pressed and the filename contains the "RatedR" string in it. If both conditions are true then a dialog box is displayed. Notice that you pass the MB_YESNO constant to the MessageBox component to specify that the box should force the user to choose yes or no. By examining the return code for the function, you can make the decision of whether or not to play the clip. If the user chooses "Yes," then no action is needed. However, if the user chooses "No," then set `DoDefault` to False and the Play is aborted.

How Video Files Are Stored

Previous examples have explained using AVI files in your applications to create video effects. What exactly is a video file and how does it work? The human brain interprets as motion a quick series of images with minor changes. Each one of these pictures is called a *frame.* If you tour Walt Disney World, you can actually watch people draw each frame of a cartoon. Thus, each frame is slightly different from the next. For smooth video, or animation, the brain prefers about 30 frames per second. More than this is not very noticeable and less frames per second gives the appearance of flicker. Think about this: a full-screen bitmap is a few hundred kilobytes. If you needed to store each frame of a video as a bitmap, that would be a lot of storage. For example, using this simple scheme you could store only about 72 seconds worth of video on a CD. If this were the case, then there wouldn't be any multimedia applications until storage capacity improved. Luckily there is a solution: *video compression.*

Instead of going though complex math in describing how video is compressed for a particular file format (such a AVI or MPEG), here is an overview of one of the techniques used. Have you ever watched a Rocky and Bullwinkle cartoon? The images freeze and the character's mouth continues to move. The animators learned that it is much easier to change part of a scene rather then the entire scene. Video compression uses a similar approach. When a frame is captured, a decision is made by the capture hardware or software. "Can I store this frame using less space by saving what is different from the previous frame, or should I save the whole thing?" Most of the time it is easier to save the parts of the scene that have changed. However, under certain circumstances, such as switching to a different camera, the overhead of describing the change would take up more space than it would to resave the entire frame. Multimedia storage has come a long way. It's now possible to store an entire full length movie on a standard CD-ROM. Future CD formats will allow CDs to hold many gigabytes of data, as compared to roughly 650M, which is today's standard.

Animation Techniques in Delphi

When you're using animation or moving graphics it's important that the motion appears smooth to the user. Unfortunately, creating a frame by simply drawing a picture, erasing it, and drawing the next frame creates animation with a lot of flicker and isn't pleasant to view. Let's look at an example using this simple approach and then improve on it.

Simplistic Animation with a Lot of Flicker

The following procedure animates a series of 10 moving ellipses that start in the middle of a paintbox and move outward at random angles. The procedure draws the ellipse, then erases the paintbox by calling the `Rectangle` method. There is also some utility code to tell you how long the procedure takes in milliseconds. Try this out and you will see that the ellipses move very fast; however, there is a lot of flicker.

```
procedure TForm1.CanvasOnlyClick(Sender: TObject);
{perform basic animation by simply drawing a frame, clearing the}
{frame and drawing the next frame                               }
var
  Radius : integer;
  RadReal : real;
  Angle,X,Y  : integer;
  Count,Count2 : integer;
  StTime,EndTime : TDATETIME;
begin
  {Get the time}
  StTime := Now;*;
  {create 10 ellipses}
  for Count2 := 1 to 10 do
  begin
     {get a random angle to send the ellipse}
     Angle   := random(360);
     {convert the angle into radians}
     RadReal := (Angle *PI)/180;
     {send it out}
     for Count := 1 to 100 do
     begin
        {calculate PaintBox coordinates}
        X := TRUNC(Count*SIN(RadReal))+100;
        Y := TRUNC(Count*COS(RadReal))+100;
        {draw the blue ellipse}
        PaintBox1.canvas.Brush.Color := clBlue;
        PaintBox1.Canvas.Ellipse(X-6,Y-6,X+6,Y+6);
        {Clear the screen white}
        PaintBox1.canvas.Brush.Color := clwhite;
        PaintBox1.canvas.Rectangle(0,0,200,200);
     end; {for count}
  end; {for count2}
  {Get stopping time and calculate difference
 EndTime := Now;
```

```
  Edit1.Text := IntToStr(Round(24.0 * 60.0 * 60.0 * 1000.0 * (EndTime -
➥StTime)));
end; {procedure}
```

Double Buffers

New Term A *double buffer* is a set of drawing surfaces. One surface is displayed, and the other is used as a drawing surface. When the drawing is complete on the drawing buffer, the buffers either switch places so that the one that was hidden is now displayed, or the hidden buffer is quickly copied onto the display buffer.

There are a few ways that you can set up a double buffer in Delphi. One is to create a bitmap in memory and use it as the temporary buffer. Draw the image on the bitmap and when each frame is drawn, use a `CopyRect` method to copy the bitmap image onto the display buffer. We have modified the ellipse procedure to use a bitmap as a temporary buffer. This procedure animates the ellipses very smoothly, however there is a huge performance hit compared to the simplistic method that we tried first. The code implementing the same ellipse animation using a bitmap double buffer follows:

```
procedure TForm1.BitmapBufferClick(Sender: TObject);
var
  Radius : integer;
  RadReal : real;
  Angle,X,Y  : integer;
  Count,Count2 : integer;
  TheBitmap : TBitmap;
  StTime,EndTime : TDATETIME;
begin
  {create the bitmap and set its dimensions}
  TheBitmap := TBitmap.Create;
  TheBitmap.Height := 200;
  TheBitmap.Width := 200;
  {Get the time}
  StTime := Now;
  {create 10 ellipses}
  for Count2 := 1 to 10 do
  begin
    {get a random angle to send the ellipse}
    Angle   := random(360);
    {convert to radians}
    RadReal := (Angle *PI)/180;
    for Count := 1 to 100 do
    begin
         X := TRUNC(Count*SIN(RadReal))+100;
         Y := TRUNC(Count*COS(RadReal))+100;
         {Clear the bitmap then draw the frame}
         TheBitmap.canvas.Brush.Color := clwhite;
         TheBitmap.canvas.Rectangle(0,0,200,200);
         TheBitmap.canvas.Brush.Color := clBlue;
         TheBitmap.Canvas.Ellipse(X-6,Y-6,X+6,Y+6);
{Copy the bitmap to the paintbox}
```

```
PaintBox1.Canvas.CopyRect(RECT(0,0,200,200),TheBitmap.Canvas,RECT(0,0,200,200));
     end;
  end;
  {Get stopping time and calculate difference
   EndTime := Now;
Edit1.Text := IntToStr(Round(24.0 * 60.0 * 60.0 * 1000.0 * (EndTime - StTime)));
➥{Free the bitmap}
  TheBitmap.Free;
end;
```

Parts of the Windows 95 GDI are very machine dependent. For example, you can increase performance on some machines by using a canvas as the second buffer instead of a bitmap. However, on other machines this slows the animation down. For demonstration purposes, we will use this technique. Always draw on one paintbox and then copy the entire image to the other paintbox using the `CopyRect` method. The result of this procedure is to produce one paintbox that has flickering animation (the one we draw directly on) and the other to have smooth and quick animation. The problem with using this method in a real application is that you would not want to display the image twice.

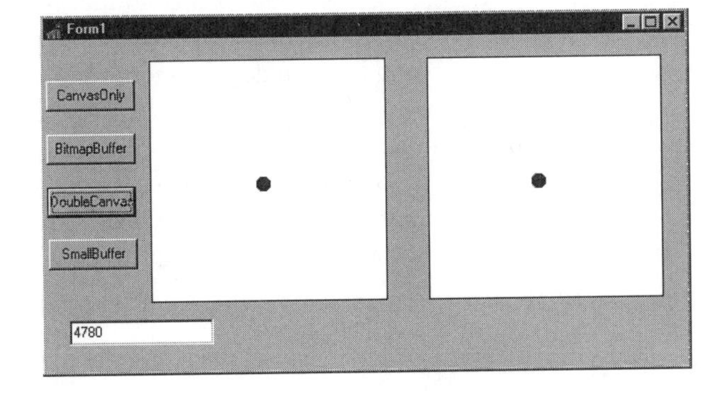

Figure 11.6.
Using two paintboxes to create a double buffer.

The following code is for animating the ellipses with two paintboxes.

```
procedure TForm1.DoubleCanvasClick(Sender: TObject);
var
  Radius : integer;
  RadReal : real;
  Angle,X,Y  : integer;
  Count,Count2 : integer;
  StTime,EndTime : TDATETIME;
begin
  {set the time the procedure begins}
  StTime := Now;
  for Count2 := 1 to 10 do
  begin
    Angle   := random(360);
    RadReal := (Angle *PI)/180;
    for Count := 1 to 100 do
    begin
         X := TRUNC(Count*SIN(RadReal))+100;
         Y := TRUNC(Count*COS(RadReal))+100;
```

```
        {clear secondary paintbox and then draw the frame}
        PaintBox2.canvas.Brush.Color := clwhite;
        PaintBox2.canvas.Rectangle(0,0,200,200);
        PaintBox2.canvas.Brush.Color := clBlue;
        PaintBox2.Canvas.Ellipse(X-6,Y-6,X+6,Y+6);
        {copy the frame to the primary paintbox}
PaintBox1.Canvas.CopyRect(RECT(0,0,200,200),PaintBox2.Canvas,RECT(0,0,200,200));
     end;
  end;
  {finish up with timings}
  EndTime := Now;
  Edit1.Text := IntToStr(Round(24.0 * 60.0 * 60.0 * 1000.0 * (EndTime -
➥StTime)));
end;
```

Don't Draw More Than You Have To

One of the problems in all the procedures you have looked at until now is that on each frame you are redrawing the entire paintbox. In the example you know that only a small portion of the frame changes, so modify your bitmap buffer procedure to operate only on a small portion of the paintbox, where the image actually changes between frames. This is the scenario where Rocky and Bullwinkle only move their lips. In the following procedure you also increase performance dramatically by drawing the ellipse outside of the loop. Using `Canvas` methods is much slower than copying portions of the canvas. The following procedure shows a close-to-optimal implementation of the ellipse animation because it draws the ellipse only once and then copies only small portions of the frame. Note that the animation may occur so fast that it is difficult to tell what is happening.

```
procedure TForm1.SmallBufferClick(Sender: TObject);
var
  Radius : integer;
  RadReal : real;
  Angle,X,Y  : integer;
  Count,Count2 : integer;
  TheBitmap : TBitmap;
  StTime,EndTime : TDATETIME;
begin
  {create a bitmap to store the ellipse}
  TheBitmap := TBitmap.Create;
  TheBitmap.Height := 20;
  TheBitmap.Width := 20;
  StTime := Now;
  {draw the ellipse in the small bitmap}
  PaintBox1.canvas.Brush.Color := clwhite;
  PaintBox1.canvas.Rectangle(0,0,200,200);
  TheBitmap.canvas.Brush.Color := clwhite;
  TheBitmap.canvas.Rectangle(0,0,20,20);
  TheBitmap.canvas.Brush.Color := clBlue;
  TheBitmap.Canvas.Ellipse(2,2,14,14);
  for Count2 := 1 to 10 do
  begin
    Angle   := random(360);
    RadReal := (Angle *PI)/180;
    for Count := 1 to 100 do
```

```
    begin
         X := TRUNC(Count*SIN(RadReal))+100;
         Y := TRUNC(Count*COS(RadReal))+100;
         {copy the small bitmap to the frame. We can get away with not erasing}
         {the buffer because the movement of the bitmap will erase the}
         {previous frame.}
PaintBox1.Canvas.CopyRect(RECT(X,Y,X+15,Y+15),TheBitmap.Canvas,RECT(1,1,15,15));
     end;
  end;
  {Clear final frame}
  PaintBox1.canvas.Brush.Color := clwhite;
  PaintBox1.canvas.Rectangle(0,0,200,200);
  {finish up timing stuff....}
  EndTime := Now;
  Edit1.Text := IntToStr(Round(24.0 * 60.0 * 60.0 * 1000.0 * (EndTime -
➥StTime)));  {clean up bitmap}
  TheBitmap.Free;
end;
```

This method of changing only part of the frame works well if only a small portion of the screen changes. However, if a large portion of the screen is changing you can actually lose performance by trying to figure out what has changed. For example, if you have ever played a game like DOOM, the whole screen is almost constantly changing. Therefore, in this scenario it would not be beneficial to try to figure out which parts of the frame should change.

Analyzing the Performance of Our Ellipse Animation Examples

Now that you have examined some different methods to produce animation in Delphi, take a closer look at how well each one performs. To use smooth animation, try to be sure that you stay close to 30 frames per second. Table 11.1 shows how well each method performed. Note that running this sort of test shows how much leeway we have in putting extra drawing and other functionality into the application before we pass the 30-frames-per-second threshold.

Table 11.1. Animation techniques.

Method	Time to execute animation	Smooth or Flicker	Frames per second
Canvas `Ellipse` method	3.79 Seconds	Flicker	263
Double buffer using a bitmap	12.24 Seconds	Smooth	81
Double buffer using a second canvas	6.90 Seconds	Smooth	145
All `CopyRects` on small portions of the image	0.330 Seconds	Smooth	3030

It's amazing how much faster it is to use the `CopyRect` method than using canvas GDI methods such as `Ellipse` and `Rectangle`. However, note that as the region to copy grows, you quickly lose performance. Currently Borland is working on an add-on that will increase performance of graphics functionality. Microsoft has released a version of this for Windows 95, and it's known as the `DirectDraw` API, which allows faster drawing than drawing through the Windows graphics device interface. This will satisfy the need for fast graphics in applications requiring extremely high performance. However, you can still do quite a bit with the canvas and bitmaps in Delphi. To prove this, create a really neat interactive animation program using only standard Delphi methods.

The Three-Dimensional, Spinning Cube

Now that you understand the concepts in creating animation in Delphi, build an interactive example. This sample application displays in a form a six-sided cube. The user can set the speed at which the cube spins on the X, Y, and Z axes. Because each user might want the cube to spin in a different way, you can't use a video file such as an AVI file.

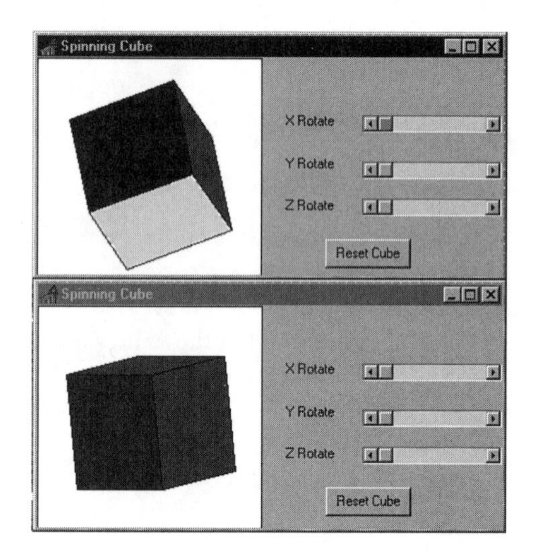

Figure 11.7.
The spinning cube.

This example illustrates the principles mentioned, plus gives a brief introduction into three-dimensional graphics. The first step in creating the cube is to know how to draw each frame. The cube consists of six faces and eight points. You define the position of each point in three-dimensional space by storing an X, Y, and Z coordinate in a record called TDPoint (for Three Dimensional point). You keep track of all these points by using an array of records.

```
Pnts : array[1..8] of TDPoint;   {Original image}
```

The points are initialized in the `InitCube` procedure (see Listing 11.6). This needs to occur only once because theses values never change. At each frame, determine how the cube is situated and figure a new set of points reflecting the coordinates of the rotated cube. This is calculated by creating a rotation matrix and then calling `ApplyMatToPoint` for each of the eight points. This leaves you with a new set of three-dimensional points. Now you can simply drop the Z value and you have X and Y coordinates for the eight corners.

You can play a little trick to determine which faces on the cube are hidden. If a cube is situated at (0,0,0) then a face is showing if the sum of its Z values is greater than 0. This only works with certain types of objects, so usually hidden surface removal is more complex, but you can do it in the simple function, `ShowSide`.

Now that you know what to draw and at which coordinates to draw it, the final task is to make the animation smooth. Each frame is triggered by an OnTimer event. The procedure reads the slider components to determine how much to increment each angle of rotation. To draw the frame, use a memory bitmap and clear it by copying another bitmap. The second bitmap is used rather than a `Rectangle` method because `CopyRect` operates quicker than `Rectangle`. You next determine which sides need to be displayed and draw them on the memory bitmap with a `polygon` method. Each side is drawn with a unique color so the final result is even more impressive. Finally, use a `CopyRect` to copy the memory bitmap onto the main form. This is an interesting example and can be easily modified to include more functionality. The full listing is shown in Listing 11.6.

TYPE **Listing 11.6. The rotating cube.**

```
unit main;
{*************************************************}
{* The 3D Rotating Cube - A Comprehensive example  *}
{* of using animation in Delphi. This application  *}
{* displays a rotating 3 dimensional cube. The user*}
{* can adjust how quickly the cube rotates on each *}
{* axis.                                           *}
{*************************************************}

interface

uses
  Windows, Messages, SysUtils, Classes, Graphics, Controls, Forms, Dialogs,
  StdCtrls, ExtCtrls;

type
  TForm1 = class(TForm)
    Label1: TLabel;
    Label2: TLabel;
    Label3: TLabel;
    Timer1: TTimer;
    ResetCube: TButton;
```

continues

Listing 11.6. continued

```
    XRot: TScrollBar;
    YRot: TScrollBar;
    ZRot: TScrollBar;
    procedure FormCreate(Sender: TObject);
    procedure FormClose(Sender: TObject; var Action: TCloseAction);
    procedure Timer1Timer(Sender: TObject);
    procedure ResetCubeClick(Sender: TObject);
  private
    { Private declarations }
  public
    { Public declarations }
  end;

var
  Form1: TForm1;

implementation

{$R *.DFM}

Type
  {Used to create a rotation matrix}
  Matrix  =  array[0..3,0..3] of real;
  {Structure to store a 3D point   }
  TDPoint =  record
     X : real;
     Y : real;
     Z : real;
  end;

var
  DoubleBuffer : TBitmap;  {We will draw here then copyrect}
  BlankBuffer  : TBitmap;  {Bitmap to store our background }
  PntsOut :array[1..8] of TDPoint; {Rotated Points}
  TPPnts : array[1..8] of TPoint;  {2D representation of pts}
  Pnts : array[1..8] of TDPoint;   {Original image}
  XAng,YAng,ZAng : real;

{*********************************************************}
{Create an array(or matrix) which sets up rotation based }
{on angles passed in terms or radians. Consult a geometry}
{book to understand the math behind rotation.            }
{*********************************************************}
procedure matrixRotate(var m:Matrix;
                       x,y,z : real);
var
    sinX, cosX,
    sinY, cosY,
    sinZ, cosZ:real; {Store here so we only need to calc once}
    C1,C2 : integer; {for the loops}

begin
    sinX := sin(x); {let's do our geometry...}
    cosX := cos(x);
```

```
    sinY := sin(y);
    cosY := cos(y);
    sinZ := sin(z);
    cosZ := cos(z);
    for C1 := 0 to 3 do  {set the matrix to the identity}
     for C2 :=0 to 3 do
       if C1 = C2 then
         M[C1,C2] := 0
        else
         M[C1,C2] := 1;
    {Take my word for it this works!....}
    M[0,0] :=  (cosZ * cosY);
    M[0,1] :=  (cosZ * -sinY * -sinX + sinZ * cosX);
    M[0,2] :=  (cosZ * -sinY * cosX + sinZ * sinX);
    M[1,0] :=  (-sinZ * cosY);
    M[1,1] :=  (-sinZ * -sinY * -sinX + cosZ * cosX);
    M[1,2] :=  (-sinZ * -sinY * cosX + cosZ * sinX);
    M[2,0] :=  (sinY);
    M[2,1] :=  (cosY * -sinX);
    M[2,2] :=  (cosY * cosX);
end;

{Apply the rotation matrix to a 3D point and return a new 3D point}
procedure ApplyMatToPoint(PointIn : TDPoint; var pointOut:TDPoint;mat : Matrix);
var
    x, y, z : real;

begin
    x :=(PointIn.x * mat[0,0]) + (PointIn.y * mat[0,1]) +
        (PointIn.z * mat[0,2]) + mat[0,3];
    y := (PointIn.x * mat[1,0]) + (PointIn.y * mat[1,1]) +
        (PointIn.z * mat[1,2]) + mat[1,3];
    z := (PointIn.x * mat[2,0]) + (PointIn.y * mat[2,1]) +
        (PointIn.z * mat[2,2]) + mat[2,3];
    PointOut.x :=  x;
    PointOut.y :=  y;
    PointOut.z :=  z;
end;

{We are using a cube which has 8 point. This is where we setup the }
{coordinates for each point. The middle of the cube is at (0,0,0)  }
procedure InitCube;
begin
  Pnts[1].X := -50;
  Pnts[1].Y := -50;
  Pnts[1].Z := -50;
  Pnts[2].X := 50;
  Pnts[2].Y := -50;
  Pnts[2].Z := -50;
  Pnts[3].X := 50;
  Pnts[3].Y := 50;
  Pnts[3].Z := -50;
  Pnts[4].X := -50;
  Pnts[4].Y := 50;
  Pnts[4].Z := -50;
  Pnts[5].X := -50;
```

continues

Listing 11.6. continued

```
  Pnts[5].Y := -50;
  Pnts[5].Z := 50;
  Pnts[6].X := 50;
  Pnts[6].Y := -50;
  Pnts[6].Z := 50;
  Pnts[7].X := 50;
  Pnts[7].Y := 50;
  Pnts[7].Z := 50;
  Pnts[8].X := -50;
  Pnts[8].Y := 50;
  Pnts[8].Z := 50;
end;

{The following function returns true if the sum of the  }
{parameters is greater than zero and false if it is      }
{less than zero. We will use this function to determine }
{Which sides of the cube to hide and which to show       }
function ShowSide(V1,V2,V3,V4 : Real) : Boolean;
begin
  if (V1+V2+V3+V4) > 0 then
    ShowSide := TRUE
   else
    ShowSide := FALSE;
end;

{We are using a double buffer. This function determines if a side}
{is visible. If it is, it draws the 2D representation on our     }
{bitmap buffer with the fill set to the color passed             }
procedure AddSide(P1,P2,P3,P4:Integer;SideColor : TColor);
begin
 if ShowSide(PntsOut[P1].Z,PntsOut[P2].Z,PntsOut[P3].Z,PntsOut[P4].Z) then
  begin
    DoubleBuffer.Canvas.Brush.Color := SideColor;
 DoubleBuffer.Canvas.Polygon([TPPnts[P1],TPPnts[P2],TPPnts[P3],TPPnts[P4],TPPnts[P1]]);
  end;
end;

{When the form loads, create and initialize our background bitmap}
{and initialize our double buffer bitmap.                        }
procedure TForm1.FormCreate(Sender: TObject);
begin
   DoubleBuffer := TBitmap.Create;
   DoubleBuffer.Height := 200;
   DoubleBuffer.Width := 200;
   BlankBuffer := TBitmap.Create;
   BlankBuffer.Height := 200;
   BlankBuffer.Width  := 200;
   BlankBuffer.Canvas.Brush.Color := clWhite;
   BlankBuffer.Canvas.rectangle(0,0,200,200);
   InitCube();
   XAng := 0;
   YAng := 0;
```

```
   ZAng := 0;
end;

{When we are done we need to clean up by freeing out bitmaps}
procedure TForm1.FormClose(Sender: TObject; var Action: TCloseAction);
begin
   BlankBuffer.Free;
   DoubleBuffer.Free;
end;

{The main procedure which draws the cube. This procedure is called  }
{by a timer that executes its OnTimer function every 20 milliseconds}
procedure TForm1.Timer1Timer(Sender: TObject);
var
  M : Matrix;              {The matrix used to rotate the cube}
  Count,Count2 : Integer; {Used to loop through points       }


begin
    XAng := XAng + XRot.Position;  {adjust the rotation angle}
    YAng := YAng + YRot.Position;  {by pulling out of the    }
    ZAng := ZAng + ZRot.Position;  {scroll bars              }
    {Adjust for degrees and build the rotation matrix}
    matrixRotate(M,(PI*XAng)/180,(PI*YAng)/180,(PI*ZAng)/180);
    {Loop through all of the points and rotate, the get 2D representation}
    for Count2:= 1 to 8 do
    begin
      ApplyMatToPoint(Pnts[Count2],PntsOut[Count2],M);
      TPPnts[Count2] :=
Point(trunc(PntsOut[Count2].X+100),trunc(PntsOut[Count2].Y+100));
    end;
    {Clear the double buffer by copyrect[ing] the Background}
  DoubleBuffer.Canvas.CopyRect(RECT(0,0,200,200),BlankBuffer.Canvas,RECT(0,0,200,200));
    {Build the cube by calling AddSide for each of the 6 sides}
    AddSide(1,2,3,4,clBlue);
    AddSide(5,6,7,8,clRed);
    AddSide(1,2,6,5,clYellow);
    AddSide(2,3,7,6,clGreen);
    AddSide(3,4,8,7,clPurple);
    AddSide(4,1,5,8,clSilver);
    {Copy the double buffer to the form}
  Form1.Canvas.CopyRect(RECT(0,0,200,200),DoubleBuffer.Canvas,RECT(0,0,200,200));
end;

{To bring the cube back to its original state, remove the rotation angles}
procedure TForm1.ResetCubeClick(Sender: TObject);
begin
  XAng := 0;
  YAng := 0;
  ZAng := 0;
end;

end.
```

Summary

The buzzword "multimedia" has created a lot of hype in the personal computer industry. In short, the use of multimedia is putting sound and video in applications. This chapter covered how to use the `PlaySound` API call to add sound effects to an application. You also covered the media player visual component, which can play all sorts of multimedia files including video. The media player component is highly configurable and can be used many different ways. For example, you examined using the component's interface and hiding the interface but maintaining the component's functionality. The last topic you covered was animation. It became clear that the media player was ideal for prerecorded video files, but there are times when you need to create smooth, on-the-fly animation. You examined how to improve performance and take advantage of certain methods that can be executed quickly. The chapter concluded with an example of a three-dimensional rotating cube that illustrates the power of using simple methods in Delphi to create animation.

Q&A

Q Can I use the MCI (media control interface) without using the media player component?

A Yes, all the multimedia API calls are available. If you have the source code for the media player component you will see the component itself uses the MCI API.

Q I used the `CopyRect` to move quickly a rectangular portion of a canvas. Are there any other ways to move parts of a canvas quickly?

A Yes, you can access the `Handle` property of a canvas, which is a handle to its device context. You can then use any of the Win32 GDI calls you operate on the picture. For example there is a call to move data to a parallelogram and you can perform various masking operations.

Workshop

Quiz

1. How does `PlaySound` know to wait until the sound has completed before executing the next instruction or to execute the next instruction while the sound is playing?
2. What does the call

   ```
   MediaPlayer1.DisplayRect := RECT(50,50,200,200);
   ```

   have on a Media Player component? *Hint:* It doesn't mean to play the video between coordinates (50,50 and 200,200).

3. How is your application notified when a media event has completed?
4. When performing animation, what is the problem with drawing a frame, erasing it, and then drawing the next frame?

Exercises

1. Write a program that continuously plays music in the background.
2. Use the Media Player component to play a video file. Give the user a set of choices as to where the video should be played (in its own windows or on the main form). Add scrollbars that let the user determine how big the picture should be.
3. Modify the rotating cube program so that the cube is rotating on a background that is a bitmap. Here is a hint: Replace the blank bitmap used to clear the frame with a real bitmap.

Week 2

Day 12

File Input/Output

File That Under...

One of the most common and valuable tasks every programmer must do at some point is work with files. A file is nothing more than an organized collection of data that is stored on hard disk, floppy disk, CD-ROM, tape, or other storage media. Obviously, database applications need to create, read, and write files, but files have many other uses too. Files can be used to store a program's setup information. They can be used to temporarily store information so that a program can use valuable system memory for other tasks and load information back in memory when needed. Files can even be used to easily pass information between programs; and of course, files are commonly used to save our work such as in a word processor or spreadsheet. Delphi handles files very well and it isn't all that difficult. The purpose of today's lesson is to walk you through the process of working with various file types and provide you with a reference of the necessary functions and procedures to make the job easier.

Today, you are going to look at attributes and file types. You learn how to work with text files, binary typed, and untyped files. You also take a look at some of the file- and directory-related functions that mimic some familiar DOS commands such as MkDir. You wrap up by talking about long filenames.

How About Them Attributes!

NEW TERM Files have special *attributes.* An attribute is a property that a file exhibits based on its setting. For example, if a file has its read-only attribute set to on, it can be read but not updated or deleted by most DOS commands or programs. Each file has an attribute byte that is used to store the attribute settings. Each setting is stored in one of the eight bits that make up the byte. Only six bits are used, two of which are used for directories and volume labels leaving us with only four to worry about when working with files. These four attributes are listed here:

File Attribute	*Delphi Constant*	*Description*
Read-only	faReadOnly	Allows files to be read from, but not updated or deleted.
Hidden	faHidden	Prevents the file from appearing on normal directory listings.
System	faSysFile	Marks a file for system use and prevents viewing in a directory listing.
Archive	faArchive	This attribute is turned off if a file has been backed up.

These attribute settings are toggled on or off as appropriate by programs using or creating the files. By default, all the attributes are turned off except for the archive bit (bit 5) when a file is created. In Delphi, as with other languages, you can change these attributes before or after you work on them as needed. Delphi provides functions such as `FileGetAttr` and `FileSetAttr` to allow us to get and set the attributes as needed. An example of where you might need this is if a file you needed to work on was read-only. You might set the read-only attribute to off, work on the file, and then set it back to on, thus protecting it from unwanted or accidental changes. Another thing worth noting here is that any combination of these attributes can be set on or off for any given file. So how does this all work? Break your attribute byte down to its binary representation and look at the bits.

Attribute Byte	*Bitmap*
Bit 0	Read-only bit
Bit 1	Hidden file bit
Bit 2	System file bit
Bit 3	Volume ID bit

Bit 4	Subdirectory bit
Bit 5	Archive bit
Bit 6	Not used
Bit 7	Not used

A newly created file's attributes would look like this:

Bit 7	*Bit 6*	*Bit 5*	*Bit 4*	*Bit 3*	*Bit 3*	*Bit 1*	*Bit 0*
0	0	1	0	0	0	0	0

In other words, 00100000 binary or 20 hex. Now say you wanted to set the read-only attribute. You could use Delphi's `FileSetAttr` function with the faReadOnly constant. The faReadOnly constant is set to 00000001 binary or 01 hex. When the filename and faReadOnly value is fed to the `FileSetAttr` function, it is `OR`'d into the Attribute byte. This example would clear the archive bit which may or may not be desirable depending on what you want to do. You'll learn how to work with multiple bits shortly.

NOTE

"Wait...Wait!" you say, "I don't know anything about binary or hex numbering systems." If this is the case, don't worry. I'll give you the information you need to work with file attributes as you go through this. You might find it helpful at some point in the future to get an article or book on computer math that covers binary and hexadecimal numbering systems in detail. If you are an old hand at this stuff, we won't bore you, we'll go through this fairly quickly covering just what we need to know for now.

Hex (short for hexadecimal) and binary are simply numbering systems like the decimal system that we use in our daily lives. What's the difference? The number of digits. Decimal has 10, 0-9. Binary has 2, 0 and 1. Finally, hex has 16, 0-9 and A-F or 0-F. Hex is commonly used in computer software development because it lends itself very well to translating to and from binary. The big deal about binary numbers and computers is that binary is the computer's native language. As we have seen with the attribute byte, one byte in the computer is often used to store up to 8 ON/OFF settings. Take the decimal number 173: in binary, 173 equals 10101101, in hex it is AD. You certainly don't want to write 10101101 when you can write AD. It is obviously much easier to remember AD than the binary equivalent. In Delphi, hex numbers are preceded by a "$", so our previous hex number would read $AD.

TIP

> In order to run Delphi, you obviously need to have Windows on your system. You can take advantage of the Windows calculator to do your number conversions and calculations. Just change the calculator to the scientific mode using the View menu. The calculator allows you to select the numbering system you want to work in. When you want to convert a number in the calculator display, simply click the option for the number system you want it converted to and it changes automatically. If you need more information on the Windows calculator, refer to its online help.

Looking at $AD or binary 10101101 (reading from right to left), you know from the attribute byte bitmap you looked at earlier that this would indicate a file with the following bits on: Read-only, System, Volume ID and Archive. Bit 8 is also set but not used. This would not be a valid attribute byte for a file you would be working on. Remember, Volume ID and Subdirectory are attributes that you will leave alone because they are taken care of when you create a volume label or subdirectory. They are not to be changed by the user or programmer. A more realistic number would be binary 100001 or $21. If you check the bitmap against this number, you will find that it shows that the Read-Only and Archive bits are set (file is Read-Only and file has not been backed up). Now take a look at how these bits are actually set. Say you wanted to set just the read-only bit of a file called JUNK.TXT. You could place the following line of code in your program:

```
FileSetAttr('JUNK.TXT',faReadOnly);
```

In the `FileSetAttr` statement, the faReadOnly constant equates to binary 00000001 or $01. This value in faReadOnly copied to the attribute byte. This example sets the Read-Only bit to 1 and all the other bits in the attribute byte to 0.

If you want to combine this constant with other constants or numbers, you can `OR` them together. When you `OR` two numbers, bit 0 of one number is `OR`'d with bit 0 of the next number, bit 1 is `OR`'d with bit 1, and so on. The `OR` function works just as it sounds. If one of the bits being `OR`'d is equal to 1, the result is 1. If neither bit is 1, then the result is 0. Following is the Truth table for the `OR` function and some examples of `OR` operations. In this case, you can achieve the same effect by adding the numbers or constants together, but it is useful to understand what happens when you `OR` numbers together.

`OR` Truth Table (Possible results for an `OR` operation)

1 OR 1 = 1
1 OR 0 = 1
0 OR 1 = 1
0 OR 0 = 0

Examples

```
10110010
OR
10010111
-------------------
10110111

10110101
OR
11100001
-------------------
```

NEW TERM

In both of the OR examples, you can see that the top numbers are different, but the bottom number stays the same. This, of course, causes the results to be different. This is called *masking*. Masking is a process that allows you to selectively view or change bits in a byte when it is used in an AND or OR operation with a predefined byte called a mask. By changing the mask (the number on the top) you can selectively turn on or off any bit or combination of bits. You can add constants and numbers or OR them together to create a mask that will be used to set more than one bit (attribute). In other words, if you wanted to set the Read-Only and Archive bits, you could do so with a statement like this: `FileSetAttr('JUNK.TXT',faReadOnly+faArchive)`. This would create a mask of 00100001.

Now, that you have two bits on, what if you want to turn one off? You simply call `FileSetAttr` again and only pass a mask containing the bits that you want to stay on, others will be turned off. The following causes the archive bit to be turned off while maintaining the Read-Only setting.

```
FileSetAttr('JUNK.TXT',faReadOnly);
```

If you use the example, all bits will be set to 0 except for the Read-Only bit (which may not be desired). This is because the faReaOnly constant has only one bit set and it is copied to the Attribute byte. The easiest way to solve our problem is to first get the attributes of a file and store them in a variable. Then you can create a mask that can be OR'd with the original settings so that you change only the bits you select. The following is code to do this:

```
Var
     FileAttr
Begin
     {Get the contents of the Attribute byte for MYFILE.TXT}
     FileAttr:=FileGetAttr('MYFILE.TXT');
     {OR  the mask (faReadOnly) with the attribute byte value that stored in
➥FileAttr
       and put the results in FileAttr}
     FileAttr:=FileAttr OR faReadOnly;
     {Set the Attribute byte to the new value stored in FileAttr}
     FileSetAttr('MYFILE.TXT',FileAttr);
end;
```

12

Look at what would happen if you created a new file and ran it through the preceding routine. You create your file called MYFILE.TXT. The attribute byte for the new file looks like this:

```
00100000   (Bit 5, the archive bit is set)
```

Retrieve the Attribute byte and store it in a variable called `FileAttr`. Next, `OR` `FileAttr` with the predefined mask, faReadOnly, storing the results in `FileAttr`. This gives you a new mask that combines the old settings with the new ones.

```
00100000
      OR
00000001
       =
00100001
```

Working in binary makes it easier to understand what bits you need to turn on and off and what the results will look like. If you convert the above to hex, you can see what is going on in your code. For example, the numbers above in hex would look like this:

```
$20 OR $01 = $21
```

The original Attribute byte contains $20 and is `OR`'d with faReadOnly (which equals $01) and the result is $21.

Now say you wanted to see if a bit was set in the Attribute byte. For this use the `AND` operator. Using the same numbers as above, you would find that none of the bits you are looking for are on. This example looks for the read-only bit.

```
00100000
     AND
00000001
       =
00000000
```

If you wanted to check the status of all the bits, you would `AND` the attribute byte with $FF or 11111111. This would look like this.

```
00100000
     AND
11111111
       =
00100000
```

As you can see, all the bits that are on in the attribute byte would be passed on through.

All this binary, hex and file attribute theory is fine, but what about in practice you ask? I knew you'd ask that question, so create a small program that allows you to view and toggle the four file attributes that were discussed (read-only, system, hidden and archive) for a specified file. This gives you chance to really see this all in action in a useful windows utility.

Figure 12.1.
File Attribute Manager screen.

First, create a new project with a single form called FILEATTR.DPR. The unit name should be ATTRSCR.PAS. Using Figure 12.1 as your guide, add the following components to the form: one Bevel, one GroupBox, three BitBtn, four CheckBox, one Label, one Edit, one DirectoryListBox, one FileListBox, and one DriveComboBox. Starting at the top, the label comes first, and next up is the editbox. Below the edit box, to the left is the DirectoryListBox with the FileListBox to its right. Below this is the the DriveComboBox. On the bottom of the form to the left is the Bevel with the three BitBtns inside. Finally, on the bottom right is the GroupBox with the four CheckBoxes inside. Now go make the necessary changes to the component properties, add some code, and get this thing running. Change the Label1 `Caption` property to `Filename:`. Next, delete all the characters from `Edit1.Text` property (for example, Edit1).

Assuming you have added the DirectoryListBox, FileListBox and DriveCombo components, you can now easily tie them together. First change the `FileList` property on the DirectoryListBox to `FileListBox1`. Notice that FileListBox1 was a choice you could select from. This makes connecting these components very easy. Next, go the DriveComboBox and change the `DirList` property to `DirectoryListBox1`. Now go to the FileListBox and change the `FileEdit` property to `Edit1`. These changes cause these components to work together as one component like in a File dialog box. You need to make a few other changes to make your utility work properly. If you want File Attribute Manager to be able to read hidden and system files and display them, you need to change a few properties in the FileListBox. Notice a property for the FileListBox called `FileType`. This property has some nested properties that you must change. Make sure the following properties are set to True: `ftReadOnly`, `ftSystem`, `ftHidden`, `ftArchive`, and `ftNormal`. The two remaining (`ftVolumeID` and `ftDirectory`) should be set to False. Change the `Caption` property for the four checkboxes to `Read Only` for CheckBox1, `Hidden File` for CheckBox2, `System` for CheckBox3, and `Archive` for CheckBox4.

Change the names of the three BitBtns to BitBtnOk, BitBtnSave and BitBtnClose. On BitBtnOk, change the `Kind` property to `bkOk`. On BitBtnSave, change to `Kind` property to `bkAll` and `BitBtnClose`, change the `Kind` property to `bkClose`. On the bkSave button, change the caption property to `&Save`. Now add some code to the buttons.

The BitBtnOk code should look like the following code:

```
procedure TForm1.BitBtnOKClick(Sender: TObject);
begin
    {Get file attributes for selected file}
    {Check to see which attributes bits are set and check appropriate boxes}
    fname:=Edit1.Text;
    AttrByte:=FileGetAttr(fname);
    If AttrByte AND faReadOnly = faReadOnly Then
       CheckBox1.Checked:=True
    else
       CheckBox1.Checked:=False;
    If AttrByte AND faHidden = faHidden then
       CheckBox2.Checked:=True
    else
       CheckBox2.Checked:=False;
    If AttrByte AND faSysFile = faSysFile then
       CheckBox3.Checked:=True
    else
       CheckBox3.Checked:=False;
    If AttrByte AND faArchive = faArchive then
       CheckBox4.Checked:=True
    else
       CheckBox4.Checked:=False;
end;
```

The BitBtnSave code should look like the following:

```
procedure TForm1.BitBtnSaveClick(Sender: TObject);
begin
     {Clear Attribute byte}
     AttrByte:=0;
     {update file attribute byte from check box settings}
     If CheckBox1.Checked = True then
        AttrByte:=AttrByte OR faReadOnly;
     If CheckBox2.Checked = True then
        AttrByte:=AttrByte OR faHidden;
     If CheckBox3.Checked = True then
        AttrByte:=AttrByte OR faSysFile;
     If CheckBox4.Checked = True then
        AttrByte:=AttrByte OR faArchive;
     {Write settings in checkboxes to file attribute byte}
     FileSetAttr(fname,AttrByte);
end;
```

The BitBtnClose code should look like the following:

```
procedure TForm1.BitBtnCloseClick(Sender: TObject);
begin
     Application.Terminate;
end;
```

You need to add the following to the Implementation section:

```
Var
   fname:string;
   AttrByte:integer;
```

The code for the OnDblClick event handler for FileListBox1 should appear as follows:

```
procedure TForm1.FileListBox1DblClick(Sender: TObject);
begin
     Form1.BitBtnOkClick(self);
```

Ok, if you have typed everything correctly into the correct sections up to here, your finished unit should appear as follows:

```
unit Attrscr;

interface

uses
 Windows, Messages, SysUtils, Classes, Graphics, Controls, Forms, Dialogs,
➥Menus, StdCtrls, Buttons, FileCtrl, ExtCtrls;

type
  TForm1 = class(TForm)
    Label1: TLabel;
    Edit1: TEdit;
    GroupBox1: TGroupBox;
    CheckBox1: TCheckBox;
    CheckBox2: TCheckBox;
    CheckBox3: TCheckBox;
    CheckBox4: TCheckBox;
    BitBtnOK: TBitBtn;
    BitBtnClose: TBitBtn;
    FileListBox1: TFileListBox;
    DirectoryListBox1: TDirectoryListBox;
    DriveComboBox1: TDriveComboBox;
    BitBtnSave: TBitBtn;
    Bevel1: TBevel;
    procedure BitBtnCloseClick(Sender: TObject);
    procedure BitBtnOKClick(Sender: TObject);
    procedure BitBtnSaveClick(Sender: TObject);
    procedure FileListBox1DblClick(Sender: TObject);
  private
    { Private declarations }
  public
    { Public declarations }
  end;

var
  Form1: TForm1;

implementation
Var
   fname:string;
   AttrByte:integer;
{$R *.DFM}
```

12

```
procedure TForm1.BitBtnCloseClick(Sender: TObject);
begin
     Application.Terminate;
end;

procedure TForm1.BitBtnOKClick(Sender: TObject);
begin
    {Get file attributes for selected file}
    {Check to see which attributes bits are set and check appropriate boxes}
    fname:=Edit1.Text;
    AttrByte:=FileGetAttr(fname);
    If AttrByte AND faReadOnly = faReadOnly Then
       CheckBox1.Checked:=True
    else
       CheckBox1.Checked:=False;
    If AttrByte AND faHidden = faHidden then
       CheckBox2.Checked:=True
    else
       CheckBox2.Checked:=False;
    If AttrByte AND faSysFile = faSysFile then
       CheckBox3.Checked:=True
    else
       CheckBox3.Checked:=False;
    If AttrByte AND faArchive = faArchive then
       CheckBox4.Checked:=True
    else
       CheckBox4.Checked:=False;
end;

procedure TForm1.BitBtnSaveClick(Sender: TObject);
begin
     {Clear Attribute byte}
     AttrByte:=0;
     {update file attribute byte from check box settings}
     If CheckBox1.Checked = True then
        AttrByte:=AttrByte OR faReadOnly;
     If CheckBox2.Checked = True then
        AttrByte:=AttrByte OR faHidden;
     If CheckBox3.Checked = True then
        AttrByte:=AttrByte OR faSysFile;
     If CheckBox4.Checked = True then
        AttrByte:=AttrByte OR faArchive;
     {Write settings in checkboxes to file attribute byte}
     FileSetAttr(fname,AttrByte);
end;

procedure TForm1.FileListBox1DblClick(Sender: TObject);
begin
 BitBtnOkClick(self);
end;

end.
```

To test the program, create a temporary file and run the File Attribute Manager. The Archive checkbox should be checked and all the other boxes are unchecked. Check Hidden File checkbox and click on Save. Do a directory listing and look for the filename. The filename should not appear in the directory listing (unless you are using a program that displays hidden files). You can then uncheck the Hidden File checkbox. Click on Save and the file again appears in a directory listing. You should have a good understanding of file attributes, so let's move on to file types.

What's Your Type?

There are two basic types of files: *text* and *binary*. There are many different ways you can store or format the data in these two file types, but they always fit into one of the two categories. So why the different types? Like anything, each file type has its advantages and disadvantages. What works well for one situation may not work well for another. Take a look at the file types and some examples of how they may be used. Keep in mind that these are examples. You are free to determine how to format and work with the data stored in a file to suite your needs.

Text Files

Most of us are familiar with text files. *Text* files are simple files containing plain ASCII characters. Data in a text file is typically stored and retrieved sequentially one line at a time, and each line ends with Carriage Return (`$D`) and Line Feed (`$A`) characters. Because data is handled sequentially, doing searches on large files or making a lot of changes to a text file can be quite tedious and inefficient. However, there are many situations, such as exporting data to a standard format, when using text files is the best choice. As a general rule, if you plan to work with data sequentially and don't need to jump to different locations in a file, a text file is probably a good choice. Look at some of the functions and procedures you need to know about for working with text files and then build a program that stores and reads data in a text file.

The first thing you need to look at is a variable type called `TextFile`. With `TextFile` you declare a variable that will be used identify the type file you wish to work with. Your declaration might look like the following:

```
Var
     MyFile : TextFile;
```

Now that you have a variable associated with the type, you need a way to pass this info to Delphi as well as the name of the file you wish to work with. This is done with a procedure called `AssignFile`. If you are familiar with Pascal, you remember the `Assign` procedure. Delphi is backward compatible with the `Assign` procedure, but you should use `AssignFile` in Delphi because it avoids scope conflicts. Use `AssignFile` like this:

```
AssignFile(MyFile,filename)
```

Where `MyFile` is the variable you defined as a text file, and `filename` is a string containing the name of the file you wish to work with. Once you have used `AssignFile`, you can refer to the file as `MyFile`.

There are few other procedures you need to know about for writing to text files. Read these descriptions and then look at the syntax and descriptions in the online help for each of these procedures. Make sure to study the following code and the comments preceding each procedure.

Procedure	*Description*
`ReWrite`	Creates and opens a new file. Any existing files with same name will be overwritten
`Writeln`	Writes a line of text to the open file with a CR/LF combination at the end.
`CloseFile`	Finishes updating the current file and closes it.

For reading text files you will need the following:

Procedure	*Description*
`Reset`	Opens an existing file. Text files are opened in read only.
`Readln`	Reads the current line of text from an open text file. Each line ends with CR/LF comination.

Ok, now that you have some definitions down, build a program that reads and writes a simple text file and see how these procedures work. Open a new project in Delphi and use Figure 12.2 as a guide to build the following Text File Demo application. From top to bottom, place Label1, Edit1, Label2, Edit2. Working from left to right, place three buttons along the bottom. Set the captions of each component to match Figure 12.2. All the code that you need to add to make this application work is in the three buttons. Add the following code to the appropriate buttons.

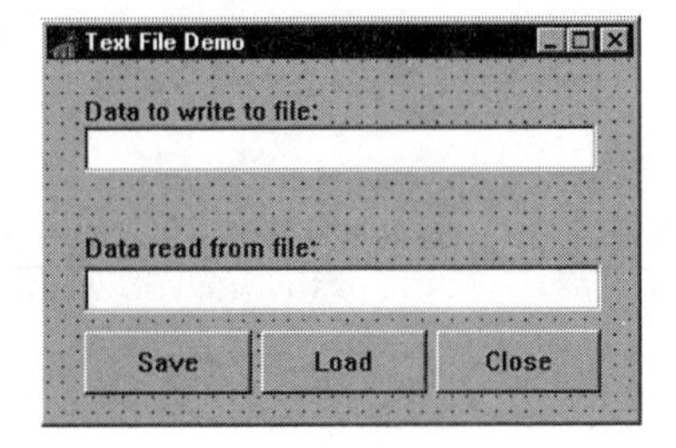

Figure 12.2.
Text File Demo.

Add this code to the Save button (button1):

```
procedure TForm1.Button1Click(Sender: TObject);
Var
   OutFile : TextFile;
   fname,OutString : string;
begin
   {Assign a filename to the variable}
   fname:='JUNKFILE.TXT';
   {Identify the filename and type as OutFile}
   AssignFile(OutFile,fname);
   {create and open a new file identified as OutFile}
   Rewrite(OutFile);
   {Get text from the write edit box}
   OutString:=Edit1.Text;
   {Write out the text in OutString to file}
   Writeln(OutFile,OutString);
   {Upadate and close the file}
   CloseFile(OutFile);
end;
```

Add this code to the Load Button (button2)

```
procedure TForm1.Button2Click(Sender: TObject);
Var
   InFile : TextFile;
   fname,InString : string;
begin
   {Assign text file name to variable}
   fname:='JUNKFILE.TXT';
   {Identify the text file as InFile}
   AssignFile(InFile,fname);
   {Open the file identified with InFile}
   Reset(Infile);
   {Read in a line of text}
   Readln(InFile,InString);
   {Store the line read in to the Read Text box}
   Edit2.Text:=InString;
   {Close the file}
   CloseFile(InFile);
end;
```

Add this code to the Close Button (Button3)

```
procedure TForm1.Button3Click(Sender: TObject);
begin
     Application.Terminate;
end;
```

The full listing should look as shown in Listing 12.1.

TYPE

Listing 12.1. Textform.

```
unit Textform;

interface

uses
 Windows, Messages, SysUtils, Classes, Graphics, Controls, Forms, Dialogs,
StdCtrls;

type
  TForm1 = class(TForm)
    Edit1: TEdit;
    Edit2: TEdit;
    Label1: TLabel;
    Label2: TLabel;
    Button1: TButton;
    Button2: TButton;
    Button3: TButton;
    procedure Button3Click(Sender: TObject);
    procedure Button1Click(Sender: TObject);
    procedure Button2Click(Sender: TObject);
  private
    { Private declarations }
  public
    { Public declarations }
  end;

var
  Form1: TForm1;

implementation

{$R *.DFM}

procedure TForm1.Button3Click(Sender: TObject);
begin
     Application.Terminate;
end;

procedure TForm1.Button1Click(Sender: TObject);
Var
   OutFile : TextFile;
   fname,OutString : string;
begin
   {Assign a filename to the variable}
   fname:='JUNKFILE.TXT';
   {Identify the filename and type as OutFile}
   AssignFile(OutFile,fname);
   {create and open a new file identified as OutFile}
   Rewrite(OutFile);
   {Get text from the write edit box}
   OutString:=Edit1.Text;
   {Write out the text in OutString to file}
   Writeln(OutFile,OutString);
   {Update and close the file}
```

```
   CloseFile(OutFile);
end;

procedure TForm1.Button2Click(Sender: TObject);
Var
   InFile : TextFile;
   fname,InString : string;
begin
   {Assign text file name to variable}
   fname:='JUNKFILE.TXT';
   {Identify the text file as InFile}
   AssignFile(InFile,fname);
   {Open the file identified with InFile}
   Reset(Infile);
   {Read in a line of text}
   Readln(InFile,InString);
   {Store the line read in to the Read Text box}
   Edit2.Text:=InString;
   {Close the file}
   CloseFile(InFile);
end;

end.
```

ANALYSIS This simple little application allows you to type text into the top edit box, press the save button, and have it written to a file called JUNKFILE.TXT. You can read the same file and have the text read from the file displayed in the bottom edit box. Take a minute or two to experiment with this application. You might even use Notepad or another editor to edit the JUNKFILE.TXT by hand just to verify the program is working properly and the way you would expect.

You have seen how to read and write a single line of text and it should be fairly obvious that you could set up a loop to read or write several lines of text. There is one catch here; you can write out to a file until you run out of disk space, but how do we know when to stop reading text in? In other words, how do you know when you are at the end of the file? Glad you asked! Delphi, like other languages, has a function to tell you when you have gone past the end of the file. That function is called `Eof`. To use `Eof`, you simply give it the file variable used with `AssignFile` and it returns a Boolean value that can be used in a determinate loop such as a while loop.

The following illustrates use of `Eof`:

```
while not Eof(InFile) do
    Begin
       Readln(InFile,MyString);
    end;
```

This loop would continue until a True is returned by `Eof`. With this in mind, write a quick-and-dirty text editor and see how it works. In this example, use the Memo, OpenDialog,

SaveDialog and MainMenu components. Drop one of each of these components onto a new form. Click the OpenDialog component and double click the `Filter` property in the object inspector to bring up the Filer Editor. Add the following two filters to the Filter Editor:

Filter Name	*Filter*
Text Files	*.txt
All Files	*.*

Do the same thing for the SaveDialog component. Using the MainMenu component, add a File menu with Open, Save, a separator line, and Exit options under it. Change the `Align` property for the Memo component to `alClient`. This causes the memo component to automatically size to fill the entire form client area. Set the Memo's `ScrollBar` property to `ssVertical`. Now just add a bit of code to these File Menu options and you have a simple text editor.

To the File | Open menu option, add

```
procedure TForm1.Open1Click(Sender: TObject);
Var
   InFile : TextFile;
   fname,InString : string;
begin
   If OpenDialog1.Execute then
   Begin
      fname:=OpenDialog1.FileName;
      AssignFile(InFile,fname);
      Reset(Infile);
      While not Eof(InFile) do
         Begin
            Readln(InFile,InString);
            Memo1.Lines.Add(InString);
         end;
      CloseFile(InFile);
      {Set filename in caption}
      Form1.Caption:=Form1.Caption + '['+fname+']';
   end;
end;
```

The preceding code uses a loop to load one line of text at a time into the Memo box until it reaches the end of the file. This is not the best way to load text into the memo component, but the idea here is to see how `Eof` works. You could have used the following line to load your file and save about 10 lines of code:

```
Memo1.Lines.LoadfromFile(OpenDialog1.FileName);
```

Using this method might appear like the following:

```
begin
  if OpenDialog1.Execute then
  begin
    Memo1.Lines.LoadfromFile(OpenDialog1.FileName);
  end;
```

To the File | Save menu option add

```
procedure TForm1.Save1Click(Sender: TObject);
Var
   OutFile : TextFile;
   fname : string;
begin
   If SaveDialog1.Execute then
     begin
        fname:=SaveDialog1.FileName;
        AssignFile(OutFile,fname);
        Rewrite(OutFile);
        {Write the contents of memo out in one block}
        Writeln(OutFile,Memo1.Text);
     end;
   CloseFile(OutFile);
   {Set filename in caption}
   Form1.Caption:=Form1.Caption + '['+fname+']';
```

The File | Save code writes out the text in the memo box as one block of text so you didn't need a loop. There are other instances that you may run into where you will need a loop to write data one line at a time out to a file. The process is similar to reading in with a loop except that you either need to know the number of lines to be written or have some other method of determining when the loop should end.

Finally, to the File | Exit menu option add

```
procedure TForm1.Exit1Click(Sender: TObject);
begin
     Application.Terminate;
end;
```

Listing 12.2 shows the complete code for the Editor.

TYPE **Listing 12.2. Edit.**

```
unit Edit;

interface

uses
 Windows, Messages, SysUtils, Classes, Graphics, Controls, Forms, Dialogs,
➥StdCtrls, Menus;

type
  TForm1 = class(TForm)
    MainMenu1: TMainMenu;
    File1: TMenuItem;
    Open1: TMenuItem;
    Save1: TMenuItem;
    N1: TMenuItem;
    Exit1: TMenuItem;
    Memo1: TMemo;
```

continues

Listing 12.2. continued

```
    OpenDialog1: TOpenDialog;
    SaveDialog1: TSaveDialog;
    procedure Open1Click(Sender: TObject);
    procedure FormCreate(Sender: TObject);
    procedure Exit1Click(Sender: TObject);
    procedure Save1Click(Sender: TObject);
  private
    { Private declarations }
  public
    { Public declarations }
  end;

var
  Form1: TForm1;

implementation

{$R *.DFM}

procedure TForm1.Open1Click(Sender: TObject);
Var
   InFile : TextFile;
   fname,InString : string;
begin
   If OpenDialog1.Execute then
   Begin
      fname:=OpenDialog1.FileName;
      AssignFile(InFile,fname);
      Reset(Infile);
      While not Eof(InFile) do
         Begin
            Readln(InFile,InString);
            Memo1.Lines.Add(InString);
         end;
      CloseFile(InFile);
      {Set filename in caption}
      Form1.Caption:=Form1.Caption + '['+fname+']';
   end;
end;

procedure TForm1.FormCreate(Sender: TObject);
begin
     {Clear text from memo box}
     Memo1.Text:='';
end;

procedure TForm1.Exit1Click(Sender: TObject);
begin
     Application.Terminate;
end;

procedure TForm1.Save1Click(Sender: TObject);
Var
   OutFile : TextFile;
   fname : string;
```

```
begin
   If SaveDialog1.Execute then
     begin
        fname:=SaveDialog1.FileName;
        AssignFile(OutFile,fname);
        Rewrite(OutFile);
        {Write the contents of memo out in one block}
        Writeln(OutFile,Memo1.Text);
     end;
   CloseFile(OutFile);
   {Set filename in caption}
   Form1.Caption:=Form1.Caption + '['+fname+']';
end;

end.
```

ANALYSIS The finished program will look like your basic Windows text editor such as Notepad, with fewer options and features of course. If you have not done so already, do a File | Project Save As and save the unit as EDIT.PAS and the project file as WINEDIT.DPR. Run the program and try loading a test text file. Make some changes to the file and save it back to a new filename. Use Notepad or another editor to create your test text files and verify files created or updated by your editor.

As mentioned earlier, there are many ways you can format and work with text files. Use your imagination and remember that there is no single right answer. You must determine what is best for the task at hand.

Binary Files

The other file type is *binary*. All non-text file types fit this category. A binary file is simply a file containing the binary information written to it by the program. In the case of ASCII characters, the ASCII code is the binary information written to the file. Unlike text files however, any file opened as binary including text files, program files, bitmaps, and so on, can be read by your program. In this mode you are responsible for determining how to handle data when it comes in.

Typed Files

This first flavor of a binary file is the *typed file*. These are files for which you have decided the on format or structure of the file and the type of data to be stored in it, such as integers, reals, strings and their lengths, and so on. A good example of this would be a simple phone/address book type program. Create a simple program to demonstrate this. Create a new project saving the unit as ADDR.PAS and the project as ADDRESS.DPR. First, create your record structure. In the implementation section, put the following code just below the `{$R *.DFM}`:

```
type
  Address = record
        Lastname: String[20];
        Firstname: String[20];
        Phone: String[15];
        StreetAddress : String[50];
        City : String[40];
        State : String[2];
        ZipCode : String[10];
  end;
```

You have created your own type called `Address`. This example only uses strings, but you could have used any other variable types (for example, integer, real, byte, and so on) in your record type. Use this new type to create some variables for your program. Next, just below the above code, add the following:

```
Var
   AddressFile : File of Address;
   AddressData : Address;
```

`AddressFile` is a File variable of type `Address`. File variables are used with many of the file I/O procedures and functions. `AddressData` is a variable of type, `Address`. Because your new type, `Address`, is a record, `AddressData` becomes a buffer with the structure of the `Address` type. This allows you to easily read or write the data in the buffer with one line of code while maintaining some order. Each record saved to disk will be the same size regardless of the data entered into it. This also known as a *fixed length record* and is the idea behind typed files.

Ok, before you get too much farther into your program, take a look at the functions and procedures you will be using to work with typed files. For more detail on these, please refer to the Delphi documentation or online help. The purpose here is to show you the functions and procedures available for the task at hand.

AssignFile

Syntax: `procedure AssignFile(var F, String);`

Purpose: Used to assign a filename to a file variable for use by other file I/O functions.

Reset

Syntax: `procedure Reset(var F [: File; RecSize: Word ] );`

Purpose: Used to open an existing file that has been assigned to a file variable with `AssignFile`.

Rewrite

Syntax: `procedure Rewrite(var F: File [; Recsize: Word ] );`

Purpose: Used to create and open a file that has been assigned to a file variable with `AssignFile`.

Seek

Syntax: `procedure Seek(var F; N: Longint);`

Purpose: Used to move to the file pointer to the specified record within the open file.

Read

Syntax: `procedure Read(F , V1 [, V2,...,Vn ] );`

Purpose: Used to read records in from a file.

Write

Syntax: `procedure Write(F, V1 [V2,...Vn]);`

Purpose: Used to write records to a file.

Eof

Syntax: `function Eof(var F): Boolean;`

Purpose: Used to determine if the program is at the end of the file. Used in conjunction with `Read`.

CloseFile

Syntax: `procedure CloseFile(var F);`

Purpose: Used to update the file with any final changes and close it.

12

Sample Project

On with the program! Earlier you created the project, added a type called `Address`, and some variables. Add the following variables just below the line containing `AddressData : Address;`

```
Fname : String;
RecSize,CurRec : Longint;
```

Now add seven edit boxes, seven labels, four buttons, and one BitBtn. Using Figure 12.3 as a guide, lay out the edit boxes and the labels starting with Edit1 and Label1 at the top and working down toward the bottom and left to right on the last line. Change the caption and name properties for the buttons as well as the BitBtn.

Listing 12.3 will be created by Delphi. Examine the code and then use it to add the code to the appropriate controls.

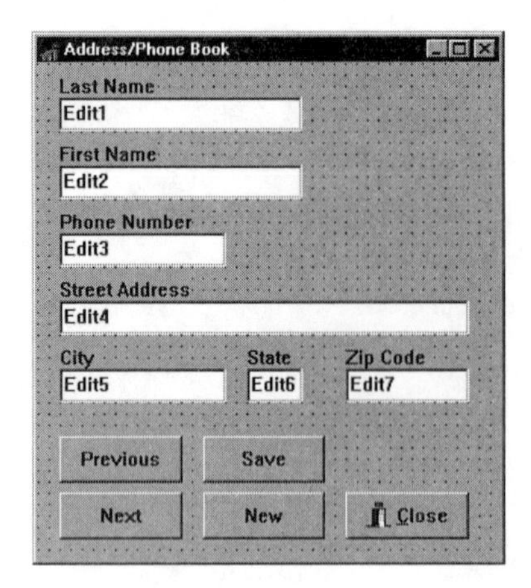

Figure 12.3.
Typed file demo–address/ phone book design.

TYPE Listing 12.3. Addr.

```
unit Addr;

interface

uses
 Windows, Messages, SysUtils, Classes, Graphics, Controls, Forms, Dialogs,
➥StdCtrls, Buttons;

type
  TForm1 = class(TForm)
    Edit1: TEdit;
    Edit2: TEdit;
    Edit3: TEdit;
    Edit4: TEdit;
    Edit5: TEdit;
    Edit6: TEdit;
    Edit7: TEdit;
    Label1: TLabel;
    Label2: TLabel;
    Label3: TLabel;
    Label4: TLabel;
    Label5: TLabel;
    Label6: TLabel;
    Label7: TLabel;
    Previous: TButton;
    Next: TButton;
    Save: TButton;
    New: TButton;
    Close: TBitBtn;
    procedure FormCreate(Sender: TObject);
    procedure NewClick(Sender: TObject);
    procedure PreviousClick(Sender: TObject);
    procedure NextClick(Sender: TObject);
    procedure SaveClick(Sender: TObject);
```

```
    procedure CloseClick(Sender: TObject);
  private
    { Private declarations }
    procedure LoadRecord;
    procedure SaveRecord;
    procedure ShowRecord;
    procedure ClearData;
  public
    { Public declarations }

  end;

var
  Form1: TForm1;

implementation
{$R *.DFM}

type
  Address = record
       Lastname: String[20];
       Firstname: String[20];
       Phone: String[15];
       StreetAddress : String[50];
       City : String[40];
       State : String[2];
       ZipCode : String[10];
  end;
Var
   AddressFile : File of Address;
   AddressData : Address;
   Fname : String;
   RecSize,CurRec : Longint;

procedure TForm1.LoadRecord;
begin
  {Load record}
  Read(AddressFile,AddressData);
  {Display record on screen}
  ShowRecord;
end;

procedure TForm1.SaveRecord;
begin
  {Copy record from screen to record}
  AddressData.Lastname:=Edit1.Text;
  AddressData.Firstname:=Edit2.Text;
  AddressData.Phone:=Edit3.Text;
  AddressData.StreetAddress:=Edit4.Text;
  AddressData.City:=Edit5.Text;
  AddressData.State:=Edit6.Text;
  AddressData.ZipCode:=Edit7.Text;
  {Write record to disk}
  Write(AddressFile,AddressData);
end;
```

continues

Listing 12.3. continued

```
procedure TForm1.ClearData;
begin
       {Clear the edit boxes}
       Edit1.Text:='';
       Edit2.Text:='';
       Edit3.Text:='';
       Edit4.Text:='';
       Edit5.Text:='';
       Edit6.Text:='';
       Edit7.Text:='';
end;
procedure TForm1.FormCreate(Sender: TObject);
begin
   {Clear the edit boxes}
   ClearData;
   {Clear Current Record Counter}
   CurRec:=0;
   {Set Filename}
   Fname:='ADDRESS.DAT';
   {Set File Variable}
   AssignFile(AddressFile,Fname);
   {Get Record Size}
   RecSize:=SizeOf(AddressData);
   {If file exists, load it}
   If FileExists(Fname) then
   Begin
       Reset(AddressFile);
       If not Eof(AddressFile) then
          begin
             Read(AddressFile,AddressData);
             ShowRecord;
          end;
   end

   {Else create it}
   else
       Begin
          ClearData;
          Rewrite(AddressFile);
       end;
end;

procedure TForm1.NewClick(Sender: TObject);
begin
    repeat
       CurRec:=CurRec+1;
       Seek(AddressFile,CurRec);
    until Eof(AddressFile);
    {Clear edit boxes}
    ClearData;
    {Create a new record}
    SaveRecord;
    {Roll back to current record}
    Seek(AddressFile,CurRec);
end;
```

```
procedure TForm1.PreviousClick(Sender: TObject);
begin
     If CurRec-1 < 0 then
     begin
     {If past beginning of file, put to first record
      and display message}
         CurRec:=0;
         Seek(AddressFile,CurRec);
         ShowMessage('This is the begining of the file');
     end
     {Otherwise, move back one record and display}
     else
     Begin
         CurRec:=CurRec-1;
         Seek(AddressFile,CurRec);
         Read(AddressFile,AddressData);
         Seek(AddressFile,CurRec);
         ShowRecord;
     end;
end;

procedure TForm1.NextClick(Sender: TObject);
begin
    {Advance to next record}
    CurRec:=CurRec+1;
    Seek(AddressFile,CurRec);
    {If not past end of file, read record and display}
    If not Eof(AddressFile) Then
       begin
         Read(AddressFile,AddressData);
         Seek(AddressFile,CurRec);
         ShowRecord;
       end
    {If past end of file, roll back to last record and
     display message}
    else
       begin
         CurRec:=CurRec-1;
         Seek(AddressFile,CurRec);
         ShowMessage('This is the end of the file');
       end;
end;

procedure TForm1.ShowRecord;
begin
  {Copy record data to edit boxes}
  Form1.Edit1.Text:=AddressData.Lastname;
  Form1.Edit2.Text:=AddressData.Firstname;
  Form1.Edit3.Text:=AddressData.Phone;
  Form1.Edit4.Text:=AddressData.StreetAddress;
  Form1.Edit5.Text:=AddressData.City;
  Form1.Edit6.Text:=AddressData.State;
  Form1.Edit7.Text:=AddressData.ZipCode;
end;

procedure TForm1.SaveClick(Sender: TObject);
```

continues

Listing 12.3. continued

```
begin
     {Save Record}
     SaveRecord;
     {Display record in edit boxes}
     ShowRecord;
end;

procedure TForm1.CloseClick(Sender: TObject);
begin
     {Save current record}
     SaveRecord;
     {Close File}
     CloseFile(AddressFile);
     {Exit application}
     Application.Terminate;
end;

end.
```

ANALYSIS You have just written your own Addresss/Phone Book database application without using a database engine. This program creates a data file called address.dat, takes input from the user, and stores it in the file in the form of records. The code in the New button clears the input fields and allows the user to enter a new record. The Save button writes the data out to the address.dat file. The Previous and Next buttons allow you to move back and forth in the database from one record to another. And of course, the Close button exits the application.

You should now be ready to test the Address/Phone book application. Run the application; you should see the screen in Figure 12.4. When the program runs for the first time, it detects whether the data file is present. In this case, it should find no file and create it (ADDRESS.DAT). Enter your name, address, and phone number into the edit boxes and select Save. To enter the next record, press the New button. The boxes clear and are ready for the next record to be entered. Enter a few more records in the same fashion, pressing Save when you are done with each record. Now test the application by moving through the records using the Previous and Next buttons. You should notice that when you get to the beginning or end of the file a message box appears and indicates that you are at the end of the record. It is obviously important to prevent or trap errors as well as attempts to move past the beginning or end of the file. Because you have added the code that does this, it also adds a nice touch to the application to notify the user that he or she is at the beginning or end as you have done here. Exit the program and then run it again. This time, it finds the data file (ADDRESS.DAT) and loads it displaying the first record. As before, you should be able to move through, edit, save, and add new records.

Now that you have created a working application, take a few minutes to go back and study the code. Read the comments in the listing to understand what is going on. In the `FormCreate` event, notice the code that checks for the existence of a data file. If one is found, it is opened

using `Reset`. The first record is loaded and displayed on the screen, otherwise it is created using `Rewrite` and you are presented with a blank screen ready to input data. Study the code and comments in each of the buttons as well as these procedures: `LoadRecord`, `SaveRecord`, `ShowRecord`, `ClearData`. Once you are comfortable with typed files, continue on.

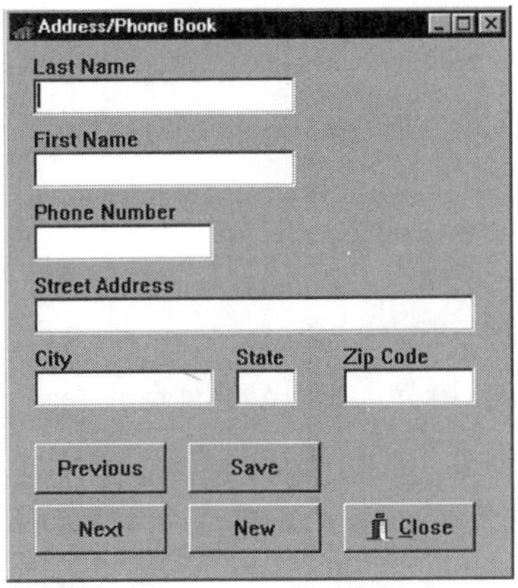

Figure 12.4.
Typed file demo–address/ phone book demo.

Untyped Files

Untyped files give you more flexibility in how you work with files. You can essentially jump to any location, change one byte or an entire block, save the data, and close the file. When you write your code, you have no rigid structure to worry about and your code can work with any type of file you want, and in any fashion you want. There is a catch however, you must write your code to determine exactly where in the file you want to work. This is done through the use of file pointers, some knowledge of the file, and some intelligence built into the program. Record sizes can vary and it is entirely up to the programmer to determine where and how big any record or piece of data is. Caution is advised when working with untyped files, but they can be very useful. What if you had a file that was quite large and you wanted to replace all the spaces with commas? You could write a simple Delphi program that would read the file into a buffer one block at a time, scan the buffer for spaces, and change them to commas as it goes and then save the changes back to disk. Again, it wouldn't matter if it was a text or binary file nor does it matter how the data was stored. The point here, is that you really have no restrictions as to how you access or work with data in untyped files. You're the boss! Before we go any further, let's look at a few more procedures and a functions that you'll be using.

BlockRead

Syntax: `BlockRead(var F: File; var Buf; Count: Word [; var Result: Word]);`

Purpose: Reads a block of data from disk into a buffer.

BlockWrite

Syntax: `BlockWrite(var f: File; var Buf; Count: Word [; var Result: Word]);`

Purpose: Writes a block of data from memory to disk.

FilePos

Syntax: `FilePos(var F): Longint;`

Purpose: Retrieves the current file pointer position.

Sample Project

These functions are discussed more, but now let's create a program to read a file and convert all spaces to commas.

Follow these steps and create the form for this application.

1. Create a new Delphi project and name save the unit as SP2CMA.PAS.
2. Save the project as SP2COMMA.DPR.
3. Add three buttons, one edit box and one label to the form.
4. Change the forms caption to read "Space to Comma Conversion."
5. Add an OpenDialog component to the form.
6. Double-click the `Filter` property and use the Filter editor to set the Filter name to "All Files" and the Filter to "*.*".
7. Set the edit box and `Label Visible` property to False.

The form should look like Figure 12.5.

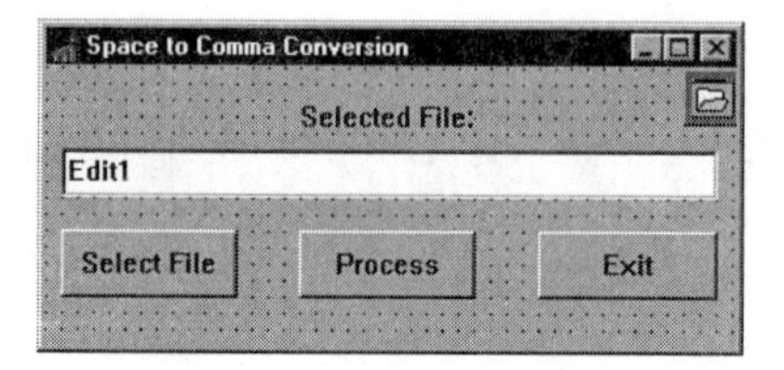

Figure 12.5.
Space to comma conversion program.

The meat of the program is in the OnClick event for the Process button. This is where code that loads data from disk, converts the spaces to commas, and saves the data back to disk. Let's take a look at some of the code.

In the following, you set up some variables needed for this operation. `InFile` is a variable of type `File` that we have already been exposed to. `Fbuffer` is an array of type `Byte` which is a 1K buffer that you can use to store the data read from the file. `FPointer` is used to store the file pointer (position in the file) so you can return to this position after a `Read` or `Write` operation.

```
Var
   InFile : File;
   FBuffer : array [0..1023] of Byte;
   FPointer : Longint;
   BytesRead : Integer;
   x : Integer;
```

Next you need to identify and prepare the file for use. You have seen `AssignFile` before, notice that you have added another paramater to the `Reset` function. This is the record size of which the default is 128 bytes. Set it to 1 for this example.

```
begin
{Set the filename to a file variable}
AssignFile(InFile,Fname);
{Set record size to 1 byte}
Reset(InFile,1);
```

Once the file is opened, you need to load it 1K at a time. Notice the `while` loop, which runs until you hit the end of the file. Also notice that on each pass through the loop you get the file pointer position. Read a block using the `BlockRead` procedure to pull a 1K block of data into the buffer. You then scan the data in the buffer one byte at a time changing all spaces to commas. After the buffer is processed, use the `Seek` procedure to place the file pointer back to the beginning of the record. This is necessary because the file pointer is moved to the start of the next block of data after a read or write operation. Then use the `BlockWrite` to save the buffer back to disk. If there is more data to process, go through the loop again, otherwise the file is updated and closed with `CloseFile`. When you are all done, you display a message saying `Processing Complete!`.

```
While Not Eof(InFile) Do
      Begin
           {Get File Position}
           FPointer:=FilePos(InFile);
           {Read a 1K Byte Block into the buffer}
           BlockRead(InFile,FBuffer,SizeOf(FBuffer),BytesRead);
           {Convert spaces to commas}
           For x:= 0 to BytesRead-1 do
           Begin
                If FBuffer[x]=32 then FBuffer[x]:=44;
           end;
           {Move Filepointer back to start of block}
           Seek(InFile,FPointer);
           {Write 1K Byte Buffer back to disk}
           BlockWrite(InFile,FBuffer,BytesRead);
      end;
      {Flush buffers to disk and close the file}
      CloseFile(InFile);
      ShowMessage('Processing Complete!');
end;
```

The preceding code will be quite fast for a couple of reasons. First, the `BlockRead` and `BlockWrite` procedures load an entire block of data in one operation. Then, processing takes place in memory (the buffer) which is much faster than reading and writing a byte at a time.

The buffer size could be set to a higher number if you wanted even more performance (especially with larger files).

Listing 12.4 is the entire listing; take a look at it and make sure to fill in the rest of the code in the correct buttons. When you are done, test it out.

Listing 12.4. Sp2cma.

```
unit Sp2cma;

interface

uses
 Windows, Messages, SysUtils, Classes, Graphics, Controls, Forms, Dialogs,
➥Menus, StdCtrls;

type
  TForm1 = class(TForm)
    Button1: TButton;
    Button2: TButton;
    Button3: TButton;
    OpenDialog1: TOpenDialog;
    Edit1: TEdit;
    Label1: TLabel;
    procedure Button2Click(Sender: TObject);
    procedure Button1Click(Sender: TObject);
    procedure Button3Click(Sender: TObject);
  private
    { Private declarations }
  public
    { Public declarations }
  end;

var
  Form1: TForm1;

implementation
Var
   Fname : String;
{$R *.DFM}
procedure TForm1.Button2Click(Sender: TObject);
Var
   InFile : File;
   FBuffer : array [0..1023] of Byte;
   FPointer : Longint;
   BytesRead : Integer;
   x : Integer;
begin
{Set the filename to a file variable}
AssignFile(InFile,Fname);
{Set record size to 1 byte}
Reset(InFile,1);
While Not Eof(InFile) Do
```

```
      Begin
           {Get File Position}
           FPointer:=FilePos(InFile);
           {Read a 1K Byte Block into the buffer}
           BlockRead(InFile,FBuffer,SizeOf(FBuffer),BytesRead);
           {Convert spaces to commas}
           For x:= 0 to BytesRead-1 do
           Begin
                If FBuffer[x]=32 then FBuffer[x]:=44;
           end;
           {Move Filepointer back to start of block}
           Seek(InFile,FPointer);
           {Write 1K Byte Buffer back to disk}
           BlockWrite(InFile,FBuffer,BytesRead);
      end;
      {Flush buffers to disk and close the file}
      CloseFile(InFile);
      ShowMessage('Processing Complete!');
end;
procedure TForm1.Button1Click(Sender: TObject);
begin
  {Display Open File Dialogbox}
  OpenDialog1.FileName := '*.*';
  if OpenDialog1.Execute then
    {Get the selected filename}
    Fname := OpenDialog1.FileName;
    {Display selected filename}
    Edit1.Text:=Fname;
    {Show the Edit box and label now that we have the filename}
    Edit1.Visible:=True;
    Label1.Visible:=True;
end;

procedure TForm1.Button3Click(Sender: TObject);
begin
     {Exit the application}
     Application.Terminate;
end;

end.
```

ANALYSIS This program reads a text file (selected by the user) into FBuffer in blocks up to 1024 bytes in size. The contents of the buffer are then scanned and the spaces are converted to commas (when the user presses the Process button). The file pointer is repositioned to the beginning of the block (because it was advanced after the `BlockRead` statement) and the changed data is written back out to the file. When the processing is done, the program displays the message, `Processing Complete!`. At this point, the user can choose to process another file or select Exit to terminate the program.

Okay, save the code then compile and run it. If all looks well, go to Notepad and create a simple text file with a sentence or two to use for testing. Switch back to the application and press the Select File button. Using the dialog box, select the text file you created. Next click the Process button. A message box should appear very quickly indicating that the program is finished. Exit the program and go back to Notepad and load the file back in. If you had no errors in the code, you should see commas where there were spaces before. You might want to test this on other files as well. To verify operation on binary files, use a large document file written in a word processor such as MS Write or Word 6 that saves files in a binary format. This covers the basics for untyped files, but only scratches the surface of what can actually be done with them. Use your imagination.

File Management, Directory Management, and Other File Support Functions

There are a number of other file I/O and management functions and procedures that you should be aware of. There isn't enough space in the scope of this book to cover them all. Familiarize yourself with the functions and procedures listed in the online help under the following three help categories:

File Management Routines
I/O Routines
Text File Routines

You have used several of the functions and procedures you will find in these areas, but several are not covered here. Many of the functions do the same types of operations in a different way. For example:

```
Var
    MyFileVar : File
Begin
    AssignFile(MyFileVar,filename);    {Create a file Variable and open a new
➥file}
    ReWrite(MyFile);
End;
```

The above routine creates a File variable and assigns a filename to it. The File variable is used by the `Rewrite` procedure to create and open the file. You could also do the same thing with the `FileCreate` function as shown in the following:

```
Var
   Handle : Integer;
Begin
   Handle :=FileCreate('Filename');
End;
```

The `FileCreate` function returns a file *handle* if the operation is successful. A file handle is nothing more than an integer value that will be used to identify the file until it is closed. If more than one file is opened, each file will have its own unique handle assigned. This file handle is used by an entire set of functions and procedures to read, write, move file position, and so on, similar to what we have already used earlier based on file variables. There are some advantages to using the procedures based on file handles versus those that use file variables. For example, the `FileOpen` function allows you to `OR` a set of constants together to set the mode in which the file is opened. See the file mode constants below.

```
fmOpenRead
fmOpenWrite
fmOpenReadWrite
fmShareCompat
fmShareExclusive
fmShareDenyWrite
fmShareDenyRead
fmShareDenyNone
```

The names are fairly descriptive, but see the online help if you need more info. They can be found under help for the SysUtils unit under Constants in the File Open Mode Constants section. If you wanted to open a file with exclusive access and deny access to all other programs or users, you would use the `fmShareExclusive`. For example:

```
MyHandle:=FileOpen(fname,fmShareExclusive);
```

Remember, you can OR these constants together to get the desired access to the file. This can be important if you are sharing files with other programs on the same system or other users on a network.

Other functions and routines you should be aware of are listed in the following table. Take a minute to look them over and see online help for more detail.

Erase	Deletes a file.
FileSize	Returns the size of a specified file.
GetDir	Returns the current directory for the specified drive.
MkDir	Creates a subdirectory.
Rename	Renames a file.
RmDir	Removes subdirectory.

There are many other functions and procedures available to you that have not been covered in here. If you have reviewed online help for the three categories dealing with files suggested earlier, you should have a good feel for what can be done with files in addition to what has been covered here.

Long Filenames

They are finally here...long filenames at last! No longer are we limited to the eight-character name with a three-character extension (8.3). Windows 95 and Windows NT allow long filenames. In Windows 95, these filenames can be up to 255 characters long, including a NULL, and allow you to be much more descriptive when naming your files. The maximum path length is 260 characters, including NULL. For backward compatibility, a short filename is created based on the first six characters of the filename. If multiple long filenames have the same first six characters and the same extension, the operating system uses an algorithm to add numbers in the filename to create a short filename compatible with older verisons of DOS and Windows. The following table shows an example:

Long Filename	*Short Filename*
LongFileName1.TXT	LONGFI~1.TXT
LongFileName2.TXT	LONGFI~2.TXT

Delphi 2 supports long filenames with changes to file-related components, functions, and procedures. You need not do anything because Delphi and the OS (Windows 95, NT) handle the details for you. You simply pass the long filename to your functions, procedures, and programs and you are done. Finally, you are not required to use the long filenames, so feel free to use the 8.3 filename as well.

Summary

Today you learned about file attributes as well has how to read and change them. You learned how to work with text files by writing a simple text editor. You then moved on and created a simple database program to store address/phone number information using typed files. You then learned about untyped files and how to open any type of file by creating a program that would open a file and replace all its spaces with commas. You learned about some of the other file management and I/O routines available. You talked about long filenames and how they are supported by Delphi 2. Quite a bit of material about working with files was covered here. With the database controls and other features of Delphi, you may not always need this type of file access. However, the information learned here may allow you to write that next conversion program, import utility, or custom file editor. At some point time, file I/O capabilities will prove to be a real asset. In any case, you are now able to save, load, scan, and process those files!

Q&A

Q Do I need to do anything special to handle long filenames?

A No, Delphi 2 functions and components have built-in support for long filenames. They recognize short or long filenames with no effort on your part.

Q How can I allow my programs to tell what a file's type is?

A You really can't. While there are standards for using file extensions to denote a file type, this standard is often not adhered to. You will have to make the determination as to how you are expecting a file to be formatted and appear and do your best to check it and handle errors that might occur. Beyond that, you just have to rely on the user choosing the right file

Q Can I also use my older Delphi (16-bit version) to do long filenames?

A Yes and no, Delphi 16 doesn't directly support long filenames; however, you can access them through Windows 95's DOS interrupt calls (int 21 services). This may turn out to be more to be more trouble than it is worth depending on your familiarity with DOS interrupts and assembly language.

Workshop

Quiz

1. What are typed files?
2. What are untyped files?
3. What attribute bit is set to make a file read only?
4. What function do you use to find the location of the file pointer?
5. What procedure is used to move the file pointer?
6. What type of files can you work with using untyped files?
7. How long can a long filename be?
8. How do Windows 95 and NT remain compatible with the old short filename standard?

Exercises

1. Add the capability in the typed files Address/Phone book program to move to the first record or the last record.

2. Write a simple program to copy files using untyped files. The program should open two files, one for input and one for output. The program should also check for the existence of input and output files to prevent errors and accidental overwriting of files without warning. The program should not allow a file to be copied over itself.

Week 2

Day 13

Databases in Delphi

A programmer will often come to a point where he asks

> I have a large amount of data that my application needs to access, and manipulate. Is there an easy way to do this?

The answer is yes. Databases provide a generic means to store data. A database engine provides the mechanism to manipulate and view the data in the database. Without databases, programmers would be forced to write complex routines to do file manipulation whenever there was a need to store and access data in an efficient manner. In essence, the programmer would be responsible for creating the database and database engine.

Databases in Delphi

Delphi has powerful built-in database support. There are visual components that enable access to tables and methods to manipulate records. This chapter explains how to create your own databases with the tools provided with Delphi and how to integrate the database into your application. Delphi has the ability to perform powerful complex database manipulation or act as a simple front end.

A database front end is a program that provides an easy-to-use interface to access and manipulate the data in a database. Delphi includes a tool that makes front-end development almost effortless by doing almost all of the development for you. This tool is called the Database Form Expert. The Database Form Expert creates a completely functional database front end without a single line of code.

The Relational Database Model

Most new databases today are relational databases. A relational database stores information in logical tables made up of rows and columns. As expected, the tables are called database tables. Take a look at a simple table.

RAD University (RADU) wants to keep records on its student population. To do this, RADU organizes its data into a table. This is shown in Table 13.1.

Table 13.1. Data in relational form.

SSN	Name	Class	Phone	GPA
185-34-2345	Ada Smith	Freshman	423-3456	3.4
123-43-2233	Joe Brown	Freshman	213-2343	2.1
432-45-2345	Ashlyn Kelly	Freshman	213-2222	4.0
234-54-2345	Ron Beagle	Sophomore	423-1234	1.9

The columns in a table are called fields, and the rows are called records. For every record in the table, there must be related information in each field.

Relational databases are used to store, manipulate, and access data. The data is stored in tables made up of logical columns and rows.

Jumping In with the Database Form Expert

Delphi comes with a powerful tool that creates a form that maps fields in a table to entry/edit fields on a form. Here is an example of how to build an application using the forms expert. This example uses one of the sample databases included with Delphi.

Using Database Form Expert

1. Start Delphi
2. Choose Database | Database Form Expert from the Main menu.
3. In the first dialog box select Create a simple form, and Create a form using TTable objects options; choose Next. (See Figure 13.1.)

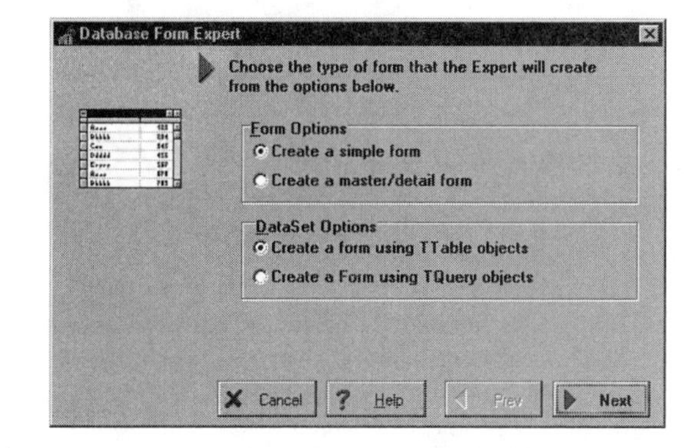

Figure 13.1.
Selecting Form and DataSet options in the Database Form Expert.

4. In the next dialog box, choose DBDEMOS in the Drive or Alias section. Selecting DBDEMOS brings up a list of tables in the list box to the left.
5. Choose EMPLOYEE.DB; click next.
6. Press the >> button to indicate that you would like to build a form showing all fields. This is shown in Figure 13.2.

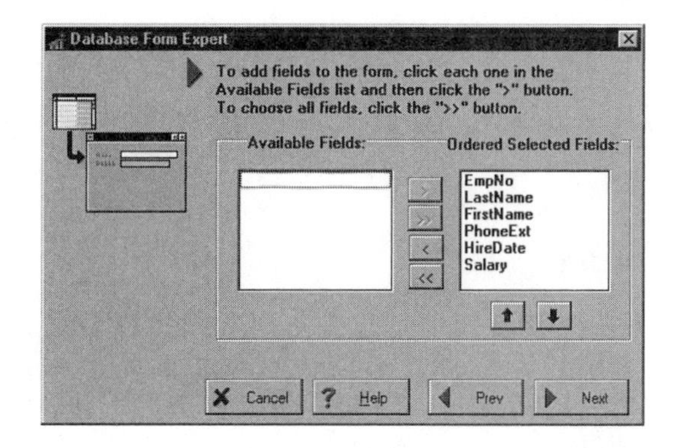

Figure 13.2.
Choosing which fields to use in the Database Form Expert.

7. Continue to choose Next, accepting all defaults until the form is created.
8. Choose Run | Run from the menu.

Congratulations! You have just created your first Delphi database application. (See Figure 13.3.)

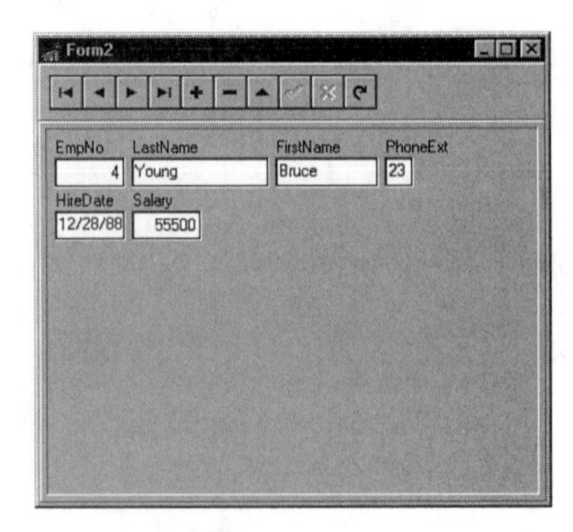

Figure 13.3.
Application built using the Forms Expert.

How Does it Work?

This sample application gives the user full control over a table containing information about employees. To manipulate the records, a database navigation tool bar is placed at the top of the application. Each button on the toolbar executes a different database function.

The button functions are described in Table 13.2.

Table 13.2. Database navigator buttons.

Icon	Function	Description
	Move First	Moves to the first record in the table
	Move Previous	Moves to the previous record in the table
	Move Next	Moves to the next record
	Move Last	Moves to the last record
	Insert	Inserts a new record at the current position
	Delete	Deletes the record that is displayed
	Edit	Allows fields in the current record to be modified

Icon	Function	Description
✓	Post Edit	Saves changes to a record
✕	Cancel Edit	Cancels changes to a record
↻	Refresh Data	Reloads the current record. This is useful if multiple applications have access to a database, and the current record may have changed.

After playing with this simple front end, choose Close to terminate the application.

Database Choices

One of the most powerful features of Delphi's database engine access is that Delphi provides a layer of abstraction between the underlying database and the database functionality. This brings up an interesting topic of "What database should I use with Delphi?" There is no right answer, and choosing a database now does not mean that later a different database cannot be installed in its place.

Database Models

There are many applications that use databases. It wouldn't make sense for the IRS to use the same type of database as Joe's Garage and Service Center. Both of these obviously need to track vastly different amounts of data and are accessed by different numbers of applications. Also, there are issues that need to be addressed by databases that are accessed by more than one application or person. For example what happens when two processes try to modify the same record at one time? Which types of security can be implemented to allow only partial data to be accessed by certain applications? These two issues are concurrence problems and security. The process of determining what type of database is appropriate for an application is known as *scaling*. The power, complexity, and functionality of a database system is often related to its physical layout and infrastructure. Next you will explore the three main classes of database layouts: stand-alone, file share, and client/server.

Stand-Alone Databases

Stand-alone databases are the simplest to deal with because a lot of issues can be ignored. A stand-alone database has its database stored in a local file system and a database engine to access it residing on the same machine. With a pure stand-alone database, the database designer does not need to handle concurrence, the condition where two people try to change the same record at one time, because this never happens. In general, a stand-alone database is not used for an application that needs excessive computing power because processing time will be spent doing data manipulation and will not be totally available to the application. Stand-alone databases are useful in development of applications that are distributed to many users, where each maintains a separate database. For example, an application that tracks miles driven in order to determine fuel reimbursement could be developed using a stand-alone database. Each person using the application would store and manipulate their own gas data on their local machine. It is not necessary for a user of this application to access any other person's data, so a local database is well suited. There are many powerful stand-alone databases. Paradox and dBASE databases can be created and manipulated with the database desktop that comes with Delphi. These can act as either stand-alone or file-share databases.

File-Share Databases

A file-share database is almost exactly like a stand-alone database except that it can be accessed by multiple clients across a network. This allows a greater deal of accessibility because the database can be accessed and manipulated by different machines. For example, take the employee database used in the previous example. If an administrator changes an employee's salary, a payroll application printing checks could see the change immediately. However, the machine that accesses the database is running the database engine locally. Another advantage of a file-share database is that there are no preconceived notions of the network. The database engine does not care if Novell, Banyan, Microsoft NT, or any other network operating system is running, because it simply sees the database as a file. A situation in which a file-share database may not be suitable is when a great deal of computation and simultaneous access needs to be performed on a database. For this, a client server database is the solution.

Client/Server Databases

The high-end solution for database access is solved through the client/server model. In this case, a dedicated machine, or server, is tasked to perform database access for a group of clients. Take the example of the IRS's database. The IRS may want to know all Social Security numbers for persons who made over $100,000 and paid less then $2,000 in taxes. In a file-share system this would bring the requesting machine to a halt while it cranks through the data. However, in a client/server model the client asks the server to perform the specified task. It is then up to the client to decide whether it wants to wait for the result or go on to do something more interesting. Meanwhile, the server has been optimized to handle requests in the fastest possible manner. Although there are many performance and flexibility advantages to a client/server architecture, there are also many disadvantages. Client/server solutions are often much more expensive than a file-share solution. Also client/server software needs a protocol in which to carry on a conversation such as TCP/IP. Although this is often flexible, it is an additional configuration and administrative function.

When developing Delphi applications that do not require backward compatibility to a database currently in use, the developer will most likely choose Paradox or dBASE because they are tightly integrated with Delphi. Also, database objects for dBASE and Delphi can be easily created and managed with the database desktop. Table 13.3 shows some statistics pertaining to the capacity of dBASE and Paradox.

Table 13.3. Comparison of Paradox and dBASE tables.

Attribute	Paradox	dBASE
Maximum Records	2 billion	1 billion
Fields per Table	255	1,024
Characters per field	Not Applicable	256
Bytes per Record	32,750	32,767

As you can see, both databases are extremely powerful and capable of holding more data than most applications will ever need. Paradox offers quite a bit more flexibility at the database level. This means that the tables have the ability to contain information other than the data contained in them. For example, Paradox allows data validation to occur at the database level. Also, password security is integrated into Paradox. These features are very useful especially if the Delphi application will not be the only application accessing the data.

Choosing which database model is right for an application is often a difficult task. Luckily, Borland's database engine is flexible enough to change databases with little effort. If this doesn't give enough flexibility, the database engine can communicate with ODBC, which can communicate with almost any database on the market today. ODBC is discussed later in the chapter, but now let's see how to create a new table using the database desktop.

Aliases

Databases can be arranged in many different ways. In Microsoft Access multiple tables are stored in one file. Paradox and dBASE use a separate file for each table. A client/server-based system such as Sybase or Microsoft SQL server stores all data on a separate machine, and communicates with clients through a special language called SQL (which will be discussed in a later chapter). In addition to the method each type of database uses to store its data, some databases require additional information. This is a very complex task for the Borland database engine to handle if it wants to communicate transparently with many different types of databases because each seems to want slightly different information. For example, a Paradox database will want to know what directory represents the database, whereas a Sybase database may need a network address for the server, database name, user ID, and password. The solution to solve this problem is the use of *aliases.* An alias contains all the information that needs to be supplied to access a database. Therefore, when creating a Paradox alias, all that needs to be supplied is the directory containing the database objects. However, when more complicated datasources are needed, additional information will be provided.

Using the Database Desktop to Create a New Table

Now that you understand the basic elements of a table, it is time to create a new sample table. The Borland Database Desktop (see Figure 13.4.) can be accessed from the Tools menu in the Delphi IDE. Choose this option to bring up the desktop.

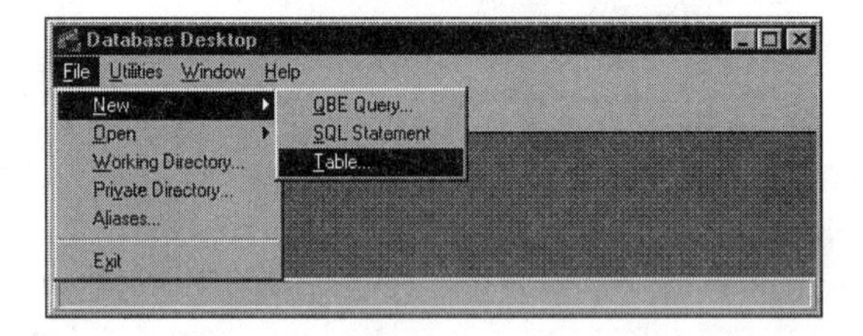

Figure 13.4.
The Borland Database Desktop.

Creating a New Table

1. Choose the File | New | Table option from the Main menu. At this point, a dialog box appears asking what type of table you want to create. For new applications, the Paradox database is most likely the easiest to work with; therefore, choose Paradox 7, and click OK.
2. The first thing that you need to decide is what data you want to store in your table, and what type of data is it. For this example consider the RADU Student Information table described earlier. Each field needs to be added in the Field Roster portion of the dialog box. To add the first field, type **`SSN`** in the `field name` field. This says that you want to add a new field called `SSN`.
3. The next piece of information needed is what type of data will be stored in the field. Social Security numbers are stored as a string of characters. Click with the right mouse button on the `Type` field to show the data types available. For a string, the Paradox type Alpha is used. Choose Alpha from the list of datatypes displayed.

4. For some datatypes, a size needs to be supplied. This tells the database the largest amount of data that can be stored in a field. For SSN, we know that all Social Security numbers are 11 characters including the dashes, so enter **11** in this field. Some datatypes such as Number do not use the size field, and the database desktop disables the size field for entries that do not use size.
5. The final piece of information that needs to be supplied to the database is whether or not a field is a key. A key simply means that the field is guaranteed to be unique for every record. Using keys in databases is extremely important; this is discussed a little later. For now, mark the SSN field as a key because you know that there will be only one entry for every student and that every student will have a unique Social Security number.
6. To define the next field in the table, press enter. Continue to define fields using the information in Table 13.4.

Table 13.4. Sample table field definition and attributes.

Field Name	Type	Size	Key
SSN	A	11	*
Name	A	30	
Class	A	10	
Phone	A	8	
GPA	N		

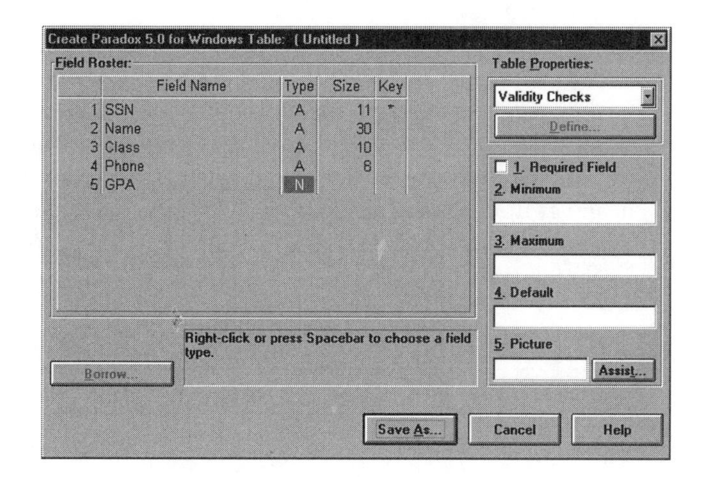

Figure 13.5.
Defining the fields using the Database Desktop.

7. Click the Save As button to save the information about the table.

8. In the Save Table as dialog box, change the Drive (or alias) listbox to indicate DBDEMOS. Enter **STUDINFO.DB** in the New file name textbox. Click OK. This saves the table. That's it! You created a new table.

Why Use Keys?

Why did you set the SSN number as a key? Keys help the database engine work efficiently. It helps if there is a definitive way to distinguish every record from all other records in a table. Paradox has a requirement that all fields that are keys be placed at the top of the definition list. Although most databases do not force tables to have a key, it's a good practice to always key each table. However, what if the table you are working on does not have a natural key? This means that there is no field in the table guaranteed to be unique for every record. Take Table 13.5, which might be used in a cooking database.

Table 13.5. Ingredients in the cooking database.

Recipe	Ingredient
Macaroni and Cheese	Macaroni
Macaroni and Cheese	Cheddar Cheese
Macaroni and Cheese	Milk
Tuna Melt	Tuna
Tuna Melt	Cheddar Cheese

You can't use Recipe as a key because there are multiple ingredients for each recipe. Also Ingredient can't be used because the same ingredient may be used in many different recipes. Luckily, most databases have a way to work around this through special data types that are administered automatically by the database engine, and the database engine guarantees that the field will be unique. In Paradox, this data type is called the Auto-Increment datatype. By defining a field as Auto-Increment, each time a record is added to the table an internal counter increases and sets the field value to that number. Table 13.6 is how you could set up the table layout for your recipe example using Auto-Increment to create a key.

Table 13.6. Cooking database field attributed with an automatic key.

Field Name	Type	Size	Key
CookBookKey	+		*
Recipe	A	30	
Ingredient	A	30	

When data is added to this table, each record automatically gets assigned a unique value. Our table now looks like Table 13.7 after data has been added.

Table 13.7. Cooking data with the key added.

CookBookKey	Recipe	Ingredient
1	Macaroni and Cheese	Macaroni
2	Macaroni and Cheese	Cheddar Cheese
3	Macaroni and Cheese	Milk
4	Tuna Melt	Tuna
5	Tuna Melt	Cheddar Cheese

There is quite a bit more information that should be provided when creating a table, however this gives a model that can be worked with, so details will be provided later on how to increase performance of the database and how to ensure that only valid information is entered.

Great, Now That I Have a Table How Do I Access It from Delphi?

We have shown the easiest way to create an application that has access to a table in Delphi: the Delphi Form Expert. Now take a closer look at what is happening behind the scenes and what steps are necessary to build an application from scratch.

The easiest way to access and manipulate databases in Delphi is by using the database visual components provided. Database visual components are stored on two tabs of the visual component library: the Data Access and Data Control tabs. The controls on the Data Access tab are used to give Delphi information about what database tables and functions should be used, whereas the Data Control tab lists visual components that can display data in a database or provide an interface to manipulate the data (such as insert, delete, and modify).

Making Delphi Aware of a Table—The TTable Component

In order to use a table the first step is to let Delphi know that you intend to interact with the table. To do this, a Table object that accesses the data in a table needs to be placed on the form. Examining the properties sheet shows that there is one property called `DatabaseName` and

TableName. These are the two minimal properties that need to be set in order for Delphi to access the table. The DatabaseName property corresponds to the database aliases that are available. The TableName specifies which table in a database should be used.

Accessing the Student Information Table

The first step in creating an application to access the Student information database that you created earlier chapter is to place a Table component on your form, and configure the DatabaseName and TableName properties.

1. Create a new application.
2. Place a TTable component on the form.The TTable component can be found on the DataAccess tab of the visual component library.
3. In the properties sheet, set DatabaseName to DBDEMOS. DBDEMOS is the alias in which the SUDINFO.DB table was saved.
4. After the DatabaseName property is set, the TableName property should indicate a listbox of all of the available tables in the database. Choose STUDINFO.DB for the database name.
5. Set the Active property to true. This immediately opens the table when the application is run. If this is set to false, the application will not be able to access any data in the table until the active property is set to True during run time.
6. Set the Name property to StudInfo.

Two other properties that can be modified at runtime are Readonly, and Exclusive. Setting Readonly to true allows the application to view only the data in the database; however, it will not be able to modify it. The Exclusive option ensures that the application is the only one accessing the data. At this point, the application has the information it needs to attach to a table. However, there is no way to manipulate the data until the table object is associated with a DataSource.

Providing the Link—The TDataSource Component

Delphi has the ability to access database information from a series of components known as DataSets, one of which is the TTable component. Data-aware controls are controls that display and manipulate data in a database that is accessed through Delphi. To provide a layer of abstraction for controls that navigate through data and display information, the TDataSource was developed. The DataSource also provides a way to detect when changes are made to data and to detect what state the DataSet, or source of data is in.

Adding the DataSource

1. Choose a DataSource component and add it to the form.
2. Set the `DataSet` property to StudInfo. This links the datasouce to the TTable component StudInfo which in turn is accessing the STUDINFO.DB table in the DBDEMOS database.
3. Set the name for the DataSource to dsStudent.

Data-Aware Controls—Seeing and Modifying the Data

At this point, you have set up everything Delphi needs to communicate with a table. However, it is now necessary to decide how the data should be displayed and how it should be manipulated. The easiest way to do this is with the data-aware controls. Most of the data-aware controls are for binding a database field to a visual component. For example, it is often necessary to have a text edit field contain the value of a field in a table. The standard data-aware controls are extremely powerful, easy to use, and Delphi comes with many to choose from. Other than the DBNavigator, all the controls on the Data Control tab are used for displaying database data. To start with, add the DBGrid control to your example.

Adding a Data-Aware Control—The DBGrid

1. Place the DBGrid control on your form. This is the first control that is added that is actually seen at run time; therefore, change the size so that it takes up a large part of the form.
2. Set the `DataSource` property to dsStudent; this links the control to the datasource.
3. What happened? As soon as the `DataSource` property is set, notice that the field names automatically appear in the grid. If there was data in the STUDINFO.DB table, this would also be displayed even at design time. However, if the `Action` property had been set to False then nothing would be seen until it is set to True.
4. Run the application. At this point, data can actually be entered into the grid. Type a SSN number, hit Tab, and type a name. Continue tabbing through the fields until a record is entered. On completion of the first record, the DBGrid control automatically puts the cursor on the next line. Continue to add a few sample records into the table. Note that if two records are entered with the same SSN, an error occurs. You will handle this gracefully a little later.
5. End the application, and add one more control: the DBEdit control. The DBEdit control displays one field of a table. Unlike the grid control that can display multiple records, the DBEdit control displays a field of the current record. The

current record is simply the record that is being accessed by the database engine at a particular moment. The DBGrind control specifies the current record by placing a triangle next to it.

6. Add a DBEdit control to the form, and set the `DataSource` property to dsStudent. Now a field needs to be specified so the control knows what to display. To set the field, set the `DataField` property to SSN.
7. Run the application. Figure 13.6 shows this application executing.

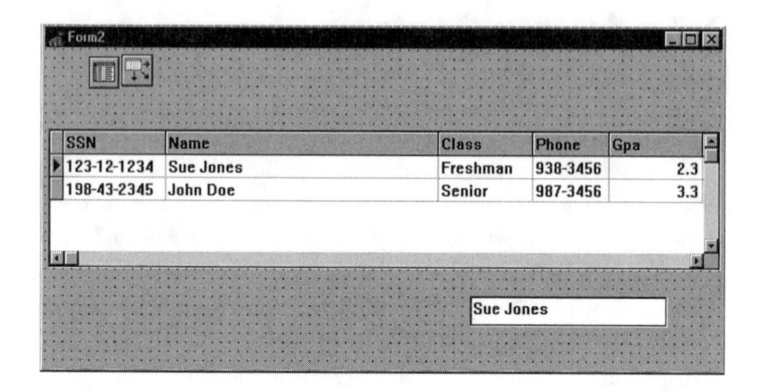

Figure 13.6.
Application using TTable, DataSource, and Data-Aware components.

Notice that when a record is moved to or clicked on in the grid, this changes the current record. This application gives some control to the user, but it would be difficult to move around in a large database. Delphi has a powerful control that allows navigation through a table: the DBNavigator. The DBNavigator is a toolbar all by itself that allows easy navigation through a table.

Adding the DBNavigator

1. Select the DBNavigator control and place it on the form. Set the `DataSource` property to dsStudent.
2. Set the `ShowHint` property to True. This causes a hint to appear when ever the cursor is placed over one of the buttons on the toolbar.
3. Run the application. Notice how easy it is to move between records, jump to the beginning or end of the database, and to edit records. Figure 13.7 shows the new application with the addition of the DBNavigator.

Figure 13.7.
Adding the Database Navigator.

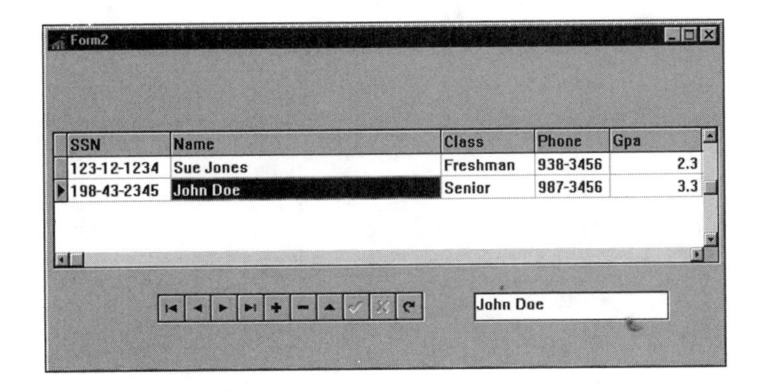

You have created a fully functional application using absolutely no code. Next you learn how database controls can be manipulated with Object Pascal from within Delphi.

Accessing Databases with Code

Now that we have examined how to access databases by manipulating visual components through the IDE, you will learn how to manipulate the components using Object Pascal. The database components offer a powerful set of events, properties, and methods that can be called from within a Delphi unit.

DataSet State

A dataset can be in one of six possible states: dsEdit, dsBrowse, dsInsert, dsInactive, dsSetKey, or dsCalcFields. The state gives information about the current interaction the application has with the dataset. To view records, the state should be in Browse mode. If an application needs to modify a record, then the DataSet must be put into dsEdit mode. Checking what state a DataSet is in can only be done at runtime by checking the `State` property. To change the state of the dataset, the `Insert`, `Edit`, `Post`, `Cancel`, or `Append` method can be used. The `Insert` method causes a new record to be inserted and that record to be put into edit mode. To edit the current record, the `Edit` method can be used.

One of the powerful features of the Delphi database engine is that it provides support to commit or rollback changes when editing a record. When a dataset is in Edit mode, changes can be made to many fields. When the changes are complete, a `Post` method can be applied to the dataset to keep and record the changes. However, if for some reason the application needs to restore a record's initial value, the `Cancel` method can be used. Listing 13.1 demonstrates how to save or rollback changes made to a record.

TYPE **Listing 13.1. Confirming a change.**

```
Var
  Save:integer;

begin
   Save :=Application.MessageBox('Save Changes?', 'CONFIRM!',mb_yesno);
   if Save = IDYES then
      Studinfo.Post {Committ Transaction}
   else
       StudInfo.Cancel {Rollback Transaction};
end; {Procedure}
```

ANALYSIS In this example a message box is displayed in which the user is asked to confirm changes to the record that is being edited. If the user chooses YES, then the `Post` method is executed on the dataset, thus saving the changes. If the user clicks No, then the `Cancel` method is used to undo any changes made during the edit. There is one flaw in this code. If the DataSet is not in dsEdit mode, and a `Post` or `Cancel` method is executed, an exception will occur. Therefore, the question is how can you check to confirm you are in Edit mode? As mentioned earlier, the `State` property tells you what mode the DataSet is in. A safer example of this code is shown in Listing 13.2.

TYPE **Listing 13.2. Confirming changes to a record, with validation of state property.**

```
Var
  Save:integer;

begin
  if Studinfo.State = dsEdit then
   begin
     Save :=Application.MessageBox('Save Changes?,'CONFIRM!',mb_yesno);
     if Save = IDYES then
         Studinfo.Post {Committ Transaction}
     else
         StudInfo.Cancel; {Rollback Transaction}
   end
  else
   Application.MessageBox('Not in Edit Mode!','Error',mb_ok);
end; {Procedure}
```

ANALYSIS These examples have shown how control over records can be accessed from code. Your application can make a logical decision of whether changes should be saved or aborted. Next you take a look at how to access the data fields.

Accessing the Fields

It is often necessary for a program to access, and modify database fields. Fortunately, Delphi makes this very easy. The `Fields` property of a DataSet describes more than the values contained in the fields. The property also contains information about the structure of the table. For example, the `Fields` property can give the name of the fields, what data type they are, the size of data, and values for the current record. TTable objects have an array of fields. This array can actually be modified using the field editor to add, delete, and modify field definitions. To start with the simplest case, if the application knows what the table definition is, fields can be accessed directly without having to determine what they represent or the data type. For example, in your Studinfo table, SSN is the first column; therefore, `StudInfo.Fields[0].AsString` equals the value of the SSN for the currently selected record. Note that the array starts at offset 0. Also note that the data type must be known to access the data correctly. If you wanted to put in a textbox, `SSN=<Current Record's Social Security Number>`, you could do it by having a statement like

```
SSN.Text := 'SSN='+Studinfo.Fields[0].AsString;
```

Assume that you made an incorrect assumption that SSN would be stored as an integer so you tried the following:

```
SSN.Text :='SSN='+IntToStr(Studinfo.Fields[0].AsInteger);
```

This compiles without any errors; however, when the statement is executed an exception occurs. How can we safeguard against this? It is possible to confirm the field name and data type of each column. This might be neccessary if a generic database manipulation program is written, and the field types are unknown. Listing 13.3 checks the data type and field name against what is expected before accessing the data.

TYPE **Listing 13.3. Confirming field name and datatype.**

```
begin
 if not(StudInfo.Fields[0].DataType=ftString) then
  begin
   Application.MessageBox('Error - Wrong Data type on Field 0','DB
➥Error',mb_ok);
   exit;
  end; {if}
 if not(comparetext(StudInfo.Fields[0].FieldName,'SSN')=0) then
  begin
   Application.MessageBox('Error - Wrong Field Name on Field 0',
                          'DB Table Error',mb_ok);
   exit;
  end; {if}
 Application.MessageBox('Field 0 Checks out: Type=ftString Name=SSN',
                        'Information',mb_ok);
end; {procedure}
```

Analysis In this example, the field type is confirmed. If the routine encounters anything other than an ftSring it displays an error message box and exits the procedure. Similarly, if the field name does not equal SSN, then an error is displayed, and the routine exits. If the procedure can get past both conditionals, then it is true that the field type and field name are valid.

Often it is difficult to access a field by the column position in a table. Therefore, Delphi allows you to access columns by their field name. To do this, address the control name followed by the `FieldByName` method and the data type. For example, to access the class field for the current record and set the text of a listbox, you could use a statement such as

```
Edit1.Text:=Studinfo.FieldByName('Class').AsString;
```

Modifying the Fields in a Table

By default, a TTable component uses all the fields in the table it is linked to. However, Delphi allows the developer to modify which fields are used, assign new fields based on calculations, and set attributes about each field. To access the field editor for the TTable component, double click on an instance of a TTable. This brings up a dialog box that allows you to add, delete, and define new fields. This dialog box also gives easy access to the TFields components. The field is based on a type inherited for TField with any specific information about the data type. For example, if one of the fields is a string, the field would be of TStringField type. Just like other components, the fields have properties and events. One advantage of this is that different fields in a table can have different properties. A good example is the case in which you want to protect one field from changes yet allow a user to modify other fields. To do this, the `ReadOnly` property for the field you want to protect could be set to TRUE. A large number of the field properties determine how data-aware controls display the data in the fields. For example there is an `Alignment` property, which determines if the data should be placed in the left, right, or center of the display field. Also, for floating point numbers a Precision value can be set to indicate what digit should be rounded.

Navigation of Records

You have already seen how the DBNavigator component can be used to move through the table. The navigator provides the functionality to move forward or backward one record, or to jump to the beginning or end of the table. This can be done within your code as well. To change the current record, five methods are available on the TTable component. These are described in Table 13.8.

Table 13.8. Dataset methods for navigation.

Method	Action
Next	Moves to the next record in the dataset.
Prior	Moves to the previous record in the dataset.
First	Moves to the first record in the dataset.
Last	Moves to the last record in the dataset.
MoveBy(I)	Moves by increments. For example MoveBy(3) moves three records forward. MoveBy(-2) moves two records backwards.

One important note about moving when a record is in Edit mode: The move causes an implicit `Post` method to occur, and the record changes are saved. There will be no way to execute a `Cancel` method for the changes. While navigating through a table, it is often necessary to know if you have hit the beginning or end of a dataset. The `EOF` (End of File) and `BOF` (Beginning of File) properties indicate if these conditions are true.

BOF Is true when an application first starts, a call to the `First` method was executed, or a `Prior` call fails because the current record is the first one in the dataset.

EOF Is true when there is no data in a dataset, a call to the `Last` method was executed, or a `Next` call fails because there are no more records.

ANALYSIS One of the typical things done to a dataset is to perform some action on every record. In the following example, the procedure moves to the first record then loops through all of the records until the `EOF` property is true. With each record, the `Edit` method is executed so that the value of the record can be changed. In the example a random dorm room is being assigned to students. To do this a random number is generated between 0 and 1. If the number is less then .5 one dorm is assigned (`StudInfo.Fields[6]`), otherwise the other dorm is assigned. After changes to the fields are made, a `Post` method is executed to save the change. This is not really necessary because a `Next` method will do the `Post` as well. The source code for this example is in Listing 13.4.

13

TYPE

Listing 13.4. Moving through a dataSet and modifying every record.

```
procedure TForm1.AssnDormsClick(Sender: TObject);
begin
  Studinfo.First; {Move to beginning of DataSet}
  StudInfo.DisableControls; { Will increase performance }
  while Not(Studinfo.EOF) do {Check for end of dataset}
    begin
```

continues

Listing 13.4. Continued

```
      StudInfo.Edit;
      {Generate a random number, assign 50% to QUAD, 50% to Hall}
      {Access Fields Directly by "Fields" Property }
      if random > 0.5 then
        StudInfo.Fields[6].AsString := 'QUAD'
       else
        StudInfo.Fields[6].AsString := 'HALL';
      StudInfo.Post; {Explicit Post (Not Really Needed)}
      StudInfo.Next; { Move to the next record }
    end; {end Loop}
    StudInfo.EnableControls; { Will increase performance }
end; {end Procedure}
```

Note that the controls can be disabled during the loop and then enabled when the loop is complete. This increases performance because the controls do not update after each iteration.

Calculated Fields

There are many circumstances in which you want to derive data from a database, but it doesn't make sense to actually store all the data. For example, if a warehouse keeps track of its inventory using a relational database where each item is a record, the number of units in stock are stored on one field, and the weight per unit is stored in another field, it doesn't make sense to store the total weight of the item. The total weight can be derived by multiplying the number of units by their weight. Therefore, if there are 120 CD-ROM drives, and each weighs two pounds, then you know that there are 240 pounds of CD-ROM drives stocked (it might be necessary to know this for shipping purposes). You may say, "This should be simple, every time the user wants to know the total weight, my Delphi application can do the multiplication and display the result." True, but what if the application requires the result to be on the form at all times just like the rest of the fields. This immediately gets more complicated because your application now has to update the field whenever navigation through the dataset occurs and needs to know how to handle inserts, deletes, and all other database events. Fortunately there is an easier way. Delphi provides an easy method to define additional fields in tables. These fields are called *calculated fields* because they are based on other fields in the table. The advantage of a calculated field is that the calculated value isn't stored in the database; however, it is derived each time a record changes and needs to access or display the field. To add calculated fields, use the fields editor, which is accessed by double clicking the TTable component. Select the Define button. You will need to supply a new field name and the data type of the field. By default, a component name is created, however this can be modified if you desire. By defining the fields, you are only setting up a place holder and letting Delphi know what type of fields they are. The next step is to insert the code to calculate the fields. Delphi executes the procedure in the OnCalcFields event handler whenever there is a need to recalculate a field. While in the OnCalcFields event handler, the dataset will be in dsCalcFields state. Only the calculated fields can be modified when in this state. It is the developer's job to ensure that all calculated fields are derived correctly in this procedure.

Look at a sample application. Joe's landscaping supply company requests a database to keep inventory of the landscape supplies (topsoil, bark chips, mulch, and so on). Joe's requirements lead us to form a table with the attributes shown in Table 13.9.

Table 13.9. Table attributes for landscaping supply example.

Name	Description
ProductCode	Key defining the product
CubicYards	The number of yards Joe has in stock
CostPerYard	The market price per yard
LbsPerYard	How much one yard weighs
MarketValue	The total market value of an item in stock
LbsInStock	The total weight of an item in stock

One way that this could be done is by creating a table with the following attributes and creating an application to access and update the data. However, there are relations between the fields. Whenever the CubicYards field changes, the total market value and pounds in stock changes. Also, if the price changes so will the market value. Therefore, if you wanted to keep this information in a standard table, the application would have to be sure to update all the relevant fields when changes are made. By using calculated fields, all this work is almost eliminated. All that needs to be done is to design the table and omit the `MarketValue` and `LbsInStock` fields from the table structure. In your application bring up the field editor and add these two fields as calculated fields. Figure 13.8 displays the field editor creating a new field MarketValue, which is a currency datatype.

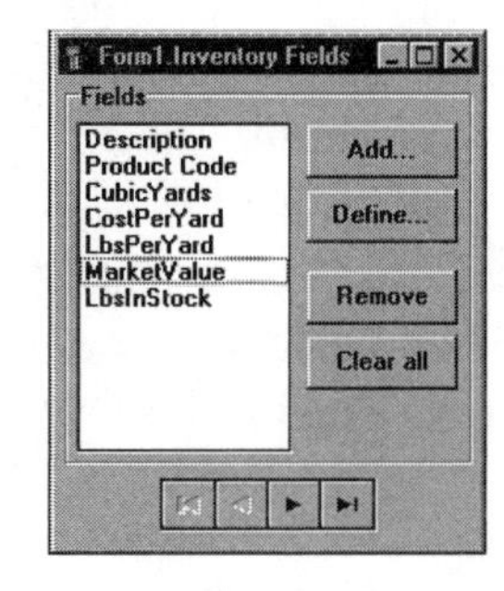

Figure 13.8.
The field editor.

The final step is to place the code behind the `OnCalcFields` event to process calculation. This procedure is shown in Listing 13.5.

TYPE **Listing 13.5. Code to calculate fields.**

```
procedure TForm1.InventoryCalcFields(DataSet: TDataset);

Var
   CurrentPrice : double; { Convert integer to float to prevent overflow}
   LbsPerYard   : double;
   YardsInStock : double;

begin
    {Put field values into local variables }
    {just to make the code a little neater}
   CurrentPrice := Inventory.FieldByName('CostPerYard').AsFloat;
   LbsPerYard   := Inventory.FieldByName('LbsPerYard').AsFloat;
   YardsInStock := Inventory.FieldByName('CubicYards').AsFloat;

   {Assign Values to the fields that are calculated}
   Inventory.FieldByName('MarketValue').AsFloat :=
      CurrentPrice * YardsInStock;
   Inventory.FieldByName('LBSInStock').AsFloat :=
      LbsPerYard   * YardsInStock;
end; {Procedure}
```

ANALYSIS In this event handler you set the local variables, `CurrentPrice`, `LbsPerYard`, and `YardsInStock` equal to their respective values in the record. The `MarketValue` and `LBSINStock` calculated fields are set based on multiplying the correct set of local variables.

Indexes

NEW TERM An index is a presorted order for the records in your table based on a particular field or fields. In the classic relational database sense, you can have a key without an index. However, in Paradox and dBASE, defining a key automatically creates an index on that field. The main advantage of an index is that it significantly speeds searching and sorting by indexed columns. Consider a sample database with 10,000 records. To find the record with its Last Name field equal to Smith could take searching up to 10,000 records. Nonetheless, on average it would search about 5,000 before it could find a match. In this sample database, if an index existed on the name field, then you would be guaranteed to find the record with a Last Name of Smith in about 14 comparisons. This is a remarkable increase in performance.

Most relational databases allow multiple indexes on tables. Before showing how to created extra indexes using the database desktop, look at why indexes are not always good. It appears that by creating an index there is a huge boost in performance, true? Yes, as far as searching and sorting are concerned. However, creating an index slows update and insert transactions, and increases the size of a table. Therefore, when creating a table and planning the indexes, try to index columns that will be searched or sorted frequently. An advantage of the database being separate from the application is that if an index needs to be added to increase performance, it can be done at any time.

I know that an index was created for the key. If I create other indexes, do all of the values in the field need to be unique? No, the key does need to be unique, but other indexes do not. How do I create indexes other than the primary key? The easiest way is with the database desktop. You can learn to do this by using the sample STUDINFO.DB table and adding an index on Name.

Adding an Index

1. Open the database desktop by using the Tools option on the Main menu.
2. In the Database Desktop, choose File | Open | Table.
3. In the Drive (or Alias) box choose DBDEMOS.
4. Choose STUDINFO.DB, and Choose OK.

   Note: If Delphi is running, and the application is accessing the table, the `Active` property needs to be set to false in the TTable object, or Paradox will not let you modify the table.
5. Choose Table | Restructure Table. This shows all the fields in the STUDINFO table.
6. In the Table Properties dropdown combobox, choose Secondary Indexes.
7. Click on Define.
8. Choose the Name field and click the button with the right arrow in it. This moves the name field into the Indexed Fields box. Click on OK.
9. You are prompted to name the index. Call it NameInd, and click OK. Figure 13.9 shows the new secondary index added to the table.
10. That's all! Choose Save, then File | Exit to leave the Database Desktop.

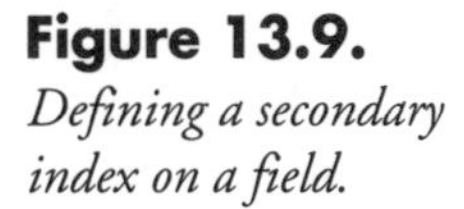
Figure 13.9.
Defining a secondary index on a field.

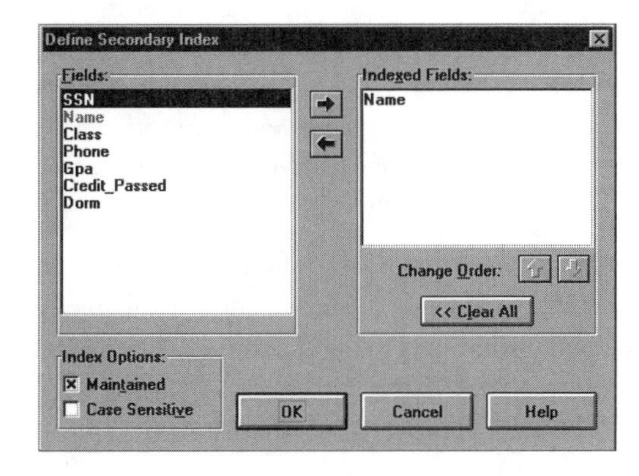

Now that a table can be indexed, how is a search in the table for a record done?

Ordering Records

When cycling through a record set the records are ordered by the current index. The IndexName property in the TTable object determines which index is in use. If no index is specified, the primary index is used to sort the records. The other way to tell Delphi what index should be used is with the IndexFieldNames property. Note that these two properties cannot both be set at the same time. When one is set Delphi automatically clears the other. Take the example where you want to add a menu item that changes the sort order of your student database from Social Security number to name. This could be accomplished by changing the IndexFieldNames property. Listing 13.6 shows how this is done.

TYPE **Listing 13.6. Changing the sort order using a menu selection.**

```
procedure TForm1.Order_By_NameClick(Sender: TObject);
begin
  Order_By_Name.Checked := True;
  Order_By_SSN.Checked := False;
  StudInfo.IndexFieldNames := 'Name';
end;
```

ANALYSIS First the Order_By_SSN menu item is unchecked. Next the Order_By_Name menu item is checked to indicate what index is being used. Finally the IndexFieldNames property is changed to sort the records in a different order.

Searching for Records

Up to this point simple navigation and modification of records has been covered. However, suppose that you wanted to access a particular record in a table. One thought that may come to mind is "Why don't I set up a loop and cycle through all the records until I find the one I want?" This would work, however you forfeit a great deal of the power the database engine provides. Using the tools provided in the TTable component, powerful searches can be performed. However, there is a major limitation in that only indexed fields can be searched.

Two techniques exist to search for records: the SetKey approach and FindKey approach. The procedure to search for values using TTable methods may seem somewhat non-intuitive. First, you have to put the table in a searchable state. To do this the SetKey method is used. Once the SetKey method is executed, the table is in dsSetKey state. For example, to place the Studinfo table in dsSetKey state, you would execute

```
Studinfo.SetKey;
```

Once a table is in a search state, set the Search field equal to a lookup value. Delphi uses this information to search for a specified value. Note that the Search field must be indexed. This is a little strange because in your code it looks like you're setting the value of the current record. However, you're in dsSetKey mode as opposed to dsEdit mode. This tells the database engine that you want to search. To take the simplest case first, search on the primary key. To find a record matching the key, set the value of the field equal to the search criteria. For example, in STUDINFO, to search for the student whose Social Security number is 432-23-2121, you would execute

```
Studinfo.FieldByName('SSN'):='432-23-2121';
```

To move to the record that you are searching for, you need to complete the search by executing the `GotoKey` method. Therefore, to conclude the search, execute

```
StudInfo.GotoKey;
```

What happens if the key is not found? The current record remains the same, and the function returns False. If the record is located, then it becomes the current record and the `GotoKey` method returns true.

This works well if you know the exact value you are trying to match. What if only part of the field is known? In that case, the `GotoNearest` method is used. `GotoNearest` takes the information that is given and finds the nearest match. Assume that you want to implement a function that will ask for part of a student's Social Security number and find the student's record. This could be implemented as in Listing 13.7.

TYPE **Listing 13.7. Searching for a Social Security number.**

```
procedure TForm1.SearchSSNClick(Sender: TObject);
begin
  StudInfo.SetKey;
  Studinfo.FieldByName('SSN').AsString := teSSNSearch.text;
  Studinfo.GotoNearest;
end;
```


ANALYSIS This procedure puts the StudInfo table into SetKey state, then sets the Social Security number equal to the one in the teSSNSearch textbox. When the `GotoNearest` method is executed, the recordset points to the record with the closest match to the Social Security number in the teSSNSearch textbox.

We are always looking for a shortcut. Delphi has two for searching on the key: the `FindKey` and `FindNearest`. When executing a `FindKey`, or `FindNearest`, Delphi encapsulates the `SetKey`, `Search Criteria` and `Goto` statements into one function. Pass the `FindKey`, or `FindNext` method an array of parameters corresponding to the key. For example, you can compress Listing 13.7 by changing the three statements into one as shown in Listing 13.8.

TYPE **Listing 13.8. Search using less code but is harder to read.**

```
procedure TForm1.SearchSSNClick(Sender: TObject);
begin
    Studinfo.FindNearest([teSSNSearch.text]);
end;
```

One advantage of the SetKey method is that it's not necessary to know the order of the indexed fields. For example, if there is a table with an index on First and Last Name, a SetKey method could be used along with the FieldByName method to set the LastName field to one value and then the FirstName field to another value. This would be followed by a GotoKey, or GotoNearest and works every time. On the other hand, if the FindKey method is used, both search values are passed as an array. For example

```
IRS.FindKey(['John','Smith']);
```

or is it...

```
IRS.FindKey(['Smith','John']);
```

You can see the dilemma. If you do not know exactly what order Delphi is expecting arguments, you will not locate the records you would like to search for.

Searching on Secondary Indexes

Searching on an index other than the primary index is accomplished by setting the IndexName property or the IndexFieldNames property exactly like you did to change the records'order. Therefore, to search for the closest Name in your Studinfo table you would execute the code in Listing 13.9.

TYPE **Listing 13.9. Searching by something other than the primary key.**

```
procedure TForm1.SearchNameClick(Sender: TObject);
begin
  StudInfo.SetKey;
  StudInfo.IndexName := 'NameInd';
  Studinfo.FieldByName('Name').AsString := teNameSearch.text;
  Studinfo.GotoNearest;
end;
```

Setting a Range of Records

ANALYSIS It is often advantageous to limit the records in your dataset by using some criteria. For example, you might want to only show the Freshman class in the Studinfo table. Another example would be if you wanted to show all the students with a grade point average above 3.6 to compose the Dean's list. These operations are range limiting because they allow you to work with a smaller subset of the data. Once a range is in place, you can assume that the rest of the records do not exist. One way to gather a range is with the `SetRange` method. Listing 13.10 shows how to choose an index by name, and set a range. The last procedure shows how to remove a range condition by using the `CancelRange` method.

TYPE **Listing 13.10. Displaying a subset of a dataset by using the `SetRange` Method.**

```
procedure TForm1.RangeFreshClick(Sender: TObject);
begin
  Studinfo.IndexName := 'ClassInd';
  StudInfo.SetRange(['Freshman'],['Freshman']);
end;

procedure TForm1.RangeDeansClick(Sender: TObject);
begin
  Studinfo.IndexName := 'GpaInd';
  StudInfo.SetRange([3.6],[5]);
end;

procedure TForm1.All1Click(Sender: TObject);
begin
  StudInfo.CancelRange;
end;
```

Controlling Input into a Table

In a perfect world, users would do everything the programmer expected them to do. Unfortunately, this never happens. End users seem to always find a way to use an application in a way that it was never intended to be used. Although an application developer will never be able to control everything that a user will do, there are some techniques that can stabilize an application and force the user to enter data and conform to the process flow that was engineered. This section discusses methods that can be used to control the data that is entered into a database.

Use Pick Components as Opposed to Open Components

To make an application as user friendly as possible, don't let the user make mistakes. Design forms with comboboxes, radio buttons, and listboxes wherever appropriate. The most dangerous data-aware controls to use are generic text editboxes and memoboxes. These allow the user to enter any data they wish. Good form design can go a long way to having happy customers or users.

Input Masks

The first thing that can be done to force the user to enter what you are looking for is by using input masks. An input mask is a property on each field component. An input mask forces a control to accept input only in a certain format. For example, if you would like the user to enter a phone number into a field on your form, some people might use (916) 873-3454, where others may use 9168733454. These are both valid numbers, however, it would be beneficial if all entries are consistent. To enforce consistence, an input mask is built using rules for what values can be placed in which field locations. For example, an input mask of 000\-00\-0000;1;_ could be used to enforce the form of a Social Security number. For example, 183-234-9829 would be allowed, but A34-34-2345 would not because the mask states that all characters must be numbers, and they must be in the form of XXX-XX-XXXX. Great, this sounds powerful, but that string looks awfully confusing. Is there an easy way to create input masks? Yes, Delphi comes with a dialog box that helps the developer build the masks. To bring up the Mask Editor, double click on the `EditMask` property of a TField object. (See Figure 13.10.) The Mask Editor has a list of common masks as well as a field to enter a new mask and test it on the fly. To see all the capabilities of masks, see the `MaskEdit` property help page for details.

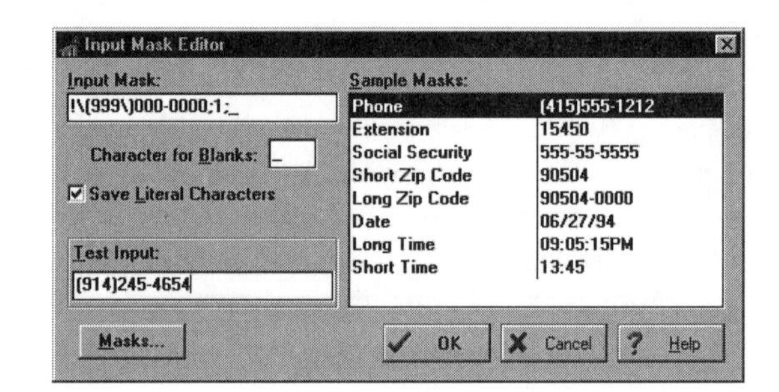

Figure 13.10.
The Mask Editor.

Database Level Constraints

The `MaskEdit` property works well at an application level; however, if a database is going to be accessed by many applications, wouldn't it be nice if some rules could be put in place such

that the data was somewhat consistent? Every database is different; however, most have some way to enforce rules on the values that can be put into fields. For simplicity, we will show how to set validation criteria in Paradox. The rules are set in the database, therefore if more than one application uses the database, the integrity will be maintained. The data validation that can be performed in a Paradox table is

- To force a value to be entered for a field
- To set the maximum value that a field can be
- To set the minimum value that a field can be
- To give a default value to a field if no value is supplied.

To set these criteria in a table, the database desktop is used. Remember that if an application that is accessing a table is opened, the `Active` property needs to be set to false, or the project should be closed. The steps to add validation criteria are as follows:

1. Go to the Database Desktop by choosing the Database Desktop option under tools.
2. Choose File | Open | Table, and select the table on which you wish to put a constraint.
3. Choose Table | Restructure Table. This brings up the list of fields in the table and each one's associated data type.
4. Be sure the table properties box is set to Validity Checks.
5. Click on the field that you wish to put a constraint on and enter the details in the dialog. For example if you wanted to put a constraint on the GPA field of your studinfo table, you would enter **`0`** in the minimum box and **`4.0`** in the maximum box.

NOTE

An application's developer will not always own the database. Therefore, a constraint may have been placed on the data outside of the application. If a Delphi application violates the validation criteria, an exception will occur.

13

The `Cancel` Method

ANALYSIS The `Cancel` method can be used as a last line of attack to control the user's input. In some cases, data validation is complex enough that it cannot be formulated into an input mask or database level constraint. For example: Joe Mathematica would like to develop a database to store his favorite prime numbers. To do this he requests an application to enter a prime number, and that the computer validate it is prime before the number is stored in a database. You provide a solution that uses a dbTextEdit box to request the user to enter his or her favorite prime number, a dbNavigator to move through the database, and a Save Changes button to commit inserts and modifications. The main task is to validate that the number is actually prime before you save it to the database. One way to do this is to execute the `Edit` method on entering the data field. Also, disable the navigator, which forces the user to click on the Save Changes button to save changes. You place the validation code in the `OnClick` event of a button. To refresh everyone's memory, a prime number is a number that cannot be divided by any number other then itself and 1. For example, 5 is prime because there are no numbers that can be multiplied to equal 5. Six is not prime because 2*3=6. In the validation code, you loop through all numbers from 2 through n-1 and check to see if the remainder is 0. If it is, you know that it is not a prime number, and you will jump out of the loop. Just a note, this is not an efficient algorithm for checking primes, as it can iterate as many times as the number. Listing 13.11 demonstrates using the `Cancel` method to confirm a number is prime.

TYPE

Listing 13.11. Confirming a number is prime using the `Cancel` method.

```
procedure TForm1.EntPrimeEnter(Sender: TObject);
begin
  Nav.Enabled := False;  {Disable the navigator}
  Primes.Edit;           {place tabel into edit mode}
end;

procedure TForm1.SaveChangesClick(Sender: TObject);

Var
 IsPrime : Boolean;
 Count : Integer;
 NumToTest : Integer;

begin
   IsPrime := True;
   Count := 2;
   NumToTest := StrToInt(EntPrime.Text);
   While (Count < NumToTest) and (IsPrime) do
     begin
       if NumToTest mod Count = 0
         then IsPrime := False; { once we find one, we are done!}
       inc(Count); { Increment the Counter}
     end; {while}
   {If the number is Prime save the number to the database}
   {otherwise roll it back using the Cancel method }
   if (IsPrime) then
      Primes.Post
     else
      begin
        Application.MessageBox('Number is not Prime!','Invalid',MB_OK);
        Primes.Cancel;
      end; {else}
```

```
   Nav.enabled := true; {Renable the Navigator}
end; {Procedure}
```

Validation Property on TFields and TTables

Three techniques to make data entry more valid have been looked at: controlling what the user can enter, database level data constraints, and forcing the user to follow a process that allows the application to check the validity of data. A final method that we will discuss involves the use of events and exceptions. Using procedures attached to On events in the field and table objects, an application can validate the data before it is stored. This is often advantageous because it gives the user slightly more freedom as to how they want to enter and edit data. Why would you need to validate at the table and field level? Because in some situations a field can be validated with only knowledge of itself. An example of this would be your prime number database. The application can determine that the number is prime without knowledge of any other data. However, if you had an application that cashiers used to log their register when they check in and out, your validation check may be that the amount coming in is greater than the amount going out. This validation could not be done until knowledge of both amounts was present.

To validate at the field level, you need to place an event handler in the `OnValidate` event. This event is called just before data is written to the database. If you want to allow the data to be written, allow the procedure to execute. Use an exception to block processing. Listing 13.12 is an example of rewriting the prime number validation using an `OnValidate` event.

TYPE **Listing 13.12. Validation using the `OnValidate` event.**

```
type
   EInvalidPrime = class(Exception);

{…}
procedure TForm1.PrimesFavPrimesValidate(Sender: TField);

Var
 IsPrime : Boolean;
 Count : Integer;
 NumToTest : Integer;

begin
 try
   IsPrime := True;
   Count := 2;
   NumToTest := StrToInt(EntPrime.Text);
   While (Count < NumToTest) and (IsPrime) do
     begin
       if NumToTest mod Count = 0
```

continues

13

Listing 13.12. Continued

```
        then IsPrime := False; { once we find one, we are done!}
      inc(Count); { Increment the Counter}
    end; {while}
  {If the number is Prime save the number to the database}
  {otherwise roll it back using the Cancel method }
  if not(IsPrime) then
     begin
       raise EInvalidPrime.Create('Number is not prime!');
     end; {else}
 except
  on EInvalidPrime do
    begin
      Application.Messagebox('Number is not prime!','Invalid',MB_OK);
      EntPrime.Text :='';
      if (Primes.State = dsInsert) or (primes.State=dsEdit)
       then Primes.cancel;
    end;
 end;
end;
```

ANALYSIS Something to note is that the `try` and `except` clauses are used to catch your exception if you detect that a number is not prime. Also, the procedure uses the `Exception.Create` method to cause a custom exception to occur. To perform record validation, the procedure would be the same; however, the code would be placed behind the `BeforePost` event.

Exception Handling

It is now apparent that your application must be aware of invalid data. Unfortunately, the application should also know what to do when errors or exceptions occur. If data can be validated what would cause an exception? Many things; these are a few of the most common.

- **Duplicate keys**—Although validation can be done to determine if a field meets criteria, it is an extra step to be sure that the key doesn't already exist. In the STUDINFO table, if two records are added with the same Social Security number, an exception occurs. This goes back to the very definition of a key. A key must be unique for every record. The database engine uses the key as a hook to know what record it is operating on. In addition, if a key is violated, then your data would be corrupt. You know that it is impossible for two people to have the same Social Security number, therefore, if two appeared in the database, it is due to human error. To keep the data meaningful, keys must be enforced.
- **Database validation error**—As mentioned earlier, constraint can be put on fields at the database level. However, what happens when one of these constrains is violated? You guessed it: an exception. Therefore, your application needs to be able to recover from invalid data exceptions gracefully and contain procedures to allow the user to fix the data.

- **Invalid state for operation**—One final error that occurs frequently is a procedure executing code based on the assumption that a table is in a particular state. This is a very dangerous assumption in an event-driven environment. Tables can be in one of six possible states: dsInactive, dsBrowse, dsEdit, dsInsert, dsSetKey, and dscalcFields. While in each state, the table behaves differently. For example, if the table is in the dsEdit state, the statement

  ```
  Studinfo.FieldByName('Class') .AsString:='Freshman';
  ```

  would set the current record's class field to that of a freshman. However, the same statement executed when in a dsSetKey state would indicate that you want to search for the first freshman. These are actually the most difficult to debug because they do not cause exceptions. Some operations *will* cause exceptions. For example, trying to execute the `Post` or `Cancel` method when in a dsBrowse state causes an exception.

Back to Abstraction

Borland's database engine can communicate with many different databases. This is useful if the application developer wants to change the underlying database structure at any time. For full flexibility and compatibility with almost *any* database, ODBC is available.

ODBC—A Further Layer of Abstraction

NEW TERM ODBC stands for *open database connectivity.* ODBC allows you to communicate with any database through a common interface by using what is known as an ODBC driver. The ODBC driver contains code that understands the specifics of a particular database and provides access to it through a standard set of API calls.

Using ODBC gives an application the greatest amount of flexibility, because, in theory, switching the type of database that an application uses would be as simple as switching ODBC drivers. In reality, there are other minor changes in the language passed to ODBC to communicate correctly with different database engines. If an application ever needs the highest level of performance with ODBC, then the application can communicate directly with the ODBC API. I warn you that this is not straightforward and provides an additional layer of complexity; however, if for optimal ODBC performance, it can be done.

Why Use ODBC

Often an application developer will want to create an application but can't scale the application initially. ODBC allows the developer to use a file-based stand-alone database for development and switch to a client/server model at a later time without a great deal of changes to the source code. This is also useful in creating a Delphi application that needs to be compatible with existing data. For example, if the current payroll system is on a Sybase SQL server, and a front end needs to be developed to access the data, Delphi can use ODBC to connect and communicate with the database. Another example of backward compatibility is if you are trying to port some applications written in a different language to Delphi. Take the example in which Visual Basic is used to create a Windows-based front end to access a Microsoft Access database. Now it comes time to develop a native, 32-bit Delphi database to access the same data. How would you do this? If you go to the Database Desktop and try to open an access file, it cannot be done.

In ODBC terminology, an ODBC driver is the library that understands how to communicate with the underlying database. ODBC drivers are often available from the database vendor or third-party software companies. An ODBC datasource is an instance of an ODBC object that uses a driver. For example, you might have a Sybase SQL server ODBC driver, and HRDATA is an ODBC datasource that is a SQL server with the Human Resource data. There can be a second datasource using the same driver. Therefore, there might be an additional datasouce, INVENT, that points to a SQL server containing information on inventory.

The ODBCAD32 utility is used to create and configure ODBC datasources. For each ODBC datasource different configuration information will be needed. For example, an Access ODBC datasource will need to be configured with the location of the .mdb file. While a SQL datasource will need to be configured with the network address of the server, and the network interface library to access the server.

To use an ODBC driver and communicate through ODBC in Delphi, a new Borland Database Engine driver needs to be created. Note that this may seem confusing because ODBC has ODBC drivers that are data drivers and the Borland Database Engine has internal drivers. A Borland database driver must be configured to access an ODBC driver. Therefore, to create a Borland database driver follow these steps:

1. Enter the Borland Database Configuration Utility.
2. Click on New ODBC Driver
3. Set the SQL link driver name to ODBC_XXXX where XXXX is the name of the BDE driver you wish to create. (See Figure 13.11.)
4. The ODBC driver to be used to access the data and a default ODBC datasource needs to be supplied.

That is all for creating the driver. To xaccess the data the easiest way in Delphi is to set up an alias using the database desktop.

Figure 13.11.
The Borland Database Configuration Utility.

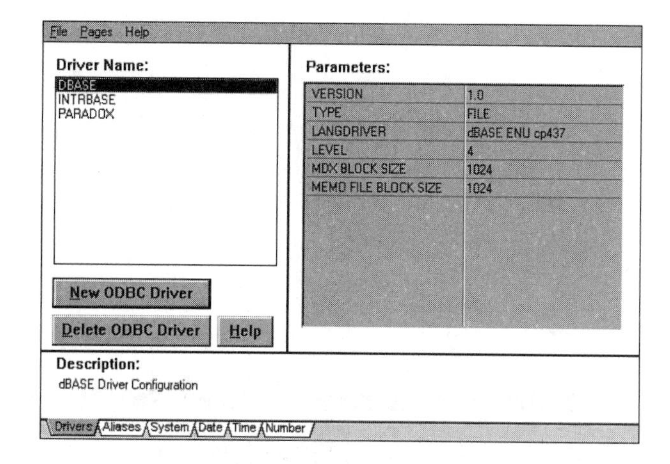

Using a Microsoft Access Database through ODBC

Define the ODBC Datasource by following these steps:

1. Run ODBCAD32.
2. At the Datasources dialog click Add.
3. This displays a list of installed ODBC data drivers. Choose Access Data *.mdb.
4. Enter a name and description for the access datasource. For this example use `TestAccess` for the datasource name.
5. Click on Select Database. This brings up a list of .mdb files.
6. Using the dialog to select the file to access.
7. Choose OK.

To define the BDE driver, follow these steps:

1. Bring up the Database Configuration Utility.
2. Click on New ODBC Drive.
3. Set the SQL link driver name to ODBC_ACCESS.
4. Set the ODBC driver to Access Data (*.mdb).
5. Set the ODBC default datasource name to **TestAccess**.
6. Click on the Aliases tab to create a new alias to use the driver.
7. Choose New Alias.
8. Name the alias **TstAccess** and choose ODBC_ACCESS as the database type.
9. Leave the BDE Configuration Utility and save the changes.

To Use the ODBC Alias in Delphi, follow these steps:

1. Create a new project and add a `TTable` component.
2. Set the `DatabaseName` property to `TstAccess`.
3. When the `TableName` property is set, a dialog box may appear requesting a user ID and password. Simply select OK.
4. Notice the tables in the access database are now available in the `TableName` property. Choose a table to work with and continue as if you are working with any other table in Delphi.

Database Security and Passwords

You have heard of computer hackers and stories of top secret data falling into the hands of the KGB after secret agents tap into data lines and decrypt the data with Cray supercomputers. These stories may seem like something out of a James Bond movie; however, data security in real world applications is nothing to be taken lightly. Data security is the process that allows certain users, groups, or processes to read or manipulate data. Take a simple example, at the Department of Motor Vehicles it is advantageous to allow all clerks to view driving records, however, only a select few should be granted the power to modify them (or else pretty soon friends and families of workers would have their tickets wiped clean). Data security may also be linked to an application. In your prime number database, the application does a powerful computation to prevent non-primes from being entered into the database. When the user awakens in the middle of the night and says "I have a favorite number that I must add to my database, 513," the user starts the computer and bypasses the Delphi front end, going directly to the Database Desktop and adds 513. Because the value is added outside the application, no validation is done (513 is not a prime number, therefore, we now have corrupted data). However, if there were some way to allow only certain users, applications, and groups to manipulate data, it would solve a lot of problems. This is why many database platforms integrate security into the database.

Security Levels

Depending on the database you are using, different levels of security are available. Although either groups, users, and application can be given access to databases, for the purpose of discussion we will limit your scope to individual users. The most common levels of security a database will use are as follows:

- None—It is very possible that anyone with physical access to the data can view it and modify it.

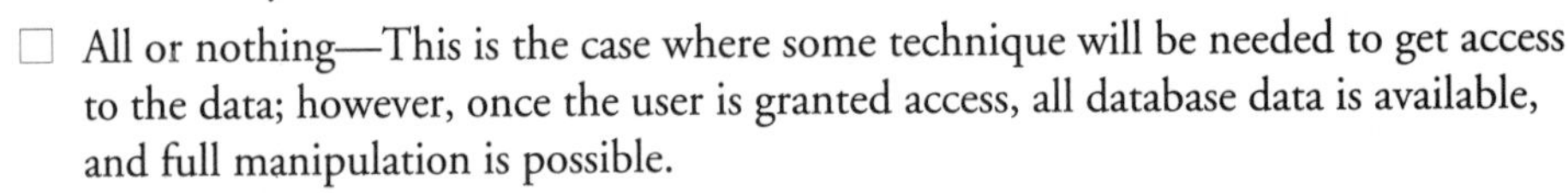

- All or nothing—This is the case where some technique will be needed to get access to the data; however, once the user is granted access, all database data is available, and full manipulation is possible.

- Multi-user, table-level access—Allowing different users to access tables in either read, update, or insert mode. Therefore, Joe may have total control over his database, but Sam would only be able to read the data.
- Multi-user, field-level access—Field-level access is the most flexible type of data security. In field-level access, users would be granted a level of access to each field in the table. Therefore, in the DMV example given earlier, a clerk could be granted update access on the Last Name field so that they could processs name changes but would be granted read-only access on the Driving Points field. Additionally, some users may not even be given read access on certain fields. For example, if a small company keeps a database of their employees, they could make the name, mail stop, and extension public information, but keep the salary and home address omitted from public access.

Authentication

NEW TERM Now that you understand how different users can be allowed different levels of access, the question becomes "How do you know what user is trying to access your data." The answer is *authentication.* Authentication is the process used to confirm that an entity is actually who they claim to be. When a user proves his identity, he has been authenticated.

In order to complete the security cycle, the database engine needs to authenticate a user and then determine what access that user has. The most common way to implement authentication is with some type of password scheme. Paradox uses a master password that defines the table owner. Secondary passwords can be defined by the table owner, and given field-level access. Another common method used by databases to perform authentication is a user ID/password combination. This is a better approach because the user's identification is not associated with his or her password. From an administration approach, this is also more secure because the database owner doesn't need to know each user's password.

Summary

In this chapter, we have covered basic database concepts and how to manipulate tables in Delphi; specifically, how to use the TTable component to gain database access. The DataSource component acts as an intermediate layer between the TTable and data-aware components. Data-aware components are a powerful set of components that can access a dataset and allow the application to view and manipulate data. Relational database design and performance issues are also discussed. Some of the information included keys and indexes. Keys are used to maintain uniqueness, and indexes are primarily for performance. We also touched on the issue of data security and how different databases implement it. In the next chapter you will learn that there are other ways to gain database access other than the TTable component. There is also a language called SQL that gives a greater deal of flexibility and functionality to the way data is accessed through the database engine.

Q&A

Q In the Studinfo table, if I wanted to allow the user to edit all fields except Social Security number, how could this be done?

A Use the `Readonly` property in the StudInfoSSN component. Fields are attached to datables and manipulated as components. By setting the `Readonly` property to true, this field cannot be modified.

Q What happens when an application attempts to violate a validity check in an application?

A An exception occurs. It is up to the developer to handle this condition gracefully. Use `try` and `except` blocks of code to handle database exceptions.

Q What if I need to store information with a many-to-one relationship. For example, if I wanted to store information about each class a student takes?

A The correct way to do this is with multiple tables. A field in your detail table will have the key to the master table. In this example the COURSE table would have a field called SSN which would link back to the main studinfo table. This is covered in detail in the next chapter.

Q I have a stand-alone file that absolutely needs security but does not have integrated security features. What can I do?

A The answer is to implement security at a different level. Either encrypt the entire database file, or save the sensitive data in encrypted form. Another method would be to store the data on a network which implements its own security. Remember that your data is only as secure as your weakest link.

Workshop

Quiz

1. If a table is in dsBrowse state, and an `Edit` method is executed, such as `Post`. What happens?
2. How can an application determine what type of data is stored in a field?
3. If an application needs to change how records are ordered, what property needs to be changed?

4. Which database models can be accessed by multiple people or applications simultaneously? Which cannot?
5. If a dataset is in dsCalculate state, what cannot be done to non-calculated fields?

Exercises

1. Create a database application that uses all the data-aware controls.
2. Modify the example that stores favorite prime numbers to also display the number squared by using calculated fields.
3. Use database level constraints to limit the maximum value of numbers stored in the prime number database. Add code to the application to display a message when too large a number is entered.

Week 2

Day 14

Introduction to SQL

This chapter covers two main topics: how to use multiple tables effectively in a relational database, and the fundamentals of Structured Query Language (SQL). Good database design cannot be enforced by a database engine. Unfortunately a database engine isn't smart enough to understand what your data means unless you explicitly explain how information is related. Relational databases use the concept that data can be stored in multiple tables, and links between the tables will be maintained by common fields. The second major topic in this chapter is on Structured Query Language (SQL). SQL allows interaction with a database by carrying on a conversation, or dialog. SQL can ask a database a question such as "Which players on the NY Mets had more than five home runs in 1995?" Also, SQL can command a database to do something. For example "Insert a new employee record with the following information," or "Delete all records from the student table where the GPA is less than 1.25." In Delphi, the TQuery component is used to execute SQL queries and statements. SQL gives an application total control over what information is requested and how the database is manipulated. Furthermore, SQL can be used to summarize data and group information.

Working With More Than One Table

One of the primary reasons that relational databases are used is that the database format is easy to understand and can be easily manipulated. In the examples that you have examined up to this point, only one table has been used, and all the needed information has been contained in the single table. However, it would be very inefficient and difficult to manage databases if data was always stored in one table. Consider the example of a university that wants to keep records on its students and the courses the students have taken. To do this with only one table, it might look like the following:

Table 14.1. Inefficient data representation for student data.

Student Number	Name	Phone	Course	Grade
12345	Jeff Smith	234-3445	CH101	C
12345	Jeff Smith	234-3445	EN333	A
12345	Jeff Smith	234-3445	NP343	A
34343	Jim Brown	543-2345	BI333	C
34343	Jim Brown	543-2345	NP343	B

This is inefficient database design because data is repeated in multiple records and is difficult to manage. There are quite a few problems with this approach. First of all, when a student changes phone numbers, every record identifying the student must be found and modified. Also, the same data is repeated many places in the database, which is a very inefficient use of space. Take this one step further and add the course descriptions to each record. Before you know it, the table is extremely large and difficult to manage. The reason the information is represented inefficiently is because the design does not take into account that there is a relationship between the students and the classes they take. Note that the following two tables represent exactly the same information but take up much less space.

Table 14.2. Student information table.

Student Number	Name	Phone Number
12345	Jeff Smith	234-3445
34343	Jim Brown	543-2345

Table 14.3. Grade table.

Student Number	Course	Grade
12345	CH101	C
12345	EN333	A
12345	NP343	A
34343	BI333	C
34343	NP343	B

These tables have a better design because the data is broken into multiple tables.

This is possible because there is a logical relationship between the data in the two tables. Note that although nothing technically would stop a developer from implementing this database with only one table, it would be poor database design because he is not taking full advantage of a relational model.

Foreign Keys

NEW TERM We have already defined a key as being a field or combination of fields in a table that makes each record unique. This is known as a *primary key.* There are also fields in tables called *foreign keys.* A foreign key means that the value is a key in a different table. An example of a foreign key would be the Student Number field in the Course Information table (the course information table would be a table listing the students enrolled in each course). The field is not unique in this table, however it will always be unique in the student information table.

Relationships

There are three main ways that tables can relate to one another. There can be a one-to-one relationship, a many-to-one relationship, or a many-to-many relationship. Let's look at each of these. Tables with true one-to-one relationships are rare because the information can often be included in the original table. However, in some cases where certain information is rarely needed, then it may make sense to keep the detail in one table and the frequently used data in another. One of the most powerful types of a relationship is a many-to-one. This means that there can be multiple references to data in a detail table. This is extremely useful because data is not repeated, and changing it in one place affects all references. The following is an example of a many to one relationship:

> The DMV keeps data on drivers and automobiles. Driver data is kept in the DRIVER table which includes a driver's license number, name, address, and

> points. Information on vehicles is stored in the AUTO table. This table tracks the Vehicle Identification Number, model, year, and the owner's driver's license number. The driver's license number in the AUTO table is a foreign key. The VIN (Vehicle Identification Number) in the auto table is a primary key, and the driver's license number in the DRIVER table is a primary key. Drivers can own more than one car; however, cars cannot have more than one owner. Therefore, there are many cars to one owner, or a many-to-one relationship.

There are also many-to-many relationships. Many-to-many relationships are often implemented with an intermediate table containing foreign keys associated with each of the tables containing the relationship. For example:

> Students take classes; therefore, every student may take more than one (many) class. Classes also have many students enrolled; therefore, there is a many-to-many relationship between students and classes. One of the tables in this database contains information on students such as ID number, name, and address. Another table describes the courses with information such as course number, description, number of credits, and pre-requisites. To indicate which students are taking what classes, there should be a third table added containing one field that is a student number, and another field that is the class. Note that from this table, you can generate either a class schedule for every student, or a student roll list for each course.

The primary objective in database design should be that information exists in only one place and that each table represents one logically related piece of the database. One final note is that there are no rules. This is not like writing a program in which if the syntax is not exact, the compiler gives an error. Data can be effectively represented in many different ways,as long as you don't forget that a database is simply a representation of data. Next, you look at linked cursors which provide an easy way to manipulate tables that are related in a many-to-one relationship.

The Importance of Using Data Modules

One of the problems in Delphi 1.0 was that it wasn't possible to save the relationships between tables in a separate unit. This forced the developer to redefine the relation between tables with each application that was developed. Throughout the rest of this chapter we will place our non-visual database visual components on a data module so that we could access them in multiple applications. Remember that you need to use the File | Use Unit command from the main menu to use components on a data module.

`MasterSource` and `MasterField` Properties

One of the most common reasons to use a many-to-one relationship is to provide detailed information in one table that is accessed from a foreign key in another table. Delphi provides an easy method to exploit this relationship by using the `MasterSource`, and `MasterField` properties on TTable objects.

The `MasterSource` and `MasterField` properties allow one table to control which record is accessible in a detail table. For example, consider a table containing student grades. This could be displayed using a DBGrid component. There could also be a set of fields that would display information about the student referenced in the current record, such as name, phone number, and dorm. To link the tables together the studinfo information table uses its `MasterSource` and `MasterField` properties to determine what record is being accessed in the Grades table. In this instance, the Student table would be considered the detail table, and the Grades table would be considered the master table.

To implement the master/detail relationship, a datasource needs to be associated with the master table. This component name is then specified on the `MasterSource` property of the detail component. One final piece of information is needed to make the association work: the field that is common to both tables needs to be specified. There are some important issues about the fields that need to be addressed. The field the master joins to in the detail table must have an index on that field in the detail table. The association is made in the `MasterField` property of the detail table. To create this association, perform the following steps:

- Add a TTable and DataSource component for both the master and the detail tables. You can use the ORDERS.DB table for the master and CUSTOMER.DB for the detail. Both of these are in the DBDEMOS database.
- Bring up the properties sheet for the detail table (CUSTOMER).
- Set the `MasterSource` property to the data source component that accesses the master table.
- Double click the `MasterFields` property; this brings up the field link designer dialog. It is necessary to pick which detail field maps to which master field. The fields must be exactly the same datatype. After the fields are linked, choose OK. This action is shown in Figure 14.1.

The sample application in Figure 14.2 uses a field link to display order information in one grid and customer information in another. For whichever order is selected, the customer detail for that order is displayed.

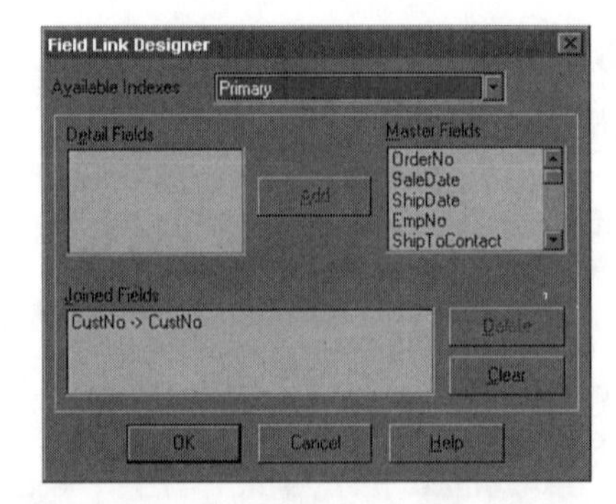

Figure 14.1.
The Field Link Designer.

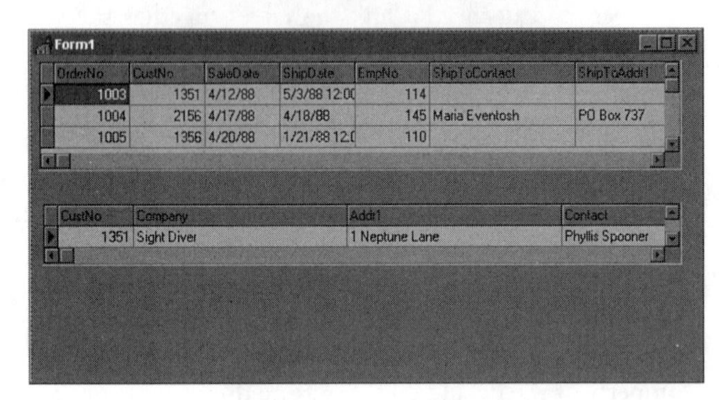

Figure 14.2.
Order application using liked fields.

Delphi allows applications to manipulate tables using the TTable component. With this component, methods exist to search for records, sort records, link tables, and move through a recordset. The shortcoming of the TTable component is that each of these tasks requires a separate method, or property definition, and it is difficult to combine operations. To solve this, Delphi also provides a secondary method to interact with a database called the TQuery visual component. The TQuery visual component allows an application to communicate with the database through a language called Structured Query Language (SQL). SQL (pronounced sequel) is extremely powerful, and if used properly can make many complex tasks simple.

What Is SQL and Where Did It Come From

Structured Query Language is nothing new; IBM developed SQL in the late 1970s. Since that time, variations and improvements have been made. However, the underlying concepts are still intact. SQL is a high-level language. An application does not tell the database engine how to perform a task, but states what the results should contain. Different database vendors have made slight changes to the SQL syntax. However, it is usually straightforward to move standard SQL between database platforms. Some database vendors have added major enhancements to SQL such as stored procedures and triggers (these are discussed in the next chapter), but for now we simply cover the basic SQL syntax.

From an object-oriented standpoint, both the TTable component and TQuery component are ancestors of a dataset class. Datasets provide a method to interact with a database and retrieve data. When using the TQuery component, different methods are used based on what action is taking place. For example, if the application is retrieving data from a database, the methods used on the TQuery visual component are different than if an application is inserting a record into a database. Unfortunately, Paradox and dBASE only offer a subset of the functionality that many SQL languages allow. The Interbase server can be used if more powerful SQL is needed (Interbase is discussed in the next chapter). Therefore, in the following introduction to SQL, the examples and list of functionality are kept basic so that everything should work with the local databases that have native support by Delphi.

Creating Queries Using SQL

NEW TERM What is a query? A *query* is a question an application asks a database and then returns records. Queries return a set of records that meet some criteria, and contain information from selected fields. So far, this does not seem so different from a `TTable` object in which fields are first edited with the field editor, and then range values are set. While this is true, SQL can do all of this in one simple statement, plus offer summarization of records, work with and link multiple tables easily, use very complex selection criteria, and much more (no you don't get a free set of steak knives if you order now!). Let's begin with the basis for all queries, the `SELECT` statement.

When talking about queries, consider every SQL statement a question. The result set is the answer with which the database engine responds. There are some SQL statements that are simply a command: "I command you to insert a record!" For this statement, you would not receive a result. However, for questions or queries a results set is the set of records returned by the database engine.

The `SELECT` statement in its simplest form is a question that requests the database engine return all the data from a table. The syntax for this would be

```
SELECT * FROM <TABLE>
```

The `SELECT` is the command. The asterisk (*) indicates that all fields should be returned, and the `FROM <TABLE>` lets the database engine know which table the data should come from. The results this query returns are equivalent to the data available in a default TTable component.

A common task that database applications need to do is limit the amount of data returned. There are two ways this can be done. Either the number of fields needs to be reduced, or the recordset needs to be reduced. Take the first scenario in which the number of fields should be reduced; to accomplish this, a set of fields can be placed between the SELECT and the FROM elements of the SELECT statement. For example:

```
SELECT Name,Address,GPA FROM STUDINFO
```

This would return a recordset containing only the Name, Address and GPA fields from the student information table. "This looks easier than using the TTable object. How can I put SQL into my Delphi application?" To execute a SQL statement in Delphi that returns a result in Delphi, the following steps must be taken:

- Add a TQuery visual component to a form or data module.
- The SQL that will be executed can be set by manipulating the SQL property in the Object Inspector or by manipulating the SQL property by using TString methods (the SQL property is an instance of the TStrings class).
- Use a data source linked to the TQuery component to access the data.
- Use the Open method to submit the query.
- Use the Close method to terminate the query.

Here is an example of executing a simple SELECT statement using a block of code.

```
Query1.SQL.Clear;
Query1.SQL.Add('SELECT  NAME,ADDRESS,GPA  from STUDINFO');
Query1.Open;
{... Do what needs to be done!....}
Query1.Close;
```

The TQuery visual component can return both live and dead result sets. The records in a live result set can be manipulated just like records accessed by a TTable visual component. A dead result set is simply a snapshot that can be navigated but not modified or manipulated. To return a live result set, the RequestLive property must be set to TRUE on the TQuery visual component and the query must conform to Delphi's "syntax requirements for a live results set."

In addition to reducing the number of fields, fields can be added. This is very similar to the calculated fields in TTables. For example, you can issue the following SQL statement which returns the price of an item plus a standard 15 percent markup.

```
SELECT Item,Description,Price,Price*1.15 FROM INVENT
```

The operators available for arithmetic manipulation on Local SQL databases are +, -, *, and /. In addition to arithmetic operators, Local SQL also supports four string manipulation functions; UPPER, LOWER, SUBSTRING, and TRIM. These functions are useful because the database engine can perform case conversions and text manipulation before the application receives the data. For example, to receive a student name in uppercase, the following query could be executed:

```
SELECT UPPER(Name) FROM studinfo
```

Part of a date can also be isolated from a date/time field by using the `EXTRACT` function. `EXTRACT` needs to know what piece of the date/time to extract and from which field to extract it. An example of using the `EXTRACT` function is

```
SELECT EXTRACT(YEAR FROM Date_Of_Birth) FROM Employee
```

It's now apparent that SQL can be used to retrieve a subset, or all the fields in a table. Many times, it is advantageous to eliminate duplicate rows. This can be achieved using the `DISTINCT` keyword. Specifying `SELECT DISTINCT <FIELDS>` returns all records that are unique in reference to the fields selected. Note that the records themselves do not need to be unique. Examine the following table that a kennel uses to keep track of which dog toy belongs to which dog.

Table 14.4. Dog breeder's table.

DogName	Breed	Toy
Ada	Beagle	Green Shoe
Ada	Beagle	Rope a Dope
Ada	Beagle	Tennis Ball
Lucky	Mix	Frisbee
Miller	Mix	Bone

If a simple `SELECT * FROM Dogs` is executed, the results set looks exactly like Table 14.4. Similarly, if a `SELECT DISTINCT * FROM Dogs` is executed the same result occurs again because all the records are unique. Now in a case in which you execute `SELECT DogName,Breed FROM Dogs`. This returns the information in Table 14.5.

Table 14.5. Results from selecting all dogs.

DogName	Breed
Ada	Beagle
Ada	Beagle
Ada	Beagle
Lucky	Mix
Miller	Mix

Note that all five records are still returned. This is because there is no `DISTINCT` clause, which makes the database return all records. Modifying this slightly so that there is a `DISTINCT` clause causes only the names of the dogs and their breed to be selected, regardless of how many toys they have. Therefore, `SELECT DISTINCT DogName,Breed FROM Dogs` returns the information in Table 14.6.

Table 14.6. Results indicating only the dogs and their breed.

DogName	Breed
Ada	Beagle
Lucky	Mix
Miller	Mix

In a case in which the owner wants to view a list of all the breeds that are being boarded, this could be done with a `SELECT DISTINCT Breed FROM Dogs`

Table 14.7. Results indicating the breeds that are boarded.

Breed
Beagle
Mix

The `DISTINCT` clause is extremely useful in narrowing a results set, if the target should be a unique set of records. In addition to the `DISTINCT` clause being used to limit the number of records returned, record criteria can also be based on the values of each record.

One of the most useful aspects of SQL is its ability to find a subset of a table using standard logic. The logical operators can reference other fields in a table as well as constants. For example, if you have a table containing data on the amount of money a store receives in a day, and the amount that was refunded to customers, it is possible to return all stores that had a loss for the day because they gave more money out then they took in. The key to limiting which records are returned is known as the `WHERE` clause.

The `WHERE` clause is used after the `FROM` clause. The clause resembles a conditional statement in object Pascal. The purpose of the `WHERE` clause is to return records meeting only a particular criterion. The format for the `WHERE` clause is

```
WHERE <BOOLEAN EXPRESSION>
```

The `<BOOLEAN EXPRESSION>` is made up of one or more logical operations that will evaluate to `TRUE` or `FALSE` for every record. The operators use field names, constants, or parameters as the operands. For example, to generate a deans list the following SQL statement could be executed:

```
SELECT * FROM studinfo WHERE GPA > 3.5
```

This would select all fields from the student information table, but would only return records for students with a GPA higher than 3.5. Multiple conditions can be used and joined together with AND and OR operators. For example, if the admissions department for a school wants to narrow their pool of applicants to those in-state students with a GPA of 3.5, and 3.7 for those who are out of state, the following SQL could be used.

```
SELECT * FROM applicant WHERE
      (State = "NY" and GPA > 3.5) or  GPA > 3.7
```

In addition to the standard =, >, and < logical operators, Local SQL also supports a LIKE operator that can be used to search for patterns in a string or to see if part of a string matches, an IN operator that determines if a value is in a set, and a BETWEEN operator, which can be used to determine if a field is between two values. We look at each of these special operators one at a time.

The LIKE operator is more flexible then the = operator because it can perform powerful wildcard searches. The two wildcard designators are the % (percent) and the _ (underscore). The percent symbol designates any characters, and the underscore represents any single character. These can be used in combination with each other. For example:

```
SELECT * FROM studinfo WHERE Name LIKE "JONES%"
```

returns records in which the name is Jones followed by anything.

```
SELECT * FROM studinfo WHERE Name LIKE "B%N"
```

returns records beginning with a "B" and end in an "N" such as Brown, Boon, and Bentin.

As mentioned, the underscore performs a wildcard search on one single letter. For example:

```
SELECT * FROM Customer WHERE State LIKE "N_"
```

This would return all states with the first letter "N", and the second letter is anything (such as NY, NH, NC, but not New Zealand). In addition to the LIKE operator, there is also an IN operator that determines if a field is in a set. For example, to determine all customers in a West Coast sales division, you could execute the following:

```
SELECT * FROM Customer WHERE State IN ("CA", "NV", "WA")
```

The BETWEEN operator is a shortcut to see if a value is in a range. For example, a white-water rafting company may use the following query to list rivers flowing at a desired rate:

```
SELECT * FROM River WHERE Flow BETWEEN 3.4 and 6.7
```


There is also no reason LIKE, IN, and BETWEEN cannot be combined with other operators. This allows you to have extremely complex and powerful selection criteria in one statement. For example:

```
SELECT * FROM Customer WHERE (State IN ("CA", "NV", "WA")) AND
      (Name LIKE "A%" OR Name LIKE "B%") AND (Purchases > 12345.44)
```

Try that one with the range method on a TTable; it would be awfully difficult. What else is different? Notice that SQL does not have the stringent indexing requirements that the TTable methods do.

Using the Database Explorer to Test Out SQL

The easiest way to test SQL statements is to use the Database Explorer. The Database Explorer has an Enter SQL tab that allows you to enter a SQL statement and then execute it by clicking on the execute SQL button (the button with a picture of a lightning bolt). The result set is shown in Figure 14.3.

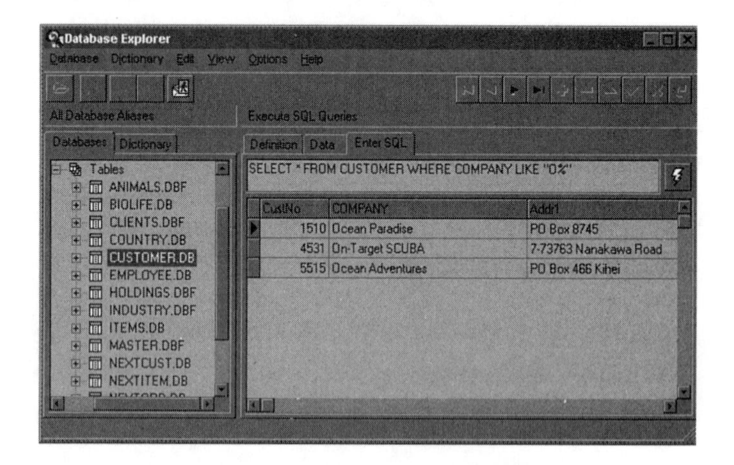

Figure 14.3.
Using the Database Explorer to execute queries.

Building a Simple Application to Perform SQL Queries

Although the Database Explorer is easy to use, you will build your own application to execute generic queries.The example shows how to use SQL from within a Delphi application. This sample program allows the user to test out the SQL language. A memo box allows any SQL query to be entered, and when the query is executed, the results are displayed in a database grid. The returned recordset can be navigated with the dbNavigator component. To create this program:

- ☐ Create a new project and add a data module in addition to the default form.
- ☐ Add the components found in Table 14.8 to the forms, and set their names as shown.

Table 14.8. Components for generic SQL application.

Component	Name	Location
Tquery	TestSQL	Data Module
TDataSource	dsTest	Data Module
TDBGrid	dbgResults	Main Form
TMemo	InputSQL	Main Form
TDBNavigator	navSQL	Main Form
TButton	ExecSQL	Main Form

☐ Arrange these components on the forms as Figure 14.4 indicates.

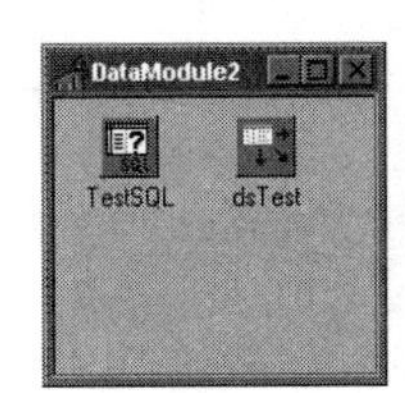

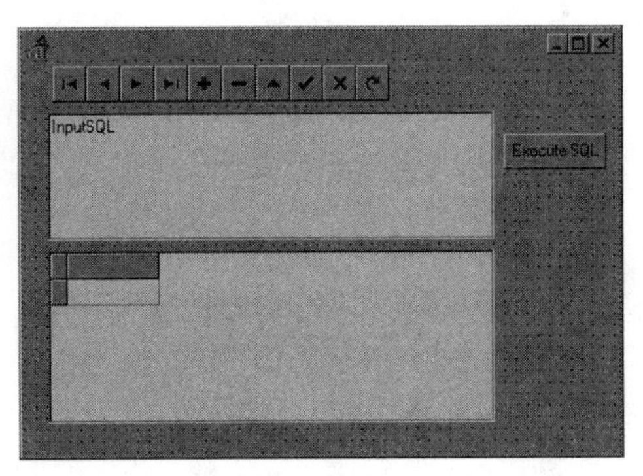

Figure 14.4.
Component layout for Generic Query tool.

☐ Link the dsTest datasource to the TestSQL query object.

☐ Click on the main form and then select File | Use Unit from the main menu. Click on Unit2 and press OK. Add DB and DBTables references to the uses section of the unit.

☐ Link the dbgResults grid and navsql navigator to the DataModule2.dsTest datasource.

☐ Set the default text in the InputSQL memo component to SELECT.

☐ Set the DatabaseName on the TestSQL query object to DBDEMOS (or any other database that you would like to experiment with SQL).

☐ The code in Listing 14.1 completes the application.

TYPE

Listing 14.1. Building a simple application to perform ad-hoc queries.

```
procedure TForm1.ExecSQLClick(Sender: TObject);
begin
  { If a query has been executed, close it before running}
  if not(DataModule2.TestSQL.state=dsInactive)
    then DataModule2.TestSQL.close;
  DataModule2.TestSQL.SQL.Clear; { Erase any old SQL Query}
  {copy SQL from Memo component}
  DataModule2.TestSQL.SQL.AddStrings(InputSQL.Lines);
  DataModule2.TestSQL.Open; {Run the query}
end;

procedure TForm1.ExitClick(Sender: TObject);
begin
   DataModule2.TestSQL.Close;
   Application.Terminate;
end;
```

ANALYSIS How does it work? The SQL that is entered into the memo component is copied into the `SQL` property of the TestSQL query component by using the `AddStrings` method. `AddStrings` copies a set of strings from one place to another. After the SQL statement is stored in the `SQL` property, the `Open` method is used to actually launch the SQL. The `Close` method is used after a query is processed to clean up and free resources.

All the queries that have been executed up to this point have been *static* queries. This means that a SQL statement is built, and executed. The SQL text is passed directly to the database engine. This is the simplest method for running queries because an application can build a query using any format and change the query easily. Delphi offers a powerful method of reusing SQL, by allowing it to except parameters. For example, the following query returns customers who live in New York:

```
SELECT * from Customers where State="NY"
```

If you wanted to make this query more generic in order to be able to find customers living in any specified state, you could use the following procedure:

```
procedure QueryState(StateIn : String);
BEGIN
  Form1.TestSQL.SQL.Clear; { Erase any old SQL Query}
  Form1.TestSQL.SQL.Add('SELECT * from Customer where STATE="'+StateIn+'"');
  Form1.TestSQL.Open; {Run the query}
END;
```

However, this would become quite tedious if you had a large number of queries that would always be the same other than some of the parameters changing. This is why Delphi supports *dynamic*, or changeable, queries. The previous example could be encapsulated into the TQuery visual component by setting the SQL parameter to

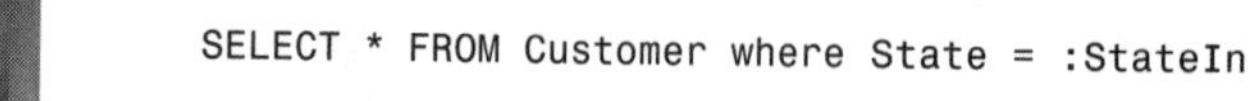

```
SELECT * FROM Customer where State = :StateIn
```

The colon before `StateIn` signifies that `StateIn` is a Delphi parameter that can be set before the query is executed. To set the parameter, simply set the `Params` property, which is an array of `TParam` objects, to the values using the `AsXXXX` method, where XXXX is the data type. Here is sample code to execute the previous query with the state parameter set:

```
TestSQL.Params[0].AsString := 'CA';
TestSQL.Open; {Run the query}
```

By using parameters, it appears that some of the legwork in building a SQL string has been eliminated. There is a way to use parameters and queries to improve performance. Lets look at this from a slightly different point of view. The database engine is given a request that needs to be satisfied. There are two steps that need to be performed. First, the database engine needs to find the most efficient way to return the results set. Secondly, it needs to actually do the work. This is like taking a trip. First you need to plan where to go, and next you actually travel there. When a parameter in a query changes, it doesn't affect how the results are returned. For example, if the query requests all records that have the state set to NY, the database engine figures that it needs to order the records by state, then move to the first record with NY and loop until a new state appears. Notice that all the steps are the same if the state changes, except for which state to search for. This has allowed Delphi to compile and optimize a query, and then run it multiple times, but has the ability to change parameters. To prepare a query, simply use the `Prepare` method on a TQuery component. For example:

```
TestSQL.Prepare; { Prepare query for optimal execution }
```

Note that a query should only be prepared once. Also note that parameter datatypes can be set by double clicking the `params` property page of the TQuery visual component. This also auto-prepares the query. A prepared query uses some database resources, therefore if a query will not be used for a while, it can be unprepared. To unprepare a query, use the `UnPrepare` method on the TQuery component.

```
TestSQL.UnPrepare; { Release some database resources }
```

Earlier in the chapter, master source and detail tables covered the concept in which one table in a relational database would reference another record. SQL offers even more flexibly in how tables can be associated. The association and linking of tables in a relational database is called a join.

Joins

NEW TERM *Joins* allow data to be connected from more than one table that is logically related. For example, look at the data in Tables 14.2 and 14.3. From a database perspective this is a great way to store and manage the data. However, now that the data is in a compact form, how could you make it look like the data in Table 14.1 The answer is a join. Joins are similar to detail/master tables in the fact that one field accessed all other fields; however, a join can operate on an entire recordset as opposed to the current record. Also not as much overhead is needed to set up a join, no extra TTables or datasources are needed. To demonstrate joins, let's examine three tables, and then show how information can be merged and extracted by using joins.

The following fictitious database is used by the Department of Motor Vehicles to track drives and automobiles.

Table 14.9. Driver—Represents data about drivers.

Driver Lic Number	Name	Address	License Class
12345	Rick	2908 Bobcat Cir	C
11111	Joe	99 Box 21	C
54321	Bob	534 Ranch Marieto	B
22222	Martha	433 Carl Drive	A

Table 14.10. Cars—Represents data about automobiles.

VIN	Make	Year	Model	Owner
10923453	Ford	1967	Mustang	22222
23459374	Buick	1992	Regal	22222
28383729	Buick	1993	Skylark	12345
34343434	Porsche	1979	911	11111

Table 14.11. Ticket—Represents data on traffic violations.

Driver	Violation	Points
22222	Speeding	5
12345	Speeding	2
22222	Signal Violation	1

The first thing that you may want to derive is a list of all cars on the street and their owner's names. To get this information, execute the following SQL query:

```
SELECT Driver.Name,Driver.Address,Cars.*
  FROM Cars,Driver
    WHERE Cars.Owner = Driver.DrivNum
```

The result of the query is the following recordset:

Table 14.12. Results from the join of Cars and Driver tables.

Name	Address	VIN	Make	Year	Model	Owner
Martha	433 Carl Drive	10923453	Ford	1967	Mustang	22222
Martha	433 Carl Drive	23459374	Buick	1992	Regal	22222
Rick	2908 Bobcat Cir	28383729	Buick	1993	Skylark	12345
Joe	99 Box 21	34343434	Porsche	1979	911	11111

What happened, and how did it work? A join can be thought of as one large recordset where every record in the first table is appended to every record in the second table to create one large table with *N* times *M* records. *N* represents the number of records in the first table and *M* represents the number of records in the second table. Next, only the records meeting a condition are kept. Usually this condition is used to keep only the records logically associated. Therefore, when the Driver and Car table are joined, the 1967 Mustang could have any of the four drivers. However, only the one matching the owner field on the SQL statement is returned. To take this apart a little further, lets look at each piece of the SQL statement.

```
SELECT Driver.Name,Driver.Address,Cars.*
```

As before, the `SELECT` statement tells the database engine which fields to return. When working with more than one table, specify the table followed by a period then the field. This removes all ambiguity as to which field to work with. In this case, you are taking the Name and Address fields from the driver table, and all fields from the Cars table. To get all fields from both tables, the `SELECT *` can still be used.

```
FROM Cars,Driver
```

Two tables are listed in the `FROM` clause. This tells the database engine which tables to use. Some database systems would let you stop here (although there is rarely a need to do this) because without the final `WHERE` clause the join should return the cross product of the two tables.

```
WHERE Cars.Owner = Driver.DrivNum
```

The `WHERE` clause is what gives the database query the crucial information of which fields are related in the two tables. A join is not limited to conditions on the `WHERE` clause. Extra limitations can be placed on one or both of the tables being joined. For example, we can modify this query so that only cars built in the 1990s are displayed.

```
SELECT Driver.Name,Driver.Address,Cars.*
   from Cars,Driver
      where (Cars.Owner = Driver.DrivNum) AND
      (Cars."Year" BETWEEN 1990 AND 1999)
```

This returns the information as shown in Table 14.13.

Table 14.13. Results also using a WHERE clause.

Name	Driver	VIN	Make	Year	Model	Owner
Martha	433 Carl Drive	23459374	Buick	1992	Regal	22222
Rick	2908 Bobcat Cir	28383729	Buick	1993	Skylark	12345

Where did Bob go? You didn't make a requirement that a driver must own a car. Therefore, because this query is based on the fact that there is one owner for every car, and it is possible for owners to own more than one car, in this case Bob didn't show up in the results set because the query requested the database to "Show all the cars and their owners."

One of the most powerful features of the Paradox database engine is that it has the ability to join tables that are of different database types. If you convert the Ticket table to dBASE, and perform the following join:

```
SELECT  * FROM TKDBASE,DRIVER
  WHERE TKDBASE.Driver =DRIVER.DrivNum
```

The database engine can still generate the correct results as shown in Table 14.14.

Table 14.14. Example of joining a dBASE and Paradox table.

DRIVER	VIOLATION	POINTS	DrivNum	Name	Address	Class
22222	Speeding	5.00	22222	Martha	433 Carl Drive	A
12345	Speeding	2.00	12345	Rick	2908 Bobcat Cir	C
22222	Signal Violation	1.00	22222	Martha	433 Carl Drive	A

Grouping Data—The GROUP BY Clause

Up to this point every piece of data that has been received has simply been the data that is stored in a database table. If data analysis needs to be done, either the application can do it, or as you will see here, the database engine can perform many tasks. For example, in your traffic ticket table, it would be a very useful thing to see the total number of points that every person has received. To do this in code without using the database engine would mean that a data type would need to be created to store information about the points each person received. Next, the application would need to loop through the table, and for every instance of a driver, add the number of points to their total points. To do this with SQL is as simple as

```
SELECT  Driver,SUM(Points)  FROM Ticket GROUP by Driver
```

This returns the results set shown in Table 15.15.

Table 14.15. Result using a `GROUP BY` clause, and the `SUM` aggregate function.

Driver	Sum of Points
12345	2.00
22222	6.00

The new features added to this query are the `SUM()` function and the `GROUP BY` clause. The `SUM()` function is called an *aggregate* function because it acts on a set of data. Other aggregate functions available on local databases are

`SUM()`—Calculates the sum of a field in a set of records.

`AVG()`—Calculates the average of a field in a set of records.

`MIN()`—Calculates the minimum value occuring in a field in a set of records.

`MAX()`—Calculates the minimum value occuring in a field in a set of records.

`COUNT()`—Returns the number of records in a record set. Note that `COUNT(*)` should return the same value as any other `COUNT()`. However, this syntax is not supported in local databases: a specific field needs to be given.

More then one aggregate function can be used in a query, for example, you can add a `COUNT(Points)` to the previous query to determine how many tickets each person has.

```
SELECT  Driver,SUM(Points),COUNT(Points)  FROM Ticket GROUP by Driver
```

This returns the results as shown in Table 14.16.

Table 14.16. Result of using two aggregate functions.

Driver	Sum of Points	Count of Points
12345	2.00	1.00
22222	6.00	2.00

The `GROUP BY` clause informs the database engine how the records should be grouped. Another way to put this is that each record is put into a record set with all records with a common value, and a function is applied to a column. Note that it is not possible to include the Violation field in this table because there can be multiple violations per driver. Because only one line for every driver is displayed, which one would it use?

There isn't a problem with using aggregate functions with a join. For example, to determine how many cars each owner drives, and the owner's name, the following query could be used:

```
SELECT Cars.Owner,Driver.Name,COUNT(Cars.Owner) FROM Cars,Driver
  WHERE Cars.Owner=Driver.DrivNum
  GROUP By Owner,Name
```

This returns the results as shown in Table 14.17.

Table 14.17. Results where a join and a GROUP BY clause are combined.

Owner	Name	Count of Owner
11111	Joe	1.00
12345	Rick	1.00
22222	Martha	2.00

There are a few things to note about this query. First, a second field was added to the group by clause. This is usually used to group by multiple fields. For example, if a query is grouped by state and city, then every city in every state would be in its own group; whereas if only city was grouped, there would be no distinction between cities in states with the same name (such as Yorktown, VA, and Yorktown, NY). In this case, the local database is not clever enough to realize that there is only one name per owner in our data, so it forces the query to group by name as well. This does not change the outcome of the query.

How does the WHERE clause effect an aggregate query? The WHERE clause limits the records used to make up groups, but not the groups themselves. To change your query to include only cars built after 1970, you could add a WHERE clause so that the query now looks like

```
SELECT Cars.Owner,Driver.Name,COUNT(Cars.Owner) FROM Cars,Driver
  WHERE (Cars.Owner=Driver.DrivNum) AND (Cars."YEAR" >= 1970)
  GROUP By Owner,Name
```

This now returns the same results as the previous query except that Martha's 1967 Mustang is not included in the count as shown in Table 14.18.

Table 14.18. Adding an additional WHERE clause.

Owner	Name	Count of Owner
11111	Joe	1.00
12345	Rick	1.00
22222	Martha	1.00

Sorting Data—The ORDER BY Clause

The ORDER BY clause is used to indicate how the recordset should be sorted. If the order in which records are returned is not important, then do not use an ORDER BY clause: it may slow down the query. To use the ORDER BY clause, simply list the fields by which the query should be sorted. For example to sort the previous query by name, you could add an ORDER BY Name clause as follows:

```
SELECT Cars.Owner,Driver.Name,COUNT(Cars.Owner) FROM Cars,Driver
  WHERE (Cars.Owner=Driver.DrivNum) AND (Cars."YEAR" >= 1970)
  GROUP By Owner,Name ORDER BY Name
```

The query now returns the records sorted by name as shown in Table 14.19.

Table 14.19. Results where the Name field is sorted using the ORDER BY clause.

Owner	Name	Count of Owner
11111	Joe	1.00
22222	Martha	1.00
12345	Rick	1.00

It is becoming apparent how powerful the SQL SELECT statment is. The previous query

Gathered information from two separate tables.

Associated fields that are logically connected

Eliminated records which did not meet a criterion

Summarized results

Sorted the output.

All in three lines of SQL!

The HAVING clause

One final clause that you will cover in the basic SELECT syntax is the HAVING clause. Remember that the WHERE clause determines which records are used to build groups. However, there is no way to use the WHERE clause to eliminate entire groups after they are calculated. For example, before the condition is added to eliminate the Cars before 1970 group, Martha is listed as owning two cars. What if the DMV would like to see all the people who own more then one car. How could this be done? The answer is that you need a way to eliminate entire groups of records after the aggregate functions have been calculated. The clause that does this is the HAVING clause. The format is simply HAVING <CONDITION> where the CONDITION is a Boolean expression that uses aggregate functions instead of fields. For example, to list all people who own more then one car, the following SQL SELECT can be issued:

```
SELECT Cars.Owner,Driver.Name,COUNT(Cars.Owner) FROM Cars,Driver
  WHERE (Cars.Owner=Driver.DrivNum)
  GROUP BY Cars.Owner,Driver.Name
  HAVING COUNT(Cars.Owner) > 1
```

As shown in Table 14.20, this returns only Martha's record because she is the only person who owns more than one car:

Table 14.20. Limiting the groups using the HAVING clause.

Owner	Name	COUNT of Owner
22222	Martha	2.00

SQL Statements for Inserting, Updating, and Deleting Records

The previous section has dealt with how to use SQL to ask the database a question. It is also possible to command the database to perform an action. The core actions are inserting, updating, and deleting records. The execution of actions that command the database to do something are implemented slightly differently in Delphi. To execute a query, the Open method is used, whereas to execute a command, the ExecSQL method is used on a TQuery visual component. This section covers the basic syntax for the UPDATE, INSERT, and DELETE SQL statements as they are used with local databases.

INSERT

The format to insert a new record into a table is

```
INSERT INTO <TABLE NAME>(FIELD1,FIELD2...)
      VALUES(VAL_OF_FIELD1,VAL_OF_FIELD2,...)
```

Only required fields and fields the application requires need to be specified. An example of inserting a new automobile into the Cars table would look like the following:

```
INSERT INTO Cars(VIN,SellYear,Make,Model,Owner)
      VALUES("88889999","1990","Nissan","Sentra","54321")
```

If the model of the car is unknown, it is still acceptable to insert it into the database. SQL can omit the field

```
INSERT INTO Cars(VIN,SellYear,Make,Owner)
      VALUES("88889999","1990","Nissan","54321")
```

INSERT statements can also use parameters in Delphi. Therefore, we could set up a generic query to insert a new automobile by passing the values as parameters. The SQL statement with parameters would appear as

```
INSERT INTO Cars(VIN,SellYear,Make,Model,Owner)
      VALUES(:VIN,:SellYear,:Make,:Model,:Owner)
```

This text would be placed into the SQL property in the TQuery component, which performs the query. To use the query in Delphi, a prepare statement increases performance.

```
InsertCar.Prepare;
```

To set the parameter, use the Params property as follows:

```
InsertCar.Params[0].AsString := '86753321';
InsertCar.Params[1].AsString := '1996';
InsertCar.Params[2].AsString := 'Bronco';
InsertCar.Params[3].AsString := 'Ford';
InsertCar.Params[4].AsString := '54321';
```

Finally, to actually execute the query, issue the ExecSQL method. Note that there is no need to use the CLOSE method.

```
InsertCar.ExecSQL;
```

The UPDATE and DELETE SQL commands are slightly more complex than the INSERT command because they can act on a recordset as opposed to one single record.

UPDATE

The UPDATE command is used to modify records that already exist in a table. It is possible to update fields based on constants, or as functions of other fields. Any number of records can be updated, from a single record to every record in a table. The syntax for the UPDATE statement is

```
UPDATE <Table>
      SET <COLUMN=EXPRESSION>,<COLUMN=EXPRESSION>,...
      WHERE <EXPRESSION TO SELECT THE RECORDS TO MODIFY>
```

For example, to modify Martha's address in the Driver table, you could execute the following SQL UPDATE statement.

```
UPDATE Driver
      SET Address='1234 Rockingham Rd'
      WHERE DrivNum='22222'
```

In this case you are only modifying one record, so the primary key can be used in the WHERE clause to select the correct record. The definition of a primary key states that no other record can have the same value for the field. Therefore, using the primary key for the WHERE clause ensures that only one record is updated.

To update all records in a table, the `WHERE` clause can be omitted. For example, if the DMV decides to do away with license classes and give everyone a class of `'A'`, they could execute the following query:

```
UPDATE Driver
      SET Class='A'
```

To update a partial set of records in a table, all the operators used in the `WHERE` clause of the `SELECT` statement can be used. To change everyone with a license of Class `'C'` to Class `'D'`, you can execute

```
UPDATE Driver
      SET Class='D'
      WHERE Class='C'
```

One other powerful aspect of the `UPDATE` statement is that fields can be modified based on functions and operations of fields that are in the record. For example, if Martha (driver 22222) takes a driving class that decreases the number of points on each of her traffic violations by 50 percent, the following SQL `UPDATE` statement can be used:

```
UPDATE Ticket
      SET Points=Points * 0.5
      WHERE Driver='22222'
```

Similarly, in the `INSERT` statement updates can use parameters and can be prepared. The final basic SQL command is the `DELETE` command which removes records from a table.

DELETE

The `DELETE` statement is very similar to the `UPDATE` statement, except that there is no `SET` clause, and all records matching the criteria are deleted instead of updated. The general syntax for the `DELETE` command is

```
DELETE FROM <TABLE>
      WHERE <EXPRESSION>
```

To delete one record from a table, use the `DELETE` statement and a `WHERE` clause set to the primary key. To delete Martha, execute

```
DELETE FROM  Driver
      WHERE DrivNum='22222'
```

As with the `UPDATE` statement, whatever logic is used in the `WHERE` clause is deleted from the table.

Database Maintenance Using SQL

In addition to queries and data manipulation, SQL can also be used for database maintenance. This includes creating, deleting, and modifying tables and indexes.

Creating Tables

To CREATE a table, execute the CREATE TABLE SQL statement. Parameters indicating the fields and their datatypes must be supplied.

For example, this SQL can be used to create the Driver table in a local database.

```
CREATE TABLE Driver(
      DrivNum          char(5),
      Name             char(20),
      Address          char(40),
      Class            char(1),
      PRIMARY KEY(DrivNum)
      )
```

If the database engine changes, there may be some small changes to the CREATE statement format. Note that after the last field is defined, a primary key can be specified.

Deleting Tables

To remove a table using SQL, the DROP command is used. The format for removing a table is

```
DROP TABLE <TABLE NAME>
```

For example, to remove the driver table you would execute

```
DROP TABLE DRIVER
```

Notice that DROP is much different than DELETE. DELETE removes records from a table. Even if all records are deleted from a table, the table still exists. Dropping a table actually removes the table.

Modifying Tables

It is possible to add and delete columns (or fields) from a table using the SQL ALTER command.

The syntax for the ALTER command is

```
ALTER TABLE <TABLE NAME>
      <ACTION> <COLUMN> <DATATYPE>
      [,<ACTION> <COLUMN><DATATYPE>,...]
```

Where `<TABLE NAME>` is the name of a table in the database, `<ACTION>` is either `ADD` or `DROP`, and `<COLUMN>` is the column that you wish to add or remove from the table. On an Add action, the datatype for the new field needs to be specified. For example, to remove the Class field from the Driver table and also add a new field, DateOfBirth, the following query can be used:

```
ALTER TABLE DRIVER DROP Class, ADD DateOfBirth Date
```

Indexes

Indexes can also be added and removed using SQL. Here are examples of creating and removing indexes:

```
CREATE INDEX NameInd ON Driver Name
```

This creates an index on the Driver table. The index name is NameInd, and the column that it indexes is Name. To remove an index, the `DROP INDEX` is used.

```
DROP INDEX Driver.NameInd
```

Removes the NameInd index from the Driver table.

Using TTable Visual Components with TQuery Visual Components

This chapter has been devoted to explaining the powers and benefits of using SQL. However, don't abandon the TTable visual component just yet. For simple navigation and table manipulation, nothing can beat the TTable object. Also let's not forget about the `Refresh` method on the TTable object. If a query is executed that modifies data in a table, then a refresh needs to be done on all TTable objects that are accessing the same table in order to reflect the changes.

Building a Simple Database Interface

SQL is an extremely powerful tool for performing searches, and limiting record sets. However, the TTable object integrates very easily with other data-aware components to allow for easy modification and navigation through the data. The two components do not preclude each other and can actually work together. In the following example, a TQuery visual component is used to search for a record that meets a criterion, and the TTable component is passed the key in its master source field. This allows the record to be manipulated completely using the DBNavigator. Examine what would need to take place if this combination of controls wasn't possible. If only TQuery components are used, the developer needs to implement all modifications, inserts, and deletes through SQL. Although this is definitely possible, and not too difficult, it is much more effort than simply dropping a TTable component on a form and linking to a dbNavigator component. If the developer only wanted to use TTable objects, then complex searching would be very difficult.

This example provides an interface to the Driver table in the DMV example that has been used in this chapter. At first glance, the application appears to be a standard database front end that uses the dbNavigator to manipulate records.

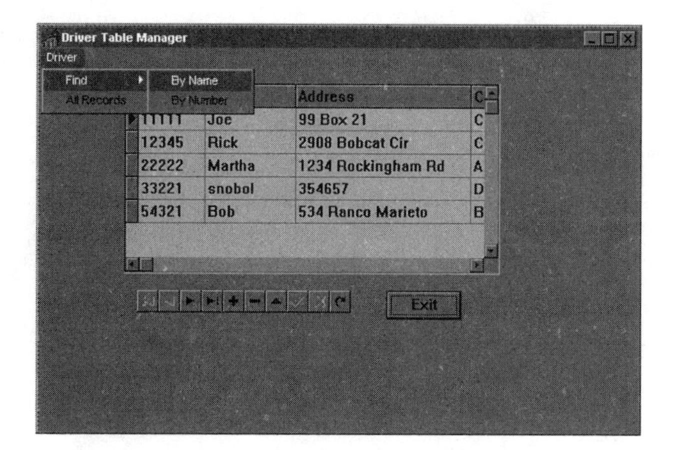

Figure 14.5.
DMV sample application.

However, there is also a menu in the application that enables the user to search by name or driver's license number. Unlike TTable searches, which are limited to keyed fields, and limited to searching on the beginning of the field, SQL can perform almost any search. In the example, you search for a substring that exists anywhere in a record. For example, searching for "artha" would produce a hit on "Martha." To link the query to the table, the `MasterSource` and `MasterField` properties need to be set on the TTable object. The `MasterSource` property is set to the component name of the TQuery component that is performing the search. Before the `MasterField` property can be linked, the key field in the `TQuery` visual component needs to be defined using the field editor. The `MasterField` property in the TTable component needs to be set to the key in the results set of the TQuery. This relationship is show in Figures 14.6 and 14.7.

14

Figure 14.6.
Property pages for TQuery component.

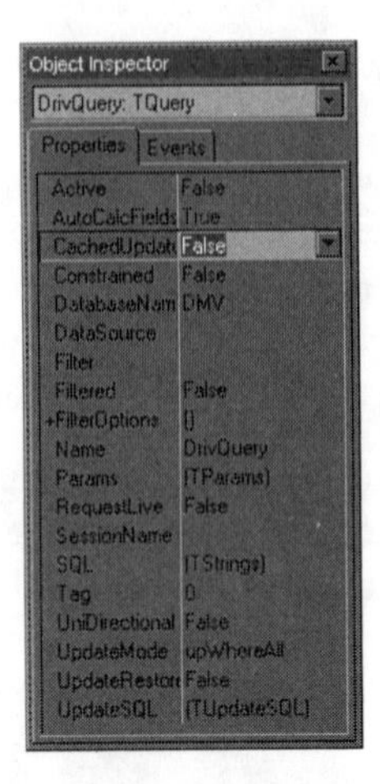

Figure 14.7.
Property pages for TTable component.

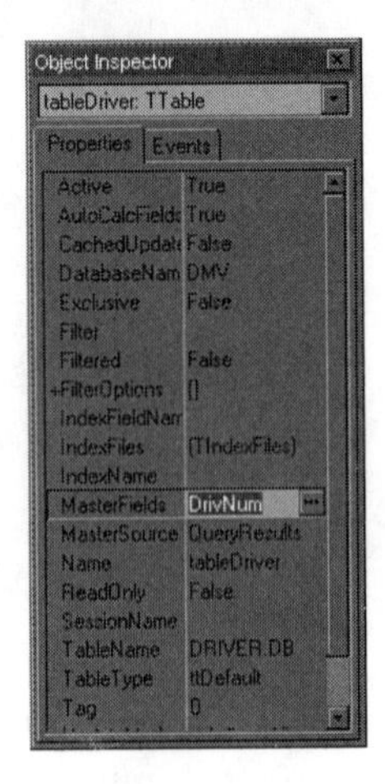

Now that the components are linked, the record selected in the query will be set to active in the TTable. For simplicity, we only allow queries to be executed that return only one record. The reason for this is that if multiple records are returned, there needs to be a mechanism to navigate through the recordset associated with the TQuery component, because the data-aware controls linked to the TTable object only see the current record. To ensure this, execute

```
if DrivQuery.RecordCount > 1 then
    begin
     Application.MessageBox('More then one match found',
                            'Please make search more explicit',mb_ok);
     DrivQuery.Close;
    end;
```

When a query executes, the RecordCount property is set to the number of records returned. If this exceeds 1, then a message is displayed, and the query closes. When a query closes, the associated TTable displays all the records in the table. Therefore, to implement the menu option All Records is simply a matter of closing the query. The final step is building and executing a query. To build the query, the format function is used. This function is very similar to the printf function in C (don't worry if you don't know C). format is used to build a string based on other variables and constants. In addition, format provides the capability to make the variables appear how the developer wants. For example, when copying a real variable into a string, the number of decimal places can be specified. The format function is given two parameters; the first is a string containing codes on how to format the result, the second is an array of variables to be used to pass the string. In the sample program, use the following command:

```
DrivQuery.SQL.Add(
 format('SELECT * FROM DRIVER WHERE Name LIKE "%%%s%%"',
     [SrchDlg.Srch.Text]));
```

This builds a string using format then sets the SQL in the component to the string that is constructed. Most of the SQL that you need to execute is constant.

```
SELECT * FROM DRIVER WHERE Name LIKE "%%"
```

The only thing that needs to be added is text sandwiched between the percent signs. For example to search for records containing the substring arth, the resulting SQL would be

```
SELECT * FROM DRIVER WHERE Name LIKE "%arth%"
```

One thing the format string does is use the percent sign to indicate that a variable needs to be inserted. Therefore, to communicate that you really do want a percent in the string, put two percent signs in quotes right next to each other ("%%"). When Delphi parses the format string, it interprets it as follows.

```
SELECT * FROM DRIVER WHERE Name LIKE "%[STRING #1 GOES HERE]%"
```

Finally, the function needs to know what variable to use for string #1. This is passed in an array as the second parameter. In our program, this is as follows:

```
[SrchDlg.Srch.Text]
```

It simply inserts the string stored in the Edit box in the search dialog. The rest of the program is straightforward and mainly uses the features of Delphi's integrated data-aware controls. (See Listing 14.2.)

TYPE

Listing 14.2. Sample DMV application.

```
program Dmv;
{ DMV - Driver Manager Interface                                   }
{ Description: This program illustrates how to use queryies and TTable}
{ Objects toether. The project consist of a main form which displays }
{ the DRIVER table which is located in the DMV database alias. The    }
{ Application has the ability to search on any part of a driver's     }
{ licence number, or name. This is accomplished by using a wild card }
{ select statment. The result set is linked to a datasource which     }
{ accesses the master source and master field properties in the TTable}
{ object, tuhus only showing the current record. Modifications,       }
{ additions and deleteions can still be made with the convenient DB   }
{ navigator.                                                          }

uses
  Forms,
  Dmv1 in 'DMV1.PAS' {main},
  Dmv2 in 'DMV2.PAS' {SrchDlg};

{$R *.RES}

begin
  Application.CreateForm(Tmain, main);
  Application.CreateForm(TSrchDlg, SrchDlg);
  Application.Run;
end.
unit Dmv1;
{ DMV1 - main unit which includes the Driver menu, dbGrid and navigator }
{ Components. When a search is executed, the dialog DMV2 will be        }
{ displayed. The query results are linked to the TTable object, to show }
{ the current record. Closing the query will show all records.         }

interface

uses
  SysUtils, WinTypes, WinProcs, Messages, Classes, Graphics, Controls,
  Forms, Dialogs, Menus, DB, Grids, DBGrids, DBTables, StdCtrls, TabNotBk,
  ExtCtrls, DBCtrls,Dmv2;

type
  Tmain = class(TForm)  { Main Form Class}
    Exit: TButton;
    dbgDriver: TDBGrid;
    DrivQuery: TQuery;
    tableDriver: TTable;
    dsDriver: TDataSource;
    QueryResults: TDataSource;
    MainMenu1: TMainMenu;
    Driver1: TMenuItem;
    Find1: TMenuItem;
    ByName1: TMenuItem;
    ByNumber1: TMenuItem;
    AllRecords1: TMenuItem;
    DBNavigator1: TDBNavigator;
    DrivQueryDrivNum: TStringField;
```

```
    procedure ExitClick(Sender: TObject);
    procedure ByName1Click(Sender: TObject);
    procedure AllRecords1Click(Sender: TObject);
    procedure ByNumber1Click(Sender: TObject);
  private
    { Private declarations }
  public
    { Public declarations }
  end;

var
  main: Tmain;
implementation

{$R *.DFM}

procedure Tmain.ExitClick(Sender: TObject);
begin
   {User would like to exit....}
   Application.Terminate;
end;

procedure Tmain.ByName1Click(Sender: TObject);
{When searching by name, we can use the format function to build the query}
{For simplicity, the application assures that only one record is returned }
begin
   {Set dialog Caption}
   SrchDlg.Caption := 'Driver Name Search';
   SrchDlg.ShowModal; {Pause, Wait for response}
   DrivQuery.SQL.Clear; {Remove any OLD SQL}
   {Build New SQL using format string Function}
   DrivQuery.SQL.Add(
     format('SELECT * FROM DRIVER WHERE Name LIKE "%%%s%%"',
     [SrchDlg.Srch.Text]));
   DrivQuery.Open; { Execute The Query }
   {If more then one record is found, reject the query}
   if DrivQuery.RecordCount > 1 then
    begin
     Application.MessageBox('More then one match found',
                             'Please make search more explicit',mb_ok);
     DrivQuery.Close;
    end;
end;

procedure Tmain.AllRecords1Click(Sender: TObject);
begin
 {Show All Records by closing the query}
 DrivQuery.Close;
end;

procedure Tmain.ByNumber1Click(Sender: TObject);
{When searching by DrivNum, we can use the format function to build the query}
{For simplicity, the application assures that only one record is returned    }
begin
   {Set dialog Caption}
   SrchDlg.Caption := 'Driver Licence Number Search';
```


continues

Listing 14.2. continued

```
    SrchDlg.ShowModal; {Pause, Wait for response}
    DrivQuery.SQL.Clear; {Remove any OLD SQL}
    {Build New SQL using format string Function}
    DrivQuery.SQL.Add(
      format('SELECT * FROM DRIVER WHERE DrivNum LIKE "%%%s%%"',
      [SrchDlg.Srch.Text]));
    DrivQuery.Open; { Execute The Query }
    {If more then one record is found, reject the query}
    if DrivQuery.RecordCount > 1 then
     begin
      Application.MessageBox('More then one match found',
                             'Please make search more explicit',mb_ok);
      DrivQuery.Close;
     end;
end;

end.
unit Dmv2;
{ DMV2 - Dialog Box to allow the user to enter a search string.  }
{ The same dialog can be used for name or number searhces, because }
{ the calling procedure can modify the form's caption before the   }
{ dialog is displayed.                                             }

interface

uses
  SysUtils, WinTypes, WinProcs, Messages, Classes, Graphics, Controls,
  Forms, Dialogs, StdCtrls;

type
  TSrchDlg = class(TForm)
    Label1: TLabel;
    Srch: TEdit;
    OK: TButton;
    procedure OKClick(Sender: TObject);
    procedure FormActivate(Sender: TObject);
  private
    { Private declarations }
  public
    { Public declarations }
  end;

var
  SrchDlg: TSrchDlg;

implementation
 uses Dmv1;

{$R *.DFM}

procedure TSrchDlg.OKClick(Sender: TObject);
begin
```

```
  Close; { Release the dialog}
end;

procedure TSrchDlg.FormActivate(Sender: TObject);
begin
  {Clear out Search Text whenever the dialog is shown}
  Srch.Text := '';
end;
end.
```

Summary

This chapter deals with how relational database tables can be used effectively by linking information through the use of keys. Delphi can take advantage of table relationships by using master and detail tables. In addition to accessing data with the TTable component, Delphi can also communicate with a database through the TQuery component. The TQuery component is used to execute SQL which can ask a question that is called a query, or perform an action such as inserting a record. Parameters can be used so that a query can be executed many times without needing to build the query each time. SQL queries are extremely powerful. In a single statement, records can be selected based on logical criteria, grouped, and sorted. In addition to queries and database manipulation, SQL can manipulate tables and indexes in a database. In short, SQL is a powerful tool that can be advantageous in many circumstances. Knowing when to use SQL and with a TQuery component, or a TTable component is often a difficult decision. Making the right decision can save a great deal of time coding. Finally, TTables and TQueries can be used together to take advantage of the strong points both have. The example at the end of the chapter demonstrates how to use the results of a query to access records with the TTable component for further data manipulation.

Q&A

Q What is the difference between the `WHERE` clause and the `HAVING` clause?

A The `WHERE` clause is used at the record level, and the `HAVING` clause is used at the group level. Both clauses are used to exclude objects from the record set. `WHERE` determines which records are used to calculate groups. Once groups have been calculated, `HAVING` determines which groups are returned.

Q I use a client/server database such as Sybase. Some queries are in stored procedures. Can I execute a stored procedure using the TQuery component, and process the results as a normal query?

A Yes. There shouldn't be a problem using this method. When the server returns a results set, it should appear exactly like a normal query recordset. Be cautious not to return a larger amount of data then is needed because this will tie up system and network resources.

Q There were limitations on using certain types of queries in Delphi 1.0; has this changed?

A Yes, there is much more support for SQL in Delphi 2. An example of this is support for subqueries and other ANSI SQL features.

Workshop

Quiz

1. In a many-to-one relationship what type of key is the column in the many table that indicates the key in the one table. (*Hint:* It is a type of key, but not in the table in which it is listed. Some would say, "It has an accent.")
2. Using the DMV tables, what SQL statement could be used to list all drivers with traffic tickets, and their cumulative points?
3. The following table lists animals in a zoo, the table name is Zoo.

Animal	Name	Age
Zebra	Joe	8
Zebra	Sally	2
Lizard	Frank	9
Cobra	Allen	1

What is wrong with the following SQL?

```
SELECT COUNT(Animal),Animal,Name,Age FROM Zoo
     GROUP BY Animal.
```

4. Using the Zoo table, what SQL statement could be used to specify the age of the oldest animal in the zoo?

Exercises

1. Modify the DMV interface program so that if multiple records are returned from a query, the user is able to select from the result set. In the example, if more than one record is returned, the program closes the query and displays a message indicating that more than one record was returned.
2. Create a query that uses the `COUNT`, `SUM`, and `AVG` aggregate functions. How do the results differ when the query is grouped by different fields?
3. Modify the DMV application so that it uses a data module for the data access components.
4. Create a Delphi application that uses the `SELECT`, `INSERT`, `UPDATE`, and `DELETE` SQL commands.

8
9
10
11
12
13
14

In Review

Week 2—Putting Delphi to Work

Week 2 brought some good material your way. Day 8 provided some real meat on event and exception handling and the benefits of both. Day 9 helped you to understand what the Visual Component Library has to offer. Day 10 gets into the fun with graphics programming. Day 11 stepped further into the visual world with multimedia and animation programming. Day 12 let you know the mechanism for doing file storage and retrieval. Day 13 provided some real insight into databases, and Day 14 capped off the week with some SQL basics.

At A Glance

Week 3—Getting Serious with Delphi

You kick off your final week on Day 15 where you learn how to set up and use the Local Interbase Server for use in developing client/server applications on a standalone system. Day 16 is an introduction to using ReportSmith and the Quick Report components to create fabulous reports with very little effort. Day 17 shows you how to create printed output without using ReportSmith or Quick Report. Next you move on to Day 18 and learn about OLE (Object Linking and Embedding). This powerful technology enables communication between applications, storing of data, sound, video, graphics and more on objects that can be saved to a file. On Day 19 you really get cooking as you learn how to write your own DLL! You even learn how to add a form to your DLL that can be used by any Windows application regardless of the language it was developed in. On Day 20 you learn how to write and implement your own visual component in Delphi. Yes, that's right! You can create your own components, no need to purchase those expensive add-on products. On Day 21, the final chapter, you explore what it takes to distribute your application to your customers. You cover the installation of your application using your own installation program, as well as Installshield.

Week 3

Day 15

Interbase

The Borland Interbase Server is a local database engine that acts like a client/server database. To be more specific, the server is a local variation of Borland's Workgroup server which can provide a true client/server database solution. There are many client/server database solutions on the market. These offer power and flexibility in data manipulation by many simultaneous users. They also offer extensions to the basic SQL system, ones allowing the database server to handle SQL requests in an optimal manner. This chapter explains how to use the Interbase server, and demonstrates some of the powers of client/server database computing. It also covers how Delphi can interact with the Interbase server and take advantage of the powerful features it offers.

When Should Interbase Be Used?

Borland's local Interbase Server allows developers to simulate a client/server computing environment without the need to buy an additional server. The local Interbase Server also simplifies the development effort because network configuration and management issues do not need to be addressed. The Interbase Server should be used if an application will be developed for a client/server environment, but the developer doesn't want to deal with the complexity of a client/server environment.

Basic Database Management: ISQL and the Server Manager

Delphi comes with a series of utility programs that manipulate Interbase Server databases. One of these is a windowed interface that enables SQL to be executed from files (called *scripts*), or typed in interactively. Another tool is used for database administration. This includes tasks such as backing up and restoring databases and administering user security. Unlike the Borland Database Desktop which makes many tasks such as building a table and adding indexes available through a nice graphical interface, WISQL provides the bare minimum. Note that there are some SQL commands that can be run through a script but not interactively.

Creating a New Database

Unlike Paradox and dBASE, where each table is stored in a separate file, Interbase stores all the database objects in one file. This file is known as the database. To create a new database called Zoo follow these steps:

1. Use the WISQL menu option File | Create Database
2. In the dialog box shown in Figure 15.1, type in the complete path and filename for the database such as c:\myib\zoo.gbs. A convention is to use .gbs extensions for local Interbase databases.

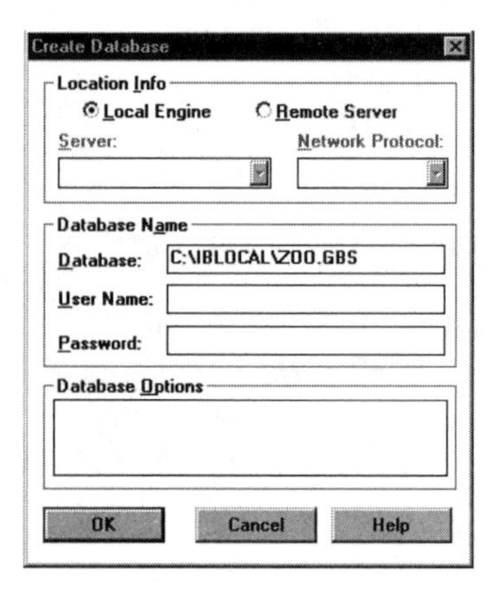

Figure 15.1.
Local Interbase Create Database dialog box.

3. If you have not changed the SYSDBA password for Interbase, enter **SYSDBA** in the User Name field and **masterkey** in the password field. Click on OK.

When a new database is created, the ISQLW program is automatically connected to the database. Now that a database has been created, SQL can be used to create database objects, populate the database with data, and manipulate the data.

Creating and Managing Users

Interbase uses a login and password pair for user authentication and database security. *Authentication* is the method that proves that a user is who they say they are. For example, when you put an ATM card into a bank machine and type your secret ID, you are authenticating yourself to the bank. Interbase uses a similar scheme. Before an application or user can access a database, they must supply a valid user and password pair. Interbase also implements security based on users. Therefore, supplying a valid ID and password not only allows you to have access to the database, but also determines what data you have access to. The SYSDBA is the master account that has the ability to grant permission to other users for simplicity, use sysdba whenever you are required to use a login and password. Later in the chapter we introduce how multiple user ids can gain different levels of access to the data. It may be necessary to modify the SYSDBA's password. To do this, bring up the Server Manager program and choose Tasks | User Security. This displays a list of active users. One of the users is SYSDBA. Double-click on this user. In the dialog box shown in Figure 15.2, type a new password, and confirm it. Choose OK.

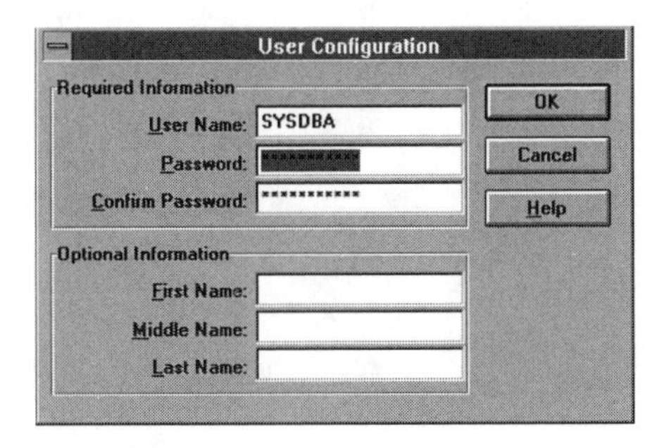

Figure 15.2.
Changing the SYSDBA's password.

NOTE

User IDs are not case sensitive; however passwords are. Therefore, when prompted for a password, be sure the case is correct.

Accessing Interbase with Delphi

To gain the full power of Interbase, we introduce a new component, the TDatabase. The TDatabase allows a connection to be maintained with the server even if data access components are closed. Also, the TDatabase allows Delphi to take advantage of the transaction processing. In addition to the TDatabase component, all the other data access components are still used. Additionally, we add the TStoredProcedure, which enables the client application to execute a special SQL procedure on the server. The purpose of this chapter is to illustrate some of the powers of client/server computing; therefore, many of the details are not Delphi specific, and actually take place on the SQL server (or local Interbase server).

We Are Back to SQL Again...

It was mentioned that many of the database maintenance capabilities are missing from the ISQL interface. It's possible to use the Borland Database Desktop to perform some database maintenance. However, to use the full power of the Interbase server, SQL can be used.

Creating Tables and Views

Interbase uses similar SQL syntax for the creation of tables that local databases use. There are many powerful features integrated into table creation. Some of these features include the ability to use defaults, support for data validation and computed fields.

The syntax of the `CREATE` statement is similar to that in the local SQL syntax (see the Interbase SQL reference for a complete description of the syntax). To create a simple table containing animals in the zoo, you might execute

```
CREATE TABLE ANIMAL (NAME CHAR(10),
        AGE INTEGER,
        BREED CHAR(20));
```

To build this table, connect to the zoo database by choosing the File | Connect To Database option and entering a valid user ID and password. Next, type in the `CREATE` statement, and then click on Run. An alternative would be to write a SQL script with the statement. One additional command would need to be placed into the script, the `CONNECT` statement. The `CONNECT` statement is almost always the first command in a SQL script because it tells the server which database to use for the following commands. The syntax of the `CONNECT` statement is

```
CONNECT <DATABASE> USER "<USER>" PASSWORD "<PASSWORD>";
```

Therefore, to use a SQL script to create the ANIMAL table, it might look like the following:

```
CONNECT "D:\IBASE\ZOO.GBS" USER "SYSDBA" PASSWORD "masterkey";

CREATE TABLE ANIMAL(NAME CHAR(10),
        AGE INTEGER,
        BREED CHAR(20));
```

The main advantage of using scripts is that multiple commands can be used in a sequence. Also, there are some commands that can only be entered through scripts.

In addition to the field definitions, constrains on the fields can be included. For example, to define which file is the primary key, the `PRIMARY KEY` clause can be added. Here the ANIMAL table is created with the `NAME` field set as the primary key.

```
CREATE TABLE ANIMAL(
        NAME CHAR(10) NOT NULL PRIMARY KEY,
        AGE INTEGER,
        BREED CHAR(20)
       );
```

Wait a second, what is that `NOT NULL` clause before the `PRIMARY KEY` clause? This tells the database that it is invalid for this field to be null. What exactly is null? Think of null as being "I don't know" as opposed to none or empty. Let's understand the need for this construction by using an example. If the ANIMAL table is populated with data, a simple `SELECT * FROM ANIMAL` can be used to list the data in the table.

```
select * from  Animal;

NAME                AGE BREED
========== =========== ====================
Fred                  4 Lion
Albert                2 Hog
Silly            <null> <null>
Willy            <null> Rhino
```

This shows that Fred and Albert are 4 and 2 respectively, but there is no known age for Silly and Willy. As expected the following statement returns:

```
select * from  Animal  where Age > 2;
Returns:
NAME                AGE BREED
========== =========== ====================
Fred                  4 Lion
```

This is true because Albert is the only one who is older than two. What do you think will happen if you execute the same query, but put a `NOT` in front of the condition? Many people would expect three records returned. They would assume that all records that don't meet the condition should be returned. Sound OK? Try it.

```
select * from  Animal  where not ( Age > 2);
Returns:
NAME                AGE BREED
========== =========== ====================
Albert                2 Hog
```

Should Silly and Willy be in the results from at least one of these queries? Not necessarily, remember that the database always attempts to return only results that are 100 percent true. The database knows that Albert's age is greater than two, so there is no problem returning him in the first query. You also know that Fred's age is not greater than two so Fred is returned in the second query. Because the ages of Silly and Willy are unknown, the database cannot certify that their age is greater than or less than two. Therefore, their data is not returned in either query. This is just one example of how null values can be somewhat confusing. A good rule of thumb is if things are not working the way they should, ask yourself, "Is a null being used anywhere?" To create the ANIMAL table with `NOT NULL` column constraints on all fields, you would execute

```
CREATE TABLE ANIMAL(
        NAME CHAR(10) NOT NULL PRIMARY KEY,
        AGE INTEGER NOT NULL,
        BREED CHAR(20) NOT NULL
       );
```

Working with the SQL Environment—The SET Statements

Think of a SQL session as an interactive conversation with the SQL server. It is possible to modify the rules of the conversation. For example, it might be helpful to display the number of records returned. The command for configuring the environment (or conversation) is `SET`. There are about ten `SET` commands for configuring the environment when using SQL scripts. For full details on using `SET`, consult the Interbase Reference. To unset an option, use the `SET <OPTION> OFF`. The example illustrates the use of `SET COUNT`.

```
CONNECT "D:\IBASE\ZOO.GBS" USER "SYSDBA" PASSWORD "masterkey";
SET COUNT;
SELECT * FROM ANIMAL;
NAME                AGE BREED
========== =========== ====================
Fred                  4 Lion
Albert                2 Hog
Silly            <null> <null>
Willy            <null> Rhino
Records affected: 4
SET COUNT OFF;
SELECT * FROM ANIMAL;
NAME                AGE BREED
========== =========== ====================
Fred                  4 Lion
Albert                2 Hog
Silly            <null> <null>
Willy            <null> Rhino
```

Comments

With almost anything having to do with programming, things can get complex very quickly. It's always a good idea to document code whenever possible. Interbase SQL uses C-style comments. Anything surrounded by `/*` and `*/` is considered a comment and is ignored. Therefore, you can use comments in SQL scripts to indicate what is happening. For example,

```
/* Find the Age of the oldest animal in the zoo */
SELECT MAX(Age) from Animal;
```

executes the SQL but ignores the comment.

Transactions

Everything in the Interbase Server is based on a transaction model. Transactions allow database manipulation statements to occur in all or nothing chunks. This means that an entire set of database manipulation statements can be treated as one large statement which either succeeds or fails. Consider the following situation:

1. A customer buys an airline ticket.
2. A seat assignment is issued.
3. The customer's credit card is processed—it's reported stolen.
4. After the customer is taken away by the police, the airline database needs to be updated to remove any changes made to it during this process. This could be quite a bit of work.

You can try to fix this problem by changing the order in which the process steps are executed.

1. A customer buys an airline ticket.
2. The customer's credit card is processed—all is well.
3. A seat assignment is requested.
4. However, all seats are booked, and the customer can't take any other flights. Once again you are stuck with the dilemma of undoing everything that has been processed.

This may not seem like that big of a deal in a simple example like this. First of all, you could check both conditions and assure that they are viable before the process is executed. However, often manipulation is done in many tables that makes it very difficult to undo what has been done. Also there is a problem if our system fails in the middle of a process. In the airline example you could have a customer booked who didn't pay, or a customer who paid but was not booked. The solution to this is to use transactions. To use a transaction in Interbase, execute the `SET TRANSACTION` command. When a transaction is complete, the `COMMIT` command is executed. If for some reason the transaction is aborted and everything set back to the way it was before the transaction started, the ROLLBACK command is used. When using WISQL, there is an implicit SET TRANSACTION done when the script begins. Therefore, all scripts should end with either a Commit or Rollback.

In addition to the implicit transaction set up in a SQL script, transactions can be set explicitly. For example:

```
SET TRANSACTION;
INSERT INTO ANIMAL VALUES('Buzz',5,'Buzzard');
COMMIT;
```

Immediately after the commit, any other client who accesses the database sees the record. This poses some interesting questions. What happens if two clients start a transaction before one of them finishes. What does the data look like? What if both clients try to insert "Buzz?" To determine how all of these conditions are handled is covered by parameters set in the SET TRANSACTION statement. If it's necessary to work with transactions within a Delphi application, a method on the TDatabase component is used. To begin a transaction, the StartTransaction method is used. At the end of a transaction, either the Commit or Rollback method is used.

The procedure in Listing 15.1 illustrates how the transaction methods can be used from a Delphi application. In this procedure, a seat assignment is made within a transaction. If everything works correctly, the transaction is committed, otherwise, the transaction is rolled back.

TYPE **Listing 15.1. Using transactions in Delphi code.**

```
procedure TForm1.AssignSeatClick(Sender: TObject);
Var
 CreditCardError : Boolean;     {Flags a credit card problem}
begin
  dbAirline.StartTransaction;   {Start the database transaction}
  SetTicket.Params[0].AsString := TicketNo.Text;
  SetTicket.Params[1].AsString := Flight.Text;
  SetTicket.Params[2].AsInteger := strtoint(Seat.Text);
  SetTicket.ExecSQl;
  {For testing, there is no credit problem.}
  CreditCardError := False;
  {****************************}
  {* PROCESS CREDIT CARD HERE *}
  {****************************}
  if CreditCardError then {If there is a problem then RollBack}
    dbAirline.Rollback
   else
    dbAirline.Commit;     {Otherwise Commit}
end;
```

15

ANALYSIS `SetTicket` is a TQuery component and `dbAirline` is a TDatabase component. You initiate the transaction by calling the `StatTransaction` method. Next you set the parameters in your query and execute the query. If no errors occur then you commit the transaction by calling the `Commit` method, otherwise you abort the transaction by executing the `Rollback` method.

Remember that other applications can't see changes made to a database until a commit is performed. This can often be confusing during development. Take an example in which an `INSERT` statement is executed from WISQL. If a File | Commit Work or explicit `Commit` command is not executed, then the Delphi application that is under development can't see the record.

Subqueries

Subqueries add even more power to the `SELECT` statement. Start with an example. In your Zoo table, an animal's name, age, and breed is listed. It's rather simple to find the age of the oldest animal in the zoo. You can simply use

```
SELECT MAX(Age) FROM ANIMAL
```

which returns

```
MAX
===========

          5
```

However, how can you list all the information about the oldest animal? If you try to execute

```
SELECT MAX(Age),Name,Breed FROM ANIMAL
```

you get an error. This is an example in which a subquery can be useful. A subquery allows the results from one query to be used in a second query. To achieve your objective, the valid query would be

```
SELECT * FROM ANIMAL WHERE AGE=
  (SELECT MAX(AGE)  FROM ANIMAL);

NAME                AGE BREED
========== =========== ====================
FRANK                 5 Snake
Buzz                  5 Buzzard
```

The Interbase Server executes the `SELECT` statement in parentheses which returns a recordset containing the value `5`. The main select is executed with the `5` being replaced in the `WHERE` clause. Therefore, the main SQL statement is transformed into

```
SELECT * FROM ANIMAL WHERE AGE=5
```

What alternatives are there? How could this have been done without a subquery? The answer is that you would have needed to do this in a two-step process. A query could be executed in a Delphi procedure in which the result is stored in a variable. This result could then be fed into the next query. It is apparent that using a subquery is much easier. In addition to an equal clause which only looks at one value, it is also possible to choose records in which a field appears in a set of records from a subquery. Take the example of a new table being introduced called ENDANGERED. This lists animal breeds on the endangered species list.

```
SELECT * FROM ENDANGERED
```

returns

```
BREED
====================
Rhino
Lion
Puffin
```

To show which animals in the zoo are on the endangered species list, you can execute

```
select * from Animal where Breed IN
 (select BREED from Endangered)
```

which returns

```
NAME                  AGE BREED
========== =========== ====================
Fred                    4 Lion
Willy              <null> Rhino
```

Note that this can also be achieved by using a `join`.

```
select Name, Age, Animal.Breed
  from Animal,Endangered
  where Animal.Breed=Endangered.Breed
```

which also returns

```
NAME                  AGE BREED
========== =========== ====================
Fred                    4 Lion
Willy              <null> Rhino
```

In addition to using sets for determining if records are contained in the set, comparisons can be made. The keywords used for comparisons are `ALL` and `ANY`. Use `ALL` to determine whether a comparison applies to all records in the subquery. Use `ANY` to determine whether the comparison is true for at least one of the records in the subquery. Here is an example in which the Animal table is updated such that

```
select * from Animal
```

returns

```
NAME              AGE BREED
========== =========== ====================
Fred                4 Lion
Albert              2 Hog
Silly               3 Snake
Willy               3 Rhino
Dirk                2 Bull Frog
FRANK               5 Snake
Leo                 2 Lion
Buzz                5 Buzzard
```

To find all the animals older than all the lions in the zoo, you can execute

```
select * from Animal where Age > ALL
   (select Age from Animal where  Breed='Lion');
```

This returns

```
NAME              AGE BREED
========== =========== ====================
FRANK               5 Snake
Buzz                5 Buzzard
```

Similarly, to find animals older than at least one lion, you can execute

```
select * from Animal where Age > ANY
   (select Age from Animal where  Breed='Lion');
```

which returns

```
NAME              AGE BREED
========== =========== ====================
Fred                4 Lion
Silly               3 Snake
Willy               3 Rhino
FRANK               5 Snake
Buzz                5 Buzzard
```

There is also nothing that limits subqueries to `SELECT` statements. `UPDATE` and `DELETE` statements can use subqueries as well. For example,

```
DELETE from Animal where Age > ALL
   (select Age from Animal where  Breed='Lion');
```

deletes all animals older than all the lions. Subqueries are extremely powerful tools for using multiple selection criteria. Insert statements can also use a query to populate a table; this syntax looks similar to a subquery, but has a different outcome.

Inserting Records Using a SELECT Statement

It would be very disappointing if the only way to get data into a table was to use the `INSERT INTO <Table> VALUES(…)` SQL command, especially if the data already existed in a table, and you need a subset to manipulate separately. Fortunately, this is made possible by using a query to insert records. If you want a table of the elderly animals in the zoo, you would first need to create a table called Old Animals. This is done with the `CREATE TABLE` statement. Next, to put all animals into the table that older than four, you would execute

```
INSERT  INTO  OLD_ANIMALS
  SELECT *  FROM ANIMAL WHERE AGE > 4;
```

This copies the records from ANIMAL into OLD_ANIMALS for those records with age greater than four.

Joins Revisited

Remember that in the last chapter you defined a join as the cross product of two tables with restrictions to limit the number of records returned. For example,

```
select * from  OLD_Animals,Endangered;
```

returns

```
NAME                   AGE BREED                BREED
========== =========== ==================== ================

FRANK                    5 Snake                Rhino
FRANK                    5 Snake                Lion
FRANK                    5 Snake                Puffin
Buzz                     5 Buzzard              Rhino
Buzz                     5 Buzzard              Lion
Buzz                     5 Buzzard              Puffin
```

It is possible to do more with joins than simply perform a natural join. A join can be based on comparative operators. For example,

```
select * from  OLD_Animals,Endangered
  WHERE OLD_ANIMALS.Breed > Endangered.Breed;
```

returns

```
NAME                   AGE BREED                BREED
========== =========== ==================== =========

FRANK                    5 Snake                Rhino
FRANK                    5 Snake                Lion
FRANK                    5 Snake                Puffin
```

which includes all combinations of records in which the `OLD_ANIMALS.BREED > ENDANGERED_BREED` based on alphanumeric comparison.

It is even possible to perform a join a table with itself. This is called a *self join*. Why in the world would a self join be necessary? Take the following example in which you

15

want to find all possible pairs of animals of the same breed. The first thing to notice is that you can alias tables. Therefore, `Animal` is listed as `An1` and `An2`. The join is made up of two clauses. First, you are joining by the `Breed`. Next you want to eliminate all pairs of the same animal. This is the statement:

```
select An1.Name,An2.Name, An1.Breed
  from Animal An1,Animal An2
  where An1.Breed=An2.Breed and An1.Name <> An2.Name;

NAME       NAME       BREED
========== ========== ====================
Leo        Fred       Lion
Fred       Leo        Lion
Silly      FRANK      Snake
FRANK      Silly      Snake
```

NEW TERM Joins to this point have been based on one-to-one matching, or the cross product of tables. There are also joins that can display records regardless of whether they meet a criteria or match a field in the second table. This type of join is called an *outer join*. There are three types of outer joins; left, right, and full. A left join is the same as a natural join except that it also includes any records in the first table that do not match any records in the second. Similarly, a right join includes all records from the second table even if they can't be joined to records in the first. Lastly, a full outer join returns the results of a natural join along with records from both tables which do not have an associated key in the other table to join with.

Example of a Left Outer Join

In this example, you list all the animals in the zoo. If the animal is on the endangered species list, it appears in the fourth column. Note the syntax for the `SELECT` statement. It uses the keywords `LEFT OUTER JOIN` to indicate the join type, and an `ON` clause to show the field on which to join.

```
SELECT * FROM
  ANIMAL LEFT OUTER JOIN ENDANGERED
  ON ANIMAL.BREED = ENDANGERED.BREED;

NAME                AGE BREED                BREED
========== =========== ==================== ===========
Fred                  4 Lion                 Lion
Albert                2 Hog                  <null>
Silly                 3 Snake                <null>
Willy                 3 Rhino                Rhino
Dirk                  2 Bull Frog            <null>
FRANK                 5 Snake                <null>
Leo                   2 Lion                 Lion
Buzz                  5 Buzzard              <null>
```

Example of a Right Outer Join

The right outer join in this example is used to show all the endangered species. If any animals of this species type exist , they appears in the first three columns. Note that the puffin is listed even though there are no puffins in the zoo.

```
SELECT * FROM
  ANIMAL RIGHT OUTER JOIN ENDANGERED
  ON ANIMAL.BREED = ENDANGERED.BREED;

NAME                AGE BREED                BREED
========== =========== ==================== ===========
Willy                 3 Rhino                Rhino
Fred                  4 Lion                 Lion
Leo                   2 Lion                 Lion
<null>           <null> <null>               Puffin
```

Example of a Full Outer Join

In the full outer join, all the animals are listed; all the endangered species are also listed. When a join can be performed, it's incorporated; however, you are guaranteed that all the records from each table are listed.

```
SELECT * FROM
  ANIMAL FULL OUTER JOIN ENDANGERED
  ON ANIMAL.BREED = ENDANGERED.BREED;

NAME                AGE BREED                BREED
========== =========== ==================== =============
Willy                 3 Rhino                Rhino
Fred                  4 Lion                 Lion
Leo                   2 Lion                 Lion
<null>           <null> <null>               Puffin
Albert                2 Hog                  <null>
Silly                 3 Snake                <null>
Dirk                  2 Bull Frog            <null>
FRANK                 5 Snake                <null>
Buzz                  5 Buzzard              <null>
```

Joins are the key to linking relational database tables. By using the wide range of joins and subqueries, almost any recordset may be returned.

Views

What is a *view*? A view is simply a query that behaves and looks like a table. For example, if you have a table consisting of university students, you could create a view called Freshman, whose records satisfy the query,

```
SELECT * from STUDENT WHERE Class = 'Freshman'
```

From that point on, there is what appears to be a table called Freshman which logically is a student information table consisting of only the freshman class. This view can then be queried, inserted, updated, or deleted (It looks almost exactly like a table). To take a slightly different look at it, you may not want to restrict records in a view, but rather restrict fields. Therefore, another view can be created called PUBLIC STUDENT which lists only name, address, and phone number, but that does not include confidential information.

Why should I use a view instead of creating a new table? There are many reasons.

- When a change is made to the table that views are based on, all the views immediately see the change. For example, if a freshman student drops out of school, the university only needs to delete them from the Student table. The FRESHMAN and PUBLIC STUDENT views automatically reflect that the record has been deleted.
- Similarly, a record can be inserted, updated, or deleted from a view, and the table the view is based on, plus all other views, sees the change.
- Database security can be based on views. There may not be problems allowing the entire world to see the PUBLIC STUDENT view; however, only a few school administrators should have access to the actual student table.

Creating Views in Interbase

To create a view, the `CREATE VIEW` SQL command is used. For example, to create a view consisting of only the name and breed of animals in the zoo, you would execute

```
CREATE VIEW  Animal_Public as
  SELECT Name,Breed from Animal;
```

Once the view is created, it looks just like a table, so you can execute a `SELECT` statement just like any other table (we even threw an `ORDER BY` clause in for anyone who had doubts).

```
SELECT * FROM ANIMAL_PUBLIC ORDER BY BREED
```

returns:

```
NAME       BREED
========== ====================
Irk        Bull Frog
Buzz       Buzzard
Albert     Hog
Fred       Lion
Leo        Lion
Willy      Rhino
FRANK      Snake
Silly      Snake
```

Using Joins with View

A join isn't limited to only one table. There is nothing to prevent a join from being used in a view. For example, the zoo might want a view listing its animals that are on the endangered species list. To do this, it can create a view called OUR ENDANGERED, which is a join of the ANIMAL table and the ENDANGERED table as follows:

```
CREATE VIEW OUR_ENDANGERED AS
  SELECT NAME,BREED,AGE FROM
  ANIMAL,ENDANGERED WHERE
  ANIMAL.BREED = ENDANGERED.BREED;
```

When a select is done on this view, the join is performed, and the results are returned. If an animal gets added to the endangered list, or if the zoo receives a new animal that is endangered, the view immediately indicates the change. Of course, a simple `SELECT` can be done on the view at any time (note that this hides the underlying join and table structure).

```
SELECT * FROM OUR_ENDANGERED
```

returns

```
NAME       BREED                        AGE
========== ==================== ===========
Leo        Lion                           2
Fred       Lion                           4
Willy      Rhino                          3
```

Using Views to Insert, Update, and Delete Data

A view is a slightly misleading term because data can actually be manipulated through a view. For example, to insert and delete a record from the ANIMAL PUBLIC view, execute

```
INSERT INTO ANIMAL_PUBLIC VALUES('Slither','Snake');
DELETE ANIMAL_PUBLIC  WHERE NAME='FRANK';
```

Now look at how this affected the underlying table.

```
SELECT * FROM ANIMAL;
```

returns

```
NAME               AGE BREED
========== =========== ====================
Fred                 4 Lion
Albert               2 Hog
Silly                3 Snake
Willy                3 Rhino
Dirk                 2 Bull Frog
Leo                  2 Lion
Buzz                 5 Buzzard
Slither         <null> Snake
```

15

Note that Frank is gone, and Slither is now listed. Why is Slither's age equal to `<null>`? There is no way to specify his age because the `Age` field isn't included in the ANIMAL PUBLIC view.

Manipulating Views Through Delphi

Views appear exactly like tables to Delphi. A TTable component linked to an Interbase database lists all the views and tables in the `TableName` property on the properties page (see Figure 15.3).

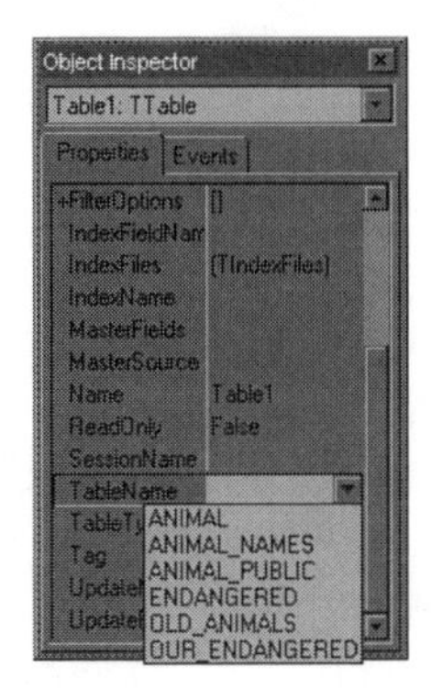

Figure 15.3.
Views are listed just as tables in the table component.

One of the anomalies the developer needs to handle is preparing for read-only views. A read-only view occurs when a view is built from a join or an aggregate function. Because the database can't "un-join" tables, it makes the views read only. Consider the following situation:

- A read-only view is linked to a TTable component.
- The TTable component is linked to a DataSource.
- The DataSource is linked to a DBNavigator component and a DBGrid.

The problem is that the DBNavigator and DBGrid components do not know that the view is read only. They allow edits, inserts, or deletes to be performed. The problem arises when they attempt to communicate with Interbase, and Interbase says that the request cannot be processed. This causes an exception to occur. Figure 15.4 shows the error message caused by a read-only exception.

To prevent this, the application developer should hide the buttons on the DBNavigator that allow write operations (all operations except navigation). Furthermore, the developer should set the `ReadOnly` property to true on the TTable component.

In addition to using the TTable component, all SQL operations can be performed on views through the TQuery component.

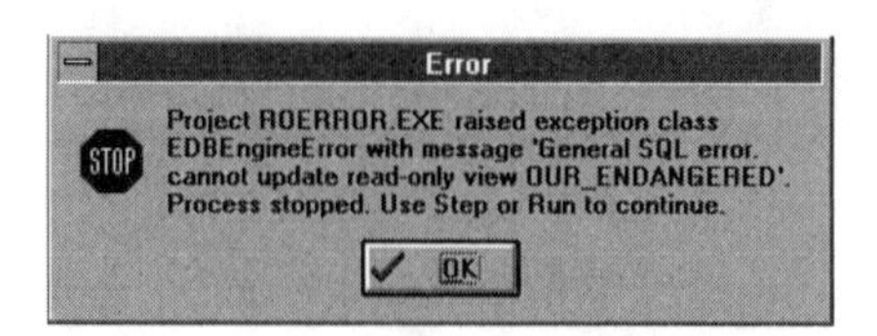

Figure 15.4.
An error dialog box from a read-only view causing an exception.

Stored Procedures

Client applications that communicate with SQL database servers form a distributed computing framework. The client takes advantage of the server's power to perform complex tasks while the client goes on to do more productive tasks. It would appear that there is a pitfall to this architecture. If there needs to be a task or routine that cannot be performed in a simple SQL statement, the data actually needs to be transferred to the client for processing. Fortunately, there is a solution. Many SQL database servers, including Interbase, allow specialized procedures to be written, which actually run on the server. This provides two main benefits. First, the server can optimize how to execute and satisfy complex SQL tasks. Secondly, this reduces the number of times that data needs to be transferred to the client for processing. In an ideal situation, the client only receives data that needs to be updated or manipulated by a user who is using the application (and of course there are exceptions).

Stored procedures can be thought of as a complete structured programming language. The language uses conditionals, loops, variables, and procedures. The syntax and exact meaning of stored procedures varies greatly from one database vendor to another, so be forewarned that after learning how to use Interbase stored procedures, Sybase or Microsoft SQL Server will *not* be trivial to learn.

Interbase supports two kinds of stored procedures. An *execute* procedure is a procedure that is passed (optional) parameters and that manipulates a database. A *select* procedure appears as a read-only table but can be passed parameters affecting how results are returned. This section explains how to create both flavors of stored procedure, the language used in stored procedures, and how to call stored procedures from Delphi.

How To Create Stored Procedures

The easiest way to create a stored procedure is to use SQL scripts. (Note: Stored procedures can not be created interactively.) In Interbase, it is necessary to change the termination character before a stored procedure is created. This allows us to include semicolons in the stored procedure to separate the commands in the procedure. To change the termination character, the `SET TERM` command is used. In the example, you change the termination character from a semicolon to a caret (^).

```
SET TERM ^ ;
```

15

NOTE

Note that the `SET TERM` command still needs to be terminated with the previous terminator. Therefore, to change the terminator back to a semicolon, you would execute

```
SET TERM ; ^
```

Once the termination character is set, you can execute the `CREATE PROCEDURE` command to actually create the stored procedure. The simplest type of procedure that you could write would be a procedure that executes one SQL statement. For example, the following script creates a procedure that inserts Ralf the rabbit into our ANIMAL table:

```
/* Create Database Connection */
CONNECT "C:\IBLOCAL\ZOO2.GBS" USER "SYSDBA" PASSWORD "masterkey";

/* Prepare Database To Create Procedure */
SET AUTODDL OFF;
SET TERM ^ ;

/* Build the Procedure */
CREATE PROCEDURE INS_RALF AS
BEGIN
  INSERT INTO ANIMAL VALUES("Ralf",10,"Rabbit");
END ^

/* Commit and cleanup */
SET TERM ; ^
COMMIT;
```

This appears to be quite a bit of overhead to create a procedure that simply inserts one record into a table. Luckily, as the complexity of the procedure increases, the overhead remains fairly constant. Examine exactly what you are doing. First, the `CONNECT` statement simply connects the script to the correct database. In order not to cause any confusion, you set the `AUTODDL` option to `OFF`. This prevents the procedure from being created before it should be. Next, the terminator is set to the caret using the `SET TERM` command. The Interbase server is now ready to accept the command that creates the procedure. Just as in Delphi, all stored procedures must begin with a `BEGIN` statement, and end with an `END` statement. A sequence of commands can appear between the `BEGIN` and `END` including other compound commands that include `BEGIN` and `END` clauses. In your example, you include only one statement that inserts a record into the ANIMAL table. Notice that the end of the procedure is terminated with a caret. This signals that you are at the end of the procedure, as opposed to terminating one of the commands contained in the procedure. To cleanup, return the terminator to a semicolon, then signal that you would like the changes to take effect by issuing a `Commit` command. This procedure is considered an execute procedure because no results are returned. Unlike Delphi, which compiles an entire unit, the Interbase server compiles each procedure independently.

Therefore, if the SQL statement to create multiple stored procedures is in one script, some may be stored, while others would fail due to syntax errors.

Before you start creating stored procedures, it is probably a good idea to know how to remove a stored procedure from the database! To remove a stored procedure, the DROP PROCEDURE statement is used. For example, to remove the INS_RALF procedure from the database, you would execute

```
DROP PROCEDURE INS_RALF;
```

Now that you have a procedure, how do you execute it? Luckily, executing a stored procedure is simpler then creating one. It uses the EXECUTE PROCEDURE statement. To execute the INS_RALF procedure, you would submit

```
EXECUTE PROCEDURE INS_RALF;
```

Now that you see how a simple execute procedure works, take a slightly more complex example which illustrates the power of stored procedures more clearly. This example procedure is used to insert a series of records into the Seating table of the Airline database. The airline program uses this procedure to allocate seats when a new flight is created. The procedure takes the flight number and the number of seats on the flight, and inserts the specified number of records into the table. The procedure sets each seat to [OPEN], which is the airline convention specifying that the seat has not been reserved. Following is the listing of the script that creates the stored procedure. Some of the concepts that are examined are parameters, local variables, and loops.

```
CONNECT "C:\iblocal\Airline.gbs" USER "SYSDBA" PASSWORD "masterkey";

/* Prepare to create procedures */
SET AUTODDL OFF;
SET TERM ^ ;

CREATE PROCEDURE
  Create_Flight(FlightNo char(8), NumSeats integer)
AS
/* Declare Local Variables */
DECLARE VARIABLE CNT INTEGER;
BEGIN
  CNT = 0;
  WHILE(CNT < :NumSeats)DO
  BEGIN
   INSERT INTO Seating(Flight,Seat,TicketNo)
     VALUES(:FlightNo,:CNT,'[OPEN]');
   CNT = CNT + 1;
  END
END;  ^

/* Clean up */
SET TERM ; ^
```

```
COMMIT;
SET AUTODDL ON;
```

Passing Parameters

Any stored procedure can access data in tables. However, it is often useful to pass the procedure parameters as is done in a Delphi procedure. One advantage of passing data in a procedure as opposed to using an intermediate table is that there isn't a need to worry about multiple applications simultaneously trying to execute a procedure, and thus overwriting data in a table used by the procedure. The syntax that Interbase uses for procedures is similar to that used in Delphi. Each parameter is listed on the `CREATE PROCEDURE` statement along with the procedure's datatype.

```
CREATE PROCEDURE
  Create_Flight(FlightNo char(8), NumSeats integer)
```

This indicates that you are passing two parameters to the `Create_Flight` procedure. The first parameter is a character string 8 bytes in length that is used to identify the flight number. The second parameter, `NumSeats`, is an integer telling the procedure how many slots to open for the specified flight. The parameters are accessed by using a colon followed by the parameter name. For example,

```
INSERT INTO Seating(Flight,Seat,TicketNo)
     VALUES(:FlightNo,:CNT,'[OPEN]');
```

uses: `FlightNo` to indicate the flight number parameter passed. To call a procedure and pass it parameters, simply execute

```
EXECUTE PROCEDURE CREATE_FLIGHT('DDF223',20);
```

This would create a new flight, DDF223, with 20 seats available. Although a procedure should be created using a SQL script, procedures can be executed anywhere. For example, a procedure can be executed interactively, from within Delphi, or even within another stored procedure (actually even within the same procedure, as stored procedures do support recursion).

Declaring Variables

In addition to the parameters that are passed, stored procedures can declare local variables as well.

```
DECLARE VARIABLE CNT INTEGER;
```

This declares the local variable of `CNT`, which is used by this procedure to loop through values. Local variables are only accessible in the procedure containing them.

Loops

Stored procedures support looping using the WHILE statement. The WHILE statement executes a statement, or compound statement, multiple times. In this example, the procedure iterates the INSERT statement until CNT is greater than or equal to the number of seats passed as a parameter.

```
CNT = 0;
WHILE(CNT < :NumSeats)DO
  BEGIN
   INSERT INTO Seating(Flight,Seat,TicketNo)
     VALUES(:FlightNo,:CNT,'[OPEN]');
   CNT = CNT + 1;
  END
```

Another Example

Examine another example of an EXECUTE stored procedure. This procedure is used to assign a seat to a person. The procedure confirms that the requested seat is available, and if it is available, it assigns it to the ticket holder. This stored procedure illustrates how parameters or information can be passed back to the caller. This procedure also depicts how conditionals can be used in a stored procedure.

```
CREATE PROCEDURE Assign_Seat(FlightNo char(8),
   SeatNum integer,TkNum char(10))
   RETURNS(Confirmed char(20))
AS
DECLARE VARIABLE Ticket Char(10);
BEGIN
   SELECT TicketNo FROM Seating
     where Flight =:FlightNo and
     Seat = :SeatNum into :Ticket;
   IF(:Ticket='[OPEN]') Then
     BEGIN
      UPDATE Seating SET TicketNo=:TkNum WHERE
        Flight =:FlightNo and Seat = :SeatNum;
      Confirmed = 'Confirmed!';
     END
   ELSE
     Confirmed = 'Seat Unavailable';
END;
```

Returning Information from an EXECUTE Procedure

It is not only possible for a stored procedure to get information from its caller, but also to return data. In this example, the procedure is returning a string indicating if the transaction was successful, or if the seat is already taken. To do this, in the CREATE PROCEDURE statement, it uses

```
RETURNS(Confirmed char(20))
```

The value in `Confirmed` at the end of the procedure is passed back to the caller.

Conditionals

This sample procedure also demonstrates how an `IF...THEN...ELSE` statement can be used to perform conditional statements. The procedure determines if a seat is taken by storing the ticket number for the specified seat into a temporary variable. If the variable is equal to `[OPEN]`, then the seat is available. When a seat is available, the procedure sets the seat number to the specified ticket, and returns a `Confirmed` message. Otherwise, the procedure returns a message to indicate that the seat is already taken. Notice that both the `IF` and `WHILE` syntax is almost exactly like Delphi's syntax for `IF` and `WHILE` statements.

Testing the Procedures Using a Script

Before you jump into a discussion about how stored procedures can be used in Delphi, we will demonstrate how they can be manipulated with scripts. Using scripts in likely the easiest way to test stored procedures and perform database maintenance. The following example shows how you test your two airline stored procedures using a script.

Our first task is to create a few flights. The airline is very small, so our planes do not hold many passengers.

```
EXECUTE PROCEDURE Create_Flight('DP109',4);
EXECUTE PROCEDURE Create_Flight('DP255',2);
```

This creates flight DP109, which can hold four passengers, and flight DP255, which can hold two passengers. Confirm that this worked.

```
SELECT * FROM Seating
```

returns

```
FLIGHT          SEAT TICKETNO
======== =========== ==========
DP109              0 [OPEN]
DP109              1 [OPEN]
DP109              2 [OPEN]
DP109              3 [OPEN]
DP255              0 [OPEN]
DP255              1 [OPEN]
```

Everything looks all right. Now assign a seat to the passenger holding ticket number T1029.

```
EXECUTE PROCEDURE Assign_Seat('DP109',2,'T1029');
```

returns

```
CONFIRMED
=====================
Confirmed!
```

So far, so good. Now try to assign another passenger to the same seat on the same flight.

```
EXECUTE PROCEDURE Assign_Seat('DP109',2,'T2222');
```

returns

```
CONFIRMED
=====================
Seat Unavailable
```

Looks good, but you still need to confirm that the first procedure actually updated the table, and that the second time the procedure is executed it didn't overwrite the first passenger.

```
SELECT * FROM Seating
```

returns

```
FLIGHT          SEAT TICKETNO
======== =========== ==========
DP109              0 [OPEN]
DP109              1 [OPEN]
DP109              2 T1029
DP109              3 [OPEN]
DP255              0 [OPEN]
DP255              1 [OPEN]
```

You're set! It appears that the two stored procedures work fine. Now for the topic of how to execute stored procedures from a Delphi application.

Using Execute Stored Procedures in Delphi

To execute a stored procedure from Delphi, the TStoredProc component must be used. The advantage of the TStoredProc component is that it can pass information to and from the stored procedure using parameters. For example, to call the `Assign_Seat` procedure from Delphi you would

- Add an instance of the TStoredProc to a form or data module.
- Set the `Database` property just as in the TQuery component
- Instead of SQL statements, the component actually uses the name of the stored procedure. After setting the database, the procedure names appear in the properties page (see figure 15.5). Note that the available stored procedures are listed. You need to choose the stored procedure you want to execute: `Assign_Seat`.

Figure 15.5.
The Object Inspector Properties tab for the TStoredProc component.

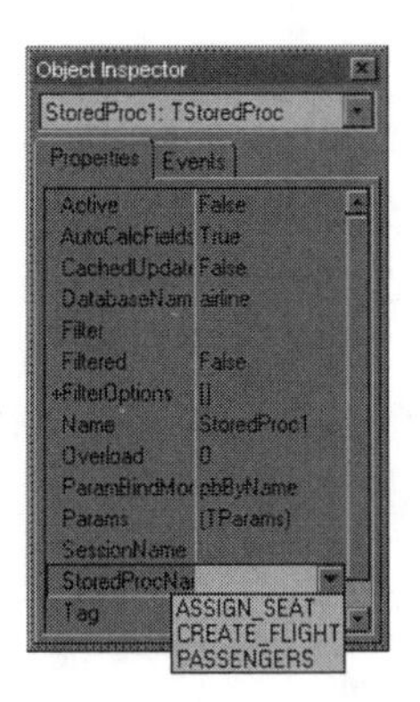

- In the application, any input parameters that need to be set should be set prior to executing the procedure. To set the parameters, either the `Params` property or the `ParamByName` method should be used.
- After input parameters are set, the `ExecProc` method is used to execute the procedure.
- Finally, any returned parameters can be read to find their returned values.

In the following example, we set a TStroredProc's input parameters from TEdit components, execute the procedure, and place the returned variable into a TEdit component.

```
spAssignSeat.Params[0].AsString := Flight.Text;
spAssignSeat.Params[1].AsInteger := strtoint(Seat.Text);
spAssignSeat.Params[2].AsString := TicketNo.Text;
spAssignSeat.ExecProc;
Status.Text := spAssignSeat.Params[3].AsString;
```

Select Stored Procedures

In addition to executing stored procedures that perform a set of tasks and can return information through parameters, there are also stored procedures that can return a complete results set. This type of stored procedure is similar to a query, therefore it is called a *select stored procedure.* The power of a select stored procedure is that it allows you to create a procedure that appears as a table to the calling SQL statement. One of the powerful features of select stored procedures is that parameters may be passed, but results can also still be manipulated using standard SQL.

Creating a Sample Select Stored Procedure

The format for creating a select stored procedure is similar to that for an execute stored procedure. The main difference is that the returned parameters are a set of rows, as opposed to a single row. An example of a select stored procedure follows. This procedure lists all the ticket holders for a specified flight. It eliminates all `[OPEN]` seats from the result set.

```
CREATE PROCEDURE Passengers(FlightNo char(8))
   RETURNS(Tickets char(10))
AS
BEGIN
  FOR SELECT TicketNo from Seating
    WHERE Flight = : FlightNo AND
     not (TicketNo="[OPEN]")
     INTO :Tickets
    DO
      SUSPEND;
END^
```

The `CREATE` statement is exactly like the `CREATE PROCEDURE` statement used to create an execute stored procedure. Although this procedure uses a `BEGIN` and `END` block (which all procedures must), there is actually only one command that performs all the functions: the `FOR SELECT` statement. The `FOR SELECT` statement performs a select with a few slight differences.

- The results are processed one record at a time.
- Results are returned as parameters. The `INTO` clause specifies what parameter should be mapped to the query result.
- A block of code can be used to process each record. This block is located after the `DO` clause. In this example, the `SUSPEND` keyword causes the procedure to simply return the record to the calling SQL statement.

Calling a Select Stored Procedure

Unlike an execute stored procedure, which needs a command to tell Interbase to execute a procedure, a select procedure is used just like a table in a `SELECT` statement. There, of course, are some major differences between a select stored procedure and a table. No insert, update, or delete, operations can be performed on a select stored procedure. However, a select stored procedure can accept parameters. For example, to call the `Passengers` procedure from WISQL, you can execute

```
SELECT TICKETS FROM Passengers('DP109')
```

which returns

```
TICKETS
==========
TT9999
TTK889
T1029
```

NOTE

Other features of the select statement can be applied to the returned rows. The following demonstrates the use of an aggregate function:

```
SELECT MAX(TICKETS) FROM Passengers('DP109')
```

returns

```
MAX
==========
TTK889
```

Implementing Select Stored Procedures in Delphi

Delphi also differentiates between select stored procedures, and execute stored procedures. An execute stored procedure must be called using a TStoredProc component, whereas a select stored procedure may be included in a SQL statement that is executed using the TQuery component. It is possible to execute a select stored procedure using a TStoredProc component, but it does not allow SQL statements to be included with the call. Therefore, you could not execute the aggregate function example using a TStoredProc component.

Sample Delphi Application

Listing 15.2 demonstrates how to execute SQL statements and stored procedures in Delphi by tying together many of the concepts covered in this chapter.

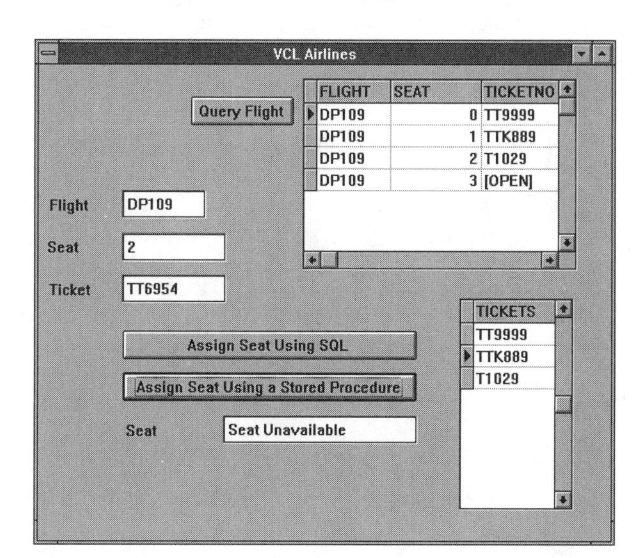

Figure 15.6.
Sample Delphi application accessing Interbase.

TYPE

Listing 15.2. AIR1.PAS.

```
unit Air1;

interface

uses
  SysUtils, WinTypes, WinProcs, Messages, Classes, Graphics, Controls,
  Forms, Dialogs, Grids, DBGrids, DB, StdCtrls, DBTables;

type
  TForm1 = class(TForm)
    Query1: TQuery;
    QueryFlight: TButton;
    DataSource1: TDataSource;
    DBGrid1: TDBGrid;
    dbAirline: TDatabase;
    Flight: TEdit;
    Label1: TLabel;
    Seat: TEdit;
    Label2: TLabel;
    TicketNo: TEdit;
    Label3: TLabel;
    SetTicket: TQuery;
    AssignSeat: TButton;
    btAssignBySP: TButton;
    spAssignSeat: TStoredProc;
    Status: TEdit;
    Label4: TLabel;
    Query2: TQuery;
    DataSource2: TDataSource;
    DBGrid2: TDBGrid;
    procedure QueryFlightClick(Sender: TObject);
    procedure Button2Click(Sender: TObject);
    procedure AssignSeatClick(Sender: TObject);
    procedure btAssignBySPClick(Sender: TObject);
  private
    { Private declarations }
  public
    { Public declarations }
  end;

var
  Form1: TForm1;

implementation

{$R *.DFM}

procedure TForm1.QueryFlightClick(Sender: TObject);
begin
    Query1.Close;
    Query1.Params[0].AsString := Flight.Text;
    Query1.Open;
    Query2.Close;
    Query2.Params[0].AsString := Flight.Text;
```

```
    Query2.Open;
end;


procedure TForm1.Button2Click(Sender: TObject);
begin
  Query1.Close;
end;

procedure TForm1.AssignSeatClick(Sender: TObject);
Var
 CreditCardError : Boolean;     {Flags a credit card problem}
begin

  dbAirline.StartTransaction;   {Start the database transaction}
  SetTicket.Params[0].AsString := TicketNo.Text;
  SetTicket.Params[1].AsString := Flight.Text;
  SetTicket.Params[2].AsInteger := strtoint(Seat.Text);
  SetTicket.ExecSQl;
  CreditCardError := False;
  {****************************}
  {* PROCESS CREDIT CARD HERE *}
  {****************************}
  if CreditCardError then {If there is a problem then RollBack}
    dbAirline.Rollback
   else
    dbAirline.Commit;     {Otherwise Commit}
end;

procedure TForm1.btAssignBySPClick(Sender: TObject);
begin
  spAssignSeat.Params[0].AsString := Flight.Text;
  spAssignSeat.Params[1].AsInteger := strtoint(Seat.Text);
  spAssignSeat.Params[2].AsString := TicketNo.Text;
  spAssignSeat.ExecProc;
  Status.Text := spAssignSeat.Params[3].AsString;
end;

end.
```

Summary

A client/server architecture is more efficient in a networked database because the data doesn't need to be passed to the client for processing. The reader should treat this chapter as an introduction to using a database server that has the look and feel of a client/server database. By no means should this chapter be thought of as a complete reference to the Interbase server, it simply gives enough information to get you on your feet. Read the reference and online help to Interbase to explore the full power that it offers. Interbase includes stored procedure, views, security, and many other features that are similar to other commercial client/server database solutions.

Q&A

Q Using Interbase, is there a way to perform a task when a record is inserted, deleted, or changed?

A Yes, *triggers* are used to perform exactly this task. A trigger can be used to maintain data integrity, keep history tables, or perform tasks that must occur when a table is changed. For more information on triggers consult the Interbase documentation.

Q What type of security does Interbase offer for different logon and passwords?

A Interbase offers complete table security in which privileges can be granted on select, insert, update, and deletion of records.

Q Can Interbase back up and restore databases?

A Yes, Interbase offers full database backup and recovery support. For more information read the reference regarding the server management tool.

Workshop

Quiz

1. Why isn't it possible to insert records into a view that is based on a join?
2. What does a right join return?
3. If a record is inserted into a table in the middle of a transaction, and the transaction is rolled back, will the record be in the table?
4. What component in Delphi is used to execute an execute stored procedure? How about a select stored procedure?

Exercises

1. Create a join that uses both aggregate functions and a join criteria other than equals (=).
2. Write a select procedure that doesn't access any tables but that returns rows.

Week 3

Day 16

ReportSmith Fundamentals

Introduction

If you have never used a report generation tool like ReportSmith or the Quick Report components, you may not even know what you are missing. When you first start writing applications, one of the things that seems to get put off to the side is reporting. The first video tape tracking program you wrote was really just an on-screen application. This is the normal progression of things. As you start getting your first real (which means paying) programming job, you may even not have to do any reports in that application either.

Eventually though, it will catch up to you. So you sit down and look at how to create printed output from that little database program you wrote. You find that the whole concept is suddenly harder than you thought it was going to be. When you print out your own reports you have to worry about things like

- Printing header and footer information on each page
- Page numbering
- How many do I print per page
- If the user changes the font, then the number of lines per page changes

How do I pick the font to use (and how do I know if they have that font on their machine)

If I add a graph to the page (a pain in itself), how does that affect the number of actual data lines of the page

In case you haven't figured it out yet, I myself have suffered through the same problems when I first started Windows programming. The answer is of course to use a commercial report construction program to help you. You can reinvent the wheel by doing it yourself, but the wheel you reinvent will be spinning in the sand most of the time. The smart money is on products like ReportSmith and Quick Report.

Both ReportSmith and Quick Report enable you to do some miraculous things as well as give your user a set of reports for their application that will blow their socks off. Too good to be true, you say; well, it gets even better. Both programs are actually even easier to use than Delphi 2 itself (this author's opinion). So let's dive in and show you how to make the most of your report writing experience. This chapter covers both ReportSmith and Quick Report. First we'll take a look at ReportSmith, and then finish the chapter by talking about Quick Report.

ReportSmith

If you have ever written or read a report (and most of you probably have), you know that there are many different types of reports. Data can be split up hundreds of different ways to give the reader the particular "slant" they want on the data.

Types of Reports

There are four major categories of reports in ReportSmith. You can see these categories by choosing File | New from the ReportSmith menu. After doing this, you see the dialog box in Figure 16.1.

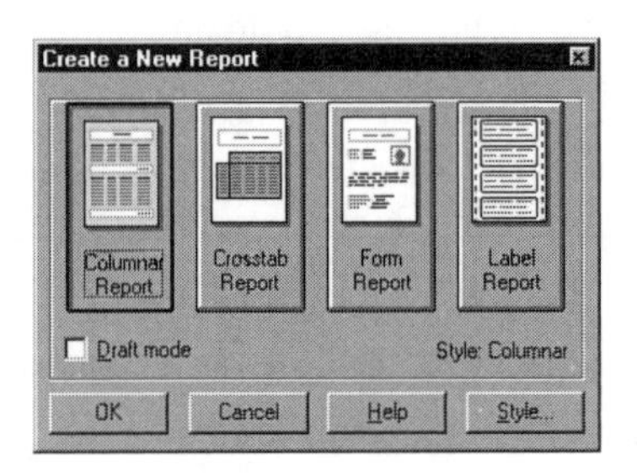

Figure 16.1.
Create a New Report dialog box.

As you can see, you have four choices for main report types: columnar, crosstab, form, and label reports. Notice the style button in the lower-right corner of the dialog box. This button enables you to pick from many subtypes of these four major report categories. The following sections take a brief look at these types.

Columnar Report

The columnar report is the type of report you would see as a white-pages directory sort of report. (See Figure 16.2.) The data is listed in columns across the page, and each column has a column heading. The report is usually titled. If the report has multiple pages, page numbers are included, usually on the lower-right corner of the page.

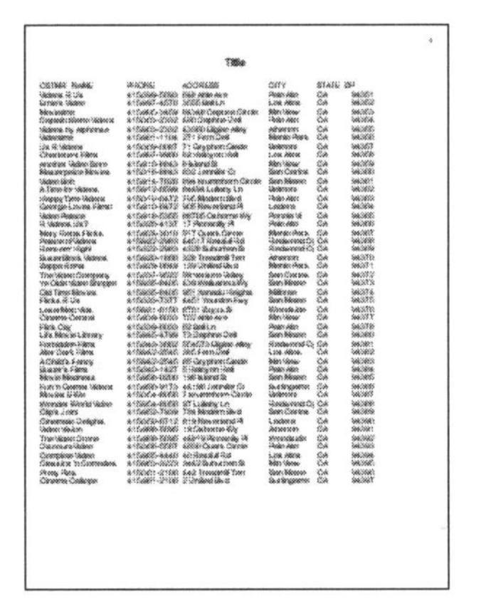

Figure 16.2.
Columnar report.

Crosstab Report

The crosstab report is a hybrid report resembling more of a spreadsheet approach. (See Figure 16.3.) This report is really called a summary report because its function is to summarize or "total up" the columns on the report.

An example of a crosstab report might be a yearly sales report in which each quarterly sales is a column, totaled at the bottom, and then the yearly sales are totaled across the page.

Form Report

In the form report, each record included in the report is displayed in free form, one record per page. (See Figure 16.4.) An example of a form report is when you are doing a report page for each of your customers. In this instance, you wouldn't want to give a report to a customer with information about another customer on it as well, so the report is limited to one customer per page.

Figure 16.3.
Crosstab report.

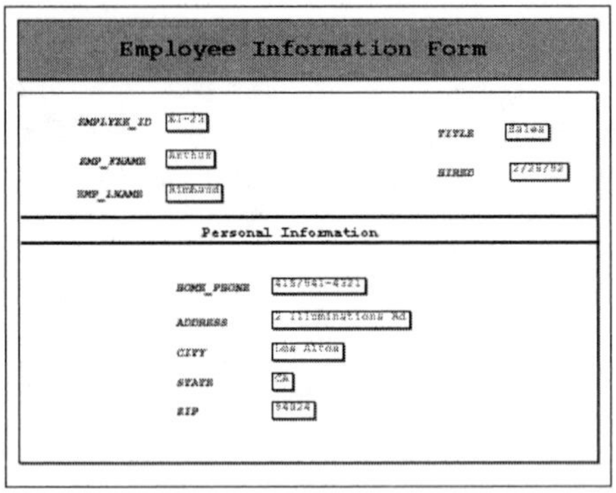

Figure 16.4.
Form report.

Labels

A label report displays data in a label format. (See Figure 16.5.) Of course this would be very useful if you were printing these reports on Avery printer labels. These types of reports are used often and in many applications. The standard use for this report is for the creation of mailing labels for customer mailing, sales, party invitations, and the like.

Before these tools existed, not only would you have to create your own labels, you would also have to tailor the report to the size labels that your customer had. With the advent of Avery laser labels and software like ReportSmith, things are easier. Once you create a label report, you can go to Page Setup, click on the Labels selection, and choose your Avery label number from the Label type and dimensions dropdown box. (See Figure 16.6.) Could things get any easier?

Figure 16.5.
Label report.

Figure 16.6.
Label types.

Custom Report Types

Besides the four standard types of reports, there are also several custom report types. These are report types that are considered more advanced but provide different views of the data (other than the four just mentioned). Look at two report types that are popular for their presentation method.

Master/Detail Report

The master/detail report provides a distinct view of your data. (See Figure 16.7.) This report is best suited to showing one-to-many relationships in your data. For example, you may want to show a salesperson's commission earnings. The earnings may come from dealing with several customers. The master/detail report would show the employee's sales by month, and the bottom of the report would show that day's sales transactions.

Another use for a master/detail report may be to look at an investor's assets (again, another one-to-many relationship where one investor may have many holdings).

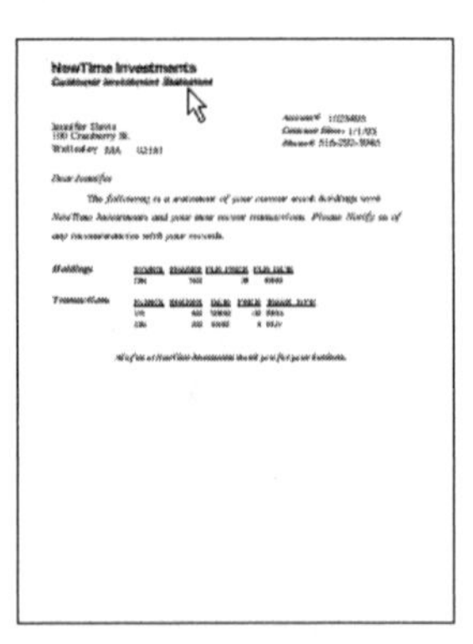

Figure 16.7.
Master/detail report.

The data for this report may very well come from several databases and from multiple queries. This is not unusual for this type of report, and provides some good data-reporting capabilities.

Summary-Only Report

The summary-only report is designed to provide a 30,000 foot view of the data. (See Figure 16.8.) This is sometimes called an *executive overview.* Say you were giving a sales report to the president of your company. He probably doesn't care what the daily sales for each of your stores but is more interested in the overall quarterly sales for the company. A summary report might provide a sales summary by region or by quarter. This would be more useful for the president to make overall business decisions. These types of reports help management keep up on the "pulse" of the company.

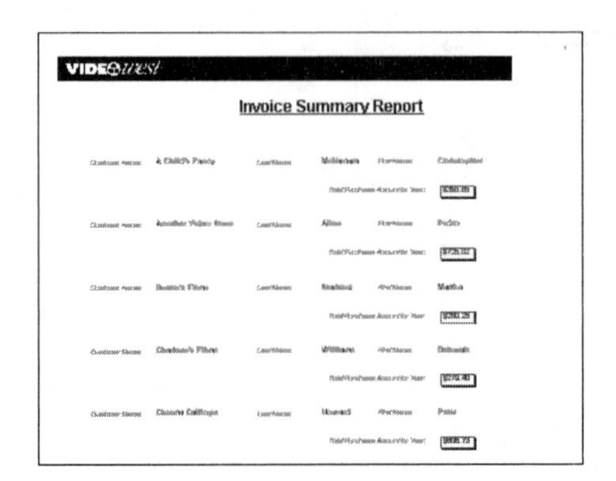

Figure 16.8.
Summary-only report.

Data Sources (ODBC, Paradox...)

Now that you have seen some of the types of reports available to you, you need to know what kind of data you can feed to ReportSmith and from what type of data sources. Currently, ReportSmith 3 supports the following data sources:

- Access
- AS/400
- Btrieve
- DB2
- dBASE
- Excel
- FoxPro
- Informix
- Ingres
- InterBase
- Oracle
- Raima
- SQLBase
- Paradox
- SQL Server
- SyBase
- Text Files
- Teradata
- Unify
- Watcom SQL

The types of databases you can connect to also depends on which version of ReportSmith you purchase. There are two versions, ReportSmith for PC Databases, and ReportSmith for SQL Databases. The ability of ReportSmith to handle this variety of connections makes it a versatile tool.

When you pick the report type in the New Report dialog box in Figure 16.1, you see the screen in Figure 16.9.

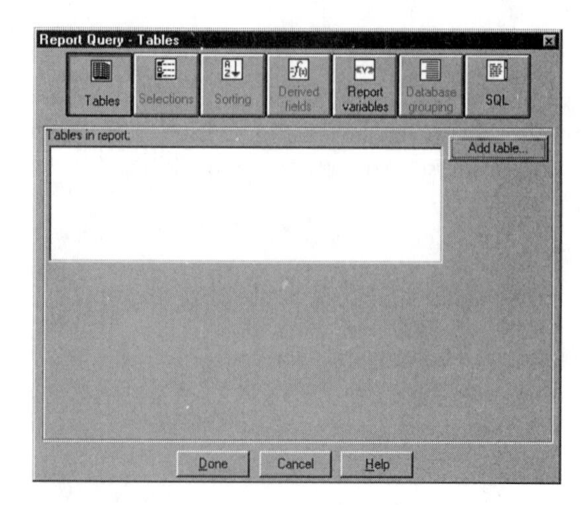

Figure 16.9.
Report Query dialog box.

Here you can cycle through the buttons from left to right to select all your options. The one you are interested in now is the Add table button. This button enables you to select the tables from which you will draw your data. When you select this button you get the following dialog box.

At this point you will be able to select the Type dropdown box in the lower-left corner of the dialog box, and see which types of databases are supported in ReportSmith. Once you pick the database type, you can then select the tables from that database.

Notice the Connections dropdown box (lower-right corner), this is for using a connection that you have previously defined. Think of this as a way to use a nickname for a commonly used database. The advantage of doing this is that your user does not have to remember the entire path to the data source, but instead has to remember just the connection name.

Connecting To Data Sources

There are three different connection methods ReportSmith can utilize to connect to the data sources mentioned earlier: ODBC, IDAPI, and native. Let's look at each one and what you can connect to with these sources.

IDAPI

The *Integrated Database Application Programming Interface (IDAPI)* is a standard interface designed by Borland to allow IDAPI-enabled applications to connect to IDAPI-enabled Borland products such as Paradox and dBase, as well as data sources supported by Borland's SQL Links product.

The next logical question is What is SQL links? SQL Links is a set of middleware drivers that allows IDAPI-enabled applications to connect to SQL databases. Once you install the SQL Links drivers and define an alias for the SQL database of choice, you can then connect to those SQL databases from applications like ReportSmith. The SQL Links product that comes with ReportSmith provides drivers for InterBase (Borland's database server product), as well as Informix.

As of the writing of this book, the data sources supporting the IDAPI interface are dBASE and Paradox in various versions. At some later date it is possible that other vendors may incorporate IDAPI support in their databases.

ODBC

For those of you that haven't dealt with ODBC, it's an interesting interface. Like IDAPI, ODBC is an interface that provides a common set of calls to access many different types of databases. There is an ODBC administrator application that gets installed into your Control Panel that allows you to configure your data sources.

As discussed in the database chapters, there are several benefits to using ODBC as your interface mechanism. From a ReportSmith perspective, the benefit is that all databases appear the same from ReportSmith's point of view. This allows you to treat a SyBase database the same as an Access database.

Through ODBC you can connect to databases like FoxPro, dBASE, Paradox, Access, and Btrieve. The real thrill here is that you can also access things that are not really "databases"; these include Excel files as well as text files. This type of connectivity gives you access to the world. The ODBC specification is open, which means that third-party vendors could also write drivers for other data sources. There are a number of companies that do just that: writing drivers for databases like Informix, DB2 and others.

There are, of course, drawbacks to using ODBC as well. All this universal interface stuff takes work. The ODBC interface has always been (and will probably continue to be) slower than using native drivers or even SQL Links drivers. This has always been the downfall of ODBC. The new 32-bit ODBC drivers have come a long way at closing the performance gap, but the gap still remains.

Native Connections

ReportSmith provides native connectivity for several database types. DB2, an IBM mainframe-oriented database product can be accessed by ReportSmith via the MDI Gateway product. MDI provides a SQL front end to the DB2 databases that allows clients (like ReportSmith SQL) to access the DB2 data as if it were a SQL database.

Ingres, Oracle, Sybase, Unify, Teradata, and SQLBase also can be connected to ReportSmith via native drivers. There are many requirements for these different databases, so please consult the ReportSmith User's Manual for the details of implementing your specific database connectivity.

Getting the Right Data into Your Reports

Now that you know how to connect to the databases, you need to get the data into your report. There are two ways of accomplishing this. The first is to place the SQL statement into ReportSmith directly. This is the most straightforward method of determining which tables and fields are going to be placed into your report and what ordering and grouping will be applied to the data. This method requires you to have a firm grasp on SQL. If you are not well-versed in the language, you can use the visual method.

ReportSmith provides a visual query builder that helps you write the SQL code to generate your report. After choosing your report type, as shown in Figure 16.9, you get the Report Query dialog box. Using this dialog box, you can perform all the functions necessary to create the SQL statement visually. Note the functions of the Report Query dialog. There are seven buttons across the top of the dialog box. The following sections look at the function of each of these.

Tables

The Tables button is used to select which tables you wish to include in your report. When this button is depressed, you can use the Add Table button in the bottom pane to add additional tables to the report. When this button is depressed, you get the Select Table To Be Added dialog box in Figure 16.10.

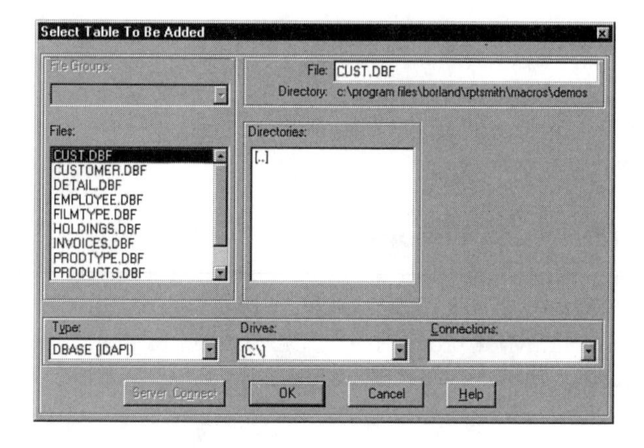

Figure 16.10.
Select Table To Be Added dialog box.

This box enables you to select tables to be added to your report by choosing them out of the listbox to the left. By changing the Type dropdown box (see Figure 16.11), you can look at other database types.

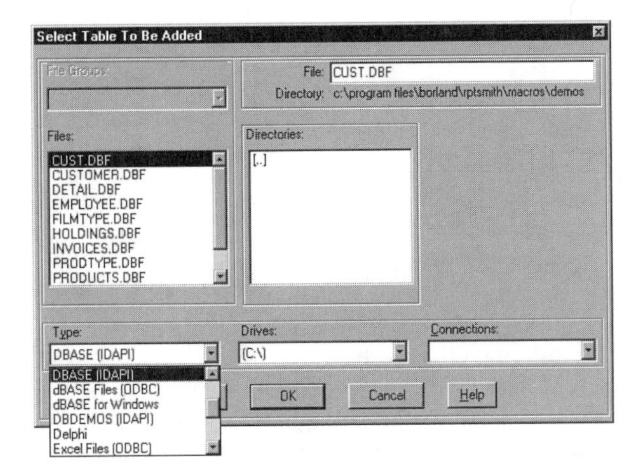

Figure 16.11.
Type dropdown box.

Once you have selected the databases to be used, you can move on to the next step. Note also that there is a Connections dropdown so you can choose a database based on its connection name, as opposed to its full file location name. The purpose of allowing you to use the Connections box is to assist you in defining an alias independent of the full file name (with path). That way your program can refer to the alias, and all you have to do is link that alias name to the actual file location.

See the installation chapter for details on how InstallShield Express can make the alias entries for you when you use their installer to build your application's setup disks.

NEW TERM If you have more than one table in your report, it is important to define the *relation* between the tables. This is the relation in a *relational database*. In order for ReportSmith to associate records in separate tables, it must know which fields are secondary keys to other tables. This is accomplished by using the Add New Link button on the bottom of the Report Query window. The Create New Table Link window appears (as seen in Figure 16.12).

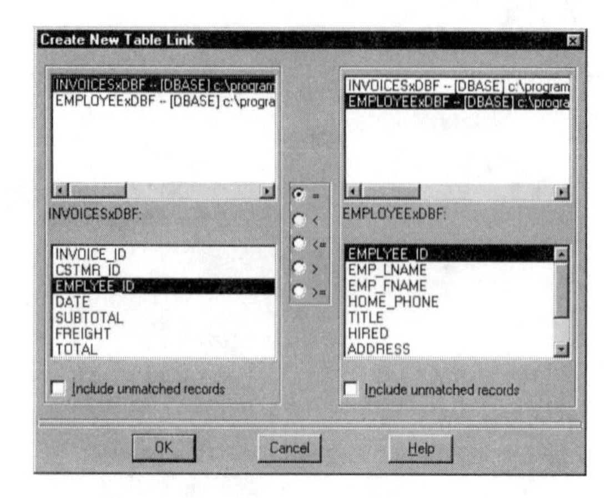

Figure 16.12.
Create New Table Link dialog box.

It's important that the fields you link in two tables contain identical data. In other words, you would not link the part description field in one table to the customer name field in another. A more likely candidate would be the part number field in a product database, to the part number field in the sales detail table. This would allow ReportSmith to print out the sales details for a customer, and access the part description (which it gets from the product table) based on the part number in the sales detail table.

By linking the fields in your tables, you are giving ReportSmith the connections it needs to take the Employee_ID from a Detail table, and print the employee's name instead of employee ID number. If you do not have those links, you cannot get supplemental data from a table, and your report will not have that user friendly aspect to it.

Selections

Now that you know what databases you are going to use, ReportSmith needs to know which records in those tables you wish to include in your report. If you press the Selections button, the bottom pane of the Report Query dialog box changes (as shown in Figure 16.13). Notice the number "1" highlighted in yellow. This is the beginning of the selection process.

Right-click the number "1" and see the dropdown box that appears. This box offers a list of things that can be done at this point.

This is a simple way for a SQL novice to build a selection statement. You can click on any portion on the selection statement and build the selection "sentence" as you go. Once you have created a selection statement, you can create additional statements by right-clicking the number "1" and choosing the Add New Selection After This Statement list choice.

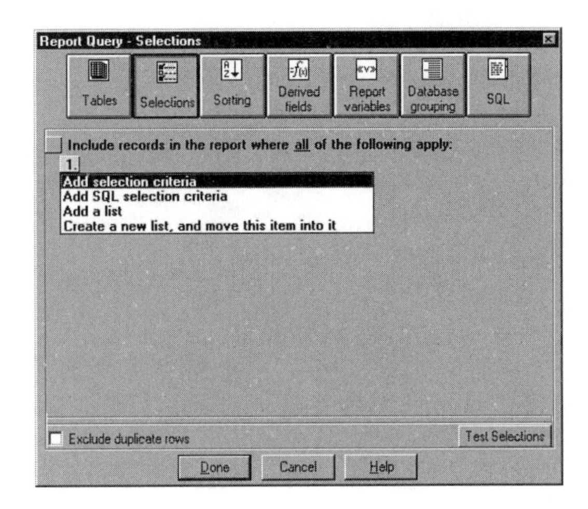

Figure 16.13.
Selection dropdown box.

Notice that after you have created one selection statement, the dropdown box changes, adding new items for deletion and manipulation of the selection statements. By using this visual building of the record selection statement, you are forgoing the more strenuous version of doing it by hand. The added benefit of using this method is that ReportSmith does allow you to use tables or variables that are not defined. You cannot misspell them, because you do not enter the names. You pick the names from a dropdown list. This lowers your chances of making a mistake.

One of the more intriguing menu items is the Convert This Item to SQL menu selection. This takes the statement you have built and turns it into a SQL statement. Once this is done, there is no way for it to be returned to a regular statement.

Sorting

The Sorting option is easy to use. You pick the fields from the lower pane and click the Insert into sort list button (as shown in Figure 16.14). This moves the item to the upper pane (which means you want the report's output sorted on that field). Once the field is in the upper pane, you can use the Ascending and Descending radio buttons to indicate how you want the data sorted. If you accidentally place an item on the sort list, you can use the Remove From Sort List button to remove the item from the list.

What you are trying to accomplish here is to determine the order in which the data will be displayed. Your user will almost always prefer to see the data either alphabetically or in number ascending or descending order. This option lets you pick the sorting method.

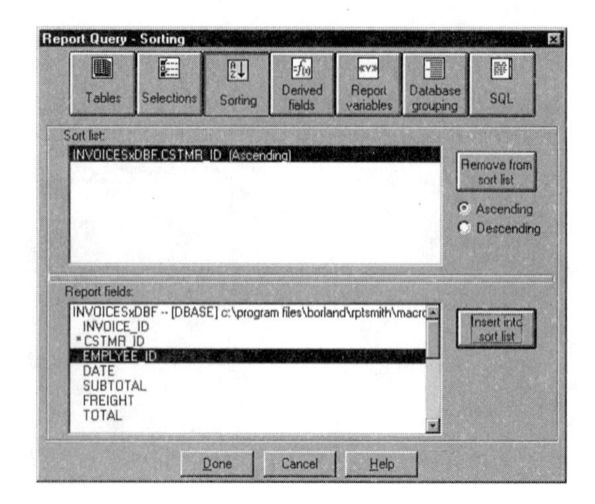

Figure 16.14.
Report Query with sorting selected.

Derived Fields

The term *derived* is synonymous with calculated. This button allows you to insert fields into your reports that are calculated based on data in your tables. When you press the Derived Fields button, the lower pane of the Report Query dialog changes to allow you to add, edit, or delete derived fields (as shown in Figure 16.15).

When you add a new derived field, the SQL statement building window appears. This window enables you to tell ReportSmith how to derive this new value of yours. It could be taking the risk factor field from the clients database and adding one to it, or something more complex.

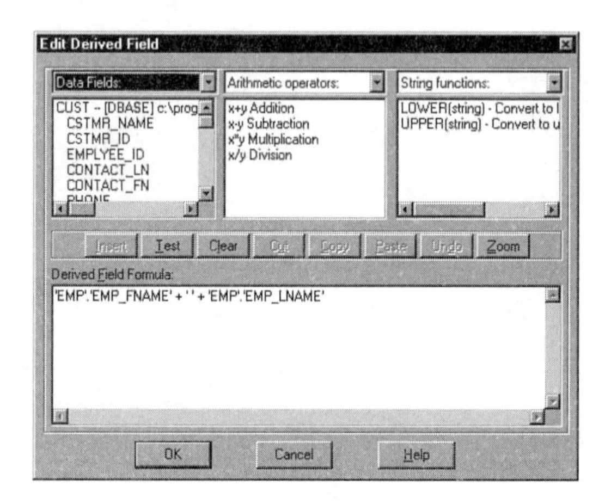

Figure 16.15.
Building the `FullName` derived field.

Derived fields perform a great service, too. An example of their use would be when you want to use a customer's name on mailing labels. If you use two fields side by side, you end up with one of two problems:

1. The overlapping name. `DanielOsier` is how my name might appear if you did not allocate enough space for a longer first name.
2. The other way it may appear is: `Dan^^^^^Osier` (with the ^ representing spaces) on the label because you allocated too much space (thinking ahead for those long names no doubt).

The answer is a derived field. In ReportSmith you define a variable called `FullName`, which holds the first name concatenated with the last name and a space between them. You then use `FullName` on the label as opposed to the first and last name. When defining a derived field, simply type the variable name into the Derived Field Name edit box, and press Add (as shown in Figure 16.16). Providing you have the Defined By SQL radio button selected, you are going to get a SQL edit dialog box. You construct the `FullName` right there.

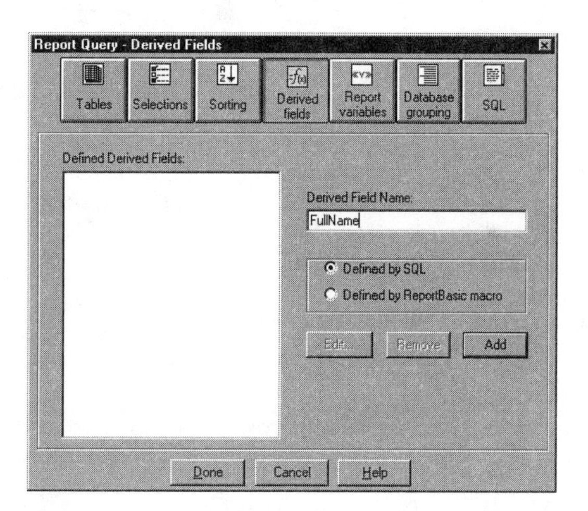

Figure 16.16.
Derived field builder.

Once it has been defined, you can press the Test button to make sure the statement is correct. Notice how we concatenated a blank space between the name parts using two quotes with a space between them. Now use the `FullName` in the report and get that perfect spacing you need to make any report look great.

Report Variables

Report variables also offer some good functionality. This function allows you to define a variable within your report, and then use that variable within your calculations and selection statements.

An example of its use is to query the user for beginning and end dates for a sales summary report and then to use those dates in selection criteria for the sales report itself. This moves the burden away from your application gathering dates and passing them to your report (always a little painful), to letting the report generator itself deal with the details.

Figure 16.17.
Report Query with Report Variables button depressed.

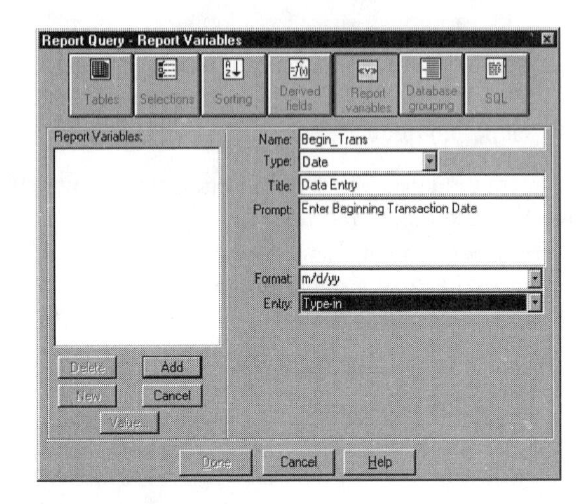

As you can see (from Figure 16.17), you have created two variables `Begin_Trans`, `End_Trans`, that the user will have to input prior to creating a report. These two report variables can then be used in the selection statement that says "select all records between the `Begin_Trans` and `End_Trans` dates."

In developing applications in the past, we have run into problems with pasing extensive amounts of data to the report generator, such as a customer's name, some set of begin and end dates, plus an employee's ID and then having the report generator do its magic. The problem was getting the data from the application to the report. Some report generators have properties you can set in their controls that act as gateways for data.

We like the way ReportSmith has opted to go. Report variables mean that much of the time we can have ReportSmith ask for those dates itself, rather than leaving it up to the application to get the data. The other benefit of this approach is that the report can be run from outside the application it is associated with because all the selection criteria is created in the report.

Database and Report Grouping

These functions allow you to group data based on some criteria prior to generating your report. An example of this might be that you have a sales database and you would like the sales summarized by department. In other words, you want to see which department is selling the most and the least. To do this, what you really need is the sales report grouped on the department number.

You can group the data two ways. By using the database grouping button, the grouping will occur on the database server. If you choose the Tools | Report Grouping command from the main menu, ReportSmith groups the data locally (See Figure 16.18). The advantage of doing the grouping on the server is that you are not taking local CPU cycles to do the grouping. All the work is happening on the server.

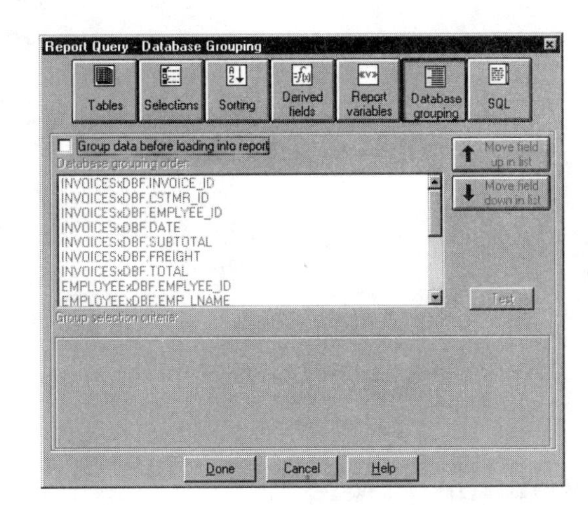

Figure 16.18.
Report Query with Database Grouping button depressed.

If the database you are accessing is on a local machine, the grouping occurs locally regardless of which grouping method you choose. You can define multiple groups for your data as well. For example, you may want to see a breakdown by salesperson (to see who is doing the best) and then break the report down further into what each salesperson has sold to each customer. This would be group within a group.

SQL

Last, but not least, the SQL button gives you the SQL statement that has been generated as a result of the choices you have made on the prior screens. This SQL statement is the culmination of all your effort. If you get the urge to forge ahead and edit the SQL statement directly, you get the warning in Figure 16.19 from ReportSmith.

This means, "If you change this perfectly formed SQL statement that ReportSmith is managing for you, ReportSmith will not be able to undo the damage if you mess it up." At this point, if you choose to continue with your quest for independence, you will not be able to use the other Report Query buttons to change the SQL statements. You will have to edit them all by hand from now on. Figure 16.20 shows the SQL edit window after you have been given the warning that was shown in Figure 16.19.

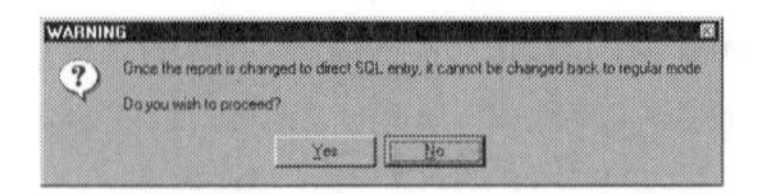

Figure 16.19.
SQL edit warning.

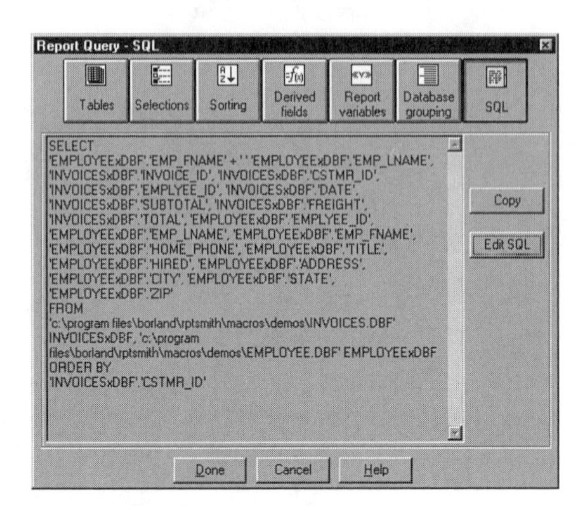

Figure 16.20.
Report Query with SQL button depressed.

Formatting Data in Your Report

Once you have the data on the page, you need to make it look good. This is where formatting your data becomes necessary. When we use the term formatting, we mean things like sizing columns, determining your actual page layout, and the like. Let's look at a couple of different items that may prove to be helpful to you. Reports usually consist of three elements: rows, columns, and fields.

Columns and Column Mode

The basis of most any report is the column. Columns let us display data in a way that is meaningful to the user. When data is displayed in columnar form, it may be necessary for you to adjust attributes of that column of data. These may include column width, font, column height, and text alignment. In these instances ReportSmith acts as any other well-written Windows 95 application. By selecting the column to manipulate by left clicking it once and then right clicking the column to get the context-sensitive menu, you see that all functions that can be performed on that column are in the pop-up menu. (See Figure 16.21.)

You may notice that even the field selection criteria is available from here. When selecting attributes like column width, notice that there is also a button for best fit. This allows you to leave the details up to ReportSmith if you wish.

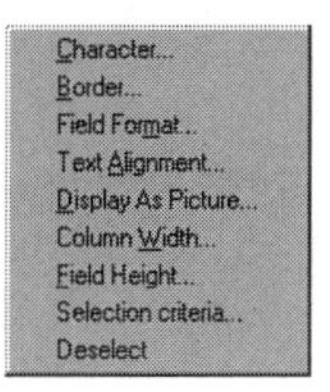

Figure 16.21.
Column pop-up menu.

When you add fields to a columnar report, one of the checkboxes on that dialog box asks if you wish to include field labels. If you say yes, you get the field name in the database as the default name on the report. These names are usually names like `Name_Last`. In these instances it is better to switch the name to something like `Last_Name`. This makes the report more readable. The labels can also be removed by selecting them and then pressing delete.

ReportSmith has a columnar mode that enables you to select a column and move it on the page. The field label associated with the column of data is moved along with the data. This mode provides a quick and easy way to order the columns in your report. When you drop your column where you want it on the page, all the other columns move over to accommodate your column in the desired position. When you are dragging the column around the page looking for a place to drop it, ReportSmith puts a vertical bar on the page to show you where the column will end up if you release the mouse button.

Rows

Rows of data in your report are a little less mysterious. If you move your cursor to the left margin of the report, your cursor changes to an arrow pointing left. If you click once next to a row of data, that row becomes highlighted. Now you can right click that row and see that you can either change the border on the row, change the row height, or deselect the row (as shown in Figure 16.22).

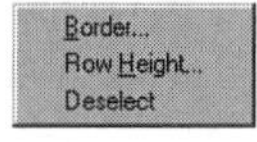

Figure 16.22.
Row pop-up menu.

If you select the row height, you can change the default row height. Notice that you can reserve the right for the row height to grow, shrink, split, or use the default height.

Fields

The field manipulation in ReportSmith is a little more exciting. If you press the field editing mode button on the toolbar, you find that you can select individual fields and adjust their properties. The difference between this mode and the columnar mode described earlier, is that in this mode ReportSmith does none of the alignment for you. It does not align and rearrange the columns to accommodate your drag-and-drops.

Field mode allows you make adjustments to your report design that ReportSmith itself could not, arranging data in ways that may seem unorthodox to someone else. The field labels will not move with the columns when you drag them. This mode allows you extreme flexibility. You can also arrange the columns of data vertically unlike the column mode where vertical alignment is automatic.

Adjustments to Your Report (Formatting)

Besides sizing and moving columns of data you can manipulate the three main portions of the report: the headers, footers, and the report body. These three can be sized and have text or data placed in them. In addition, the appearance of these sections can be enhanced.

Headers and Footers

The header and footer for your report can be added by selecting Insert | Header/Footer. The dialog box that appears allows you to add a header or footer for the entire report, the page, or a report group you have created. (See Figure 16.23.)

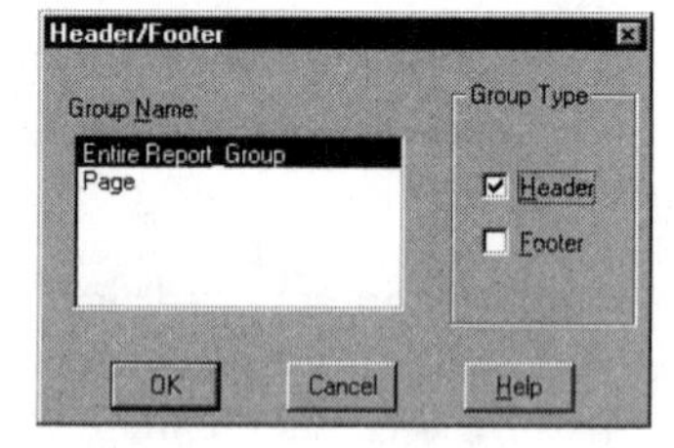

Figure 16.23. *Header/Footer dialog box.*

Select the item you wish to change (report, page, or group). Once that is selected, use the check boxes to the right and select whether a header and/or footer is desired. After you press the OK button to close the dialog box, notice that on the report you now have gray boxed areas (the headers and footers) for your selection. Remember where and how often the different headers and footers appear.

- Report header—Appears only at the top of the first page of the report. If the report is multiple pages, this header does not appear on subsequent pages of the report. Data that might be placed in the report header could be the report title, the date the report is generated, and company addressing and logo information.
- Report footer—Appears only at the bottom of the first page of the report. If the report is multiple pages, this header does not appear on subsequent pages of the report. Data that might be placed in the report footer may include grand totals for all the groups in the report, or advertisements such as "Report generated by Dan's Super program ++."

- Page header—Appears at the top of all report pages. On the first page, it appears below the report header; on subsequent pages it appears at the top of the page. The page header data may include the date the report was run or other data a customer would like to have available on each page of the report.
- Page footer—Appears at the bottom of each page. On the last page of the report, the page footer appears above the report footer. Page footers traditionally include the report page number (although the page number might be placed in the page header if desired).
- Group header—Appears before each detail section holding the related data. If no report or page header exists in the report, and you have selected a page feed after each group, the group header appears to be a page header. A group header would usually contain field labels for data contained in the accompanying detail section.
- Group footer—Appears after each detail section of related data. The footer appears on the last page of the report just above the report header, if one is present. The group footer would usually contain subtotal information for data contained in the detail section preceding it. (Grand total information for all groups in the report would go in the report footer).

Figure 16.24 shows a report with all the right combinations of header/footer information in place. ReportSmith offers a rich set of styling tools to make your reports shine.

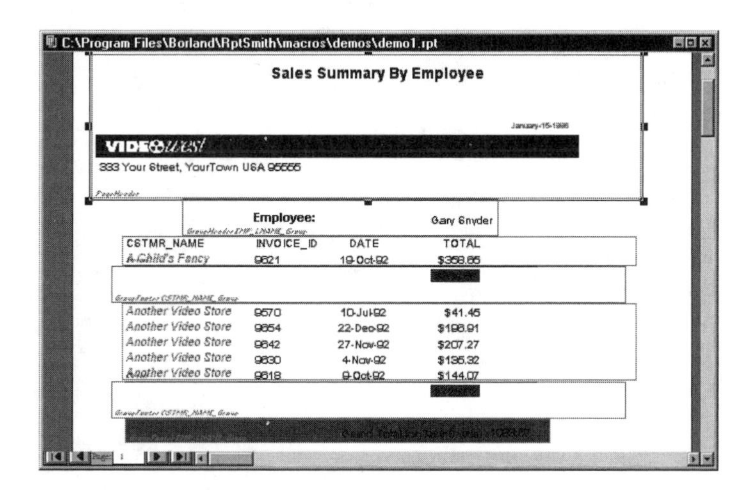

Figure 16.24.
Typical report with all header/footer combinations in place.

Run for the Borders

Once the header/footer is created, it can be sized by simply clicking once on the section and then using the sizing handles to resize the item as shown in. If you right-click on the header/ footer, from there you can also place a border around the object. Notice the wide variety of border options available to you (see Figure 16.25).

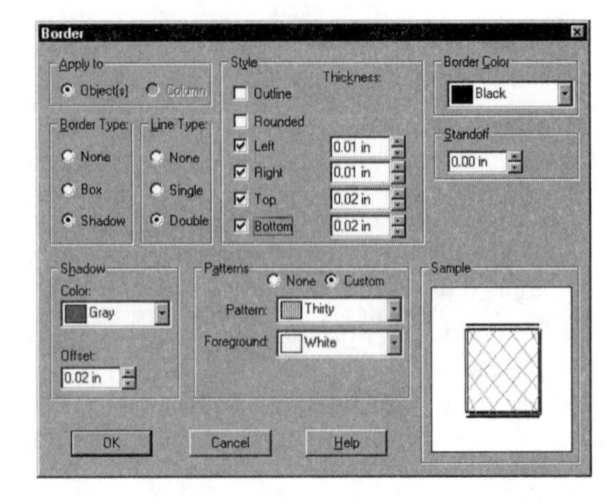

Figure 16.25.
Borders dialog box.

The body of the report has the same options. Besides being able to place a border around the body area, you can also fill the interior of the report using the custom radio button in the pattern frame of the border dialog box. This can really give your reports some flair by highlighting data with colored or patterned boxes.

Number and Date Formatting

In order for your report to really have that professional look, it is important to have your ducks in a row, as well as your numbers. To format numbers in ReportSmith is both easy and powerful.

Right click the field you wish to format, then choose Field Format. You should see a dialog box like Figure 16.26.

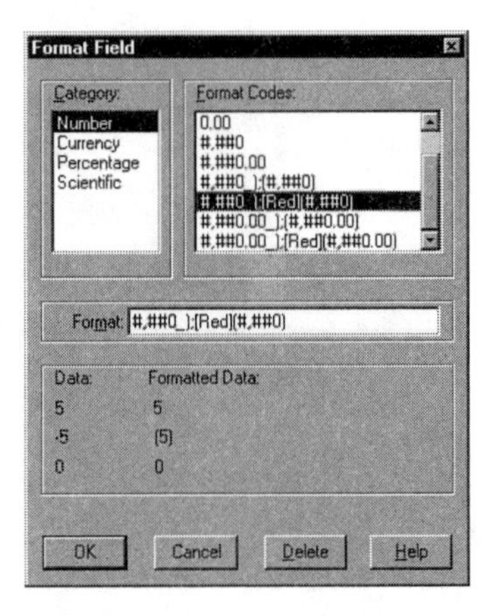

Figure 16.26.
Field Format dialog box.

At this point, if you are formatting a number, you could use either one of the predefined *format codes* (also called *masks*). These codes are telling ReportSmith how to format the number. For instance, a code of "`#,##0.00`" means

- always display the number with two decimal places (the two zeros after the decimal)
- always display a number to the left of the decimal point even if the number being formatted is less than zero (from the zero to the left of the decimal point)
- display additional digits in the tens, hundreds place only if there is a significant digit to display (from the # in the mask)
- place a comma after the thousands place in the number (from the comma in the code)

As you can see, you can easily build very complex masks to format the number any way you wish. Many currency formats are available as well. Using the $ (dollar sign), you can specify dollar amounts. In your code you can have three sections: one for positive numbers, one for negative numbers, and one for zero. If you enter the mask `$#,##0.00_);[Red]($#,##0.00);"No Data"`, this means use `$#,##0.00_)` for positive numbers; `[Red]($#,##0.00)` for negative numbers (which displays the negative number in red and in parentheses); and display the string `"No Data"` for a zero in the report.

To format a date/time field, you first need to place one on your report. If your data fields do not have dates in them, use the Insert | Fields | System Fields selection, and pick one of the date/time formats from the listbox (as shown in Figure 16.27).

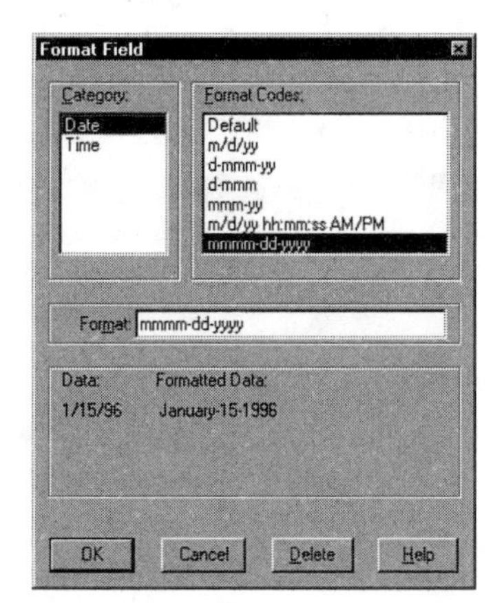

Figure 16.27.
Date/Time Field Format dialog box.

This allows you to place a date/time field in your report. Once the field is on your report, you can right click it. If you pick field format, you get a date/time formatting dialog box. This enables you to format the date and/or time to your exact specifications. This uses the same concept of a mask or code to apply to the data.

Hiding Sections and Pagination

You can also format entire sections of data in ReportSmith. By choosing Format | Section you can choose to hide or display each section in the report as well as how the pagination occurs (as shown in Figure 16.28).

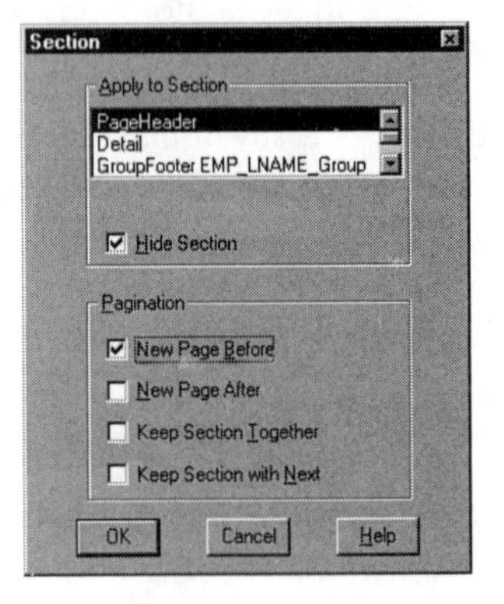

Figure 16.28.
Section dialog box.

One of the especially useful items is selecting New Page After for a group section. This would be used if you were generating a sales report grouped by salesperson. By choosing New Page After you would be generating a new page after each salesperson's report group was printed. This would give you an individual sheet to give to each employee, so they would understand their sales figures.

Alignment Palette

The Alignment palette is available to help you get that report layout just perfect. When you choose Tools | Alignment you get the floating alignment toolbar. This toolbar offers a number of ways for you to align objects in your report.

The VCL Control (Using ReportSmith with Delphi 2)

The ReportSmith VCL component provides a simple-to-use interface between Delphi 2 and ReportSmith. The Report VC is found on the Data Access Tab on the VCL toolbar. By placing the Visual Component on your form, you now have direct access to ReportSmith. Look at the property sheet in Figure 16.29, to get an idea of some of the things you can do.

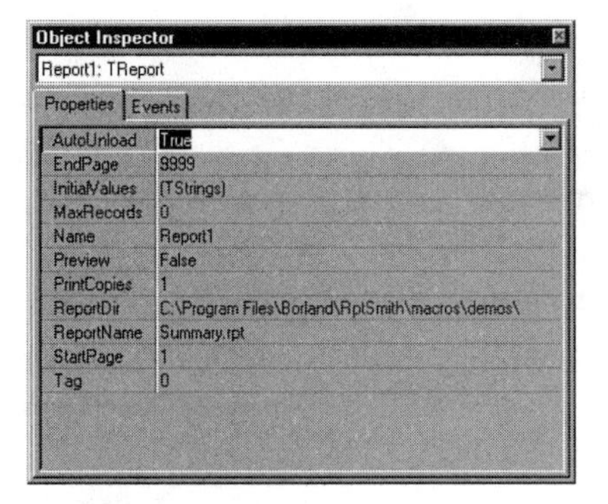

Figure 16.29.
Object Inspector's Properties tab for Report Visual Component.

You can either set the properties for the Report Visual Component at design time by using the Object Inspector or at runtime using Delphi code statements. The properties are

- `AutoUnLoad`—If this set to `True`, ReportSmith runtime removes itself from memory after running the specified report. If set to `False`, then it stays in memory. You might want ReportSmith runtime to remain in memory if you think the user is going to run a number of reports, and you want the reports to come up fast. If you think the user will only run one report, you might want to set this property to `True`, and free up valuable memory. If you do not unload the runtime, you should call the `CloseApplication` method at the end of your report printing to unload the ReportSmith runtime.
- `EndPage`—This is the last page of the report that you want to print. This is usually left at 9999 so that all pages are printed. For huge reports, this allows you to give a sample printing to the customer without all 10,000 pages being printed (save a tree).
- `InitialValues`—This property allows you to create and set the value of ReportSmith report variables. You could create a variable called `Employee_ID` and feed a value for this variable to the ReportSmith runtime. The report could then pick this value up and use it as part of some data selection criteria.
- `MaxRecords`—This tells the ReportSmith runtime the maximum number of records to use in report generation. This allows you to keep your report from picking all three million records in your customer's database and subsequently taking all day to generate one report.
- `Name`—This is the name of the VC object on your form. The default name for the first instance is Report1.
- `Preview`—Set this to `True` if you want the user to preview the report in a window prior to printing. If this is set to `False`, the ReportSmith runtime sends the report to the printer immediately upon creating the report.

- `PrintCopies`—Determines the number of copies of the report sent to the printer.
- `ReportDir`—This is a reference to the directory in which the report file(s) reside.
- `ReportName`—This is the name of the report file that you want the ReportSmith runtime to execute.
- `StartPage`—You can alter the page the ReportSmith runtime starts with. This is usually left at 1.
- `Tag`—The tag field has no particular meaning to ReportSmith. See the Delphi documentation for uses of this property.

If you want to set these properties in code instead of visually, you can certainly do so. Here is how you would access the Report Visual Component programmatically.

```
Begin
  Report1.AutoUnLoad := FALSE;
  Report1.REportDir := "c:\temp";
  Report1.ReportName := "MyReport.Rpt";
  Report1.InitialValues.Add('@MyRptVar1=<3>');
  Report1.InitialValues.Add('@MyRptVar2=<test>');
  Report1.StartPage := 2;
  Report1.EndPage := 5;
  Report1.Preview := TRUE;
  Report1.Printcopies := 3;
  Report1.MaxRecords := 1000;
  Report1.Run;
  Report1.CloseApplication
end;
```

No matter how you set the properties, the result is the same. Notice how we use the `Add` method for the `InitialValues` property to add values. This could also be done by clicking the property in the Object Inspector and bringing up the string list editor. The Report visual component is a fast and easy way to access ReportSmith from within Delphi 2.

Runtime ReportSmith Viewer

ReportSmith provides a runtime viewer for ReportSmith reports. This viewer may be distributed with your reports as well as part of your Delphi 2 applications containing reports. If you use the InstallShield Express that comes with Delphi 2, the ReportSmith runtime viewer is made part of your distribution disks if you include reporting capability in your application.

Customizing With ReportBasic

Although ReportSmith has many items that can be adjusted from the menuing system, there are still many operations that can only be performed programmatically. Borland has provided ReportBasic as the mechanism to customize ReportSmith's behavior. ReportBasic is a

full-featured language that provides expression operators, data types including arrays, and even trappable errors.

You can create macros using the ReportBasic language and embed them in your report. These macros can then be called from within your report at runtime. The language is very similar to Visual Basic. The ReportBasic command reference is a book in itself, and we could not cover the material here. Please refer to the ReportSmith documentation for assistance with ReportBasic.

Quick Report

As you have seen, ReportSmith provides an incredible amount of functionality. The only shortcoming (if you could even call it that) is that ReportSmith requires extra files present in order for it to work. It also requires some memory and other system resources to do its job.

Borland has realized that ReportSmith may be overkill for your particular needs. You may only need a simple, one-page columnar report. Quick Report to the rescue!

Components

Quick Report offers a number of native Delphi components that allow you to create fairly complex reports without the need for external tools. Quick Report works on the premise of report banding. In our ReportSmith reports, we had report, page and section headers and footers, as well as detail sections. Each one of these could really be considered bands. Quick Report provides a QRBand component that can act as any type of band.

Here is a brief overview of each visual component and what its function is:

- `TQuickReport`—This is the master control mechanism for the entire report. Every report must have one of these VCs on them. This item must have a DataSource component from which to get its data.
- `TQRPrinter`—A low-level print object that has some cool features like a print preview function.
- `TQRBand`—This is the banding component mentioned earlier. By adjusting its `BandType` property, it can become a header, footer, detail section, or any number of other section types.
- `QTRGroup`—This component is how you create a group using Quick Report. Remember in ReportSmith you used the Report Grouping functions; this component is Quick Reports equivalent function. You can create groups, then use a `TQRBand` to create a summary band or to total data.
- `QTRLabel`—This is how you place text on a band.

- `TQRDBText`—This is used to add a database field to your report. It is a data-aware control that hooks to your DataSource.
- `TQRDBCalc`—This component allows you to perform simple calculations on fields in your database such as summing and counting. This is where you get the summary fields to put into your summary band.
- `TQRShape`—This component allows you to draw basic shapes on your reports.
- `TQRSysData`—This is similar to the System Variables function found in ReportSmith. You can print out things like time, date, page numbers, and so on.
- `TQRPreview`—This component is what allows you to preview your report prior to printing. You do not have to use this component if you are only printing. This component is simply a window to your report. Stretch it out in a form and that component becomes the preview window. Very nice!

Sample Applications

If you open the demo.dpr project file located in the QuickRpt directory, you can see the true power of the dark side of the force. Just kidding. This demo is really cool, and shows you all the different report combinations. See Figure 16.30 for the demo example.

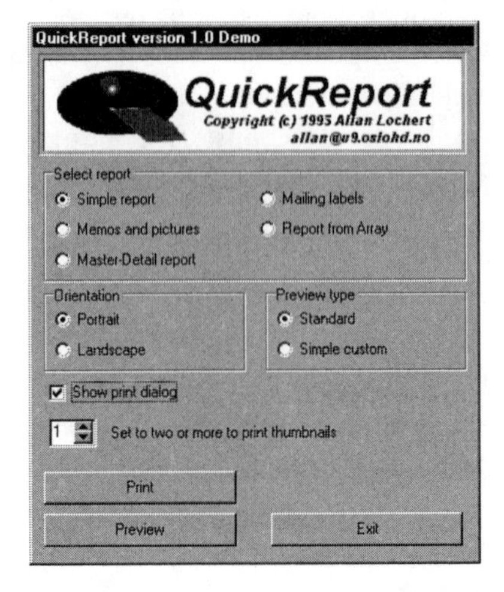

Figure 16.30.
Quick Report demo application.

Take some time to look through and dissect the application to see how it calls the different reports. It is a fascinating add-on to Delphi 2.

Summary

In this chapter you have learned how ReportSmith's functionality accents Delphi's. You have gone over how ReportSmith can attach to multiple database types, how you can use the Report Query dialog box to set up your entire report, and how (if you feel brave) you can enter your own SQL statements and directly manipulate the data. We have talked about formatting your report to make it look its best, how to add graphs to your reports to make them look snazzier, and relaying information in a more meaningful way to the end user.

Just as important as using ReportSmith, you have seen how the ReportSmith VCL component allows you to integrate the functionality of ReportSmith into Delphi in a seamless fashion. Lastly, we have discussed the concept of views (as they apply to ReportSmith), and the benefits they provide. I hope this chapter has helped you to realize the potential of ReportSmith and the benefits that it can provide. Remember though, that the best way to learn is to play with ReportSmith and Quick Reports. Tear apart the sample reports to see what makes them tick. Experimentation is the key to knowledge!

Q&A

Q Why did Borland include both ReportSmith and Quick Report? Isn't that overkill?

A Not really. Both products offer different functionality at different levels. Quick Report has less sophistication, but at a much smaller footprint. ReportSmith, on the other hand, does everything for a price. We need both.

Q I know what I need in my report, but I can't visualize the design. Is this normal?

A Yes! Most people have a tough time generating reports that make sense to others. The best way to create reports is by working with your customer for specifics. It may take time. Many customers require frequent revisions to the report style until it is right.

Workshop

Quiz

1. What is the main purpose of summary bands in Quick Report? What is the ReportSmith equivalent?
2. Can reports be run outside the Delphi environment without the ReportSmith development environment? If yes, how?
3. Why does ReportBasic exist in ReportSmith? What function does it serve?

Exercises

1. Create a simple report using ReportSmith. Re-create the same report in your application using Quick Report. Take note of the differences between the methods for each. This may help you draw a conclusion as to which tool you prefer, if any.
2. Create a report that utilizes all three header/footer types (report, page, and group). You will need to create a simple report grouping first. Try adding summary fields to the group and report footers, and get some totals for data. You will need to use one of the data sources that has numerical data in it, so you have something to total.

Week 3

Day 17

Printing

Printing is today's topic. Although we increasingly live in an electronic world in which we send faxes and e-mail and use computers for slide presentations, there always comes a time where you must print out text or graphics from a program, such as the one that generates form letters and customized flyers.

As you learn about printing, you will not use ReportSmith. You will learn two ways to print directly from Delphi programs, which can save on overhead if you do not need the features of a report writer or another printing add-on. You will learn about the basic printing methods, in which you send one line or string of text at a time to the printer, as with a simple DOS-based program in Pascal. This chapter also examines the printer objects available in Delphi. Using the printer object, you can print text. You will see how to use the printer dialog boxes and how to print graphics. This chapter covers all the basic information that you need to know to add full print capabilities to your applications without the need for add-ons, report generators, and so on.

Basic Printing with Pascal

If you are familiar with printing in Pascal or other languages, this is nothing new. Basic printing simply involves creating a file variable, which you learned about on Day 12, "File Input/Output," and assigning it to the printer. Then you use a `writeln` statement to send the text to the printer. This type of printing is primitive compared to all the features built into Windows, but you occasionally might want to print this way. Suppose, for example, that a computer is hooked up to a line printer for the purpose of saving readings as they are gathered in a factory. If the computer has a hardware failure, all the readings gathered up to that point are on the printout. Likewise, you might want to print a simple list that does not require graphics, fonts, and other formatting available in Windows. The following code uses a `writeln` statement to print:

```
var
  P : TextFile;
begin
   AssignPrn(P);
   rewrite(P);
   writeln(P,'This is a test of printing');
   -CloseFile(P);
end;
```

As you can see, a variable called `P` of type `TextFile` is declared. A variation of `Assign` is used here: `AssignPrn`. It assigns the variable to the printer port, treating like a file. Next, the printer port must be opened, so `rewrite` is used. Text is sent out to the printer with the `writeln` procedure, and the printer port is closed with `CloseFile`. It is important to close the printer port to complete the operation. Any text left in memory is sent to the printer, and the port is closed—just like a file.

To see how this works, create a program for selecting a text file and sending it to the printer. Add two buttons, an `OpenDialog` component and a label to the form. Use the `OpenDialog` filter property to add a .txt filter. Look at Figure 17.1 as you design the screen. Then fill in the code that refers to Listing 17.1. Save the project as FILE2PRN.DPR and the unit to FILEPRN.PAS.

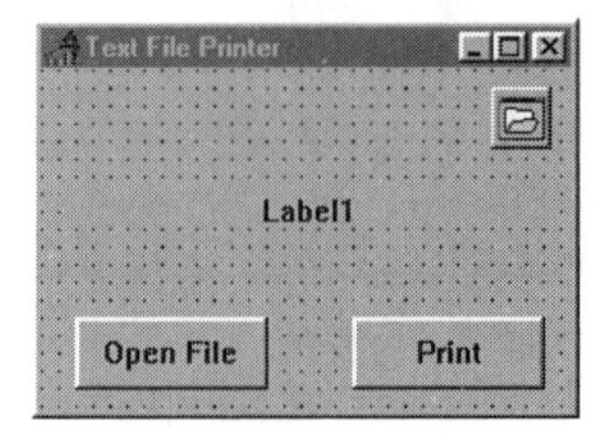

Figure 17.1.
Text file transfer—FILE2PRN.DPR.

You need to add `Printers` to the uses statement to have access to the printer functions.

TYPE Listing 17.1. Text file printer.

```
unit Fileprn;

interface

uses
 Windows, Messages, SysUtils, Classes, Graphics, Controls, Forms, Dialogs,
StdCtrls,Printers;

type
  TForm1 = class(TForm)
    Button1: TButton;
    OpenDialog1: TOpenDialog;
    Button2: TButton;
    Label1: TLabel;
    procedure Button1Click(Sender: TObject);
    procedure Button2Click(Sender: TObject);
  private
    { Private declarations }
  public
    { Public declarations }
  end;

var
  Form1: TForm1;

implementation

{$R *.DFM}
Var
   Fname : String;

procedure TForm1.Button1Click(Sender: TObject);
begin
  if OpenDialog1.Execute then
  begin
    Fname:=OpenDialog1.FileName;
    Label1.Caption:='Ready to print ' + Fname;
  end;
end;

procedure TForm1.Button2Click(Sender: TObject);
Var
   P,F : TextFile;
   TempStr : String;
begin
```

continues

Listing 17.1. continued

```
    AssignFile(F,Fname);
    Reset;
    AssignPrn(P);
    Rewrite(P);
    Label1.Caption:='Now Printing '+ Fname;
    While Not Eof(F) Do
    begin
         Readln(F,TempStr);
         Writeln(P,TempStr);
    end;
    CloseFile;
    CloseFile(P);
    Label1.Caption:='Printing Complete!';
end;

end.
```

This program enables you to use the File Open dialog box to choose a file for printing. It reads the file one line at a time and sends each line to the printer. Give it a try by printing some text files.

Printing with Delphi's TPrinter Object

It is not possible to go through all the printer object properties, methods, and so on. This section, though, develops a few programs that demonstrate the printer object's use. You will see how to add printer capabilities to your applications.

In Delphi, you use the `TPrinter` object to access the Windows printer interface. Delphi's `Printers` unit contains the `Printer` variable, which is declared as an instance of the `TPrinter` object:

```
Printer : TPrinter;
```

To use the `TPrinter` object, you must add the `Printers` unit to the `uses` clause of your code. Unlike some of the other commonly used units, `Printers` is not added by Delphi.

```
uses
 Windows, Messages, SysUtils, Classes, Graphics, Controls, Forms, Dialogs,
StdCtrls,Printers;
```

Once you do this, you can use `Printer` to reference properties in the `TPrinter` object.

Using the TPrinter Object

Before you can use the `TPrinter` object, you need to understand some properties and methods.

`Canvas`	Declared as an instance of the `TCanvas` object. The `Canvas` is where the page or document is built in memory before it is printed. The `Canvas` has properties, including `Pen` and `Brush`, that enable you to draw and put text on it.
`TextOut`	A method of the `TCanvas` object, it enables text to be sent to the `Canvas`.
`BeginDoc`	Used to start a print job.
`EndDoc`	Used to end a print job. Actual printing does not occur until a call to `EndDoc` is made.
`PageHeight`	Returns the page height in pixels.
`NewPage`	Forces a new page on the printer and resets the `Pen` property value of the Canvas back to (0, 0).
`PageNumber`	Returns the number of the page currently being printed.

Suppose, for example, that you want to print text using the printer object. You might have code that looks like

```
Printer.BeginDoc;
Printer.Canvas.TextOut(10,10,'I am printing through the printer object');
Printer.EndDoc;
```

This code causes the text `I am printing through the printer object` to be printed starting at the tenth pixel to the right and the tenth pixel down on the canvas. `BeginDoc` starts the print job. The text is sent to the canvas with `Canvas TextOut` property. `EndDoc` causes the text to be printed and ends the print job.

These properties and methods only scratch the surface of what is available, but they are enough to create the file printing program that you wrote earlier with the printer object. Load the FILE2PRN.DPR project, and resave it as FILE2POB.DPR. Resave the unit as FILEPOBJ.PAS. Edit the code in the Print button—in this case, Button2. The program reads the file one line at a time as before, but it now calculates the position on the canvas to which the text should be sent and puts it on the canvas to be printed. Listing 17.2 shows the revised File Print program. The comments will help you understand the code. If you made a copy of the old file to FILEOBJ.PAS, modify the code in the print button (Button2)so that it looks like the code in Listing 17.2. You can change the `Caption` property if you want to read `Text File Printer using the TPrinter Object.`

TYPE **Listing 17.2. Text file printer using the `TPrinter` object.**

```
unit Filepobj;

interface
```

continues

Listing 17.2. continued

```
uses
 Windows, Messages, SysUtils, Classes, Graphics, Controls, Forms, Dialogs,
 ➥StdCtrls,Printers;

type
  TForm1 = class(TForm)
    Button1: TButton;
    OpenDialog1: TOpenDialog;
    Button2: TButton;
    Label1: TLabel;
    procedure Button1Click(Sender: TObject);
    procedure Button2Click(Sender: TObject);
  private
    { Private declarations }
  public
    { Public declarations }
  end;

var
  Form1: TForm1;

implementation

{$R *.DFM}
Var
   Fname : String;

procedure TForm1.Button1Click(Sender: TObject);
begin
  if OpenDialog1.Execute then
  begin
    Fname:=OpenDialog1.FileName;
    Label1.Caption:='Ready to print ' + Fname;
  end;
end;

procedure TForm1.Button2Click(Sender: TObject);
Var
   F : TextFile;
   TempStr,PageNum : String;
   Ctr,x,PHeight,LineSpace: Integer;
begin
   Ctr:=1;
   {Open the text file to be printed}
   AssignFile(F,Fname);
   Reset;
   {Start printing}
   Printer.BeginDoc;
   {Get the Page Height}
   PHeight:=Printer.PageHeight;
   {Calculate distance to space lines based on a 60 line page}
   LineSpace:=PHeight DIV 60;
   {Get the current page being printed}
   PageNum:=IntToStr(Printer.PageNumber);
```

```
    {Update label with current page number}
    Label1.Caption:='Now Printing '+ Fname + ' Page ' + PageNum;
    While Not Eof Do
    begin
         {Read a line of text from the text file into TempStr}
         Readln(F,TempStr);
         {Send the contents of TempStr to the printer}
         Printer.Canvas.TextOut(0,x,TempStr);
         {Increment x the appropriate number of pixels to print the next line }
         x:=x+LineSpace;
         {Count the number of lines printed}
         Ctr:=Ctr+1;
         {If 60 lines have been printed, start a new page, get page number and
          and reset our counters}
         If Ctr > 59 then
         begin
             Printer.NewPage;
             x:=0;
             Ctr:=0;
             PageNum:=IntToStr(Printer.PageNumber);
             Label1.Caption:='Now Printing '+ Fname + ' Page ' + PageNum;
         end;
    end;
    {Close the text file and cause the job to print}
    CloseFile;
    Printer.EndDoc;
    Label1.Caption:='Printing Complete!' + ' Pages printed = '+ PageNum;
end;

end.
```


Make sure that you save your work before you test the new version of the text file printer. The program behaves much as before, except that it is now printing through the printer object. There are also a few changes to the status messages.

This method of printing enables you to add graphics to a document easily. You can also add code to change the page orientation, font sizes, styles, and much more. You get this extra capability without having to write much code. You simply tell the printer object what to print and how it should be printed.

Using the `TPrinterDialog` and `TPrinterSetupDialog` Components

You have seen commercial applications in which dialog boxes are used to choose the print options, such as the number of copies, collating, and the page orientation. In Windows with Delphi, it does not take much to do those things. Just put the TPrinterDialog component on the page and add a few lines of code. Your application now has printer dialog boxes for the user. The code that activates this looks like

```
if PrintDialog1.Execute then
   Begin
       {your print code}
  end;
```

When this code is executed, the standard Windows Print dialog box appears, giving the user choices for the pending print job. After the user makes his choices, the print job is completed by using the specified settings—except for the number of copies, which requires a loop. For the most part, it is as simple as that.

To see how this works, modify the file print program to enable Print Dialog support. Make a copy of the previous version by saving it to new filenames. First, load FILE2POB.DPR. Select Save Project As... and name it PRINTDLG.DPR. Select Save File As... and name it PRNDLG.PAS. Once you make a few simple changes, you can test the Print Dialog features. From the Dialogs tab, select the PrintDialog component and drop it on the form. Modify the code in the Print button to look like the code in Listing 17.3.

TYPE **Listing 17.3. Adding Print Dialog support.**

```
Var
   F : TextFile;
   TempStr,PageNum : String;
   Ctr,x,PHeight,LineSpace: Integer;
begin
   Ctr:=1;
   {Open the text file to be printed}
   AssignFile(F,Fname);
   Reset(F);
   if PrintDialog1.Execute then
   Begin
     {Start printing}
     Printer.BeginDoc;
     {Get the Page Height}
     PHeight:=Printer.PageHeight;
     {Calculate distance to space lines based on a 60 line page}
     LineSpace:=PHeight DIV 60;
     {Get the current page being printed}
     PageNum:=IntToStr(Printer.PageNumber);
     {Update label with current page number}
     Label1.Caption:='Now Printing '+ Fname + ' Page ' + PageNum;
     While Not Eof(F) Do
     begin
        {Read a line of text from the text file into TempStr}
        Readln(F,TempStr);
        {Send the contents of TempStr to the printer}
        Printer.Canvas.TextOut(0,x,TempStr);
```

```
        {Increment x the appropriate number of pixels to print the next line }
        x:=x+LineSpace;
        {Count the number of lines printed}
        Ctr:=Ctr+1;
        {If 60 lines have been printed, start a new page, get page number and
         and reset our counters}
        If Ctr > 59 then
        begin
            Printer.NewPage;
            x:=0;
            Ctr:=0;
            PageNum:=IntToStr(Printer.PageNumber);
            Label1.Caption:='Now Printing '+ Fname + ' Page ' + PageNum;
        end;
     end;
    {Close the text file and cause the job to print}
    CloseFile;
    Printer.EndDoc;
    Label1.Caption:='Printing Complete!' + ' Pages printed = '+ PageNum;
  end;
end;
```

17

The only difference from the previous program is the `if PrintDialog` and `begin...end` statements:

```
if PrintDialog1.Execute then
begin
           {print code...}
end;
```

When you run the program and select print, the Print dialog box appears (see Figure 17.2). It waits for the user to make his choices before the job is printed. You can get to the Properties dialog box by pressing the Properties button (see Figure 17.3).

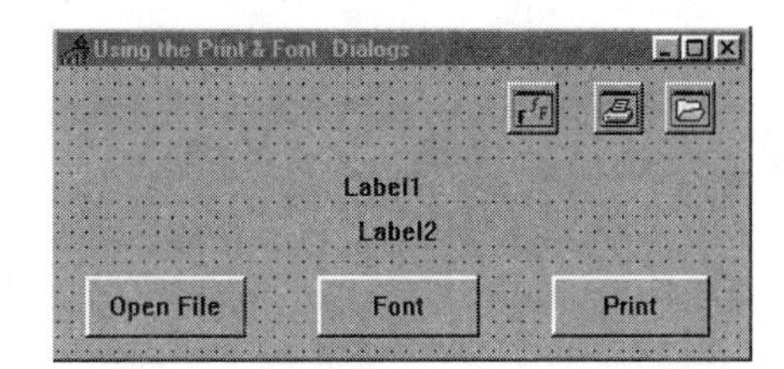

Figure 17.2.
The Print dialog box.

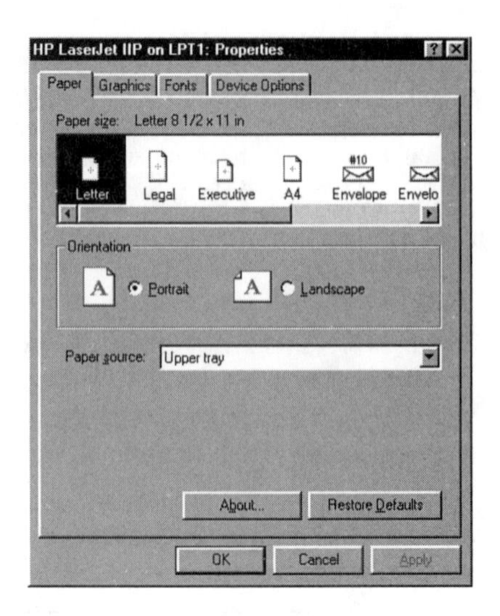

Figure 17.3.
The Properties dialog box.

Fonts and Font Sizes

Changing fonts and font sizes is easy, too. Suppose, for example, that you want to change the font size to 18 and the font to Times New Roman. The `Font` property of the canvas enables you to do just that. By adding the following lines of code to the print routine in your program, you can easily change the font to fit your needs:

```
{Set Font Size}
Printer.Canvas.Font.Size:=18;
{Set Font Type to Times Roman}
Printer.Canvas.Font.Name:='Times New Roman';
```

One problem remains, though. The original program was based on the default 10-point system font and assumed that there were 60 lines per page. When you change fonts and font sizes, the old code will not work so well. To eliminate this problem, add code that uses the font size to calculate how many lines can fit on a page. The following code, for example, adds 10 lines to the font size and calculates the `LinesPerPage` variable so that there is space between the lines when the `LineSpace` variable is calculated:

```
{Calculate the lines per page based on the font size}
LinesPerPage:=PHeight Div FontSize+10;
{Calculate distance to space lines based on the lines per page}
LineSpace:=PHeight DIV LinesPerPage;
```

The new variables that are added to accommodate these changes are `FontSize` and `LinesPerPage`. Add these changes to the Print button code. Make sure that the code looks like the code in Listing 17.4.

TYPE Listing 17.4. Print button code.

```
procedure TForm1.Button2Click(Sender: TObject);
Var
   F : TextFile;
   TempStr,PageNum : String;
   Ctr,x,PHeight,LineSpace,LinesPerPage,FontSize: Integer;
begin
   Ctr:=1;
   {Open the text file to be printed}
   AssignFile(F,Fname);
   Reset(F);
   if PrintDialog1.Execute then
   Begin
     {Start printing}
     Printer.BeginDoc;
     {Get the Page Height}
     PHeight:=Printer.PageHeight;
     {Set the Font to 18}
     Printer.Canvas.Font.Size:=18;
     {Set Font Type to Times Roman}
     Printer.Canvas.Font.Name:='Times New Roman';
     {Calculate the number of lines per page based on the font
      adding 10 to leave some room between lines}
     LinesPerPage:=PHeight Div FontSize+10;
     {Calculate distance to space lines based on the lines per page}
     LineSpace:=PHeight DIV LinesPerPage;
     {Get the current page being printed}
     PageNum:=IntToStr(Printer.PageNumber);
     {Update label with current page number}
     Label1.Caption:='Now Printing '+ Fname + ' Page ' + PageNum;
     While Not EofF Do
     begin
        {Read a line of text from the text file into TempStr}
        Readln(F,TempStr);
        {Send the contents of TempStr to the printer}
        Printer.Canvas.TextOut(0,x,TempStr);
        {Increment x the appropriate number of pixels to print the next line }
        x:=x+LineSpace;
        {Count the number of lines printed}
        Ctr:=Ctr+1;
        {If LinesPerPage have been printed, start a new page, get page number
         and reset our counters}
        If Ctr > LinesPerPage-1 then
        begin
            Printer.NewPage;
            x:=0;
            Ctr:=0;
            PageNum:=IntToStr(Printer.PageNumber);
            Label1.Caption:='Now Printing '+ Fname + ' Page ' + PageNum;
        end;
     end;
    {Close the text file and cause the job to print}
    CloseFile;
    Printer.EndDoc;
```

continues

17

Listing 17.4. continued

```
    Label1.Caption:='Printing Complete!' + ' Pages printed = '+ PageNum;
  end;
end;
```

Save your code and try it out. The program prints text files in 18 point Times New Roman, calculates the number of lines of text that can be printed on a page, and starts a new page at the appropriate place. Using this technique, you can allow the user to choose the font by means of a Font dialog box. You get the font information from the user, instead of hard coding it in the program as you do here. Finish up this program by adding the Font dialog box to enable the user to select the font, the font size, the font style, and so on. Add a new button called Font. Likewise, add code to enable the program to print the number of copies selected by the user.

To change the font settings, you can use the `Font` property and its properties to get information from the Font dialog box and to apply it to the canvas. `Printer.Canvas.Font.Size:=FontDialog1.Font.Size;` sets the font size from the Font dialog box settings. `Printer.Canvas.Font.Name:='Times New Roman';` sets the font to Times New Roman. `Printer.Canvas.Font.Type:=FontDialog1.Font.Type;` sets the type from the Font dialog box.

For the number of copies, you must create a loop that encompasses the print code and executes it the number of times specified by the user. To get the number of copies specified by the user, do the following:. `NumCopies:=PrintDialog1.Copies`. The number of copies are stored in Variable, `NumCopies` for later use.

To make these changes, modify the code in the Print button so that it looks like the code in Listing 17.5. Add a second label to the form just below Label1. Pay close attention to the code, for some lines have been moved to make the loops work properly. The comments are useful.

TYPE **Listing 17.5. Print button with font and number of copies code.**

```
procedure TForm1.Button2Click(Sender: TObject);
Var
   F : TextFile;
   TempStr,PageNum : String;
   Ctr,x,PHeight,LineSpace,LinesPerPage,FontSize,CopyNum,NumCopies: Integer;
begin
   if PrintDialog1.Execute then
   Begin
     Ctr:=1;
     {Open the text file to be printed}
     AssignFile(F,Fname);
     {Get the number of copies to print from the Print Dialog}
```

```
      NumCopies:=PrintDialog1.Copies;
      {Loop through and print for each copy to be printed}
      for CopyNum:=1 to NumCopies do
      begin
        {Open file at beginning}
        Reset(F);
        {Clear the counters for next pass}
        x:=0;Ctr:=0;
        {Start printing}
        Printer.BeginDoc;
        {Get the Page Height}
        PHeight:=Printer.PageHeight;
        {Set the Font size from the Font Dialog}
        Printer.Canvas.Font.Size:=FontDialog1.Font.Size;
        {Set the font name from the Font Dialog}
        Printer.Canvas.Font.Name:=FontDialog1.Font.Name;
        {Set the font style from the Font Dialog}
        Printer.Canvas.Font.Style:=FontDialog1.Font.Style;
        {Calculate the number of lines per page based on the font
        adding 10 to leave some room between lines}
        LinesPerPage:=PHeight Div FontSize+10;
        {Calculate distance to space lines based on the lines per page}
        LineSpace:=PHeight DIV LinesPerPage;
        {Get the current page being printed}
        PageNum:=IntToStr(Printer.PageNumber);
        {Update label with current page number}
        Label1.Caption:='Now Printing '+ Fname + ' Page ' + PageNum;
        While Not Eof(F) Do
          begin
           {Read a line of text from the text file into TempStr}
           Readln(F,TempStr);
           {Send the contents of TempStr to the printer}
           Printer.Canvas.TextOut(0,x,TempStr);
           {Increment x the appropriate number of pixels to print the next line }
           x:=x+LineSpace;
           {Count the number of lines printed}
           Ctr:=Ctr+1;
           {If LinesPerPage have been printed, start a new page, get page number
            and reset our counters}
           If Ctr > LinesPerPage-1 then
           begin
               Printer.NewPage;
               x:=0;
               Ctr:=0;
               PageNum:=IntToStr(Printer.PageNumber);
               Label1.Caption:='Now Printing '+ Fname + ' Page ' + PageNum;
           end;
          end;
        {Close the text file and cause the job to print}
        CloseFile;
        Printer.EndDoc;
        Label1.Caption:='Printing Complete!' + ' Pages printed = '+ PageNum;
        Label2.Caption:='Number of Copies = ' + IntToStr(NumCopies);
      end;
    end;
end;
```

17

These changes read the settings from the Font dialog box, shown in Figure 17.4, and use them for the print job. The print job is printed the number of times specified by the user in the Print dialog box.

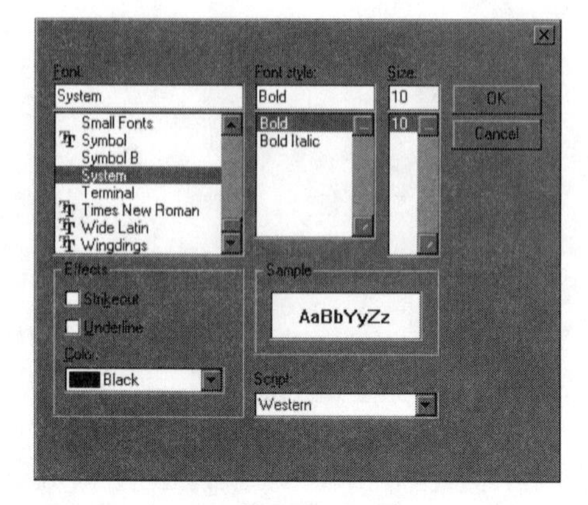

Figure 17.4.
The Font dialog box.

You can look over the properties that are available to you by using the online help. When you have made the changes to the program, it should look the code in Listing 17.6.

TYPE Listing 17.6. Using the Print and Font dialog boxes.

```
unit Prndlg;

interface

uses
 Windows, Messages, SysUtils, Classes, Graphics, Controls, Forms, Dialogs,
 ➥StdCtrls,Printers;

type
  TForm1 = class(TForm)
    Button1: TButton;
    OpenDialog1: TOpenDialog;
    Button2: TButton;
    Label1: TLabel;
    PrintDialog1: TPrintDialog;
    FontDialog1: TFontDialog;
    Button3: TButton;
    Label2: TLabel;
    procedure Button1Click(Sender: TObject);
    procedure Button2Click(Sender: TObject);
    procedure Button3Click(Sender: TObject);
  private
    { Private declarations }
  public
    { Public declarations }
  end;
```

```
var
  Form1: TForm1;

implementation

{$R *.DFM}
Var
   Fname : String;

procedure TForm1.Button1Click(Sender: TObject);
begin
  if OpenDialog1.Execute then
  begin
    Fname:=OpenDialog1.FileName;
    Label1.Caption:='Ready to print ' + Fname;
  end;
end;

procedure TForm1.Button2Click(Sender: TObject);
Var
   F : TextFile;
   TempStr,PageNum : String;
   Ctr,x,PHeight,LineSpace,LinesPerPage,FontSize,CopyNum,NumCopies: Integer;
begin
   if PrintDialog1.Execute then
   Begin
     Ctr:=1;
     {Open the text file to be printed}
     AssignFile(F,Fname);
     {Get the number of copies to print from the Print Dialog}
     NumCopies:=PrintDialog1.Copies;
     {Loop through and print for each copy to be printed}
     for CopyNum:=1 to NumCopies do
     begin
       {Open file at beginning}
       Reset(F);
       {Clear the counters for next pass}
       x:=0;Ctr:=0;
       {Start printing}
       Printer.BeginDoc;
       {Get the Page Height}
       PHeight:=Printer.PageHeight;
       {Set the Font size from the Font Dialog}
       Printer.Canvas.Font.Size:=FontDialog1.Font.Size;
       {Set the font name from the Font Dialog}
       Printer.Canvas.Font.Name:=FontDialog1.Font.Name;
       {Set the font style from the Font Dialog}
       Printer.Canvas.Font.Style:=FontDialog1.Font.Style;
       {Calculate the number of lines per page based on the font
       adding 10 to leave some room between lines}
       LinesPerPage:=PHeight Div FontSize+10;
       {Calculate distance to space lines based on the lines per page}
       LineSpace:=PHeight DIV LinesPerPage;
       {Get the current page being printed}
       PageNum:=IntToStr(Printer.PageNumber);
       {Update label with current page number}
```

17

continues

Listing 17.6. continued

```
          Label1.Caption:='Now Printing '+ Fname + ' Page ' + PageNum;
          While Not Eof Do
            begin
             {Read a line of text from the text file into TempStr}
             Readln(F,TempStr);
             {Send the contents of TempStr to the printer}
             Printer.Canvas.TextOut(0,x,TempStr);
             {Increment x the appropriate number of pixels to print the next line }
             x:=x+LineSpace;
             {Count the number of lines printed}
             Ctr:=Ctr+1;
             {If LinesPerPage have been printed, start a new page, get page number
              and reset our counters}
             If Ctr > LinesPerPage-1 then
             begin
                 Printer.NewPage;
                 x:=0;
                 Ctr:=0;
                 PageNum:=IntToStr(Printer.PageNumber);
                 Label1.Caption:='Now Printing '+ Fname + ' Page ' + PageNum;
             end;
            end;
          {Close the text file and cause the job to print}
          CloseFile(F);
          Printer.EndDoc;
          Label1.Caption:='Printing Complete!' + ' Pages printed = '+ PageNum;
          Label2.Caption:='Number of Copies = ' + IntToStr(NumCopies);
        end;
      end;
   end;
   procedure TForm1.Button3Click(Sender: TObject);
   begin
        FontDialog1.Execute;
   end;

   end.
```

ANALYSIS The code in Listing 17.6 enables the user to select a file to be printed via a Windows Open dialog box. The Font button enables user selection of the font to be used when printed via the standard Windows Font dialog box. Next, the Print button displays the standard Windows Print dialog box enabling access to all the features usually found there. As you can see, the majority of the code is found in the Print Button OnClick event.

The final program form should look like Figure 17.5.

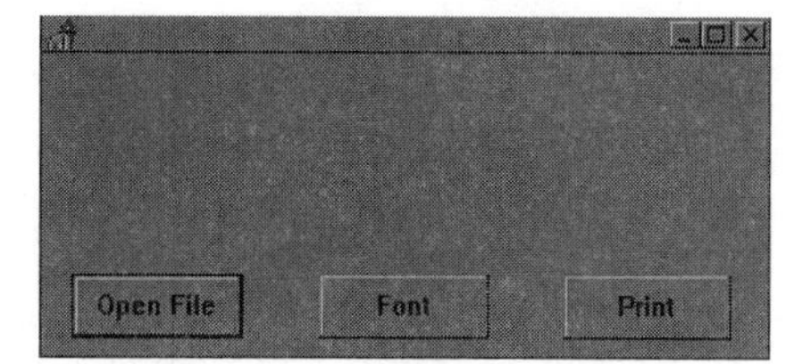

Figure 17.5.
The Printer Object, Print, and Font dialog box.

Sending Graphics to the Printer

You have printed text using the old-fashioned method, and you have sent text through the `TPrinter` object. What about graphics? You might want to create logos, charts, and other nontext information. This section shows you how to create just about any printed graphic. You are limited only by the type of the printer that you are using.

Sending graphics to the printer is about the same as sending it to the screen. You use the `TPrinter` object's `Canvas` and its properties and methods to draw or place graphics on the canvas. In fact, you can design graphics by first sending them to the screen. When you know what they will look like, modify the code to send them to the printer.

Consider the following code, for example. It draws a circle on the surface of Form1 in the upper left corner.

```
begin
     {Set the width of the pen to be 5 pixels wide}
     Form1.Canvas.Pen.Width:=5;
     {Draw an ellipse with the upper left corner at 0,0
      and the lower right corner at 200,200}
     Form1.Canvas.Ellipse(0, 0, 200, 200);
end;
```

This code draws the same circle in the same location on the printer canvas and sends it to the printer:

```
begin
     {Start the print job}
     Printer.BeginDoc;
     {Set the width of the pen to be 5 pixels wide}
     Printer.Canvas.Pen.Width:=5;
     {Draw an ellipse with the upper left corner at 0,0
      and the lower right corner at 200,200}
     Printer.Canvas.Ellipse(0, 0, 200, 200);
     {complete and print the print job}
     Printer.EndDoc;
end;
```

By adding the `BeginDoc` and `EndDoc` lines and by changing `Form1` to `Printer` to point to the printer `canvas` instead of the form `canvas`, you can send the same graphics to the printer. You can create a small program with a Screen button and a Printer button to test this code.

Day 10, "Introduction to Graphics," discussed pixels, pens, and brushes and drawing shapes with `Ellipse`, `LineTo`, and `Rectangle`. You can apply what you learned about graphics to the printer canvas. You can send almost any graphic to the printer as easily as you can to the screen.

Now create a program that enables the user to use a File Open dialog box to select a graphics file—such as a bitmap (.bmp) or Windows metafile (.wmf)—to display it on the screen, and to send it to the printer. Delphi makes this task easy. You use an image component to store the graphic on the screen and the `CopyRect` method to move the image to the printer canvas, which sends the image to the printer. In this program, you will enable the user to select a divisor for changing the size of the finished printout. You also add code to print the graphic in the center of the page.

First, create the form shown in Figure 17.6 with the following components:

2 buttons
1 image component
1 OpenDialog component
1 panel
2 labels
1 SpinEdit component from the Samples tab

Create a new project. Call it PRINTPIC.DPR, and call the unit PICPRINT.PAS. Lay out the form as shown in Figure 17.6. Change the caption of the form to Image Printer. Change the button captions to Load Picture and Print. Add filters to the OpenDialog component for graphics files (.bmp and .wmf) and all files. For the SpinEdit component, set `MinValue` to 1 and `MaxValue` to 10. Change the Label1 caption to Size Divisor and Label2 caption to Graphic Area. Change the `Image1.Stretch` property to True so that the image is resized to fit in the image box, if possible, when it is loaded. Likewise, make sure that the `AutoSize` property is set to False.

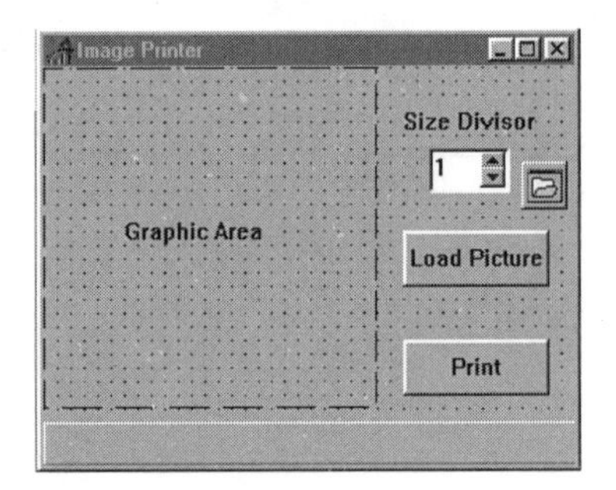

Figure 17.6.
The Image Printer form.

NOTE

When you place the image box on the form, make it a reasonably sized square on the form and position it so that its `Top` and `Left` properties are both set to 0. If you have trouble, set them to 0 in the Object Inspector; the box will snap into position. The positioning is important.

To load the image, execute the `LoadFromFile` method for the image box that you placed on the form. In this case, feed the filename from `OpenDialog` as a parameter to the `LoadFromFile` method. The image is loaded and displayed.

```
If OpenDialog1.Execute then
        Image1.Picture.LoadFromFile(OpenDialog1.FileName);
```


To print the image, you need to know where the center of the canvas is so that we can place the image in the center. The following code gets the center *x,y*-coordinates by gettting the printer page height and width then by dividing the height and width by 2. It then stores the values in the `CenterX` and `CenterY` variables.

```
{Find Center on the Canvas}
     PHeight:=Printer.PageHeight;
     PWidth:=Printer.PageWidth;
     CenterX:=PWidth Div 2;
     CenterY:=PHeight Div 2;
```

You calculate the placement coordinates based on the user input divisor. First, get the user input value from the `SpinEdit` control's `Value` property. To place the image, you need to know the *x,y*-coordinates of the Top,Left and Bottom,Right positions. The variables are shown in the following table:

Variable	*Position*
X1	Left
Y1	Top
X2	Right
Y2	Bottom

The following code calculates the center position based on the divisor selected by the user:

```
{Calculate center position with the user set size divisor}
     SDiv:=SpinEdit1.Value;
     X1:=CenterX-(PWidth Div (SDiv*2));
     Y1:=CenterY-(PHeight Div (SDiv*2));
     X2:=CenterX+(PWidth Div (SDiv*2));
     Y2:=CenterY+(PHeight Div (SDiv*2));
```

The user input divisor is multiplied by two. This product is then divided into the page width or height. This quotient is subtracted from or added to the `CenterX` and `CenterY` values to determine the center position. If the user selects the default divisor—1—the image is printed centered on the page, and it takes up the full page. If the printer page measures 2000 by 2000 pixels, the center position is 1000,1000. For example,

```
X1 = 1000 - (2000 Div (1*2))    or    X1 = 1000 - 1000    or    X1 = 0
```

This sets the X1 (Left) position to 0, which is the far left position on the page.

```
X2 = 1000 + (2000 Div (1*2))    or    X2 =  1000 + 1000    or    X2 = 2000
```

This sets the X2 (Right) position to 2000, which is the far right position.

This gives the settings for an image that takes up the full page. By changing the divisor, the user can reduce the size of the printed image. You use the `Div` operator for division because you are working with integers and want to avoid remainder values. With this formula, the image is always printed in the center of the page, regardless of the user input divisor.

To put the graphic on the printer canvas, you need to use the `CopyRect` method, which copies a rectangular area from one canvas to another.

```
procedure CopyRect(Dest: TRect; Canvas: TCanvas; Source: TRect);
```

The destination and source rectangles are passed as variables of type `Trect`. In this case, the source canvas is the canvas of Form1.

You position the image box at 0,0 because the `CopyRect` statement takes the image from the form canvas—not directly from the Image box. If you set the image box to 0,0 in the form client area, you do not have to worry about offsets in the calculations. If you move the image box to another location with no offset values calculated in, you might lose part or all of the of the image because it would be out of the rectangular area that you are copying.

Because `CopyRect` takes two variables of type `TRect`, you must declare two variables of this type and put the data in them. To declare the variables,

```
Var
       PrnRect, ImgRect : TRect;
```

`TRect` is defined as a record in the Windows unit as follows:

```
TRect = record
  case Integer of
    0: (Left, Top, Right, Bottom: Integer);
    1: (TopLeft, BottomRight: TPoint);
end;
```

You feed it four values. Next, you use the `Rect` function to store data in the new variables. The `Rect` function takes the `X1,Y1,X2,Y2`—or Top,Left,Right,Bottom—coordinates as parameters and returns the data as a record of type `TRect` to the variables. For example,

```
    {Store the desired Printer Canvas Rect Size in PrnRect}
    PrnRect:=Rect(X1,Y1,X2,Y2);
```

```
{Get the Image Box Canvas Rect Size in ImgRect}
ImgRect:=Rect(0,0,Image1.Width,Image1.Height);
```

Once you assign the values to `PrnRect` and `ImgRect`, use the variables in the `CopyRect` method statement to copy the image to the printer canvas:

```
{Copy the image from image box to printer canvas}
Printer.Canvas.CopyRect(PrnRect,Form1.Canvas,ImgRect );
```

With a few exceptions—such as hiding the label that marks the graphics area when the graphic is displayed and updating the panel with the program status—you now know how to make a working image printer. Listing 17.7 shows the completed code for the Image Printer program. Take some to study the comments. Input the code in the proper places and test the program.

TYPE **Listing 17.7. `Picprint`.**

```
unit Picprint;

interface

uses
 Windows, Messages, SysUtils, Classes, Graphics, Controls, Forms,
➥Dialogs,Printers,StdCtrls, ExtCtrls, Spin;

type
  TForm1 = class(TForm)
    Button1: TButton;
    Button2: TButton;
    OpenDialog1: TOpenDialog;
    Image1: TImage;
    SpinEdit1: TSpinEdit;
    Panel1: TPanel;
    Label1: TLabel;
    Label2: TLabel;
    procedure Button1Click(Sender: TObject);
    procedure Button2Click(Sender: TObject);
  private
    { Private declarations }
  public
    { Public declarations }
  end;

var
  Form1: TForm1;

implementation

{$R *.DFM}

Var
   PHeight,PWidth : Integer;
```

continues

Listing 17.7. continued

```
procedure TForm1.Button1Click(Sender: TObject);
Var
     PrnRect,ImgRect:TRect;
     CenterX,CenterY,X1,Y1,X2,Y2,SDiv : Integer;
begin
     Panel1.Caption:='Printing...';
     Printer.BeginDoc;
     {Find Center on the Canvas}
     PHeight:=Printer.PageHeight;
     PWidth:=Printer.PageWidth;
     CenterX:=PWidth Div 2;
     CenterY:=PHeight Div 2;
     {Calculate center position with the user set size divisor}
     SDiv:=SpinEdit1.Value;
     X1:=CenterX-(PWidth Div (SDiv*2));
     Y1:=CenterY-(PHeight Div (SDiv*2));
     X2:=CenterX+(PWidth Div (SDiv*2));
     Y2:=CenterY+(PHeight Div (SDiv*2));
     {Store the desired Printer Canvas Rect Size in PrnRect}
     PrnRect:=Rect(X1,Y1,X2,Y2);
     {Get the Image Box Canvas Rect Size in ImgRect}
     ImgRect:=Rect(0,0,Image1.Width,Image1.Height);
     {Copy the image from image box to printer canvas}
     Printer.Canvas.CopyRect(PrnRect,Form1.Canvas,ImgRect );
     Printer.EndDoc;
     Panel1.Caption:='Printing Complete!';
end;
procedure TForm1.Button2Click(Sender: TObject);
begin
     {Load a graphic to image box on Form}
     If OpenDialog1.Execute then
     begin
          Label2.Visible:=False;
          Image1.Picture.LoadFromFile(OpenDialog1.FileName);
     end;
end;

end.
```

ANALYSIS The code in Listing 17.7 allows the user to select an image file by clicking the Load Picture button. The picture is displayed in the form in the Image component. Next, the picture may be printed by clicking the Print button. When the Print button is clicked, the code copies the image from the form canvas and sends it to the printer.

At this point, you should be able to run the program, select a graphics image (bitmap or metafile), and display it on the screen. You can select a number from 1 to 10 for the size divisor and print the image. Your image is sized and centered on the page if everything has been set up correctly. Once you successfully load and print a few graphics files, pat yourself on the back for a job well done.

Summary

Today you learned about basic printing techniques, in which you treat the printer port as a file and use `writeln` statements to send text to the printer. To demonstrate this, you created a program that reads a text file and sends each line to the printer.

You also learned how to accomplish the same task by using the `TPrinter` object, which gives you the flexibility to change fonts, font sizes, and so on. You saw how to use the printer dialog boxes to enable users to make printing selections. You learned how to draw on the printer canvas as though you were drawing on the screen and to send it to the printer.

Finally, you learned how to load a graphics image onto the screen and to send it to the printer. Although this chapter covered only the basics of printing text and graphics, you can apply what you learned here to future projects in Delphi.

Q&A

Q I tried to print an icon using the Image Printer. Although it loaded, it will not properly size or center the screen or paper. Why?

A An icon, unlike a bitmap or metafile, is not a resizable graphic in the image box. The icon simply displays in the top left corner of the image box and prints the same way on the page. When you copied the rectangular image from the image box to the printer canvas, you took the size of the image box. The icon used only a portion of this space. The program is working properly; you just cannot see the image box that contains the icon. The image changes in size and moves towards the center when lager numbers are specified in the divisor.

Q What about printing with the API functions?

A You can use API functions to do printing, but the purpose of the Delphi Printer Object is to shield the user from the hassles of using the API calls. Using the printer object also makes your code more portable, because the API can change between versions of Windows.

Q How can I tell if my print job is printing?

A Use the `Printing` property of the `TPrinter` object. If `Printing` is set to True, the print job has been called with `BeginDoc` but `EndDoc` has not yet been called. The code might look like this:

```
If Printer.Printing then
    {your code here}
```

Q How can I abort a print job?

A By using the `Abort` method of the `TPrinter` object, you can add code to a button or your code to abort a print job. The following line of code causes the print job to abort:

```
Printer.Abort;
```

Workshop

Quiz

1. Do you need to use the Printer Object to send text to the printer?
2. To use the printer functions, what must you add in the interface section of the program?
3. Name the two important methods used to print with the Printer Object. (Hint: The print job cannot start or complete without them.)
4. Drawing on the printer canvas is much like drawing on a form canvas. True or False.
5. How do you activate the Print dialog box in your program? Show the code.
6. What code is used to activate the Properties dialog box?
7. What method is used to copy an image from the form canvas to the printer canvas?
8. How do you print a small circle or ellipse using the `TPrinter` object?

Exercises

1. Write a simple program that enables the user to input the name, street address, city, state, and zip code for the return address and the mailing address and to print them to fit on a standard letter-sized envelope. If your printer does not take envelopes, print the addresses on a sheet of paper. *Hint:* The Top,Left corner of the envelope is 0,0.
2. Modify the Image Printer program to enable the user to select among the center, top left, and lower right positions for printing the image.

Week 3

Day 18

OLE 2, A Primer

Introduction

One of the first things any beginning OLE 2 programmer should learn is the proper pronunciation of the technology. Because, as most of you know, it's better to look and sound like you know what you're doing than actually doing anything. So, when you're talking with colleagues never reference OLE 2.0 as "Oh El Eee 2." People will talk. The accepted pronunciation of OLE 2.0 is Olé 2. (Uttering this password could gain you free membership to the Geek of the Month Club.)

Microsoft Object Technology Strategy

To understand the importance of OLE, it might help to have an idea of how Microsoft views objects. This view dictates how Microsoft treats object-oriented technology and how it is integrated into the end-user products as well as programming and support tools. In talking about objects we will discuss two areas of interest: OOP and OOSS. Although we have discussed OOP in an earlier chapter, it is important to differentiate between OOP and OOSS even though they share a common ancestry. Although you are using a Borland product (Delphi 2.x), you must delve into what Microsoft has in store for the developer community because they lay the OLE foundation we all use. We will discuss how Delphi 2 has tapped into the power of OLE 2, and what that means to you.

Object-Oriented Programming (OOP): A Good and Necessary Step

Before discussing OOP, remember the Grady Booch definition of an object from *Software Engineering with Ada*: "an entity that has a state; that is, it has some value...the behavior of an object is defined by the actions it suffers and vice versa...every object is actually an instance of some class of objects." Because you have already read Day 7, we can assume you understand some the basic principles surrounding OOP.

The problem with OOP is that it defines a source code (programming language) standard. This means that the objects are dependent on both the language and the specific compiler. You may ask, "Why should I care?" Because there is an incredible dependency implied here. The "gotcha" is that the applications that interact with your newly upgraded application need to be recompiled and redistributed simultaneously with your new application. This may be realistic with three or four applications running on a single machine at a single site but is nearly impossible to accomplish if your software is on tens, hundreds, or thousands of systems in a distributed environment (networked). To make matters worse, consider that your new application may interact with applications from several other vendors, and you may not even have access to their code for recompilation.

Objective Oriented System Software (OOSS): A Better Second Step

There must be a way to achieve compatibility with other objects (preferably all) without having to worry about whether your object was written in C++, Ada, Delphi 2, or on Windows NT or Windows 3.1. Well, you're in luck. We give you the OOSS.

New Term Object-oriented system software defines a *binary* standard that defines how objects interact with each other. This accomplishes a great deal. Because the standard is a binary one, it assures that all objects created to the standard are able to interoperate freely, regardless of the operating system they run under, the language the object was written in, or the company that created the object.

This standard allows for the creation of what is termed *component software.* Component-based software development employees reuse components to develop new applications. Rather than inventing the functionality of Excel in your application, you use the functionality of Excel itself. By using many components from other applications, your role is more of an integrator rather than a programmer.

This addresses several critical needs.

- The need for a single, well-defined object model that promotes objects that can communicate between applications even if the applications are on different machines (distributed computing)
- The need to integrate components written by diverse companies in many languages in a smooth, seamless fashion
- The need to be able to upgrade a single object component without disturbing the operation of the distributed system.

So What's Your Point?

You may ask, "How is Microsoft going to help me achieve this state of object 'nerdvana'?" The following is the strategy that Microsoft is using for delivering object technology innovations:

- Deliver value today. OLE provides the foundation for component-based software. Microsoft is using, and will continue to use, OLE as its strategic object technology throughout its operating systems, development tools, and its end-user applications.
- Provide the most open solution. Microsoft will ensure that all future enhancements to OLE are published through the Open Process. The Open Process is a method whereby Microsoft distributes and discusses preliminary technology specifications with software architects, OEMs, hardware and software vendors, and corporate developers. This happens at least one year prior to the release of a new technology. These Open Process members can then provide feedback or alternative approaches to the problem and help to shape the end product into something that is as useful as possible. This also allows the participants early access to the technologies so their products can take full advantage of these new technologies when produced. This particular aspect allows companies like Borland to have a say in what future enhancements are out into OLE.
- Provide the most comprehensive cross-platform support. Microsoft has vowed to ensure that OLE works across multiple platforms and incorporates many of the market-driven standards.
- Protect existing customer investments. Many users and developers alike are afraid that their investment will be obsolete in just a few years (or less). Future versions of

Windows will provide extensive OLE services. Also, today's OLE applications will inherit tomorrow's capabilities.

All of Microsoft's product line supports OLE, including MS Office suite, as well as their programming languages.

The real bonus here (from my perspective) is that Borland can use this OLE base as a stepping stone to achieve the next level of consciousness. When you combine the solid code base of Microsoft with the proven creativity of Borland, the benefactor is you, the developer. The developer ends up with great tools on a solid base.

I hope that this introduction has given you a better feel for how Microsoft treats the world of objects and where they are going with it. Next, let's explore OLE in particular.

Prehistoric OLE (1.0)

OLE 1.0 was a new and wonderful technology. It was introduced as part of Windows 3.1 and provided for both object linking and embedding. This meant that the user could now create complex compound documents capable of containing objects from a variety of sources. Embedded objects could be edited by simply double-clicking on the item. For instance, an Excel spreadsheet embedded in a Word document could be double-clicked, and an Excel spreadsheet would come up in a separate window with the spreadsheet loaded and allow you to edit it. When you were done editing, Excel would allow you to save the changes back to the embedded Excel object in the Word document.

Another feature was object linking. This allowed a spreadsheet to be linked into a Word document (basically this was nothing more than a pointer to the spreadsheet within the Word document). If the data in the original spreadsheet is updated, then the next time the Word document was loaded, the link would update the document and reflect the changes. Think of the benefits for the manager who had a Word document with the embedded Excel spreadsheets from his or her employees. Tell your workers to update their data Monday by 10:00 a.m., bring up your document at 10:05 a.m. (all the data being self-updating) and print out the current statistics for the week. Give it to your boss, and look like a pro. It always comes back to image: "It's much better to look good than to feel good," but with OLE you can have both!

OLE 1.0 provided much needed relief for the weary end user who desperately needed a way to decrease the "manual" in manual labor.

The Revolution: OLE 2.0

So you say you want a revolution? Well, you have one. OLE 2.0 has come a long way in helping us solve some of the key problems in component-based software.

OLE Component Object Model

Every structure needs a foundation. OLE 2.0's foundation is the Common Object Model. The *Common Object Model (COM)* is a system software object model that allows complete interoperability between components that are written by different companies and in different languages. The modularity of these components is the key to their success. These components can be purchased, upgraded, or replaced individually or in groups without affecting the performance of the whole (sort of like the Borg, if you're a *Star Trek* fan). All are part of the collective contributing to the good of the whole (resistance is futile).

COM is the backbone or nerve center of OLE. COM's primary responsibility is to ensure that components behave in a well-known and predictable manner. This should be done with the smallest cost to the programmer, maximizing the options in component implementation. The COM accomplishes this by defining a binary interface (which we spoke of earlier) that is completely independent of the programming language used in implementing the component. A component written to comply with the binary COM interface specifications can communicate with another component without really knowing any specific information about the other component's implementation.

OLE relies on COM to provide all the basic communication between components. Again, this is an example of the object mentality. OLE uses the functionality of COM instead of reinventing the wheel. Remember, reuse is a programmer's best friend! This communication by COM is what allows you to embed a Visio drawing in a Word document. Word knows nothing of Visio's implementation; the products are even from different companies, yet COM allows the two to talk enough to get the job done.

OLE Automation

NEW TERM Automation is a wonderful new feature integrated into OLE 2.0 that allows you to access and manipulate another application's objects from outside that application. These objects that are exposed for external use are called *OLE automation objects.* The types of objects that can be exposed are as varied as the Windows applications themselves. A word processor could expose a document, paragraph, or sentence as an automation object. A spreadsheet could as easily expose a spreadsheet, chart, cell, or range of cells.

The major difference between the usual OLE objects and automation objects is that automation objects can only be accessed programmatically, as shown in Figure 18.1. This could be accomplished using a programming language like Delphi, Visual Basic, or a macro-based language like VBA in Access 3.0. These objects are not exposed to the end user and are primarily used to automate tasks that may be repetitive in nature. Usually, there would be no user intervention in the task performed between your application and the exposed object.

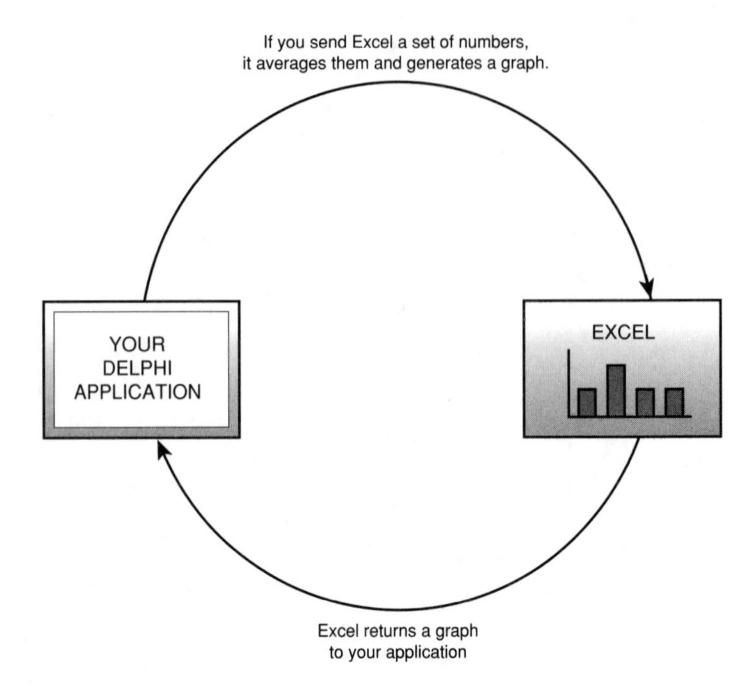

Figure 18.1.
Automation at work.

The result of this programmatic interface is that automation objects can't really be linked or embedded into your application, they can only be accessed by pre-programmed remote control. Why? Because they are created and used by pre-programmed code, and are therefore temporary in nature. They may only exist for a small portion of the execution time of your program.

There are two types of automation servers: in-process and out-of-process. Delphi supports the creation of both types of servers. An in-process server is a DLL that exports automation objects. Because the automation objects come from a DLL as opposed to another application, the objects are part of the client application. The benefit of using an in-process server is that the automation server runs in the same address space as the client application, so the calls do not have to be regulated or "marshalled." This regulation adds a huge overhead to each call made to the automation server.

An out-of-process server is a stand-alone executable that exports automation objects. An example of this would be Microsoft Word. Word has a number of objects it exposes as automation objects. There is an example later in this chapter using Word as an automation server.

Classes, Documents, and Items

OLE automation relies on three different types of information to function properly. An OLE class determines the server application that created the automation object. For instance, if the object class is a .doc document, it was created using Word.

The OLE documents refer to the source file containing the data for the OLE object. Any OLE document object must be a linked document (versus embedded), because a linked document's data must reside in a file.

The last item is an OLE item. The item determines which portion of a document contains the data that is going to be linked or embedded into another. This is a way in which you can actually have things smaller than an entire document linked into another. Items are how you downsize.

OLE Custom Controls

OLE custom controls are software components (again the modular mentality) that you can purchased off the shelf or write yourself. You use these controls to provide additional functionality to your application. There are a number of custom controls available, ranging from button and listbox controls to complex network management and interface controls. Delphi 2 has several sample OCXs included with the product. You can find them on the OCX tab within the Delphi 2 development environment.

Many of the custom controls in use now have been implemented as VBXs. The VBX is just a special form of DLL. The OLE custom control (which has an extension of .ocx) is a major improvement over the VBX. The VBX is a 16-bit implementation whereas the OLE control supports both 16 and 32 bit and is platform independent. The OLE custom control specification is equally applicable to Windows, Windows NT and successors, and to the Apple Macintosh. It even encompasses the potentially difficult issue of internationalization (for example, how do you spell the name of the color property—color, colour, couleur, colore?). This gives the OLE control a distinct advantage in the new 32-bit market.

Every OLE custom control possesses three sets of attributes:

- Properties—Named attributes such as color, font, or caption.
- Events—Actions occurring based on an external action directed to the control from outside the control itself. This could be the user clicking the OLE control or pressing a key while the control is in focus.
- Methods—Functions in the control itself that allow external code to change the control's behavior or appearance. This could be as simple as modifying the current text entry in a text control.

These three sets of attributes improve the flexibility of OLE controls to "become" whatever you need them to be. This is the beauty of OLE custom controls. This flexibility allows the software developer to create applications whose existence is almost solely based on other OLE controls (see Figure 18.2). It makes the job more an integration effort rather than a creation effort.

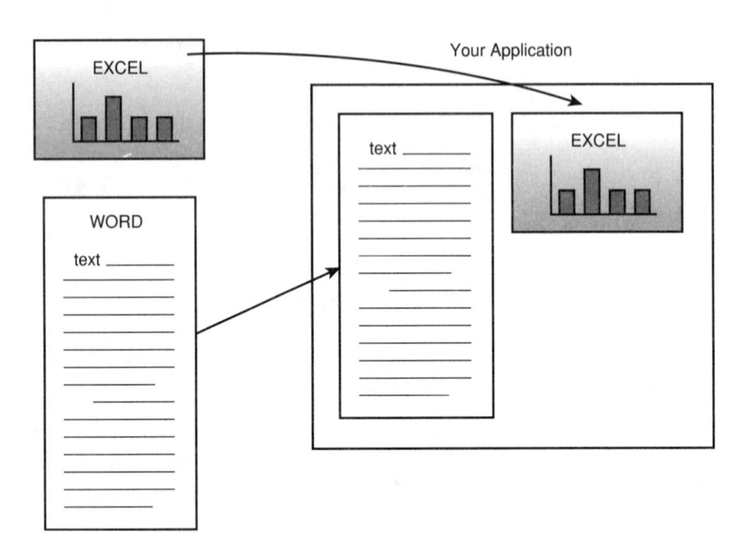

Figure 18.2.
OLE + OLE = App.

OLE Drag-and-Drop

The drag-and-drop features of OLE are used almost without notice. Taking a file from the Explorer and dropping it into Notepad is a prime example. This allows the user a great deal of flexibility and control. Maybe you don't want to use Notepad. You can drag foo.txt from the Explorer over to WordPad and use it instead. Delphi 2 supports the drag-and-drop capability.

OLE Component Management

Because of the autonomous nature of OLE (having individual components), you may upgrade or replace an OLE component without having to recompile all the applications that rely on that component. Remember that everyone deals with OLE components through a defined set of interfaces. The internal structure is not visible to the developer. This means that as long as the interface remains consistent, the internals of the component could be rewritten completely and the user would never know the difference.

OLE Documents

An OLE document is a form of compound document that can incorporate data created in any OLE-enabled application. For instance, an OLE-enabled word processor (like Microsoft Word) can accept tables and charts from an OLE-enabled spreadsheet (like Microsoft Excel). OLE Documents enable users to convey their ideas more effectively by incorporating many different types of information into any business document. In addition to incorporating static information like charts and tables, OLE documents can also incorporate live data such as sound, video, and animation. OLE documents also make users more productive by simplifying the process of creating compound documents. The following sections describe features specific to OLE documents.

OLE (Object Linking and Embedding)

This feature was supported in OLE 1.0 as we discussed earlier. It is still supported in OLE 2.0. This supports the object strategy of keeping old investments safe and adding new functionality to the OLE specification.

OLE Visual Editing

To us, visual editing is probably the greatest feature of OLE 2. Visual editing allows users to create robust, compound documents easily, incorporating text, graphics, sound, video, and many other diverse objects. Instead of constantly switching between applications to create different parts of a compound document, users can work within a single application that holds the context of their document. As the user begins to edit an object that originated in another application, such as a spreadsheet or graphic, the menus and tools of the container application automatically change to the menu and tools of that object's native application. The user can then edit the object in the context of the document without worrying about activating and switching to another application. Notice Figure 18.3 in which the Excel spreadsheet has been activated inside the Word document. The Word menu has changed to incorporate the Excel menu choices.

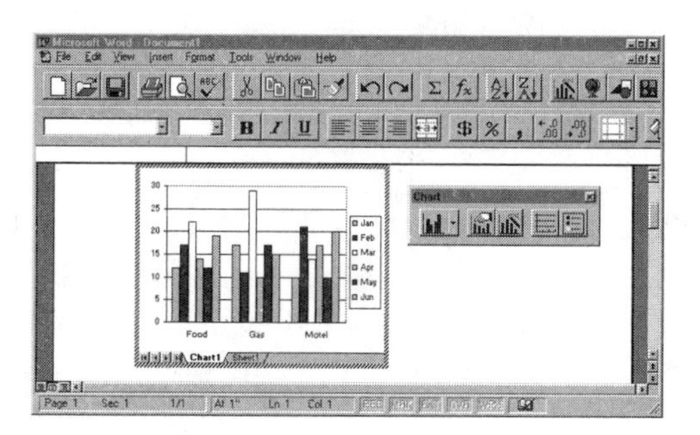

Figure 18.3.
Visual editing.

NEW TERM This particular feature provides a smooth path for users to follow when creating a compound document. Visual editing is also referred to as *in place activation.* This term makes sense because the menus and toolbars change as the OLE server is activated for the particular object being edited. This provides a similar look and feel for the user—always a plus.

Object Conversion

Objects can be converted to different types so that different applications can be used with the same object. For example, an object created with one brand of spreadsheet can be converted so that it can be interpreted by a different spreadsheet application for editing.

Nested Object Support

In a truly object-based system, you should be able to nest objects in multiple layers within other objects. Users should be able to access and manipulate those objects that are nested inside other objects, and establish links to them. It just so happens that OLE 2.0 provides all these features! This again adds to the flexibility of object-based software.

Optimized (Persistent) Object Storage

Using OLE 1, the entire object had to be loaded from disk into memory, even if you only wanted to draw the object's border on the screen. This was a huge waste of our two most precious resources: memory and CPU cycles. This problem has been overcome in OLE 2. In OLE 2 objects remain on disk until needed and are not loaded into memory each time the container application is opened. The great part is that now an OLE 2 object need only load the portion of itself required at that point in time.

A relevant example of this would be a Word document with an embedded Excel spreadsheet that would only load the spreadsheet if you are editing the page on which that spreadsheet resides. This also helps speed the responsiveness of your application because you're not carrying the entire document around with you—only a portion. Also, OLE has complete transacted object storage that supports commits and rollbacks (no, we aren't talking about InterBase) of objects to disk. This ensures that data integrity is maintained as objects are stored in the file system.

Storage-Independent Links

This feature allows objects to update each other's information. Not a big deal, right? It is when those objects are embedded in other documents. Simply put, my Excel spreadsheet (embedded in a Word document) can exchange data with another Excel spreadsheet (embedded in yet another document). All this occurs even though neither embedded object exists as a straight disk file. Pretty cool.

OLE 2.0 opens new doors for programmers who want to complete complex software applications in a short period of time. It allows the mere mortal programmer to include the power of Excel in his or her application without having to write it! This is why component-based software development tools like Delphi have sold so well, and OCX (again, the extension given to an OLE custom control) enabled Delphi 2, will sell even better. There is a large ROI (return on investment) here. A little integration work with a huge payoff.

The Price

Of course there is a little investment up front on your part. You have to study and understand OLE. Hundreds of hours of mind-numbing work and you might begin to glean a faint understanding of where OLE is headed. The details of OLE are at least as complicated as the details of Windows programming.

OLE 2.0 Sans Delphi Components

You may choose to use only the raw OLE API when constructing your application. What you are up against if you try the "I write everything myself" mentality is that the raw OLE API makes little to no assumptions about your application. This is more a curse than a blessing. Using the raw API allows you more flexibility but it also does very little of the work for you. It only gives you the core structure and defines many of the standard interfaces. The rest of the job is up to you. Definitely puts the "manual" in manual labor.

The benefit of using the raw OLE API is that you have a lot of choices. You need to decide which of the standard interfaces you need, and how they communicate with the rest of your program. You even have a choice of programming language. We recommend Delphi 2 of course, but an OLE 2 application could be written in C++, Ada, BASIC, Assembly, and so on. Programming the OLE 2.0 API gives you the ultimate in flexibility. It's sort of like playing SimCity; you create the culture from the ground up.

In our humble opinion, it is always better to let someone else do the work for you. You can then concentrate on making your killer application.

OLE 2 Using Delphi 2

There are a number of significant achievements in Delphi 2, not the least of which is the OLE 2.0 support. Borland does a good job at hiding most of OLE behind the environment. Unless you want to dabble in the raw stuff, you don't have to. Let's look at the three major areas in which Delphi 2 makes a good contribution toward OLE functionality: linking and embedding, automation, and OCX control support.

Linking and Embedding and OLE Containers

The entire concept of linking and embedding was that you could include the functionality of another application in Delphi. That way you could use the functionality of a spreadsheet without having to write one.

Delphi supports this concept by offering you the OLE container. This visual control gives you the ability to embed an OLE object on a Delphi form. After placing the control on a form, you can stretch it to occupy the correct amount of space on the form. This is the client area in which the OLE container displays the object. Now that you have the receptacle there, put something in it.

There are several ways to get an OLE server item into your new OLE container. The easiest by far is to use the Object Inspector. By selecting the `ObjectClass` or `ObjectDoc` properties and then pressing the ... button, you see the Insert Object dialog box. (See Figure 18.4.)

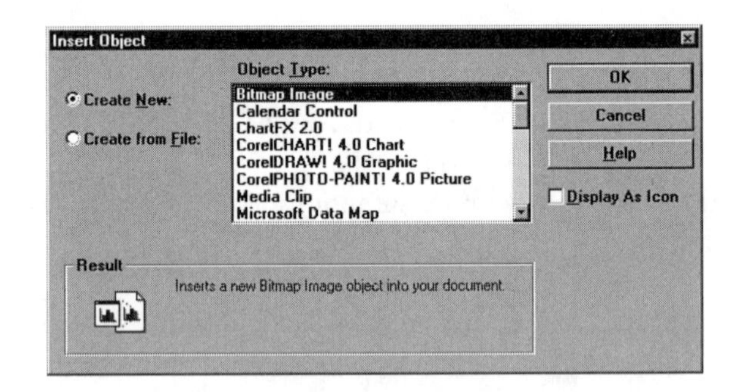

Figure 18.4.
Insert Object dialog box with Create New selected.

This dialog box enables you to insert any registered OLE object into your OLE container object. Notice that you can either create the object from disk, or create a new object based the OLE object type you have selected. If you leave the Create New radio button pushed, you can select an object type from the listbox as shown in Figure 18.4. When you press Enter, notice that the application type you have selected causes that application to be launched. This enables you to create or alter the contents of the object. Once you are finished, you see that under the File menu on that application there is a new selection, Exit & Return to XXX, where XXX is the name of the form you placed on the OLE container. Now your OLE container should be displaying that object in your OLE control.

If you choose the Create From File option in the dialog box in Figure 18.4, the dialog box changes slightly, as seen in Figure 18.5.

Now you see that you must choose a file to import into your OLE container. The application that is placed in your OLE container depends on the document's extension. If the file is a .doc file, then Word will be the editing and display mechanism for the object. Notice how the object (possibly a Word Document) is shown within the OLE container control area on your form.

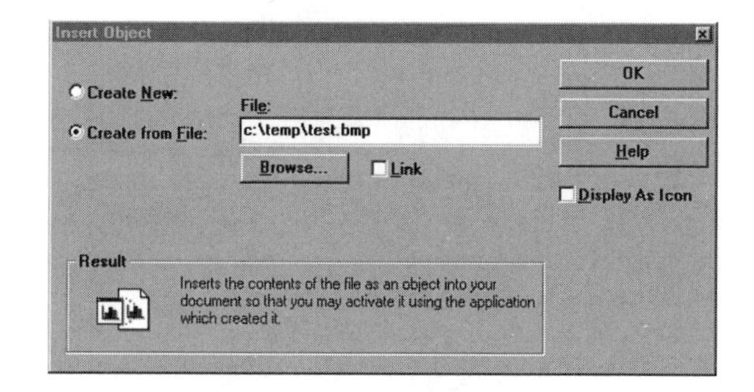

Figure 18.5.
Insert Object dialog box with Create from File: selected.

When you run your application, the object shows up on the form right where your OLE container object is placed. If you have enabled in-place editing by setting the `AllowInPlace` property to `TRUE`, when you double click the object, the server application allows you to edit the document.

You don't really have to place an object in the OLE container at design time. This would truly limit the flexibility of the container. During runtime you can also make several different calls to place an OLE object into the container. This is done using calls like `InsertOLEObjectDlg()`, which prompt the user for an object just like it did for you at design time when you pressed the … button.

Try it. Follow these steps:

1. Open a new project.
2. On the initial form place an OLE container control that covers most of the form.
3. Place a button on the form.
4. Double click the button to bring up the code window for that button.
5. Add the code necessary to make your code look like

```
procedure TForm1.Button1Click(Sender: TObject);
var
  OLEPointer: Pointer;
begin
  if InsertOLEObjectDlg(Form1, 0, OLEPointer) then
  begin
    OLEContainer1.PInitInfo := OLEPointer;
    ReleaseOLEInitInfo(OLEPointer);
  end;
end;
```

6. Run the application.

When you press the button on the running application, you get the same Insert Object dialog box that you got at runtime. The `InsertOLEObjectDlg()` call activates the Insert Object dialog box. The OLEPointer was created because that holds a pointer to the OLE object that you have selected in the dialog box.

18

After you get a pointer to the OLE object, set the `PInitInfo` property of the OLE container control. The `ReleaseOLEInitInfo()` function then releases the memory that was used for the OLEPointer to store the initialization information. Now you have a real OLE application.

Once your OLE container has something in it, you can save that information to a file, and then read in back out later. This is done using the `SaveToFile()` and `LoadFromFile()` functions. These functions are designed specifically to save and retrieve OLE data. Try using this function by following these steps:

1. Add two more buttons titled Load and Save to the form you created earlier.
2. Double click the Save button, and make the code there look like

   ```
   procedure TForm1.Button2Click(Sender: TObject);
   begin
   OleContiner1.SaveToFile ('C:\Junk.OLE');
   end;
   ```

3. Then double-click the Load button and make the code there look like

   ```
   procedure TForm1.Button3Click(Sender: TObject);
   begin
   OleContainer1.LoadFromFile ('C:\Junk.OLE');
   end;
   ```

4. Run the application (it will look like Figure 18.6).
5. Press Button1 and insert a new object (like a Paintbrush file).
6. After you edit the object, press the Save button. There should now be a file called C:\Junk.OLE on your hard drive.
7. Press Create again and create a new paintbrush picture. After that is complete, press Load and the old picture should appear. This one gets loaded into the OLE container on top of the one already there.

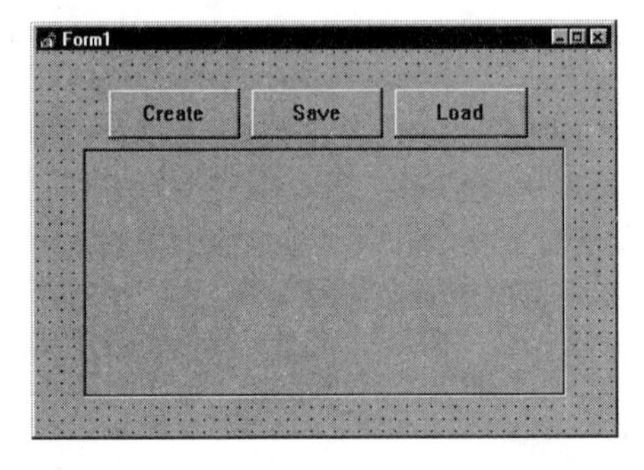

Figure 18.6.
The OLE test application.

When you insert the object from the Insert Object dialog box using the Create From File radio button, there is also a checkbox for Link. When an object is linked, it is automatically updated whenever the source file on your hard drive is modified. When Link is unchecked,

you are embedding the object, and changes made to the original are not reflected in your OLE container.

There are many other properties as well as methods that can be employed. There isn't the room here to look at them all. This is merely a teaser to help you get interested in the potential of the OLE container control. The best way to learn is to play. Try the control and see how it works. You really can't break anything by adding OLE objects to your application, so try it!

OLE Automation

OLE automation is a powerful ally to have in the war on programming. As programs become more complex, it is harder to be expert in every aspect of program design. Many people specialize in database applications, while others do games. OLE automation helps you tap the power from others' applications in an effort to leverage their work to your benefit. OLE automation allows you to control the execution of another application that is an OLE automation server.

This application must specifically expose objects for your use and control. A prime example of this would be a Delphi application controlling Microsoft Word to create a form letter. Based on the input in the Delphi application, a unique form letter is generated in Word. Try it by following these steps:

1. Create a new project.
2. Add five edit box controls named and labeled NameBox, AddressBox, CityBox, StateBox, and ZipCodeBox.
3. Add to the form a button labeled "Make Form Letter."
4. Double-click the button, and make your code look like the following:

```
uses OleAuto;

procedure TForm1.Button1Click(Sender: TObject);

var
 MsWord: Variant;
  L: Integer;

begin
  try
      MsWord := CreateOleObject('Word.Basic');
    except
      ShowMessage('Could not start up Microsoft Word.');
    Exit;
  end;
MsWord.AppShow;
MSWord.FileNew;
MSWord.Insert(NameBox.Text + #13);
MSWord.Insert(AddressBox.Text + #13);
```

```
    MSWord.Insert(CityBox.Text + ', ' + StateBox.Text + #13);
    MSWord.Insert(ZipCodeBox.Text + #13 + #13);
    MSWord.Insert('Dear Mr. ' + NameBox.Text + #13 + #13);
    MSWord.Insert('     Have a nice day.' + #13 + #13);
    MSWord.Insert('Sincerely,' + #13);
    MSWord.Insert('               Danny O' + #13);
    end;
```

5. Make sure that you don't forget the `Uses` statement above the procedure call.
6. Run the program.
7. When you fill in the blanks with the required information and press the button, the application starts Word if it is not already running (by executing the `CreateOLEObject()` call).
   - Makes the application visible (with `AppShow` call). By default the applications called are hidden, assuming you wish to do processing in the background.
   - Creates a new document by executing the `FileNew` procedure.
   - Then you have a series of `Insert` commands that place text into the Word document. Notice that each one of these statements is followed by a #13 (Return key). If you just placed a very long string into the Word document it would wrap as a normal user typed sentence does.

This is a simple example of the power of OLE automation. You can control any application that exposes its functionality as an automation server.

Finally, there is an example of a true automation server and client found in the \demos\oleauto\autoserv directory. Here you can find two programs. One is a multi-file text editor that is also an automation server, and the second is an automation client that can control the server. The first is MemoEdit.DPR, which is the automation server, and the next is AutoDemo.DPR, which is the automation client.

If you look at the code in `MemoEdit`, you will find that there is a special way objects are exposed for others to use. The heart of the declaration is the code in the `AutoMemo` unit. See the partial listing following:

```
type
  TMemoApp = class(TAutoObject)
  private
    function GetMemo(Index: Integer): Variant;
    function GetMemoCount: Integer;
  automated
    procedure CascadeWindows;
    function NewMemo: Variant;
    function OpenMemo(const FileName: string): Variant;
    procedure TileWindows;
    property MemoCount: Integer read GetMemoCount;
    property Memos[Index: Integer]: Variant read GetMemo;
  end;
```

As you can see, the word "automated" sticks out rather well. Here is where the class is defined; notice the base class, `TAutoObject`. Borland thinks of it all, huh? This is a high-level interface that would really be ugly to implement in some other language.

Once `MemoEdit` exposes the functions and procedures shown above, the AutoDemo application can utilize those to control an instance of AutoMemo. Run the AutoDemo program and see how fast the response is between the two applications.

The AutoDemo application creates an OLE instance of the AutoMemo application in its `FormCreate` procedure.

```
procedure TMainForm.FormCreate(Sender: TObject);
begin
  try
    MemoEdit := CreateOleObject('MemoEdit.Application');
  except
    MessageDlg(
      'An instance of the "MemoEdit.Application" OLE
Automation class ' +
      'could not be created. Make sure that the MemoEdit
application has ' +
      'been registered using a "MemoEdit /regserver" command
line.',
      mtError, [mbOk], 0);
    Halt;
  end;
end;
```

The same method (`CreateOLEObject`) you used to create an OLE Word object in the previous example is used here to create an instance of MemoEdit. Notice that if object creation does not go as planned, a message is displayed telling the user that the server has registered.

Look at each button, and see how the exposed elements are called by this application. See how effortless it is to control the AutoMemo application. The tiling of the windows is a simple call.

```
procedure TMainForm.TileButtonClick(Sender: TObject);
begin
  MemoEdit.TileWindows;
end;
```

This is the magic of OLE automation. Take some time to look through this example and understand how it works. If you want to write your own OLE automation server, you can use the automation expert to create your own OLE automation server (as shown in Figure 18.7). Choose New from the File menu, and then Automation object. The Automation Expert pops up and asks you for the class name you wish to use as well as the application name (OLE class name), and a description.

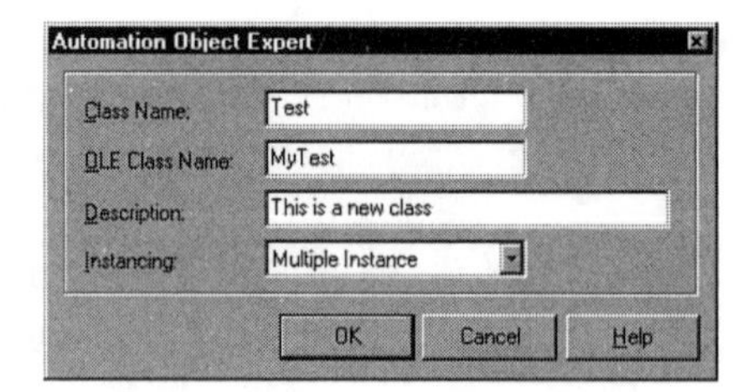

Figure 18.7.
The Automation Object Expert.

When you fill in the blanks and press Enter you get the following code:

```
unit Unit1;

interface

uses
  OleAuto;

type
  Test = class(TAutoObject)
  private
    { Private declarations }
  automated
    { Automated declarations }
  end;

implementation

procedure Registerest;
const
  AutoClassInfo: TAutoClassInfo = (
    AutoClass: Test;
    ProgID: 'MyTest';
    ClassID: '{31FC9AC0-5285-11CF-BA43-00AA004B40BB}';
    Description: 'This is a new class';
    Instancing: acMultiInstance);
begin
  Automation.RegisterClass(AutoClassInfo);
end;

initialization
  Registerest;
end.
```

Notice it created your Test type based on the `TAutoObject` class. Also see how it created the `Registerest` procedure so that the first time this is run the registration information will be placed in the Registry. The ClassID with the weird string is a unique number in time and space that is generated for each OLE object. This ClassID is how objects find each other. The automation expert runs the algorithm for you that generates the number and places it into the code for you. Now you can add your own procedures and functions in the automated section of the class definition.

The instancing of an automation server is crucial. Notice the line `Instancing: acMultiInstance`. This means that one automation server can export multiple instances of the OLE objects. The DLL (or in-process) servers are always multiple instance servers. There is also a single instance server where every time another instance of the OLE object is needed, a new server is started. The last instance type is internal. This means that the OLE objects are internal to the program, are not registered, and therefore external applications do not have access to them.

When you create your automation servers you also must remember that you are somewhat constrained as to the data types you pass around. The standard data types are SmallInt, Integer, Single, Double, Currency, TDateTime, String, WordBool, and Variant. This still gives you enough variety to get the job done.

OCX Custom Controls

New Term

An *OLE custom control* is an OLE 2 object with an extended interface that lets it behave like a control for Windows.

OLE custom controls are a set of extensions to the existing OLE 2 compound document specifications. It builds on the concepts of embedded objects, in-place activation, and OLE automation to meet the specific interaction requirements between controls and control containers. These extensions are defined in the "OLE Controls and Control Containers Guidelines, Version 1.1" found on the Microsoft Developer's CD. This document defines how OLE controls interact with their environment and the minimal functionality that an OLE control must support.

OCXs are more than just editable embedded objects. They transform end-user events such as mouse clicks and keystrokes into programmatic notifications to the container, which can use those transformed events to execute other code.

An OCX is similar only in appearance to a Delphi visual control. They appear similar because you interact with both types of control through the Object Inspector where you view their properties and events.

The reason an OCX looks similar is because when you import an OCX to use in the development environment, Delphi generates a component wrapper around it so it is usable in the environment. In essence it makes Delphi think it is a visual component. Now you can use that OCX in your projects.

The OCX tab on the component bar has several sample OCXs in it. You can add these to your forms and use them just the same as a visual component. Place the ChartFX OCX onto a blank form. Stretch it out and notice how it starts off by showing sample data until real data is added. You can change the properties at design time and watch the graph change. The OCX concept offers many benefits over the old VBX component. Try them out.

Summary

We can only begin to scratch the surface of OLE in this chapter (or book for that matter). OLE is a complex and rich subject worthy of in-depth study. We highly recommend looking at the OLE tutorials that come with Delphi 2. Even though OLE has been getting a bad rap for being slow, as the machines get faster and the software more optimized, I think that will change. It seems that OLE is the wave *to* the future, and your knowledge is the surfboard.

Q&A

Q I thought linking was a continuous updating mechanism, but you said it only updates during application loading. Is there any way of updating while remaining in the application?

A Yes! You can update a link while in an application if it is supported by the application (usually through a Link|Update menu selection).

Q I have not seen much about OCX controls. How can I get more information?

A The Microsoft Developer's Network CD (a quarterly subscription service from Microsoft) is the single largest wealth of information we have ever seen in one place. It gives you access to thousands of articles, white papers, and specifications dealing with many issues including OCX technology.

Workshop

Quiz

1. Describe the difference between drag and drop and embedding.
2. What are the inherent limitations of VBX technology?
3. What is the major benefit of OLE automation?

Exercises

1. Demonstrate to yourself the concepts of linking and embedding on your favorite application (Word, Excel, and so on.)
2. To demonstrate drag-and-drop to yourself (if you have not already used it), open Explorer and drag a worthless text file onto the Recycle Bin (make sure to retrieve it if it was an important file).

3. Try importing several different document types into the OLE container (by file) and see which applications are called on to edit those objects when you run your application.
4. In the AutoDemo application, try to add the Arrange Icons functionality to the automation server. Remember that once this is complete, you will have to minimize and rearrange all the window icons in order for this function to do anything. Also, try adding a minimize all button to the AutoDemo, and see if you can get that to work.

Day 19

Using and Writing DLLs

The goal of this chapter is to teach you how to create your own DLL (Dynamic Link Library) using Delphi. For some reason that escapes me, this topic has been left out of some of the beginning level books on Delphi. Writing a DLL in C or C++ can be a bit tedious because of the amount of setup code as well as resource files that need to be created (not to mention the compiler and linker options that must be set) all to get one little DLL. Delphi, by contrast, makes creating a DLL quite easy! While you won't be learning some of the more advanced topics involving DLLs, you will learn the basic information needed to create 16- or 32-bit DLLs. By the end of this chapter, you will know what a DLL is, why you would want to write one, and most importantly, all the necessary steps involved in creating and using your own DLL with Delphi! In fact, as you go through this, you will build a DLL from the ground up and learn how to call it from a separate Delphi program. You then move on and learn how to add resources such as forms to the DLL. This is where Delphi really shines in the creation of DLLs. Believe me, writing a simple DLL in C/C++ is time-consuming enough (compared to Delphi); creating one with forms and other resources would keep you quite busy for a while!

What Is a DLL and Why Write One?

New Term So, you ask, what is the DLL thing? Well, DLL stands for *dynamic link library*. Great, what does that mean? A dynamic link library is a special type of executable file used to store functions and resources in a file separate from your executable. Usually, you might write a program and create functions, resources, and so on and they get linked into your executable file. This is called *statically linked*. When you use routines in a DLL, this is called *dynamically linked* because the code is linked at runtime. A DLL allows useful, commonly used functions and resources to be made available to many applications at one time while only having one copy of the code loaded on disk and in memory. A DLL is typically not loaded into memory until it is needed, but once in memory, any program that needs to use it simply makes a call to it for the needed function or resources.

OK, Now I Know What a DLL Is, Why Would I Write One?

Now that you know what a DLL is, let's discuss why you would want to write one. There are several reasons why you might want to write a DLL. Over time, you will undoubtedly create handy routines, resources, and so on, that you will want to reuse in your programs. You could move these handy creations to a DLL and make them available to all your applications. Assume you created a handy string-parsing routine, or an encryption routine, or some fancy dialog box that you like to use in your programs. Put it all in a DLL and you never have to cut and paste or write them again. Why not put this stuff in your own unit that you can include in all your projects. That is an option and may be the better one for some situations, but a DLL may be a better solution if the code contained in it is used often and by a number of your applications. Assume that you have a number of programs that might be running on the same system at the same time. With your DLL, they will only load the code once! (See Figure 19.1.) This reduces disk and memory space. Another benefit to putting your code into a DLL is that it can be used by applications developed in other languages such as C, Visual Basic, and Access Basic, as well as any other language or development system that can make calls to DLLs. Windows API calls are stored in DLLs. You might think of writing a DLL as a way to extend the Windows API on the user's PC…well, it sounded good!

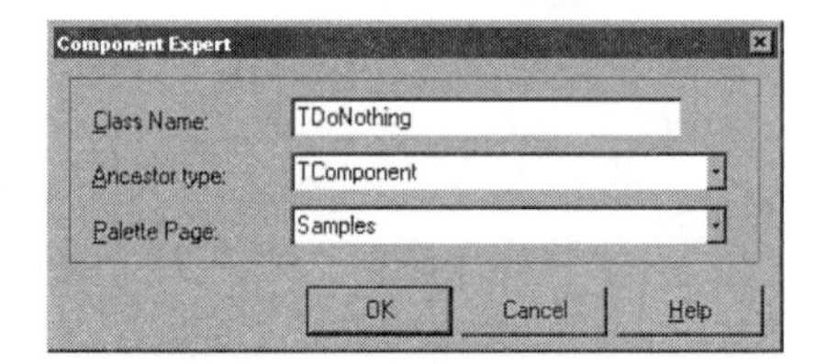

Figure 19.1.
Application and DLL memory usage.

OK, now that you have looked at what a DLL is and why you might want to write your own, you're ready to move on to actually writing your own. You'll walk step by step through the process of creating your own DLL, but first, you need to set up a few things.

Setting Up the Code to Create the DLL

Before you can create some functions for your DLL, you must do some setup. Delphi actually does a lot of the work for you as it creates some of the necessary files that you don't actually need to see or worry about. You only need to worry about the source code in one file, the PROJECT.DPR. These steps walk you through this process while trying to keep things simple and organized. Let's get started!

1. Start Delphi if it is not already running, and choose File | New. Select the DLL item.
2. Create a directory in which to store the source code for the DLL. This is optional, but it keeps things organized and makes it easier to see what belongs to your project.
3. Save the project to the directory created in Step 2 by doing a File | Save Project As. Select the directory in which save the file and enter the desired filename. Call it MYDLL.DPR.
4. Add the Exports clause just above the `begin...end` block.

If all went well, you should have a file called MYDLL.DPR that looks like this:

```
library mydll;

{ Important note about DLL memory management: ShareMem must be the
  first unit in your library's USES clause AND your project's (select
  View-Project Source) USES clause if your DLL exports any procedures or
  functions that pass strings as parameters or function results. This
  applies to all strings passed to and from your DLL—even those that
  are nested in records and classes. ShareMem is the interface unit to
  the DELPHIMM.DLL shared memory manager, which must be deployed along
  with your DLL. To avoid using DELPHIMM.DLL, pass string information
  using PChar or ShortString parameters. }

uses
  SysUtils,
  Classes;

exports

begin
end.
```

Before you add code to this, there are a few things you should know about DLLs. All variables in the DLL are private to that DLL including global variables. This is because a DLL has its own data segment. This means that your programs and DLLs may not share variables. You

19

will need to pass and return values that need to be shared. Also, if you plan to do any assembly language programming, you need to be aware of the fact that your DLL will not have its own stack segment. This can cause problems for your program if it makes assumptions that the SS and DS registers contain the same value. If you are going to use strictly Delphi functions in your DLL, you should not need to worry about this because Delphi will never generate code that assumes that DS=SS.

Now add some code to this. You'll add a simple encryption function that when called by a windows program and passed a null-terminated string, will run through a loop that performs an exclusive OR operation on each character with the value 159. The results are passed back as a null-terminated string. This has an interesting effect on your data. The function scrambles or encrypts it. When run through the function a second time, it unscrambles or decrypts your data. The function looks like this:

```
function Encrypt(eptr : PChar):PChar;
Var
   x : integer;
   l : word;
   estr : string;
   ch : char;
begin
     {Convert the null terminated string to
      a pascal style string}
     estr:=StrPas(eptr);
     {Get the length of the string}
     l:=StrLen(eptr);
     {Encrypt the string using a simple
      exclusive or method}
     for x:=1 to l do
     begin
          ch:=estr[x];
          ch:=Chr(Ord(ch) xor 159);
          estr[x]:=ch;
     end;
     {Convert the pascal style string
      back to a null terminated string}
     StrPcopy(eptr,estr);
     {Return the string to the calling function}
     Encrypt:=eptr;
end;
```

NOTE

When you write a function or procedure that you want to put in a DLL, it is recommended that you test it in a regular program. This makes testing and debugging much easier than jumping back and forth between your DLL and a program that calls it. When your function is fully debugged and tested, then you can move it over to a DLL.

You may want to take a minute to study the function and read the comments to get a feel for how the function works. When you are done, move on to exporting the function.

Exporting the DLL Functions

Now that you have a function that is ready for use in your DLL, you need to add the word "export" to the end of the function declaration. This tells the system that it will be made available to programs outside your DLL. This is done by causing the compiler to use the `far` call model for this function. It looks like this:

```
function Encrypt(eptr : PChar):PChar; export;
```

You also need to add the `exports` clause to your code. This allows you to list your functions and procedures that are to be exported. Think of this as a lookup table. The `exports` clause can also include one of the following:

- `index`—Used to assign an ordinal number to the function for exporting from the DLL. If an index is not assigned, the compiler generates one automatically. `Index` is not used by Win32; you should use `name` instead. `Index` is listed here for your information because you'll be converting from Delphi 1.0.
- `name`—Used to assign a name to the function to be exported. If you don't assign a name, Delphi uses the function's name after converting it to uppercase. `Name` is the only lookup option supported in Win32.
- `resident`—Causes the exports information to stay in memory after a DLL is loaded. If functions are going to be called by name from the calling function, this speeds up the process for Windows to look up a DLL.

The `exports` clause looks like this:

```
Exports
  Encrypt;
```

OK, now look at your program in its complete form.

```
Library Mydll;

uses
    SysUtils;

{$R *.RES}

function Encrypt(eptr : PChar):PChar; export;
Var
   x : integer;
   l : word;
   estr : string;
   ch : char;
```

```
begin
     {Convert the null terminated string to
      a pascal style string}
     estr:=StrPas(eptr);
     {Get the length of the string}
     l:=StrLen(eptr);
     {Encrypt the string using a simple
      exclusive or method}
     for x:=1 to l do
     begin
          ch:=estr[x];
          ch:=Chr(Ord(ch) xor 159);
          estr[x]:=ch;
     end;
     {Convert the pascal style string
      back to a null terminated string}
     StrPcopy(eptr,estr);
     {Return the string to the calling function}
     Encrypt:=eptr;
end;
{Provides lookup info calling programs}
Exports
  Encrypt;
begin
end.
```

Notice the `uses` clause with the `SysUtils` unit included. This was added by Delphi. You'll need to use functions in the `SysUtils` unit such as `StrPcopy`, `StrLen`, and so on. Of course if you need to use functions and procedures in another unit, you'll need to add those units to the `uses` clause as well.

Compiling the DLL

If you haven't already, enter the code listing into the MYDLL.DPR window as discussed earlier. Make sure to save the project when you are done. At this point, you have done everything necessary to prepare the program to compile as a DLL. Select Compile | Build All. This creates MYDLL.DLL in the directory to which you saved your DLL source code. If you examine the DLL, you will notice that it is quite a bit smaller than a typical Delphi application. This is because you have not included all the libraries required to create normal Delphi programs. You are now ready to test your program, so go write a small program to call your DLL and display the results each time the DLL is called.

Accessing the Functions and Procedures in the DLL

Accessing your DLL, or any other for that matter, is quite easy. You simply declare the function properly and it becomes available for use as if it were part of your application. Create

a new project and do a File | Save Project As. Save the project file as TESTDLL.DPR. Save the unit file as DLLTEST.PAS. Now, in DLLTEST.PAS, put the following in the implementation section:

```
{ Import routine from DLL. Takes password and returns an encrypted string}
function Encrypt(eptr : PChar) : PChar;
  far; external 'MYDLL';
```

Notice the `far` and `external` directives at the end of the function. These directives are important in allowing your program to find and access the function in your DLL.

- `far`—Tells the compiler that it must use the `far` call model to be able to access the function or procedure.
- `external`—Tells the compiler that the procedure is not part of this program. This allows the program to compile without looking for code it will never find.

  In addition to `far` and `external`, you may also choose how you want to import the function; by `name`, `new name`, or `ordinal number`. These are optional.
- `name`—Imports and looks up the function by name in the DLL. In other words, if the function name in your declaration is `Encrypt`, that is what will be looked up.

Example:

```
function Encrypt(eptr : PChar) : PChar;  far; external 'MYDLL';
```

- `new name`—Imports by a specified name rather than the function identifier. This is used if you want to refer to the function in your program by a name other than its name in the DLL. You might want to call the function `MyEncrypt` when it is actually called `Encrypt`.

Example:

```
function Encrypt(eptr : PChar) : PChar;  far; external 'MYDLL' name
'MyEncrypt';
```

- `ordinal number`—Imports the function by ordinal number. This is the fastest way to look up a function because the program does not need to use the lookup table in the DLL. Win32 ignores the ordinal number references and lookup by name.

Example:

```
function Encrypt(eptr : PChar) : PChar;  far; external 'MYDLL' index 1;
```

Now that you have that down, finish your program and test your DLL. Drop an edit control and a button onto to the form. Position them and size them to your liking. You might want to add a button to exit the program as well (this is optional because you can always use the control box to close your application). Double-click the button you set up to execute your routine. Add the following code:

```
Var
   RetCode : Integer;
   Source,Dest : PChar;
   MyStr : string;
   begin
     {Allocate space your null terminated string}
     Source:=StrAlloc(100);
     {Get the text from the edit box}
     MyStr:=Edit1.Text;
     {Convert your string to a null terminated string}
     StrPcopy(Source,MyStr);
     {Pass your null terminated string to the DLL
      for encryption and put the returned contents
      in the edit box}
     Edit1.Text:=StrPas(Encrypt(Source));
   end;
```

This code does the following:

- Reads the text in the edit box.
- Converts the text to a null-terminated string.
- Sends the null-terminated string to your function in the DLL.
- Captures the returned string and converts it back to a Pascal-style string.
- Updates the edit box with the new string.

Do a Save Project As, naming the unit DLLTEST.PAS and the project TESTDLL.DPR.

When you are finished, your code should look like this:

```
unit Dlltest;

interface

uses
 Windows, Messages, SysUtils, Classes, Graphics, Controls, Forms, Dialogs,
➥StdCtrls;

type
  TForm1 = class(TForm)
    Button1: TButton;
    Edit1: TEdit;
    Label1: TLabel;
    Button2: TButton;
    procedure Button1Click(Sender: TObject);
    procedure Button2Click(Sender: TObject);
  private
    { Private declarations }
  public
    { Public declarations }
  end;

var
  Form1: TForm1;
```

```
implementation

{$R *.DFM}

{ Import routine from DLL. Takes password and returns the processed string}
  function Encrypt(eptr : PChar) : PChar;
  far; external 'MYDLL';

procedure TForm1.Button1Click(Sender: TObject);
Var
   RetCode : Integer;
   Source,Dest : PChar;
   MyStr : string;
   begin
     {Allocate space your null terminated string}
     Source:=StrAlloc(100);
     {Get the text from the edit box}
     MyStr:=Edit1.Text;
     {Convert your string to a null terminated string}
     StrPcopy(Source,MyStr);
     {Pass your null terminated string to the DLL
      for encryption and put the returned contents
      in the edit box}
     Edit1.Text:=StrPas(Encrypt(Source));
   end;
procedure TForm1.Button2Click(Sender: TObject);
begin
     Application.Terminate;
end;

end.
```

Once you have this typed in and debugged, you should be able to type any text you want into the text box. Click the button containing code to call the DLL and see the text in the edit box change. The first time you click, the text will be scrambled. The second time you click it will be unscrambled. This certainly is not the most secure encryption routine around, but it can be fun and useful in keeping the casual user from seeing your data. Enough on encryption though, we are focused on writing DLLs. You have just completed writing your first DLL as well as a program that calls and tests it.

Calling the DLL in Another Language

Now that you have tested your DLL and are satisfied that it works, what if you want to call it from another language? As a programmer, it will be up to you to find out what the requirements are for calling a DLL in the language you are using. For the sake of an example, look at how you could call the DLL from Visual Basic. VB seems like a natural here because many Delphi programmers have come from Visual Basic. The important thing to remember is that programming languages do not always have the same data types. Sure, you will usually have the basic types such as integer, long integer, and so on, but strings are often handled differently as well as other types that may be found in one language and not another. Because of this, you will have to know what data types need to be sent to a DLL function that you wish to call and what will be returned. You must then determine how to declare the external function (DLL function) properly so that it will work. You may also need to convert or move the data to a data type you can work with in the language you are using. In any case, Visual Basic does not handle pointers, so you need to declare your function to send the string in by value and expect a long integer back. You also need to use a Windows API call to transfer the data at the pointer location to a Visual Basic string. We put the following two `declare` statements in the `declarations` portion of your VB program. Comments are included explaining what each `declare` is used for.

```
'Declare for MYDLL.DLL
Declare Function Encrypt Lib "mydll.dll" (ByVal lpString As String) As Long
'Declare for lstrcpy which copies the data at the pointer address
'to a visual basic string since VB does not handle pointers
Declare Function lstrcpy Lib "Kernel" (ByVal lpString1 As Any, ByVal lpString2
➥As Any) As Long
```

With that taken care of, assume you have created a text box and a button to use for testing the program. The text box is called Text1. Here is the code that would be put in the button Click event. This code is also commented for your convenience.

```
Sub Command1_Click ()
    Dim MyString As String
    Dim StrPtr As Long
    'Get the string for the text box
    MyString = Text1.Text
    'Send your string the Encrypt Function in MYDLL.DLL
    'and receive a pointer back
    StrPtr = Encrypt(MyString)
    'Copy the data at the pointer to your VB string
    StrPtr = lstrcpy(MyString, StrPtr)
    'Put the modified string back in the text box
    Text1.Text = MyString
End Sub
```

If you have Visual Basic, take a few minutes to enter this program and try it out. You'll find that it works just as well as your Delphi counterpart. This really demonstrates the power of putting functions and procedures in a DLL.

Calling a DLL from a DLL

You may be scratching your head by now as you read the section heading above. Calling a DLL from a DLL? Why in the heck would I want to do that? Well, actually this idea is not that far-fetched. Assume that you have a DLL that you have written containing many numeric operations and arithmetic functions. Now you are writing another DLL that does other types of functions, and one of your routines needs a function that you know is in your

MYNUM.DLL file. All you would need to do is a little setup and call it from the current DLL. Now you ask, but if I wrote both of them, why not include them in one DLL? Well, you could do that. What if you are going to have both of the DLLs loaded on the system your program is running on anyway? Well, in that case, why spend the time to cut, paste, recompile, and so on? You know your handy little function is already compiled and debugged; just call it from where you and and you only need to debug the new DLL. At some point it may make sense to merge the DLLs. It just depends on what you want and need to do. Now assume that you have this DLL that you didn't write. You know how to use all its functions and it has become a favorite of yours. You are writing your own DLL and you decide that you need to use one of those functions in your DLL. You now have no choice. You will have to call that DLL from your DLL. Also remember that Windows API calls are in DLLs, so you may eventually need to do this anyway. The bottom line here is that calling a DLL from a DLL is something that you should realize may be necessary and/or useful at some point. Luckily, this is very easy to do. If you understand what you have done up to this point, you will find this very simple. You might want to take a short two- or three-minute break and think about how this might be done, then come back and take a look at a simple example of how it is done.

Calling a DLL from a DLL is very easy. I won't bore you with all the setup details again; you already know how to do that. I'll show you the code for two new DLLs and a program that tests them. Your first DLL (NUMDLL.DLL) has two functions, one to increment an integer and one to decrement an integer and then return the result. The second DLL (NUM2DLL.DLL) has a function that adds three to an integer and returns the result. Your NUM2DLL calls the `increment` function from the NUM2LL.DLL and uses it to increment your integer three times by using a loop. After the loop is complete, it returns the new value. These are simple operations that would not require a DLL or the techniques that are being used here, but the real point is calling a DLL from a DLL. So, we'll focus on calling another DLL. When you are done with this book, you can put some code in these DLLs that actually does something worthwhile, like activate a routine that displays a bitmap of a spreadsheet so the boss doesn't see what you were really doing. Hey, now there's an idea!

Following is the code for NUMDLL.DLL. There's nothing special here, just a DLL with an `Increment` and `Decrement` function.

```
Library Numdll;

{$R *.RES}

function Increment(num : Integer):integer;export;
Begin
     num:=num+1;
     Increment:=num;
end;
function Decrement(num : Integer):integer;export;
Begin
     num:=num-1;
     Decrement:=num;
```

```
end;

Exports
     Increment,
     Decrement;
begin
end.
```

Here is the code for NUM2DLL.DLL. The only thing special here is that the function that you want to call in the other DLL is declared as if you were calling it from a normal program.

```
Library Num2dll;

{$R *.RES}

function Increment(num1 : integer):integer;far;external 'numdll';

function AddThree(num2 : integer):integer;export;
Var
   x : integer;
begin
   For x:=1 to 3 do
   begin
        num2:=Increment(num2);
   end;
   AddThree:=num2;
end;
Exports
    AddThree;
begin
end.
```

Finally, create the the code to test this. Design a form that looks like Figure 19.2 and add the code appropriately as it appears in Listing 19.2. Do a File | Project Save As and call it NUMTEST.DPR.

Figure 19.2.
Add Three DLL—calling a DLL test.

Your program doesn't even need to know about NUMDLL.DLL. When you make a call to NUM2DDL.DLL, it makes the call to NUMDLL.DLL.

```
unit Getnum;

interface

uses
```

```
 Windows, Messages, SysUtils, Classes, Graphics, Controls, Forms, Dialogs,
➥StdCtrls;

type
  TForm1 = class(TForm)
    Button1: TButton;
    Edit1: TEdit;
    procedure Button1Click(Sender: TObject);
  private
    { Private declarations }
  public
    { Public declarations }
  end;

var
  Form1: TForm1;

implementation

{$R *.DFM}

function AddThree(num : integer):integer;far;external 'num2dll';

procedure TForm1.Button1Click(Sender: TObject);
Var
   MyNum : Integer;
   MyStr : String;
begin
     MyStr:=Edit1.Text;
     MyNum:=StrToInt(MyStr);
     Edit1.Text:=IntToStr(AddThree(MyNum));
end;

end.
```

By now, you should have a pretty good grasp on what is involved in creating your own DLL with functions and procedures. Now is a good time to point out that you can write some pretty compact and efficient code in your DLLs if you put your mind to it. In MYDLL.DLL, you created a DLL that actually used some string functions. This required us to include the SysUtils unit in the `uses` clause. This is handy and convenient but cost us an additional 15K or so of memory. A well-written DLL should be compact, fast, and bulletproof. These topics are out of the scope of this chapter and in some cases, out of the scope of the book. The main point I want to convey to you is that you spend some time thinking out the best way to implement your code in a DLL. Use exception handling (as you see in the next section when you add forms to a DLL) to make sure your DLL doesn't exit without cleaning up after itself. Use standard Pascal code or inline assembler if possible to keep memory requirements down. Think out, test, and optimize your code where speed is important. Finally, if you do need to include a unit for some functions or procedures that you don't want to reinvent or don't know how to, then by all means do so. All these routines are here for you to use. Just use good judgment and be aware of the cost. You are now ready to move on and learn how to add forms to DLLs, a very cool and easy thing to do!

Adding Forms to a DLL

Now for the good stuff: adding a form to your DLL. This may seem like a pretty complicated task (and it would be in C/C++) but it is fairly simple in Delphi once you know the steps. It helps to have a basic understanding of object-oriented programming (OOP) to fully understand what is going on, but we will take a close look at the program as we go and talk about these concepts. Adding a form or other resource to your DLL is a very powerful feature. You can create some nice functions and procedures that display or take information via forms, dialog boxes, and so on, and store them in a DLL. Then, of course, you can use them in Delphi, VB, C/C++, etc.

Creating DLLs with Functions and Forms

Some of the steps are a bit different than when you create a DLL without forms, so walk through this step by step so you can see the differences. The steps required are listed; follow along reading the comments to understand what the various portions of code do.

1. Start Delphi if it is not already running, do a File | New, and select the DLL item.
2. Create a directory in which to store the source code for the DLL. This is optional, but it keeps things organized and makes it easier to see what belongs to your project.
3. This time add a new form by doing a File | New Form and add some components to it. Add two buttons, one label, and an edit box. (See Listing 19.1.)
4. Add the appropriate code to the components. (See Listing 19.1.)
5. Add a function that activates the form or executes some code. (See Listing 19.1.)
6. Add the declaration for the function just before the `Implementation` section. (See Listing 19.1.)
7. Save the project. Choose File | Save Project As and save as GETKEY.DPR. Save the unit as INPUT.PAS.
8. Choose View | Project Source.
9. Add the `Exports` clause to the bottom before the main `begin` at the bottom of the listing. (See Listing 19.2.)
10. Delete any code between the main `begin...end` block. (See Listing 19.2.)

Go ahead and make your code look like the listings and then take a closer look at what is going on.

TYPE **Listing 19.1. INPUT.PAS**

```
unit Input;

interface

uses
 Windows, Messages, SysUtils, Classes, Graphics, Controls, Forms, Dialogs,
➥StdCtrls, Buttons;

type
  TForm1 = class(TForm)
    Edit1: TEdit;
    Label1: TLabel;
    BitBtn1: TBitBtn;
    BitBtn2: TBitBtn;
    procedure FormCreate(Sender: TObject);
  private
    { Private declarations }
  public
    { Public declarations }
  end;

var
  Form1: TForm1;

{Export function for use outside the DLL}
function Get_Key(Dummy : integer) : Integer;export;

implementation

{$R *.DFM}

Function Get_Key(Dummy : integer) : Integer;
Var
   KeyForm : TForm1;
   TempStr : String;
   RetCode : Integer;
Begin
    {Create an instance of your form}
    KeyForm:=TForm1.Create(Application);
    {Clear the edit box}
    KeyForm.Edit1.Text:='';
    {Set the initial return value to -1 indicating error}
    Get_Key:=-1;
    Try
      with KeyForm do
         {If OK button pressed, Get char from edit box}
         if ShowModal = mrOk Then
           Begin
             TempStr:=KeyForm.Edit1.Text;
             {Set retrun value to value in edit box}
             RetCode:=Ord(TempStr[1]);
             Get_Key:=RetCode;
           end
           {If Cancel pressed, set return value to 0}
```

continues

Listing 19.1. continued

```
           Else
             Get_Key:=0;
    finally
             {Remove the instance of your form from memory}
             KeyForm.Free;
  end;
end;
procedure TForm1.FormCreate(Sender: TObject);
begin

end;

end.
```

TYPE

Listing 19.2. GETKEY.DPR

```
Library Getkey;

uses
  Forms,SysUtils,
  Input in 'INPUT.PAS' {Form1};

{$R *.RES}
{Encryption Function}
function Encrypt(eptr : PChar;EncryptKey : Integer):PChar; export;
Var
   x : integer;
   l : word;
   estr : string;
   ch : char;
begin
     {Convert the null terminated string to
      a pascal style string}
     estr:=StrPas(eptr);
     {Get the length of the string}
     l:=StrLen(eptr);
     {Encrypt the string using a simple
      exclusive or method}
     for x:=1 to l do
     begin
          ch:=estr[x];
          ch:=Chr(Ord(ch) xor EncryptKey);
          estr[x]:=ch;
     end;
     {Convert the pascal style string
      back to a null terminated string}
     StrPcopy(eptr,estr);
     {Return the string to the calling function}
     Encrypt:=eptr;
end;
```

```
{Provides lookup info calling programs}
Exports
  Get_Key,
  Encrypt;
begin
end.
```

Start with the code in the form unit (INPUT.PAS) in Listing 19.1. You should notice a lot of the normal code put there by Delphi when you create a form. There are also a few things that need to be added to make the form work in your DLL. First, declare the function that you will be calling.

```
{Export function for use outside the DLL}
function Get_Key(Dummy : integer) : Integer;export;
```

As with your first DLL, notice the `export` at the end of the declaration. This tells the compiler that it will be made available to other programs.

Now move on to the actual function where you see a few new things. First, you set a variable called `KeyForm` of type `Tform1`.

```
Var
      KeyForm : Tform1;
```

Next, you use this variable to create an instance of your form so it can be displayed. You do this with the following code. This is where OOP enters the scene.

```
KeyForm:=TForm1.Create(Application);
```

NOTE

> As you start creating your own DLLs with forms, keep in mind that you must have created the instance of your form before you can access anything on it.

Now take a look at the entire function.

```
Function Get_Key(Dummy : integer) : Integer;
Var
   KeyForm : TForm1;
   TempStr : String;
   RetCode : Integer;
Begin
    {Create an instance of your form}
    KeyForm:=TForm1.Create(Application);
    {Clear the edit box}
    KeyForm.Edit1.Text:="'';
    {Set the intial return value to -1 indicating error}
    Get_Key:=-1;
    Try
```

```
    with KeyForm do
       {If OK button pressed, Get char from edit box}
       if ShowModal = mrOk Then
         Begin
           TempStr:=KeyForm.Edit1.Text;
           {Set retrun value to value in edit box}
           RetCode:=Ord(TempStr[1]);
           Get_Key:=RetCode;
         end
         {If Cancel pressed, set return value to 0}
         Else
           Get_Key:=0;
  finally
           {Remove the instance of your form from memory}
           KeyForm.Free;
end;
```

The function is defined to take an integer (which is not used currently) and pass back an integer containing the ASCII code for the character entered in the editbox. Next notice the line with the following:

```
if ShowModal = mrOk Then
```

The BitBtn components used in your example have a property called `ModalResult` to pass back the to the form, which can be read by the `ShowModal` function. The constants used in your example are `mrOk` and `mrCancel`, which are set in the OK button and Cancel button `ModalResult` properties, respectively. When the button is clicked, it passes the `ModalResult` set at design time back to the form. This allows us to determine which button was pressed. When the `ShowModal` function returns a true in the statement `if ShowModal = mrOk Then`, the code associated with that statement is executed. In this case, you go get the character from the editbox, get its ASCII value, and send the value back to the calling program. If the results of the statement are false, you fall through to the `else` and set the return value to 0. Next you need to do some cleanup and exit. For this, do the following:

```
KeyForm.Free
```

This releases the resources used by the object (our form) that you created and exits the function. Also notice the `Try` and `Finally` keywords in the previous code example for `Function Get_Key(Dummy : integer) : Integer;`. This gives us some protection in your routine (remember the exception handling earlier in the book?). If an exception is raised during your DLL's execution, you release the form from memory and exit.

That's all you need to worry about in the form unit. Now move on to the project source file (GETKEY.DPR). As with the regular DLL, you need to change the header from `Program Getkey` to `Library Getkey`. You also notice that the `uses` clause is included this time.

```
Library Getkey;

uses
  Forms,SysUtils,
  Input in 'INPUT.PAS' {Form1};
```

If you followed the instructions to this point for making a DLL with a form, Delphi will have updated the `uses` clause for you. You also want the `Encrypt` function included from the first DLL example. This function as well as others could have also be put in a unit and made available with an entry in the `uses` clause. The final thing to note is that you must add an entry to the `Exports` section for the function that activates your form. In this case, it looks like this:

```
Exports
  Get_Key,
  Encrypt;
begin
end.
```

That's all there is to it! At this point, if you have followed the instructions and made sure that your code looks like that in Listings 19.1 and 19.2, you should be able to successfully compile your first DLL with a form in it! With that in mind, go create a program to test it.

Accessing Forms in DLLs

Accessing forms in a DLL is no different than calling any other DLL function. All the work has been done in the DLL code. You simply call the procedure or function, passing parameters if needed, and the DLL function displays the form. Once the form has done its job, it exits and passes back information if necessary and goes away. Build a simple program to call the new DLL and use the form and function that you have stored there.

Create a new project called TESTFORM.DPR. Save the project and name UNIT1.PAS as T1FORM.PAS. Obviously, you can call these anything you like, but these are names used in the listings and it is less confusing if you use the same. On the form, add three buttons, three labels, and one editbox. Set up the properties and make the form look something like Figure 19.3.

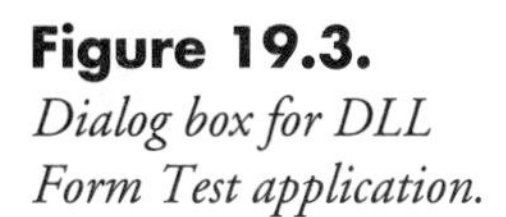

Figure 19.3.
Dialog box for DLL Form Test application.

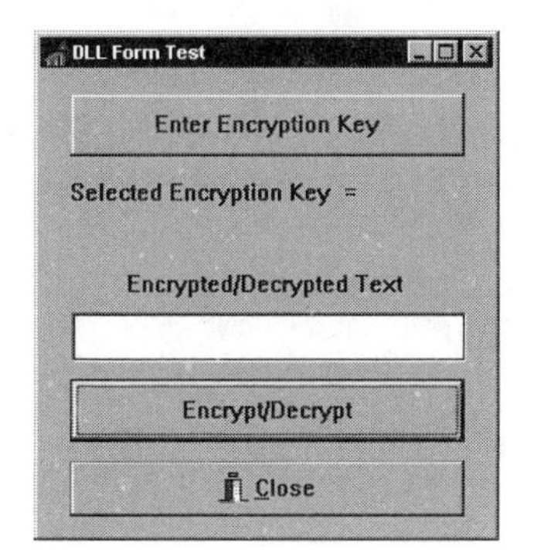

Using the code example that follows, enter the code in the appropriate places. Make sure to set the caption properties on the buttons and labels appropriately.

```
unit T1form;

interface

uses
  SysUtils, WinTypes, WinProcs, Messages, Classes, Graphics, Controls,
  Forms, Dialogs, StdCtrls, Buttons;

type
  TForm1 = class(TForm)
    Label1: TLabel;
    Button1: TButton;
    Edit2: TEdit;
    Label2: TLabel;
    BitBtn2: TBitBtn;
    Button2: TButton;
    Label3: TLabel;
    procedure BitBtn2Click(Sender: TObject);
    procedure Button1Click(Sender: TObject);
    procedure Button2Click(Sender: TObject);
    procedure FormCreate(Sender: TObject);
  private
    { Private declarations }
  public
    { Public declarations }
  end;

var
  Form1: TForm1;
  EKey : Integer;
implementation

{$R *.DFM}

function Get_Key(Dummy : Integer) : Integer;far;external 'GETKEY';
function Encrypt(eptr : PChar;EncryptKey : integer) : PChar;far;external
'GETKEY';

{Close Button}
procedure TForm1.BitBtn2Click(Sender: TObject);
begin
     halt;
end;

{Encrypt/Decrypt Button Code}
procedure TForm1.Button1Click(Sender: TObject);
Var
   Source : PChar;
   MyStr : String;
begin
   Source:=StrAlloc(100);
   MyStr:=Edit2.Text;
   StrPcopy(Source,MyStr);
   Edit2.Text:=StrPas(Encrypt(Source,EKey));
```

```
end;

{Enter Encryption Key Button Code}
procedure TForm1.Button2Click(Sender: TObject);
begin
     EKey:=Get_Key(0);
     Label3.Caption:=Chr(EKey);
     Button1.Default:=True;
     Button2.Default:=False;
end;


end.
```

As you might expect, you enter the declaration in the code to tell your program that you will be calling functions that are not available in your code. These follow the `resource filename` directive (`{$R *.DFM}`) like this:

```
{$R *.DFM}

function Get_Key(Dummy : Integer) : Integer;far;external 'GETKEY';
function Encrypt(eptr : PChar;EncryptKey : integer) : PChar;far;external
➥'GETKEY';
```

Once you have entered the code and compiled the program, you should see the screen in Figure 19.3. Pressing the Enter Encryption key displays the form in Figure 19.4.

Figure 19.4.
The Encryption Key Input Screen.

Enter **`A`** in the editbox and press OK. The form disapears and you return to the screen shown in Figure 19.3. Next, enter **`testing`** in the editbox. When you press the Encrypt/Decrypt button, you should see something like `5$25(/&` in the edit box. When you press Encrypt/Decrypt again, you should see `testing`. Now press the Enter Encryption key button again. This time change the character to a "G". Press the Encrypt/Decrypt button again. This time the text should change to `3"43.)`. Press Encrypt/Decrypt one more time and it should become `testing` again. If you experiment enough, you will find certain combinations of strings and encryption key characters that will mess up your string when you attempt to restore it or won't display the actual characters in the editbox. This is due to the nature of the XOR encryption algorithm. If a combination of characters generates the correct character in your string, it can cut your string short, thus affecting its restoration. Also, some of the characters may translate to something that looks like ¦. This is because the editbox doesn't display all symbols available in the ASCII or Extended ASCII character set. This is nothing to worry about; the actual character value is still in memory. When you click again, the string should return to normal.

Calling a DLL Function with a Form from Visual Basic

If you have done development in Visual Basic, I wanted to take this opportunity to show you that the work you do on DLLs in Delphi is not wasted. You can use your DLLs written in Delphi in other languages. If you don't have Visual Basic, you can skip this section and go right to the summary.

Even though calling a DLL with a form in it is no different than calling a regular function, create a simple Visual Basic program to call your `Get_Key` function and make sure that you can actually call it from something else. If you don't have Visual Basic, you can just follow along.

Create a Visual Basic form with a button and two labels in the general declarations section, and add the following declaration:

```
Declare Function Get_Key Lib "Getkey.dll" (ByVal EKey As Integer) As Integer
```

Add the following code to the button:

```
Sub Command1_Click ()
    Dim ch As Integer
    ch = Get_Key(0)
    Label2.Caption = Chr$(ch)
End Sub
```

When you run the program and click the button, the program should call the DLL `Get_Key` function and display the form on the screen. At this point, you should see your Encryption Key Input Screen form that you created earlier (see Figure 19.4). When you enter a character and press OK, the form closes, returns the ASCII character code back to the Visual Basic program, and displays it in the label.

This pretty much wraps up our discussion of writing DLLs in Delphi. I think by now you can see that this is a pretty powerful feature and not all that difficult, especially if you have come from Visual Basic or a similar environment that doesn't allow the creation of DLLs. If you still use other languages, you can now use Delphi to extend their capabilities by creating your own DLLs!

Summary

In this chapter we discussed DLLs and what they are. We also talked about why you would want to write one. We then moved on to learn how to set up the code to write your own DLL. From there, you learned how to add a function to the DLL. Next you learned how to export the functions, making them avialable to other programs or DLLs. After creating your DLLs,

you needed to test them, so you developed your own program and learned how to import (call) your DLL functions in your DLL. You learned how to call your DLL functions from another programming language (VB). You moved on to learn how to add a form to a DLL and call it from Delphi and VB.

Q&A

Q How large will MYDLL.DLL be with a form in it?

A You will add approximately 200K to the your DLL because of the forms unit. Additional units add on to this number.

Q Do I need to load and unload my DLLs?

A No, your DLL will be loaded into memory if it is not found in memory and unloaded when not needed anymore.

Q My programs can't find my DLLs, what gives?

A Your DLL must either be in the directory your program is running from, the \WINDOWS\SYSTEM directory, or someplace in the search path.

Workshop

Quiz

1. What is a DLL?
2. Why use a DLL?
3. What is the `Exports` statement used for?
4. Where and how do you declare a DLL function so you can use it in your own program?
5. How do you show or activate the form in your DLL?

Exercises

1. Add a function to MYDLL.DLL to accept an integer, increment it, and return it as an integer. Create a small program to test it.
2. Add a form to the GETKEY.DLL that displays a string that has been passed to it and exits upon pressing an OK button.

Week 3

Day 20

Writing Your Own Visual Components

By now you have a good understanding of Delphi. You can summarize it as a rich set of programming building blocks that you can use to develop applications rapidly, as well as the necessary tools for communicating and tying the building blocks together. These building blocks are the *visual components,* which enable rapid application development. You could write a Delphi application without using any visual components—you could use pure Win32 API calls in an application. Developing applications is easy, though, because of the visual component library. Today, you will learn many of the important concepts in writing a visual component. You will see sample visual components, which can help you write your own visual components.

Why Write a Visual Component?

Visual components are so powerful because they hide all the implementation details from the developer. Just as a driver does not have to understand how rack-and-pinion steering works in his car in order to drive, an applications developer does not have to know how a visual component works in order to use it. He simply needs to know how to communicate with it. There are several reasons why you might want to write your own visual components.

Reuse Code

The interface to a visual component is built into the Delphi programming environment. Therefore, if you use an object frequently, you can turn it into a visual component and add it to the toolbar. This makes using the component easier and includes the implementation in the library.

Modify Current Visual Components

Because Delphi is an object-oriented language and a visual component is an object, you can create a visual component that is a subclass of an existing one. Suppose, for example, that you love to use blue circles in your applications. You want to take advantage of all the properties, events, and methods of the TShape component, but you always change the shape parameter to a circle and the color of the brush to blue. One solution is to create a subclass of TShape called TBlueCircle. This adds to the library a component that is a blue circle by default when it is placed on a form.

Make Money

If you have to add specialized functionality to your application, you can buy a third-party component. This is one of the biggest advantages of a component-based system. For example, if you need networking capabilities, you can either write the networking routines yourself or buy a set of components that provide network capability. Likewise, you can create a component that provides additional functionality and sell it to other applications developers. When you sell the library, you provide a compiled version of the product. Therefore, your customer does not see the source code or the implementation details of the product. When the component is added to a form, however, he can use the friendly interface to communicate with the component through the IDE.

See Changes in Behavior During Development

If you compile a piece of code into a visual component, you can see changes in its appearance during development. For example, when you set the value of the `Shape` property to a circle on the TShape component, the shape on the form changes into a circle. This happens before the component is compiled. This is extremely useful in components that are visible. During development, you can get a sense of how the application will look at runtime.

Building and Installing a Component

The first component that you will build only compiles and installs on the toolbar. You can add the TDoNothing component to a form even though it does not do anything. You can, of course, remove the component from the toolbar.

Using the Component Expert

In this example, you use the powerful Component Expert, which is included with Delphi. All components must be inherited from other components. If you want to start from scratch, you must create a subclass of the `TComponent` class. The Component Expert takes three pieces of information:

- The name of the new component that you want to create
- The class that the component is inherited from
- The toolbar that the component should be installed on

The steps are

1. Choose Component, New from the main Delphi menu. This brings up the Component Expert dialog box.
2. In the dialog box, specify `TDoNothing` for the class name, `TComponent` for the ancestor type, and Samples for the palette page (see Figure 20.1). Click OK.

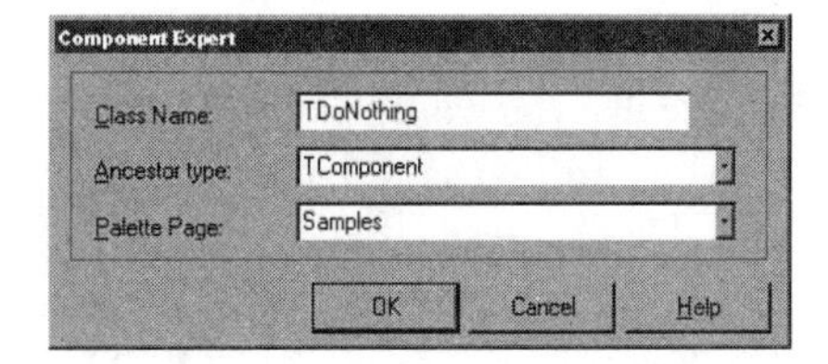

Figure 20.1.
The Component Expert for `TDoNothing`.

Delphi creates the shell of a unit that compiles to a visual component. Save the unit with a meaningful name, such as NOTHING.PAS. Listing 20.1 is the code that the expert produces.

TYPE **Listing 20.1. The shell of a visual component.**

```
unit nothing;

interface

uses
  SysUtils, Windows, Messages, Classes, Graphics, Controls, Forms, Dialogs;

type
  TDoNothing = class(TComponent)
  private
    { Private declarations }
  protected
    { Protected declarations }
  public
    { Public declarations }
  published
    { Published declarations }
  end;

procedure Register;

implementation

procedure Register;
begin
  RegisterComponents('Samples', [TDoNothing]);
end;

end.
```

ANALYSIS Usually, you would modify the shell to add custom functionality to the component. There are two parts to the component library: the `TDoNothing` class and the `Register` procedure. Delphi uses all the code associated with the class to determine how the component functions. It also calls the `Register` procedure to place the component on the toolbar. In this case, it simply installs the component on the Samples tab of the IDE.

Compiling and Installing from Source Code

To compile and install the component, follow these steps:

1. Choose Component, Install from the main Delphi Menu. This brings up the Install Components dialog box.
2. Click the Add button on the Install Components dialog box. This brings up the Add Module dialog box.

3. Type the path name and the filename—NOTHING.PAS—or choose Browse to find the source file. Click OK. The Install Components dialog box now shows `nothing` in the Installed units list box. (See Figure 20.2.)

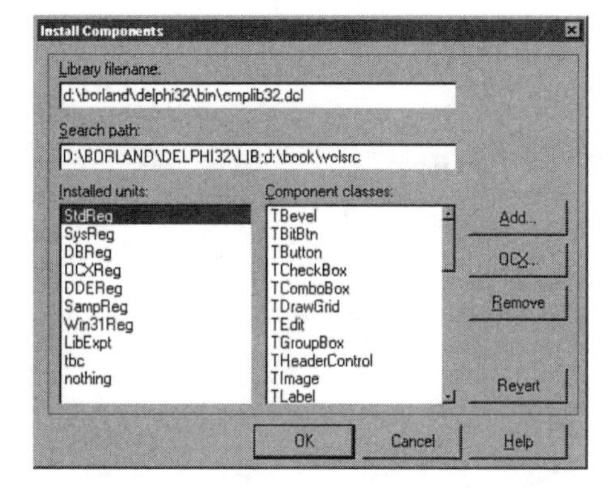

Figure 20.2.
The Install Components dialog box.

4. Click OK to compile and install the component.

Look at the Samples toolbar. Notice there's a new component on it. Put the mouse over the component so that the hint shows. The new component is a DoNothing component. Create a new application and add the component to the form. When you click the component to view the properties and events pages, you see that there are two properties (see Figure 20.3). The `Name` property defaults to DoNothing1, and the `Tag` property defaults to 0. There are no events on the events page. This is a fully functional visual component even though it does not do anything.

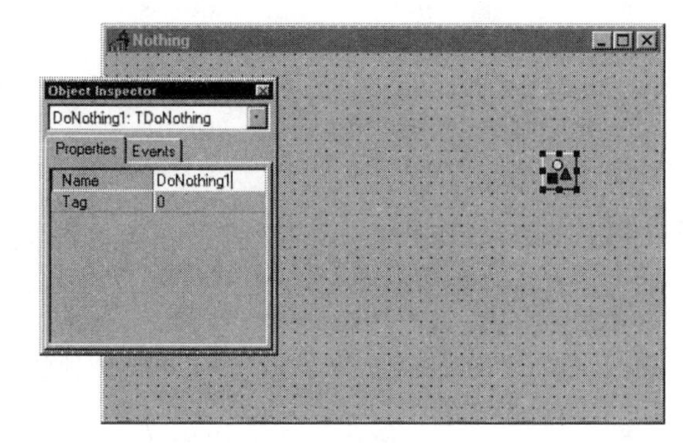

Figure 20.3.
The application and properties page with the DoNothing component.

Removing the Component

You sometimes need to remove a component from the toolbar or uninstall it from Delphi. For example, an upgraded version of a visual component might become available, or you might want to remove a component that you do not use. The TDoNothing component that you just created is essentially useless. To remove it, follow these steps:

1. Choose Component, Install from the main menu. This brings up the Install Components dialog box.
2. In the Installed Units list box, click the `nothing` unit. The TDoNothing component type is displayed in the Component Classes list box.
3. Select Remove and click OK to remove the TDoNothing component from the toolbar.

Installing a Component from a Compiled Library

When you installed the .pas source code file into Delphi, it created a compiled version of the component called NOTHING.DCU. If you wanted to sell your DoNothing library, you would distribute the .dcu file so that customers could not see the source code. Installing a compiled library is the same as installing from source code except that you specify the NOTHING.DCU file in the Add Module dialog box.

Adding a Bitmap for a Component

A bitmap represents a visual component it on the Component toolbar. It is taken from a Delphi resource file with the same name as the .dcu file and a 24×24-bitmap resource for each component in the library. The resource name must correspond to the class name of the component. To build the resource file, you can use the image editor tool and design your own bitmap.

Writing a Visual Component

An applications developer uses components by placing them on a form or by using the `Create` method. After you create a component, you can manipulate it by setting properties, calling methods, and responding to events. You do not have to worry about how properties and methods work. The component calls its event handler when a particular event occurs. When you write a component, you must write the implementation details for properties and methods and call event handlers when the event should occur. To do this, define a class that becomes the component and fill in the necessary details.

Private, Protected, Public, and Published

Delphi uses object classes to create visual components. Different parts of the object class definition are declared in different protected regions. Variables, procedures, and functions can have four types of access.

`Private`Only procedures and functions defined within the class definition and all routines in the same unit have access.

`Protected` procedures and functions defined in the class definition and procedures and functions in descendant classes have access.

`Public`All procedures and functions have access.

`Published`Public access with a hook into the Delphi IDE to display the information in the property and event pages.

Properties

A developer in Delphi uses the properties of a component to read or set certain attributes—similar to the data fields stored in a class. Properties, however, can trigger code to be executed. For example, when you change the `Shape` property on the TShape component, the component actually changes shape. There must be a mechanism that tells the component to change shape when the property is changed. In other words, a property can take on two personalities. It can be a piece of data that affects how a component works, or it can trigger an action.

Methods

Methods are procedures and functions that a class has made public. Although you can use properties to call a function or a procedure, use them only if it is logical to do so. Methods, on the other hand, can be used any time. Another difference is that properties are usually set with one piece of data. Methods can take multiple parameters and can return multiple pieces of data through `VAR` variable declarations.

Events

Events enable developers or users to enhance the component when something happens—that is, when an event occurs. For example, the `OnClick` event means in effect, "If you want to do something when the user clicks this, tell me what procedure to execute." It is the job of the component designer to call the component user's events when necessary.

Building a Useful Component—TMult

You can now create a visual component that performs a task and includes at least one property, method, and event. Think of it as the "Hello, World!" of component design. It is impractical to use this component in real applications, but it demonstrates the basic concepts of component design. It is also an example of deriving a component from the top of the component hierarchy. All components have TComponent in their family tree. TMult is a direct descendant of TComponent.

Creating TMult

The TMult component has two properties of type `integer` that can be set at design time or runtime. The component has one method, `DoMult`. When it is executed, the two values in the properties are multiplied and the result is placed in a third property called `Res`. One event in the TMult component, `OnTooBig`, is also implemented. If either number is set greater than 100 when the `DoMult` method is called, the component calls the code to which the user has pointed in the event page. TMult is an example of a purely functional component—it has no graphical parts. Standard components that are purely functional include TTimer, TDatabase, and Ttable.

TMult contains the following properties:

`Val1` The first value to multiply. It is available at design time and runtime.

`Val2` The second value to multiply. It is available at design time and runtime.

`Res` The value obtained by multiplying `Val1` and `Val2`. `Val1` is multiplied by `Val2`. It is available only at runtime.

TMult contains one method, `DoMult`, which implements the multiplication of `Val1` and `Val2`. TMult's event, `OnTooBig`, calls the user's event handler (if one exists) when `Val1` is multiplied by `Val2` and either value is greater than 100.

Building TMult

The first step is to create a unit that has the standard shell for all components. To do this, use the Component Expert as before. Figure 20.4 shows how you should fill in the Component Expert for TMult.

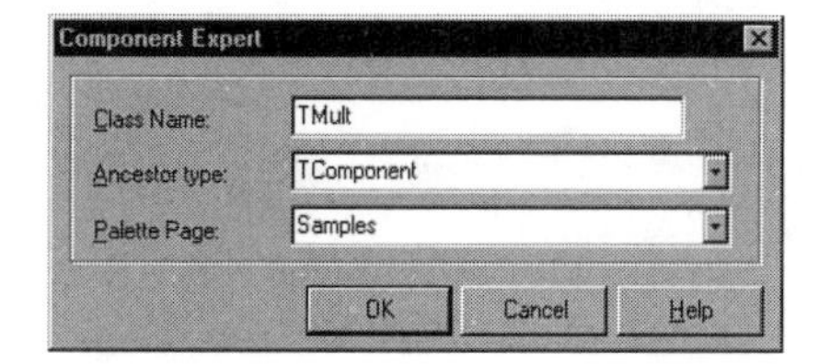

Figure 20.4.
Component expert parameters for TMult.

The code generated includes a shell for the `TMult` class declaration and one procedure for registering the function. To develop the component's properties, method, and event, you must modify the class definition and provide the corresponding procedures and functions. The first step is to save the shell with a meaningful name. In this case, use TMULTIPLY.PAS.

Adding Properties to TMult

TMult has three properties: `Val1`, `Val2`, and `Res`. `Val1` and `Val2` are available at design time and runtime, whereas `Res` is available only at runtime. Because each property holds data, you must define variables in the `TMult` class to hold data. Users do not access the variables directly but, instead, through a specialized call. Therefore, the variables that hold data for the three properties are declared in the `Private` section of the class definition—which means that only functions and procedures within the class can access the data. By convention, the names of the variables begins with `F`, followed by the name of the property. In this case, all the properties are integers, so they are declared as type `integer`. The class declaration is

```
type
  TMult = class(TComponent)
Private
   FVal1 : integer;
   FVal2 : integer;
   FRes  : integer;
Protected
Public
Published
end;
```

Now you must declare the properties themselves. Use the `property` key word in the class definition. The property definition typically appears in one of two places. If a property will be available at design time, it must be declared in the `Published` section of the declaration. If it is available only at runtime, it is placed in the `Public` section. In this case, the properties are stored as simple data types and no special action is performed when the data is read or written. Therefore, it is possible to use direct access to read and write the property. With *direct access,* you tell Delphi to set or return data from a variable when a property is read or written. `read` and `write` methods define the variables. Here are the property definitions for the three properties:

```
type
  TMult = class(TComponent)
Private
   FVal1 : integer;
   FVal2 : integer;
   FRes  : integer;
protected
public
   Property Res:integer read FRes;     {Property to Obtain Result}
published
   property Val1:integer read FVal1 Write FVal1 default 1; {Operand 1}
   property Val2:integer read FVal2 Write FVal2 default 1; {Operand 2}
end;  {TMult}
```

Because the `Res` property is read-only, you do not need a direct access method to write to the `FRes` variable.

`Val1` and `Val2` are set by default to 1, which is misleading. The default that a property shows is actually set in another step of creating the component—adding a constructor. Delphi uses the default value on the property line to determine whether it should save the value when a user saves a form file. When a user adds this component to a form and leaves `Val1` set to 1, the value is not saved in the .dfm file. If the value is anything else, though, it is saved.

You have declared the properties for the component. If you installed the component now, `Val1` and `Val2` would appear in the Properties box. You have a few more steps to follow to make the component function.

Adding the Constructor

A constructor is called when a class is created. It is often responsible for the dynamic memory allocation or resource gathering that a class needs. The constructor also sets defaults for the variables in a class. When a component is added to a form at design time or runtime, the constructor is called. To declare the constructor in the class definition, add a `constructor` line in the `Public` portion of the class declaration. By convention, `Create` is used as the name of the constructor procedure.

```
{...}
public
constructor Create(AOwner : TComponent); override;{Main Constructor}
{...}
```

The constructor is passed one parameter—the component that owns it. It is different from the parent property. You must specify that you want to override the default constructor for the ancestor class, `TComponent`. In the implementation portion of the unit, you add the associated code for the contructor. For example,

```
constructor TMult.Create(AOwner: TComponent);
BEGIN
```

```
  inherited Create(AOwner); {Call constructor for parent class}
  FVal1 := 1;                       {Set Default for Value1}
  FVal2 := 1;                       {Set Default for Value2}
END; {End constructor}
```

For any parent-specific construction to be performed, you must first call the inherited `Create` procedure. In this case, the only additional step is to set default values for `Val1` and `Val2` that correspond to the default section of the property declaration.

Adding a Method

A method is simpler to implement than a property. To declare a method, place a procedure or function in the `public` portion of the class definition and write the associated procedure or function. In this case, you add the `DoMult` method.

```
{...}

public
 procedure DoMult;                                {Method to multiply}

{...}

procedure TMult.DoMult;
Begin
  Res := FVal1 * FVal2
End;
```

Your component now works, so a user can add it to a form, and set values for `Val1` and `Val2` at design time and runtime. During execution, the `DoMult` method can be called to perform the multiplication.

Adding an Event

An event enables a user to have specialized code executed when something happens. For your component, you can add an event that is triggered whenever `Val1` or `Val2` is greater than 100 and `DoMult` is executed. You can modify that code so that the `Res` property remains unchanged when this happens.

In Delphi, an event is simply a specialized property—a property that is a pointer to a function. Everything else that applies to properties applies to functions.

One final piece of information that the component needs to provide is when to call the user's event handler. This is simple. Whenever it is time to trigger an event, test whether the user has defined an event handler. If he has, call the event. You must add the declarations to the class definition.

```
{...}
Private
```

```
   FTooBig : TNotifyEvent;
   {…}
published
   Property OnTooBig:TNotifyEvent read FTooBig write FTooBig;  {Event}
   {…}
end;  {TMult}
 {…}
```

ANALYSIS The TNotifyEvent type, which is used to define FTooBig and OnTooBig, is a generic function pointer type that passes one parameter of type component—usually Self. The final step is to modify the TMult.DoMult procedure so that it calls the event handler if either number is too large. Before you call the event handler, you check whether an event is defined. To do this, you use the assigned function. assigned returns TRUE if an event is defined for the event handler and FALSE if it is not.

Listing 20.2 shows all the code for the component.

TYPE **Listing 20.2. The TMult component.**

```
unit TMultiply;

interface

uses
  SysUtils, WinTypes, WinProcs, Messages, Classes, Graphics, Controls,
  Forms, Dialogs, StdCtrls;

type
  TMult = class(TComponent)
Private
   FTooBig : TNotifyEvent;
   FVal1 : integer;
   FVal2 : integer;
   FRes  : integer;
protected
public
   constructor Create(AOwner : TComponent); override;{Main Constructor}
   procedure DoMult;                                {Method to multiply}
   Property Res:integer read FRes write FRes;     {Property to Obtain Result}
published
   property Val1:integer read FVal1 Write FVal1 default 1; {Operand 1}
   property Val2:integer read FVal2 Write FVal2 default 1; {Operand 2}
   Property OnTooBig:TNotifyEvent read FTooBig write FTooBig;  {Event}
end;  {TMult}

procedure Register;

implementation
{***********************************************}
constructor TMult.Create(AOwner: TComponent);
BEGIN
  inherited Create(AOwner);
```

```
  FVal1 := 1;
  FVal2 := 1;
End;
{*********************************************}
procedure TMult.DoMult;
Begin
 if (Val1 < 100) and (Val2  < 100) then
  Res := FVal1 * FVal2
 else
  if assigned(FTooBig) then OnTooBig(Self);
End;
{*********************************************}
procedure Register;
begin
  RegisterComponents('Samples', [TMult]);
end;
{*********************************************}
end.
```

Testing the Component

ANALYSIS You can install this component by following the procedure described earlier in the chapter. Feel free to create an icon for the toolbar. After the component has been installed, you can test it by creating an application that uses it. The test application for this component consists of three edit boxes and one button. A user can place numbers in the first two edit boxes. When he clicks the button, the numbers are multiplied using the component and the result is placed in the third box. You can add an event handler that displays a dialog box stating that at least one of the numbers is too large if the `OnTooBig` event is triggered.

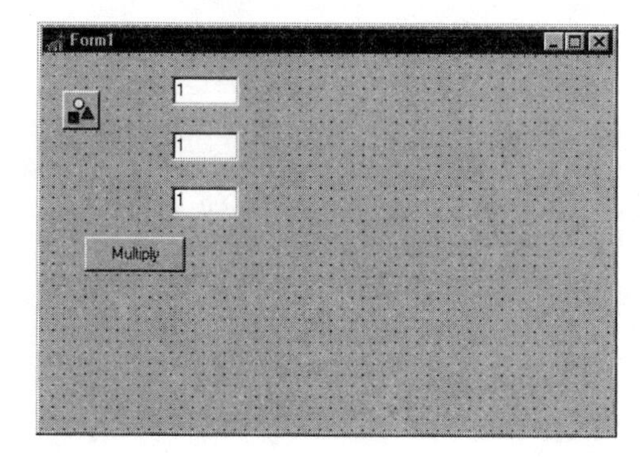

Figure 20.5.
Component layout for TMult test application.

Listing 20.3 shows the code for the test application. Figure 20.5 displays the component layout.

TYPE **Listing 20.3. Main unit for testing TMult.**

```
unit main;

interface

uses
  SysUtils, Windows, Messages, Classes, Graphics, Controls, Forms, Dialogs,
  StdCtrls, TMultiply;

type
  TForm1 = class(TForm)
    Mult1: TMult;
    EdVal1: TEdit;
    EdVal2: TEdit;
    EdResult: TEdit;
    Button1: TButton;
    procedure Button1Click(Sender: TObject);
    procedure Mult1TooBig(Sender: TObject);
  private
    { Private declarations }
  public
    { Public declarations }
  end;

var
  Form1: TForm1;

implementation

{$R *.DFM}

procedure TForm1.Button1Click(Sender: TObject);
begin
   { Set Properties }
   Mult1.Val1 := StrToInt(EdVal1.Text);
   Mult1.Val2 := StrToInt(EdVal2.Text);
   { Execute The Method}
   Mult1.DoMult;
   { Capture the result }
   EdResult.Text := IntToStr(Mult1.Res);
end;

procedure TForm1.Mult1TooBig(Sender: TObject);
begin
   Application.MessageBox('Boy what a wimpy component!',
                          'Component Says it is Too Big',
                          MB_OK);
end;
end.
```

Figure 20.6 shows, the event handler is called when a number greater than 100 is multiplied in the TMult component.

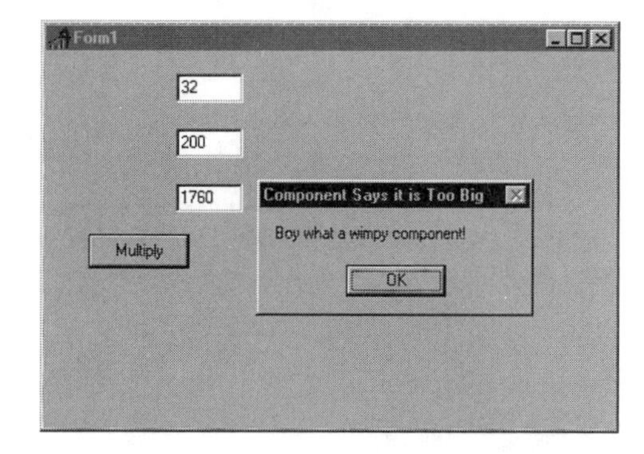

Figure 20.6.
The TMult test application event handler.

Using Procedures to Get and Set Property Values

The TMult component relies on an awkward two-step process for obtaining the product of two numbers. Whenever you change the value of `Val1` or `Val2`, `Res` should be recalculated automatically. To do this, you can call a procedure whenever the property is set. Likewise, you can call a function that returns the value of the property whenever it is read.

An *access method* is the process of calling a procedure or function when a property is accessed. To use access methods, you replace the direct storage variable name with the name of the function used to manipulate the data on the property declaration. To implement access methods in the `TMult` method, you must make the following changes to the class declaration:

```
{…}
type
  TMult = class(TComponent)
Private
   FTooBig : TNotifyEvent;
   FVal1 : integer;
   FVal2 : integer;
   FRes  : integer;
   {**********  Move DoMult to Private Area *******}
   procedure DoMult;
   {**********  Add SetVal1 and SetVal2 Definition *******}

   procedure SetVal1(InVal : Integer);    {To Set Value1}
   procedure SetVal2(InVal : Integer);    {To Set Value2}
protected
public
   constructor Create(AOwner : TComponent); override;{Main Constructor}
   Property Res:integer read FRes write FRes;     {Property to Obtain Result}
published
   {**********  Set access methods *******}
   property Val1:integer read FVal1 Write SetVal1 default 1; {Operand 1}
   property Val2:integer read FVal2 Write SetVal2 default 1; {Operand 2}
   Property OnTooBig:TNotifyEvent read FTooBig write FTooBig;  {Event}
end;  {TMult}
{…}
```

20

```
{*********************************************}
procedure TMult.SetVal1(InVal : Integer);
Begin
  FVal1 := InVal;
  DoMult;
End;
{*********************************************}
procedure TMult.SetVal2(InVal : Integer);
Begin
  FVal2 := InVal;
  DoMult;
End;
{…}
end.
```

In the test program, you no longer need to call the `DoMult` method. In fact, if you attempt to call `DoMult`, the application does not compile because it has been moved to the private region. The functionality otherwise remains the same.

Modifying an Existing Component—TButClock

TMult demonstrates many of the issues involved in writing components, but it does not demonstrate how a component can be derived from an existing component. One of the key advantages of an object-oriented programming language is that an object can be derived from a parent class. For example, if you want a component that is a green button, you do not have to write all the code that makes a button look like a button and that provides hooks for all the possible user interactions. A generic button already exists.

With inheritance, you can derive a new class that has all the functionality of a parent class with the addition of a customized feature or enhancement. In the following example, you create a component called TButClock. It acts exactly like a standard button except that the `Caption` property is automatically overwritten with the current time.

To modify an existing component, you use the Component Expert to create the shell of the component and override any functionality that should be added. In this example, you embed a component within a component—the timer component is embedded in TMult. When the component is created in the constructor routine, the timer is allocated and activated to fire every second. When the timer calls its `OnTimer` event, the `LoopTime` procedure updates the caption. If the component is destroyed, the destructor is called; it frees the timer and returns any system resources.

The Header and Class Definition

The header and class definition for this example are built from the standard Component Expert. Additions to the shell include a constructor, a destructor, a private timer, and a private procedure. The constructor and destructor specify that you want to override the default code that is called when the component is created or deleted. The `MainTimer` timer notifies the component every second, and the `LoopTimer` is the procedure that is called by the timer to update the `Caption` property. `TButClock` is inherited from `Tbutton`. One final note is that `ExtCtrls` needs to be added to the USES list. Listing 20.4 shows the class definition and the UNIT heading for the button clock component.

TYPE

Listing 20.4. Unit heading and class declaration for TButClock.

```
unit tbc;

interface

uses
  SysUtils, Windows, Messages, Classes, Graphics, Controls, Forms, Dialogs,
  StdCtrls,ExtCtrls;

type
  TButClock = class(TButton)
  private
    { Private declarations }
    MainTimer : TTimer;
    procedure LoopTime(Sender:TObject);
  protected
    { Protected declarations }
  public
    constructor Create(AOwner :TComponent);override;
    destructor Destroy;override;
    { Public declarations }
  published
    { Published declarations }
  end;

procedure Register;

implementation
```

20

The Constructor

The constructor first executes any necessary code from its parent. In this case, the object is a descendent of `TButton`, so it is important that the button does whatever allocation or initialization is necessary for it to function properly. After you call the inherited constructor, you create `MainTimer` by calling its `create` method. You then need to set three properties on the timer:

- `MainTimer` must be enabled so that it calls `OnTimer` events.
- The interval needs to be set; 1000 milliseconds is convenient.
- The `OnTimer` event must have its procedure declared.

Because an event handler in a component is simply a pointer to a function, you can set the event routine at runtime.

```
constructor TButClock.Create(AOwner :TComponent);
begin
    inherited Create(AOwner);
    MainTimer := TTimer.Create(AOwner);
    MainTimer.Enabled := True;
    MainTimer.Interval := 1000;
    MainTimer.OnTimer := LoopTime;
end;
```

The Destructor

For the destructor, destroy the timer that you created and call parent class destructor to ensure any other necessary clean up is done.

```
destructor TButClock.Destroy;
begin
    MainTimer.Destroy;
    inherited Destroy;
end;
```

The `LoopTime` Procedure

The timer is created and set to call the `LoopTime` procedure in the component's constructor. Therefore, the only thing that must be done in the `LoopTime` procedure is to query the current time and set the `Caption` property to it. To query the time, use the `Now` function call. To convert this to a string, use the `TimeToStr` call.

```
procedure TButClock.LoopTime(Sender : TObject);
begin

    Caption := TimeToStr(Now);end;
```

The `Register` Procedure

You finish the component with the `Register` procedure, which states that the TButClock component should be placed on the Samples page of the visual component library.

```
procedure Register;
begin
  RegisterComponents('Samples', [TButClock]);
end;
end.
```

Using the Button Clock

After you build the button clock component, it is ready for use. When you add the component to a form at design time, it actually keeps time even before the program is compiled. You did not modify the functionality of the `Caption` property so that it can be read; it indicates the current time. You have not prevented the user from writing to the `Caption` field. Whatever he writes to the `Caption` property, is overwritten with the current time when the `OnTimer` event is triggered in the next second. Figure 20.7 shows an application using the button clock component.

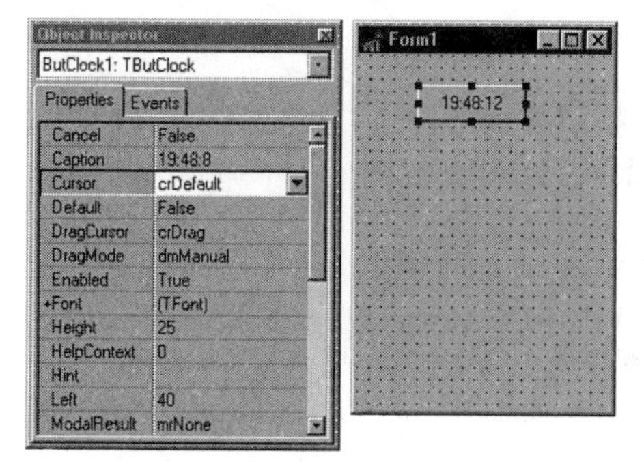

Figure 20.7.
Using the button clock.

A Graphical Example—TBlueScreen

The following example shows how a graphical component is developed. A graphical component is a component that can be placed on a form and manipulated but that does not have a window handle. All graphical components are descendants of the `TGraphicComponent` class. The `TGraphicComponent` type provides a Delphi canvas and the associated hooks for manipulating it. It is the job of the component developer to draw on the canvas and process other properties, events, and methods. The following example describes the pieces of a useful graphical visual component, TBlueScreen.

In the movie *E.T.*, Elliot makes his bicycle fly above the city. The scene was filmed against a blue screen. Later the blue was filtered out, and the background was put in. The actor playing Elliot actually rode a bicycle down a sound stage that was painted blue, and a computer replaced the blue with the background. In this example, you do the same thing with a visual component. The TBlueScreen visual component takes two bitmaps as properties. It displays the foreground bitmap superimposed on the background bitmap. The result is displayed on the visual component. The foreground bitmap is replaced with the background bitmap wherever a particular color is seen. This color is typically blue, but your component enables any color to be used as the mask.

The main concept in developing a graphical component is to implement an effective `Paint` procedure. The `Paint` procedure is called by Delphi whenever the component needs to redraw itself. This example uses Win32 APIs to mask one image onto another. These APIs are not included in the Win3.1 API.

The Header and Class Definition

The header is standard, except that you must add `CommCtrl` to the uses section. `CommCtrl` contains the code for image lists that are used to implement the blue screen effect. The `TBlueScreen` class inherits the `Height` and `Width` properties of its parent class. The class also declares three new properties: `ForegroundBitmap`, `BackgroundBitmap`, and `MaskColor`. These properties store their values in three variables—`FForegroundBitmap`, `FBackgroundBitmap`, and `FMaskColor`—which are declared in the `private` section of the declaration. `ForegroundBitmap` and `BackgroundBitmap` are available only at runtime. `ForegroundBitmap`, `BackgroundBitmap`, and `MaskColor` use direct access to read the value of the property, and they use a `Set` procedure. Then the property is written to. You specify that the `Paint` procedure should be overridden. Consequently, you handle `paint` events in a special procedure. Listing 20.5 show the unit heading and the class declaration.

TYPE Listing 20.5. Blue screen unit heading and class declaration.

```
unit bluescr;

{*******************************}
{* Bluescreen Custom Control   *}
{*******************************}

interface

uses
  SysUtils, Windows, Messages, Classes, Graphics, Controls, Forms, Dialogs,
  CommCtrl;

type
  TBlueScreen = class(TGraphicControl)
  private
     FMaskColor : TColor;
     FBackgroundBitmap : TBitmap;
     FForegroundBitmap : TBitmap;
     procedure SetBackgroundBitmap(InBitmap : TBitmap);
     procedure SetForegroundBitmap(InBitmap : TBitmap);
```

```
     procedure SetMaskColor(InColor : TColor);
    { Private declarations }
  protected
    { Protected declarations }
    Procedure Paint; Override;
  public
    { Public declarations }
    constructor Create(AOwner:TComponent);override;
    property BackgroundBitmap : TBitmap read FBackgroundBitmap write
SetBackgroundBitmap;
    property ForegroundBitmap : TBitmap read FForegroundBitmap write
SetForegroundBitmap;

  published
    {Get inherited Properties}
    property Height default 50;
    property Width default 50;
    property MaskColor:TColor read FMaskColor write SetMaskColor;   { Published
declarations }
  end;

procedure Register;

implementation
```

The Constructor

The constructor is called when a component is added to a form and when the program creates the component at runtime. The constructor is used to set up the initialization and default settings. In this case, the default width, height, and mask color for the component are set. The two bitmaps are set to `nil` to test whether the property has been set.

```
constructor TBlueScreen.Create(AOwner:TComponent);
Begin
  inherited Create(AOwner);
  Width := 50;
  Height := 50;
  FBackgroundBitmap := nil;
  FForegroundBitmap := nil;
  FMaskColor := 0;
end;
```


The Set Procedures

The `BackgroundBitmap`, `Foregroundbitmap`, and `MaskColor` properties all use procedures when the property is set. In each case, the procedure sets the private property variable and causes the component to repaint itself. If this is not done, the component does not redraw when the `BackgroundBitmap`, `Foregroundbitmap`, or `MaskColor` is modified. The component only repaints itself when it is invalidated.

```
procedure TBlueScreen.SetBackgroundBitmap(InBitmap : TBitmap);
begin
  FBackgroundBitmap := InBitmap;
  Paint;
end;

procedure TBlueScreen.SetForegroundBitmap(InBitmap : TBitmap);
begin
  FForegroundBitmap := InBitmap;
  Paint;
end;

procedure TBlueScreen.SetMaskColor(InColor : TColor);
begin
  FMaskColor := InColor;
 Paint;
end;
```

The `Paint` Procedure

The real magic in this component comes from the `Paint` procedure. It is called when a part of the component becomes invalidated or when the routine is called explicitly. The steps in the `Paint` procedure are

1. It calls the inherited `Paint` routine to perform any functionality that the parent would perform.
2. It checks whether a background bitmap has been specified. If one has been specified, `Paint` performs a `StretchDraw` to copy the background bitmap to the component.
3. It checks whether a foreground bitmap has been specified. If one has not been specified, the remaining steps are skipped. No foreground image is displayed.
4. It copies the foreground bitmap to a temporary bitmap so that it is not destroyed.
5. It creates an image list—a new concept introduced in the Win32 API. An image list enables you to define a list of images that can be drawn or masked. In this case, you use the `ILC_MASK` flag to state that you want to use a masked image list. You must specify the dimensions that define the size of the image list.
6. It adds the copy of the foreground bitmap to the image list. You specify in the `MaskColor` property which color should be masked. After the image is added, the `ImageList_AddMasked` function returns an index to it.
7. It calls the `ImageList_Draw` function to draw the superimposed image.
8. It destroys the image list and frees the temporary bitmap.

```
procedure TBlueScreen.Paint;
var
  Index   : integer;
```

```
  ImgList : HIMAGELIST;
  TmpBitmap : TBitmap;
begin
  inherited Paint;
  if BackgroundBitmap <> nil then
    Canvas.StretchDraw(RECT(0,0,Width,Height),BackGroundBitmap);
  if ForegroundBitmap <> nil then
    begin
      {The bitmap will actually be masked, therefore make a copy}
      {so that we do not destroy the user's bitmap              }
      TmpBitmap := TBitmap.Create;;
      TmpBitmap.Width := FForeGroundBitmap.Width;
      TmpBitmap.Height := FForeGroundBitmap.Height;
      TmpBitmap.Canvas.Draw(0,0,FForeGroundBitmap);
      ImgList := ImageList_Create(ForegroundBitmap.Width,
                                  ForegroundBitmap.Height,
                                  ILC_MASK,1,1);
      Index := ImageList_AddMasked(ImgList,TmpBitmap.Handle,MaskColor);
      ImageList_Draw(ImgList,Index,Canvas.Handle,0,0,ILD_TRANSPARENT);
      ImageList_Destroy(ImgList);
      TmpBitmap.free;
    end;
end;
```

The `Register` Procedure

You finish the component with the `Register` procedure, which states that the TBlueScreen component should be placed on the Samples page of the visual component library.

```
procedure Register;
begin
  RegisterComponents('Samples', [TBlueScreen]);
end;

end.
```

Using TBlueScreen

Although creating the TBlueScreen component is complex, using it is extremely easy. This illustrates the power of components. You can hide the complexity of the implementation from the user. To test this component in a simple application, create a new project that superimposes one image onto another. The form layout for this sample includes two TImage components, one TBlueScreen component, and a button component. Label components provide descriptions, but they are optional.

Load the image that you want to use as the background into one of the TImage components by double-clicking it and choosing a bitmap file. Load the foreground image into the other TImage component. For the sake of simplicity, make the dimensions of the TImage and TBlueScreen components the same as the dimensions of the bitmaps. When the user clicks the button, TBlueScreen superimposes the images. Figure 20.8 shows the layout of the component.

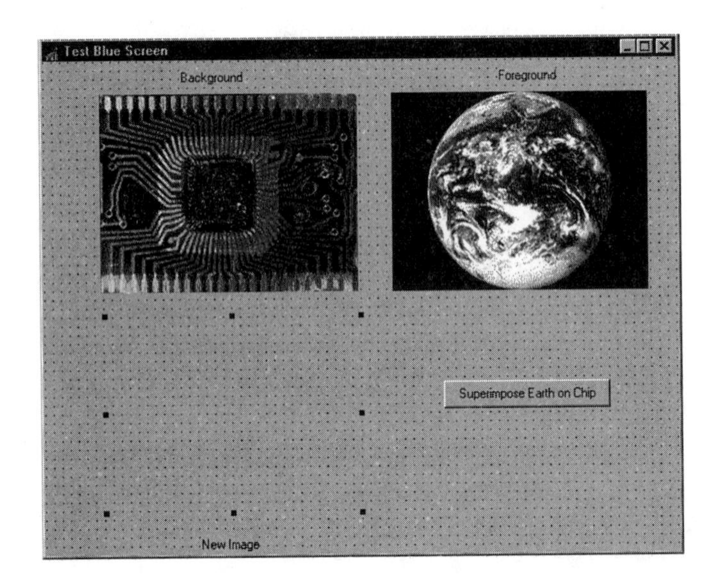

Figure 20.8.
Component layout for testing TBlueScreen.

Other than the dimensions, the only property that must be set at design time is the color of the mask. In the bitmap that I chose for the foreground—the earth on a black background—I set `MaskColor` to 0 so that the black is masked out and replaced with the background bitmap. To finish up, you need to add only two lines of code, which are added to the OnClick event of the button. Here is the `OnClick` procedure:

```
procedure TForm1.Button1Click(Sender: TObject);
begin
  BlueScreen1.Foregroundbitmap := fg.picture.bitmap;
  BlueScreen1.backgroundbitmap := bg.picture.bitmap;
end;
```

This code sets the background bitmap property equal to the bitmap contained in the foreground image component. Likewise, it sets the background bitmap property equal to the bitmap in the background image component. When the program is run, both the background and foreground images are displayed. If the button is clicked, the properties for the TBlueScreen component are set and cause an immediate repaint to occur. The component then draws the `fg` image on top of the `bg` image (see Figure 20.9).

Figure 20.9.
Using the TBlueScreen component to superimpose the earth on a computer chip.

Declaring a New Event—UserPlot

When you worked with TMult, you saw how to add an event to a component. You made some assumptions, though. You declared the property as a `TNotifyEvent` type. For passing other parameters to or from an event, Delphi declared `TNotify` as a pointer to a function that is passed a `TObject` as a parameter. If an event must use other parameters, you can declare the appropriate type. The following example shows how to declare a new event type. It is used to create an event that passes a real number to the event handler and returns a different real number by using a `var` parameter.

Depending on the types of applications that you design, the following component might be useful. It is often necessary to plot a mathematical function graphically. Many components enable you to create a graph by supplying a set of points, but none enable you simply to supply the function that you want to plot. This component does exactly that. An event called OnUserFunc is defined. It passes an `X` value and wants a `Y` value returned. The range and scale factors are set as properties. Therefore, if you want to plot the function `Y=X2` function, you add the component to your form and the following code to the `OnUserFunc` event:

```
procedure TForm1.FuncGraph1UserFunc(X: Real; var Y: Real);
begin
  Y := X * X;
end;
```

The TFuncGraph component handles all the scaling and transforms the coordinates. Essentially, you need to type only one line of code. The other examples in this chapter showed you how to implement most of this component. The entire code for TFuncGraph appears in Listing 20.6. The following sections focus on how to define a new event type and how to create an event based on the new type.

TYPE Listing 20.6. The FuncGraph component.

```
unit UserPlot;

interface

uses
  SysUtils, Windows, Messages, Classes, Graphics, Controls, Forms, Dialogs;

type
  TUserPlotFunc = procedure(X : real ; var Y : real) of object;
  TFuncGraph = class(TGraphicControl)
  private
    { Private declarations }
    FRangeMinX : integer;
    FRangeMaxX : integer;
    FRangeMinY : integer;
    FRangeMaxY : integer;
    FUserFunc  : TUserPlotFunc;
  protected
    { Protected declarations }
    procedure paint; override;
  public
    { Public declarations }
    constructor Create(Aowner : TComponent); override;
  published
    property RangeMinX : integer read FRangeMinX write FRangeMinX;
    property RangeMaxX : integer read FRangeMaxX write FRangeMaxX;
    property RangeMinY : integer read FRangeMinY write FRangeMinY;
    property RangeMaxY : integer read FRangeMaxY write FRangeMaxY;
    property OnUserFunc : TUserPlotFunc read FUserFunc write FUserFunc;
    property Width default 50;
    property Height default 50;

    { Published declarations }
  end;

procedure Register;

implementation

constructor TFuncGraph.Create(Aowner : TComponent);
begin
{simply set default width and height and range}
   inherited Create(AOwner);
   Height :=  50;
```

```
   Width  :=  50;
   FRangeMaxX := 1;
   FRangeMaxY := 1;
end;

procedure TFuncGraph.Paint;
var
  X,Y   : integer; {Real Pixels}
  RX,RY : real;    {Users Coordinates}

begin
  inherited Paint;
  Canvas.Rectangle(0,0,Width,Height);
  For X := 1 to Width do
   begin
     {convert X into user's X    }
     {Note the Width cannot be 0 }
     RX := FRangeMinX + (((FRangeMaxX - FRangeMinX)/Width)*X);

     {If the component user has assigned a plot function}
     {call the function, otherwise set RY = 0           }
     if assigned(FUserFunc) then
       FUserFunc(RX,RY)
      else
       RY := 0;

     {Now convert RY back into pixel coordinates}
     Y := round((1-((RY-FRangeMinY)/(FRangeMaxY-FRangeMinY)))* Height);
     if X = 1 then
       Canvas.MoveTo(X,Y)
      else
       Canvas.LineTo(X,Y);
   end;

end;

procedure Register;
begin
  RegisterComponents('Additional', [TFuncGraph]);
end;

end.
```

20

Creating a New Event Type

ANALYSIS The key to this component is to enable the user to define an arbitrary function to plot. You do this by implementing a new event type, `TUserPlotFunc`, whose definition is

```
TUserPlotFunc = procedure(X : real ; var Y : real) of object;
```

This type is declared in the `type` section of the unit. Note that `TUserPlotFunc` is a procedure—which looks strange in the `type` section. This means that you can declare a variable that is a pointer to a procedure that takes the arguments defined in the type declaration. Once the type is set up, you define a published property of `TUserPlotFunc` to create an event that uses the defined parameters.

```
published
   property OnUserFunc : TUserPlotFunc read FUserFunc write FUserFunc;
```

When the component is installed, a new event called `OnUserFunc` is listed. If the user double-clicks the event, Delphi creates a new procedure with the correct parameters.

```
procedure TForm1.FuncGraph1UserFunc(X: Real; var Y: Real);
begin

end;
```

Calling the Event

To call the user's event handler from your component, call the variable that points to the procedure and pass the necessary parameters. Make sure that a valid event is defined. To check whether an event is defined, call the `assigned` function. Here is an example of calling the user's function:

```
if assigned(FUserFunc) then
       FUserFunc(RX,RY)
```

Using TFuncGraph

Figure 20.10 shows how powerful a custom event can be. By typing only eight lines of code, as seen in Listing 20.7, you can graph four mathematical functions. This is rapid application development.

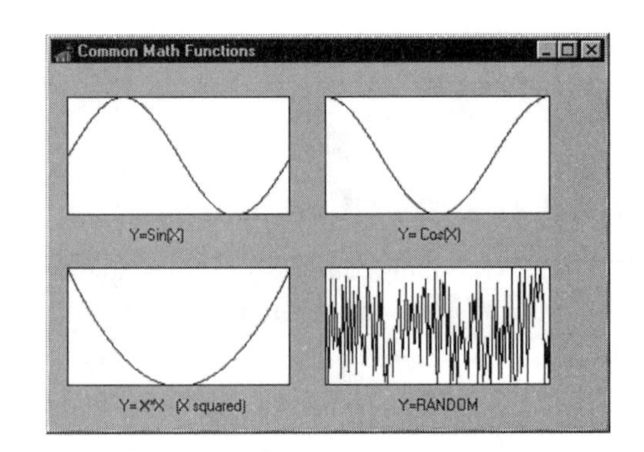

Figure 20.10.
Using the TFuncGraph component to graph four mathematical functions.

TYPE **Listing 20.7. Test program for TFuncGraph.**

```
unit math2;

interface

uses
  SysUtils, Windows, Messages, Classes, Graphics, Controls, Forms, Dialogs,
  UserPlot, StdCtrls;

type
  TForm1 = class(TForm)
    FuncGraph1: TFuncGraph;
    FuncGraph2: TFuncGraph;
    FuncGraph3: TFuncGraph;
    FuncGraph4: TFuncGraph;
    Label1: TLabel;
    Label2: TLabel;
    Label3: TLabel;
    Label4: TLabel;
    procedure FuncGraph1UserFunc(X: Real; var Y: Real);
    procedure FuncGraph2UserFunc(X: Real; var Y: Real);
    procedure FuncGraph3UserFunc(X: Real; var Y: Real);
    procedure FuncGraph4UserFunc(X: Real; var Y: Real);
  private
    { Private declarations }
  public
    { Public declarations }
  end;

var
  Form1: TForm1;

implementation

{$R *.DFM}

procedure TForm1.FuncGraph1UserFunc(X: Real; var Y: Real);
  var Rads : real;

begin
  Rads := X * (3.1415/180);
  Y := sin(Rads) * 100;
end;

procedure TForm1.FuncGraph2UserFunc(X: Real; var Y: Real);
  var Rads : real;
begin
  Rads := X * (3.1415/180);
  Y := cos(Rads) * 100;
end;

procedure TForm1.FuncGraph3UserFunc(X: Real; var Y: Real);
begin
  Y := X * X;
```

```
end;

procedure TForm1.FuncGraph4UserFunc(X: Real; var Y: Real);
begin
  Y := random(100);
end;

end.
```

Summary

The building blocks of Delphi's RAD environment rely on the visual component library's ease of use; the implementation is hidden. Today you learned how to build your own components. Compared to other RAD languages, Delphi is unique because components are written in its native language. The component developer's main job is to define an interface to a new component and to implement its details. Delphi makes this easy and includes a Component Expert to get you started. Writing components is easy and rewarding. Consult the component writer's guide; it has a wealth of information.

Q&A

Q Can I create a component and not inherit any ancestor class?

A No. Every component must be a descendent of a class—even the most basic class, `TComponent`.

Q How do I distribute a component that I developed?

A When you install a .pas component, Delphi compiles the component into a .dcu file. The compiled version can also be installed. For commercial distribution, give your customers the .dcu file.

Q Can I integrate help into my component?

A Yes. Delphi gives many hooks for help. Review the component writer's guide for details.

Workshop

Quiz

1. Are properties in components simply variables, or is it possible to link code to properties in a component?

2. What is the difference between properties that are available during development and those that are available only at runtime?
3. What is the difference between published and public?
4. What is the difference between how an event is defined and how a property is defined?

Exercises

1. Add a property to the TButClock component that enables a user to specify an alarm time. Also add an OnAlarm event that is called when the specified time is reached.
2. Modify the TBlueScreen component so that the user can either choose a mask color or have it automatically selected as the color of the pixel in a position whose coordinates are specified as properties.
3. Add a method to the TBlueScreen component that enables the user to save the image as a bitmap.
4. Rewrite the TButClock visual component to use multithreading, as opposed to a timer.

Week 3

Day 21

Developing Your Own Installation Program

In 1981, IBM introduced the IBM PC and PC-DOS; clones followed shortly afterward. Installing a program usually involved nothing more than copying files to a disk or a subdirectory and running the executable or batch file. In those days, some programs had install programs that simply copied the files for you into a subdirectory. As time went on, users could select options that were added to configuration files—.dat, .cfg, and so on. There was no standard for setting up and installing programs. Every programmer had their own way of keeping track of user settings and other information needed by the program. When you wanted clean your hard disk, you often had a difficult time determining which files were needed. The AUTOEXEC.BAT and CONFIG.SYS files contained lines that applied to particular programs.

Windows brought .ini files and SETUP.EXE programs—not a bad idea at the time. Windows even provided API functions, which you could use to create, read, and write .ini files easily. This development helped standardize naming conventions, access methods, formatting, and even the location of files, but it still was not enough; .ini files had their own problems. Some programmers used the WIN.INI and SYSTEM.INI files, whereas others used their own application-specific .ini files. Some used both.

All those .ini files and Windows applications made cleaning a hard disk even more complex. In DOS, you had to delete the application directory and its contents and maybe a few lines in the CONFIG.SYS and AUTOEXEC.BAT files. In Windows, if you delete an application's files and directories, remnants often remain in the WIN.INI and SYSTEM.INI files from the application's installer. This causes clutter, confusion, and unpredictable effects in Windows. Applications that watch installs and enable you to uninstall programs are available, but you cannot not always trust them to work. Many Windows programs share DLLs and other resources. To work properly, uninstall programs must be installed before other applications. Because they can't possibly have a complete database of every Windows program, they cannot uninstall every program properly unless they monitored its installation.

Windows NT and its Registry came to the rescue first. For Windows 95, Microsoft requires developers to use the Registry, follow a given set of standards, and provide complete install and uninstall programs—otherwise, they may not display the Windows 95 logo on their software. This is good for developers because they have standards to follow. It is good for end users because they now have an easy, orderly method for installing and uninstalling their software.

Today's topic is the requirements that an application must satisfy to earn the Windows 95 logo. You learn what the Registry is and how to use it. You write your own install and uninstall program using the Registry. You also learn about using a third-party product to create applications that meet the Windows 95 logo requirements, regardless of the method you used to create your installer and uninstaller.

Meeting the Windows 95 Logo Requirements

The Windows 95 logo requirements are technical requirements that developers must follow when they create software or hardware. This section introduces you to the some of the important concepts. To help you design applications, you should consult *Programmer's Guide to Microsoft Windows 95* and *Windows Interface Guidelines for Software Design* from Microsoft Press. The requirements are occasionally updated, so be sure to obtain the latest information from Microsoft. When you write an application that meets the requirements, you must apply to Mircosoft before it can display the logo.

Obviously, you do not have to write applications that satisfy all the Windows 95 logo requirements. If you are writing freeware, shareware, or your own personal software, it might not be worth the effort. Even so, it does not hurt to follow the standards as much as possible.

That way, if you decide to market your application later, you will not have as much work to do to earn the logo.

Microsoft looks at applications in four main categories:

- File-based applications
- Nonfile-based applications that run exclusively in full mode —not windowed
- Utilities—including file and disk utilities and virus scanning and cleaning programs
- Development tools

The following requirements apply to all applications:

- The application must use the Win32 API.
- The application must follow the Windows 95 look and feel for the user interface.
- The application must be tested and successfully run on both Windows 95 and Windows NT and adjusted as necessary to compensate for differences in features between the two.
- The application must support long filenames, displaying them appropriately in dialog boxes, controls, and so on.
- The application must support plug-and-play.

There are more requirements regarding the use of OLE, MAPI (messaging application programming interface), and UNC (universal naming convention). In addition, an application must provide install and unistall programs, and it must use the Registry rather than the WIN.INI and SYSTEM.INI files. When you do obtain a complete list of the current requirements and start designing your application, you will find that Delphi's VCL makes most of the work a breeze, because many of the tasks are already done.

New Term The *Registry* is a hierarchical database used by Windows to store system hardware and software, and program and user settings. Windows 95 and Windows NT store information in the Registry that would be stored in .ini files in Windows 3.1.

The Registry

The Registry is a database that stores information about system hardware configuration, Windows, and Windows applications. Almost everything that is found in an .ini file in Windows 3.1 goes in the Windows 95 or Windows NT registry. The Registry is organized in a hierarchical format. It is quite complex, containing many levels of keys, subkeys, and values. This chapter focuses on the Registry and the install and uninstall program that you will write. You should acquire a copy of the Windows 95 Resource Kit and a good reference book on the Win32 API. The Microsoft Developer's Network CDs also contain information the Registry.

The Registry breaks its data into two categories: computer-specific and user-specific. Computer-specific information includes anything related to the hardware and its settings as well as installed applications and their settings. User-specific information includes desktop preferences, user profiles, user-selected printers, and network settings. Six main registry keys contain all the subkeys and entries—many entries are nested several levels deep.

The four computer-specific top-level keys are

`Hkey_Local_Machine`	Information about the computer, including installed hardware and software settings
`HKey_Current_Config`	Information about current hardware
`HKey_Dyn_Data`	Dynamic status information used by plug-and-play routines
`Hkey_Classes_Root`	Information on OLE, drag-and-drop, shortcuts, and the Windows 95 user interface

The two user-specific top-level keys are

`Hkey_Users`	User information, including desktop settings and application settings
`Hkey_Current_User`	Information for the user who is currently logged in

To work with the Registry, you need to know how to view it, change it manually, and verify that changes are recorded properly. This is easy. From the Run menu in Windows 95 or Windows NT, enter `REGEDIT.EXE`. This brings up the Registry Editor, which enables you to view and edit the Registry.

WARNING

You should never make changes to the Registry unless you know what you are doing. Make sure that you back up the Registry and your data before you test your application or give it to other users.

TIP

To back up the Registry, copy SYSTEM.DAT in the Windows subdirectory to a safe place. This is a hidden file, so you need something that can see it, such as Windows Explorer in Windows 95.

When the Registry Editor pops up, it looks like Figure 21.1. You move through the Registry just as you do through the directory structure with Windows Explorer. Look at the Registry menu options. Notice that you can export and import the entire Registry or just portions of between text files. The Registry Edit menu shows the editing functions relating to the highlighted entry. If you need more information on the Registry Editor, refer to the online

help. Today, you will use REGEDIT to verify that your program is working correctly. If you make a typing error, you can use REGEDIT to fix the mistake.

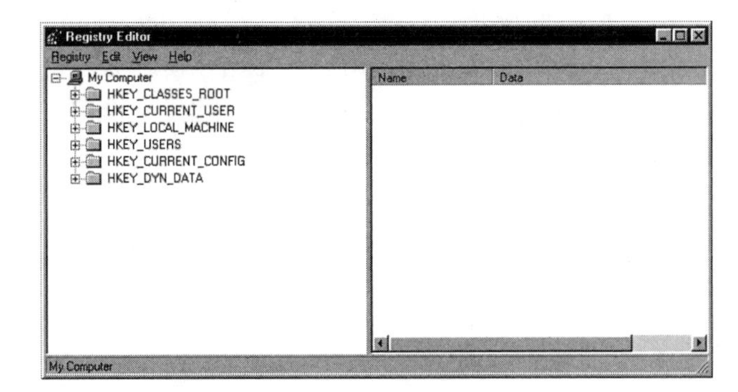

Figure 21.1
The Registry Editor.

The following information, for example, was exported from the hardware section with REGEDIT:

```
[HKEY_LOCAL_MACHINE\hardware]

[HKEY_LOCAL_MACHINE\hardware\devicemap]

[HKEY_LOCAL_MACHINE\hardware\devicemap\serialcomm]
"COM1"="COM1"
"COM2"="COM2"

[HKEY_LOCAL_MACHINE\hardware\DESCRIPTION]

[HKEY_LOCAL_MACHINE\hardware\DESCRIPTION\System]

[HKEY_LOCAL_MACHINE\hardware\DESCRIPTION\System\FloatingPointProcessor]

[HKEY_LOCAL_MACHINE\hardware\DESCRIPTION\System\FloatingPointProcessor\0]
```

Some information is stored as a subkey, whereas other information is stored in the values within a subkey. For example,

```
[HKEY_LOCAL_MACHINE\hardware\devicemap\serialcomm]
"COM1"="COM1"
"COM2"="COM2"
```

Make sure that you are comfortable with the Registry before you attempt to write code that modifies the Registry.

Writing the Install and Uninstall Program

Before you write your simple installer, take a look at what Microsoft recommends to satisfy the Windows 95 logo requirements. An installer should

- ☐ Provide a standard Windows GUI
- ☐ Provide the ability to uninstall the application and related files safely
- ☐ Check the hardware and software configuration
- ☐ Check available space on the hard disk space
- ☐ Copy the application and required files to the hard disk, creating subdirectories as needed
- ☐ Modify the Registry and files as needed to make the application function properly
- ☐ Provide users with installation options, such as typical, compact, custom, and silent (unattended)
- ☐ Provide common default settings
- ☐ Ask for a disk only once during the installation
- ☐ Beep and prompt for next disk when ready
- ☐ Display a progress indicator that shows the user how much has been done in the installation process
- ☐ Provide a user with the ability to cancel the installation before completion
- ☐ Keep a log of all the installed files and changes to the user's system
- ☐ Clean up when an install is canceled or when the uninstall program is run
- ☐ Remove any files, Registry entries, shortcuts, and other changes made during the installation

These are most of the important requirements. Check with Microsoft for the latest requirements and information. The simple installer that you will write does not meet all these requirements—only a few, such as copying a file to disk and making a Registry entry. The purpose here is to introduce you to some of the details behind installers. After seeing all that, you might want to obtain a third-party install program generator.

With Delphi, you can easily make some API calls to work with the Registry. `RegCreateKey` creates a new key in the Registry.

```
function RegCreateKey(Key: HKey; SubKey: PChar; var Result: HKey): Longint;
```

If a key already exists with the same name, it is opened. If you pass a subkey containing subkeys, some of which exist and some of which do not exist, the subkeys that exist are opened and the subkeys that do not exist are created. When the subkey information is passed, it appears similiar to a file and directory pathname. For example,

```
MySubKey:='SOFTWARE\MyCompany\MyApp';
     RetCode:=RegCreateKey(HKEY_LOCAL_MACHINE,MySubKey,Result);
```

The SOFTWARE subkey exists, but the MyCompany and MyApp subkeys do not. SOFTWARE is opened, and the others are created.

`RegOpenKey` opens a key or subkey. As with `RegCreateKey`, you must provide the key and subkey information. If the key does not exist, an error is returned. For example,

```
function RegOpenKey(Key: HKey; SubKey: PChar; var Result: HKey): Longint;
```

`RegCloseKey` closes a key after you are done working with it. You use the handle returned in the result after you use `RegCreateKey` or `RegOpenKey`. For example,

```
function RegCloseKey(Key: HKey): Longint;
```

`RegDeleteKey` deletes a subkey. When you delete a subkey, all of its subkeys are deleted as well. For example,

```
function RegDeleteKey(Key: HKey; SubKey: PChar): Longint;
```

NOTE

While you can read and change most of the Registry information, the `Hkey_Dyn_Data` keys and values contain Plug and Play status information about system devices. This is read-only information.

These API functions are actually intended for use with Windows 3.1. However, they work well for updating the Registry in Windows 95 and Windows NT because of their backward compatibility. They are also easy to work with and understand. As you become more experienced with the Win32 API and Delphi, you might want to investigate the Win32 Registry functions.

Now you can build a simple program that checks available disk space, creates a subdirectory, copies a file from a floppy to the new subdirectory, and adds Registry entries about the program. The program also contains an uninstall option, which you can activate by passing `/U` on the command line.

Create a new project. Name the project MYSETUP.DPR and the unit INSTALL.PAS. Use Figure 21.2 as an example of how to lay out the form. Set the form's properties so that it is centered on startup and is not sizable.

WARNING

Make sure that you have a backup of your Registry file before you run code that will modify its contents.

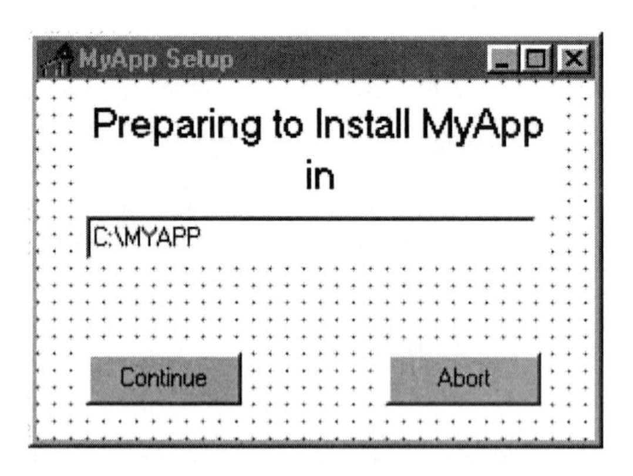

Figure 21.2
The MyApp Setup screen.

Use Listing 21.1 to update your program.

TYPE **Listing 21.1. Install.**

```
unit install;

interface

uses
  Windows, Messages, SysUtils, Classes, Graphics, Controls, Forms, Dialogs,
  StdCtrls, FileCtrl;

type
  TForm1 = class(TForm)
    Button1: TButton;
    Label1: TLabel;
    Edit1: TEdit;
    Button2: TButton;
    procedure Button2Click(Sender: TObject);
    procedure Button1Click(Sender: TObject);
    procedure FormCreate(Sender: TObject);
  private
    { Private declarations }
  public
    { Public declarations }
  end;

var
  Form1: TForm1;

implementation

{$R *.DFM}
Var
    MySubKey : PChar;
    RetCode : Longint;

procedure TForm1.Button2Click(Sender: TObject);
begin
```

```
    Application.Terminate;
end;

procedure TForm1.Button1Click(Sender: TObject);
Var
   {storage for free disk space value}
   DskSpc : Longint;
   {Predefined disk space minimum}
   MinDSpace : Longint;
   {File Variables to use in copy routine}
   InFile,OutFile : File;
   {variable to keep track of records read and written}
   NumRecsRead,NumRecsWritten : integer;
   {Buffer used to copy file}
   Buf : array[1..4096] of Byte;
   Result : HKey;
begin
     {Check Disk space of drive c:}
     MinDSpace:=1024000; {1 meg minimum disk space}
     DskSpc:=DiskFree(3);{get disk space on c}
     If DskSpc<MinDSpace then
     begin
          ShowMessage('Not enough Diskspace, setup aborting');
          Application.Terminate;
     end;
     {Create directory}
      mkdir('c:\myapp');
     {----------------Start Copy Routine--------------}

     AssignFile(InFile,'A:\MYAPP.EXE');
     AssignFile(OutFile,'C:\MYAPP\MYAPP.EXE');
     {Open files and Set record size to 1 byte}
     Reset(InFile,1);
     Rewrite(OutFile,1);
     While Not Eof(InFile) Do
     Begin
           {Read a 4K Byte Block into the buffer}
           BlockRead(InFile,Buf,SizeOf(Buf),NumRecsRead);
           {Write a 4K Byte Buffer to new file}
           BlockWrite(OutFile,Buf,NumRecsRead);
     end;
        {Flush buffers to disk and close the file}
        CloseFile(InFile);
        CloseFile(Outfile);
     {----------------End Copy Routine--------------}
     {Make Registery Entry}
     MySubKey:='SOFTWARE\MyCompany\MyApp\1.0';
     RetCode:=RegCreateKey(HKEY_LOCAL_MACHINE,MySubKey,Result);
     If RetCode = ERROR_SUCCESS then
        RegCloseKey(Result)
     else
        begin
             ShowMessage('Registery Update Failed!');
             Application.Terminate;
        end;
     ShowMessage('Installation Complete');
```

continues

Listing 21.1. continued

```
     Application.Terminate;
end;
procedure TForm1.FormCreate(Sender: TObject);
Var
    F : File;
begin
     {Check for command line option /U, if so uninstall
      otherwise fall through and get ready to install}
     If (ParamCount > 0) and (ParamStr(1) = '/U') then
         begin
             AssignFile(F,'C:\MYAPP\MYAPP.EXE');
             Erase;
             RmDir('C:\MYAPP');
             MySubKey:='SOFTWARE\MyCompany';
             RetCode:=RegDeleteKey(HKEY_LOCAL_MACHINE,MySubKey);
             If RetCode=ERROR_SUCCESS then
             begin
                ShowMessage('MYAPP Successfully Uninstalled');
                Application.Terminate;
             end;
         end;
end;
end.
```

ANALYSIS Take a look at what we did in Listing 21.1. The various sections of code are commented so that you can follow along easily. We'll concentrate our study on the code that affects the Registry, but you should look at each section of code mentioned. The bulk of your program is contained in the code for Button1, the Continue Button; Button2 is the abort button and only contains a line of code to terminate the program. After declaring variables in Button1, the first thing you do is check the free disk space. Set a variable for 1M and check the free disk space. If you have less than 1M of free disk space, the program displays a message and aborts. If you have enough disk space, the program continues by first creating the application directory, C:\MYAPP in this case.

Next the program copies the application MYAPP.EXE to C:\MYAPP using knowledge gained about file I/O on Day 12, "File Input/Output." Now you get into the meat of the program, updating the Registry. Take a close look at the code that makes your Registry entry.

First, you stuff the Registry entry info into a string.

```
MySubKey:='SOFTWARE\MyCompany\MyApp\1.0';
```

Next you make an API call to enter the information into the Registry.

```
RetCode:=RegCreateKey(HKEY_LOCAL_MACHINE,MySubKey,Result);
```

The following `If...Then...Else` statement checks for the Registry update's success. If the code is successful, it drops through and continues. Otherwise, the program displays an error message and then terminates.

```
If RetCode = ERROR_SUCCESS then
   RegCloseKey(Result)
else
   begin
        ShowMessage('Registery Update Failed!');
        Application.Terminate;
   end;
```

Finally, the program displays the success message and exits.

```
ShowMessage('Installation Complete');
Application.Terminate;
```

That takes care of the install portion of the program. Remember that we said it would also have an uninstall option? Well, it does. To activate the uninstall portion of the program, you must specify a `/U` as a command-line parameter. Do this by putting some code into the form Create event because it executes when the program starts. Take a look.

The following `If…Then` statement checks for parameters on the command line.

```
If (ParamCount > 0) and (ParamStr(1) = '/U') then
```

If the `/U` is found, it erases the file MYAPP.EXE from the C:\MYAPP directory.

```
begin
    AssignFile(F,'C:\MYAPP\MYAPP.EXE');
    Erase;
```

Next it removes the C:\MYAPP directory.

```
    RmDir('C:\MYAPP');
```

Here you remove the registry entry that was added when MYAPP.EXE was installed.

```
    MySubKey:='SOFTWARE\MyCompany';
```

Finally, check the return code of the Registry entry deletion process and display a success message when complete and then exit the application.

```
   RetCode:=RegDeleteKey(HKEY_LOCAL_MACHINE,MySubKey);
    If RetCode=ERROR_SUCCESS then
    begin
       ShowMessage('MYAPP Successfully Uninstalled');
       Application.Terminate;
    end;
end;
```

As you can see writing a simple installer and updating the registry is not a big deal, but you do have to quite a bit more work to do that what we did here if you want a nice, user-friendly installer.

NOTE

> You hard-coded the drive and directory values. Therefore, you might have to change the code to fit your needs if you plan to use a drive other than drive A or a directory other than C:\MYAPP.

If you have taken all the precautions and saved your Registry file to a safe place, you can run the program and see it in action. To do this, copy a small executable that you are familiar with to a blank formatted floppy. Rename the executable MYAPP.EXE. Then compile and run the program. The application's form appears. Press the Continue button. The floppy drive light should come on as the program copies the file to the new directory—C:\MYAPP. A message box should indicate that the installation was successful.

To verify, check whether the directory C:\MYAPP exists. It should contain the application MYAPP.EXE, which you copied and renamed to the disk in drive A. Next, check whether the Registry was updated correctly. Use the Run option to run `REGEDIT`. When `REGEDIT` pops up, open

```
HKEY_LOCAL_MACHINE/SOFTWARE
```

You should see MyCompany as a subkey. You can open each subkey until you get down to the version number:

```
HKEY_LOCAL_MACHINE/SOFTWARE/MyCompany/MyApp/1.0
```

This is displayed in a tree format in `REGEDIT`. When you are satisfied that the installation works properly, you should test the uninstall portion of the code. Run the program again, but this time use the `/U` parameter on the command line. You can do this in Delphi by adding `/U` to the parameters section under the Run menu option and then running the program. The file and directory are deleted, and the entries are removed from the Registry. To verify this, search for the directory and use `REGEDIT` to view the Registry.

To make this installer satisfy the Windows 95 logo requirements, you need to do much more work. This program falls severely short of a good installer. You have not compressed files, stored values such as a path in the Registry to make the entries useful, provided indicators of installation progress, or created a folder or group with shortcuts or icons. You now have, however, an idea of what creating an installer involves. Writing a decent installer actually warrants a book of its own.

For many people, creating an installer and uninstaller from scratch does not make sense. You should use a third-party install program generator to create your installers. They help ensure that your applications have a consistent look and feel during the install process. They also save you time and hassles. There is no need to reinvent the wheel, so to speak, unless you plan to write your own commercial installer.

Using a Commercial Install Program Generator

Several third-party tools are available—just scan the advertisements in any Delphi, Visual Basic, or other Windows developer magazine. This section discusses InstallShield, which many programs on the market use. You have probably installed programs that use InstallShield. It provides gauges on the screen that track of the progress of the entire installation and the current disk. With InstallShield, you can build a simple script, create a list of files to be installed, add messages, and compile an installer in no time.

The version of InstallShield discussed in this section is version 3, which runs on Windows 3.1, Windows 95, and Windows NT 3.5 or higher. If you want to be more elaborate, you might need a Windows resource editor (such as Borland's Resource Workshop) and a C++ compiler (such as Borland's C++ 4.0 or higher).

InstallShield 3.0 offers

- A scripting language that enables you to customize the installer for your needs
- Sample scripts
- Support for user dialog boxes
- Bitmaps for displaying graphics and information for the user
- Updates to text files, including AUTOEXEC.BAT and CONFIG.SYS
- Registry updates
- Create and uninstall options
- The capability to access the Windows API or DLLs from a script

InstallShield's scripting language looks like a cross between C and Pascal, but you do not need to understand either one to use it. You should feel comfortable with InstallShield after you familiarize yourself with the commands and syntax of the scripting language. You can customize the sample scripts that come with the package to fit your needs. The manual is packed with all the information that you need to get going quickly. The product also has a royalty-free license agreement, so you can ship your installers with as many programs as you like.

The beginning of an InstallShield script has a constant declarations section. For example,

```
declare

// Constant declarations.
#define SPACE_REQUIRED          100000          // Disk space in bytes.
#define APP_NAME                "My Application"
#define PROGRAM_FOLDER_NAME     "My Application Folder"
#define APPBASE_PATH            "Program Files\\MyCompany\\Myapp1\\"
#define APPBASE_PATH_WIN32S     "Programf\\MyCompany\\Myapp1\\"
#define COMPANY_NAME            "MyCompany"
```

```
#define PRODUCT_NAME              "MyApp"
#define PRODUCT_VERSION           "1.0"
#define DEINSTALL_KEY             "Sample1DeinstKey"
#define UNINSTALL_NAME            "Sample1App"
#define PRODUCT_KEY               "myapp.exe"
```

By making changes that apply to your application in the declarations section of a sample script, you can create an installer quickly. Code for creating program groups and Registry entries, checking disk space, creating subdirectories, and decompressing and copying files is provided in the sample script. You use the constant names, but set your own values. After you set up the constants, the sample scripts will compile. After you compile a list of files to be installed and move them to a floppy disk, your installer is ready for use.

You can make only small changes to the sample scripts at first. Then, as you become more familiar with the product and the scripting language, you can customize your installers as much as you want. The scripting language is powerful; it has a wealth of functions for doing just about anything you might need in an installer. You can run other DOS or Windows applications from the installer. The language is also extensible through its capability to call functions in DLLs and the Windows API. This means that you can write your own functions and routines in Delphi to extend its power and capability. The manual is well written and has information on creating DLLs with Borland and Microsoft C++ compilers.

The five basic steps in creating the installer and the installation disks are

1. Create a script or update a template as needed for your application. Compile it to SETUP.INS and transfer it to disk 1.
2. Compress and split up your files. Copy them to the appropriate disk.
3. Compress any temporary resources or files that needed by the installer to _SETUP.LIB. Copy them to disk 1.
4. Copy the appropriate compressed InstallShield executables and DLLs to disk 1.
5. Create a list of all the files that must be installed. Compile it to SETUP.PKG and copy it to disk 1.

Listing 21.2 shows a complete generic InstallShield script. It was provided by Stirling Software, and most of the work is done for you. You can modify it as needed when you create your installer. It can help you create professional-looking, production-ready installers.

TYPE **Listing 21.2. InstallShield 3.0 Script**

```
/*-----------------------------------------------------------------------*\
 *
 *  IIIIIII SSSSSS
 *    II    SS                      InstallShield (R)
 *    II    SSSSSS          1990-1995, Stirling Technologies, Inc.
 *    II        SS                All Rights Reserved.
 *  IIIIIII SSSSSS
 *
```

```
 *
 *  This code is intended as a supplement to InstallShield documentation
 *  and is provided AS IS.
 *
 *
 *    File Name:  SETUP.RUL
 *
 *  Description:  InstallShield Professional Edition
 *                32-bit Template One script.
 *
 *
 *       Author:  Stirling Technologies, Inc.       Date: 10-20-95
 *
 *     Comments:  This template script performs a basic installation to a
 *                Windows 95 or Windows NT platform.  The installation
 *                includes components: Application Program Files, Sample and
 *                Template Files, Online Help Files, and Multimedia Tutorial
 *                Files.  With minor modifications, this template can be
 *                adapted to create new, customized installations.
 *
 *
 *
\*---------------------------------------------------------------------------*/

declare

// Constant declarations.
#define SPACE_REQUIRED          100000          // Disk space in bytes.
#define APP_NAME                "My Application"
#define PROGRAM_FOLDER_NAME     "My Application Folder"
#define APPBASE_PATH            "Program Files\\MyCompany\\Myapp1\\"
#define APPBASE_PATH_WIN32S     "Programf\\MyCompany\\Myapp1\\"
#define COMPANY_NAME            "MyCompany"
#define PRODUCT_NAME            "MyApp"
#define PRODUCT_VERSION         "1.0"
#define DEINSTALL_KEY           "Sample1DeinstKey"
#define UNINSTALL_NAME          "Sample1App"
#define PRODUCT_KEY             "myapp.exe"

        // Global variable declarations.
        STRING  svFolder, svDir, szMsg, szFileSet, szTitle, svUninstLogFile;
        STRING  svTarget, szProgram, szParam, szTemp, szAppPath;
        BOOL    bSpaceOk, bWinNT, bWin32s, bIsShellExplorer;
        NUMBER  nResult;

        // Function declarations.
        prototype SetupScreen();
        prototype CheckRequirements();

program

StartHere:
        Disable( BACKGROUND );

        // Set installation info., which is required for registry entries.
        InstallationInfo(   COMPANY_NAME, PRODUCT_NAME, PRODUCT_VERSION,
➥PRODUCT_KEY );
```

```
     // Set up the installation screen.
     SetupScreen();
     Enable( DIALOGCACHE );


// Create a Welcome dialog.
WelcomeDlg:
     Disable( BACKBUTTON );
     Welcome( "", 0 );
     Enable( BACKBUTTON );

     // Test target system for proper configuration.
     CheckRequirements();


// Ask user for a destination location for the installation.--
GetTargetDirectory:
     if (bWin32s) then
        svTarget = TARGETDISK ^ APPBASE_PATH_WIN32S;
     else
        svTarget = TARGETDISK ^ APPBASE_PATH;
     endif;
     if ( AskDestPath( "", szMsg,
                       svTarget, 0 ) = 12 ) then
        goto WelcomeDlg;
     endif;

     // Perform space check of target drive.
     bSpaceOk = TRUE;
     if (GetDiskSpace( svTarget ) < SPACE_REQUIRED) then
        szMsg = "There is not enough space available on the disk\n" +
                "'" + svTarget + "' \n" +
                "Please free up some space or change the target location\n" +
                "to a different disk";
        MessageBox( szMsg, WARNING );
        bSpaceOk = FALSE;
     endif;

      // If not enough space, ask user to try again.
     if (bSpaceOk = FALSE) goto GetTargetDirectory;

     // Set the App Paths key for the main program.
     szAppPath = svTarget ^ "PROGRAM";
     RegDBSetItem( REGDB_APPPATH, szAppPath );
     szProgram = svTarget ^ "PROGRAM\\myapp.exe";
     RegDBSetItem( REGDB_APPPATH_DEFAULT, szProgram );

SetupFilesToTransfer:
     szFileSet = "General";
     TARGETDIR = svTarget;

     // Define the file set.
     FileSetBeginDefine( szFileSet );

        SetStatusWindow( -1, "Copying program files..." );
        CompressGet( "DATA.Z", "*.*", INCLUDE_SUBDIR );

     FileSetEndDefine( szFileSet );
```

```
TransferFiles:
     // Prepare InstallShield to record deinstallation information.
     DeinstallStart( svTarget, svUninstLogFile, DEINSTALL_KEY, 0 );
     RegDBSetItem( REGDB_UNINSTALL_NAME, UNINSTALL_NAME );

     // Set up progress indicator and information gauge.
     Disable( DIALOGCACHE );
     Enable( STATUSDLG );

     StatusUpdate( ON, 90 );

     // Perform the file set.
     SetStatusWindow( 0, "Copying program files..." );
     nResult = FileSetPerformEz( szFileSet, 0 );

     switch (nResult)

     case FS_DONE: // Successful completion.

     case FS_CREATEDIR: // Create directory error.
          MessageBox( "Unable to create a directory under " + TARGETDIR +
                    ➥"."+
                     "Please check write access to this directory.", SEVERE
                    ➥);
          exit;

     default: // Group all other errors under default label.
          NumToStr( szTemp, nResult );
          MessageBox( "General file transfer error."+
                      "Please check your target location and try again."+
                      "\n\n Error Number:"+szTemp +
                      "\n Related File: "+ERRORFILENAME,
                      SEVERE );
          exit;
     endswitch;

     Delay( 1 );
     Disable( STATUSDLG );

// Create program folders and icons.
InstallProgramItems:
     SetStatusWindow( 95, "Creating Program Folder and Icons...." );

     if ((bWinNT || bWin32s) && !bIsShellExplorer ) then
        AppCommand( PROGMAN, CMD_RESTORE );
        svFolder = PROGRAM_FOLDER_NAME;
        CreateProgramFolder( svFolder );
        ShowProgramFolder( svFolder, 0 );
        LongPathToShortPath( svTarget );
        Delay(1);
     endif;

     szProgram = svTarget ^ "PROGRAM\\MYAPP.EXE";
     if ((bWinNT || bWin32s) && !bIsShellExplorer ) then
        AddFolderIcon( svFolder, APP_NAME, szProgram,
                       svTarget ^ "PROGRAM",
                       "", 0, "", REPLACE );
        Delay( 1 );
```

21

```
            szProgram = svTarget ^ "PROGRAM\\MYAPP.EXE";
            szParam   = svTarget ^ "EXAMPLES\\EG1.DOC";
            AddFolderIcon( svFolder, "Example1", szProgram + " " + szParam,
                           svTarget ^ "Examples",
                           "", 0, "", REPLACE );
            Delay( 1 );

            szProgram = svTarget ^ "PROGRAM\\MYAPP.EXE";
            szParam   = svTarget ^ "EXAMPLES\\EG2.DOC";
            AddFolderIcon( svFolder, "Example2", szProgram + " " + szParam,
                           svTarget ^ "Examples",
                           "", 0, "", REPLACE );
            Delay( 1 );

            szParam = svTarget ^ "HELP\\MYAPP.HLP";
            AddFolderIcon( svFolder, "On-Line Help", "WINHELP.EXE" + " " +
                         ➥szParam,
                           svTarget ^ "Help","", 0, "", REPLACE );
            Delay( 1 );

            szParam   = svTarget ^ "README.TXT";
            AddFolderIcon( svFolder, "Readme ", "NOTEPAD.EXE " + szParam,
                           svTarget,
                           "", 0, "", REPLACE );
            Delay( 1 );

            // Global variable UNINST stores the name and location of the
            // uninstaller file.
            szProgram = UNINST;
            LongPathToShortPath( szProgram );
            LongPathToShortPath( svUninstLogFile );
            szProgram = szProgram + " -f" + svUninstLogFile;
            AddFolderIcon( svFolder, "unInstallShield", szProgram,
                           WINDIR, "", 0, "", REPLACE );
         else

            LongPathToQuote( szProgram, TRUE );
            AddFolderIcon( "", APP_NAME, szProgram,
                           svTarget ^ "PROGRAM",
                           "", 0, "", REPLACE );
         endif;

         Delay( 1 );

      // Announce setup complete and offer to read README file.e
      FinalInstallProcess:
         SetStatusWindow( 100, "Installation complete." );

         if (AskYesNo( "Do you want to view the README file now?", YES ) = YES)
            then LaunchApp( "NOTEPAD.EXE", svTarget ^ "README.TXT" );
            Delay( 2 );
         endif;

         szMsg = "Setup is complete.  You may run the installed program "+
                 "by double-clicking on the program icon.";
         MessageBox( szMsg, INFORMATION );

         exit;
```

```
/*------------------------------------------------------------------------*\
 *
 * Function:  SetupScreen
 *
 *  Purpose:  This function will set up the screen look.  This includes
 *            colors, fonts, text to be displayed, etc.
 *
 *
 *    Input:
 *
 *  Returns:
 *
 * Comments:
\*------------------------------------------------------------------------*/
function SetupScreen()
        number nDx, nDy;
begin
        GetExtents( nDx, nDy );

        Enable( FULLWINDOWMODE );
        Enable( INDVFILESTATUS );
        Enable( BITMAP256COLORS );

        SetTitle( "Installing " + APP_NAME, 24, WHITE );

        SetColor( BACKGROUND, BK_BLUE ); // Dark blue.
        SetColor( STATUSBAR, BLUE );     // Bright blue.
        SetTitle( "Setup", 0, BACKGROUNDCAPTION ); // Caption bar text.

        Enable( BACKGROUND );

        Delay( 1 );

end;


/*------------------------------------------------------------------------*\
 *
 * Function:  CheckRequirements
 *
 *  Purpose:  This function will check all minimum requirements for the
 *            application being installed.  If any fail, then the user
 *            is informed and the installation is terminated.
 *
 *
 *    Input:
 *
 *  Returns:
 *
 * Comments:
\*------------------------------------------------------------------------*/
function CheckRequirements()
number nvDx, nvDy;
number nvResult;
STRING svResult;

begin
```

```
        // Check screen resolution.
        GetExtents( nvDx, nvDy );
        if (nvDy < 480) then
           MessageBox( "This program requires VGA or better resolution.",
                       WARNING );
           exit;
        endif;

        // Determine the target system's operating system.
        GetSystemInfo( OS, nvResult, svResult );
        bWinNT  = FALSE;
        bWin32s = FALSE;
        bIsShellExplorer = FALSE;

        if (nvResult =  IS_WINDOWSNT) then
           bWinNT = TRUE; // Running Windows NT.

           // Check to see if NT is using EXPLORER Shell
           if( QueryShellMgr( svResult ) = 0 ) then
               if( StrCompare( svResult, "EXPLORER.EXE" ) = 0 ) then
                   bIsShellExplorer = TRUE;
               endif;
           endif;

        elseif (nvResult =  IS_WIN32S) then
           bWin32s = TRUE; // Running Win32s.
        endif;

end;
```

Analysis The comments and descriptive command names make the code easy to follow. The intent here is not to teach you InstallShield script programming but to give an idea of what a script looks like and what you need to worry about. As mentioned earlier, you would only need to update some application-specific information in the declarations and the rest of the programming has been done for you. As you study the script code, you should see comments and descriptive commands; then you can easily spot the following:

- Constant declarations
- Global variables
- Program start
- Setup code
- Welcome Dialog Code
- Check system requirements (Windows 95?, NT?, etc.)
- Ask for destination location code
- Perform disk space check code. If low on disk space, ask for new location or instruct user to free some space.
- Store application path in the registry.
- Transfer files
- Display and update progress indicators

- Indicate successful installation
- Create folders and icons
- Store uninstall information

This is just a high-level view of the script; you should refer to the InstallShield documentation if you need more information.

InstallShield 3.0 is useful in creating install programs for any Windows applications regardless of the languages they are written in. Stirling Software has recently created InstallShield Express Lite for Delphi, a Windows application for creating installers for your Delphi applications. InstallShield Express Lite for Delphi presents you with what looks like a yellow notepad that has a check list on it. You click each item and are presented with dialog boxes that ask for information. You point and click your way through the selections, enter application names, your company name, files to be installed, registry entries, and so on. You can create a disk image and do a test run. When you are satisfied, the files are transferred to setup disks and your application is ready to ship. Literally, you can create an installer in about 10 minutes and not write a single line of code. That's right, no script to write as with InstallShield 3.0. And now for the best news of all, InstallShield Express Lite for Delphi ships with Delphi 2.0! Whether you use the InstallShield Express or other InstallShield product, you will easily be able to produce high-quality installers that meet the Windows 95 logo requirements with little or no coding in a very short amount of time.

Summary

Today you learned about the Windows 95 logo requirements that applications and installers must meet. You saw how important the Registry is and how eliminates the need for .ini files. You wrote a simple installer that checked available disk space, created a directory, copied files to the new directory, and made Registry entries. You enabled the program to uninstall the files and clean up the Registry entries. You also learned about InstallShield, a third-party install program generator that simplifies the process of making professional installers. You are now ready to create your own installer and uninstaller package. What are you waiting for? Go make your first million!

Q&A

Q What if I need to update or create .ini files?

A You can still use the `TIniFile` object in Delphi to work with .ini files. It should be used only for backward compatibility or in cases where the Registry is not suitable for the task. Use of .ini files can disqualify your application for the Windows 95 logo. Refer to Delphi's online help and documentation for information on the topic.

Q What if I want my install program to update the Windows 95 Add/Remove Programs section in Control Panel so that I can uninstall it easily later?

A This is simple, provided that your program has an uninstall feature or that you have written a separate uninstaller. Add the following entries to the Registry:

```
HKEY_LOCAL_MACHINE
\SOFTWARE\Microsoft\Windows\CurrentVersion\Uninstall\Application Name
  DisplayName=Product Name
  UninstallString=path and filename with any necessary command line
  parameters.
```

Your uninstall code must remove these entries from the Registry when it is done.

Workshop

Quiz

1. When Microsoft reviews requests to display the the Windows 95 logo, what are the four main categories of programs that it considers?
2. List three requirements that fit programs in all four categories.
3. What function do you use to add a Registry entry?
4. What function do you use to delete a Registry entry?
5. Why should you use the Registry versus .ini files?
6. How many main registry keys are there?
7. What is the name of the Registry file in Windows 95? Does it show up in a normal directory listing?

Exercises

1. Modify the install program that you created earlier so that the name of the file, the directory, and the path information are not hard-coded. Make the program get the necessary information from a file called SETUP.LST. The program should be able to install multiple files listed in SETUP.LST. Make the form go full screen, and give it a blue background. Make it look more professional.
2. Use `REGEDIT` to export a copy of the Registry. Consult the online help for information. Then export the contents of only one main key.

In Review

Week 3—Getting Serious with Delphi

Week 3 started with an introduction to the bigger world of client/server with Interbase on Day 15. ReportSmith and Quick Reports were the topics of discussion on Day 16. Day 17 showed you how to print in Delphi without using ReportSmith. Day 18 was a bullish chapter on OLE and its purpose. Day 19 taught you how to write your own DLL: a powerful capability. Day 20 showed you how to construct your own VCL to extend the Delphi environment, and you finished Week 3 with an installation overview on Day 21.

Quiz Question Answers

Day 1

1. The first benefit is that you can, with a minimum amount of work, rapidly prototype front ends to show customers. The second benefit is that you do not have to throw that work away as you would if you used one of those demo front-end builders. You can turn your demo into the end product. That means time not wasted. Even another benefit is that a RAD environment offers is a highly integrated, high-level toolset to maximize your productivity.
2. Visual components differ in many ways from OCXs. One way is that VCs compile right into your executable because they are native Delphi code. OCXs must be included separately with your finished product.

Day 2

1. Syntax highlighting is a feature offered in the Delphi development environment in which the editor understands the Delphi language. Through this understanding it is able to color code different portions of your code (comments are gray, reserved words blue). You can change the colors used to highlight the code. The benefit of this feature is to point out mistakes and make the code easier to read.
2. By using the Component | Install menu selection from the Delphi main menu.

Day 3

1. Constants cannot change their value during the execution of the application, whereas variables are designed to do exactly that.
2. Because our mathematical equations in code must act the same as the real world of math; otherwise the computer would generate incorrect answers.
3. Typed constants are basically variables that are pre-initialized. The benefit here is that, with pre-initialization, your variable starts out life fulfilled!

Day 4

1. 100 times. The outer loop goes 10 times around, and for each one of those times the inner loop runs through 10 iterations. 10X10=100.
2. `While...do` tests the condition prior to entering the loop.
3. A function is designed to return a single value, whereas a procedure is designed to return zero or more values.
4. Passing around large data structures has a large overhead. It is more memory efficient to pass a pointer around.

Day 5

1. .pas, .dpr, .dof, .dem, and .res are created at design time; .dcu and .exe are created at compile time.
2. Unit heading, interface part, implementation part, initialization part, and finalization part.
3. To add a new form to your project, you can select the new form button from the SpeedMenu or do File | New Form menu option. To remove a form from the project, you can use the Project Manager user interface to select the form and then

click on the remove unit button. You can also select the form you wish to remove and use the Remove File From Project icon on the SpeedMenu or you can use the File | Remove From Project menu option.

4. When you delete a form from a project, the associated .pas or .dfm files are not deleted, their references in the project source file are just removed.

Day 6

1. The right mouse button brings up context-sensitive menus that apply to the object you are right clicking. This helps you see what functions can be performed on this object at this time.
2. Those specific size windows are designed to go well with specific screen resolutions for maximum visibility and usefulness. Also, if we all use them, it helps reinforce the uniformity of the environment.
3. So the user does not have to spend a lot of time learning how to navigate your menu bar, but rather can spend it learning your application itself.

Day 7

1. The goals are modifiability, efficiency, reliability, and understandability.
2. It supports information hiding by creating units. Units allow you to hide the implementation details of an application and present an interface to the data.
3. Because in the real world you have objects that are based on other objects. In Delphi you can create a `Car` class, and then create child objects that inherit the `Car` class properties, but also add their own. The result could be a convertible class, a race car class, and so on.

Day 8

1. Graphical programs respond to Win32 events. A `readln` statement is part of console input that doesn't exist in a graphical application.
2. A processor (the chip) can only execute one instruction at a time. Multiple tasks running simultaneously are given processor time slices, which gives the appearance of simultaneous processing. If a computer has more than one CPU and an operating system that knows how to use multiple processors effectively (such as Windows NT), then the computer can perform more than one task at a time because each processor can be executing instructions in parallel.

3. We can use a `try…except` block to catch the exception, and then again raise the exception using a `raise exception` statement.
4. Delphi provides the capability to define and raise your own exceptions. This is useful because it allows a single model for handling errors and exceptions.
5. The Finalization section of a Delphi application contains code to be executed before the application terminates. Similarly, the Initialization section executes code while the application is being loaded.

Day 9

1. The user can view a visual component at runtime if the visible property is set to true. A nonvisual component is visible at design time, but not at runtime.
2. Nested properties are properties within properties. You can spot a property with nested properties because it has a plus sign to the left of it. If you click the plus sign, it expands to show the nested properties. Properties can be nested several levels.
3. A method is a function or procedure declared inside a component or object that can be called to affect the behavior or appearance of that object.
4. Components and objects have events associated with them that, when activated, execute associated event handlers (sections of code). An example of a common event would be a mouse click.
5. MaskEdit.
6. Timer.

Day 10

1. The triangle would not erase itself and would leave a trail as it moved across the window.
2. The easiest way to perform clipping in a rectangular region is to use a PaintBox visual component. The PaintBox visual component prevents anything from being drawn outside the paintbox.
3. Red, green, and blue can be used to create almost any color by combining the proper amounts of each color. The `RGB()` function can be used to create a color composed of red, green, and blue components. A palette is the set of colors that are currently available in a drawing environment.
4. Image visual components can encapsulate a bitmap object. Bitmap objects have a `LoadBitmap` method that can be used to load a bitmap from a file into the bitmap,

which in turn loads the image into the image component. The `CopyRect` method can be used to copy a portion of any canvas (including a canvas in a bitmap) to any other canvas (including the canvas of a PaintBox).

Day 11

1. `PlaySound` accepts a set of parameters that determine how a sound is played and where the source of the sound is located. One of these parameters determines if the sound is played synchronously or asynchronously. If the sound is played synchronously then the application waits until the sound has been played. The asynchronous setting allows the sound to play while the application continues to execute.
2. It means to set the display region between pixels 50,50 and 250,250. The first set indicates the location (50,50) and the second set indicates the width and height (200,200).
3. When a media player method completes, an OnNotify event is sent to the media player. Any special code that needs to be executed at the completion of a media event can be placed in the OnNotify event handler.
4. Drawing directly on a canvas causes a flickering effect. To achieve smoother animation, draw on a bitmap and then copy the image to the visual canvas.

Day 12

1. Typed files are files that are formatted a particular way and store a particular type of data in specific fields.
2. Untyped files are files with no particular format or data type.
3. The read-only bit: bit 0.
4. `FilePos(var F): Longint;`
5. `Seek(var F; N: Longint);`
6. Any file type.
7. 255 characters.
8. A unique short filename based on the first six characters of the long filename is created when a long filename is created.

Day 13

1. An exception will occur if you attempt to execute an edit method while a table is in a dsBrowse state.

2. Fields can be accessed as components. The TField component has a `DataType` property that indicates what type of data a particular field contains.
3. The `IndexName` property on a TTable component can be set to a secondary index to order the records by the index specified.
4. Both file share and client/server databases support multiple applications accessing the database simultaneously. Some true stand-alone databases only allow a single application to access it.
5. Regular fields cannot be updated when a dataset is in a dsCalculate state. Only calculated fields can be updated while in this state, however all fields can be read.

Day 14

1. A field indicating a key in a different table is called a *foreign key*.
2. `SELECT Driver.DrivNum,Sum(Points) from Driver, Ticket` where `Driver.DrivNum = Ticket.Driver Group By Driver.DrivNum` can be used to list the drivers with tickets and their accumulated points.
3. The statement groups by animal type; however, it has different names for animals of the same type. Therefore, it is not possible to show the names and the number of each animal.
4. `SELECT MAX(Age) from Zoo` can be used to specify the age of the oldest animal.

Day 15

1. Inserting records into a view based on a join is not possible because there is no way to split the record or un-join the inserted data.
2. A right join returns all the records associated in one of the tables being joined regardless whether a match occurs in the table to which it is being joined.
3. The record will not be in the table. All modifications performed within a transaction will be erased if a rollback is performed.
4. A TStoredProcedure component is used to execute an `Execute` stored procedure and a TQuery component is used to return a result set with a `Select` stored procedure.

Day 16

1. Summary bands are used to summarize data from a detail section. In ReportSmith you have summary fields that are used to do the same thing.

2. Yes. There is a ReportSmith runtime viewer that allows the user to run to report outside of Delphi.
3. ReportBasic extends the functionality of ReportSmith to allow you to do things that Borland may not have thought of. ReportBasic makes the tool even that much more flexible.

Day 17

1. No, you can open the printer port like you would a file and use the Pascal procedure to send text to the printer.
2. You must add `Printers` to the Uses clause.
3. `BeginDoc` and `EndDoc`.
4. True.
5.
```
if PrintDialog1.Execute then
   Begin
      {your print code}
  end;
```
6. There is no code to execute the Properties dialog box; it is accessed from the Print dialog box.
7. `CopyRect`.
8. You simply draw the circle on the Printer canvas just as you would a screen-related canvas such as a form.

```
begin
     {Start the print job}
     Printer.BeginDoc;
     {Set the width of the pen to be 5 pixels wide}
     Printer.Canvas.Pen.Width:=5;
     {Draw an ellipse with the upper left corner at 0,0
      and the lower right corner at 200,200}
     Printer.Canvas.Ellipse(0, 0, 200, 200);
     {complete and print the print job}
     Printer.EndDoc;
end;
```

Day 18

1. Drag-and-drop is the capability of applications to handle objects without having to do a File | Open and pull them in. Instead you can drop the object on the application and it opens that object directly. Object embedding involves placing a copy of an OLE object into another document or application.
2. The major limitation is that VBX is a 16-bit technology. The problem with that is VBXs will not survive well in the 32-bit Windows 95/NT environment. This means that VBXs are slower and less efficient than their 32-bit OCX counterparts.
3. OLE automation allows your application to control other OLE server enables applications. This is a huge benefit because instead of reinventing the wheel, you can drive someone else's car!

Day 19

1. Dynamic Link Library (DLL)—a special type of executable file containing functions, procedures, and resources that you can load at runtime.
2. Although you can, this is usually handled automatically by Windows.
3. Exports is used in a DLL to make the routines visible and available to other applications.
4. DLL functions are declared in the implementation part of the calling program as an external function or procedure.
5. The calling program simply calls a routine that uses the form and it created and displayed by the DLL.

Day 20

1. When a component user sets a property it can trigger a procedure that processes all the applicable logic.
2. Properties available at development can be set by using the Object Inspector. Properties available at runtime can only be set by using object Pascal code.
3. A public property is available to any code at runtime. Specifying a property as published will make it appear in the Object Inspector and thus be available at development time.
4. Both properties and events are declared identically, however events are defined as special event types that make the object inspector list them on the events page.

Day 21

1. File-based applications, nonfile-based applications that run exclusively in full mode not windowed, utilities including file and disk utilities and virus scanning and cleaning programs, and development tools.
2. a. The application must use the Win32 API.

   b. The application must follow the Windows 95 look and feel for the user interface.

   c. The application must be tested and successfully run on both Windows 95 and Windows NT and adjusted as necessary to compensate for differences in features between the two.
3. `function RegCreateKey(Key: HKey; SubKey: PChar; var Result: HKey): Longint;`
4. `function RegDeleteKey(Key: HKey; SubKey: PChar): Longint;`
5. One reason is because it is a requirement for the Windows 95 logo. Another reason is that it a safer place to store your programs configuration information than .ini files because .ini files are easily deleted.
6. Six; they are `Hkey_Local`, `Hkey_Current_Config`, `Hkey_Dyn_Data`, `Hkey_Classes_Root`, `Hkey_Users` and `Hkey_Current_User`.
7. The Registry filename is SYSTEM.DAT. It does not appear in a normal directory listing because it is a hidden file.

ASCII Chart

Dec	Hex	Char
000	00	NUL
001	01	SOH
002	02	STX
003	03	ETX
004	04	EOT
005	05	ENQ
006	06	ACK
007	07	BEL
008	08	BS
009	09	HT
010	0A	LF
011	0B	VT
012	0C	FF
013	0D	CR
014	0E	SO
015	0F	SI
016	10	DLE
017	11	DC1
018	12	DC2
019	13	DC3
020	14	DC4
021	15	NAK
022	16	SYN
023	17	ETB
024	18	CAN
025	19	EM
026	1A	SUB
027	1B	ESC
028	1C	FS
029	1D	GS
030	1E	RS
031	1F	US
032	20	SP
033	21	!
034	22	“
035	23	#
036	24	$
037	25	%
038	26	&
039	27	‘
040	28	(
041	29	)
042	2A	*
043	2B	+
044	2C	,
045	2D	-
046	2E	.
047	2F	/
048	30	0
049	31	1
050	32	2
051	33	3
052	34	4
053	35	5
054	36	6
055	37	7

Dec	Hex	Char
056	38	8
057	39	9
058	3A	:
059	3B	;
060	3C	<
061	3D	=
062	3E	>
063	3F	?
064	40	@
065	41	A
066	42	B
067	43	C
068	44	D
069	45	E
070	46	F
071	47	G
072	48	H
073	49	I
074	4A	J
075	4B	K
076	4C	L
077	4D	M
078	4E	N
079	4F	O
080	50	P
081	51	Q
082	52	R
083	53	S
084	54	T
085	55	U
086	56	V
087	57	W
088	58	X
089	59	Y
090	5A	Z
091	5B	[
092	5C	\
093	5D	]
094	5E	^
095	5F	–
096	60	`
097	61	a
098	62	b
099	63	c
100	64	d
101	65	e
102	66	f
103	67	g
104	68	h
105	69	i
106	6A	j
107	6B	k
108	6C	l
109	6D	m
110	6E	n
111	6F	o

Dec	Hex	Char
112	70	p
113	71	q
114	72	r
115	73	s
116	74	t
117	75	u
118	76	v
119	77	w
120	78	x
121	79	y
122	7A	z
123	7B	{
124	7C	¦
125	7D	}
126	7E	~
127	7F	Δ
128	80	Ç
129	81	ü
130	82	é
131	83	â
132	84	ä
133	85	à
134	86	å
135	87	ç
136	88	ê
137	89	ë
138	8A	è
139	8B	ï
140	8C	î
141	8D	ì
142	8E	Ä
143	8F	Å
144	90	É
145	91	æ
146	92	Æ
147	93	ô
148	94	ö
149	95	ò
150	96	û
151	97	ù
152	98	ÿ
153	99	Ö
154	9A	Ü
155	9B	¢
156	9C	£
157	9D	¥
158	9E	₧
159	9F	ƒ
160	A0	á
161	A1	í
162	A2	ó
163	A3	ú
164	A4	ñ
165	A5	Ñ
166	A6	ª
167	A7	º

Dec	Hex	Char	Dec	Hex	Char
168	A8	¿	196	C4	─
169	A9	⌐	197	C5	┼
170	AA	¬	198	C6	╞
171	AB	½	199	C7	╟
172	AC	¼	200	C8	╚
173	AD	¡	201	C9	╔
174	AE	«	202	CA	╩
175	AF	»	203	CB	╦
176	B0	░	204	CC	╠
177	B1	▒	205	CD	═
178	B2	▓	206	CE	╬
179	B3	│	207	CF	╧
180	B4	┤	208	D0	╨
181	B5	╡	209	D1	╤
182	B6	╢	210	D2	╥
183	B7	╖	211	D3	╙
184	B8	╕	212	D4	╘
185	B9	╣	213	D5	╒
186	BA	║	214	D6	╓
187	BB	╗	215	D7	╫
188	BC	╝	216	D8	╪
189	BD	╜	217	D9	┘
190	BE	╛	218	DA	┌
191	BF	┐	219	DB	█
192	C0	└	220	DC	▄
193	C1	┴	221	DD	▌
194	C2	┬	222	DE	▐
195	C3	├	223	DF	▀

Dec	Hex	Char
224	E0	α
225	E1	β
226	E2	Γ
227	E3	π
228	E4	Σ
229	E5	σ
230	E6	μ
231	E7	γ
232	E8	Φ
233	E9	θ
234	EA	Ω
235	EB	δ
236	EC	∞
237	ED	ø
238	EE	∈
239	EF	∩
240	F0	≡
241	F1	±
242	F2	≥
243	F3	≤
244	F4	⌠
245	F5	⌡
246	F6	÷
247	F7	≈
248	F8	°
249	F9	•
250	FA	·
251	FB	√
252	FC	η
253	FD	²
254	FE	■
255	FF	

ANSI Chart

Dec	Hex	Char
000	00	null
001	01	☺
002	02	☻
003	03	♥
004	04	♦
005	05	♣
006	06	♠
007	07	•
008	08	◘
009	09	○
010	0A	◙
011	0B	♂
012	0C	♀
013	0D	♪
014	0E	♫
015	0F	☼
016	10	►
017	11	◄
018	12	↕
019	13	‼
020	14	¶
021	15	§
022	16	▬
023	17	↨
024	18	↑
025	19	↓
026	1A	→
027	1B	←
028	1C	∟
029	1D	↔
030	1E	▲
031	1F	▼
032	20	space
033	21	!
034	22	"
035	23	#
036	24	$
037	25	%
038	26	&
039	27	'
040	28	(
041	29	)
042	2A	*
043	2B	+
044	2C	,
045	2D	-
046	2E	.
047	2F	/
048	30	0
049	31	1
050	32	2
051	33	3
052	34	4
053	35	5
054	36	6
055	37	7
056	38	8
057	39	9
058	3A	:
059	3B	;
060	3C	<
061	3D	=

Dec	Hex	Char	Dec	Hex	Char
062	3E	>	092	5C	\
063	3F	?	093	5D	]
064	40	@	094	5E	^
065	41	A	095	5F	–
066	42	B	096	60	`
067	43	C	097	61	a
068	44	D	098	62	b
069	45	E	099	63	c
070	46	F	100	64	d
071	47	G	101	65	e
072	48	H	102	66	f
073	49	I	103	67	g
074	4A	J	104	68	h
075	4B	K	105	69	i
076	4C	L	106	6A	j
077	4D	M	107	6B	k
078	4E	N	108	6C	l
079	4F	O	109	6D	m
080	50	P	110	6E	n
081	51	Q	111	6F	o
082	52	R	112	70	p
083	53	S	113	71	q
084	54	T	114	72	r
085	55	U	115	73	s
086	56	V	116	74	t
087	57	W	117	75	u
088	58	X	118	76	v
089	59	Y	119	77	w
090	5A	Z	120	78	x
091	5B	[	121	79	y

Dec	Hex	Char
122	7A	z
123	7B	{
124	7C	|
125	7D	}
126	7E	~
127	7F	Δ
128	80	Ç
129	81	ü
130	82	‚
131	83	ƒ
132	84	„
133	85	…
134	86	†
135	87	‡
136	88	ˆ
137	89	‰
138	8A	Š
139	8B	‹
140	8C	Œ
141	8D	ì
142	8E	Ä
143	8F	Å
144	90	É
145	91	‘
146	92	’
147	93	“
148	94	”
149	95	•
150	96	–
151	97	—
152	98	˜
153	99	™
154	9A	š
155	9B	›
156	9C	œ
157	9D	¥
158	9E	₧
159	9F	Ÿ
160	A0	
161	A1	¡
162	A2	¢
163	A3	£
164	A4	¤
165	A5	¥
166	A6	¦
167	A7	§
168	A8	¨
169	A9	©
170	AA	ª
171	AB	«
172	AC	¬
173	AD	-
174	AE	®
175	AF	¯
176	B0	°
177	B1	±
178	B2	^{2}
179	B3	^{3}
180	B4	´
181	B5	µ
182	B6	¶
183	B7	·

Dec	Hex	Char	Dec	Hex	Char
184	B8	¸	214	D6	Ö
185	B9	¹	215	D7	×
186	BA	º	216	D8	Ø
187	BB	»	217	D9	Ù
188	BC	¼	218	DA	Ú
189	BD	½	219	DB	Û
190	BE	¾	220	DC	Ü
191	BF	¿	221	DD	Ý
192	C0	À	222	DE	Þ
193	C1	Á	223	DF	ß
194	C2	Â	224	E0	à
195	C3	Ã	225	E1	á
196	C4	Ä	226	E2	â
197	C5	Å	227	E3	ã
198	C6	Æ	228	E4	ä
199	C7	Ç	229	E5	å
200	C8	È	230	E6	æ
201	C9	É	231	E7	ç
202	CA	Ê	232	E8	è
203	CB	Ë	233	E9	é
204	CC	Ì	234	EA	ê
205	CD	Í	235	EB	ë
206	CE	Î	236	EC	ì
207	CF	Ï	237	ED	í
208	D0	Ð	238	EE	î
209	D1	Ñ	239	EF	ï
210	D2	Ò	240	F0	ð
211	D3	Ó	241	F1	ñ
212	D4	Ô	242	F2	ò
213	D5	Õ	243	F3	ó

Dec	Hex	Char
244	F4	ô
245	F5	õ
246	F6	ö
247	F7	÷
248	F8	ø
249	F9	ù
250	FA	ú
251	FB	û
252	FC	ü
253	FD	ý
254	FE	þ
255	FF	ÿ

Symbols

A

C

D

E

F

G

H

J-K

L

M

P

Q

R

S

T

U

V

W-Z

Book ISBN 0-672-30863-0